This book is a milestone for today's evangelicals. It is not the first, and will certainly not be the last, book on the identity and mission of evangelicals in Europe, yet it has all the ingredients and information needed to refresh our interest in this topic and to challenge our views on our own form of Christianity. Between evangelical traditional self-definition, through religious inclusivism (Protestant, Catholics and Orthodox forms of evangelicalism) and present day challenges, evangelicalism attracts newcomers and contradicts expectations, and remains a form of always renewed, adapted and personally active Christian faith. Understanding the dynamics of European evangelicalism, with its Western, Central and Eastern European cultural nuances, is the important topic of this volume and the authors, as well as the editors, undertook this great task in order to inform us as well as possible about the importance of being earnest in our Christian beliefs and life. Congratulations to all and all the best recommendations for its readers.

Octavian D. Baban, PhD
Adjunct Professor of New Testament and Head of Department,
Baptist Theological Institute of Bucharest, Romania

This timely book clarifies what evangelicals are and surveys their presence in Europe today. It describes a spiritual phenomenon that is often misunderstood and is the perfect introduction to one of the most vital movements in the church today.

Gerald Bray, DLitt
Director of Research,
Latimer Trust, Cambridge, UK

Evangelicals are hard to define, but even harder to deny. This book provides an update on evangelical identity from a European perspective. While public opinion too easily confuses evangelical Christianity with right-wing American politics, Christian nationalism and fundamentalism, this book shows that these are fringes and not the core. The core identity of evangelicals is not defined by politics (least of all current politics) but by a theology deeply rooted in traditional Christianity, and therefore overlaps in many ways with Catholic and Orthodox Christianity. The growing mutual understanding between evangelicals and Orthodox Christianity is one of the surprising aspects of this book. Reading it should help to overcome the all-too-familiar but often inaccurate clichés about evangelicals that seem to survive mainly in the publicly funded media and among liberal-minded church officials. For evangelicals, the book deals with some issues, such as nationalism and racism, that they do indeed need to address. It is also an eye-opener for German evangelicals: their struggles and intellectual battles are different from those in other countries and still largely tied to the historical-critical biblical scholarship taught in German state universities.

The book is highly informative, well researched, eye-opening and at times provocative: those who want to understand evangelicals from the inside (and find an explanation for why evangelical Christianity is so difficult to place and describe) will not be disappointed.

Roland Deines, PhD
Vice Rector for Research, Professor of Biblical Theology and Ancient Judaism,
Internationale Hochschule Liebenzell, Germany

This is an essential read for anyone seeking to understand the rich tapestry of evangelicalism across the continent. This book masterfully captures the unity and diversity within the movement, offering profound insights into its theological, cultural and missional dimensions. A must-read for theologians, pastors and lay leaders alike, it challenges and inspires readers to embrace the dynamic and transformative power of the gospel in a pluralistic world. Highly recommended!

Connie Duarte and Jan Wessels
General Secretaries, European Evangelical Alliance

Far from trying to offer a "one-size-fits-all" box for evangelicalism, this landmark collection of articles offers a balanced, varied, contextual and academic presentation of the tradition and current state of the movement. The tone and scholarly level of the contributions, the selection of topics and the variety of authors will be appreciated by academics, leaders and critical thinkers. The general public will also benefit from important correctives of common misconceptions. The specific focus on Europe and on the current varieties of evangelicalism adds a precious dimension of contextualization. We come away informed and appreciative of the common denominators, the rich variety and the evolving tensions that cohabitate in the ever-changing label of "evangelical."

Marvin Oxenham, PhD
General Secretary,
European Council for Theological Education

Like many other terms, "evangelicalism" changes with time and context. Terms like this lose or even twist in meaning if they are not redefined in changed historical, philosophical, cultural and theological contexts. The present book is a creative and theologically solid attempt to understand European evangelicalism in a changed environment. After reading it, I feel more strongly that I want to be identified as part of the European evangelical family.

Einike Pilli, PhD
Rector, Estonian Free Church Theological Seminary
Chair of the Theology and Education Commission, European Baptist Federation

This is a remarkable volume that shows the strong connections that evangelicals have across Europe. The fact that it emerges from a conference in Prague, which brought together eighty evangelical theologians from all over Europe, is impressive. The authors of the chapters in the first section thoughtfully and carefully deal with a range of crucial contemporary theological issues. That is followed by perceptive descriptions of evangelical movements in fourteen representative European countries. Finally, there are five chapters with illuminating sociological analyses. No previous study has covered the European evangelical landscape in such a far-reaching way. It is a book to be read by anyone who is interested in Christian witness in Europe and who wishes to be both informed and challenged.

Ian Randall, PhD
Senior Research Associate,
Cambridge Centre for Christianity Worldwide, UK

This handbook supplies us finally with an answer to the question: what does "evangelical" mean? In thirty research-based, clearly written and insightful chapters this book presents the theology, the history, the spread and the relevance of European evangelicalism. Without being apologetic, misconceptions of evangelicalism are done away with and the unity in diversity in this movement is convincingly demonstrated. I expect this handbook to be an incentive for ongoing and fruitful research.

Herman Selderhuis, PhD
Professor of Church History,
Theological University Apeldoorn, Netherlands

At a time when, once more, the value of an "evangelical" identity is being called into question, here is a volume that demonstrates why and how such failures of confidence should be resisted. These diverse articles reveal a movement that is well able to reflect upon itself and faithfully reimagine its essential concerns within the European context.

Nigel G. Wright, PhD
Principal Emeritus,
Spurgeon's College, London, UK

Evangelicalism in Europe

GLOBAL LIBRARY

Evangelicalism in Europe

Unity in Diversity

Edited by
Frank Hinkelmann and Pieter J. Lalleman

© 2025 Frank Hinkelmann and Pieter J. Lalleman

Published 2025 by Langham Global Library
An imprint of Langham Publishing
www.langhampublishing.org

Langham Publishing and its imprints are a ministry of Langham Partnership

Langham Partnership
PO Box 296, Carlisle, Cumbria, CA3 9WZ, UK
www.langham.org

ISBNs:
978-1-78641-123-5 Print
978-1-78641-248-5 ePub
978-1-78641-249-2 PDF

Frank Hinkelmann and Pieter J. Lalleman hereby assert their moral right to be identified as the Authors of the General Editors' part in the Work in accordance with sections 77 and 78 of the Copyright, Designs and Patents Act 1988.

All rights reserved. No part of this publication may be reproduced, stored in a retrieval system or transmitted, in any form or by any means, electronic, mechanical, photocopying, recording or otherwise, without the prior written permission of the publisher or the Copyright Licensing Agency.

Requests to reuse content from Langham Publishing are processed through PLSclear. Please visit www.plsclear.com to complete your request.

All Scripture quotations, unless otherwise indicated, are taken from the Holy Bible, New International Version®, NIV®. Copyright ©1973, 1978, 1984, 2011 by Biblica, Inc.™ Used by permission of Zondervan.

Scripture quotations marked (ESV) are from The Holy Bible, English Standard Version® (ESV®), copyright © 2001 by Crossway, a publishing ministry of Good News Publishers. Used by permission. All rights reserved.

Scripture quotations marked (CJB) taken from the Complete Jewish Bible by David H. Stern. Copyright © 1998. All rights reserved. Used by permission of Messianic Jewish Publishers, 6120 Day Long Lane, Clarksville, MD 21029. www.messianicjewish.net.

British Library Cataloguing-in-Publication Data
A catalogue record for this book is available from the British Library

ISBN: 978-1-78641-123-5

Cover & Book Design: projectluz.com

Langham Partnership actively supports theological dialogue and an author's right to publish but does not necessarily endorse the views and opinions set forth here or in works referenced within this publication, nor can we guarantee technical and grammatical correctness. Langham Partnership does not accept any responsibility or liability to persons or property as a consequence of the reading, use or interpretation of its published content.

Contents

Foreword xiii

Identity, Unity and Diversity. xiii

Introduction 1
Frank Hinkelmann and Pieter J. Lalleman

Part 1: Evangelical Theology

1. What Defines Evangelicalism? 5
Frank Hinkelmann

2. Evangelicals and the Authority of Scripture 25
Hetty Lalleman

3. Evangelicals and the World. 47
Joshua T. Searle

4. Evangelical Identity and Orthodox Perception: A Romanian Contextual Analysis. 65
Cristian Sonea

5. Evangelicals and Other Christian Traditions: An Insider's Perspective. 79
Tim Grass

6. The Challenge of Post-Evangelicalism and the Search for the Non-Negotiable. 97
Martin P. Grünholz

7. Nationalist and/or Populist Political Movements: How do Evangelicals Vote and Respond? 115
Evert van de Poll

8. The Place of Mission in Evangelical Identity 137
McTair Wall

9. British Evangelicals: Towards a Public Theology of Racial Justice . . 151
Israel Oluwole Olofinjana

10. The Elephant in The Room: Sexual Ethics and the Boundaries of Evangelicalism. 163
David Sandifer

Part 2: Evangelicals in Various Countries

11   Evangelicalism in Austria 187
     Frank Hinkelmann

12   Evangelicalism in Croatia 201
     Danijel Časni

13   Evangelicalism in the Czech Republic......................... 215
     Pavel Černý

14   Evangelicalism in France..................................... 229
     Sébastien Fath

15   Evangelicalism in Germany 241
     Frank Hinkelmann

16   Evangelicalism in the Republic of Ireland..................... 255
     Patrick Mitchel

17   Evangelicalism in Italy...................................... 273
     Leonardo De Chirico

18   Evangelicalism in Norway..................................... 287
     Lars Dahle

19   Evangelicalism in Portugal 301
     Timóteo Cavaco

20   Evangelicalism in Romania.................................... 313
     Marcel Măcelaru

21   Evangelicalism in French-Speaking Switzerland 333
     Monique Cuany

22   Evangelicalism in German-Speaking Switzerland................ 347
     Stefan Schweyer and Paul Bruderer

23   Evangelicalism in Ukraine.................................... 359
     Sergii Sannikov

24   Evangelicalism in the United Kingdom......................... 373
     David Hilborn

Part 3: Sociological Analyses

25 Evangelicals in Central and Eastern Europe: The Case of Poland... 397
    Natalia Zawiejska

26 Evangelicals in Portugal: Plural and Growing Communities....... 413
    Elsa Correia Pereira

27 Evangelicals in Southern Europe: Sociological Perspectives 429
    Sébastien Fath

28 Evangelicalism in Northern Europe, Especially in Sweden:
    A Sociological Perspective................................... 443
    Per Ewert

29 Evangelicalism in Western Europe Today:
    Some Sociological Remarks 457
    Jelle Creemers

    About the Authors 469

Foreword

Identity, Unity and Diversity

In August 2024, the Fellowship of European Evangelical Theologians held its biennial conference in Prague, Czech Republic. The conference was organized in close cooperation with the Fellowship of Evangelical Theologians in the Czech Republic as well as with the European Evangelical Alliance (EEA). The cooperation with EEA was a novelty that came about due not only to this partner's awareness of the need for theological reflection in general, but also to the importance of the theme of the conference: "Evangelical identity in Europe – unity in diversity."

For several reasons, we were convinced that a theological discussion on evangelical identity recommended itself and was even urgent. The first reason was the fiftieth anniversary of the first Lausanne Congress, which was a landmark in the history of the evangelical movement. What has been realised since that conference? Where are we now? What has changed over the last fifty years?

Another reason for choosing this theme was the growing diversity of evangelicals in Europe. In the past, the evangelicals were well represented in Western and Northern Europe. In the last decades, people from Southern Europe entered the scene and even more from the East, from post-Communist countries. Their situation differs from that of their brothers and sisters from the North and the West. This background often affects their concerns and the selection of theological topics which they emphasize as characteristic of their identity. Some would now even speak of evangelical identities instead of identity. At the conference we also heard that in many countries immigration from outside Europe is having a profound influence on the evangelical scene.

The last reason why we thought it necessary to reflect on evangelical identity was the fact that many people nowadays identify "evangelical" with a political movement. For them, it is the same as conservative, radical and fundamentalist (see Frank Hinkelmann's contribution "What Defines Evangelicalism?" in this volume). Needless to say that European theologians and leaders who identify as evangelicals cannot escape defining their position in this respect.

During the conference, the theme was addressed in three main papers and five workshops. You will find the text of the main papers and of some of the contributions to the workshops in this volume. In addition, there were short papers about the history and sociology of evangelicals in various countries and regions of Europe. Readers will find many more such papers in this volume, so that they will have a good, though still not complete, overview of the local developments and preferences.

The conference was highly appreciated by most participants. They praised the good ambiance and the quality of the papers. The conference was not intended to come up with the formulation of a resolution on what should be understood by "evangelical" today or a sharp definition of evangelical identity. The discussion will be continued and it is my hope that this volume will be a worthy contribution to the ongoing debate.

Yet there was a clear sense of unity among those present in Prague. Apparently, mutual recognition did not depend on complete agreement on the characteristics of evangelical identity. Maybe this is related to the fact that being an evangelical is not a goal in itself. As the term "evangelical" indicates, faithfulness to the gospel of Jesus Christ and rejoicing over its good news are the main thing. We are evangelicals because we love the gospel and the God of the gospel. This leads to a sense of unity which can well accommodate diversity and even appreciate it as an expression of the richness of God's work.

Gert Kwakkel
Chairman, Executive Committee,
Fellowship of European Evangelical Theologians

Introduction

Frank Hinkelmann and Pieter J. Lalleman

This handbook *Evangelicalism in Europe: Unity in Diversity* is the result of a joint conference organized by the Fellowship of European Evangelical Theologians (FEET) and the European Evangelical Alliance (EEA) in Prague (Czech Republic) in August 2024. Almost eighty evangelical theologians from all over Europe met in Prague to discuss the history and shape of the evangelical movement in Europe in its unity and diversity. For this publication, we have asked some additional authors for contributions from their national contexts.

The book consists of three parts, the first of which focuses on theological issues. It deals with fundamental aspects such as the question of what the term "evangelical" actually means (Frank Hinkelmann, Austria), the question of "Evangelicals and Authority" (Hetty Lalleman, UK/Netherlands), "Evangelicals and the World" (Joshua Searle, Germany), and "Evangelicals and Others" (from a Romanian Orthodox perspective Christian Sonea, Romania). The latter essay has a response from an evangelical perspective (Tim Grass, UK). In additional contributions, Martin Grünholz (Germany) takes up the question of Post-evangelicalism, Evert van de Poll (Netherlands) looks at the relationship between "Evangelicals and populist movements," McTair Wall (France) examines the topic of "Evangelicals and mission," Israel Olofinjana (UK) analyses the relationship between the evangelical movement in Europe and Christians from the Global South and David Sandifer (Netherlands) discusses the extent to which sexual ethics represents a watershed for evangelicals.

The second main part of the volume consists of the histories and current circumstances of the evangelical movement in a number of countries and in different regions of Europe. These histories are examined and explored in greater depth. The diversity of the evangelical movement becomes particularly evident in this section.

The third and final part of the book focuses on sociological issues. Natalia Zawiejska (Poland) and Elsa Pareira (Portugal) present the evangelical landscape in their respective countries. The contributions by Sébastien Fath (France), Per Ewert (Sweden) and Jelle Creemers (Belgium) offer an overview sociological perspective of evangelicalism in Southern, Northern and Western Europe respectively.

We are grateful to Langham Publishing, particularly to our friend Roman Soloviy, for the ready acceptance of this book for publication. It is our hope that the volume will give the reader a concise insight into the theology, history and the present situation of the evangelical movement in Europe in its unity in diversity.

Part 1

Evangelical Theology

1

What Defines Evangelicalism?

Frank Hinkelmann

Introduction

Emotive Term Evangelical[1] – this is the succinct German title of a book published in the 1990s. The original English title sounds much less emotionally charged: *Who Are the Evangelicals? Tracing the Roots of Today's Movements.* However, the German title aptly describes the current situation: evangelicals are unpopular with the (media) public,[2] are perceived as a threat and are often equated with radical Islamic preachers, if not with terrorists from the so-called Islamic State (IS).[3] At best, they are regarded as sectarian fundamentalists.[4] Anyone who enters the term "evangelical" into a Google search will easily get the impression from the links suggested that evangelicals can be categorized

---

1. Derek J. Tidball, *Reizwort Evangelikal. Entwicklung einer Frömmigkeitsbewegung* (Stuttgart, Edition Anker, 1999); original Derek J. Tidball, *Who Are the Evangelicals? Tracing the Roots of the Modern Movement* (Grand Rapids: Zondervan, 1994).

2. Cf. www.taz.de/!5048455/ where Friederike Gräff stated: "Evangelicals are the bogeymen among Christians" and a few lines further on: "Evangelicals are unpopular in wide circles for various reasons . . ." All translations from the German are mine.

3. So wrote Thorsten Denkler in the *Süddeutsche Zeitung* on 13 June 2016, after an IS supporter carried out an attack in a gay bar in Orlando in which around fifty people died. Denkler wrote: "He could just as easily have been an evangelical Christian for this act." See www.sueddeutsche.de/politik/schiesserei-in-orlando-warum-orlando-kein-angriff-auf-die-offene-gesellschaft-war-1.3031086.

4. According to Gerfried Sperl in the *Austrian Standard*, who wrote: "They exist in Norway, Denmark and Sweden: small fundamentalist sects that have emerged from Protestant movements, which are summarized as 'evangelicals' in the USA and Latin America." See http://derstandard.at/1310512027578/Der-Fundamentalismus-hinter-dem-Massaker.

as "radical,"⁵ "arch-conservative"⁶ or "fundamentalist"⁷ – in any case either dangerous or naive.⁸ In the words of a German newspaper, evangelicals are "homophobic, self-righteous [and] intellectually poor."⁹ In addition, the media often equate evangelicals with the politics and political style of US president Donald J. Trump. In the USA, "evangelical" is now regularly used as a political term and no longer as a religious term.

As early as 1999 the evangelical theologian John Stott quoted the American professor James Davison Hunter, who listed the keywords used by American academics to characterize evangelicals as "right-wing zealots," "religious nuts," "a misanthropic cult," "fanatics," "demagogues," "anti-intellectual and simplistic" while our message is considered "vicious," "cynical," "narrow," "divisive" and "irrational."¹⁰ The situation has not improved since then and there is thus no denying that the term evangelical has been given a "bad rap" in the Western world. A non-evangelical public associates it with both beliefs and behaviour that most evangelical Christians would neither identify with nor recognize as describing them.

This chapter aims to explain both this historical origin of the term evangelical and the theological meaning of this disputed term,¹¹ in order to provide a preliminary definition.

The Historical Origin of the Term "Evangelical"

The word evangelical became popular with the Reformation of the sixteenth century as a translation of the German term "evangelisch." In its original meaning, it was understood as a synonym for the English term "Protestant" and was

---

5. Cf. https://chrismon.de/artikel/2016/32085/radikale-christen-deutschland and www.derbund.ch/evangelikale-in-bern-radikale-christen-sorgen-fuer-aerger-in-familiensied-lung-259016388617.

6. Cf. www.prosieben.at/serien/galileo/news/evangelikale-christen-bibel-auslegung-kirche-konservativ-glauben-lehre-353631.

7. Cf. https://saekulare-gruene.de/der-christliche-fundamentalismus-in-deutschland-ein-positionspapier.

8. Cf. also the multi-part ARTE programme "Evangelikale – Mit Gott an die Macht," www.arte.tv/de/videos/RC-023779/evangelikale-mit-gott-an-die-macht.

9. Quoted from https://taz.de/Christlicher-Fundamentalismus/!5048455.

10. John Stott, *Evangelical Truth. A Personal Plea for Unity* (Leicester: IVP, 1999), 16.

11. Cf. Andrew Atherstone and David Ceri Jones, "Evangelicals and Evangelicalisms: Contested Identities" in *The Routledge Research Companion to the History of Evangelicalism*, ed. Andrew Atherstone and David Ceri Jones (London: Routledge, 2020), 1–21.

used to describe both Lutheran and Reformed followers of the Reformation.[12] However, over the course of the following two centuries "Protestant" came to be used in English for followers of the Reformation churches.[13] It was only from the 1730s onwards that the term evangelical went through a reinterpretation.[14] In the wake of the preaching of John Wesley and George Whitefield,[15] an "evangelical revival"[16] emerged, first in Great Britain and soon also in North America, which not only affected the Church of England but also spread to dissenters and other groups.[17] Subsequently, "evangelicals" were regarded as Christians who emphasized the personal appropriation of salvation, the gathering of all believers, a sanctified way of life and evangelism and mission.[18]

A second definition draws on the ground-breaking work of David Bebbington, who defined the evangelical movement with the following four characteristics: biblicism, crucicentrism, conversionism and activism. Mark A. Noll, a leading American historian of the evangelical movement, summarized Bebbington's definition as follows:

- Conversion, or "the belief that lives need to be changed";
- the Bible, or "the belief that all spiritual truth is to be found in its pages";
- activism, or the dedication of all believers, including laypeople, to lives of service for God, especially as manifest in evangelism (spread-

---

12. Cf. Denton Lotz, "The Evangelization of the World in this Generation." The Resurgence of a Missionary Idea Among the Conservative Evangelicals (Hamburg: Unpublished Dissertation, 1970), 66-67. I think it is wrong to regard the Reformers as early evangelicals, as Michael Reeves, for example, suggests. However, Reeves deliberately starts from a theological and not a historical definition. Cf. Michael Reeves, *Gospel People. A Call for Evangelical Integrity* (Wheaton: Crossway Books, 2022), 131-34.

13. Fritz Laubach, *Aufbruch der Evangelikalen* (Wuppertal: Brockhaus, 1972), 13.

14. This date, introduced by David Bebbington, has been accepted by the majority of scholars. Cf. Timothy Larsen, "The Reception Given 'Evangelicalism in Modern Britain' Since its Publication in 1989" in *The Emergence of Evangelicalism. Exploring Historical Continuities*, ed. Michael A. G. Haykin and Kenneth J. Stewart (Nottingham: IVP, 2008), 23-24.

15. Cf. Mark Noll, *The Rise of Evangelicalism. The Age of Edwards, Whitefield and the Wesleys* (Leicester: IVP, 2004).

16. Tidball, *Evangelicals*, 32.

17. Cf. especially Noll, *Rise*; David W. Bebbington, *Evangelicalism in Modern Britain. A History from the 1730s to the 1980s* (London: Unwin Hyman, 1989), 20-74; Mark A. Noll, *Das Christentum in Nordamerika*. Kirchengeschichte in Einzeldarstellungen IV/5 (Leipzig: EVA, 2000), 79-96; George Rawlyk and Mark A. Noll (eds), *Amazing Grace. Evangelicalism in Australia, Britain, Canada and the United States* (Grand Rapids: Baker, 1993).

18. Laubach, *Aufbruch*, 13-14; Friedhelm Jung, *Die deutsche Evangelikale Bewegung. Grundzüge ihrer Geschichte und Theologie* (Bonn: VKW, 1994), 5-6.

ing the good news) and mission (taking the gospel to other societies);
- crucicentrism, or the conviction that the death of Christ was the crucial matter in providing atonement for sin (that is, providing reconciliation between a holy God and sinful humans.[19]

However, it should be borne in mind that Bebbington never intended to define the term evangelical in general terms; rather, he understood his fourfold definition as a description of the historical situation in Great Britain during the eighteenth century. This is why some scholars see the need for additions to Bebbington's definition. Steve R. Holmes therefore drew the following conclusion:

> All these various attempts to capture the definition of "evangelical" fail because the word is a descriptor which is uncontrolled in use but is profoundly historically determined . . . [the term evangelical] began to be used in its currently popular sense in the UK around the middle of the eighteenth century to refer in general to those who embraced and energetically promulgated, a new, highly experiential, ethically rigorous, ecclesiologically diverse and doctrinally conservative form of protestant Christianity.
>
> To claim to be "evangelical" is, in common English protestant usage, to assert some sort of continuity with this tradition . . . Academic definitions of evangelical identity have, therefore, inevitably been descriptive and essentially historical. The only way we can meaningfully determine what is to be "evangelical" is to examine the range of people and organizations who have claimed the word as a self-denomination and uncover what they share in common.[20]

I am not sure we should follow Holmes' suggestion to define the term evangelical by examining the convictions held by those claiming to be evangelical. Instead, I believe there are different, more convincing ways to determine both who is an evangelical and what it means to be evangelical.

---

19. Noll, *Rise*, 16.

20. Steve R. Holmes, "Evangelical Theology and Identity" in *21st Century Evangelicals: Reflections on Research by the Evangelical Alliance*, ed. Greg Smith (Watford: Instant Apostle, 2015), 24–25.

The Question of Evangelical Identity

Reinhard Hempelmann offers a systematic and denominational classification of the evangelical spectrum, thus providing a definition of evangelical identity. He speaks of different types of evangelical movements that touch, overlap and in some cases also differ significantly.

1. The classical type, which is concretized in the Evangelical Alliance (founded in 1846), the Pietist movement and the Lausanne Movement, and primarily connects established church members and free church members. This strand ties in with the "pre-fundamentalist" Alliance movement and represents the mainstream of the evangelical movement.

2. The fundamentalist type, characterized by an understanding of the Bible that assumes the absolute inerrancy and infallibility of "all Scripture in every respect" (cf. Chicago Declaration).[21] It is also characterized by its strongly defensive and dissociative character in relation to historical-critical biblical research, the teaching of evolution and ethical issues (abortion, pornography, feminism, etc.). Since a fundamentalist understanding of Scripture can develop different forms of piety from within itself, the fundamentalist type differentiates itself in various directions.

3. The missionary-socially oriented type, which emphasizes the need for holistic evangelism, in which evangelism and social responsibility are accentuated in their close relationship. This type is widespread in the Third World among "socially concerned evangelicals," among others . . . It is expressed, for example, in projects that are interested in contextualizing evangelism and mission.

4. The Pentecostal-charismatic type, which is characterized by a piety related to the Holy Spirit and the gifts of grace and which in turn has differentiated itself in many ways and developed at least three different directions: Pentecostal church movements, inner-church renewal groups, neo-charismatic centres and mission agencies, which see themselves as independent of denominations, but are theologically and in their piety practice very close to the Pentecostal movement.[22]

---

21. See https://library.dts.edu/Pages/TL/Special/ICBI_1.pdf.

22. Reinhard Hempelmann, *Evangelikale Bewegungen: Beiträge zur Resonanz des konservativen Protestantismus* (EZW-Texte 206; Berlin: Evangelische Zentralstelle für Weltanschauungsfragen, 2009), 10–11.

It is obvious that anyone who takes a closer look at the evangelical spectrum will be struck by its diversity. However, we still might not need to agree with the conclusion of Hansjörg Kägi that we need to drop the term:

> "Evangelicalism" has become such a large catch-all that it seems impossible at first to even adequately clarify what it contains. In addition, the term evangelicalism is also emotionally charged. Time and again, reports appear about "evangelicalism" or evangelical causes that are either tendentious or show how difficult it is to deal with "evangelicalism" as a large movement. It is not uncommon for evangelicals to be held responsible for things that only apply to a very small part of evangelicalism or rather to fundamentalism.[23]

Instead of giving up using the term evangelical, it seems to be more appropriate to search for a theologically determined definition of the term. Andrew Atherstone and David Ceri Jones commented correctly: "In every generation, from the eighteenth century to present, evangelical identity has been contested."[24] At the same time, as one looks at evangelicalism today, one certainly has to consider what Timothy Larsen pointed to in regard to the global use of the term evangelical by many groups such as the *Evangelical Theological Society* (USA), the *African Evangelical Alliance*, the *Journal of Asian Evangelical Theology*, the *Fellowship of European Evangelical Theologians*, the *World Evangelical Alliance*, the *Korea Evangelical Theological Society*, the *Evangelical Theological Seminary* in Cairo and the *National Association of Evangelicals in America*:

> While the word "evangelical" will undoubtedly not mean exactly the same thing in such diverse locations, the members of these organizations are indeed part of a cross-pollinating international movement. It is routine for an individual in good standing with one of these groups (or numerous more that have not been named) to be sought after for service in any of the others, thus revealing

---

23. Hansjörg Kägi, *Die Evangelikalen – Eine Übersicht über Geschichte und Theologie der Bewegung*. Sonderdruck des Artikels von Pfr. Dr. Hansjörg Kägi, "Evangelikalismus – Versuch eines Überblicks über Geschichte und Theologie," in *Basileia – Festschrift für Eduard Bues*, ed. Hans Dürr and Christoph Ramstein (Basel: Mitenand, 1993) mit Ergänzungen des Autors. idea schweiz Dokumentation 143 (1993), 7.

24. Atherstone and Jones, "Evangelicals," 3.

the sense that they are fellow believers of the same species, local variations notwithstanding.[25]

The Theological Meaning of the Term "Evangelical"

"Evangelicalism is probably the most over-defined religious movement in the world,"[26] says Mark Smith in regard to the British scene, but this is not necessarily also true for other European contexts. And while we can speak of different evangelical identities during the centuries and depending on the local contexts, as the above examples from the German context illustrate, we cannot overlook the fact that the evangelical movement is first and foremost a movement of piety based on shared theological convictions.[27] Anyone who wants to do justice to the evangelical movement and thus to the term evangelical should therefore first and foremost strive for a theological clarification. As James Packer stated,

> You cannot add to evangelical theology without subtracting from it. By augmenting it, you cannot enrich it; you can only impoverish it . . . What is more than evangelical is less than evangelical. Evangelical theology, by its very nature, cannot be supplemented; it can only be denied.[28]

Our theological definition must be embedded in the wider historical and intellectual-historical context of the past centuries.[29] Even if the roots of the movements lie in the period of the Reformation, the Enlightenment and Modernism were to develop far-reaching interactions with the evangelical movement. Joel

---

25. Timothy Larsen, "Defining and Locating Evangelicalism," in *The Cambridge Companion to Evangelical Theology*, ed. Timothy Larsen and Daniel J. Treier (Cambridge: Cambridge University Press, 2007), 3.

26. Mark Smith, "British Evangelical Identities: Locating the Discussions," in *British Evangelical identities Past and Present: Aspects of the History and Sociology of Evangelicalism in Britain and Ireland*, ed. Mark Smith (Milton Keynes: Paternoster, 2008), 1–2.

27. Cf. Martin Greschat, *Die christliche Mitgift Europas – Traditionen der Zukunft* (Stuttgart: Kohlhammer, 2000), 180–82; Gisa Bauer, *Evangelikale Bewegung und evangelische Kirche in der Bundesrepublik Deutschland. Geschichte eines Grundsatzkonflikts* (1945 bis 1989) (Arbeiten zur Kirchlichen Zeitgeschichte, Reihe B: Darstellungen 53; Göttingen: Vandenhoeck & Ruprecht, 2012), 663.

28. Quoted in John Stott, *Christ the Controversialist. A Study in Some Essentials of Evangelical Religion* (London: Tyndale Press, 1970), 32–33.

29. E.g. Erich Geldbach, "Evangelikalismus. Versuch einer historischen Typologie," in *Die Kirchen und ihre Konservativen. „Traditionalismus" und „Evangelikalismus" in den Konfessionen*, ed. Reinhard Frieling (Bensheimer Hefte 62; Göttingen: Vandenhoeck & Ruprecht, 1984), 52–83.

A. Carpenter rightly speaks of a "symbiotic relationship" between the evangelical movement and modernity[30] and Martin E. Marty sees evangelicalism as "the characteristically Protestant way of dealing with modernity."[31] Critics of evangelicalism make it too easy for themselves – and it is also historically inaccurate – if they understand the evangelical movement solely as a backward or retrograde counter-movement to the Enlightenment and to modernity, which rejects the modern, liberal and secular social majority consensus or zeitgeist.[32] It is good that, especially in anglophone scholarship this approach is widely recognized as outdated.[33] In a society increasingly characterized by the compartmentalization of life, the evangelical movement offers a strong personal religious experience. Modern society emphasizes the voluntary nature and freedom of choice of the individual, an aspect that evangelicals also emphasize and which is reflected in their theological convictions. The German church historian Martin Greschat was therefore correct to conclude:

> The evangelical form of piety, in which the personal choice and decision of the individual is of fundamental importance, is in a very favourable position not only to survive but even to succeed in the face of modern developments. In a society that has elevated individual choice to a rule and norm at all levels, the evangelical demand for choice appears decidedly modern.[34]

At the same time, it is the shared beliefs (besides shared experience and a shared piety) that form the actual unifying "strand" of the evangelical movement.[35] In the following, we will therefore present some theological definitions from both the German-speaking and the English-speaking world. We will begin with a definition by the German church historian Friedhelm Jung,

---

30. Joel A. Carpenter, *Revive Us Again. The Reawakening of American Fundamentalism* (New York: Oxford University Press, 1997), 234–35, with reference to Martin E. Marty.

31. Martin E. Marty, "The Revival of Evangelicalism and Southern Religion," in *Varieties of Southern Evangelicalism*, ed. David E. Harrell Jr. (Macon: Mercer University Press, 1981), 9.

32. Cf. Martin Urban, *Ach Gott die Kirche! Protestantischer Fundamentalismus und 500 Jahre Reformation* (München: dtv, 2016), 204–5. Gisa Bauer concluded her study on German evangelicalism: "In conclusion, it should be noted that despite the tendencies towards pluralisation within the evangelical movement since the 1980s, the 'old' themes of criticism of theology and pluralism, criticism of the church and the Enlightenment are still part of evangelical rhetoric and argumentation and of evangelical identity today." Bauer, *Evangelikale Bewegung*, 660.

33. Cf. Carpenter, *Revive*, 234.

34. Greschat, *Mitgift Europas*, 184.

35. Robert K. Johnston, "Evangelikale Theologie" in *Die Religion in Geschichte und Gegenwart*. 4th ed. Volume 2. C – E (Tübingen: Mohr Siebeck, 1999), 1699.

himself an evangelical, who drew primarily on attempts at definitions from within the German-speaking world:[36]

1. The emphasis on the absolute authority of the Holy Scriptures for doctrine and life. The Bible is regarded as the Word of God, inspired by the Holy Spirit, with no agreement among evangelicals on the nature of inspiration.

2. Conversion and rebirth through faith in Jesus Christ, to which the Bible and the three early church symbols bear witness, are necessary for the attainment of eternal salvation.

3. The cultivation of spiritual fellowship among all believers in Jesus Christ. Evangelicals are convinced that God has an *ecclesia invisibilis* among all churches and congregations, which will only be fully revealed at the parousia of Christ.

4. Evangelicals regard the sanctification of personal life and mission through the proclamation of the gospel and *diakonia* as the primary mission of God for their lives.

5. The expectation of the visible return of Jesus Christ and the hope of eternal life in the kingdom of God make evangelicals cautious about all attempts to establish an earthly kingdom of peace through human power alone.[37]

In comparison to Bebbington's quadrilateral, Jung did not take up the christological focus while he added sanctification, the *ecclesia invisibilis* and the parousia, although the latter conviction only became widespread during the nineteenth century.

Martin Greschat, himself not an evangelical, presented a further description of the term evangelical. For him, the basic convictions of evangelical piety include:

1. The central role of the Bible as the authority par excellence;

2. The doctrine of the redemption of mankind through Christ's sacrificial death on the cross;

3. A personal faith that has experienced the truth of this statement with all its senses – which is expressed in terms such as repentance,

---

36. Jung, *Evangelikale Bewegung*, 231–32 note 25.
37. Jung, *Evangelikale Bewegung*, 8.

conversion and rebirth and from which a life of discipleship and sanctification in close union with Jesus Christ arises;

4. The fellowship of like-minded people in one's own group, denomination or church, to which, however, fellowship with the awakened in other denominations or denominations always belongs. In this respect, evangelical piety is cross-denominational and . . . can be characterized as ecumenical. This includes

5. the emphasis on mission and evangelization. And finally,

6. the expectation of the imminent return of Christ on earth is important, both for judgment and for reigning with the pious.[38]

Greschat took up all elements of Bebbington's quadrilateral and added – similar to Jung – the inter-denominational aspect of fellowship as well as the issue of the parousia.

Timothy Larsen, an evangelical historian at Wheaton College, Illinois, offers the following description of what an evangelical is:

1. an orthodox Protestant

2. who stands in the tradition of the global Christian networks arising from the eighteenth-century revival movements associated with John Wesley and George Whitefield;

3. who has a preeminent place for the Bible in their Christian life as the divinely inspired, final authority in matters of faith and practice;

4. who stresses reconciliation with God through the atoning work of Jesus Christ on the cross;

5. and who stresses the work of the Holy Spirit in the life of an individual to bring about conversion and an ongoing life of fellowship with God and service to God and others, including the duty of all believers to participate in the task of proclaiming the gospel to all people.[39]

While Larsen takes up the key points of Bebbington's quadrilateral, he puts special emphasis on the historical roots of the evangelical movement. In addition, he is the first to add to his definition a denominational boundary by saying that only a "Protestant" can be an evangelical. He explains this as follows:

---

38. Greschat, *Mitgift Europas*, 181. The quotation is from the essay "Die Bedeutung evangelikaler Frömmigkeit im internationalen Kontext" (180–94).

39. Larsen, "Defining," 1.

an argument could be made that St. Francis of Assisi was an evangelical. St. Francis, after all, had a clear, dramatic conversion experience; he was so committed to activism that he pioneered friars out itinerating amongst the people; preaching the gospel; and ministering to physical needs rather than being cloistered monks; his biblicism was so thorough that his Rule was made up mostly of straight quotations from Scripture; his crucicentrism was so profound that it reached its culmination in the stigmata. For all I know, St. Francis might have been a better Christian and more committed to the distinctives of the quadrilateral (generally conceived) than any evangelical as defined in this chapter who ever lived, but a definition of evangelicalism that would include medieval Roman Catholic saints would not be serviceable for delineating the scope of scholarly projects.[40]

This point Larsen made is worth considering. While other definitions have not specifically mentioned this aspect, we can assume that their authors took it for granted that the term "evangelical" predominantly describes a movement within Protestantism. Larsen continues by showing that during the eighteenth and nineteenth centuries evangelicalism often "cultivated an explicitly anti-Catholic stance."[41] While this is true – with some noteworthy exceptions – from a historical perspective, a question needs to be raised whether this distinction should be part of a theological definition.

While the definitions presented thus far all came from church historians, the next one comes from the Marburg theologian Roland Werner under the heading "purposefully Protestant." Unlike Larsen, Werner intentionally brings the ecumenical dimension into consideration:

1. "Being evangelical" means nothing more than believing "orthodoxly" in Jesus Christ. Evangelical Christians are characterized by the fact that they take the historical core of the Christian faith seriously, preserve it and want to apply it as a standard for faith and life. In this respect, the evangelical movement is a movement that wants to penetrate the roots of Christianity and in this sense represents a renewal movement from the historical core . . .

2. "Being evangelical" means wanting to follow Christ personally. By referring directly to the Bible, evangelical Christians take up the call

---

40. Larsen, "Defining," 2.
41. Larsen, "Defining," 4.

to repentance that was at the heart of Jesus's preaching: "The time is fulfilled, and the kingdom of God is at hand; repent and believe in the gospel" (Mark 1:15), seriously and personally. For them, faith in Christ can only ever lead to consciously choosing to follow Christ . . .

3. "Evangelicals" seek the unity of believers in common prayer and witness. This has been a characteristic of the evangelical movement from the very beginning. As a result, it developed the potential to work across churches. It is therefore not surprising that the evangelical Catholics movement exists in the USA, for example, and that the charismatic branch of the evangelicals has not only reached the Roman Catholic Church but also extends into the Orthodox churches . . .

4. "Evangelicals" want to make a difference in this world. The dynamism of the evangelical part of Christianity is related to its conviction that the Great Commission (Matt 28:18–20) is to be taken seriously as a legacy of Jesus. They also see themselves as "in the world," but not "of the world" (John 17), as "co-workers with God" (1 Cor 3:9), i.e. as active co-creators of God's good and salutary plans in this world.[42]

What is noteworthy about this definition is that Werner speaks of evangelicals as Christians who are "purposefully Protestant" (*evangelisch*), but at the same time also refers to cross-confessional connections of evangelicals with so-called "evangelical Catholics" as well as Orthodoxy.

Finally, reference should be made to the Anglican evangelical theologian James I. Packer, who in 1978 summarized what he called "evangelical fundamentals":

1. The supremacy of Holy Scripture
2. The majesty of Jesus Christ
3. The lordship of the Holy Spirit
4. The necessity of conversion
5. The priority of evangelism

---

42. Roland Werner, "Zielgerichtet evangelisch" in *Der E-Faktor. Evangelikale und die Zukunft der Kirche*, ed. Ulrich Eggers and Markus Spieker (Wuppertal: Brockhaus, 2005), 33–34.

6. The importance of fellowship[43]

However, when John Stott quotes Packer's definition, he also poses a legitimate question:

> Is it altogether appropriate, I ask myself, that an activity like evangelism, an experience like conversion and an observation like the need for fellowship, even with their theological underpinnings, should be set alongside such towering truths as the authority of Scripture, the majesty of Jesus Christ and the lordship of the Holy Spirit? They seem to belong to different categories. Perhaps I'm asking for no more than a reshuffling of the cards. Yet it seems to me important, when we are trying to define our essential evangelical identity, that we distinguish between divine and human activity, between the primary and the secondary, between what belongs to the centre and what lies somewhere between the centre and the circumference.[44]

Michael Reeves summarizes Stott's own approach as follows:

> John Stott believed that this Trinitarian, theology-led description of evangelicalism could be made even clearer and simpler. He therefore amended Packer's list, bringing everything – the theological and the practical – under three essential marks:
>
> 1. Bible: the revelation of God the Father
> 2. Cross: the redemption of God the Son
> 3. Spirit: the ministry of God the Spirit
>
> Here, the evangelical concerns for conversion, evangelism and fellowship . . . are clearly made, not additions to the theology, but an extension and application of it. And it is not that Stott crassly shoehorned everything into three simply for the look of being Trinitarian. He saw that evangelicals want to be clear about which God they worship . . . They also want to be clear that their theology

---

43. Jim Packer, "The Evangelical Anglican Identity Problem: An Analysis by Jim Packer (1978)" in J. I. Packer and N. T. Wright, *Anglican Evangelical Identity: Yesterday and Today* (London: Latimer Trust, 2008), 47–51. Alister McGrath seems to have picked up Packer's definition, see Alister McGrath, *Evangelicalism and the Future of Christianity* (London: Hodder & Stoughton, 1993), 49–80; a few years later, however, he returned to a slightly adapted form of Bebbington's definition, see McGrath, *A Passion For Truth: The Intellectual Coherence of Evangelicalism* (Leicester: IVP, 1996), 22.

44. Stott, *Evangelical Truth*, 28.

derives from Scripture. And lastly, they actually need to be clear on two things about the gospel: the unique, redemptive work of Christ and the ongoing, regenerative work of the Spirit.[45]

A Working Definition

In the following, I want to present my own definition of the term "evangelical" based on the ones discussed above as well as other ones. This definition is based on the historical and intellectual development of the evangelical movement in both the Anglo-Saxon and the German-speaking worlds; it is further nourished by its theological character, whose roots lie in the revival movements of the eighteenth and nineteenth centuries and, in the German-speaking area, especially in Pietism and Neo-Pietism; and it includes the global character of the evangelical movement, a movement that today has its largest and growing number of followers in the Global South.[46] This definition is not to be understood in contrast to the other definitions given, but rather endeavours to summarize the current yield and state of basic theological conviction of the evangelical movement.[47]

Evangelicals believe:

1. that the Holy Scriptures are the revelation of God the Father, that they are fully inspired and are to be regarded as binding for doctrine and life;

2. that the substitutionary death of Jesus Christ, the Son of God, on the cross is the only basis for redemption and reconciliation between the holy God and sinful humans;

3. that as a work of God, the Holy Spirit indwells every born-again follower of Jesus, empowering and equipping them with his gifts.

The three further focal points of evangelical faith conviction are the result of the work of God, the Holy Spirit, in the life of a Christian. Evangelicals therefore also believe:

---

45. Reeves, *Gospel People*, 129.

46. Cf. on the Global South especially Philip Jenkins, *New Faces of Christianity: Believing the Bible in the Global South* (New York: Oxford University Press, 2006); Todd M. Johnson and Gina A. Zurlo, *World Christian Encyclopedia* 3rd ed. (Edinburgh: Edinburgh University Press, 2020).

47. The following is a revised and expanded version of chapter 7 of my book Frank Hinkelmann, *Evangelikale in Deutschland, Österreich und der Schweiz. Ursprung, Bedeutung und Rezeption eines Begriffs* (Bonn: VKW, 2016), 133–42.

1. that conversion and rebirth through faith in Jesus Christ form the starting point of a life with God (becoming a Christian), which is necessary for the attainment of eternal salvation;
2. that every Christian is a follower of Jesus and that this includes a mission to proclaim the gospel in word and deed as well as a way of life that is guided by the ethical standards of the Holy Scriptures;
3. that there is a fellowship of all Christians that transcends denominational boundaries, while at the same time emphasizing the binding affiliation to a local congregation.

In the following, these six points will be briefly elaborated and explained.

1. Evangelicals believe that the Holy Scriptures are the revelation of God the Father, that they are fully inspired and are to be regarded as binding for doctrine and life.

Holy Scripture is regarded as the revealed word of God the Father and therefore as the only and binding standard for the teaching and life of a Christian, without a normative form of interpretation being established. Since a priesthood of all believers is advocated, the interpretation is not bound to any ecclesiastical denomination. Unlike the Roman Catholic Church, the evangelical movement has no magisterium.[48] The Holy Scriptures are considered to be inspired, but there is no uniform doctrine of inspiration. For this reason, evangelicals also have very different understandings of inspiration. The same applies to the understanding of Scripture. While one wing of evangelicalism believes in the infallibility and inerrancy of the word of God, others reject these concepts. However, the authority of Scripture remains the basis of an evangelical understanding of Scripture.

At the same time, a liberal understanding of Scripture, which in part denies the inspiration of Scripture, as well as a post-evangelical understanding of Scripture, in which contemporary culture is often elevated to the standard for understanding and interpreting Scripture, exclude a person from being part of the evangelical movement.

---

48. Cf. the document of the Second Vatican Council, *Dogmatic Constitution on Divine Revelation* (Verbum dei) from 18 November 1965.

2. Evangelicals believe that the substitutionary death of Jesus Christ, the Son of God, on the cross is the only basis for redemption and reconciliation between the holy God and sinful humans.

Every person is born a sinner and cannot find redemption through their own efforts. Sin is not understood as a trivial matter, but as a fundamental condition that separates the fallen human being from God. God responded to this fundamental failure of humanity to fulfil its purpose by sending his Son Jesus Christ, who lived on earth, died on the cross and rose from the dead on the Easter morning. It is only through this substitutionary act of Jesus that reconciliation between the holy God and sinful humans has become possible. God's invitation to reconciliation is extended to every human being.

This theological conviction also means that people who reject the atoning death of Jesus or see the cross merely as an expression of devotion and declaration of God's love alone do not belong to the evangelical movement.

3. Evangelicals believe that as a work of God, the Holy Spirit indwells every born-again follower of Jesus, empowering and equipping them with his gifts.

When a person is born again, they receive the Holy Spirit, who lives in the Christian from then on. The New Testament describes the Holy Spirit as a helper and comforter who enables Christians to become more like Jesus, who equips Christians with gifts and gives them both knowledge and strength. At the same time, there are different understandings within the evangelical movement regarding the spiritual gifts. While the vast majority of evangelicals believe that all spiritual gifts today are still sovereignly bestowed by the Holy Spirit and that God can work signs and wonders through his Spirit, others see the so-called "sign-gifts" as extinct. Anyone who denies the reality and work of the Holy Spirit cannot belong to the evangelical movement.

The other focal points of evangelical faith are expressions and results of this work of the Holy Spirit in the life of a Christian. Therefore:

4. Evangelicals believe that conversion and rebirth through faith in Jesus Christ form the starting point of a life with God (becoming a Christian), which is necessary for the attainment of eternal salvation.

At the beginning of a life with God is the rebirth of man and woman, their conversion. They experience the forgiveness of their sin through Jesus Christ and are henceforth a redeemed Christian and child of God. As a sign of being born again, a Christian receives the Holy Spirit.

Both the rebirth and the reception of forgiveness can be received directly from God by every person in a personal prayer. This is where the evangelical position differs from the conviction that ascribes the sole mediation of salvation to sacraments and church institutions and also from autonomous tendencies to earn salvation through one's own performance or works. Evangelicals see good works as the fruits of faith that confirm conversion.

5. Evangelicals believe that every Christian is a follower of Jesus and that this includes a mission to proclaim the gospel in word and deed as well as a way of life that is guided by the ethical standards of the Holy Scriptures.

God not only redeems Christians to save them from eternal damnation and being a Christian is more than an end in itself. As a follower of Jesus, glorifying and worshipping God is the primary focus. Prayer and Bible reading therefore play an important role for evangelicals. Evangelicals also advocate the universal priesthood of all believers.[49] This includes a lifestyle and a way of life that is aligned with the ethical standards of the Holy Scriptures. Evangelicals want to pass on the love of God that they have experienced to others, both through words (preaching) and deeds (social commitment in and for society), but without imposing their faith on others. The emphasis here is on a holistic approach without abandoning the proclamation of the gospel.

At the same time, this excludes a one-sided focusing of Christian action on social action at the expense of the proclamation of the gospel, as well as a "withdrawal from the world" that rejects any responsibility for creation and reduces the message of the gospel solely to the salvation of souls.

6. Evangelicals believe that there is a fellowship of all Christians that transcends denominational boundaries, while at the same time emphasizing the binding affiliation to a local congregation.

For evangelicals, the local church occupies an important role. This is where spiritual fellowship becomes visible and where it should be lived out in accordance with the New Testament doctrine of the priesthood of all believers with the participation of the faithful. At the same time, evangelicals also recognize that there is an *ecclesia invisibilis* (an invisible church) consisting of all believ-

---

49. Lutherans and Reformed Christians do give the pastor/minister a special place, but all Protestants have abandoned the catholic sacramental understanding of the role of the priest.

ers beyond denominational boundaries. This is why they consciously seek fellowship with Christians of other denominations.

In many respects, the evangelical movement is therefore the oldest "ecumenical" movement[50] that allows Christians to become part of a trans-denominational movement on the foundation of shared theological convictions and the reality of faith experienced together, without this necessarily having to find expression in an organizational union. This is where the evangelical movement, with its theologically evolved understanding, surpasses the confessions and beliefs of churches and denominations, while numerous important questions that need to be clarified and defined by a church are deliberately left open.

Adiaphora

The above shows that there are numerous topics on which evangelicals arrive at different convictions due to their theological convictions and their denominational character. Stott offers a helpful list of the so-called "adiaphora" (middle ground) among evangelicals:

1. Baptism: should we baptize only adult believers or their infants as well? And by immersion or affusion?
2. The Lord's supper: how should we define our sharing in the body and blood of Christ (1 Cor 10:16)?
3. Church government: should it be episcopal, presbyterian or congregationalist?
4. Worship: is there a place for liturgy, or should all public prayer be extempore? Can we combine the formal and the informal?
5. Charismata: are any not available today? And of those which are, which are the most important?
6. Women: which ministries are open to them and which are closed? What does masculine "headship" mean, and how does it apply today?
7. Ecumenism: what degree of involvement with non-evangelical churches is appropriate?
8. Old Testament prophecy: how are we to understand its fulfilment?

---

50. Cf. Ruth Rouse, "Voluntary Movements and the Changing Ecumenical Climate," in *A History of the Ecumenical Movement 1517–1948*, ed. Ruth Rouse and Stephen Neill (London: SPCK, 1967), 321.

9. Sanctification: what degree of holiness is possible for the people of God on earth?
10. The state: what should be the relations between church and state?
11. Mission: are "mission" and "evangelism" synonymous? What is the place of the quest for social justice?
12. Eschatology: how do we understand the tribulation, the rapture, the millennium, the parousia and our final destination?[51]

Summary

"Evangelicalism lacks a single pope, or a curia . . . there is no 'evangelical high court,' and thus ultimately no mechanism for settling the ongoing disputes about identity which have wracked the movement since its inceptions."[52] Yet there are good reasons to speak of an evangelical movement, which is primarily a trans-denominational and transnational piety movement that originated in the eighteenth and nineteenth centuries, and which was influenced as much by British puritanism and the Great Awakening as it was influenced by Pietism and the revival movements of previous centuries. Today the evangelical movement is a global movement with an estimated membership of 650 million believers; the vast majority of evangelicals now live in the Global South and no longer in the so-called Christian West. The theological definition of the term "evangelical" given here summarizes its foundational theological convictions. Evangelicals are united by these common theological convictions that transcend denominational and national borders.

Bibliography

Bebbington, David W. *Evangelicalism in Modern Britain. A History from the 1730s to the 1980s*. London: Unwin Hyman, 1989.

Hinkelmann, Frank. *Evangelikale in Deutschland, Österreich und der Schweiz. Ursprung, Bedeutung und Rezeption eines Begriffs*. Bonn: VKW, 2016.

Holmes, Steve R. "Evangelical Theology and Identity." Pages 23–36 in *21st Century Evangelicals. Reflections on Research by the Evangelical Alliance*. Edited by Greg Smith. Watford: Instant Apostle, 2015.

---

51. Stott, *Evangelical Truth*, 142–43.
52. Atherstone and Jones, "Evangelicals," 20.

Jung, Friedhelm. *Deutsche Evangelikale Bewegung. Grundzüge ihrer Geschichte und Theologie*. Bonn: VKW, 1994.

Larsen, Timothy. "Defining and Locating Evangelicalism." Pages 1–14 in *The Cambridge Companion to Evangelical Theology*. Edited by Timothy Larsen and Daniel J. Treier. Cambridge: Cambridge University Press, 2007.

McGrath, Alister. *Evangelicalism and the Future of Christianity*. London: Hodder & Stoughton, 1993.

Noll, Mark A. *The Rise of Evangelicalism. The Age of Edwards, Whitefield and the Wesleys. A History of Evangelicalism 1*. Leicester: IVP, 2004.

Packer, James I. *The Evangelical Anglican Identity Problem. An Analysis*. Oxford: Latimer House, 1978.

Reeves, Michael. *Gospel People. A Call for Evangelical Integrity*. Wheaton: Crossway Books, 2022.

Stott, John. *Evangelical Truth. A Personal Plea for Unity*. Leicester: IVP, 1999.

2

Evangelicals and the Authority of Scripture

Hetty Lalleman

What Are Evangelicals?

The word "evangelical" is used in many different ways and its use varies from country to country. For instance, in Germany the mainstream church is called "evangelisch" and churches like the Baptists are called "evangelisch-freikirchlich" or "free evangelical." Originally, "evangelisch" was understood as the German translation of the English term "evangelical." In the Netherlands many new, often more charismatic, more or less independent churches, call themselves "evangelical church." In this country, most Reformed/Calvinistic churches do not see themselves as evangelical because they identify the word "evangelical" with free churches and charismatic groups, whereas they stand in the long tradition that goes back to Calvin. In Great Britain, however, the evangelical movement has been around for a few centuries and it is described in David Bebbington's famous book *Evangelicalism in Modern Britain* (1989).[1] Bebbington writes about evangelicals in Britain:

> Evangelical religion is a popular Protestant movement that has existed in Britain since the 1730s. It is not to be equated with any single Christian denomination, for it influenced the existing churches during the eighteenth century and generated many more in subsequent years.[2]

---

[1]. David W. Bebbington, *Evangelicalism in Modern Britain: A History from the 1730s to the 1980s* (London: Unwin Hyman, 1989).

[2]. Bebbington, *Evangelicalism*, 1.

The word evangelical became "the standard description of the doctrines of ministers in the revival movement, whether inside or outside the Church of England."[3] Bebbington mentions several preachers from the early days of this revival movement, who are also known on the Continent, such as George Whitefield (converted in 1735) and Charles and John Wesley (1738).

Bebbington's book contains his famous, and often repeated, characterization of evangelicalism as a movement that believes in "*conversionism*, the belief that lives need to be changed; *activism*, the expression of the gospel in effort; *biblicism*, a particular regard for the Bible; and what may be called *crucicentrism*, a stress on the sacrifice of Christ on the cross. Together they form a quadrilateral of priorities that is the basis of Evangelicalism."[4] Famous though it is, many scholars think Bebbington's definition needs some broadening. Thus John R. W. Stott prefers a trinitarian focus, stating that conversion and evangelism are elaborations of the work of the Trinity. He suggests that "our evangelical priorities" are to be limited to "three, namely the revealing initiative of God the Father, the redeeming work of God the Son, and the transforming ministry of God the Holy Spirit."[5] Similarly, Kevin J. Vanhoozer comments on Bebbington's characterization that evangelical theology is "essentially *Trinity-centric*" and that it is unfortunate that in lists like Bebbington's only crucicentrism is mentioned.[6]

In this chapter I will assess the place of the Bible in the evangelical movement, which Bebbington characterizes as "biblicism." How do we regard the Bible, how do we use it in theology and how does it function in the church? In doing this I am heavily dependent on the wisdom of recent evangelical scholars and creedal statements. I have not tried to hide the fact that the original audience of my material was formed by the members of FEET, the Fellowship of European Evangelical Theologians. It is therefore fitting to begin with a few quotes from the great evangelical leader of the second half of the last century, Stott, who was also the founder of FEET.[7] Stott states: ". . . we evangelical people are first and foremost Bible people, affirming the great truths of revelation, inspiration and authority."[8] And he acknowledges the importance of Scripture

---

3. Bebbington, *Evangelicalism*, 1.

4. Bebbington, *Evangelicalism*, 3.

5. John Stott, *Evangelical Truth: A Personal Plea for Unity, Integrity and Faithfulness* (Carlisle: Langham Global Library, 2013), 11.

6. Kevin J. Vanhoozer and Daniel J. Treier, *Theology and the Mirror of Scripture: A Mere Evangelical Account* (London: Apollos, 2016), 52.

7. See below.

8. Stott, *Evangelical Truth*, 44.

as follows: "Because Scripture is the revelation of God by the inspiration of the Spirit, it has authority over us"[9] and by stating that "... supreme authority resides neither in the church, not in the individual, but in Christ and the biblical witness to him."[10] These words mean that the authority of the Bible cannot be replaced by the authority of the church (as in the Roman Catholic tradition) nor by the direct guidance of the Spirit illuminating individuals apart from the church or the Bible, nor by human ratio.

The Lausanne Covenant 1974 – Fifty Years Ago

A major influence on the development of evangelical practice in the twentieth century, the content of which is still being explored, is the Lausanne Covenant whose main author is Stott and which was published after the conference in the eponymous town in 1974. Although its influence on the theory and practice of evangelical mission and social action is tremendous, its balanced statements on the Bible have been heard less and deserve more attention.[11] Under the heading "The Authority and Power of the Bible," the Covenant describes the status and importance of the Bible as follows:

> We affirm the divine inspiration, truthfulness and authority of both Old and New Testament Scriptures in their entirety as the only written word of God, without error in all that it affirms, and the only infallible rule of faith and practice. We also affirm the power of God's word to accomplish his purpose of salvation. The message of the Bible is addressed to all men and women. For God's revelation in Christ and in Scripture is unchangeable. Through it the Holy Spirit still speaks today. He illumines the minds of God's people in every culture to perceive its truth freshly through their own eyes and thus discloses to the whole Church ever more of the many-colored wisdom of God.[12]

---

9. Stott, *Evangelical Truth*, 35.

10. Stott, *Evangelical Truth*, 20.

11. Cf. the absence of the Bible as subject in, for instance, Margunn Serigstad Dahle, Lars Dahle and Knud Jørgensen (eds), *The Lausanne Movement: A Range of Perspectives* (Regnum Edinburgh Centenary Series 22; Oxford: Regnum, 2014) and Robert A. Hunt, "The History of the Lausanne Movement, 1974–2010," *International Bulletin of Missionary Research* 35 (2011): 81–84.

12. See https://lausanne.org/statement/lausanne-covenant#the-authority-and-power-of-the-bible.

Subsequent Lausanne Statements

After Lausanne 1974, three further Lausanne Congresses have been held: in Manila (1989), in South Africa (2010) and in Seoul (2024). The second Lausanne Congress in Manila again concentrated on mission and evangelism, the church and the world, and less on the place of the Bible, although it definitely acknowledges the authority of Scripture.[13] The Lausanne Congress in South Africa resulted in a document entitled "The Cape Town Commitment: A Confession of Faith and a Call to Action." This Commitment has much more to say about the place of the Bible as the word of God and it expresses the authority of Scripture as follows:[14]

> WE LOVE GOD'S WORD
>
> We love God's Word in the Scriptures of the Old and New Testament . . . We receive the whole Bible as the Word of God, inspired by God's Spirit, spoken and written through human authors. We submit to it as supremely and uniquely authoritative, governing our belief and our behaviour. We testify to the power of God's Word to accomplish his purpose of salvation. We affirm that the Bible is the final written word of God, not surpassed by any further revelation, but we also rejoice that the Holy Spirit illumines the minds of God's people so that the Bible continues to speak God's truth in fresh ways to people in every culture.

The Cape Town Commitment emphasizes that the Bible tells an "overarching narrative," which

> provides our coherent biblical worldview and shapes our theology. At the centre of this story are the climactic saving events of the cross and resurrection of Christ which constitute the heart of the gospel.

It also emphasizes the truth of everything the Bible teaches:

> The whole Bible teaches us the whole counsel of God, the truth that God intends us to know. We submit to it as true and trustworthy in all it affirms, for it is the Word of the God who cannot lie and will not fail.

---

13. See https://lausanne.org/statement/the-manila-manifesto.
14. See https://lausanne.org/statement/ctcommitment, par. 6.

This paragraph speaks out against

> a dominant relativism that denies that any absolute truth exists or can be known. If we love the Bible, then we must rise to the defence of its truth claims. We must find fresh ways to articulate biblical authority in all cultures.

The document also claims that studying the Word of God should result in biblical living.

At this stage it is helpful to see how Christopher Wright, who worked closely with Stott and who is the main author of the Cape Town Commitment, explains the main differences between Lausanne 1974 and Cape Town 2010 with regard to the view of the authority of Scripture. Wright writes:

> When I was working on the Cape Town Commitment for Lausanne 2010, I wanted to do three main things somewhat differently from earlier evangelical statements of faith (including the 1974 Covenant):
> 1. To avoid too many abstract nouns and passive verbs and write in a more narrative style, with the governing idea being that our faith flows from covenantal love for God in response to what he has done for us;
> 2. to aim for a "whole Bible" approach, by including the Old Testament part of the "big story," and not just New Testament proof texts, as was common before;
> 3. to avoid the dichotomy of "doctrine" and "ethics" – by writing in such a way that the ethical response was an intrinsic part of the commitment of faith. ("If you love me, keep my commandments.") So the Bible section gives some primary reasons why we do love God's word, including the God the Bible reveals, the story it tells and the truth it reveals – but also, the life it demands.[15]

These words of Wright show that, in essence, the various Lausanne documents do not differ in their high view of Scripture, but that the Cape Town Commitment deliberately uses a more "personal" language, with words such as "our" and "love" ("We love God's Word"). It even phrases its view of Scripture in terms of a marriage: "We love the Bible as a bride loves her husband's letters, not for the paper they are, but for the person who speaks through them." As a result

---

15. Personal email from Wright to me, 25 February 2024.

the Cape Town statement sounds less rationalistic than its 1974 predecessor, which was also significantly shorter. Cape Town focuses on making the Bible relevant in different cultures and on the necessity to live according to its truth.

The 1974 Lausanne statement was clearly written in the time when modernism was prevalent, when facts and "objective" statements were relevant and people used "prooftexts" from the Bible to clarify their points of view in discussions with each other and non-believers. In the twenty-first century people are mainly interested in personal stories, in narratives that reveal what is in people's hearts and in their personal experiences. The Cape Town Commitment relates to this cultural trend by emphasizing the "overarching narrative" of the Bible. At the same time, it takes a stand against a cultural relativism which is averse to "objective truth" by emphasizing the Bible's truth and reliability and the reality of God acting in history.

In the 2024 Seoul document the introduction to the section on the Bible is as follows:

> A pillar of the Lausanne Movement from its inception has been an unwavering commitment to the Bible as God's authoritative word, the only rule of faith and practise for the church, its mission, and the Christian life. However, this high view of Scripture has not always produced the kind of faithful biblical interpretation that upholds the gospel and strengthens the mission of the church to make Christlike disciples. Worse, the often-conflicting interpretations threaten the church's effectiveness to bear witness to God's glory and gospel truth. Affirmations of a high view of Scripture therefore require a way of reading the Bible that is attentive to its historical, literary, and canonical contexts, illuminated by the Holy Spirit, and guided by the interpretive tradition of the church. The crucial affirmations about the Bible that the church needs most today concern not only the Bible's nature but its interpretation: how to read the Bible faithfully with the communion of saints of all times and places.[16]

Compared to the Cape Town Commitment, the Seoul Statement introduces an emphasis on the need to read the biblical texts both in their canonical context and "guided by the interpretive tradition of the church" of the past and the present. In section 22 the Seoul text says:

---

16. See https://lausanne.org/statement/the-seoul-statement, in the original document this passage is in italics.

> We affirm the necessary and positive role of tradition which passes on a continuity of faithful reading from past generations who were led by the same Spirit and believed in the same gospel of Jesus Christ through the same Scriptures. For an evangelical approach to interpretation to be faithful, it must honour this tradition and let it be a Spirit-enabled guide in our reading of the Bible.

And section 24 states:

> We therefore affirm the need for the global collaboration of all members of Christ's body, and for attention to the ancient creeds, confessions and ecclesial traditions. Reading and listening in the communion of saints, guided by the Spirit, across space and time, serve to keep local communities anchored to the faith that was once for all delivered to the saints. For the church to flourish in the coming decades, we must form ourselves into faithful Bible reading and listening communities that faithfully declare and display in many ways and places the one lordship of Christ. (Jude 3)

The two sections I just quoted seem to react against an individualistic reading of Scripture, disconnected from any church and from the tradition. Thus Seoul takes a counter-cultural stand in our overtly individualistic society, the influence of which is felt in all areas of society and church life. The Seoul Statement contains a strong emphasis on the "communion of saints" throughout the ages, including the ancient creeds. As we will see below, this is the same emphasis that we find in the work of Vanhoozer, who states that "sola scriptura" does not mean "solo scriptura."[17]

FEET

A positive side-effect of the Lausanne Congress on World Evangelization in 1974 was the founding of the Fellowship of European Evangelical Theologians (FEET). Howard Marshall, chair of FEET 1992–2002, transcribed for me a note from John Stott saying that after the Lausanne Congress a group of European theologians met elsewhere in Switzerland "and decided to arrange a European Evangelical Theological Conference." This took place in September 1976 and "FEET was duly constituted." Stott joined its Advisory Council. His note continues: "FEET was founded 'to promote evangelical theology in Europe in a

---

17. Kevin J. Vanhoozer, *Biblical Authority after Babel: Retrieving the Solas in the Spirit of Mere Protestant Christianity* (Grand Rapids: Brazos, 2018), 120–21, 129–30.

spirit of loyalty to the Bible. By this it seeks to serve the renewal of theological thinking in our churches."

There are of course many more evangelical theologians in Europe than those represented in FEET or in the European Evangelical Alliance (EEA),[18] but I have highlighted Stott's definition of the aim of FEET because it contains three important elements which may still help us today in reflecting on evangelical theology in general and on evangelicals and the authority of Scripture in particular. Thus, in this chapter I will discuss the three concepts Stott mentioned: loyalty to the Bible, the renewal of theological thinking and of our churches.

Loyalty to the Bible

The EEA expresses its view of Scripture as follows: "THE BIBLE (Holy Scripture) is the inspired and authoritative Word of God."[19] FEET has in its "basis of faith" the following statement about the Bible:

> The doctrinal basis of the Fellowship shall be the following doctrines of the Christian faith, based on the revelation of the triune God given in the Scriptures of the Old and New Testaments: The divine inspiration of Holy Scripture and its consequent entire trustworthiness and supreme authority in all matters of faith and conduct.[20]

It may strike some readers that neither organization uses the word inerrancy. To see if this term is dispensable, we will listen to various evangelical theologians who defend a high view of Scripture without recurrence to the term inerrancy. The first is Andrew McGowan, a long-standing member of FEET. In his book *The Divine Spiration of Scripture,* McGowan deals extensively with the discussion about inerrancy which is so prominent in the United States. He refers to FEET, which does not mention the inerrancy of the Bible, but "the entire trustworthiness and supreme authority" of Scripture. McGowan defines the "divine inspiration," or "divine spiration" of Scripture as he calls it, as follows:

---

18. The conference in Prague (2024), where this material was first presented, was a joint conference of FEET and the EEA.

19. EEA Vision and Mission Statement document 2017, www.europeanea.org/wp-content/uploads/2018/02/EEA_Vision_Values_Mission.pdf.

20. See https://feet-europe.org/about, par. 3.

> The doctrine of divine spiration[21] (inspiration) is the affirmation that at certain times and in certain places, God the Holy Spirit caused men [sic] to write books and his supervisory action was such that although these books are truly the work of human beings, they are also the Word of God. The church, under the guidance of the Holy Spirit, ultimately came to recognize that there are sixty-six books that God caused to be written in this way over a long period of time.[22]

Elsewhere McGowan states that God

> did not give us an inerrant autographical text, because he did not intend to do so. He gave us a text that reflects the humanity of its authors but that, at the same time, clearly evidences its origin in the divine speaking. Through the instrumentality of the Holy Spirit, God is perfectly able to use these Scriptures to accomplish his purposes.[23]

Instead of using the word "inerrancy," which reflects mainly an American discussion, McGowan uses the word "infallibility" as an "evangelical alternative."[24] He writes:

> In Europe, the word "infallibility" has generally been used by evangelicals rather than the word "inerrancy." It has the sense of purpose, meaning that God will infallibly achieve what he has determined to achieve in and through his Word.[25]

This explanation on the one hand emphasizes that the Bible is unlike any other book, whereas on the other hand it is clear that God worked with and through human beings. Evangelicals do not believe in a Bible that came immediately down from heaven. For us the human character of the Bible is not a weakness or a mistake, but it is the mode in which God chose to reveal himself throughout

---

21. A. T. B. McGowan, *The Divine Spiration of Scripture: Challenging evangelical perspectives* (Nottingham: Apollos, 2007), 41, states that "*theopneustos*" basically means that God "breathed out" his words and that human beings expressed what he wanted to say. Therefore he prefers the word "spiration" over "inspiration." The authors were guided by God, but the word "*theopneustos*" does not concentrate on this. Instead, the word emphasizes "the authority in God rather than in the Scriptures themselves. We might speak, then, of the authority of God speaking by his Spirit in and through the Scriptures" (43).
22. McGowan, *Divine Spiration*, 43.
23. McGowan, *Divine Spiration*, 124.
24. McGowan, *Divine Spiration*, 124.
25. McGowan, *Divine Spiration*, 162.

the ages. Moreover, his full and perfect revelation of himself came in the person of his Son Jesus Christ. We believe in Jesus as our Saviour and Lord, we believe in a person, not in a book. The Bible is not the "fourth person of the Trinity."

The Bible is the trustworthy record of what God has chosen to reveal to us in creation and history. God gave his words through human beings and we believe that what we received in these sixty-six books is enough to know everything we need in order to believe in God the Father, God the Son and God the Holy Spirit, and God's salvation work in history.

Through the work of the Holy Spirit these words, written by very diverse human beings over a long period of time, form a document with a remarkably coherent message: God the Creator loves people and wants to redeem people so that they may live to glorify his Name. God the Son made it possible for us to have free access to the Father by dying for our sins on the cross. He rose from the death and by his resurrection his authority was affirmed and his work of reconciliation completed. The Holy Spirit brings home this message to the hearts of human beings, who are lost without God.

The second is – again – John Stott, the creator of FEET. In *Evangelical Truth* he pleads for a "reverent" approach to Scripture as necessary for evangelicals. We need to study the Bible thoroughly in its historical and cultural context, but we also believe that the Bible "is unlike every other book."[26] We listen to the Bible in "humility," Stott states, so that the Word of God can correct us and lead us, through the illumination of the Holy Spirit.[27] As we saw above, Stott clearly emphasizes the authority of Scripture. However, he distances himself from American fundamentalism, which tends to view biblical inspiration as a "somewhat mechanical process, in which the human authors were passive and played no active role."[28]

The third is Hans Burger, who in a recent book emphasizes the importance of soteriology, or more precise Christology, in defining the position of Scripture. Christology should precede our discussions about Scripture, he argues: "Theologically, the *solus Christus* precedes the *sola Scriptura* . . ."[29] Burger states that "it is important to differentiate between the 'Word of God' and the 'word of God.'" Jesus Christ, the incarnation of God, is "the fulfilment, embodiment, and realization of what God has to say. In him, God communicates a fullness

---

26. Stott, *Evangelical Truth*, 34.
27. Stott, *Evangelical Truth*, 35.
28. Stott, *Evangelical Truth*, 6.
29. Hans Burger, *Jesus Christ, Hermeneutics, and Scripture: From Epistemology to Soteriology* (Eugene: Cascade, 2024), 4.

of life and knowledge . . . Accordingly, as the personal incarnation of what God has to say, he is the key to understanding the Scriptures."[30]

Burger argues that "the 'Word of God' as the second person of the Trinity can never be reduced to a book or a text. The Word of God is a person . . ."

> Christ precedes Scripture: because of Christ, we receive Scripture; in the light of Christ, we understand Scripture; what is in Christ, is communicated by Scripture; the role of Scripture in the Christian life and theology depends on Christ himself. This is not to play off Scripture against Jesus Christ: Christ is the Christ of the Scriptures. Only by remaining in the word can we remain in the Word.[31]

And a little later he continues:

> I understand the authority of Scripture as part of God's authority: the powerful, judging and sustaining authority of God's king, Jesus Christ. How Jesus Christ exercises his authority in our lives, is by uniting us with himself, giving us his Word and his Spirit.[32]

Burger here makes an important point which tends to be overlooked in the discussion about the authority of Scripture. The Bible is not a textbook with statements about faith, but a dynamic, living testimony of God's work in creation and history, culminating in the full revelation of God in Jesus Christ, the Word with a capital letter. And it is the Holy Spirit who brings this text to life.

Burger's Christocentric reading of the Bible makes a vital point about the impossibility of reading and studying Scripture outside the context of faith, the context of the church. By contrast, Matthieu Richelle, in his introduction to the Old Testament, or Hebrew Scriptures, as he calls them, explains the art of exegesis in great detail, with many useful practical examples to clarify the theory. However, his book offers no theological view or discussion of the value of the Bible. "I have written this book in an irenic, ecumenical, and interreligious spirit," Richelle states.[33] With Burger I think that it is not possible to read and interpret the Bible in a non-confessional, non-theological way without missing the essential meaning of the text. Yet many evangelical scholars regularly find themselves more or less caught between the academy with its

---

30. Burger, *Jesus Christ*, 212.
31. Burger, *Jesus Christ*, 213, with a general reference to Ingolf U. Dalferth.
32. Burger, *Jesus Christ*, 218.
33. Matthieu Richelle, *Interpreting Israel's Scriptures: A Practical Guide to the Exegesis of the Hebrew Bible / Old Testament* (Peabody: Hendrickson Academic, 2022), 5.

so-called "value-free, objective research" of the Bible on the one hand and the confession of the church and their personal conviction on the other hand.

A fourth scholar who does not use the term inerrancy is the American Kevin Vanhoozer, who discusses the three "solas" of the Reformers in depth in *Biblical Authority after Babel*. His chapter on *Sola Scriptura* emphasizes the authority of the Bible for the church and the believers. Vanhoozer states: "Scripture is *sufficient for everything for which it was divinely given* . . ." "Scripture is enough to learn Christ and the Christian life."[34]

Another non-European, Michael F. Bird, uses the words "veracity" and "divine truthfulness" to characterize the Bible: "God's Word is true as it correlates with God's intent for what Scripture is to achieve, because he is faithful to his world and his Word."[35] and "God's Word will never mislead us and it is a safe and reliable guide in all matters to which it speaks."[36]

Finally I return to Wright, who wrote:

> I believe 21st-century missiology will have to wrestle with a *doctrine of scripture* that moves beyond the way evangelical scholarship has tended to defend the inspiration and authority of the Bible with the concepts and methods of modernity itself, towards a more dynamic understanding of the authority and role of the Bible in a post-modern world. And I think this will be one of the biggest challenges for Christian theology in the 21st century, since there is no mission without the authority of Christ himself, and our access to that authority depends upon the Scriptures. *So, a major missiological task for Evangelical theology will be a fresh articulation of the authority of the Bible and its relation to Christ's authorization of our mission.*[37]

In a personal conversation Wright explained to me what he meant by these words.[38] The authority of Scripture provides the framework of our theological thinking, which is based on the authority of Christ, but Scripture does not

---

34. Vanhoozer, *Biblical Authority*, 114.

35. Michael F. Bird, "Inerrancy is not necessary for evangelicalism outside the USA," in *Five Views on Biblical Inerrancy*, ed. James R. A. Merrick and Stephen M. Garrett (Grand Rapids: Zondervan, 2013), 145–73, here 158.

36. Bird, "Inerrancy," 163.

37. Christopher J. H. Wright, "Christ and the Mosaic of Pluralisms," in *Global Missiology for the 21st Century: The Iguassu Dialogue*, ed. William D. Taylor (Grand Rapids: Baker, 2001), 71–99, here 76; italics original.

38. At the Tyndale Fellowship Conference, 4 July 2024.

deal with every subject we encounter in our world. So we need to define how to respond to current issues in line with and from within the framework of the authority of Christ.

At this point, we can conclude this survey of evangelical views by returning to Lausanne 2010. Evangelical identity can only be sustained by a high view of Scripture as it is phrased in the Cape Town Commitment:

> We submit to it [the Bible] as supremely and uniquely authoritative, governing our belief and our behaviour. We testify to the power of God's Word to accomplish his purpose of salvation. We affirm that the Bible is the final written word of God, not surpassed by any further revelation, but we also rejoice that the Holy Spirit illumines the minds of God's people so that the Bible continues to speak God's truth in fresh ways to people in every culture.[39]

The Importance of Creative Theological Thinking

For our second main point we move to the use of the Bible in theology. The constitution of FEET contains the following words about evangelical theology:

> The object of the Fellowship is the advancement of the Christian religion in the whole of Europe through the promotion and encouragement of the study of evangelical Christian theology in a spirit of loyalty to the Bible with a view to serving the renewal of theological thinking and fellowship, strengthening the work of the Churches, and promoting the task of theological research and education locally.[40]

Why is theology important to the evangelical movement? For evangelical academics, this question does not need answering. Of course theology is important. But in many evangelical churches, theology was, and probably still is, not only seen as irrelevant but also as a suspect activity. I can illustrate these concerns by sharing some of my own experiences as a theological student (from the age of 18).[41] I concentrate on the area of Old Testament studies, which gradually became my field of expertise. "There is a danger of losing your faith," I was warned when people heard I was going to study theology at a secular

---

39. See https://lausanne.org/statement/ctcommitment.
40. See https://feet-europe.org/about, par. 2.
41. At Utrecht State University, where the Department of Theology has since closed.

university. By God's grace, that did not happen. But the Bible, to me the most important book on earth, was certainly critically discussed and a variety of viewpoints was presented in the literature we had to read as students. Many of these views clashed with an evangelical view of Scripture.

When I started my theological studies, biblical scholarship at the university was solely focused on the historical-critical method, which was seen as *the* method to understand the message of the Bible. Although the beginnings of the historical-critical method lay in the distant past, few people in academia doubted its eternal truth and value. With hindsight most of us understand how this method was a child of the Enlightenment, emphasizing objective facts and evolution. Of the books I had to study for my master's degree, Hans-Joachim Kraus' *Geschichte der historisch-kritischen Erforschung des Alten Testaments* is a typical and unforgotten example.[42] In six hundred pages, Kraus gives a very detailed and thorough overview of the history of the historical-critical method, with Julius Wellhausen's *Prolegomena zur Geschichte Israels* (1878) producing results such as the division of the authorship of the Pentateuch in the four sources J, E, D and P. In fact, Wellhausen's source analysis was one of the first things I already learned as a new student. There was no discussion about these "certain outcomes of scholarship"; Wellhausen was right!

As an evangelical student, I missed two things in these and other theories about the origins of the Old Testament: first, a connection with the church. Worse, in fact several of these historical-critical scholars, such as Graf and Kuenen, had drifted away from the church. Second, there was no way to discover the *message* of a passage in Scripture. The splitting of a text into several sources resulted in "cut-and-paste" work, but it did not help to discover any meaning in the text, let alone to preach it in a church context.

Towards the end of my studies, around 1980, a new method was slowly making its appearance in the Netherlands: instead of *diachronic* exegesis (searching for historical layers in a text), *synchronic* exegesis developed. Narrative exegesis arrived on the scene. A Bible passage was read as a unity, and repetitions of words were seen as functional, not as proof of different sources. In fact, knowledge of the historical origins of the text was no longer regarded as essential for our understanding of the text. I remember my sense of relief that finally the Bible was read as we had it in front of us.

---

42. Hans-Joachim Kraus, *Geschichte der historisch-kritischen Erforschung des Alten Testaments* (Neukirchen-Vluyn: Neukirchener Verlag, 1956; 4th ed., 1988).

This chapter cannot begin to cover the developments in biblical research since then.[43] Just a comment on post-modern attempts to "deconstruct" the text, which in their extreme form result in losing the meaning of the text entirely. Marshall writes about deconstructionism: "There are some obvious examples of 'deconstruction' which hardly seem compatible with an acceptance of the Bible as Scripture and indeed seem to be bent on its destruction."[44]

Personal View

To me, the *value* of the historical-critical approach to biblical studies is that scholars tried to define the historical setting of biblical texts and to get as much information about their author(s) as possible. However, historical-critical scholars often linked the issue of the historicity or non-historicity, as was often the case, with the validity of a text. The *value* of the Bible was measured by its historicity: Joshua could not have conquered Jericho in the way the Bible describes it, so the story is not "true." In Wellhausen's view, later texts (like P) were more theologically advanced than what he saw as the "primitive" ones and therefore more valuable than older ones (like E).

Now we need to be careful here: not every Old Testament scholar who used (uses) the historical-critical method was (is) liberal in their theology. I have known many who were Christians and believed in the cross and the resurrection of Jesus Christ. And conversely, scholars who use narrative exegesis do not necessarily believe that anything happened in history. They may appreciate the beauty of Old Testament stories, but history is not their point of interest.[45] I am convinced that we need to find a balance, paying attention both to the historical background and the final form of the text.[46]

Personally, I have found much encouragement in meeting other theologians in the *evangelical* tradition who sought for alternatives to historical-critical scholarship. My participation in the conferences of the Tyndale Fellowship,

---

43. For a good, practical overview, see Wright, "Christ and the Mosaic," which explores the pros and cons of author-centred approaches (like the historical-critical method), text-centred approaches (like narrative exegesis) and reader-centred approaches (like feminist readings).

44. I. Howard Marshall, "Evangelicalism and Biblical Interpretation" in *The Futures of Evangelicalism*, ed. Craig Bartholomew, Robin Parry and Andrew West (Leicester: IVP, 2003, 100–23), here 120 fn 31.

45. An example is the Dutch Old Testament scholar Jan Fokkelman, whose presupposition is that the world of the text creates a world in itself but tells us nothing about historical reality or about a God who reveals himself. See, for example, J. P. Fokkelman, *Oog in oog met Jakob*, 2nd ed. (Zoetermeer: Meinema, 1999).

46. Cf. Marshall, "Evangelicalism," esp. 109–10.

experiencing the healthy climate of thorough academic research *and* a reverent view of the Bible, in a setting where people read the Scriptures and prayed together – these experiences have stimulated my development as a theologian in the evangelical tradition. I am thankful for them, as I am for FEET, a similar environment which combines prayer, Bible reading and thorough research. What evangelical biblical scholars have done and are still doing, in organizations such as the Tyndale Fellowship and FEET, is to engage critically with and evaluate the various methods used in biblical scholarship.[47] Yet they also try to offer creative ways of reading Scripture as the word of God. Here I can only give some examples of what, in my opinion, are important evangelical contributions to biblical scholarship. Old Testament commentaries by evangelical scholars often offer a combination of historical comments and a narrative approach. I have, for example, profited much from David Firth's commentaries, such as the technical volume on 1 and 2 Samuel and the popular one on Joshua.[48] In fact, the series in which these respective books appeared contain many valuable volumes.

Our Different Cultural and Historical Backgrounds

If we as evangelicals do not always see eye to eye on the above issues, it seems to me that this is caused (among other things) by the various settings and the different cultures in which we operate. I will try to illustrate this claim by means of some examples from the research on the Pentateuch and Isaiah.

A recently updated German evangelical introduction to the study of the Old Testament still very much interacts with the historical-critical debate, in which evangelicals define their own point of view by trying to be true to what the Bible itself says about the authorship of its books.[49] Thus the book defends the conservative position that the Book of Isaiah is a unity and that the eighth-century prophet was well equipped to prophesy about later times

---

47. An older result of such work is David W. Baker and Bill T. Arnold (eds), *The Face of Old Testament Studies. A Survey of Contemporary Approaches* (Grand Rapids: Baker Academic and Leicester: Apollos, 1999). See also David G. Firth and Jamie A. Grant (eds), *Words and the Word: Explorations in Biblical Interpretation and Literary Theory* (Nottingham: Apollos, 2008), which contains contributions by a range of evangelical scholars who accept biblical narratives as skilful compositions which nonetheless contain historical elements.

48. David G. Firth, *1 & 2 Samuel* (Apollos OTC; Nottingham: Apollos, 2009); David G. Firth, *The Message of Joshua* (The Bible Speaks Today; Nottingham: IVP, 2015). In the latter, Firth writes on p. 23: "... we can describe Joshua as a work of narrated history."

49. Manfred Dreytza, Walter Hilbrands and Hartmut Schmid, *Das Studium des Alten Testaments: Eine Einführung in die Methoden der Exegese*, 3rd ed. (Wuppertal: Brockhaus, 2024).

in chapters 40–66. That the context of the German evangelicals is shaped by the debate with mainstream German historical criticism is also visible in the recent introduction to the Old Testament edited by Hendrik Koorevaar and Walter Hilbrands, to which many evangelical scholars, mainly from Germany, Belgium and the Netherlands, contributed – including myself. The book offers a thorough alternative to traditional historical-critical, often German, research.[50]

A very different approach is found in the *Central and Eastern European Bible Commentary*, published by the same company as the present book.[51] The authors do not say much about authorship, but without much discussion state that the Pentateuch was written with the use of different sources and that its final form probably dates from the Persian period (538–333BC).[52] Likewise, Tamás Czövek writes: "Like all ancient books, Genesis was compiled by the final editor(s) after a long process. This was probably completed around 400 BC using various sources and traditions."[53] And about Isaiah we read:

> Chapters 1–39 are about the ministry of Isaiah, the son of Amoz, who lived and prophesied in Jerusalem in the second half of the eighth century BC. . . .
>
> The tone of chapters 40–55 is substantially different . . .
>
> The anonymous prophet who speaks in this section [40–55, HL] . . .

The third part of the book is attributed to "Third Isaiah."[54] These evangelical scholars in Central and Eastern Europe have been and are obviously working in a setting which is different from the German one and their concerns are different. The emphasis in the *Central and Eastern European Commentary* is clearly on the theological significance of the Bible for the life of the church and individual Christians. In this respect I see similarities with England, where the Tyndale Fellowship has stopped discussing the traditional, German, histori-

---

50. Walter Hilbrands and Hendrik J. Koorevaar (eds), *Einleitung in das Alte Testament. Ein historisch-kanonischer Ansatz*, 3rd ed. (Petzenkirchen: Verlag für Glaube, Theologie und Gemeinde, 2024).

51. Its general introduction states that "The commentary is written in the spirit of the Lausanne Covenant, with contributions reflecting a range of theological diversity in the context of Central and Eastern Europe." Corneliu Constantineanu (ed.), *Central and Eastern European Bible Commentary* (Carlisle: Langham Global Library, 2022), x.

52. Viktor Ber, "The Pentateuch" in *Central and Eastern European Bible Commentary*, ed. Corneliu Constantineanu (Carlisle: Langham Global Library, 2022), 1–3, here 1.

53. Tamás Czövek, "Genesis" in Constantineanu, *Bible Commentary*, 4–66, here 4.

54. Bohdan Hroboň and Tchavdar S. Hadjiev, "Isaiah" in Constantineanu, *Bible Commentary*, 699–753, here 699–700.

cal-critical scholarship. On the other hand, my impression is that evangelical theologians in France are closer to the situation and approach of the German evangelical theologians. As for the applications in the *Central and Eastern European Commentary*, written from a post-Communist perspective, they are excellent. The church in Western Europe can certainly learn a great deal from them. Think of the role of God's Word in the life of the church and the interaction with governments that are anti-Christian, as Western Europe is fast becoming a non-religious, secular society.

These differences in approach highlight the fact that as evangelicals we should listen to one another and hear each other out. We can hopefully agree that both interaction with contemporary exegetical models *and* contemporary applications of the biblical texts are needed.

In past and present times, many evangelicals have turned their back to the theological enterprise altogether – or never even started it in the first place. Alister McGrath addresses this indifference to academic theology among evangelicals, criticizing them for focusing on pragmatic issues and not on academic research.[55] Yet whereas McGrath blames pragmatism, elitism and the influence of fundamentalism, McGowan sees the separation between church and academy as a consequence of liberal theology.[56] However that may be, McGrath defines an evangelical theologian as not standing "above the community of faith, but someone who is deeply involved in its life of worship, prayer, adoration and evangelism. For evangelicalism, the theologian is one who is called to serve the community of faith from within."[57] As an example of a relevant evangelical theologian, who never had an academic or institutional status, but who through his thinking, speaking and writing shaped many in the evangelical world, McGrath mentions John Stott. He was a deep thinker, who addressed issues the churches were concerned about, thus bridging the gap between theology and the church. McGrath comments: "The best intellectuals may exist and operate outside the academy!"[58]

---

55. Alister E. McGrath, "Theology and the Futures of Evangelicalism," in *The Futures of Evangelicalism*, 15–39.

56. McGowan, *Spiration*, 13.

57. McGrath, "Theology," 26.

58. McGrath, "Theology," 2.

How Relevant is Our Theology?

Apart from shallow and anti-intellectual, evangelical thinking also tends to be individualistic. When an evangelical believer reads the Bible, the only question tends to be: "What does that text tell *me*, about myself?" I am arguing that we need solid, sound, evangelical theology for many reasons: to play our part as evangelicals in the academic world; to support intellectuals and academics in the church who work in other disciplines; to support our young people who are everywhere confronted with anti-Christian and secular views; and to equip the church with solid teaching in a secularized world. As for this last point, social media presents a huge variety of materials, not just conspiracy theories but also "new insights" into the origins of Christianity and the Bible which "the church has hidden" thus far but which are now at last revealed. I know from experience how easily church members are influenced by what they read online, as if what is presented there has more authority than the Bible itself.

The focus of contemporary theological discussions seems mainly to be on ethical issues, often dictated by secularization and political and societal developments. However, there is much more that evangelical theologians should address, such as the missionary role of the church, the essence of the gospel, and God's work in history, in the present time and in the future. I am convinced that evangelical theologians can make a difference in the church by teaching about God's worldwide mission, thus counterbalancing the individualism of Western, White and wealthy believers.

The Church

After the above, I only mention a few things about the relation between the church, theology and the Bible. I want to repeat the importance of the church as the context for reading and interpreting the Bible, as is clearly expressed in the Seoul Statement,[59] with the help of Vanhoozer, who makes the point that *sola scriptura* does not mean *solo scriptura*. "*Sola Scriptura* functions properly only in the context of the whole church."[60] The Protestant/evangelical belief in the priesthood of all believers runs the risk of believers reading the Bible only with an eye on themselves, directly applying the text to themselves as if they are the ultimate interpreter. Such individualism leads to "naïve biblicism."[61] Instead, we need the tradition of the church and the wisdom of human interpreters in

---

59. See above.
60. Vanhoozer, "Biblical Authority," 130.
61. Vanhoozer, "Biblical Authority," 145, also 120–21.

the past, who were led by the Holy Spirit, in order to interpret and understand Scripture well. We can think here of the Creed of Nicea and that of Chalcedon, and of church fathers such as Augustine, whose value was acknowledged by the Reformers.[62] The community of believers past and present is led by the Holy Spirit to read and interpret Scripture and to apply it to the life of the church. A biblical precedent for this approach is Acts 15, the story about the meeting in Jerusalem, where we read: "It seemed good to the Holy Spirit and to us . . ." (verse 28). The Spirit enlightens the hearts and minds of the church gathered together.[63] Another example of the need for non-individualistic interpretation of Scripture is the story of how Philip, sent by the Spirit, explains a passage from Isaiah to an Ethiopian eunuch. This man was able to read Scripture, he knew the language, he had been to Jerusalem, and yet he needed a helper to achieve understanding.[64]

Conclusion

With respect to the Bible as the authoritative word of God, evangelicals will need to own the contents of the various Lausanne statements since 1974 if we want to call ourselves truly "evangelical" theologians: the view that the whole Bible is the "Word of God, inspired by God's Spirit, spoken and written through human authors. We submit to it as supremely and uniquely authoritative, governing our believe and our behaviour."[65] We also do well to notice the transition from a modern to a postmodern approach to this issue in the Lausanne texts.

As evangelical scholars we need one another to deepen our understanding of the Scriptures. We need a thoroughly biblical theology, which equips us to teach the church and to broaden its understanding of God's work in the past, present and future. We read the Bible with the whole of the church past and present. This is a task we undertake in great thankfulness to God who gave us his words, which the Spirit brings to life. These Spirit-filled words help us to grow closer to Jesus Christ, our Lord and Saviour.

---

62. Vanhoozer, "Biblical Authority," 134–35.
63. Vanhoozer, "Biblical Authority," 130–31.
64. Vanhoozer, "Biblical Authority," 118, 124.
65. *Cape Town Commitment*, 2010.

Bibliography

Bebbington, D. W. *Evangelicalism in Modern Britain: A History from the 1730s to the 1980s*. London: Unwin Hyman, 1989.

Burger, Hans. *Jesus Christ, Hermeneutics, and Scripture: From Epistemology to Soteriology*. Eugene: Wipf and Stock, 2024.

Constantineanu, Corneliu, ed. *Central and Eastern European Bible Commentary*. Carlisle: Langham Global Library, 2022.

Firth, David G., and Jamie A. Grant. *Words and the Word: Explorations in Biblical Interpretation and Literary Theory*. Nottingham: Apollos/IVP, 2008.

Marshall, I. Howard. "Evangelicalism and Biblical Interpretation." Pages 100–23 in *The Futures of Evangelicalism*. Edited by Craig Bartholomew, Robin Parry and Andrew West. Leicester: IVP, 2003.

McGowan, Andrew. *The Divine Spiration of Scripture: Challenging Evangelical Perspectives*. Nottingham: Apollos/IVP, 2007.

Stott, John R. W. *Evangelical Truth* [1999]; now published together with the 2010 *Cape Town Commitment*. Carlisle: Langham Global Library, 2013.

Vanhoozer, Kevin J. *Biblical Authority after Babel: Retrieving the Solas in the Spirit of Mere Protestant Christianity*. Grand Rapids: Brazos, 2016.

Wright, Christopher J. H. "Christ and the Mosaic of Pluralisms." Pages 71–99 in *Global Missiology for the 21st Century: The Iguassu Dialogue*. Edited by William D. Taylor. Grand Rapids: Baker, 2001.

3

Evangelicals and the World

Joshua T. Searle

Introduction

As evangelicals our fundamental conviction is that *only* the crucified and risen Christ can bring salvation and healing to the world: there is "no other name under heaven . . . by which we must be saved" (Acts 4:12). Yet our commitment to Christ should not make us indifferent to the world. As an evangelical Christian, I am persuaded that it is God's intention that the gospel of Christ should penetrate every sphere of life and that God is just as concerned with those spheres that we arbitrarily designate as "secular" as he is with the "sacred" dimensions of life. The whole world belongs to God, who desires the salvation of all people, not just those who adhere to a Christian system of belief or who are affiliated to a church. God wills that "all people should be saved and come to a knowledge of the truth" (1 Tim 2:4).

Nevertheless, it must be admitted that this conviction has not been accepted by all evangelicals – either in history or in the present day. Many have extolled the apparent virtue of withdrawal from the world or been satisfied with a marginal existence. In some contexts where to be an evangelical meant a constant struggle for survival in the face of hostile state or church authorities, this posture could perhaps be justified on pragmatic grounds.[1] Yet the projection of this experience of marginalization to Europe today engenders, in my view, a false idealization of withdrawal from the world as the most faithful mode of Christian existence. For evangelicals who insist on withdrawing from the world and focusing solely on religious matters, no active mission in the

---

1. This isolationist position was typical of evangelical churches in the Soviet Union. See Walter Sawatsky, *Soviet Evangelicals since World War II* (Eugene: Wipf and Stock, 2007).

fullest sense is possible. All that remains is contentment with one's marginal status and living without the hope of making an impact on the world for the sake of the gospel. In such a condition, Christians are condemned to live passively and inertly, waiting for the "end times."

Against this passive separatist posture, my aim in this chapter is to encourage my fellow European evangelicals to recognize active engagement with the world not as a sign of compromise to the secular *Zeitgeist*. Rather, engagement with the world should be regarded as an expression of our identification with the incarnate Christ, who came, full of grace and truth, to make his dwelling in the world and to redeem it in the power of God's truth and love.[2] I am convinced that in our current European context – to which commentators have attached adjectives like "post-modern," "post-secular" and "post-Christendom" – the clear lines that used to divide the church from the world have now largely lost their meaning. It is no longer plausible to posit the church as an ideal concept that is separated from the world, since "the line between church and world passes right through each Christian heart."[3] The church, including evangelical churches, consists of people whose lives are shaped (either consciously or unconsciously) by powerful forces in contemporary culture, such as the media, arts and politics. It is essential for evangelicals to understand that "Christian lives are structured not only by the church and its narratives, but also by the world."[4]

Since their earliest origins to the present day, evangelicals have implicitly understood their embeddedness in their host cultures. Evangelicals are inevitably part of the broader societal landscape, both shaping and being shaped by the world around them. This chapter aims to elucidate the relationship between evangelicals and the world by addressing the complexities, challenges and opportunities that inevitably arise out of this dynamic interaction. I write as a missiologist whose basic concern is to equip the European evangelical community to witness effectively to the saving message of the gospel of Christ. Therefore, my interest in the evangelical–world relationship is not merely a

---

2. The missional significance of the doctrine of the incarnation has become increasingly emphasized in recent decades since the 1991 publication of David Bosch's monumental work, *Transforming Mission: Paradigm Shifts in Theology of Mission: 20th Anniversary Edition* (Maryknoll: Orbis, 2011). See also Pieter Verster, *The Triune God and Mission: A Theology of Mission* (Eugene: Wipf and Stock, 2022), 58–59.

3. James Wm. McClendon Jr., *Ethics: Systematic Theology Volume 1* (Nashville: Abingdon, 1986), 17.

4. Terrence W. Tilley, *Postmodern Theologies: The Challenge of Religious Diversity* (Maryknoll: Orbis, 1995), 147.

matter of historical or antiquarian interest. My aim is to develop a biblically informed approach to evangelical public engagement, drawing mainly on the Anabaptist vision and the Lausanne Covenant. The approach that I advocate seeks to persuade my fellow evangelicals not to follow prevailing social trends, but to discern the activity and purposes of God in the midst of cultural change and to participate intelligently and reflectively in these purposes in order to be able to reach more people with the gospel.

In the first part of the chapter I seek to clarify the key terms, "evangelicals" and "the world," in order to ensure that I employ them consistently. The main section of the chapter then begins with a critical summary of St Augustine's notion of the Two Cities, which has been foundational in shaping evangelical thinking about the church–world relationship. The chapter argues for prioritizing the kingdom of God as the central framework for evangelical interaction with the world, moving away from a church-focused approach. Building on this argument, in the next section the focus of the chapter shifts to the Lausanne Covenant. It is now over fifty years since the 1974 International Congress on World Evangelization in Lausanne, when the famous Lausanne Covenant was formulated. In my view, the Covenant retains its relevance today and continues to offer one of the most concise, judicious and insightful accounts of how evangelicals ought to engage with the world. Building on these insights, I conclude with a model of engagement with the contemporary world, which I offer for the consideration of my fellow European evangelicals as an interpretive tool for understanding how to apply our evangelical convictions towards the task of participating in the *missio Dei* in our European context today.

Clarification of the Key Terms

The initial difficulty encountered by anyone wishing to understand the relationship between "evangelicals" and the "world" is the wide variety of meanings attached to these contested terms. Thus, it is necessary to introduce certain general considerations of these key words before entering upon a closer examination of their interrelation.

Evangelicals

The term "evangelical" has been used in numerous contexts with varying degrees of accuracy to denote an emphasis on the forgiveness of sins through the saving power of the cross of Christ which constitutes the "good news"

(Greek *euangelion*).[5] In the early sixteenth century the word "evangelical" acquired a more specific meaning in relation to the Protestant Reformation. After Martin Luther, evangelicalism became associated with the belief that the saving work of Christ must be personally appropriated through a conscious decision to turn away from sin and towards new life in Christ. Justification of sin and salvation to eternal life were regarded as the unmerited rewards of repentant sinners for their faith in Christ, rather than the achievements of human effort or "good works." Moreover, evangelicalism imposed an obligation on its adherents not merely to appropriate the gift of salvation for themselves, but to share and proclaim the message of the availability of salvation in Christ.

Throughout its history, evangelicalism has undergone many renewals and transformations, such as the Pietist movement, the Great Awakenings, the fundamentalist–modernist controversy and, more recently, the charismatic movement. These transformations have shaped not only the self-identity of evangelicals, but also the position that evangelicals have taken towards the world.

It is important to note the diversity of evangelical faith and practice throughout the world. There are clearly huge cultural variations between the faith and practice of evangelical Christians in China, South Africa, Nigeria, Brazil, the United States of America and Germany. Even within these national contexts, there is considerable variation. In order to maintain a clear focus, this chapter will draw primarily on European expressions of evangelicalism.

The World

Within the semantic field of evangelicalism, there are certain words that are infused with substantial meaning and evoke strong and often contrasting reactions. One such word is "world." For some, "world" evokes a sphere of reality that is categorically opposed to the kingdom of God. For many evangelicals, the world is suffused with malevolent connotations and regarded as a byword for sin and debauchery. This association of the world with evil and immorality has its origins in the Bible, in which the depiction of a sinful and fallen world is widespread. This notion is particularly prevalent in the Johannine texts in which salvation history is interpreted as a struggle between Christ

---

5. The scope of this chapter precludes offering a summary of the many definitions of evangelicalism. For an authoritative account of evangelical identity, see Andrew Atherstone and David Ceri Jones, "Evangelicals and Evangelicalisms: Contested Identities," in *The Routledge Research Companion to the History of Evangelicalism*, ed. Atherstone and Ceri Jones (London: Routledge, 2018), 1–21.

and the world, which is ruled and enslaved by the evil one (John 16:33; 1 John 4:3; 5:19). When some evangelicals speak about, for example, "the one world church" or "the world's false religions" or "the apostate world order" or "the One World Government," the word "world" is used to signify an entity that is categorically opposed to God.[6]

Hence, in evangelical discourses the word "world" is often used to describe a system that is in conflict with the purposes of God. Moreover, to be opposed to the world meant, by implication, to be in harmony with God. In the social imaginary of evangelicals, the world is commonly regarded as that sphere in which "humanity and the spiritual world are organized over against God."[7] This perception was reinforced by Christ's famous rebuff to Pilate in John 18:36 ("my kingdom is not of this world") and by the Johannine notion of the kind of faith which "overcomes the world" (1 John 5:4). The apostle James was likewise adamant that "whosoever . . . wishes to be a friend of the world makes himself the enemy of God" (Jas 4:4). In an even more explicit denunciation of "the world," John declared that "the whole world lies in the power of the evil one" (1 John 5:19). Drawing from such verses, the Lausanne Covenant likewise states that, "'The world' means secular or Christ-less society, and 'worldliness' is any form of surrender to its values and ideologies."[8]

While the New Testament recognizes the fallen nature of the world and warns against conforming to its sinful patterns (Rom 12:2), it also portrays the world as the object of God's love, redemption and restoration through Christ. John 3:16 ("For God so loved the world that he gave his only Son, that whoever believes in him should not perish but have eternal life") famously emphasizes God's love for the world and the compassionate motivations that led the Father to send his Son into the world in order to bring salvation and eternal life to the world's inhabitants. Moreover, Romans 1:20 ("For his invisible attributes, namely, his eternal power and divine nature, have been clearly perceived, ever since the creation of the world, in the things that have been made. So they are without excuse") echoes the Psalms in highlighting the beauty and order of the world as a reflection of God's divine nature. The New Testament also expresses the ultimate hope that through the atoning sacrifice of Christ on the cross, God will bring all things in the world into a reconciled unity to himself

---

6. Joshua T. Searle, *The Scarlet Woman and the Red Hand: Evangelical Apocalyptic Belief in the Northern Ireland Troubles* (Eugene: Pickwick, 2014), 214–17.

7. This is how C. K. Barrett defined the word "world" in John 18:36. Barrett, *The Gospel according to John* (2nd ed.; London: SPCK, 1978), 536.

8. John R. W. Stott, *The Lausanne Covenant: Complete Text with Study Guide* (Peabody: Hendrickson, 2012), 78.

(Col 1:20; Eph 1:10). The tension between the contrasting depictions of the world as both the object of God's judgement and the focus of God's reconciling work in Christ is the hermeneutical key to understanding the wide variety of evangelical approaches to the world.

A Tale of Two Cities: The Influence of Augustine

The conflict between the world being both the focus of God's judgment and the arena of his redemption is evident in Augustine of Hippo's concept of the Two Cities, which has profoundly influenced how evangelicals view the secular world. The idea of the "City of God" (*civitas Dei*) and the "City of the World" (*civitas terrena*), as formulated by Augustine, posits an ontological distinction between the celestial realm and the terrestrial realm. The City of God represents the realm of the divine, embodying eternal truth, justice and love. Its citizens include those who are aligned with God's will and seek salvation and righteousness. By contrast, the City of the World represents the temporal, profane domain of sinful human beings and is characterized by sin, conflict, selflove and the lust for power (*libido dominandi*).[9] It encompasses human society with its imperfections, injustices and moral shortcomings which result from the Fall. Augustine saw this city as subject to decay and ultimately ordained for destruction.[10] He believed that the two cities coexist in the world, intertwined yet ultimately on divergent paths.[11] While believers are called to live in the City of the World and to engage "dispassionately" (*sine affectu*)[12] with temporal affairs, their ultimate allegiance should be to the City of God.

This model has had a profound influence on how evangelicals have understood their duties and responsibilities in relation to the world, most notably in the case of Martin Luther. Based on Augustine's distinction between the two cities, Luther believed that Christians should engage with the secular world while maintaining a primary allegiance to the spiritual realm.[13] He encouraged believers to carry out their vocations in the world diligently and ethically, viewing all aspects of life, whether secular or spiritual, as opportunities to serve

---

9. Veronica Roberts Ogle, *Politics and the Earthly City in Augustine's City of God* (Cambridge: Cambridge University Press, 2021), 53.

10. This worldly city, Augustine maintains (*City of God* XV.17), "has its beginning and end on earth, where there is no hope of anything beyond what can be seen in this world."

11. Augustine, *City of God* XIV.28.

12. Augustine, *City of God* IX.4.

13. Luther, "Temporal Authority: To What Extent It Should Be Obeyed," in *Luther: Selected Political Writings*, ed. J. M. Porter (Eugene: Wipf and Stock, 2003), 51–70.

God.[14] Luther's teachings on the priesthood of all believers endowed secular callings with a sacred purpose, since what mattered for salvation was not one's role in the church, but one's personal relationship with God.[15]

Augustine's distinction between the earthly and heavenly cities also had a profound impact on the thinking of John Calvin concerning Christian engagement with the secular world. Calvin developed a robust theology of vocation, social responsibility and active participation in earthly affairs, while maintaining a focus on the eternal values of the heavenly city.[16] He acknowledged that God's grace is not just available for the elect, but is also evident in the wider world. In his *Institutes of the Christian Religion*, Calvin discussed several aspects of God's providence that allowed for the maintenance of order and morality in society.[17] Subsequent Reformed theologians, such as Abraham Kuyper, Herman Bavinck and Louis Berkhof, expanded on Calvin's ideas and explicitly articulated the concept of common grace.[18] They differentiated between common grace and special grace, maintaining that common grace is God's general favour toward all humanity, whereas special grace is accessible only to the elect.[19]

Augustine and his evangelical successors, such as Luther and especially Calvin, thereby conferred a certain dignity on secular vocations. They encouraged Christians to take ownership of their faith and to participate actively in the world while maintaining their ultimate allegiance to God. Nevertheless, one problem with Augustine that was not completely resolved by the Reformation and which continues to beset evangelicals today has been a tendency to regard the church and the kingdom of God as practically synonymous.[20] Augustine's perspective inadvertently promotes ecclesiocentrism, suggesting that the church encompasses all aspects of God's kingdom and implying that the world, mired in sin, is impervious to theological interpretation in its own right. This view risks neglecting the entirety of God's redemptive work in the world, beyond the confines of the visible church. By focusing too much on

---

14. Jonathan D. Beeke, *Duplex Regnum Christi: Christ's Twofold Kingdom in Reformed Theology* (Leiden: Brill, 2020), 42–55.

15. Alister E. McGrath, *Christian History: An Introduction* (Oxford: Wiley, 2013), 169.

16. Matthew J. Tuininga, *Calvin's Political Theology and the Public Engagement of the Church: Christ's Two Kingdoms* (Cambridge: Cambridge University Press, 2017), 12.

17. Calvin, *Institutes* II.ii.13; II.vii.10; IV.xx.16; IV.x.15.

18. Malcolm B. Yarnell III, *The Formation of Christian Doctrine* (Nashville: B&H Academic, 2007), 49.

19. Charles Partee, *The Theology of John Calvin* (Louisville: Westminster John Knox, 2008), 117–18.

20. Joshua T. Searle, *Theology After Christendom: Forming Prophets for a Post-Christian World* (Eugene: Cascade, 2018), 126–30.

the church as the primary representation of the kingdom, many evangelicals have tended to downplay the significance of other spheres of life where God's redemptive work can be perceived. This has led to the misunderstanding that the kingdom is primarily an ecclesiastical reality, rather than a comprehensive domain where God's sovereignty is recognized and lived out in the world – including in domains that today are regarded as secular, such as culture, politics, law and economics.

Moreover, Augustine's distinction between the City of God and the City of the World introduced a problematic dualism into Christian thinking about the world that often painted the secular world in a negative light. Augustine's negative characterization of the City of the World has created the perception that the secular world is largely corrupt and devoid of inherent value or purpose.[21] This depiction of the world as inherently sinful and, by implication, of no inherent theological value, found powerful expression in the famous allegorical novel, *The Pilgrim's Progress*, by John Bunyan. With the aid of arresting images such as the "City of Destruction" and "Vanity Fair," Bunyan characterizes the world as a perilous and deceptive realm filled with temptations and distractions that challenge the pilgrim on their journey to salvation in the "Celestial City."[22]

By primarily associating the kingdom of God with the church and its visible manifestations, Augustine's theology laid the foundation of evangelical theology, which for centuries assumed that redemption was mainly an individual or ecclesiastical matter rather than a holistic transformation that includes society, culture and the world at large. This perspective has sometimes led evangelicals to overlook the potential for God's grace, justice and love being actively manifested in secular fields like politics, arts, education and social ethics. One way of remedying this problem is to reassert the central place of the kingdom of God in evangelical engagement with the secular world. A kingdom-focused theology encourages evangelicals to integrate their faith and everyday work by regarding vocations such as politics, the arts and education, not as trivial distractions, but as mission fields that offer opportunities to spread the gospel.

---

21. Mark Aloysius, *Arendt and Augustine A Pedagogy of Desiring and Thinking for Politics* (London: Taylor and Francis, 2024), 10.

22. John Bunyan, *The Pilgrim's Progress*, ed. Roger Sharrock (New York: Penguin, 1987), 79. See also N. H. Keeble "'Come ye out from among them, and be ye separate': Bunyan and the Writing of Dissent," in *The Oxford Handbook of John Bunyan*, ed. M. Davies and W. Owens (Oxford: Oxford University Press, 2018), 133–48.

The Kingdom of God as the Starting Point of Evangelical Engagement with the World

Some expressions of the evangelical tradition have reduced the gospel to a personal arrangement that God makes with individuals in order to guarantee the eternal security of individual souls.[23] As a result, it has been assumed that the saving work of Christ is concerned solely with the post-mortem destiny of individuals.[24] Salvation, from this perspective, is seen in terms of a transaction, rather than a personal transformation or world transfiguration. This interpretation regards the kingdom of God as a synonym for heaven, by which is meant a destination to which individual souls attain after death, rather than as the transfiguring presence of God in the present world.[25]

Against this limited view, other evangelicals have maintained that the gospel proclamation must be understood in terms of the kingdom of God, which has implications that extend to the whole world. The kingdom, according to this interpretation, is the sphere of God's reign in the world through which every aspect of creation and culture is redeemed and transfigured under the sovereign rule of Christ and the activity of the Holy Spirit.[26] The kingdom can be described as the meeting point between Christian vision and social reality.[27] The kingdom denotes not primarily a destination at which one arrives after death, but the healing of creation, involving the liberation of the entire cosmos from its bondage to the natural laws of death, decay and corruption (Rom 8:22–24; 1 Cor 15:53–54). Salvation is the universal emancipation of every aspect of life in accordance with the vision of God's coming kingdom.[28] Salvation is a holistic process of healing and restoration; the gospel penetrates the whole world with its redeeming light.[29] From this perspective, the essential message of Christianity concerns neither the forgiveness of personal sins (*pace* evangelical fundamentalism) nor the deliverance of society from structural

---

23. Scot McKnight, *The King Jesus Gospel: The Original Good News Revisited* (Grand Rapids: Zondervan, 2016).

24. Ross Clifford and Philip Johnson, *The Cross Is Not Enough: Living as Witnesses to the Resurrection* (Grand Rapids: Baker, 2012).

25. Dallas Willard criticises such approaches as "Gospels of Sin Management." See chapter 2 of Willard, *The Divine Conspiracy: Rediscovering Our Hidden Life in God* (San Francisco: Harper, 2009).

26. Nicholas Perrin, *The Kingdom of God: A Biblical Theology* (Grand Rapids: Zondervan, 2019).

27. Joshua T. Searle and Mykhailo N. Cherenkov, *A Future and a Hope: Mission, Theological Education and the Transformation of Post-Soviet Society* (Eugene: Wipf and Stock, 2014), 7.

28. McClendon, *Doctrine: Systematic Theology Volume 2* (Nashville: Abingdon, 1994), 427.

29. McClendon, *Ethics*, 230.

sin (*pace* liberal theology, social gospel, liberation theology, etc.). Rather, the gospel is a message concerning *the regeneration of life*, resulting from a new birth in the spirit (John 3:7; 2 Cor 5:17; 1 Pet 1:3; Jas 1:18).[30] The coming of God's kingdom propels the world towards its *telos* or ultimate destination. This ultimate objective denotes a condition of grace-filled freedom in which the world is covered with the glory of God and the kingdoms of this world are transfigured into a God-glorifying community of peace and justice.

"Deep and Costly Penetration of the World": The Lausanne Covenant and Holistic Gospel Witness

The scope of this kingdom-centred vision of salvation is not restricted to the church but encompasses the whole of God's creation. To use a fashionable word, this evangelistic vision of world salvation in Christ is "holistic" – in the sense that it addresses the spiritual, social, economic and physical needs of individuals and communities. This holistic approach to mission found powerful expression in the influential Lausanne Covenant of 1974, which insists that, "World evangelization requires the whole church to take the whole gospel to the whole world."[31] The Lausanne Covenant includes several expressions of regret at the false division between social concern and gospel proclamation that had, in its view, harmed the cause of the gospel in the world:

> We express penitence both for our neglect and for having sometimes regarded evangelism and social concern as mutually exclusive. Although reconciliation with other people is not reconciliation with God, nor is social action evangelism, nor is political liberation salvation, nevertheless we affirm that evangelism and sociopolitical involvement are both part of our Christian duty.[32]

The text even decries the exclusive focus on evangelism to the neglect of social responsibility as a "travesty of the gospel."[33] Against such a divided approach, the Lausanne Covenant makes a compelling biblical case for integral or holistic mission. The call to holistic witness, including serious evangelical engagement with the world is nowhere more apparent than in this clear statement:

---

30. Searle, *Theology After Christendom*, 116–17.
31. Stott, *Lausanne Covenant*, 51.
32. Stott, *Lausanne Covenant*, 45.
33. Stott, *Lausanne Covenant*, 46.

> We affirm that Christ sends his redeemed people into the world as the Father sent him, and that this calls for a similar deep and costly penetration of the world. We need to break out of our ecclesiastical ghettos and permeate non-Christian society.[34]

Lausanne emphasizes that the mission of the church is not solely about preaching the gospel for personal salvation but involves a comprehensive engagement with the whole person and society. The text further exhorts evangelicals to engage deeply with urgent social, cultural and ethical issues in the world, such as poverty, injustice and religious pluralism. Lausanne interprets such engagement as an indispensable means of witnessing to God's redemptive work in the world.[35]

The Lausanne Covenant develops this point by expanding the definition of "conversion" – a concept that has been central to the evangelical movement from its origins to the present day. Far from being merely a personal or individual matter regarding one's eternal destiny, true conversion, according to Lausanne, leads to a changed life that includes active participation in the mission of God: "Conversion involves at least three new relationships – obedience to Christ, membership of a church and responsible service to the world."[36] Challenging the idea that conversion can be divorced from social and ethical implications, the Lausanne Covenant affirms that evangelicals are called to express their faith through actions that reflect God's love and justice in the world. This expanded definition of conversion is predicated on an evangelical theology of world engagement which maintains that, "God is constantly present and active in his world."[37] Eschewing the narrow ecclesiocentrism of many expressions of evangelicalism, the Covenant states plainly that, "God is not just interested in the Church but in the world."[38]

Engaging with the world means not simply a unilateral proclamation of the gospel message from the church to the world, but also a willingness to listen and learn from the world. Evangelicals, according to Lausanne, need "to listen sensitively (to the world) in order to understand."[39] This points to an essential aspect of evangelical engagement with the world that has often been overlooked: namely, that the relationship between the church and the

---

34. Stott, *Lausanne Covenant*, 51.
35. Stott, *Lausanne Covenant*, 45, 49, 63.
36. Stott, *Lausanne Covenant*, 43–44.
37. Stott, *Lausanne Covenant*, 85.
38. Stott, *Lausanne Covenant*, 47.
39. Stott, *Lausanne Covenant*, 39.

world is not one-sided, but interactive and dynamic. The church's mission to the world is a movement in two directions.[40] The church ceases to be a holy place that is rigidly separated from the secular world. Mission is not about reaching out from religious sanctuaries in order to grab a few converts into the church; it is, rather, a dangerous and costly call to vulnerable, sacrificial living in order to transform the kingdoms of this world into the kingdom of God after the pattern of Revelation 11:15: "The kingdoms of this world are become the kingdoms of our Lord, and of his Christ; and he shall reign for ever and ever." From this perspective, mission signifies not merely a movement from the church into the world, but also a constant Christian presence in the world. This presence is expressed not only through evangelistic activity, but also through the sacrament of living. Mission is not only a course of action; it is also a way of thinking and being and implies a critical disposition towards the world and a creative awareness of the presence of God's kingdom in the world. God's mission in the world is expressed in imperatives to the Christian community to proclaim and encourage, send and convert, to go and teach, as well as in non-binding forms, such as being, living, sympathizing, loving, salting and shining the light of Christ in places of darkness.[41]

Dangers of Evangelical Engagement with the World: Avoiding Politicization

The Lausanne Covenant initiated a shift in mission from a narrow focus on individual conversions to a broader emphasis on holistic transformation and a willingness to engage in deep dialogue with the world. In my view, this represents an important and commendable development. Nevertheless, while acclaiming this necessary expansion of the scope of evangelical mission, it is essential to retain a clear focus on the proclamation of the gospel, as it was originally proclaimed by Christ. We must avoid the danger, identified by Lesslie Newbigin, of reshaping mission into nothing more than "action for the humanization in the secular life of the world."[42] It is also essential to avoid the absorption of evangelicalism into political agendas. While maintaining the

---

40. Searle, *Theology After Christendom*, 92.
41. Searle, *Theology After Christendom*, 93.
42. Lesslie Newbigin, *The Open Secret: An Introduction to the Theology of Mission* (London: SPCK, 1978), 10. David Bosch criticised this one-sided emphasis on socio-political transformation, claiming that such an approach to mission produced a "diluted gospel." See Martin Reppenhagen and Darrell L. Guder, "The Continuing Transformation of Mission: David J. Bosch's Living Legacy: 1991–2011," in Bosch, *Transforming Mission*, 535–36.

hope for the transformation of the world in the power of God's truth, evangelicals in Europe must ensure that they do not allow the church to degenerate into a vehicle for worldly political activism.

In their engagement with the world, it is essential that evangelicals respect the freedom and dignity of all people, especially those outside the church. Since the gospel, including gospel morality, cannot be imposed by political or religious authorities, evangelicals should reject any attempt by governments to co-opt them to their political agendas – even and especially when such governments claim to be "Christian." Unfortunately, there are several examples in the world today of evangelical Christians working in collusion with authoritarian political regimes to impose Christian moral norms on society by passing legislation that discriminates against minorities on grounds such as gender, race, ethnicity, religion or sexual orientation.[43]

Throughout history evangelicals have often been targeted by oppressive decrees imposed by Christian legislators who equated dissent with blasphemy and nonconformity with treason.[44] In the sphere of politics and religion, Christianity, without freedom and dignity, is emptied of its Christian content and assumes dehumanizing and unjust forms of domination and control. All forms of theocracy are hostile to evangelical convictions concerning the freedom and dignity of all human beings. Evangelicals should be especially suspicious of so-called "Christian" state authorities that violate people's freedom with supposedly good intentions under the banner of maintaining "Christian values" or defending "Christian civilization." Governments and churches that have attempted to "Christianize" the population top-down have not only violated people's dignity and freedom, but have also proved ineffective and even counter-productive. Worldly activism (for example, political lobbying on contentious issues, such as abortion, migration, transgenderism or support for Israel or Palestine) is no substitute for costly witness. Evangelicals should not seek to

---

43. This attempt to impose gospel morality through the exercise of political power could be referred to as the "Constantinian temptation." John Howard Yoder warned against this temptation. See Yoder, *The Priestly Kingdom: Social Ethics as Gospel* (Notre Dame: University of Notre Dame Press, 1984), 142–43. The scope of this chapter does not allow a discussion of examples of state authorities co-opting evangelicals to serve their ideological purposes. For more on this, see David P. Gushee, *Defending Democracy from Its Christian Enemies* (Grand Rapids: Eerdmans, 2023).

44. See, for example, Karen Smith, "Baptists," in *The Oxford History of Protestant Dissenting Traditions, Volume II: The Long Eighteenth Century c.1689–c.1828*, ed. Andrew C. Thompson (Oxford: Oxford University Press, 2018), 54–76.

take sides in the contemporary "culture wars" but should offer an alternative to the polarized thinking that characterizes social and political life.[45]

This alternative consists not in the acquisition of political power, but in the prophetic witness to the gospel of freedom. In today's secularized European societies the question we should ask is, "how does the church witness to the rule of God without itself ruling?"[46] Christ calls his church not to establish a theocracy but to become "a community of *voluntary* commitment, willing for the sake of its calling to take upon itself the hostility of the given society."[47] As evangelicals, the fruitfulness of our witness to Christ depends not on our political status or power, but on the power of the gospel. Our witness to the world is necessarily precarious, since we will inevitably be in the minority. This is the assumption throughout the New Testament. As missiologist Stefan Paas notes,

> The New Testament images of the church do not convey a community that is destined to somehow rule the world . . . but a community that leads a precarious life within the world.[48]

Christ's command to his disciples was to preach the gospel and to build the kingdom through love and service, rather than through force and domination. In Christ, God reveals himself to the world not in power and authority but in freedom and sacrificial love. The gospel summons people to a free response to the initiatives of divine grace.

The Need for Critical Engagement with the World

Without being actively hostile to the state, evangelical involvement with political power should always be viewed from a hermeneutic of suspicion. Suspicion towards political power, however, does not imply a commitment to a sectarian ethic, which assumes that withdrawal from the world and retreat into the

---

45. Russell D. Moore, *Onward: Engaging the Culture Without Losing the Gospel* (Nashville: B&H, 2015), 12–13.

46. This is a central question in Nigel G. Wright, *Disavowing Constantine: Mission, Church, and the Social Order in the Theologies of John Howard Yoder and Jürgen Moltmann* (Eugene: Wipf and Stock, 2007).

47. John Howard Yoder, *The Politics of Jesus: Vicit Agnus Noster* (Grand Rapids: Eerdmans, 1980), 45. No reference to Yoder can go without comment in the light of his extensive sexual abuse of women as documented in Rachel Waltner Goossen, "Defanging the Beast: Mennonite Responses to John Howard Yoder's Sexual Abuse," *Mennonite Quarterly Review* 89 (2015): 7–80. Nevertheless, his works currently remain in the scholarly domain and are cited here in full recognition of the problematic nature of such citations.

48. Stefan Paas, *Church Planting in the Secular West Learning from the European Experience* (Grand Rapids: Eerdmans, 2016), 116.

church is the only way to preserve the integrity of one's faith.[49] In the emerging postmodern society the clearly demarcated lines that used to divide the church from the world have lost their meaning, which makes the sectarian posture of complete withdrawal not only undesirable, but even untenable.[50] A free and faithful approach to Christian witness involves not uncritical rejection of the world, but critical engagement with the world.[51] This posture will provide a powerful missional stimulus for the church's participation in the great commission. When this missional impulse is lacking, the power of the gospel can be distorted into a form of complacency and private piety that reduces the good news of the coming kingdom to a self-help aid for personal comfort and worldly happiness.

Evangelical missional engagement with the world must have a robust biblical-theological basis. Specifically, Christian engagement with the contemporary world must be informed by a theological perspective on the kingdom of God and its righteousness. The gospel message is, therefore, a free invitation to participate in the dawning reality of the new reign of freedom, which has been inaugurated by the incarnation of Christ and his death and resurrection. Through the Holy Spirit, Christ is creating a new community of freedom and truth which is set apart from the falsehoods that govern life in the world. The community that Christ is building in the world is one in which the humble are exalted, the poor are dignified, and the values of solidarity, hospitality and justice pervade all relationships. Jesus's proclamation of the availability of the kingdom of God is a call to live in the awareness of another world, where the values that govern relationships are radically antithetical to the social norms that prevail in this world.[52]

In order to engage effectively with the world, European evangelicals require a theology that deconstructs the false dichotomies of church versus world and sacred versus secular. This theology informs our public engagement and transforms our practice by helping us to see that the gospel takes root not just in the religious sphere, but in the life of the world, often in the most surprising and unexpected places. In our engagement with the world, we aim not for the

---

49. I have written about this issue in relation to evangelical communities in the former USSR in chapter 5 of my co-authored book (with Mykhailo Cherenkov), *A Future and a Hope*, 100–34.

50. McClendon, *Ethics*, 17.

51. See chapter 4 of Searle, *Theology After Christendom*, in which I argue for a reformulation of mission away from evangelization and towards solidarity.

52. Dallas Willard and Don Simpson, *Revolution of Character: Discovering Christ's Pattern for Spiritual Transformation* (Nottingham: IVP, 2006), 9.

Christianization of society, but rather for the socialization of gospel, meaning the interfusion of gospel values and social realities. This does not involve the accommodation of the gospel to social conventions; rather, it involves the penetration of the gospel into the world and the transfiguration of every aspect of human life.

Crucially, the success of this kind of mission is expressed not in the triumph of evangelical Christianity over society, but in compassion for and involvement in society. Solidarity with the world, not numerical conversions to church subcultures, is what matters. What is preserved here is the social responsibility and the desire to influence and change, but without the naive optimism of Christendom-laden assumptions concerning the top-down Christianization of society.[53] The guiding principle of our engagement with the world should be, as Elaine Graham maintains, the "salvation of the world, and not the survival of the Church."[54] This approach, which prioritizes solidarity with the godforsaken world, requires "a deep sympathy with the integrity of the godless and a compassionate identification with the godforsaken."[55]

A proper understanding of solidarity helps us to perceive that the sectarian division between the church and the world was based not on the biblical principle of incarnational mission, but on the secular principle of the division of life into clearly demarcated spheres of influence. The ethic of separation from the world was motivated by fear, including the fear of sin and fear of the supposed compromises to the integrity of the gospel that would ensue unless the church retained its sacramental character and institutional identity. Any theological perspective that is determined by fear cannot be truly theological, since the animating principle of theology is love and "there is no fear in love, because perfect love casts out fear" (1 John 4:18). Moving beyond fear, evangelical engagement with the world must be informed by the hope of the gospel and the desire to share this hope with those who have not yet received this good news.

Conclusion

I believe that the time has come for bold and innovative thinking about the way European evangelicals relate to the world. In the present condition of politi-

---

53. Joshua T. Searle, *Church Without Walls: Post-Soviet Baptists after the Ukrainian Revolution* (Oxford: Whitley, 2016).

54. Elaine Graham, *Between a Rock and a Hard Place: Public Theology in a Post-Secular Age* (London: SCM, 2013), 223.

55. Graham, *Rock and Hard Place*, 232.

cal instability and social disruption it is becoming increasingly apparent that a new vision of Christian engagement is required for these changing times. There is still hope for the church in the secularized societies of Europe, but the aims and structures of church must be subordinated to the kingdom of God. I believe that in order for Christian witness to the world to have a meaningful impact in today's secular society, we need to regard Christianity not as a religion of private salvation but as a movement of universal compassion. My hope is that European evangelicals will be the spearhead of a new movement within global Christianity that learns to recognize the work of Christ in the world today, and, second, to participate with Christ in the power of the Holy Spirit to accomplish the Father's purposes in the world.

This world-orientation requires a coming of age of evangelical theology. Christianity awaits its renewal in the new spiritual configurations of the emerging postmodern and post-Christendom context of European society. Theologians have a vital role to play in this process of renewal, but they must recognize that their task lies not in the preservation of the church, but in the striving for the realization of the kingdom of God as a visible reality in the world. Our aim should be, in the words of Dietrich Bonhoeffer, nothing less than the "realization in our world of the divine and cosmic reality which is given in Christ."[56] In order to realize the gift of Christ's presence in the world, there needs to be a new awareness of the transforming power of the gospel that extends to every sphere of life. Fostering this kind of awareness is how I envisage the task of evangelical missiology in Europe today.

The implications of this shift for the church are significant. The church must be re-imagined in order to ensure its faithfulness to the gospel in these momentous times of cultural change. The church in post-Christendom Europe can become a powerful movement of the gospel, but only if the church is willing to undergo radical transformation, which involves a reorientation from separation to solidarity. At their best, churches are inclusive and boundary-pushing communities that offer a foretaste of heaven on earth. They are the emancipatory communities in which people are released from the iron cage of bureaucratization that regulates life in the world. Churches engage the world by offering a compelling alternative to the coldness and formality that govern inter-human relations in the world. Churches, by contrast, should be communities of warmth, compassion, hospitality and welcome, where strangers and outsiders feel at home and where humane values of dignity and care are

---

56. Bonhoeffer, quoted in Larry L. Rasmussen, *Dietrich Bonhoeffer: Reality and Resistance* (Louisville: Westminster John Knox, 2005), 216.

recognized and affirmed. Creativity should be valued over productivity and meaning prized over utility.

Church, in the ideal scenario, is the site of life in which God manifests himself among his people. The church is not synonymous with the kingdom, but if churches express their common life in *koinonia* (compassionate fellowship) towards each other and in *agape* (sacrificial love) towards the world, then such churches can rightly claim to be beachheads of the kingdom – as places "in which the reign of God begins to be made manifest here and now."[57] Instead of separation and isolation, the evangelical churches of Europe will become a catalyst for a gospel movement of Christian compassion that expresses itself in a new vision of church without walls. And God will delight in this.

Bibliography

Bosch, David. *Transforming Mission: Paradigm Shifts in Theology of Mission [1991] 20th Anniversary Edition*. Maryknoll: Orbis, 2011.

Clifford, Ross, and Philip Johnson. *The Cross Is Not Enough: Living as Witnesses to the Resurrection*. Grand Rapids: Baker, 2012.

Graham, Elaine. *Between a Rock and a Hard Place: Public Theology in a Post-Secular Age*. London: SCM, 2013.

Moore, Russell D. *Onward: Engaging the Culture Without Losing the Gospel*. Nashville: B&H, 2015.

Newbigin, Lesslie. *The Open Secret: An Introduction to the Theology of Mission*. London: SPCK, 1978.

Paas, Stefan. *Church Planting in the Secular West Learning from the European Experience*. Grand Rapids: Eerdmans, 2016.

Searle, Joshua T. *Theology After Christendom: Forming Prophets for a Post-Christian World*. Eugene: Cascade, 2018.

Stott, John R. W. *The Lausanne Covenant: Complete Text with Study Guide*. Peabody: Hendrickson, 2012.

Willard, Dallas. *The Divine Conspiracy: Rediscovering Our Hidden Life in God*. San Francisco: Harper, 2009.

Wright, Nigel G. *Disavowing Constantine: Mission, Church, and the Social Order in the Theologies of John Howard Yoder and Jürgen Moltmann*. Eugene: Wipf and Stock, 2007.

Yoder, John Howard. *The Priestly Kingdom: Social Ethics as Gospel*. Notre Dame: University of Notre Dame Press, 1984.

---

57. Glen H. Stassen and David P. Gushee, *Kingdom Ethics: Following Jesus in Contemporary Context* (Downers Grove: IVP, 2003), 230.

4

Evangelical Identity and Orthodox Perception

A Romanian Contextual Analysis

Cristian Sonea

Introduction

This chapter offers a historical examination of the perspective of the Orthodox Church on evangelicals in Romania. The analysis is based on contributions from key Orthodox figures such as Bishop Grigorie Comșa, Grigorie Leu and Petru Deheleanu. In addition, the research incorporates the insights of Petru I. David, a well-known figure in Romanian Orthodox theology whose influence extended before and after 1989. The chapter also refers to the forthcoming *Handbook of Orthodox Missiology*, Volume 2, which will provide a contemporary context and continuity in the study of Orthodox missiology and its approach to the evangelical movement. I will outline the evolution of Orthodox attitudes towards evangelicals, tracing the historical and theological developments that have shaped these perceptions over time.

In the Romanian context, evangelicals are often grouped under the term "Neo-Protestants," a designation that includes Pentecostals, Baptists, Brethren and others. This term, however, has its roots in the Communist era and carries certain connotations that may not fully capture the diversity and theological richness of evangelicalism as understood globally. From the Orthodox perspective, evangelicalism is seen as a broad movement within Protestant Christianity that emerged after the Reformation and is characterized by specific beliefs and practices. The term "evangelical" itself, derived from the English "evangelicalism," is preferred by some Romanian religious scholars over "Neo-Protestant" to better describe the post-Reformation Christian communities connected to both the Magisterial Reformation and the Radical Reformation.

Historically, the Orthodox Church in Romania has viewed the emergence of evangelical groups with suspicion, often perceiving them as agents of proselytism aiming to convert Orthodox Christians to a different faith. This perspective is deeply rooted in the Orthodox understanding of the church as the one true body of Christ, where any division or new movement is seen as a potential threat to the unity and purity of the faith.

Evangelicals, on the other hand, have often regarded the Orthodox Church as overly ritualistic and even non-Christian due to its emphasis on tradition, sacraments and veneration of saints. This mutual distrust was exacerbated during the Communist era, when both groups faced persecution but were often pitted against each other by the state in order to prevent a unified Christian front against the regime.

Nineteenth Century: The Mission for Autocephaly Recognition

In the nineteenth century, following the liberation of the Balkan states from Ottoman rule with the help of the Tsarist Empire, the Romanian Orthodox Church faced the dual challenge of asserting its autocephaly and establishing its identity within the newly formed national states. As Romania, along with other Balkan countries, sought recognition for the Orthodox Church, tensions arose with the Ecumenical Patriarchate. The quest of the Romanian Orthodox Church for autocephaly culminated in its recognition in 1885, a pivotal moment that shaped its theological and missiological orientation. During this period, the primary mission of the Church was one of recognition, striving to consolidate its place in the pan-Orthodox world and under the new political regimes.[1]

The "Sectarian" Challenge

Early in the twentieth century evangelical movements began to establish themselves in Romania. These movements, often referred to as "sects" by the

---

1. Ioan Ică Jr., "The Modern and Contemporay Orthodox Theology. Moments, Figures, Development, Interpretation," in *Orthodox Theology in the 20th Century and Early 21st Century: A Romanian Orthodox Perspective*, ed. Viorel Ioniță (București: Basilica, 2013), 21.

Orthodox Church, were viewed with suspicion and hostility. The response of the Church to this growing challenge was the development of a defensive missiology, heavily influenced by what came to be known as "sectology." This approach was characterized by a polemical stance against evangelicals, with efforts concentrated on protecting Orthodox believers from what were perceived as heterodox influences.

The "Great Union" of 1918 is a cornerstone in Romanian history, marking the unification of Transylvania, Banat, Crișana and Maramureș with the Kingdom of Romania. This historic moment was not only a political achievement, but also one deeply rooted in the cultural and spiritual fabric of the Romanian nation. During this period, the Orthodox Church and the Greek Catholic Church had crucial roles. Both religious institutions were seen as guardians of the Romanian identity, which was inextricably linked to the Romanian language, ethnicity and Eastern Christian faith. The Orthodox Church, in particular, was seen as the cornerstone of Romanian national identity, especially in the context of the centuries-long struggle against foreign domination and cultural assimilation by neighbouring empires.

The Greek Catholic Church, although in communion with Rome, shared the same Eastern rites and liturgical traditions as the Orthodox Church, making it a significant cultural and national force in Transylvania. The Greek Catholic clergy and faithful played an active role in the national movement that led to unification in 1918. Their involvement was driven by a desire to preserve and assert Romanian identity in a region where Romanian culture and faith had often been suppressed.

The perception of evangelical missions as a threat to Romanian identity stems from this close link between faith and nationality. Evangelical groups were often associated with Western influences and were seen as attempts to undermine the fundamental elements of the Romanian nation – language, ethnicity and Eastern Christian faith. For many Romanians, especially those involved in the national movement, these missions were not only religious in nature but were also perceived as cultural and political encroachments that could weaken the cohesion of the Romanian people.

A key figure in this period was bishop Grigorie Comșa of Arad (1925–1935), who was instrumental in combating the spread of evangelical groups.[2] Comșa organized extensive anti-sectarian missions, particularly in Transylvania, a region with a diverse religious landscape. He published anti-sectarian

---

2. Grigorie Comșa, *Noul ghid pentru combaterea și cunoașterea sectelor religioase* (Arad: Tiparul Tipografiei Diecezane, 1927).

sermons, brochures and articles in Orthodox publications such as *Telegraful Român* and *Revista Teologică* of Sibiu, as well as *Biserica și Școala* of Arad. Grigorie Leu's book on confessions and sects laid the groundwork for the anti-sectarian studies, providing a historical and missionary perspective on the various religious groups deemed to be "sects" by the Orthodox Church.[3] After the war this work was further developed by Petru Deheleanu, a professor at the Theological Academy of Arad, who in 1948 wrote the *Manual de Sectologie (Handbook of Sectology)*.[4] His handbook, which was considered the most comprehensive of its time, employed a methodical approach based on "thesis, antithesis and synthesis" to address the challenges posed by these groups and became a cornerstone in Orthodox anti-sectarian literature.

According to Roland Clark, the interwar period was a period of deep-seated suspicion and opposition from the side of the Orthodox Church. While overseeing the spiritual life of its adherents, it was apprehensive about the rise of evangelical groups, often labelled as "Repenters." These groups were viewed as a disruptive influence on the traditional religious and social order.[5]

Fascism, "Sectology," Survival, Modernity

The interwar period saw the rise of the Iron Guard, a fascist movement that sought to intertwine Eastern Orthodox Christianity with an ultra-nationalistic, anti-Semitic and anti-Communist ideology. While the Iron Guard presented itself as a defender of Orthodoxy, its relationship with the Church hierarchy was fraught with tension. The movement often attacked the Church leadership, labelling them as the "satanic generation" because of their perceived compromises.[6] People such as Vasile Ispir, who criticized the Iron Guard's misuse of Christian symbols for political ends, became embroiled in these conflicts. During the period of Iron Guard government, Romanian nationalism and Orthodoxy were so closely interconnected that even being Greek Catholic raised questions about one's nationality. Only being Orthodox was seen as synonymous with being Romanian. Thus, when asked if a Greek Catholic could

---

3. Grigorie Leu, *Confesiuni și secte. Studiu istoric misionar* (București: Basilica, 1929).

4. Petru Deheleanu, *Manual de Sectologie* (Arad: Editura Seminariului Teologic, 1948).

5. Roland Clark, *Sectarianism and Renewal in 1920s Romania. The Limits of Orthodoxy and Nation-Building* (London: Bloomsbury Academic, 2021), 102–39.

6. Ilie I. Imbrescu, *Ucenicul Harului Divin: Apostrofare Unui Teolog, Biserica și Mișcarea Legionară* (București: Cartea Românească, 1940), 141.

be considered Romanian, the response often was that they could be a "good Romanian" but not a Romanian in the full sense of the word.

The nationalist and exclusivist ideology promoted by the Iron Guard had a huge impact on perceptions of national identity and this situation caused an increase in the tensions between the religious denominations. As a result, attitudes towards evangelicals were characterized by resentment. This led to the further development of the discipline of "sectology" and to more structured and widespread religious missions explicitly aimed at countering the influence of so-called "sects."

After World War II, the Communist regime aimed to establish an atheist society. The Romanian Orthodox Church was forced into a defensive stance, focusing on survival rather than expansion or active mission work. The Church's missionary activity was largely restricted to the ecclesiastical sphere, as public religious expressions were heavily curtailed.

In the post-Communist era, after 1990, the Romanian Orthodox Church continued to navigate the challenges of modernity while addressing its historical relationship with the evangelicals. The legacy of the "sectology" remained influential, as the Church sought to balance its traditional defensive attitude with the need to engage with contemporary religious dynamics and to counteract the influence of evangelical movements. The book by Petru I. David, an influential theologian from Bucharest, entitled *Călăuza creștină. Sectologie* (*Christian Guide. Sectology*), published in 1987 and revised in 1994, exemplifies the attempt to reconcile past practices with the demands of a rapidly changing society. His later work, *Invazia sectelor* (*The Invasion of the Sects*), reflects an apologetic and sectological perspective aimed at defending traditional Orthodox faith against what are perceived as heretical or schismatic influences from neo-Protestant and evangelical movements. Published in three volumes in 1997–2000, *The Invasion of the Sects* underscores the ongoing concern of the Romanian Orthodox Church about the perceived threats to doctrinal integrity and religious unity posed by these movements.

In the first volume, evangelicals are categorized under "neo-Protestant proselytism" and described as a "malady of the twentieth century" that represents a harmful influence on Orthodox Christianity.[7] The second volume expands on this perspective by addressing the apocalyptic spectrum associated with certain evangelical communities, thereby emphasizing the perceived

---

7. Petru I. David, *Invazia sectelor. De la erezii vechi la secte religioase ale timpului nostru*, vol. 1 (București: Crist-1, 1997), 512.

dangers of non-Orthodox religious movements.[8] The third volume delves into dogmatic issues, providing an apologetic analysis of evangelical teachings, contrasting them with Orthodox doctrine and highlighting significant theological differences, particularly concerning revelation, the church, the sacraments and eschatology.[9]

In conclusion, the Orthodox relationship with evangelicals, as seen through the writings of David, is characterized by a rigid defence of Orthodox tradition against the perceived "invasion" of sects, with a strong emphasis on safeguarding and preserving the purity of Orthodox doctrine and practice.[10]

The Present-Day Relationship

Romanian Orthodox theologians acknowledge the existence of several fundamental religious concepts and forms of faith that they share with various evangelical movements, despite the existence of significant disagreement about how these are interpreted.[11] The agreements and disagreements can be illustrated with reference to the classic quadrilateral by means of which David W. Bebbington identified four key characteristics of evangelicalism: biblicism, crucicentrism, conversionism and activism.[12]

Conversionism is the belief that humans are born in a state of enmity with God and must undergo a spiritual rebirth or conversion to reconcile them with the Creator. Evangelicals frequently emphasize the importance of a personal decision to "turn to God" and undergo a spiritual rebirth or "be born again" through the work of the Holy Spirit. This is seen as a fundamental renewal of life oriented towards the eternal kingdom of God. Orthodox theologians

---

8. Petru I. David, *Invazia sectelor. „Proorocii" timpului, dascăli mincinoși, antihriștii evanghelizatori!*, vol. 2 (Constanța: Europolis, 1999), 391.

9. Petru I. David, *Invazia sectelor. Obsesia chipului fiarei apocaliptice la sfârșit de mileniu II*, vol. 3 (Constanța: Europolis, 2000), 350.

10. David, *Invazia sectelor* 1:9–13.

11. The data for this section are taken from *Misiologie Ortodoxă* Volume II (*Orthodox Missiology* Volume II), a comprehensive handbook designed for theological faculties under the patronage of the Romanian Orthodox Patriarchate. The volume, coordinated by Professor emeritus Valer Bel and Professor Cristian Sonea, carries the blessing of His Beatitude Patriarch Daniel and will be published by the Basilica Publishing House of the Romanian Orthodox Patriarchate. In addition, the section offers a synthesis of the chapter entitled "The Orthodox Church and Evangelicals in Eastern Europe. Between pastoral tensions and social reconciliation." This chapter, written by Cristian Sonea and the evangelical theologian Teofil Stanciu, appeared in *Christianity and Transforming States: Mapping Varied Christian Experiences and Responses*.

12. David W. Bebbington, *Evangelicalism in Modern Britain: A History from the 1730s to the 1980s* (London: Unwin Hyman, 1989), 2–17.

observe that this emphasis on conversion highlights a key distinction when compared to Orthodox Christianity, which views salvation as a process that encompasses both personal faith and participation in the sacramental life of the Church, as well as a constant state of conversion.[13]

The activism of evangelicalism is its strong commitment to evangelism and the conviction that each believer bears the personal responsibility to disseminate the gospel. This activism is frequently driven by an urgent sense of mission, rooted in the anticipation of Christ's return. The Orthodox Church regards this missionary fervour with a combination of respect and caution, acknowledging its intensity but also expressing concern over the potential for proselytism, which has historically resulted in tensions between evangelical and Orthodox communities.[14]

Biblicism means that evangelicals adhere strictly to the principle of *sola scriptura* which holds that the Bible is the sole authority for divine revelation and is therefore considered infallible. This is in contrast with the Orthodox view, which holds that Scripture forms part of tradition. The emphasis on biblical authority, particularly evident in American evangelicalism, serves to differentiate evangelical theology from the approach to Scripture observed in Orthodoxy. However, both traditions acknowledge the authority of the Bible in matters of morality.[15]

Evangelical crucicentrism emphasizes the importance of the doctrine of the atoning sacrifice of Jesus Christ on the cross. This crucicentric perspective interprets Christ's death primarily through legal and moral lenses, emphasizing substitutionary atonement as the key to understanding salvation. Orthodox theology, while also emphasizing the importance of Christ's sacrifice, tends to view it within a broader framework of *theosis* (deification), where salvation is seen as a process of participation in the divine life.

Overall, the Orthodox Church views evangelicalism as a dynamic and diverse movement, rather than a unified entity. It is characterized by constant change and internal diversification. This is exemplified by the numerous branches or groups within evangelicalism that have been identified by evangelical scholars. These categories include:

---

13. Cristian Sonea, "Fenomenul penticostalismului," in Valer Ber and Cristian Sonea (eds), *Misiologie ortodoxă: manual pentru facultățile de teologie din Patriarhia Română* vol. 2, Cursuri, manuale și tratate de teologie ortodoxă (București: Basilica, 2024), 130.

14. Sonea, "Fenomenul penticostalismului," 134.

15. Sonea, "Fenomenul penticostalismului," 135.

Fundamentalist evangelicals: a movement characterized by a literal interpretation of the Bible and a strong emphasis on its inerrancy. Fundamentalists often adopt a polemical stance towards other Christian groups, including Orthodox Christians. Their various eschatological views, such as premillennialism and dispensationalism, also serve to differentiate them from Orthodox teachings.

Old evangelicals: a group characterized by a focus on mass evangelism, with an emphasis on personal conversion experiences and the emotional aspects of faith. The tradition is exemplified by people such as Billy Graham, who are perceived by Orthodox observers as embodying an overly individualistic approach that contrasts with the communal and liturgical focus of Orthodoxy.

New evangelicals: a movement that emerged in the 1950s in response to Fundamentalism. They emphasize the social implications of the gospel. This group comprises activists who are concerned with issues of peace and justice. They often engage in political action, which can sometimes align with Orthodox concerns for social ethics. However, there are instances when their methodology and emphasis diverge from those of the Orthodox tradition.

Charismatic evangelicals: These believers are typically associated with the Pentecostal movement, which places a strong emphasis on the work of the Holy Spirit, spiritual gifts and charismatic worship practices. The Orthodox Church acknowledges the presence of the Holy Spirit but may be cautious about the more ecstatic and experiential aspects of Pentecostalism.

Ecumenical evangelicals: This subgroup is committed to constructive dialogue with other Christian traditions, including Orthodoxy. Such endeavours at dialogue are regarded favourably by the Orthodox Church, particularly when they demonstrate respect for doctrinal divergences and strive for mutual comprehension rather than the propagation of one's own beliefs.[16]

The perspective of the Orthodox Church on evangelical missionary activity is rooted in a complex interplay of theological, ecclesiological and pastoral concerns. This perspective is thoroughly examined by Valer Bel and David Pestroiu, who outline a range of objections to evangelical approaches that Orthodox Christianity views as incompatible with its teachings and practices.[17]

---

16. Sonea, "Fenomenul penticostalismului," 138.

17. Valer Bel and David Pestroiu, "Obiecțiuni heterodoxe la adresa misiunii Bisericii Ortodoxe și concepția organizațiilor para-eclesiale despre misiunea ei," in Ber and Sonea, *Misiologie ortodoxă* 2, 98.

In conclusion, the Orthodox perspective on evangelicalism is shaped by both historical experiences and theological analysis. While the Orthodox Church acknowledges the fervour and dedication of evangelicals to the Christian faith, it is also aware that considerable theological and ecclesiological divergences exist.

Orthodox Criticism of Evangelicals
Evangelical Proselytism

The Orthodox Church views the missionary efforts of evangelical groups, especially those that operate outside of established ecclesial structures, with suspicion and concern. These organizations are often accused of engaging in proselytism rather than true Christian mission. From the Orthodox standpoint, proselytism involves an aggressive and often manipulative attempt to convert individuals, particularly those who are already members of the Orthodox Church. This approach is seen as particularly problematic because it targets Orthodox Christians under the assumption that they are "Christians by birth, not by conversion," implying that they lack a genuine, personal faith and therefore need to be "truly" converted.[18]

The Orthodox Church perceives this strategy as destructive, especially in traditionally Orthodox countries, where it can undermine the unity of the Church and lead to spiritual confusion among believers. The growth of evangelical communities in Orthodox countries is not seen as a sign of spiritual revival but as a troubling indicator of the inroads made by what the Orthodox consider to be a form of religious colonialism.

From the Orthodox perspective, the evangelical approach to mission is fundamentally flawed to the point of being a "counter-witness" to Christian faith. This is because, in the eyes of Orthodox theologians, evangelicals lead people away from the Church and its sacramental life, which they view as essential for salvation. The Orthodox Church believes that it alone has preserved the fullness of Christian truth and any movement that draws believers away from this truth is seen as spiritually dangerous.

This perception of evangelicals as counter-witnesses is rooted in a deep concern for the spiritual well-being of Orthodox Christians who might be drawn into evangelical communities. The Orthodox Church views itself as the true Church established by Christ and any movement that challenges this

---

18. Bel and Pestroiu, "Obiecțiuni heterodoxe," 101.

self-understanding is not only seen as theologically erroneous but also as a threat to the souls of its members.[19]

The Nature of the Church

Central to the Orthodox critique is the stark contrast in how the two traditions understand the nature of the Church. The Orthodox Church views itself as the one, holy, catholic and apostolic church, a mystical body that transcends the merely human and institutional, encompassing both the visible and invisible aspects of Christian life. This understanding is deeply sacramental, with the church seen as the body of Christ, intimately connected to the divine through the sacraments, particularly the eucharist.

Evangelical ecclesiology is seen as reductive because it often describes the church as a voluntary association of believers who come together primarily for worship and mutual support. This view is seen as lacking the sacramental depth that characterizes the church in the Orthodox ecclesiology. Evangelicals are perceived as downplaying or even rejecting the sacramental and hierarchical structure of the church, which in Orthodox theology is essential for maintaining the integrity of the Christian faith and the continuity of apostolic tradition.[20]

This divergence has practical implications for how each tradition understands and practises mission. The Orthodox Church sees its mission as inseparable from its sacramental life; it is through the sacraments of the Church that believers are united with Christ and incorporated into his body. Evangelicals are often accused of promoting an individualistic form of faith that emphasizes personal conversion over communal sacramental participation.

The Role of the Sacraments

A significant point of contention is the role of the sacraments. In Orthodox theology, the sacraments, particularly the Eucharist, are central to the life of the Church. The Eucharist is not merely a symbolic act but a real participation in the body and blood of Christ, which unites believers with him and with one another in the most profound way.

Evangelicals are perceived as having a diminished view of the sacraments. For many evangelicals, sacraments like baptism and the eucharist are merely symbolic acts that follow personal faith rather than essential means of grace.

---

19. Bel and Pestroiu, "Obiecțiuni heterodoxe," 102.
20. Bel and Pestroiu, "Obiecțiuni heterodoxe," 103.

The Orthodox critique this view as a significant departure from the Christian tradition as understood and practiced by the church from the earliest times. This sacramental deficiency weakens the evangelical understanding of the church and its mission, reducing the Christian life to a matter of individual belief and moral behaviour rather than a communal participation in the divine life through the sacraments.[21]

From Criticism to Empathy: "Brothers Waiting for Our Love"

Notwithstanding the aforementioned points of criticism, the Orthodox response to evangelicalism is not characterized by outright rejection or hostility. Conversely, there is an emphasis on viewing those involved in evangelical proselytism as "brothers waiting for our love." This phrase encapsulates a call to engage with evangelicals and other non-Orthodox Christians not as adversaries, but as fellow human beings and potential partners in the broader Christian mission.[22] The Orthodox Church advocates a response to evangelical proselytism that is grounded in love, dialogue and a profound comprehension of the other's perspective. This approach is predicated on the conviction that authentic Christian mission must perpetually reflect the love of Christ and the unity of all humanity in God's creation.

The Orthodox mission is defined as a form of testimony that is expressed through the sacraments, liturgical practices and the moral and spiritual conduct of the community. This mission is not concerned with coercing others into conversion; rather, it is about extending an invitation to them to become part of the life of the Church. This invitation is to be extended on the basis of a witness that is both authentic and respectful of their freedom.

The Orthodox perspective encourages dialogue with evangelical Christians, recognizing that, despite significant theological differences, there is a shared commitment to Christ that can be the basis for mutual understanding and cooperation. This dialogue is seen as an opportunity to share the richness of the Orthodox tradition while also learning from the experiences and insights of others.

---

21. Bel and Pestroiu, "Obiecțiuni heterodoxe," 104.
22. Bel and Pestroiu, "Obiecțiuni heterodoxe," 105.

Collaboration

Despite the historical tensions that were presented, there have been notable instances where Orthodox and evangelical communities have found common ground, particularly in response to social and moral issues that challenge the core values of the Christian faith in the region. A significant area of collaboration between Orthodox and evangelicals in Romania has been in the defence of traditional Christian values, particularly concerning the family, marriage and religious education.

Religious education in public schools: After the fall of Communism, the reintroduction of religious education in Romanian public schools became a pivotal issue. Both Orthodox and evangelical communities recognized the importance of a strong religious presence in the education system, seeing it as essential for preserving Christian moral values in the next generation. When secularist NGOs challenged the inclusion of religion as a compulsory subject, both groups united to defend its place in the curriculum. They encouraged parents across denominational lines to opt-in for religious education for their children, resulting in a significant majority of students being enrolled in these classes. The success of this campaign demonstrated the potential for joint action in areas of shared concern.[23]

The Bodnariu family case (2015–2016): Both groups also collaborated in the case of the Bodnariu family, a Romanian-Norwegian Pentecostal family whose children were taken into custody by the Norwegian authorities under controversial circumstances. The case garnered widespread attention, initially within the evangelical community but soon expanded to include the Orthodox Church. The Romanian Orthodox Patriarchate publicly expressed its concern for the family and numerous protests were organized across various denominations, both in Romania and among the Romanian diaspora.[24]

Referendum for the family (2018): The most significant example of Orthodox-evangelical collaboration was during the 2018 referendum on the definition of marriage in Romania. The referendum sought to amend the constitution to define marriage explicitly as a union between one man and one woman, thus preventing the legalization of same-sex marriage. Although the referendum ultimately failed due to low voter turnout, it represented an unprecedented

---

23. Cristian Sonea and Teofil Stanciu, "The Romanian Orthodox Church and the Evangelicals: Conflicts and Collaboration," in *Christianity and Transforming States: Mapping Varied Christian Experiences and Responses*, ed. David Emmanuel Singh (Minneapolis: Fortress Press, 2024), 289–91.

24. Sonea and Stanciu, "Romanian Orthodox," 293–95.

level of cooperation between Orthodox, evangelical and other religious communities. The shared belief in the sanctity of heterosexual marriage as ordained by God provided a strong basis for this alliance, demonstrating that, despite their theological differences, these communities could come together to defend what they perceive as fundamental Christian values.[25]

Towards a New Paradigm of Collaboration

These instances of collaboration suggest that there is a growing recognition among Orthodox and evangelical leaders of the need for a more sustained and structured dialogue. The challenges posed by secularization, moral relativism and the erosion of traditional values in Eastern Europe create a context in which these two Christian traditions have more in common than what divides them. For the collaboration to move beyond isolated instances, it is essential to establish ongoing theological and social dialogues that address both the common ground and the differences between the traditions. Mutual respect and understanding are crucial, as is the willingness to engage in joint actions that reflect shared Christian values. The history of tensions between Orthodox and evangelicals cannot be ignored but neither should it be a barrier to future collaboration. Instead, these historical experiences can serve as a foundation for a deeper, more meaningful partnership, in which both traditions can contribute to the common good of society while respecting their unique theological identities.

The convergence seen in recent years, especially in defence of the family and religious education, can be seen as providential, suggesting that the Holy Spirit may be guiding these communities toward a new kind of unity, one that does not require the removal of denominational boundaries but encourages collaboration across them in the face of common challenges.

Bibliography

Bel, Valer, and David Pestroiu. "Obiecțiuni heterodoxe la adresa misiunii Bisericii Ortodoxe și concepția organizațiilor para-eclesiale despre misiunea ei." Pages 99–123 in Valer Bel and Cristian Sonea, eds. *Misiologie ortodoxă II [Orthodox Missiology] Vol. II: manual pentru facultățile de teologie din Patriarhia Română.* Vol. 2. Cursuri, anual și tratate de teologie ortodoxă. București: Basilica, 2024.

---

25. Sonea and Stanciu, "Romanian Orthodox," 296–300.

Clark, Roland. *Sectarianism and Renewal in 1920s Romania. The Limits of Orthodoxy and Nation-Building*. London: Bloomsbury Academic, 2021.
Comșa, Grigorie. *Noul ghid pentru combaterea și cunoașterea sectelor religioase*. Arad: Tiparul Tipografiei Diecezane, 1927.
David, Petru I. *Călăuza creștină: sectologie: pentru cunoașterea și apărarea dreptei credințe în fața prozelitismului sectant*. 2nd ed. Curtea de Argeș: Editura Episcopiei Argeșului, 1994.
———. *Invazia sectelor. Vol. 1: De la erezii vechi la secte religioase ale timpului nostru*. București: Crist-1, 1997.
———. *Invazia sectelor. Vol. 2: "Proorocii" timpului, dascăli mincinoși, antihriștii evanghelizatori!*. Constanța: Europolis, 1999.
———. *Invazia sectelor. Vol. 3: Obsesia chipului fiarei apocaliptice la sfârșit de mileniu II*. Constanța: Europolis, 2000.
Ioniță, Viorel, ed. *Orthodox Theology in the 20th Century and Early 21st Century: A Romanian Orthodox Perspective*. București: Basilica, 2013.
Sonea, Cristian. "Fenomenul penticostalismului." Pages 129–40 in *Misiologie ortodoxă II [Orthodox Missiology] Vol. II: manual pentru facultățile de teologie din Patriarhia Română*. Vol. 2. Edited by Valer Ber and Cristian Sonea. Cursuri, manuale și tratate de teologie ortodoxă. București: Basilica, 2024.
Sonea, Cristian, and Teofil Stanciu. "The Orthodox Church and Evangelicals in Eastern Europe. Between pastoral tensions and social reconciliation." Pages 283–302 in *Christianity and Transforming States: Mapping Varied Christian Experiences and Responses*. Edited by David Singh. Philadelphia: Fortress, 2024.

5

Evangelicals and Other Christian Traditions

An Insider's Perspective

Tim Grass

Introduction

This chapter explores what it means to be evangelical, before examining how evangelicals view other Christian traditions. This is because how we see ourselves shapes how we see others. Throughout, I shall ask questions and raise issues for consideration, because our relationship to other Christian traditions will vary according to the context and form of encounter. The aim is to sketch out some stable frameworks within which each of us can develop an approach to members of other Christian traditions which is thoughtful, faithful to Christ, and contextually grounded. In doing so, I shall engage with the other side of the coin, as presented in this volume by the Orthodox missiologist Fr Cristian Sonea.

As to my own perspective, I was brought up in rural England in fairly fundamentalist churches and switched from a university to an evangelical theological institution in order to study where my soul would not be endangered. As a pastor, I disliked having to stand apart from ecumenical activities in our town, especially as other evangelical leaders did not see the need to do so. Completing a doctorate in theology and beginning to teach, I became aware that a number of evangelicals were converting to Orthodoxy around that time and so began to engage with Orthodox Christians. This engagement has taken place in a variety of contexts, but primarily through the Evangelical Alliance in Britain, the Ecumenical Institute at Bossey and the Lausanne-Orthodox Initiative, which I served for six years as facilitator.[1]

What an Evangelical Is

What does it mean to be an evangelical? Who do we think we are? Let me suggest three ways in which we may define this.[2] First, we could analyse statements of evangelical belief, such as those produced by national Evangelical Alliances, the Lausanne Movement and other evangelical bodies. On that basis, we could define evangelicals as those who affirm these beliefs as true. However, evangelicals have often criticized those whose Christianity is solely a matter of head knowledge.

A second answer stresses the need for inward experience. An evangelical is not only someone who believes particular things, but someone who has a particular approach to personal faith and its practical outworking. On this definition, being evangelical is about spirituality (including prayer, engagement with Scripture and the sacraments or "ordinances" of baptism and the Lord's supper[3]) and discipleship as well as doctrine.[4] But this requires us to consider how to relate to others who claim the same experience and define themselves as "evangelical." Many Roman Catholics now do so: since Vatican II, many find that they can sustain and maintain evangelical faith within their church

---

1. For one interpretation of the history of relationships between evangelicals and Orthodox, see Tim Grass, "Evangelicals and Eastern Christianity," in *The Routledge Research Companion to the History of Evangelicalism*, ed. Andrew Atherstone and David Ceri Jones (Abingdon: Routledge, 2019), 110–26. A brief outline of the development and approach of the Lausanne-Orthodox Initiative is provided in Mark Oxbrow and Tim Grass, "Introduction," in *Living the Gospel of Jesus Christ: Orthodox and Evangelical Approaches to Discipleship and Christian Formation*, ed. Mark Oxbrow and Tim Grass (Oxford: Regnum, 2021), 1–8. From a North American standpoint, see Bradley Nassif, "Orthodoxy and Evangelicalism: An Emerging Global Dialogue," in *The Evangelical Theology of the Orthodox Church*, ed. Bradley Nassif (Yonkers: St Vladimir's Seminary Press, 2021), 265–75.

2. For a survey of attempts to define "evangelical," "evangelicals" and "evangelicalism," alert to the different ways that historians and theologians approach the challenge, see Andrew Atherstone and David Ceri Jones, "Evangelicals and Evangelicalisms: Contested Identities," in Atherstone and Jones, *Routledge Research Companion*, 1–21.

3. Their "obligation and perpetuity" was affirmed in the ninth article of the basis of faith adopted by the World Evangelical Alliance at its founding in 1846: Ian Randall and David Hilborn, *One Body in Christ: The History and Significance of the Evangelical Alliance* (Carlisle: Paternoster, 2001), 358. They are not mentioned in the basis of faith of the World Evangelical Fellowship, founded in 1951.

4. For an authoritative exposition of evangelical spirituality, see Ian Randall, *What a Friend we have in Jesus: The Evangelical Tradition* (London: Darton, Longman & Todd, 2005).

rather than by leaving it.[5] A recent survey commissioned by the Evangelical Alliance in Northern Ireland concluded that 38 percent of Roman Catholics in the province call themselves evangelical (that is a little less than the 47 percent of Protestants who do so).[6] There are Orthodox believers who do so too: Brad Nassif has argued that Orthodoxy is at its heart evangelical and that the evangelical movement may be viewed as a recall to emphases which Orthodoxy should never have let go.[7] Now, how far can this approach go? What about non-Trinitarians who claim to be evangelical, for instance in "Oneness" Pentecostal churches, or Mormons who testify to their "burning heart experience" and sing classic evangelical hymns? What does our response to such examples tell us about how we understand what it means to be evangelical? My own conviction is that conversion involves entering into relationship with God the Holy Trinity, on the basis of trust in the work of Christ for us. I could not regard non-Trinitarians, or those who do not affirm the work of Christ as the sole basis for our acceptance with God, as evangelicals.

A third way of looking at evangelicalism, a sociological approach, sees it as being about networks – relationships and communities: evangelicals are those who associate with, or see themselves as part of, groups which are characterized by particular emphases in theology, spirituality and practice. I recall the former General Secretary of the World Council of Churches, Konrad Raiser,

---

5. David E. Bjork, *Unfamiliar Paths: The Challenge of Recognizing the Work of Christ in Strange Clothing. A Case Study from France* (Pasadena: William Carey Library, 1997), 103. On evangelical-Roman Catholic relationships, see Thomas P. Rausch, ed., *Catholics and Evangelicals: Do They Share a Common Future?* (New York / Mahwah: Paulist Press, 2000); Leonardo De Chirico, "Evangelical Theological Perspectives on Post-Vatican II Roman Catholicism" (PhD thesis, King's College London, 2002; published under the same title, Frankfurt am Main / Oxford: Peter Lang, 2003); Mark A. Noll and Carolyn Nystrom, *Is the Reformation Over? An Evangelical Assessment of Contemporary Roman Catholicism* (Grand Rapids: Baker, 2005); Timothy George, "Evangelicals and Roman Catholics," in *Evangelicals Around the World: A Global Handbook for the 21st Century*, ed. Brian C. Stiller, Todd M. Johnson, Karen Stiller and Mark Hutchinson (Nashville: Thomas Nelson for the World Evangelical Alliance, 2015), 68–71; "'Scripture and Tradition' and 'the Church in Salvation': Catholics and Evangelicals explore Challenges and Opportunities: A Report of the International Consultation between the Catholic Church and the World Evangelical Alliance (2009–2016)," www.christianunity.va/content/unitacristiani/en/dialoghi/sezione-occidentale/evangelici/dialogo/documenti-di-dialogo/testo-in-inglese.html; Groupe national de conversations catholiques-évangéliques, *Évangéliser aujourd'hui. Des catholiques et des évangéliques s'interpellent* (Charols/Paris: Excelsis/Salvator, 2017); John Maiden, "Evangelicals and Rome," in Atherstone and Jones, *Routledge Research Companion*, 93–109.

6. Declan McSweeney, "Northern Ireland's Evangelical Catholics reveal a 'more varied and complex' Religious Situation," *Catholic Herald*, 12 March 2024, https://catholicherald.co.uk/northern-irelands-evangelical-catholics-reveal-a-more-varied-and-complex-religious-situation. The survey was commissioned by the Evangelical Alliance in Northern Ireland.

7. Nassif, *Evangelical Theology*, 17–18, 148–49.

saying that in his view, an evangelical was anyone who self-identified as such. This approach is problematic, not least because some who hold traditional evangelical views have not wished to self-identify as evangelical; conversely, some who do self-identify as evangelical do not hold to what are generally regarded as evangelical convictions.[8] But it reminds us that being evangelical is something which we practise with others. We cannot define evangelicalism in terms of individuals alone any more than we can define being a Christian in terms of individuals alone. God's purpose involves adopting us into a community which reflects, and by grace participates in, the love between the persons of the Trinity.

Having considered various approaches to the question of definition, which are not mutually exclusive, we should now examine three significant definitions of what it means to be evangelical. The first and the best known in the English-speaking world is that of David Bebbington: evangelicals are conversionist, activist, Bible-centred and cross-centred.[9] Sonea has offered a brief response in this volume, from an Orthodox perspective.[10] Bebbington's definition does not seek to answer all the concerns we may have and some have found it too broad. But we should remember that he was highlighting what he regarded as the key characteristics of evangelicals: he was describing, not prescribing. And his concern is not with doctrine in itself, but with the ways that doctrinal convictions played out in culture, practice and spirituality.[11] At least two national alliances, in Ireland and France, offer statements of belief which look to be drawing on Bebbington's hallmarks.[12]

---

8. See Mark Noll, "What is 'Evangelical'?" in *The Oxford Handbook of Evangelical Theology*, ed. Gerald McDermott (Oxford: Oxford University Press, 2010), 19–32. In 1976 a Southern Baptist leader, Foy Valentine, famously declared that his denomination was not evangelical, calling the term a "Yankee word": Timothy George, "Evangelicals and Others," *First Things* 160 (2006), www.firstthings.com/article/2006/02/evangelicals-and-others.

9. D. W. Bebbington, *Evangelicalism in Modern Britain* (London: Unwin Hyman, 1989), ch. 1 (especially 3–20). As an Orthodox theologian, Nassif works with this definition, for example *Evangelical Theology*, 164. The Baptist historian Derek Tidball expounds the same four points by way of elaborating on John Stott's definition of evangelicals as Bible people and gospel people: *Who are the Evangelicals? Tracing the Roots of Today's Movements* (London: Marshall Pickering, 1994), 12–13.

10. See pages 65-78 above.

11. Mark Smith, "British Evangelical Identities: Locating the Discussion," in *British Evangelical Identities Past and Present*, 1: *Aspects of the History and Sociology of Evangelicalism in Britain and Ireland*, ed. Mark Smith (Bletchley: Paternoster, 2008), 3.

12. "Evangelical Alliance Ireland," www.evangelical.ie; Conseil national des évangéliques de France, "Les évangéliques: ce qu'ils croient," www.lecnef.org/page/445845-ce-qu-ils-croient.

Timothy Larsen's definition, whilst also offered from a historian's perspective, is arguably sharper than Bebbington's. An evangelical is:

1. an orthodox Protestant
2. who stands in the tradition of the global Christian networks arising from the eighteenth-century revival movements associated with John Wesley and George Whitefield;
3. who has a preeminent place for the Bible in her or his Christian life as the divinely inspired, final authority in matters of faith and practice;
4. who stresses reconciliation with God through the atoning work of Jesus Christ on the cross;
5. and who stresses the work of the Holy Spirit in the life of an individual to bring about conversion and an ongoing life of fellowship with God and service to God and others, including the duty of all believers to participate in the task of proclaiming the gospel to all people.[13]

Larsen is not defining what it means to be Christian, but what it means to be evangelical and where to find the community which goes by that name. His first point is a helpful reminder that historically, evangelicalism often flourished at times and in places where there was a resurgence of Roman Catholicism, or at least a fear of that happening.[14] However, the definition raises a problem. In some countries the term "Protestant" has carried political connotations from which evangelicals have sought to distance themselves: this was true in Spain during the latter part of the nineteenth century and today affects the "new fellowships" in Ireland formed of converts from a Roman Catholic background.

A third definition has been offered by the theologian Alister McGrath. Once again it is descriptive rather than prescriptive, but as well as being doctrinal in nature it is, in his term, "existential," setting out how we experience the living Christ. McGrath lists six core evangelical convictions:

---

13. Timothy Larsen, "Defining and locating Evangelicalism," in *The Cambridge Companion to Evangelical Theology*, ed. Timothy Larsen and Daniel J. Treier (Cambridge: Cambridge University Press, 2007), 1–14, 1.

14. John Maiden, "Evangelicals and Rome," 94–97; Sarah Scholl, "The *Réveil* and Catholicism," in *The Genevan Réveil in International Perspective*, ed. Jean Decorvet, Tim Grass, and Kenneth J. Stewart (Eugene: Pickwick, 2023), 487–99 (French edition: *Le Réveil de Genève. Perspectives internationales* [St-Legier, CH: Éditions HET-PRO, 2024]).

1. The supreme authority of Scripture as a source of knowledge of God and a guide to Christian living.
2. The majesty of Jesus Christ, both as incarnate God and Lord, and as the saviour of sinful humanity.
3. The lordship of the Holy Spirit.
4. The need for personal conversion.
5. The priority of evangelism for both individual Christians and the church as a whole.
6. The importance of the Christian community for spiritual nourishment, fellowship and growth.[15]

He goes on to stress that evangelicalism is not simply a matter of doctrine but of what he calls "ethos": an approach to Christian devotion and practice which is shaped by biblical principles.[16]

All three definitions focus on evangelical distinctives, rather than on fundamental convictions which evangelicals hold in common with other Christian traditions. Whilst they constitute valuable analytical tools, for the purposes of mission and ministry we need to formulate definitions which are biblically rooted and historically, culturally and contextually sensitive.[17] Whilst that may mean that what suits one period or culture is not necessarily suited to another, attention to local and temporal considerations can be balanced by aligning definitions as far as possible with historic and catholic expressions of fundamental Christian truth, most notably the Nicene Creed of 381 as the only creed confessed by both East and West.[18] This would assist in building relationships with those in other Christian traditions without minimizing divergent understandings.

---

15. Alister McGrath, *Evangelicalism and the Future of Christianity* (London: Hodder & Stoughton, [1993]), 51. He is drawing on *Evangelical Affirmations*, ed. Kenneth S. Kantzer and Carl F. H. Henry (Grand Rapids: Zondervan, 1990), 27–38, and J. I. Packer, *The Evangelical Anglican Identity Problem: An Analysis* (Oxford: Latimer House, 1978), 20–23. Curiously, in a later work McGrath, in offering a "working definition" of evangelicalism, reverts to a version of Bebbington's quadrilateral: Alister E. McGrath, *A Passion for Truth: The Intellectual Coherence of Evangelicalism* (Leicester: IVP, 1996), 22.

16. McGrath, *Evangelicalism and Future*, 52.

17. For the impact of changing contexts on evangelicals globally, see Mark A. Noll, "Evangelical Identity, Power, and Culture in the 'Great' Nineteenth Century," in *Christianity Reborn: The Global Expansion of Evangelicalism in the Twentieth Century*, ed. Donald M. Lewis (Studies in the History of Christian Mission; Grand Rapids: Eerdmans, 2004), 34–35.

18. For this purpose, I would not use the Apostles' Creed, since it was never adopted in the East.

As we formulate our own definitions of what it means to be evangelical, certain issues need to be borne in mind. First of all, what words or phrases do our own languages use to denote evangelicals and evangelicalism? The German terms include *evangelisch, evangelikal* and the Swiss *biblisch-erneuert* ("biblically renewed").[19] In various parts of Eastern Europe some refer to "neo-Protestants" or "repenters." Cristian Sonea has explained the context in which these terms were used in Romania and how they can be unhelpful in encounter today.[20] These terms do not all mean quite the same thing. Some of them are loaded with cultural and perhaps even theological baggage. So it may not be evidence of theological compromise to seek alternatives. Even the English term "evangelical" has recently proved problematic for those in the USA who rejected its identification by some quarters of the media, as well as the evangelical constituency, with the policy objectives and cultural style of Donald Trump.

Second, in affirming the necessity of conversion to Christ, we must remember that not all evangelicals have the same experience of conversion. For some it is dramatic, but that is also true of some who are not evangelicals. Evangelicals do not have a monopoly on sudden conversions. Other evangelicals experience conversion in a manner more like that of Timothy, who appears to have come to faith gradually within a Christian family (2 Tim 1:5; 3:15). Related to this, the way evangelicals have conceptualized their experience owes much to the context in which evangelicalism arose and developed. It can be argued that the classic evangelical conversion narrative owes more than has sometimes been acknowledged to contemporary thinking about epistemology, especially the ideas of John Locke (1632–1704).[21]

Finally, as people with good news, we ought to formulate our definition in accordance with the root of the word "evangelical," *euangelion* ("good news"). What was that good news that Jesus and then the apostles proclaimed? How do we understand and present it? And how, therefore, do we define ourselves as a community shaped by it?

---

19. See Erich Geldbach, "'Evangelisch,' 'Evangelikal' & Pietism: Some Remarks on Early Evangelicalism and Globalization from a German Perspective," in *A Global Faith: Essays on Evangelicalism and Globalization*, ed. Mark Hutchinson and Ogbu Kalu (Sydney: Centre for the Study of Australian Christianity, 1998), 156–58.

20. See pages 65-66 above.

21. For Locke's influence on key early evangelical thinkers, see Bebbington, *Evangelicalism in Britain*, 48, 49, 53–54.

Evangelical Attitudes towards Other Christian Traditions

At the beginning of this section a cautionary note should be sounded: how often do evangelicals at the local level, even church leaders, think deeply about this issue? This is partly because ecumenism is often perceived as irrelevant to "real" church life. This idea has roots in early evangelicalism, which sought to transcend denominational barriers through shared experience. Yet, whilst space does not permit dealing with the topic here, evangelicals have often been to the fore in global ecumenical ventures.[22] Having said that, let us list some approaches adopted towards members of other Christian traditions, approaches which also affect relations within the evangelical community.

Rejection

The attitude that writes off other churches as "dead" or nations with no real evangelical presence as "unreached" is often dismissed as old-fashioned, unjust and exclusive, but like many caricatures, it contains sufficient truth to make it plausible. There are congregations in which even the most charitable observer is unable to discern any sign of interest in spiritual things and there are countries where it is arguable that the Christian message has rarely been heard as good news.

Yet we should be cautious towards this approach, remembering that rejection of other Christians is sometimes a response to being rejected by them. A consequence of such rejection is the attempt to win others to evangelical faith. This may be regarded as proselytism, as Sonea points out.[23] However, whilst the accusation may not infrequently be justified at the local level, there needs to be an awareness on both sides of the differing perspectives of each tradition on what constitutes nominal Christianity, from which individuals need to be converted.[24] Evangelicals have been fully involved in ecumenical work on this problem,[25] but as a movement we need to find ways of helping

---

22. On evangelicals and institutional ecumenism, see *Dictionary of the Ecumenical Movement*, ed. Nicholas Lossky et al., 2nd ed. (Geneva: World Council of Churches, 2002); William J. Abraham, "Church and Churches: Ecumenism," in McDermott, *Oxford Handbook of Evangelical Theology*, 296–309.

23. See pages 73–74.

24. This difference proved significant at the Lausanne Movement consultation on Nominal Christianity which took place in Rome during 2018: for the statement which resulted, see https://lausanne.org/statement/missing-christians-global-call.

25. See World Council of Churches, "Towards Common Witness," www.oikoumene.org/resources/documents/towards-common-witness; Mark Oxbrow and Tim Grass (eds), *The Mission of God: Studies in Orthodox and Evangelical Mission* (Oxford: Regnum, 2015), especially

our co-religionists who are more separatist, aggressive or confrontational in their approach to other traditions to take on board what has been learned through this process.

Seeking to Be Accepted by Others

This approach can lead to downplaying differences, but it is risky in other ways too. What if we place too much hope in becoming accepted? For example, George Eldon Ladd (1911–1982) sought to be accepted as a New Testament scholar by the mainstream scholarly community and was devastated to receive a negative review of his *Jesus and the Kingdom* by an influential form critic, Norman Perrin.[26] On the other hand, sometimes evangelicals do need to give more attention to how others perceive them. Some of us have mistaken rudeness and disrespect for faithfulness to the Lord. We need to listen to how we are perceived by others and reflect on the charges they lay against us.

Dialogue

Evangelical involvement in dialogue with other Christian traditions has developed massively in the last half-century, for a range of reasons,[27] but it has to go deeper than "being nice to each other" (as an Orthodox challenged me). We need a thought-out approach to our practice of dialogue. The practice of the Lausanne-Orthodox Initiative has been to set dialogue in the context of relationship-building, where it becomes possible to speak the truth in love (Eph 4:15). Speaking the truth may involve each tradition asking "hard questions" of the other, an approach which has proved fruitful in the International Roman Catholic – Pentecostal Dialogue.[28] A dialogue in which such questions are deemed out of order can only be superficial, and since those questions are

---

the essays in Section 2.

26. For Ladd's somewhat tragic story, see John D'Elia, *A Place at the Table: George Eldon Ladd and the Rehabilitation of Evangelical Scholarship in America* (New York: Oxford University Press, 2008).

27. These include the renewal of scholarly confidence among evangelicals, changing understandings of what it means to be evangelical, developments in Roman Catholic thinking and practice, the spread of the charismatic movement, the impact of Western secularisation and concomitant changes in moral attitudes, and the awareness of shared suffering under Communist regimes; see Noll and Nystrom, *Is the Reformation Over?*, ch. 3.

28. This approach is outlined by Jelle Creemers, "Dance to the Beat of your own Drum: Classical Pentecostals in Ecumenical Dialogue," *Journal of the European Pentecostal Theological Association* 35.1 (2015): 66.

bound to be in our minds, it is healthier and serves God's truth better if they are given voice and an opportunity is provided for them to be answered.

Balancing it is the approach known as "receptive ecumenism," which sets out to learn from others rather than teaching them.[29] We cannot assume that all in other Christian traditions are themselves converted (neither are all in our own tradition) but we should be open to discovering that they are "brothers waiting for our love," in Sonea's words.[30] Even where we cannot discover that, we can engage with them on the basis that they bear the name of Christian, appealing to them to enter into the reality which the name expresses.

Collaboration

As Sonea demonstrates, it is often possible to engage with non-evangelicals in such spheres as Bible translation and distribution, practical diaconal service or advocacy on behalf of groups in society who have nobody to speak for them.[31] Indeed, we may and should work for the good of society with those outside the Christian constituency also. Francis Schaeffer referred to this rather negatively as "co-belligerence" but "collaboration" is a more positive and constructive term.[32]

Critical Fellowship

We work together where possible but are honest about our differences where it is not; we can do this because our relationship is based on seeing the presence of Christ in the other. This has a practical consequence which is not often mentioned in ecumenical discussion: if we recognize a non-evangelical as a sister or brother in Christ, that lays upon us certain obligations, which are

---

29. See Callan Slipper, *Enriched by the Other: A Spiritual Guide to Receptive Ecumenism* (Grove Spirituality Series 139; Cambridge: Grove Books, 2016), 18–25; Churches Together in England, "Receptive Ecumenism," https://cte.org.uk/about/ecumenism-explained/receptive-ecumenism/; Durham University, Centre for Catholic Studies, "Receptive Ecumenism," www.durham.ac.uk/research/institutes-and-centres/catholic-studies/research/constructive-catholic-theology-/receptive-ecumenism-/.

30. See page 75 above.

31. See pages 76-77 above.

32. Francis A. Schaeffer, *The Church at the End of the Twentieth Century* (London: Norfolk Press, 1970), 46–47.

summed up by the apostle John in terms of willingness to lay down our life for our brothers and sisters because Christ laid down his life for us (1 John 3:16).[33]

An Evangelical Approach

The approach we adopt as individuals may not always coincide with the approach adopted by the church to which we belong, partly because the issues are not identical. For example, a church may have concerns about who should be welcomed to share in communion, whereas individuals do not have the responsibility of deciding that matter: their relationships with other individuals involve different areas.

At this point, we need to take up our understanding of what it means to be evangelical: how does it affect which of the approaches to other traditions we choose? It will be helpful to look at some factors which may shape our thinking.

- Do we see evangelicalism as a way of being Lutheran, Anglican, Methodist or Baptist – or as a separate tradition which stands alongside them? The British historian W. R. Ward argued that we should see evangelicalism as a renewal movement *within* European churches, part of a wider quest for "heart religion" during the seventeenth and eighteenth centuries.[34] Historically, it was almost a century before the term "evangelical" was used of a distinct party within the churches and longer still before the term was used as part of denominational titles in English.[35] However, if we believe that evangelicalism is complete in itself as a separate tradition, possessing all the theological and spiritual resources needed for faithful discipleship, and is not merely a renewal movement within existing

---

33. We might also add conversion, as does Patrick Mitchel, "The Influence of Vatican II on the Protestant Churches in Ireland," in *Ireland and Vatican II: Essays Theological, Pastoral and Educational*, ed. Niall Col (Dublin: Columba Press, 2015), 178. However, my concern here is with approaches adopted by those who remain within evangelical churches.

34. See W. R. Ward, *Early Evangelicalism: A Global Intellectual History, 1670–1789* (Cambridge: Cambridge University Press, 2006). His approach is paralleled by Timothy George, "Evangelicals and Others," who sees evangelicalism as "a renewal movement within historic Christian orthodoxy with deep roots in the early Church, the Reformation of the sixteenth century, and the great awakenings of the eighteenth century." For the wider context, see also Ted A. Campbell, *The Religion of the Heart: A Study of European Religious Life in the Seventeenth and Eighteenth Centuries* (Columbia: University of South Carolina Press, 1991).

35. See Mark Noll, "Introduction," in Mark Noll, David W. Bebbington and George M. Marsden, *Evangelicals: Who They Have Been, Are Now, and Could Be* (Grand Rapids: Eerdmans, 2019), 10.

traditions, we may have less desire or sense of need to build relationships with members of other Christian traditions.

- What has been our experience of other traditions? Have they rejected us, tried to make us conform or been open to our contribution?[36] How much do we draw on them in worship (what we sing, how we pray, which Bible translations we use)? If we have come to evangelicalism from another tradition, what did we bring with us?
- Whatever definition of being evangelical we adopt, we are unlikely to lay equal stress on each aspect of it. Where we lay the stress and how we do so, will help to shape our attitude to other traditions. Rob Warner has drawn attention to the variation within English evangelicalism between those who stress the Bible and the cross, and those who stress conversion and activism, and has shown how this has influenced the drawing of boundaries delineating what is regarded as the evangelical constituency.[37] Activists are, of course, less cautious about relating to other Christian traditions, perhaps partly because they are working in fields where collaboration presents fewer obstacles.
- Where do we encounter non-evangelicals? Our approach is likely to vary according to context: for example, we may work happily with Roman Catholics in a food bank but find it impossible to worship together.
- What about our ecclesiology? Do we believe in a pure church or a mixed one, a church you enter by choice, often by requesting baptism as a believer, or one which embraces the baptized inhabitants of a particular territory? Those in the believers' church traditions often struggle more with relating to other Christian traditions than those who adhere to the territorial traditions arising from the Magisterial Reformation. In Britain, for example, Baptists have often been ambivalent towards institutional ecumenism, while the Brethren and others have usually stood apart from it.
- Territorial ecclesiology may play out in a different way, when evangelicals are on the receiving end of an approach which equates

---

36. Sonea draws attention to the way that the Communist government in Romania played off the two traditions against one another so that they would not unite against it: Page 66 above.

37. Rob Warner, "Evangelical Bases of Faith and Fundamentalizing Tendencies," in *Evangelicalism and Fundamentalism in Modern Britain*, ed. David Bebbington and David Ceri Jones (Oxford: Oxford University Press, 2013), 328–47; more fully, Rob Warner, *Reinventing English Evangelicalism, 1966–2001: A Theological and Sociological Study* (Carlisle: Paternoster, 2007).

adherence to a particular Christian tradition with nationality, as in Franco's project of National Catholicism, or Orthodoxy in Romania, and are forced to react against it.[38] This leads to suspicion of evangelicalism as a foreign import which is subversive of the social and cultural order, and forces evangelicals to justify their national allegiance, potentially at the expense of an awareness that they belong to a transnational Christian movement. It also leads to an assumption by other traditions that evangelicals are voluntarist in their ecclesiology,[39] when there is a diversity of evangelical ecclesiologies.

- What scope do we have for independent existence as a community? It may be that there is no evangelical congregation anywhere near; official restrictions may make it difficult or impossible to establish specifically evangelical congregations; or we believe that God has called us to serve within a non-evangelical congregation or context. Such circumstances force us either to choose an unbiblical isolation or to relate to non-evangelicals in the most constructive and faithful ways possible.
- For some evangelicals, their understanding of biblical prophecy helps to shape their approach. Those who believe that the institutional ecumenical movement is a foreshadowing of the beast and the false prophet in the Book of Revelation will react differently from those who do not. Sonea's discussion of Romanian sectology texts which portray evangelicals as forerunners of the beast is a salutary challenge to the tendency of some evangelicals to view Orthodox (and others) in the same terms.[40] Such people will see no point in relating to other Christian traditions because, they assert, these will all be destroyed. So they call on believers in those traditions to "come out of Babylon" (Rev 18:4).
- Sometimes we may be fighting old battles. In a changing context, the truths which need to be stressed may not be those which needed to be stressed when there was general acceptance of the teaching of Scripture. Things have moved on since the World Council of Churches convened its first assembly at Amsterdam in 1948. Today the greatest divide is not between evangelicals and Orthodox, or evangelicals and Catholics, but between those who affirm Christ as

---

38. See pages 67-68 above.
39. See page 74 above.
40. See pages 69-70 above.

Son of God, Saviour and Lord, and those who do not. A defining moment for evangelical-Orthodox relations was the World Council of Churches assembly in Canberra in 1991, when they discovered that they shared similar concerns over theological error.[41]

- We cannot treat all members of any Christian tradition as identical. In personal encounter, we need to listen to others so that we understand what they actually think, say and do, rather than assuming that "all Catholics believe X" or "all Orthodox do Y"; after all, we dislike it when someone says, "all evangelicals say Z." Open listening creates space in which conversation partners can recognize where the Holy Spirit is at work creating and sustaining faith in Christ.

Looking for Strengths and Weaknesses in Other Traditions

In line with my aim to pose questions rather than provide all the answers, let me outline the spirit in which we might evaluate other Christian traditions. Whatever our understanding of what it means to be evangelical, we must acknowledge that we owe much to other traditions in the church, such as our understanding of the Trinity and Christology. Don Fairbairn, an American evangelical who has taught in Russia, wrote that Orthodoxy focuses on the "who" and the "what" of salvation, whereas evangelicalism and Catholicism focus on the "how."[42] Now, if the "how" is about how we come to know the "who" and thus enjoy the "what," the "who" and "what" questions must be treated as the most fundamental: who is this Jesus we are inviting people to come to know? What has he done, what is he doing and what will he do? The "who" is implied, rather than explicitly stated, in Bebbington's hallmarks, and more explicit in the definitions offered by Larsen and McGrath; but it is compellingly elucidated in the Nicene Creed, hence the value of using this.

A second point follows from recognizing our debt to other traditions. If truths which we as evangelicals rejoice to proclaim were elaborated by people whose understanding of Christian commitment and of corporate worship was different from our own, what does that say to us? At the very least, we must acknowledge that the Holy Spirit was at work in those settings and arguably through aspects of them which we find difficult to accept.

---

41. See "Report of the Orthodox-Evangelical Meeting, 8–12 February 1993, Bernhauser Forst, Stuttgart, Germany," *International Review of Mission* 83 (1993): 631–34.

42. Donald Fairbairn, *Eastern Orthodoxy Through Western Eyes* (Louisville: Westminster John Knox, 2002), 111.

Third, what do we make of the fifth-century Vincentian Canon, that Christian teaching is that which is believed *ubique, semper et ab omnibus* ("always, everywhere and by all")? The church has been around for two millennia but evangelicals have not. That surely forces us to recognize that the evangelical tradition cannot be regarded as self-sufficient.

As in theology, so in biblical study:

> ... there is a *history* of biblical interpretation, there is a *tradition* of understanding the Bible to which all Christians, scholars and others, should give *reverent* attention. God truly speaks to individuals as they open their hearts and minds to him and listen to his Word, but they must never forget that they are set within the Church to which God has been pleased to give light and understanding over the centuries.[43]

As we look for strengths in other traditions, we need to cultivate a due humility before the word of God, as we recall that the Lord has always more light and truth to bring out from it, and that we are part of the church which is called to be *semper reformanda*, always being reformed in submission to God's revelation. We also need to be humble in listening to those of other traditions, as they point out to us aspects of our own where we have not been sufficiently faithful to that. This is why Father Cristian's critique of Bebbington's hallmarks is particularly valuable.

Inevitably we are likely to measure members of other Christian traditions against our own definition of what it means to be evangelical. For example, if we believe that the heart of evangelical faith is expressed in those four characteristics Bebbington listed, we shall measure other traditions against them. Are they Bible-centred? Are they Christ-centred? Are they converted? Are they active in living out their faith? Let us take one of these hallmarks as an example of how we might undertake this exercise. What does it mean to be Bible-centred? Does it mean adhering to a particular expression of the doctrine of Scripture? Consider what role Scripture plays in our gatherings for worship: how much is it read? Does it form the substance of our preaching? How does Scripture shape our own lives? In summary, we might evaluate other traditions – *and our own* – by asking whether they allow the Bible to function as the living and

---

43. John Cockerton, *Essentials of Evangelical Spirituality* (Grove Spirituality Series 49; Bramcote, Nottingham: Grove Books, 1994), 5.

active word of God (Heb 4:12). In the words of John Stott, "The hallmark of authentic evangelicalism is not subscription but submission."[44]

Conclusion

This chapter has raised issues to think about as we consider how to explain in our context what it means to be evangelical and what this might mean for our evaluation of – and relationships with – other Christian traditions. In a sense, we must always relativize evangelical formulations precisely in order to move towards greater faithfulness to the revelation of God. All of us stand under the word of God as applied by the Holy Spirit to our individual and corporate existence, and if allowed free course it will detect those aspects of our tradition which fail to do justice to the revealed will and purpose of our unchanging God.

By contrast, evangelicals are changing; other Christian traditions are changing (even Orthodoxy, which understands itself to be the one, holy, catholic and apostolic church confessed in the creeds); and the times are changing. We must therefore constantly update our approach to other Christian traditions in order to remain faithful to God's unchanging gospel. And this should be a priority for us. If the whole church is commissioned to take the whole gospel to the whole world, we must work at relating to Christians in other traditions and cooperating with them where we can: otherwise, our obedience to that mandate is impaired. Part of God's church can never do the job on its own.

Bibliography

Atherstone, Andrew, and David Ceri Jones, eds. *The Routledge Research Companion to the History of Evangelicalism*. Abingdon: Routledge, 2019.
Bebbington, D. W. *Evangelicalism in Modern Britain*. London: Unwin Hyman, 1989.
Fairbairn, Donald. *Eastern Orthodoxy through Western Eyes*. Louisville: Westminster John Knox, 2002.
Larsen, Timothy, and Daniel J. Treier, eds. *The Cambridge Companion to Evangelical Theology*. Cambridge: Cambridge University Press, 2007.
McDermott, Gerald R., ed. *The Oxford Handbook of Evangelical Theology*. Oxford: Oxford University Press, 2010.
McGrath, Alister. *Evangelicalism and the Future of Christianity*. London: Hodder & Stoughton, 1993.

---

44. John Stott, *Evangelical Truth: A Personal Plea for Unity, Integrity and Faithfulness* (Downers Grove: IVP, 2003), 61.

Nassif, Bradley. *The Evangelical Theology of the Orthodox Church.* Yonkers: St Vladimir's Seminary Press, 2021.

Noll, Mark A., and Carolyn Nystrom. *Is the Reformation Over? An Evangelical Assessment of Contemporary Roman Catholicism.* Grand Rapids: Baker, 2005.

Oxbrow, Mark, and Tim Grass, eds. *The Mission of God: Studies in Orthodox and Evangelical Mission.* Oxford: Regnum, 2015.

Stiller, Brian C., Todd M. Johnson, Karen Stiller and Mark Hutchinson, eds. *Evangelicals around the World: A Global Handbook for the 21st Century.* Nashville: Thomas Nelson for the World Evangelical Alliance, 2015.

Stott, John. *Evangelical Truth: A Personal Plea for Unity, Integrity and Faithfulness.* Downers Grove: IVP, 2003.

6

The Challenge of Post-Evangelicalism and the Search for the Non-Negotiable

Martin P. Grünholz

Introduction

We live in a secular age. This realization is not new. What is new is that the wave of people abandoning their faith and leaving the church is not only affecting the major Protestant and Catholic churches, but increasingly also the evangelical movement. Yet this shift away from evangelicalism, which has become quite strong during the past ten years, is not a form of secularization but of deconstruction. It is generally called post-evangelicalism.

Post-Evangelicals and Post-Christians

Post evangelicalism raises serious questions for the evangelical movement, which is questioned, criticized, examined and sometimes discarded. As a prominent German post-evangelical, Thorsten Dietz, argues in his book *People with a Mission*, it is less a question of a widespread exodus from evangelical churches and networks, but rather an intensive discussion about how much diversity evangelicalism can tolerate.[1] And Dietz writes:

---

1. Thorsten Dietz, *Menschen mit Mission: Eine Landkarte der evangelikalen Welt* (Holzgerlingen: SCM R. Brockhaus, 2022), 321–29.

My suggestion at this point is to regard post-evangelicals neither as liberal apostates nor as fugitives from fundamentalism. It is too early for summarising assessments of the spectrum. All simple interpretations either as apostasy or as a movement of spiritual growth are unlikely to do justice to the diversity of the field.[2]

Post-evangelicals see themselves as a movement, a community of thought and learning, in which so-called unhealthy practices and theological convictions are discarded or adapted. The end of this process of deconstruction is thus not necessarily apostasy from the Christian faith, nor does post-evangelicalism construct a precise theological foundation.

The term post-evangelicalism goes back to a book first published in 1995 by Dave Tomlinson, a long-time vicar in the Church of England and now chaplain at St Ethelburga's Centre for Reconciliation and Peace in London.[3] Although the evangelical movement was still growing at the time, Tomlinson criticized the fact that its doctrine and its practice were drifting further and further apart and that evangelicals were losing touch with mainstream society. In his view, a claim to truth and an understanding of the Bible were being advocated that were ideologically narrow and not in line with academic scholarship. In practice, the evangelical commitment to social justice was falling short. Tomlinson claimed that we need a Christianity for a new age, which he saw in a post-evangelical movement. His criticism and the concept of post-evangelicalism only found significant resonance after the new edition of the book in 2014. Interestingly, Tomlinson already distinguished between post-evangelical and ex-evangelical. He understood the latter as a "ceasing to be" while he understood post-evangelical as "following on from."[4] Looking at current groups and so-called "dropout networks," it is obvious that not everyone has followed this conceptual distinction. The boundary between post-evangelical, ex-evangelical and ex-Christian is rather blurred and must be considered carefully on a case-by-case basis.

Someone who did give up Christianity altogether is Joshua Harris, the author of the book *I Kissed Dating Goodbye*, which was published in 1997, sold over 1.2 million copies worldwide and was recognized and discussed internationally.[5] The long-time pastor of the USA megachurch Covenant Life Church, Gaithersburg, Maryland, initially resigned from the pastorate in 2015,

---

2. Dietz, *Menschen mit Mission*, 321; all translations from German are my own.
3. Dave Tomlinson, *The Post-Evangelical* (London: SPCK, 2014).
4. Tomlinson, *Post-Evangelical*, 6.
5. Joshua Harris, *I Kissed Dating Goodbye* (Sisters: Multnomah Books, 1997).

expressed doubts about his own book the following year and finally banned further sales of the book in 2018. In July 2019, he publicly declared that he and his wife Shannon were divorcing due to "significant changes [that] have taken place in both of us."[6] He then told *The Guardian* that he had lost his faith and no longer considered himself a Christian.[7]

The longer the post-evangelical movement exists, the harsher its criticism of classic evangelicalism is becoming:

> To follow Jesus in the twenty-first century is to follow him out of certain evangelical norms. To deconstruct these temples of idolatry, and to call others to do the same. In the interviews and research I conducted for this book, many different evangelical norms came up as issues that Christians are deconstructing today. Some of the big ones were politics, purity culture, a "flat" reading of the Bible, treatment and exclusion of the LGBTQ+ community, the doctrine of hell, and hypocrisy ... [W]e will look at how to best move forward when there are clearly parts of Christianity (namely evangelicalism) that need to be deconstructed.[8]

This accusation of "evangelical idolatry" and the call to deconstruct evangelicalism are not coming from outside critics but from within: from post-evangelical Christians, co-workers, pastors, theologians and others who see themselves as a kind of drop-outs yet usually publish their books in publishing houses that are known as evangelical and discuss their issues in podcasts and blogs. Their polemics concern the foundations of the Christian faith, not just a specific theological tradition. As Volker Gäckle writes:

> The debate began with the question of how to evaluate same-sex sexuality and has now landed on much more central theological questions: Is there a final judgement by God? Is faith in Jesus Christ the decisive criterion for salvation and lostness? Is the Holy Scripture a reliable and trustworthy basis for the faith and life of the church, even from a historical perspective? Pietism argued about this with the ecumenical missionary movement and liberal

---

6. See www.instagram.com/p/B0CtVRingGj/.

7. See www.theguardian.com/world/2019/jul/29/author-christian-relationship-guide-joshua-harris-says-marriage-over. Kevin DeYoung offers a good statement and classification www.thegospelcoalition.org/article/reflections-josh-harris-deconversion/.

8. Preston Ulmer, *Deconstruct Faith, Discover Jesus: How Questioning Your Religion Can Lead You to a Healthy and Holy God* (Colorado Springs: NavPress, 2023), 72, 77; German: *Anders als geglaubt* (Holzgerlingen: SCM R. Brockhaus, 2024), 103, 110–11.

theology at church congresses and synods in the 1960s and 1970s. Today we are arguing about similar issues in our own community.⁹

What is Evangelical?

In order to better understand the issues, we need to approach the origins of post-evangelicalism from two sides: a historical and a theological one.

Historically, the term evangelical occurred for the first time in English with William Tyndale in 1531, who spoke of "evangelical truth."[10] This referred to the truth of the gospel and trust in this gospel alone. In the English-speaking world, the term "Evangelical Church" became established and was often used as a synonym for "Protestant Church" as based on the Reformation in the sixteenth century. However, the term underwent a change in the following centuries. First in the USA, where evangelical churches increasingly began to distinguish themselves from the "mainline Protestants," who followed liberal theology and biblical criticism in the ways of Enlightenment theology. A famous point in the evolution of the term evangelical were the global campaigns by Billy Graham, who consistently spoke of "evangelical" to distinguish himself from the mainline Protestant churches. In the English-speaking context the theologians Martin Lloyd-Jones and John Stott, and in the German-speaking context the long-standing chairman of the German Evangelical Alliance, Fritz Laubach, helped to coin the term as a concept of identity. In historical and sociological understanding, the term was linked to the Reformation, in Germany to Pietism as an inner-church renewal movement, internationally to revivalist movements such as "The Great Awakening" and to the Evangelical Alliance, founded in London in 1846.

However, viewing the evangelical movement solely from this historical perspective would not do justice to its self-image because its very plurality cannot be captured in this way alone. As the President of the Union School of Theology, Michael Reeves, argues in *Gospel People*:

> If "evangelicalism" is merely a sociological category and means nothing more than the common traits of all who wear the label, of course evangelicalism will look a shallow thing. If "evangelical"

---

9. Volker Gäckle, "Windstille, Wandel und Gottes Wirken," *Lebendige Gemeinde* 4 (2021): 16. Professor Gäckle is Rector of the evangelical Liebenzell International College.

10. Phil Johnson, "The History of Evangelicalism," *Pulpit Magazine* 3 (2009), https://web.archive.org/web/20100616020408/http://www.shepherdsfellowship.org/pulpit/Posts.aspx?ID=4111.

theology is stretched to fit all that, then it is the product not of historic and biblical doctrines but of whatever theology is currently doing the rounds. In that case "evangelicalism" must be vacuous and faddish.[11]

In 1989, the historian David Bebbington summarized the four core elements of the evangelical movement in what became known as the Bebbington Quadrilateral. He argued that evangelicals 1) see themselves as faithful to the Bible, emphasizing the trustworthiness of the Bible and 2) standing for substitutionary atonement as a central element of the doctrine of justification. 3) They are convinced of the need for personal conversion and therefore evangelize, actively working to spread the gospel so that as many people as possible are saved, 4) and they value social action.[12] Bebbington understands the evangelical movement as a sociological entity that is closely organized around theological positions.

Particularly in view of the post-evangelical movement, it is evident that a historically defined identity of evangelicalism is not enough and should not even be the priority, because having common roots does not mean agreement on theological identity. The strength of evangelicalism lies precisely in the fact that it has a common theological foundation as a Bible-based movement, independent of sociological structures, institutions or just a common history. Reeves therefore also argues in favour of seeing the true evangelical movement as anchored in a clear theology with three essential doctrines: "1. revelation by the Father in the Bible. 2. redemption through the Son in the gospel. 3. the rebirth through the Spirit in our hearts."[13] In other words, evangelicals are deliberately trinitarian. In this respect he follows John Stott, who said: "I maintain that the evangelical faith is nothing other than the historic Christian faith: the original, biblical, apostolic Christianity."[14]

---

11. Michael Reeves, *Gospel People. A Call for Evangelical Integrity* (Wheaton: Crossway, 2022), 145.

12. David W. Bebbington, *Evangelicalism in Modern Britain. A History from the 1730s to the 1980s* (London: Unwin Hyman, 1989), 2–17.

13. Reeves, *Gospel People*, 16.

14. Michael Reeves and John Stott, *The Reformation: What You Need to Know and Why* (Peabody: Hendrickson, 2017), 31.

Deconstruction

It is precisely from these theological convictions that post-evangelicals are breaking away. And when they do, they often use a term that is closely associated with them, namely "deconstruction." Deconstruction may be a buzzword, but it is not a recent innovation. Its philosophical roots lie with René Descartes (1596–1650) and his methodological doubt, which gave rise to modern philosophy, especially to the rationalist and empiricist questioning of Immanuel Kant (1724–1804), who exaggerated reason. The French philosopher Jacques Derrida (1930–2004) is considered the founder and main representative of deconstructionism.[15] The term was first applied to Christianity in 2008 by the Strasbourg philosopher Jean-Luc Nancy (1940–2021) in his book *Deconstruction of Christianity*.[16] Nancy was concerned with dismantling fixed systems in order to create new room for manoeuvre; he left it open whether and in what form something would subsequently be reconstructed or reassembled.

Deconstruction is a matter of testing convictions on the basis of their viability, which is often done on the basis of practical benefits. A deconstruction of faith can begin with simple questions such as "That doesn't make sense to me," moving on to more fundamental doubts such as "Faith doesn't 'work' for me" to profound questioning: "Faith doesn't do me any good." This approach does not necessarily lead to a loss of faith but there are many documented reports of people who have gone through a deconstruction process and ultimately de-converted, lost their faith, particularly as a result of podcasts and books such as the ones mentioned above. The theologian Markus Voss describes a number of such harrowing reports of loss of faith in a video.[17] If one follows the podcasts, blogs and books of prominent post-evangelical representatives, it is shocking to realize how many of them are gradually taking the path from deconstruction to de-conversion.

---

15. A good introduction to the philosophical theory of deconstructivism is provided by P. Zima, *Die Dekonstruktion* (2nd ed.; Tübingen: Francke, 2016).

16. Jean-Luc Nancy, *Dis-Enclosure. The Deconstruction of Christianity* (Oxford: Oxford University Press, 2008).

17. Markus Voss, „Dekonstruktion durch Worthaus" (2023), https://youtu.be/aLp3Xdh4fxo?si=0drHdKLPlK5KH5w5. Worthaus is an online media centre that has been in existence from 2010; it has since had a significant influence on the postmodern movement in Germany. In addition to many guest speakers, the main speakers are Thorsten Dietz and Siegfried Zimmer.

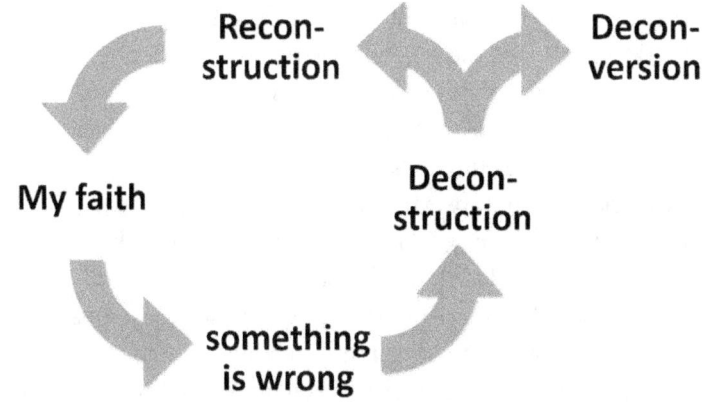

However, the biographies of Rebecca McLaughlin, Natha and Alisa Childers show that a deconstruction process can also have a positive outcome.[18] For example, Childers writes:

> The progressive wave that slammed me against the Rock of Ages had broken apart my deeply ingrained assumptions about Jesus, God, and the Bible. But that same Rock of Ages slowly but surely began to rearrange the pieces, discarding a few and putting the right ones back where they belonged. This is my account of the reconstruction of my faith.[19]

After a phase of questioning their faith, these people came into contact with the gospel of the grace of Jesus in a completely new way and were gripped by it. Their books are both biographically and argumentatively strong testimonies to a reconstruction of faith in the evangelical tradition. The central point is personal contact with Jesus and dealing with good arguments from biblical theology and from apologetics.

Post-Evangelical Positions

In German-speaking countries, the theologian Martin Benz has had much influence with his book *Wenn der Glaube nicht mehr passt. Ein Umzugshelfer* (*When faith no longer fits. A help to move*) and his podcast entitled "Movecast."

---

18. Rebecca McLaughlin, *Confronting Christianity: 12 Hard Questions for the World's Largest Religion* (Wheaton: Crossway, 2019); Natha, *Überrascht von Furcht* (4th ed.; Biel: Crosspaint, 2022); Alisa Childers, *Another Gospel? A Lifelong Christian Seeks Truth in Response to Progressive Christianity* (Carol Stream: Tyndale House, 2020).

19. Childers, *Another Gospel*, 9.

Benz listed a variety of topics that simply no longer "fit" for post-evangelicals in our time. He mentioned the general understanding of Scripture, the infallibility of God's word and the understanding of inspiration, and more specifically the violence in Scripture, the understanding of the cross as substitutionary atonement, redemption and eternal damnation; also evangelical positions on sexual ethics, especially on homosexuality and LGBTQI+; experiences of hypocrisy and abuse of power among Christians and a general lack of mercy and love, combined with strict black and white thinking.[20]

A central point of criticism that is raised by almost all post-evangelicals is sexual ethics. It is often the trigger and starting point for change, or the pivot at which a profound change that has taken place finally becomes visible. Criticism is levelled at the entire spectrum of sexual ethics, from the rejection of premarital and extramarital sex, and purity culture, to abortion, divorce and remarriage. The important American post-evangelical, David P. Gushee, a former member of the Southern Baptist Convention and professor of ethics in Louisville, had to leave the university due to what he saw as too narrow a position on sexual ethics. Gushee is now a professor at Mercer University in Atlanta, which sees itself as taking a lead in the field of post-evangelical theology.[21] In 2020 Gushee wrote: "Something that went terribly wrong in many evangelical contexts was the turn to sexual purity as the main way to state the moral norm, and the gendering of responsibility for it . . . The purity movement was linked to evangelical patriarchalism."[22]

But where sexual ethics is seen as problematic, the issues of course do not remain limited to this field of ethics alone, but the whole field of ethics and its concept is up for debate. It is striking that many post-evangelical tendencies emanate from ethicists who are in favour of fundamental changes of direction. The prime example in Germany is the proposal for a "Transformative Ethics. An ethics for thinking for oneself" which was largely shaped and promoted by the professors Tobias Faix and Thorsten Dietz. In the accompanying podcast, "Map and Territory," Dietz said:

> Very conservative, traditional, fundamentalist ethics try to lock people into norms, into grids, into boxes and have zero sense of autonomy, of self-determination, of self-efficacy. It is simply

---

20. Martin Benz, *Wenn der Glaube nicht mehr passt. Ein Umzugshelfer* (Neukirchen-Vluyn: Neukirchener Verlagsgesellschaft, 2022), 47–172.

21. See www.reflab.ch/david-gushee-und-die-postevangelikalen-eine-globale-reise/.

22. Donald P. Gushee, *After Evangelicalism; The Path to a New Christianity* (Louisville: Westminster John Knox, 2020), 122–23.

pure heteronomy, pure heteronomy. And when people break down because of this, there's nothing you can do, it's God's will. That is hostile to life. It doesn't do justice to the liberating God of the Bible, it's merciless, it's hard-hearted. We are absolutely committed to strengthening Christian freedom, freedom as self-determination and autonomy.[23]

And surely, where ethics are re-thought, the question of doctrine naturally also arises. If biblical norms and commandments are up for discussion, why not other theological convictions? In 2023, Jakob Friedrichs, who made a significant contribution to the spread of post-evangelical thought in Germany, wrote in his book on Easter: "So if it is important to you to believe in Jesus as the Son of a virgin, then do it. With joy. But if this idea rather alienates you, then do not. And please no less joyfully."[24] The virgin birth, although biblically attested and bindingly recognized in the ecumenical confessions of the Nicene and the *Apostolicum*, is presented as an option that one can choose to believe but does not have to.

Consequently, the whole question of the deity of Jesus is also up for debate. It is also asserted that Jesus did not claim to be the Son of God. He did not see himself as part of a divine plan of salvation and redemption that deliberately headed for Golgotha and found its fulfilment in the planned triumph on the Easter morning. In a book published only a few weeks before the drafting of this chapter, the post-evangelical theologian and podcaster, Jason Liesendahl, wrote about Jesus in terms of a process theology to which many post-evangelical theologians tend:

> Jesus was a human being. He was a devout Jew. It is possible that in his early years he had an experience with God that we do not know about, which shaped him for the rest of his life. That is why Jesus dedicated his life to the cause of God . . . Perhaps it was not only Jesus who died on the cross, but also faith in God in Jesus. And in the friends of Jesus.[25]

It is only logical that the doctrine of the substitutionary atonement on the cross of Golgotha is also under attack by post-evangelicals. On the statement

---

23. Thorsten Dietz, "Karte & Gebiet. Podcast einer Ethik zu Selberdenken"; Hartmut Rosa, "Gibt es ein gutes Leben in der Moderne?" Folge 35, 26.04.2024: 1:08:44 – 1:09:23, https://open.spotify.com/episode/4uC6vWzFyQlOXJiCDhZO9U?si=AzRSXhEURpafFYsIm3Qklg.

24. Jakob Friedrichs, *Ist das Gott oder kann das weg?* (Aßlar: Gerth Medien, 2020), 18.

25. Jason Liesendahl, *Gott kann auch nicht alles. Einführung in die Prozesstheologie* (Trier: ruach.jetzt, 2024), 40–42.

that "Jesus was the Son of God and the Saviour of the world, he came to die and he performed many miracles," Siegfried Zimmer of Worthaus commented: "It almost makes me vomit."[26] In the follow-up lecture, Dietz adds jokingly, "This substitutionary atonement theory – where is it in the New Testament? Search, search, search . . . it's not to be found."[27] In a provocative and exaggerated podcast, Friedrichs even referred to the doctrine of substitutionary atonement with offensive words that were censored by the editors of this book.[28]

Reference must also be made to changes in the field of eschatology. Post-evangelical publications strongly criticize the traditional understanding of heaven and hell, damnation and resurrection. Here, too, there is a striking proximity to process theology, as can be seen in Liesendahl, among others, who writes:

> In process theology, there is a great deal of scepticism towards this otherworldly reward-punishment system. There is even debate about the extent to which there can even be an afterlife in the sense of a personal consciousness . . . Will God's bait be successful in the end and bring the sticky process of healing the world to a good end? I honestly find that unlikely. But maybe God is good for surprises.[29]

By now it will be clear that post-evangelical positions differ greatly from evangelical convictions and that they essentially represent a different theology. The evangelical understanding of revelation and history, of the historicity and hermeneutics of the Bible, and in particular the doctrine of inspiration that regards the entire Bible as authoritative Holy Scripture, are strongly criticized and rejected. Gushee, for example, comments:

> Despite its profound meaning, the Bible cannot quite bear the weight evangelicals expect it to bear . . . Some scriptural texts consistently demonstrate that they are inspired by God because they prove so useful for teaching. A healthy post-evangelical approach to the Bible will heighten realism about the fact that the Bible is

---

26. Siegfried Zimmer, "Der Prozess vor Pilatus (Mk 15, 1–15) | 9.4.2.," https://youtu.be/w2lVEExi164?si=TPlmYbQ9X0zM5Crk&t=3327 at 55:20.

27. Thorsten Dietz, "Der Prozess: Warum ist Jesus gestorben? Worthaus 9.4.3, 10.6.2019": 1:10:20–1:10:30, www.youtube.com/watch?v=HDwUUbBOJeU.

28. Jakob Friedrichs, "Wofür starb Jesus? Teil 1, Hossa Talk #34 (20.03.2016)," https://hossa-talk.de/34-das-kreuz-wofuer-starb-jesus-teil-1/ at 56:40.

29. Liesendahl, *Gott kann auch nicht alles*, 194–95.

always an interpreted text, and that we flawed, limited people are the interpreters.[30]

For post-evangelicals, the Bible is not fully inspired but only in parts. The distinguishing criterion is usefulness. Post-evangelicals place themselves explicitly "beyond sola scriptura," as Gushee admits openly: "Beyond sola scriptura. Post-evangelicals are no longer able to accept exaggerated claims about the inerrancy and all-sufficiency of the Bible. If we hang in there with Christianity, we will need a new approach to listening for God's voice and discerning God's will."[31]

Post-evangelical theology is therefore very different from evangelical theology. While the two have a common historical origin, their theological positions are incompatible, despite the fact that post-evangelicals like to see themselves as bridge-builders between evangelicals and liberals, or evangelicals and science, or evangelicals and society.

Legitimate Concerns: Doubt and Discipleship

As with all criticism, and especially when it is voiced not just by individuals but by a larger number of representatives of the previously joint movement, there are of course justified arguments which should not be ignored. The fact that many post-evangelicals have biographical fractures and wounds can and must be recognized and taken seriously. Evangelicals are and remain sinners who must live from God's grace and forgiveness. In the name of evangelicalism, errors, false teachings and abuses have happened and continue to take place. Hurt must be taken seriously and addressed; sin must be exposed and named, for example where abuse has taken place. Where failure becomes recognizable, it is important to name it clearly, admit guilt and bring it before God and with people for clarification and forgiveness.

However, evangelicalism as a whole cannot be held responsible for the sins of individuals.[32] Not all violations and false teachings committed in the context or under the label "evangelical" can be attributed to evangelicalism.

From a practical theological perspective, Cedric Grossmann and Benjamin Carstens have provided practical recommendations for congregations and those affected, to ensure that such incidents, which often raise massive ques-

---

30. Gushee, *After Evangelicalism*, 43.
31. Gushee, *After Evangelicalism*, 45.
32. See also Reeves, *Gospel People*, 106.

tions in individuals, do not lead to a deconstruction of faith (or a preliminary stage of it), but to a reconstruction of faith. Their suggestions can only be mentioned briefly here:

- For congregations: don't fight with prohibitions; create a church culture that allows doubt; listen and share experiences.
- For those affected: focus on Jesus Christ; learn to live with unclarities and ambiguities; doubt your own doubts; protect your own heart; take children as role models.[33]

It will be crucial to seek honest answers to honest questions and to accompany people through a sometimes lengthy process of recovery. In particular, the beauty of Christian friendships will take on a whole new significance. When working with individuals in pastoral counselling, home groups and local churches, a great deal of empathy and pastoral wisdom is needed to accompany those affected when they have doubts and to guide them through their deconstruction processes. It is important to take people seriously, especially in and with their doubts. At the same time, it is important not to attempt to deal with all doubts at the same time, but to have one uncertainty at a time.

Going through a process of deconstruction naturally puts everything to the test. Yet both for individuals and for organizations such processes can also have a healing effect, namely when the reconstruction process results in a faith that is more stable and authentic than before and when issues are placed at the right level.

A. Childers and Tim Barnett end their book *The Deconstruction of Christianity* with the abiding hope in the living God.[34] Sometimes we find ourselves, like Peter and the other disciples, inwardly on Holy Saturday: full of questions, full of doubt, full of guilt and sin. Some questions also remain – but there are so many answers that we just do not know yet. When we find ourselves on Holy Saturday, Easter Sunday is just around the corner! A. Childers testifies:

> Slowly and steadily, God began to rebuild my faith. The questions that had knocked the foundation out from under my beliefs – the ones I had never thought to ask, the ones I didn't know existed – were not simply being answered. They were being dwarfed by sub-

---

33. Cedric Grossmann and Benjamin Carstens, "Dekonstruktion – Zerstörung oder Rettung des Glaubens?," www.wiedenest.de/artikel/dekonstruktion-zerstoerung-oder-rettung-des-glaubens.

34. Alisa Childers and Tim Barnett, *The Deconstruction of Christianity. What It Is, Why It's Destructive, and How to Respond* (Carol Stream: Tyndale House, 2023), 199–255.

stantial evidence and impenetrable logic so robust that I felt like a kid in a candy store – who had just found out that candy exists.[35]

We all need this result of reconstruction, renewal, consolidation and strengthening! All the more so that we can rediscover our identity as children of God in order to be courageous witnesses of the gospel in our world and times.

Limits of Our Concern: Distinction of Truths

In order to distinguish justified from unjustified concerns and accusations, and to define evangelicalism over against post-evangelicalism, we need some systematic criteria to separate different levels from one another so that we can evaluate them one by one. In my opinion, we need a hierarchy of truths as a theological triage because not all issues are equally important.

(spiritual) Opinions
e.g. style of music in church service...

Doctrinal statements
e.g. eschatology; understanding of baptism; women's ordination...

Truths of faith
Early church confessions (Apostolicum; Nicaenum; Athanasianum) especially substitutionary atonement; Bible as a revelation of God

The Foundation: Truths of the Faith

The decisive foundation of the Christian faith is formed by the truths of faith. These are the foundations and have highest priority, as the basis that determines whether someone is part of the Christian church in its 2,000-year-old form or

---

35. Childers, *Another Gospel*, 227.

not. Of central importance is the gospel that Jesus Christ died for us and for our sins and was bodily resurrected in order to reconcile us with God (Rom 3:21–26; 1 Cor 15:3–5; 2 Cor 5:19–21). These truths of faith find expression in the teaching of the Bible as God's revelation, in our redemption through the Son Jesus Christ and the rebirth and gathering into the church through the Holy Spirit.

This belief is reflected in the understanding of Scripture and the three authoritative early church confessions (the *Apostolicum*, the *Niceno-Constantinopolitanum* and the *Athanasianum*). Irrespective of the existence of different denominations, this is all about issues on which all churches and congregations throughout the ages agree. We are convinced that this foundation is not the result of human agreement but a work of the Holy Spirit, who founded the church at Pentecost (Acts 2; 15:28) and filled the apostles with authority and divine inspiration (2 Tim 3:16; 2 Pet 1:21).

Doctrinal Statements

The level of doctrinal statements is important although not of the same priority as the fundamental truths of faith. Topics such as a specific end-time doctrine (Rev 20), a specific baptismal practice (Rom 6), the understanding of the Lord's Supper (1 Cor 11) and ecclesiological questions about ministries in the church (1 Tim 2–3) are highly relevant and often have a very strong identity-forming effect on a Christian denomination.

Doctrinal issues can and must be discussed at a fundamental level, but different doctrinal statements do not prevent us from having fellowship with Christians of other convictions, provided that the truths of the faith are shared. In accordance with Ephesians 4:36, Christian organizations, institutions and networks often work together because they agree on the first level truth – for example, the basis of faith of the Evangelical Alliance – whilst giving each other freedom in other areas.

Opinions

All of us also have (theological) opinions. For example, it is normal for believers to favour different styles of music, just as there are different opinions about clothing styles and other outward appearances, especially between the generations. The same goes for opinions on politics, culture and society. When opinions are spiritually exaggerated and elevated to truths of faith, the situation quickly becomes difficult. In these areas there can be a genuine dialogue with each other, whereby believers can try to convince others with arguments. But in the sphere of opinions it is important to create freedom. We should not open a front on the wrong issues and bring guilt upon ourselves through hardheartedness or stubborn behaviour: "If anyone is inclined to be contentious, we have no such practice, nor do the churches of God" (1 Cor 11:16 ESV).

Hopeful Outlook: The Non-Negotiable

With this theological triage in mind, we can now ask again what evangelical theology stands for and how we can respond to the challenges posed by post-evangelicals as described in paragraph 5. To what do we hold on to as non-negotiable? Let us begin with the foundation, namely the doctrine of the infallible, divine inspiration of the Bible as Holy Scripture. Just as the Lausanne Covenant states: "We affirm the divine inspiration, truthfulness and authority of both Old and New Testament Scriptures in their entirety as the only written word of God, without error in all that it affirms, and the only infallible rule of faith and practice."[36] The Bible is enough! What we need is a return to this basic principle of the apostles and of theology, so that we adhere to what the Reformation understood by "sola scriptura." As J. I. Packer wrote very aptly: "I listen to Scripture to hear God preaching and instructing me in matters theological and practical, matters of belief and matters of behavior, matters of doctrine, matters of doxology, matters of devotion, matters of orthodoxy (right belief), and matters of orthopraxy (right living)."[37] We must retain this basic attitude and regain it where necessary.

In dogmatics we must adhere to a proclamation of the gospel that is bound to salvation history and confession. Our doctrine must be rooted in Scripture and unfold from there. As Harald Seubert explains:

> If we do not speak and teach from God's revelation in Christ and his word, statements on contemporary issues will remain phraselike, vague and ultimately void. This leads to a declaration of bankruptcy. The church is trapped in its own bubble when it aligns itself with the spirit of the age, precisely because it does not teach and

---

36. *Lausanne Covenant, Article 2: The Authority and Power of the Bible*, https://lausanne.org/statement/lausanne-covenant.
37. James I. Packer, *Engaging the Written Word of God* (Peabody: Hendrickson, 2012), 162.

proclaim profoundly from the centre, breadth and depth, from the word of the cross and the liberating power of the gospel.[38]

For this reason, substitutionary atonement is at the heart of our doctrine. It is not optional or merely one of many aspects of the New Testament message but it is the inner core of the gospel. This is why the European Evangelical Alliance affirms it in Articles 4 and 5 of its Statement of Faith:

> 4. The substitutionary sacrifice of the incarnate Son of God as the sole and all sufficient ground of redemption from the guilt and power of sin, and from its eternal consequences.
>
> 5. The justification of the sinner solely by the grace of God through faith in Christ crucified and risen from the dead.[39]

In this way we rely on the salvation that objectively happened and was given to us on the cross on Golgotha. We do not rely on an individual conviction based on experience, but on the *extra nos* of justification by grace alone through faith alone. Hence we agree with Ingolf Dalferth when he warns: "It is therefore not our experience that is the beginning of theology, but that without God nothing can be experienced . . . Experience-based theology comes to an end with death."[40]

Once we have this approach to doctrine, based on Scripture, we can also develop a theocentric ethics based on natural law. As John Lennox explained in his ethics: "The moral law is not a set of impersonal rules and regulations: it is the declared will of the tri-personal Creator. The human race's obedience, therefore, is always, ultimately, not merely a question of conforming to a law, but of obeying a person."[41] The late German professor of ethics Helmut Burkhardt therefore began his theocentric ethics with a basic definition: "The right thing to do is to act in accordance with God's will."[42]

---

38. Harald Seubert, "Heilsgeschichte und der dreieinige Gott," *Diakrisis* 43.3 (2022): 132–41, 132; https://ksbb-bayern.de/wp-content/uploads/2023/02/Heilsgeschichte-und-der-dreieinige-Gott.pdf.

39. EEA Statement of Faith, Articles 4 and 5, www.europeanea.org/wp-content/uploads/2019/11/2019-11_EEA-basis_of_faith_english.pdf.

40. Ingolf Dalferth, *Sünde. Die Entdeckung der Menschlichkeit* (3rd ed.; Leipzig: EVA, 2024), 425.

41. David Gooding and John Lennox, *Doing What's Right: Whose System of Ethics is Good Enough?* (The Quest for Reality and Significance Book 4; Belfast: Myrtlefield House), 95.

42. Helmut Burkhardt, *Einführung in die Ethik Band 1. Grund und Norm sittlichen Handelns. Fundamentalethik* (Gießen: Brunnen, 1996), 49.

This leads us to the conflict-ridden minefield of sexual ethics. When social norms are changing, Christian theology must find appropriate answers, but it must not allow itself to be driven by these changes. What the evangelical movement needs is a Protestant theology of the body. Carl R. Truman writes:

> Moreover, the church must rediscover natural law and a theology of the body . . . Simply put, it is the idea that the world in which we live is not simply a morally neutral "stuff" but has a moral order in itself. Our body in particular is not a vessel that we merely inhabit and animate. It is a deep and meaningful integral part of our identity, our self.⁴³

And the New Testament scholar, Joel White, adds:

> A Christian sexual ethic that is aligned [with biblical standards] does not have to embarrass us; on the contrary, it can also inspire us – especially in our time, which has become disorientated and unstable for many. A biblically-based sexual ethic is not bad news about what God wants to withhold from us, but good news about how beautiful life can be when we discover God's design for intimate togetherness.⁴⁴

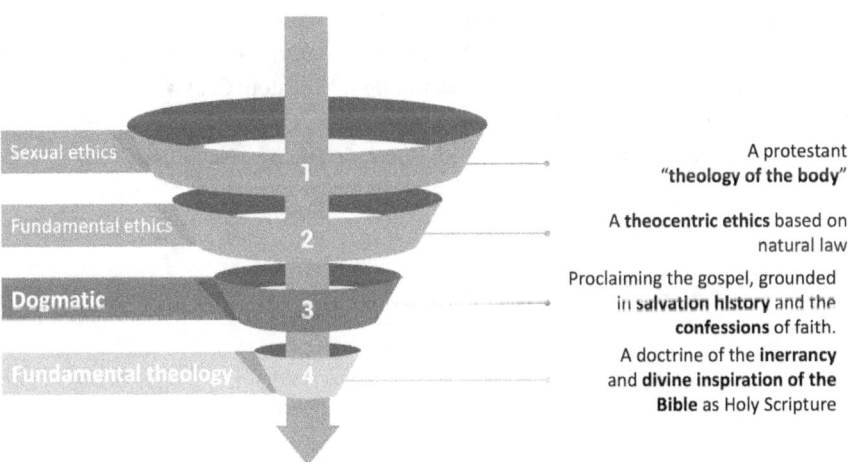

---

43. Carl R. Trueman, *Strange New World. How Thinkers and Activists Redefined Identity and Sparked the Sexual Revolution* (Wheaton: Crossway, 2022), 182.

44. Joel White, *Was sich Gott dabei gedacht hat. Eine biblische Basis einer christlichen Sexualethik* (Holzgerlingen: SCM R. Brockhaus, 2021), 23.

The evangelical movement is certainly not perfect. But amid the current challenges from within the movement and the rapid changes in society, the evangelical movement stands in the tradition from the Book of Acts to the twenty-first century and does its best to proclaim and embody the teachings of its Lord, Jesus Christ, in a biblically faithful way. This is something we must hold on to and continue to work on.

Bibliography

Childers, Alisa. *Another Gospel? A Lifelong Christian Seeks Truth in Response to Progressive Christianity*. Carol Stream: Tyndale House, 2020.

Childers, Alisa, and Tim Barnett. *The Deconstruction of Christianity. What It Is, Why It's Destructive, and How to Respond*. Carol Stream: Tyndale House, 2023.

Dietz, Thorsten. *Menschen mit Mission. Eine Landkarte der evangelikalen Welt*. Holzgerlingen: SCM R. Brockhaus, 2022.

McLaughlin, Rebecca. *Confronting Christianity: 12 Hard Questions for the World's Largest Religion*. Wheaton: Crossway, 2019.

Reeves, Michael. *Gospel People. A Call for Evangelical Integrity*. Wheaton: Crossway, 2022.

Tomlinson, Dave. *The Post-Evangelical*. London: SPCK, 2014.

Trueman, Carl R. *Strange New World. How Thinkers and Activists Redefined Identity and Sparked the Sexual Revolution*. Wheaton: Crossway, 2022.

———. *The Rise and Triumph of the Modern Self: Cultural Amnesia, Expressive Individualism, and the Road to Sexual Revolution*. Wheaton: Crossway 2020.

Ulmer, Preston. *Deconstruct Faith, Discover Jesus. How Questioning Your Religion Can Lead You to a Healthy and Holy God*. Colorado Springs: Navpress, 2023.

7

Nationalist and/or Populist Political Movements

How do Evangelicals Vote and Respond?

Evert van de Poll

Introduction – the Context, Swing to the Right

The focus of this chapter is the growing attraction of nationalist and populist political movements among the Christian electorate, including evangelical Protestants. Various evangelical leaders are concerned and critical towards this trend, which raises the question whether or not a nationalist political stance is compatible with evangelical identity. We will look at the trend of nationalism, different understandings of what is a nation, and where nationalism comes in in the changing political landscape all over Europe. We shall also bring to light the differences and overlap with populism. Then we will analyse the position of evangelical Protestants and analyse why so many vote for parties with a nationalist outlook. Finally we will outline an evangelical response, based on biblical considerations.

The Trend and the European Parliament

The elections for the European Parliament on 9 June 2024, as well as recent parliamentary elections in the Netherlands, France, Great Britain and other countries, have illustrated a change in the political landscape that is taking place across the continent. Besides the traditional parties, divided into right-wing, centre and left-wing, new political formations have emerged which are transforming the political landscape. Most notable is the growing appeal of nationalist parties and movements, many of which have a populist outlook. The combined result of the latter in elections varies from 10 to 35 percent nationally, and even more in some regions.[1]

In the media these parties are often collectively designated as "extreme-right," "radical-right," "populist" or "nationalist," but in actual fact they vary from country to country. As for their political agendas, there is considerable overlap with traditional or so-called moderate right-wing parties on the one hand, and social-democratic parties on the other hand. Yet what they have in common is a concern for the sovereignty and the economic interests of their own nation, and for the cultural identity of its native population, over and against economic immigration, multiculturality, and the open borders and free-trade liberalism of "Brussels" and "Europe."

In the European Parliament, these parties are allied in three groups: the largest one is "Patriots for Europe" with 84 seats,[2] followed by the "European Conservatives and Reformists" (ECR) with 78 seats[3] and "Europe of Sovereign Nations" (ESN) with 25 seats.[4] Together they comprise 23.2 percent of the parliament (187 out of 720 seats). These numbers do not include the representatives of similar parties who are among the 32 non-attached MEPs or have joined the European People's Party.[5]

---

1. A case in point is Great Britain. During the general elections on 4 July 2024, the Reform UK Party led by the Brexit campaigner Nigel Farage obtained almost 15 percent of the votes. Due to the "first past the post" system, the party only obtained four out of the 650 seats in the House of Commons. In comparison, the social democratic Labour Party obtained 411 out of the 650 seats (63 percent) but they won only 33.7 percent of the votes, against 23.7 percent for the Conservatives.

2. The formation of the parliamentary group *Patriots for Europe* was initiated by the Hungarian prime minister, Viktor Orban (Fidesz). Its members are MEPs from France, Hungary (two parties), Italy, Spain, Portugal, Czech Republic (two parties), Austria, Netherlands, Belgium, Denmark, Greece and Latvia. The president is Jordan Bardella of the French *Rassemblement national*.

3. The group *European Conservatives and Reformists* (ECR) includes MEPs from Belgium, Bulgaria, Croatia, Cyprus, Czechia, Denmark, Sweden, Finland, Greece, Italy, Latvia (two parties), Lithuania (three parties), Luxemburg, Netherlands, Poland (two parties), Romania (two parties) and some independent MEPs from France and Estonia.

4. The group *Europe of Sovereign Nations* includes MEPs from Bulgaria, Czechia, France, Germany, Hungary, Lithuania, Poland and Slovakia.

5. The European People's Party is the largest group in the European Parliament. It includes mainly Christian Democrats, but also moderate right-wing MEPs such as *Les Republicains* of France.

Nationalism
Definition(s)

All these parties are invariably called nationalist and/or populist. But what exactly does that mean? We can define nationalism in a general sense as a strong sense of belonging to a certain people in a certain country; an attachment to its history and its national institutions; and also to what is considered the collective identity of this people and this country. This sense of belonging primarily concerns the nation in the sense of a people, an ethnic group, which is not the same as the modern nation-state.

Social scientists do not agree on a clear definition of nationalism. Secular commentators have put forward a variety of distinctions between nationalism and patriotism, or types of nationalism, to distinguish between what is acceptable and what is not. There is also much disagreement about the historical roots of nationalism. Some see it as dating from the French Revolution or the development of German Romanticism, while others trace it back to the Reformation or even to the medieval period. Perhaps the most insightful definition is that of Scottish social scientist Anthony Smith, one of the founders of nationalism studies. In an interview with *The Ukranian Week*, he summarized his definition as follows:

> The core doctrine of nationalism is a very abstract one. It says that the world is divided into nations, and that each has its character, its destiny, its history. It says that people belong, or should belong to a nation, that nations should be free and express themselves fully, and that a world of peace and justice is the one that's founded on free nations.
>
> What has happened is that in each case, this doctrine has been married to other ideas of particular nations, particular ethnic communities, particular political communities, which change the tenor and the tone of that core doctrine. For example, in Poland they had an idea that Poland was a crucified Christ, which had to be resurrected. Nowhere is this part of the doctrine of nationalism. Some nationalisms may be liberal or bourgeois, in Czechia for example. Other nationalisms may be anti-imperialist, anticolonial, or perhaps working class or peasant nationalisms, depending on the situation of that particular group.[6]

---

6. Interview with Anthony Smith, *The Ukrainian Week*, Sept. 2008, about his book *The Cultural Foundation of Nations* (2007).

This definition helps us to see that nationalism has various expressions, and that it may be fused with diverse and even competing political objectives.

Different Understandings of Nation

At the heart of the issue of nationalism are different understandings of what a nation is and what nationality means. Anthony Smith defines a nation as "a named population sharing a historic territory, common symbols and historical memories, a mass public culture, a common economy and common legal rights and duties for its members." He finds that nationalism builds on pre-existing kinship, religious and belief systems of the ethnic groups that form the background of modern nations. These "ethnie," as he calls them, are "units of population with common ancestry myths and historical memories, elements of shared culture, some link with a historic territory and some measure of solidarity, at least among their elites."[7]

The question becomes whether or not this ethnic and symbolic background should have a bearing on what a nation means to us today. At this juncture, there are fundamental disagreements. In a recent interview, the Dutch political scientist Eric Hendriks who lives in Budapest, explained:

> Conservatives, particularly here in Hungary, have a different, more romantic understanding of the nation than left-liberal circles in the Netherlands, in which Dutchness is often reduced to a matter of bureaucratic-legal registration. In the left-liberal ideal, the nation is an open field of individuals within a "neutral" legal framework. [Here in Hungary] in contrast, there is the romantic notion of nationhood – which grounds the nation within a cultural or ethnohistorical destiny. This understanding developed in the Romantic period and used to be common throughout Europe. Hungarian conservatives see their nation as consisting of substantial historical units: from the Magyar to several other ethnicities, cultures and religious groups.[8]

Hendriks goes on to explain why leftwing liberals want to strip the concept of nationhood of its deep grounding in a historical people and a shared culture, and instead reduce it to a legal and official category. Their argument is that if

---

7. Anthony D. Smith, *Nations and Nationalism in a Global Era*, 57.

8. Eric Hendriks, "Naties in Europa. Boedapest: kruispunt voor liberalen, conservatieven en postliberalen," *Groen*, Journal of the *Wetenschappelijk instituut* of the Dutch political party *Christen Unie* (December 2023): 15; my translation.

you hold a Dutch passport, you are Dutch. This allows new Dutch people to immediately become fully Dutch – to belong completely on an abstract level. The advantage of this liberal view is that it is maximally open and inclusive. It leaves as much room as possible for religious and (sub)cultural pluralism in society. In this framework, what holds the nation-state together should be no more than what is legally and morally necessary to keep the playing field open and tolerant.

But then Hendriks asks: is Dutch citizenship really just a legal-bureaucratic category, a passport, a formal framework on the leftwing liberal model? Or is it a civic-republican practice with duties and a shared ethos, an existential unity, a community of destiny that extends through the ages, as conservatives hold?

Hendriks concludes by saying that "each of the two models and the various intermediate forms – more or less culturalist, more or less demanding, more substantial or more legal, more romantic or more liberal – all have issues. And none is equally applicable in every country."[9]

Civic and Ethnic Nationalism (Ignatieff)

The distinction between a cultural-Romantic and the leftwing liberal vision of what a nation is, runs parallel to the distinction between civic and ethnic nationalism proposed by several authors like Michael Ignatieff. Civic nationalism, which Ignatieff and others find acceptable, holds that a nation should be composed of all those who subscribe to its political creed, irrespective of race, ethnicity, colour or religion. According to this view, what holds a nation together are not its common roots but the rule of law.

Ethnic nationalism, according to Ignatieff, finds that national belonging is the overriding form of belonging, based on the people's pre-existing ethnic characteristics, their language, religion, customs and tradition. In the nineteenth century the peoples of Europe that lived under imperial regimes were inspired by this nationalism, which is currently gaining ground in many European countries. Ignatieff warns that the stronger the sense of belonging to one's own group, the more hostile, the more violent, the feelings towards outsiders, the "other."[10]

---

9. Hendriks, "Naties in Europa," 20.
10. Michael Ignatieff, *Blood and Belonging: Journeys into the New Nationalism* (New York: Farrar, Strauss & Giroux, 1994), 1–6, 189.

However, this neat distinction does not always accord with reality. Anthony Smith brings out the fact that even nations based on common citizenship do remember the ethnic tradition that has shaped them in the past.[11]

Nationalism and Liberation – Two Sides of the Coin

In the past, a large part of Europe consisted of multi-ethnic and multicultural kingdoms and empires: Holy Roman, Austro-Hungarian, Ottoman, Russian. However, during the last centuries the trend has been that each nation (people) wanted to be independent in its own nation-state. Some states now correspond to a single nation or ethnic people, whilst others include significant ethnic minorities which may strive for autonomy or even independence. This trend explains why there is so much apprehension towards the idea of a federal European Union. Nations (peoples) have fought so hard to gain their sovereignty that they are very reluctant, to say the least, to accept a new supranational layer of governance "above" them.

Nationalism was a major drive to liberate states and unite people in a common cause in the 1989 revolutions in Central and Eastern Europe. These were not just rebellions against an illegitimate regime but also nationalist revolutions against Soviet domination. Today, the same nationalism is a potent force to rally the people of Ukraine, Poland and the Baltic States to defend their country against Russian imperialism. On the other hand, the same drive was also responsible for multiple claims to sovereignty which caused conflict and war in the ethno-federal setting of the former Yugoslavia from 1992 onwards.[12]

Ethnic nationalism is open to idolatry because it requires loyalty to the state, the people and the race, the motherland, the fatherland, King and country. Even in states where the initial struggle was viewed positively, nations that affirm their identity can be tempted by self-absorption, narrowness of spirit and xenophobia. In multicultural states the situation is complicated by the fact that ethnicity may be fluid and many people now have more than one ethnic identity.[13]

---

11. Anthony D. Smith, "Gastronomy or geology?," 19.

12. This is brought out by Valerie Bunce, "The National Idea: Imperial Legacies and Post-Communist Pathways," *East European Politics and Societies* 19.3 (2005): 412.

13. For this section I am indebted to Rosemary Caldwell, "Populism, patriotism and hospitality," in Jeff Fountain (ed.), *Hope, Healing and Hospitality. The 2017 State of Europe Report* (Amsterdam: Seismos Press/Schuman Centre for European Studies, 2018), 10–15.

Populism and How It Relates to Nationalism

A political concept closely related to nationalism is populism, a term derived from the Latin word *populus*, "people." The Oxford English dictionary gives a neutral definition: populism is "support for the concerns of ordinary people." In our time this term refers to political leaders and movements who claim to express "the will of the people" and who aim to defend it against opposing forces. Often the term also implies an approach to politics which oversimplifies more complex issues. "Populists have always used crude stereotypes and sweeping statements in their rhetoric."[14]

The difficulty of the label is that most leaders themselves do not identify as populist; it is a negative label given to them by academics and media. It is used pejoratively, much like the labels nationalism, far-right and extreme right. The movements to which these labels refer rather identify as patriotic, sovereigntist, anti-austerity, illiberal or post-liberal, democrats or freedom party.

Two Oppositions

Populism can be characterized by two oppositions. First a "vertical" opposition of "the people" against elites who do not defend their interests. They might be EU technocrats, the current government, financial institutions, multinational companies, or all of these together. And second a "horizontal" opposition of the native people against incomers who threaten their economic position and the society to which they are attached; immigrants and the growing immigrant communities, especially the Muslims among them.

Populist Movements – Left and Right

As a result of these oppositions, populist leaders and their voters tend to be in favour of direct democracy (in the form of a referendum); they also tend to be intolerant towards the ruling elites and political parties on the other end of the spectrum, arguing that they do not represent "the people"; and they favour a strong state, even an authoritarian form of governance. The British theologian and social theorist John Milbank explains:

> More precisely, a populist movement pursues causes that tend to centre on a way of life that is perceived as threatened. Not so

---

14. Samuel Abraham, "No alternative to liberal democracy," *New Eastern Europe* 2 (2017): 7–13, here 8.

much equality is demanded as the right to go on quietly flourishing in a particular way to which people are attached. Sometimes, this means that it is the values and lifestyles of the modestly successful, the upper working-classes and the lower middle-classes that are being defended against both more freewheeling wealthy elites and the more anarchic, gregarious forces of working-class life . . . As to structures, populism characteristically cares little about formal democracy or the rights of minorities. Typically, it looks to a strong leader to deliver it from forces seen as perverse, though they may sometimes be inevitable. These can be the incursion of foreigners or drastic changes in the general way of life of a people. It tends to Caesarism.[15]

Populist politicians are Eurosceptic: they oppose the way in which the EU currently functions and the economic globalization of which the EU is seen as an agent.

Although populism is usually a right-wing movement, there are also left-wing forms of populism such as *Sumar* (formerly *Podemos*) in Spain, the *Bündnis Sarah Wagenknecht* in Germany, *La France Insoumise* in France. Some would also add the *Socialistische Partij* in the Netherlands is populist.

Populism and Democracy

Supporters argue that populism constitutes the essence of democratic politics, and that it is liberalism, and the liberal elite, that is the problem.

According to opponents, populism's main danger is that it is a moralist ideology that rejects any division of interests or opinions within "the people." It rejects the legitimacy of opponents and weakens the rights of minorities. This uncompromising stand leads to a polarized political culture, dividing the people into "us" who are good and "them" who are a bad. Some call it "an illiberal democratic response to undemocratic liberalism."[16]

---

15. John Milbank, "The Problem of Populism and the Promise of a Christian Politics," ABC News, 16 February 2017, www.abc.net.au/religion/the-problem-of-populism-and-the-promise-of-a-christian-politics/10096050. For a fuller treatment of the same subject, see his chapter "Virtue against sovereignty," in *Virtues in the Public Sphere: Citizenship, Civic Friendship and Duty*, ed. James Arthur (London: Routledge, 2020), 3–27.

16. See the discussion in Cas Mudde and Cristóbal Rovira Kaltwasse, "Populism," in Michael Freeden, Lyman Tower Sargent and Marc Stears (eds), *The Oxford Handbook of Political Ideologies* (Oxford: Oxford University Press, 2013), 500–6.

Populism and Nationalism: Different and Overlapping

Rosemary Caldwell helpfully describes the relation between populism and nationalism as follows:

> There is a close connection between European populist parties and nationalism, often combined with authoritarianism. Their xenophobic nature comes from a concept of the nation that relies on an ethnic and chauvinistic definition of the people and rejects the multicultural nature of many modern European societies.[17]

In left-wing and progressive circles, as well as in the media, nationalism and populism are often portrayed as identical and collectively labelled as "ultra" or "extreme" right-wing. But that is an oversimplification. Not all right-wing parties which emphasize national identity and economic sovereignty are therefore populist. A "my nation-first" kind of political agenda is not necessarily populist in the sense of anti-elite, against representative democracy, and in favour of an autocratic regime. Being patriotic does not automatically mean that one is against immigration and against allowing non-native communities to express themselves in society. Similarly, not all patriotic political leaders oppose European integration and even the European Union, as long as national sovereignty is maintained.

Similarly, populist movements are not by definition nationalistic. Left-wing populism has a mainly economic agenda. It opposes austerity measures and the borderless free market of neo-liberalism. It also expresses a sort of economic nationalism versus the supranational policies imposed by the EU and the European Central Bank. German journalist Matthias Krupa speaks of an emerging "left-wing nationalism" which "condemns the EU as the cold-hearted perpetrator of endless neoliberalism."[18] But these parties are not at all attached to national identity nor to the traditional culture of the nation.

However, right-wing populist movements are invariably nationalistic. When they talk about the "people," they mean the native population. Playing on feelings of "us against them," calling for protection of the national economy, and depicting the ruling elite as well as the immigrant newcomers as threats to the economic and cultural security of "the people," they foster an exclusive, if not a militant nationalism.

---

17. Caldwell, "Populism, patriotism and hospitality," 12.
18. Matthias Krupa, "Nationalism on the Left," *Die Zeit Online*, September 2015, www.zeit.de/politik/ausland/2015-09/left-wing-nationalism-europe.

Nationalism in the Political Landscape: GAL versus TAN

So far, I have approached the issue of nationalism in a rather theoretical way. In practice, the issue is complicated because a nationalist political agenda never stands alone; it is always combined with certain positions on other issues. Therefore, we should take a look at the political landscape at large, to see where nationalism comes in and also where an anti-nationalist stance comes in. In fact, the upsurge of nationalism and the reactions it provokes illustrate well how the political landscape across Europe is changing profoundly.

Political scientists are now complementing the traditional left-right model with a new one, called GAL–TAN. The capital letters stand for Green–Alternative–Libertarian and Traditional–Authoritarian–Nationalist respectively. The traditional model of right-left is based on social-economic views. The new model is helpful for two reasons. First, moderate right-wing and moderate left-wing movements have become comparable with respect to the social and economic issues that divided them in the past; it is now better to qualify them together as centrist. Second, new issues now dominate the political discussion and the intentions of voters, such as the environment, European integration, immigration, bureaucracy, legislation on medical ethics, gender, discrimination and multiculturality.

The political scientists have noted that certain issues tend to go together. On the one hand there is a cluster of "Green" environmental challenges, Alternatives to the consumerist economy and Liberal (if not libertarian) cultural values and ways of life; hence the acronym GAL. On the other hand, there is a cluster of attachment to Traditional values, an emphasis on the Authority of the state and its institutions, in particular the police, often linked with a call for strong political leadership, and a national orientation (hence the acronym TAN).

As people have rallied around the new issues, new political movements, parties and groupings have emerged. Some existing mainstream parties have morphed and now position themselves as more GAL or more TAN.[19] The principal issues that divide these two types of movements are the immigration of non-Europeans and European integration.

---

19. More about the GAL–TAN scale in Tarik Abou-Chadi, "Niche party success and mainstream party policy shifts, how green and radical right parties differ in their impact," *British Journal of Political Science* 46.2 (2016): 417–36.

Threefold Security Versus Universalism

TAN-parties are Eurosceptic and strongly opposed to (economic) immigration. We can summarize the priorities of "TAN-parties" as three securities: first *economic* security (jobs, purchasing power), second *physical* security (authority, police) and third *cultural* security (maintaining "our" norms, values and way of life in a multi-ethnic society).

While nationalism is usually linked to parties with a TAN agenda, it can also be present in left-wing populist parties, especially those who are critical of the economic agenda of the EU. However, nationalism is largely absent from most "progressive" and "liberal" movements with a GAL agenda. By and large, the latter favour universalism as an alternative to nationalism. Universalism here means the universal value of human rights, the belief that all cultures are equally valid in a multicultural society, and preference for Europeanism, a federal Europe, which is in fact universalism on the scale of our continent.

In summary, both nationalism and the alternatives to nationalism are part of a wider package of political priorities. This makes it complicated for anyone to take position on this single issue.

The Position of Christians
Christians Politically Disinherited

In the present, changing political landscape, Christians are forced to reorient themselves. Shall they remain faithful to the political stream for which they have always voted or will they join an emerging political formation, to influence it from within? We see that the GAL–TAN divide cuts right through the political orientation of Christians, including evangelical Protestants. Some prioritize "creation care" and related environmental issues, so they are attracted to GAL parties; but they run into conflict with the cultural liberalism that is very present in green movements. Other Christians are concerned about upholding traditional Christian values in legislation and defending the Christian heritage, so they are attracted to TAN parties; but they are uncomfortable with the overt anti-foreigner attitude of these movements.

One way to cope with these discrepancies is to create Christian movements within these parties in order to influence their internal discussions, but it remains to be seen whether this is an effective way to wield influence and whether this will be accepted at all.

Since the end of the nineteenth century Christians in many countries formed "Christian" political parties or movements in order to develop a distinctive political vision, based on the social teaching of Catholic and Protestant churches. This enabled them to play a role in the pluralist liberal democracy and to affirm the values and issues that are important to them. However, as a result of secularization the traditional Christian-democratic parties are in decline. Moreover, they have adapted their approach to the changing political landscape by adopting either a GAL or a TAN kind of agenda. This situation makes the value of having a Christian party questionable and leaves Christians politically disinherited.

Evangelicals and Nationalist Parties Today: Two Views

Election surveys in several countries indicate that many practising Christians are attracted by TAN parties.[20] Is this compatible with the principles of the Christian faith? With respect to this question, there is debate going on in the church at large, evolving around two different views. The first view is expressed by the official discourse of many church leaders, of mission agencies and Christian humanitarian organizations – at any rate in Western Europe. They generally denounce nationalism and populist parties, and they recall universal moral values such as human dignity and social justice. They call for hospitality to immigrants and emphasize the value of European collaboration and integration.

On the other hand, many church members do not follow these directives. Almost invisibly, they vote for populist or far-right politicians who take a strong stance against immigration and defend traditional cultural values. Initially these politicians mainly gained support among nominal Christians, for whom Christianity is more a matter of cultural identity than of personal faith, but they are now also attracting practising Christians.

The *Rassemblement national* (RN) in France is a case in point. Sociologist Pascal Perrineau has shown that the RN has deeply penetrated the nominally Catholic population for whom "Christianity" is the same as the traditional cul-

---

20. Some examples: 1) a survey among conservative Christians in the Netherlands: Eduard Sloot, "De PVV is ook onder christenen de grootste partij, maar het verschilt sterk per kerkverband" (*Nederlands Dagblad*, 21 December 2023); 2) a similar report on the political stance of conservative Catholics in France, which is comparable to that of many French evangelicals: Paul Airiau, "Des catholiques trouvent dans l'extrême droite actuelle l'expression d'une contestation" (*La Croix*, 20 June 2024), www.la-croix.com/religion/des-catholiques-trouvent-dans-l-extreme-droite-actuelle-lexpression-dune-contestation-20240627; 3) the conclusion of the German author Hannsjörg Hemminger, that "many Evangelicals lean towards the AfD – but more often they are apolitical" ("Die Union ist keine Heimat mehr," *Zeitzeichen, Evangelische Kommentare zu Religion und Gesellschaft*, 2018, https://zeitzeichen.net/archiv/2018_April_evangelikale-und-die-afd).

ture, but that practising Catholics long resisted voting for the RN.[21] However, the latest indications are that more and more practising Christians in France support the RN or another TAN-type movement. We can assume that other countries show similar trends, as far as Catholics are concerned.

Motivations

There is now some research as to why both nominal and practising Christians vote for parties with a TAN-type agenda. We do not know of any research among evangelical Protestants, but we have sufficient indications to suggest that their attitudes and voting are fairly similar to those of other Christians. We can observe four main motivations.

Agreement with the Political Priorities of TAN Parties

The main motivation is that they agree with the priorities of these parties mentioned above: Euroscepticism, anti-immigration and concern for threefold security: economic, physical and cultural.

Solidarity with Israel, Stand Against Antisemitism

Evangelical Christians have a tradition of solidarity with the Jewish people, support for the State of Israel and taking position against antisemitism. These points are still important for many evangelicals in deciding for which party they shall vote. It is remarkable that these issues have "switched sides," so to say: the traditional antisemitism of right-wing nationalists has largely disappeared. Contemporary TAN-kind parties are generally pro-Israel and opposed to antisemitism. On the other hand, many GAL-type parties have abandoned the traditional left-wing support for the Jewish people and the State of Israel. Instead, they see the Muslims in their country as well as the Palestinians in and around Israel as the "victims," and the State of Israel as a colonizing power. In some of these parties, this leads to a vehement antizionism, which often amounts to outright antisemitism. This switch affects evangelical Protestant voters, in favour of a TAN party.

Opposition to Cultural Liberalism

Christians voting for TAN parties are attracted by their positive stance on Christian cultural heritage. Many Christians are concerned about the decline

---

21. Pascal Perrineau, *La France au Front: essai sur l'avenir du Front national* (Paris: Fayard, 2014).

of Christianity as a religion and the demise of the "Christian" character of the society in which they grew up. This explains why they are attracted by political leaders who seem to be defending traditional values based on traditional Christian moral teaching. The French historian and religious scientist Paul Airiau detects that increasing numbers of traditional or conservative Catholics, including the Catholic movement of charismatic renewal, are attracted by nationalist right-wing parties such as the *Rassemblement national* led by Marine Le Pen and *Reconquête* led by Eric Zemmour. What he observes among Catholics can also be seen among evangelicals, many of whom share the same conservative political outlook and the same traditional views on family, life and other ethical issues. Therefore, in the following quotes, I have changed "Catholic" into "Christian."

> The entire Christian electorate is undergoing a process of moving to the right. This is a way to protest against the legislative changes in the area of morality.
>
> Moreover, there is a strong sense of identity. These Christians speak about our country being culturally Christian, and that it would lose its identity if it were completely torn away from Christianity. This vision insists on a national, almost ethnic dimension, which until now was counterbalanced by the Christian values of fraternity, reasonableness and charity towards all the needy, including refugees.
>
> Moreover, gender issues play an important role in the thinking of these Christians . . . They contest the so-called cultural liberalism that is promoted by progressive and left-wing parties. The progressive idea of the left is that the human being and sexual identity are not given by nature, but social and cultural constructs. Against the traditional family, made up of a father, a mother and children, they promote the absolute freedom of the individual, outside any framework considered to be natural. So, individuals have the absolute freedom to do what they want with themselves, particularly in the name of human rights.
>
> The Christian current to the right, on the other hand, affirms the existence of a stable human nature comprising two sexes articulated to each other.[22]

---

22. Airiau, "Des catholiques"; my translation.

Concern about Christian Heritage and Growing Public Influence of Islam

Finally, we see concern about the preservation of the cultural and moral heritage of Christianity and opposition to the growing influence of Islam and Muslim religious practice in the public sphere. Paul Auriau observes:

> There has also been a shift towards a discourse on the need for immigrants to integrate in terms of assimilation to "our" culture, and the exclusion of those who do not want to integrate. There is also the fear of Islam flooding in.[23]

Instrumentalizing the "Christian" Cultural Identity – West versus Central and East

It should be noted, however, that many leaders of nationalist or TAN parties are non-religious or only nominal church members – at least in Western Europe. Nor do all of them take the same position as evangelicals and other conservative Christians on ethical issues; in fact, they often find themselves at odds with conservative church leaders on these issues.

Nationalist leaders and their movements are generally opposed to signs of Islam in the public sphere such as minarets and calls for prayer, prayer in the workplace, serving halal meat in public schools, wearing dress that shows religious affiliation such as burkas or veils, and so on. The emphasis on the "Christian" cultural identity of the native population is combined with opposition to the culture and religion of people with a non-European background. The French sociologist Olivier Roy points out that the leadership of the *Rassemblement national* often finds itself at odds with the Catholic Church.[24] The RN is an amalgam of secularist, Christian and neo-pagan currents, which tends to see the church as too liberal on issues of immigration, and yet, interestingly, too conservative on family values and sexuality. The RN can therefore dismiss the church as an element of the French establishment. Roy finds that the leaders of the RN and of similar movements in other countries are "instrumentalizing Christianity for political ends." For them, religion matters first and foremost as a marker of identity, enabling them to distinguish between the good "us" and the bad "them." They defend the cultural heritage and would subsidize the restoration of cathedrals, *non pas pour les prières mais pour les pierres*, not

---

23. Airiau, "Des catholiques."
24. Olivier Roy, "The French National Front: From Christian Identity to Laïcité," in Nadia Marzouki et al. (eds), *Saving the People: How Populists Hijack Religion* (London: Hurst, 2016), 79–93.

because of their prayers but because of their stones, their architectural value. Christianity as national and cultural identity is so "thin" that, as Roy puts it, that it can be easily "hijacked." He goes on to say:

> The claim to defend the Christian identity of a nation has the dual purposes of building nostalgia for a golden national past and depicting Islam as a religion that is intrinsically foreign to "our" European culture. Nationalist and/or populist movements that employ Christianity to this end are "Christian" largely to the extent that they reject Islam.[25]

The same cannot be said in general of nationalist political leaders in Central Europe (Poland, Slovakia, Croatia and Hungary). Many of them are personally committed to traditional values rooted in the Christian history of their country and some are practising Christians. Generally speaking, they oppose the liberal or libertarian ethical values which in the West are called "European values." For the same reason, the constitutions of several countries in this part of Europe explicitly define marriage as the union of a man and a woman.

In this respect, some right-wing nationalist leaders call themselves "illiberal," in particular Hungarian prime-minister Viktor Orban. "Illiberal" is a term coined by academics in Central Europe to denote the rejection, not of a liberal economy or of liberal democracy as such, but of the "progressive" liberalist values of Western liberal democracies. Samuel Abraham, rector of the Bratislava International School of Liberal Arts and editor of the journal *Kritika & Kontext*, sums up the "illiberal" critique as follows:

> From the right, liberal democracy is denigrated for undermining moral values, religious beliefs and the spirit of patriotism. The religious right views liberals as immoral for allowing abortion and favouring same sex marriage. Some of the political left also dismiss liberal democracy, as a cynical cover up for prevailing and growing economic disparity.[26]

Abraham shows that critics of West-European liberal democracy span from the right to the left of the political spectrum. Most of them, however belong to a TAN-kind of political movement. Their alternative is a strong state that cares

---

25. Roy, "French National Front," 86.
26. Abraham, "No alternative," 9. This issue of *New Eastern Europe* is entirely devoted to the topic of liberal democracy and its alternatives, illiberal or other, in Central and Eastern Europe.

for the economically weak, defends the nation as a whole, enhances traditional moral values and defends the Christian roots and heritage of the country.

Instrumentalizing Christianity, Should Christian Voters Be Blamed for the Same?

We return to leaders of TAN-kind of parties who are not committed to the Christian faith and are instrumentalizing the Christian heritage for political ends. Should Christians who vote for them be blamed for doing the same? I do not think so. Many Christians who vote for such parties are sincerely concerned about the demise of traditional Christian values in the multicultural, multireligious and largely secularized society today. Their attachment to the Christian heritage is not a matter of political expediency but rooted in their Christian faith. In their view, voting for a TAN-kind of party is better than supporting the programme of another party when it comes to defending these values and this heritage.

Evangelical Response

How can or should churches respond to the upsurge of nationalism in general, and in particular to the way in which it plays a key-role in populist movements? Here are some possible ways of reflection and action, which leave it to each of us to respond in a concrete way.

Biblical Teaching on Nationhood and Identity

To begin with, there is an urgent need for consistent biblical teaching on the relation between nationhood and faith identity in our churches and organizations, and how to live together as different neighbouring nations. We can only briefly touch on this, by making three points:

The Particular and the Universal

There are two lines in the Bible that should be kept in balance: the particular line of Israel and the other nations, tribes and peoples, each of which has a specific identity and historical experience – and the universal line that all people share the same human dignity as created in the image of God and that all people are the object of salvation through Jesus Christ. These lines are clearly visible in Paul's address to the philosophers on the Areopagus:

> And he made from one man every nation of mankind to live on all the face of the earth, having determined allotted periods and the boundaries of their dwelling place, that they should seek God, and perhaps feel their way toward him and find him. Yet he is actually not far from each one of us. (Acts 17:26–27)

These are the two lines of national people Israel on the one hand and the spiritual people of the church that run parallel, even in the final consummation of the new creation.[27]

Positive and Negative Side of Nationhood
In her article on nationalism, Rosemary Caldwell insists that we should maintain the balance between the two ways in which the Bible speaks about nationhood. On the one hand, tribes, peoples and nations have a place in God's purposes, providing a sense of common identity, security and purpose. It is through the diversity of nations, languages and countries that humanity fulfils its cultural mandate. The differences between cultures create boundaries and a certain degree of dispersion of the human family, but this is precisely how God restrains the will of some to dominate others, and how he prevents the potentially limitless evil of a fallen human race once peoples are unified through empire.[28]

On the other hand, from Genesis 11 onwards the biblical authors also depict the nations negatively. The pride and arrogance exhibited in the building of the tower of Babel result in the Lord's discipline: division and mutual incomprehension. The blessed state of the human family, characterized by unity and coherence, has become a relationship of irritation, alienation and insecurity.

When articulating a biblical view on nationhood, we should therefore strike a balance between the positive aspect of diversity of cultures in response to the culture mandate and the negative aspect of fragmentation, division, competition and rivalry. The nations are the communities that arise in the course of human history, now affected by sin, but also upheld by both the blessing and judgement of God's sovereign rule over human life on earth.

---

27. Notice that the New Jerusalem, picture of the new creation, bears the name of the capital of Israel and has the names of 24 Jews on its gates and foundation stones, while her king is Jesus Messiah, the Jewish King of the Jews. The gates are open for all nations. Apparently, nationhood is part of the new creation (Revelation 22).

28. Caldwell, "Populism, patriotism and hospitality." Missiologist Christopher J. H. Wright makes the same point in *The Mission of God* (Nottingham: IVP, 2004), 216.

National Identity and Faith Identity in Christ

Furthermore, there is a balance to be maintained between national identity and faith identity in Christ. Christians have a "dual nationality," so to speak. They are called to live out their eternal Christian identity that transcends ethnic and cultural boundaries, within the earthly community, the people to which they belong ethnically, culturally and/or politically.

Distinctions of nation (or peoplehood), ethnic origin, gender and social status cease to be relevant to their standing before God or one another (Gal 3:28; Col 3:11). That is the universal aspect of the gospel and of the church, the body of Christ.

But this is not to say that the "local" collective human identities no longer exist, or that they become irrelevant. The church is not a replacement of nations, but coexists with them. The distinctive ethnic and cultural identities of believers remain. Paul is still aware of himself as being part of the Jewish people: ethnically, culturally and even religiously. He follows the traditions of his people, but he insists that these should not be imposed on non-Jewish believers. There is diversity of expressions of the Christian life, simply because of the diversity of nations, or peoples. (In biblical languages these terms mean the same.) Unity in Christ is not uniformity, it presupposes the diversity of tribes, peoples, nations and their cultures.

Patriotism: Inclusive and Peaceful Nationalism

What are the conditions for Christian support of nationalism, rightly understood? Our Christian identity is incompatible with a form of nationalism which recognizes only the good of its own people and seeks only its own fulfilment, neglecting the rights of others. The antidote to such nationalism is patriotism, a love of one's own country that recognizes the same rights of every other nation. Patriotism is a good basis for seeking collaboration and mutual exchange between different nations.

Christians will oppose *exclusive* nationalism, in which people of other ethnic and cultural origin are rejected, and *militant* nationalism, that wants to impose itself on other nations. Instead, Christians can support an *inclusive* and *peaceful* nationalism, which is the same as patriotism. It cares for refugees and welcomes migrants who want to become part of and contribute to the ongoing historical experience of the nation. A patriotic love for one's country is quite compatible with the European idea of collaboration and integration.

Biblical Social Values: Hospitality and Integration

Faced with the rise of nationalism and the rejection of newcomers, we need to emphasize the fundamental biblical social values: the dignity of each human being as created in the image of God; solidarity between rich and poor; hospitality for refugees and asylum seekers who are fleeing oppression, war, natural catastrophes or ecological disasters. In the Old Testament, "strangers" were welcome to live in Israel and to participate in the life and the religion of Israel. In so doing, they become part of its national history and its future. We could translate this principle by the term "inclusive patriotism," which means that there is a place for immigrants who want to integrate in our society and contribute to the ongoing story of our nation.

The "Neighbourly Love" of a Responsible Society

An important principle of both Catholic and Reformed Protestant social teaching is that the commandment to love our neighbours also applies to the relations between different peoples, countries and states. The Christian Democratic movement of the twentieth century called this the principle of the responsible society. "Our" people and "our" country have a responsibility towards neighbouring people and countries; the practice of solidarity extends beyond our own borders.

Here we have the essence of the European ideal. Nations in Europe are neighbours, part of a family of nations or cultures. Given their common roots, their common (Christian) religious heritage (Christianity) and their common historical experience, they have the responsibility to collaborate for the common good of the whole of Europe. This was the founding principle of the process of European integration that has resulted in the current European Union.

Connect with the Voters of Populist/Patriotic Parties

Churches have a responsibility towards those who vote for populist parties. Mainline political parties have lost contact with these voters. And churches too have largely lost contact with them, even though many of them are nominal church members, while quite a few of them are practising Christians. Can they share their views in the faith community?

Do pastors who are critical of TAN kind of parties listen to the concerns of the people who vote for them, including the members of their own congregation?

Christian Heritage as a Bridge

We saw that the attachment of populist leaders and their voters to the Christian cultural heritage has more to do with Christian culture than with Christian faith. But should we therefore ignore or even refute this attachment? We too are concerned about the preservation of the Christian heritage and we can make this a common cause. We can then use this concern as a bridge to communicate what the Christian faith really means.

Whilst we are right to be concerned at the resurgence of nationalism across Europe, this is also a moment for the church to engage creatively with this new political landscape, to speak prophetically into this contested space, and to point uncompromisingly to the only one who truly brings freedom, liberty and hope to Europe: Jesus Christ.

Bibliography

Abraham, Samuel. "No alternative to liberal democracy." *New Eastern Europe* 2 (2017): 7–13.

Caldwell, Rosemary. "Populism, patriotism and hospitality." Pages 10–15 in *Hope, Healing and Hospitality. The 2017 State of Europe Report*. Edited by Jeff Fountain. Amsterdam: Seismos Press/Schuman Centre for European Studies, 2018.

Grand'Maison, J. *Nationalisme et religion*. Montreal: Beauchemin, 1970.

Hendriks, Eric. "Naties in Europa. Boedapest: kruispunt voor liberalen, conservatieven en postliberalen." *Groen*, Journal of the *Wetenschappelijk instituut* of the Dutch political party *ChristenUnie* (December 2023): 12–17.

Ignatieff, Michael. *Blood and Belonging: Journeys into the New Nationalisms*. New York: Farrar, Strauss & Giroux, 1994.

Krupa, Matthias. "Nationalism on the Left." *Zeit Online*, September 2015. www.zeit. de/politik/ausland/2015-09/left-wing-nationalism-europe.

Marzouki, Nadia, Duncan McDonnell and Olivier Roy, eds. *Saving the People: How Populists Hijack Religion*. London: Hurst, 2016.

Memory, Jim, and others. "Nationalism in Europe Revisited" and other articles on this theme. *Vista*, e-magazine with research-based information on mission in Europe 45 (2024). https://vistajournal.online/latest-articles.

Mudde, Cas. *Populist Radical Right Parties in Europe*. Cambridge: Cambridge University Press, 2007.

Smith, Anthony D. "Gastronomy or Geology? The Role of Nationalism in the Reconstruction of Nations." *Nations and Nationalism* 1.1 (1994): 3–23.

———. *Nations and Nationalism in a Global Era*. Cambridge: Polity Press, 1995.

———. *The Cultural Foundation of Nations: Hierarchy, Covenant, and Republic*. London: Wiley-Blackwell, 2007.

8

The Place of Mission in Evangelical Identity

McTair Wall

Introduction

David Bebbington characterizes mission as the lifeblood of evangelicals from the start.[1] As evangelicals deconstruct and reconstruct their missional identity, in keeping with the spirit of the times, they need to reflect on this characteristic aspect of their DNA. This chapter is an attempt to engage with some aspects of the evangelical missional identity in the complex and diverse European context.[2] We will use Christopher Wright's definition of the term "missional" as "an adjective denoting something that is related to or characterized by mission."[3]

We begin with how evangelicals have traditionally been characterized or have characterized themselves in relation to mission. We then discuss developments in this portrait over the last fifty years, especially in relation to the holistic turn in missions and its relation to the rise of the theology of the mission of God. This allows us to reflect on some areas that need to be addressed as evangelicals write and enact their future story in missional terms. We seek to demonstrate that even though evangelical missional identity is deeply rooted in

---

1. David W. Bebbington, *The Evangelical Quadrilateral: Volume 1: Characterizing the British Gospel Movement* (Waco: Baylor University Press, 2021), 15.
2. Where I use "evangelicals" in what follows, I mean European evangelicals.
3. According to Wright, "*Missional* is simply an adjective denoting something that is related to or characterized by mission, or has the qualities, attributes or dynamics of mission. Missional is to the word *mission* what covenantal is to *covenant*, or fictional to *fiction*." Christopher J. H. Wright, *The Mission of God: Unlocking the Bible's Grand Narrative* (Nottingham: IVP, 2006), 24.

a rich biblical and theological soil, it is not a static identity, but open to growth and adaptation to its environment.

Characterizations of Evangelical Missional Identity

From the very start, evangelicalism had a strong missional ethos. The term evangelicalism itself came to prominence as a result of the great awakening movements of the eighteenth and nineteenth centuries in the context of missional fervour.[4] A brief look at the missional theology and engagements of evangelicals, as expressed in the World Evangelical Alliance (WEA), the Lausanne Movement and the Bebbington quadrilateral, will help us to appreciate the contours of evangelical missional identity.

The Historic Missional Ethos of the WEA

In a volume that was conceived in partnership with the European Evangelical Alliance (EEA), it is only appropriate to refer to the long and rich missional perspective of the WEA, which has its roots in Europe. The historic missional ethos of the WEA is stated clearly in its Global Witness Commission:

> The World Evangelical Alliance, from its inception in London England in 1846, had missions and evangelism as part of its core ethos. The first edition of the Alliance's journal "Evangelical Christendom" carried news of missionary work around the world. As the world changed and the WEA adapted to meet the concerns of Evangelical churches around the world, its concern for missions and evangelism remained constant. A rebirth of the Alliance in 1951 saw four commissions established, two of which were the Evangelism Commission and Missionary Commission.[5]

The theology behind this strong commitment to mission is best seen in the statement of faith of the WEA,[6] in which the missional dimension of evangelical convictions occupies the central place. We notice that mission is grounded in

---

4. The historical chapters in this volume demonstrate this point.
5. See https://worldea.org/what-we-do/global-witness.
6. See https://worldea.org/who-we-are/statement-of-faith/. For the original statement and missional ethos of the WEA, see J. W. Ewing, *Godly Fellowship: A Centenary Tribute to the Life and Work of the World Evangelical Alliance 1846–1946* (London: Marshall, Morgan and Scott, 1946; reprinted in the World of Theology Series 23; Bonn: Culture and Science Publications, 2022), 17–18.

"the supreme authority" of Scripture "in all matters of faith and conduct." This means that Scripture is fundamental for articulating all matters of missional faith and practice. Other elements of the statement also resonate strongly with the missional impulse of the WEA, such as the "vicarious and atoning death" of Jesus as the basis of mission, "the salvation of lost and sinful man through the shed blood of the Lord Jesus Christ by faith" and the Holy Spirit's enabling of believers to bear witness to Christ.

The Lausanne Covenant

The 1974 Lausanne Covenant, written under the influence of John Stott, offers what is called today "missional theology," in that it rereads the theological foundations of the evangelical faith through a missiological lens. It firstly grounds the witness and mission of God's people in the person and missional purposes of God (art. 1), as seen in the missional authority and narrative development of Scripture (art. 2), in the uniqueness of Christ and his gift of forgiveness to all who turn to him in faith, and in the centrality of Christ's death and resurrection for all who believe (art. 3). The Lausanne Covenant goes on to suggest the need for a more holistic approach to mission (art. 4–5), a more missional ecclesiology (art. 6) and a greater unity and collaborative spirit among evangelicals in representing Christ in the whole world (art. 7–8). It continues with a call to renew evangelical commitment to making Christ known where he is not known, through words and deeds (art. 9). For this to happen, there is a need to pay greater attention to the relationship of gospel and culture (art. 10), to better prepare leaders to take up the task of mission (art. 11), and to awaken to the fact that believers are involved in a deep spiritual conflict of cosmic significance (art. 12–13). This is why they need the power of the Holy Spirit to enable them to pursue their witness until the return of Christ (art. 14–15). We shall return to the strong influence of the Lausanne Movement on the development of evangelical missional identity worldwide.

Bebbington's Evangelical Quadrilateral

These various perspectives on the evangelical commitment to global mission have been captured in the now classic Bebbington quadrilateral of evangelical identity: biblicism, crucicentrism, conversionism and missional activism. Bebbington has demonstrated that his "Weberian" typology of evangelical identity has global validity and cannot be limited to Great Britain.[7] In 1983 Bebbington explained his quadrilateral in the following missional way:

> Firstly, they [the evangelicals] were conversionist. They believed that people needed to have their lives changed by receiving the gospel. Secondly, they were activist. They insisted that true Christians must put effort into spreading the gospel. Thirdly, they were biblicist. They regarded the Bible as the sole source of the gospel. And fourth, they were crucicentric. They saw the doctrine of the cross as the focus of the gospel.[8]

It should be noted that this particular formulation of the quadrilateral focuses on mission and gospel.[9] It begins with the need for "conversion" and a changed life by "receiving the gospel," which is communicated in the context of the mission to reach outsiders. It continues with active efforts in specifically "spreading the gospel." In the later book *Evangelicalism in Modern Britain* and in later articulations of this hallmark of evangelicalism, the notion of activism is broadened to "the expression of the gospel in efforts," but Bebbington has not lost sight of the particular commitment of evangelicals as bearers of the good news.[10] Also, without losing sight of the emphasis on biblical authority in general, this earlier formulation refers to the Bible as the "source of the gospel." Finally, the cross is the "focus of the gospel" that needs to be communicated by the people of God sent out into the world.

This formulation of the missionary zeal that characterizes evangelical identity finds a more "theological" expression in Bebbington's publications after 1989, where his quadrilateral begins with the Bible, followed by the cross, then personal conversion and finally activity in missionary communication.[11] This suggests that for Bebbington, evangelical identity is no less than a missional identity that is focused on the gospel, its embodiment and its communication in the various contexts in which it finds expression. But this identity is influ-

---

7. See Bebbington, *Evangelical Quadrilateral: Volume 1*, 3–4.

8. David W. Bebbington, "The Gospel in the Nineteenth Century," *Vox Evangelica* 13 (1983): 19; cf. Bebbington, *Evangelical Quadrilateral: Volume 1*, 1–8.

9. This order is maintained in the seminal work, David W. Bebbington, *Evangelicalism in Modern Britain: A History from the 1830s to the 1980s* (London: Unwin Hyman, 1989), 2–17, 270.

10. Bebbington, *Evangelicalism in Modern Britain*, 2.

11. See David W. Bebbington, *The Dominance of Evangelicalism: The Age of Spurgeon and Moody* (Downers Grove: IVP, 2005), 23–40; Bebbington, *Evangelical Quadrilateral: Volume 1*, 4–8, 36–39; David W. Bebbington, *The Evangelical Quadrilateral: Volume 2: The Denominational Mosaic of the British Gospel Movement* (Waco: Baylor University Press, 2021).

enced by and in dialogue with the cultural milieu in which it is forged.[12] Hence, European expressions of evangelical missional identity can be best appreciated through a study of the cultural milieu in which they occur.[13]

The Holistic Turn

While mission was the lifeblood of evangelicals from the start, it is noteworthy that their understanding of what constitutes mission has mutated over the last fifty years. The traditional portrayal of evangelical missional identity strongly emphasized evangelism and church planting in cross-cultural contexts. However, there has always been a concern for the development of the whole person and society in general, following the lead of the father of the modern evangelical mission movement, William Carey, who gave himself also to medical work, education, social reform and Bible translation.[14] But more recently this concern seems to vary from context to context in Europe, depending on local influences on evangelical identity. What is more, holistic concerns were seen as supporting the primary focus of evangelism, church-planting and other Word-centred ministries. This seems to indicate that before the rise of the Lausanne Movement, evangelicals embraced a more "minimalist" self-understanding of their missional identity, at least theologically.[15] In other words, whereas holistic missional thinking and practice do not seem to have suffered the pitting of "evangelism" against "social action" in some regions of evangelicalism, following the early twentieth-century modernist-fundamentalist divide,[16] the "theology of holistic mission" took time to develop.

This formalized theology came about with the rise of the Lausanne Movement and the synergy of dialogue between Western and Majority World evangelicalism.[17] A major influence on the holistic formulation of mission theology

---

12. Bebbington, *Evangelical Quadrilateral: Volume 1*, 8–12.

13. This is clear in the regional chapters in this volume and in discussions with theologians from different parts of Europe. I am thankful for the useful exchange with evangelical theologians from across Europe at the 2024 FEET conference in Prague.

14. See e.g. Thomas Schirrmacher, ed. *William Carey: Theologian, Linguist, Social Reformer* (World of Theology Series 4; Bonn: Culture and Science Publishing, 2013).

15. Cf. Hannes Wiher, "50 Years of the Lausanne Movement," *Evangelical Review of Theology* 48.3 (2024): 209–10.

16. I am grateful to Rolf Kjøde for these observations at the 2024 FEET conference in Prague.

17. See Hannes Wiher, *Holistic Mission: An Historical and Theological Study of Its Development, 1966–2011* (World of Theology Series 25; Bonn: Culture and Science Publishing, 2022), 15–43; Wiher, "50 Years of the Lausanne Movement."

at the first Lausanne Congress in 1974 came from Majority World church leaders. The Latin American theologians Samuel Escobar and René Padilla drew the attention of Western leaders to the need for an integration of evangelism and social justice in missional engagement both in theology and in practice.[18] The result of this open dialogue, and the beginning of a more holistic understanding of mission, can be seen throughout the Lausanne Covenant, for example in article 5 on "The Christian social responsibility," where we read that "evangelism and socio-political involvement are both part of our Christian duty" (cf. art. 10).

However, this was only the beginning. It was re-emphasized in the twenty-one articles of the Lausanne Movement's 1989 Manila Manifesto, which repeatedly affirms the need for a holistic and integral gospel witness. Article 8, for example, says: "We affirm that we must demonstrate God's love visibly by caring for those who are deprived of justice, dignity, food and shelter" (cf. art. 9, 16, 18, 20).

This holistic seedling came to full blossom under the influence of Christopher Wright in the 2010 Cape Town Commitment. Part 1, Section 7, Paragraph A (I, 7, A), sets the pace for the rest of the Commitment this way:

> Integral mission means discerning, proclaiming, and living out, the biblical truth that the gospel is God's good news, through the cross and resurrection of Jesus Christ, for individual persons, and for society, and for creation. All three are broken and suffering because of sin; all three are included in the redeeming love and mission of God; all three must be part of the comprehensive mission of God's people. (cf. II, B-C)

The second part of the Cape Town Commitment is concerned with the whole gospel, for the whole church, for the whole person and for the whole world. It is noticeable that in this document evangelicals talk about the whole of creation and its care for the first time in the context of the mission of the church. We will return to this point later.

The fourth Lausanne Congress, held in Seoul, Korea, in September 2024, speaks about a holistic gospel that needs to be "declared and demonstrated" in all sectors of society and in all areas that concern the human person and human communities. This comes out in the Movement's "State of the Great Commis-

---

18. David R. Swartz, "Lausanne 1974: A Latin American Challenge to North American Missiology," in Schwarz, *Facing West: American Evangelicals in an Age of World Christianity* (New York: Oxford University Press, 2020), 97–131.

sion Report," which sets the stage for the way mission should be pursued as evangelicals look ahead to 2050.[19] For the European context, the document is particularly interested in six challenges facing evangelicals in their attempts to re-engage Europe with the gospel: restoring truth and trust, reshaping morality, rebuilding community, reconnecting digitally, respecting creation, and being attentive to demography.[20] One cannot help but notice that there is something "indirect" about many of these concerns, which can be seen as "pre-evangelistic" ways of preparing people to embrace the gospel. The report suggests that in light of the fact that evangelical Protestantism is largely marginalized in the European context, the turn to other ways of communicating the good news has become necessary. It emphasizes finding contextualized ways of rebuilding trust with Europeans, the need for coherence between what evangelicals proclaim and what they actually do. That is, whole-life evangelism, the need for both objective and subjective embodiment of the truth, going public with evangelical faith as those sent out into the world, caring for the whole person and for all of creation. The goal is to "show and tell," in contextualized ways, about the "plausibility structures of our faith."[21]

Influence of the Mission-of-God Theology

To better appreciate these developments in evangelical missional identity, one must also pay attention to the influence of the mission-of-God theology (*missio Dei*) that has dominated the field in numerous ways over the past fifty years. This is not the place to discuss the history of this subject; others have done

---

19. The report is based on the research of 150 experts from global Christianity who highlight the need to address twenty-five "gaps" in evangelical mission theology and engagement in light of the new challenges in societies around the world: Global ageing population, new middle class, next generation, Islam, secularism, least reached peoples, Bible in a digital age, church forms in a digital age, discipleship in a digital age, evangelism in a digital age, AI and transhumanism, sexuality and gender, wholistic health, polycentric missions, polycentric resource mobilisation, integrity and anti-corruption, integrated spirituality and mission, developing leaders of character, people on the move, urban communities, digital communities, ethnicism and racism, Christianity, radical politics and religious freedom, caring for creation and the vulnerable, societal trust and influence of Christianity.
A summary can be found at https://congress.lausanne.org/the-25-collaborate-session-gaps/.

20. Lausanne Movement, *State of the Great Commission: A Report on the Current and Future State*, 2024, 423–32; online at https://lausanne.org/report/europe; cf. Jim Memory, *Europe 2021: A Missiological Report*, https://www.ecmi.org/de/europe-2021-a-missiological-report.

21. *State of the Great Commission*, 426. It is too early to engage the Seoul Statement of the Lausanne Movement which has received much criticism for the way missiological questions are treated.

in-depth studies on it.²² What interests us is how developments in evangelical missional identity have been impacted by the *missio-Dei*-theology. We will note areas where this theology forms the basis for developments in ecclesiology, hermeneutics, theology and ethics.²³

The Rise of Missional Ecclesiology

First, the mission-of-God theology is an attempt to move from an more ecclesiocentric conception of mission to a theocentric one. The result of this move is that evangelicals had to come to grips once again with the *missio ecclesiae* (mission of the church). This prepared the way for what became known as "missional ecclesiology." This affirms the church as instrument and participant in the divine mission, and as missional at its very core, as opposed to seeing mission as just a ministry of the church. It partly follows the lead of the Vatican II document, *Ad Gentes*, which declares that the church is by nature "missionary" because God is a missionary God.²⁴ But it was Lesslie Newbigin's influence on missional ecclesiology that particularly challenged the European evangelical concept of the relation between church and mission. Newbigin believed that Western Protestant ecclesiology needed to be reformulated in light of the new mission situation of Europe.²⁵ His challenge was taken up by John Stott[26] and Christopher Wright,²⁷ which gave rise, more recently, to the

---

22. See e.g. John Flett, *The Witness of God: The Trinity, Missio Dei, Karl Barth, and the Nature of Christian Community* (Grand Rapids: Eerdmans, 2010); Hannes Wiher, "God's Mission and the Church's Mission," in *The Church in Mission: Foundations and Global Case Studies*, ed. Bertil Esktröm (Pasadena: William Carey, 2016), 67–93; Rolf Kjøde, "Missio Dei: Is There Any Common Ground?," *Mission Studies* 39 (2022): 219–46.

23. Due to space constraints, we cannot discuss these areas in any depth.

24. Second Vatican Council, *Ad Gentes* (1965): "The pilgrim Church is missionary by her very nature, since it is from the mission of the Son and the mission of the Holy Spirit that she draws her origin, in accordance with the decree of God the Father" (I, § 2), www.vatican.va/archive/hist_councils/ii_ vatican_council/documents/vat-ii_decree_19651207_ad-gentes_en.html.

25. See Goheen, "'As the Father Has Sent Me, I Am Sending You': Lesslie Newbigin's Missionary Ecclesiology," *International Review of Mission* 91.362 (2002): 354–69; cf. Lesslie Newbigin, *The Household of God. Lecture on the Nature of the Church* (London: SCM, 1953); Lesslie Newbigin, *The Gospel in a Pluralist Society* (Grand Rapids: Eerdmans, 1989).

26. John Stott, *The Living Church: Convictions of a Lifelong Pastor* (Downers Grove: IVP, 2007).

27. Christopher J. H. Wright, *The Mission of God's People: A Biblical Theology of the Church's Mission* (Grand Rapids: Zondervan, 2010).

missional ecclesiology of the Cape Town Commitment.[28] This turn toward a missional ecclesiology among evangelicals is still gaining momentum, but it has a long way to go, both in theological articulation and in practice in the various contexts.[29]

Missional Hermeneutics

The renewed interest in mission studies caused by the theology of the mission of God was also felt in biblical hermeneutics. The crisis that occasioned the birth of *missio-Dei*-theology pushed missiologists and biblical scholars to explore the biblical teaching on mission afresh. In the 1980s and 1990s, early contributions to the need for a missiological approach to Scripture, especially by David Bosch, marked the beginnings of a new interest in biblical hermeneutics.[30] This gave rise to the discipline of "missional hermeneutics" in the 2000s, especially under the influence of Christopher Wright, who argues for the redemptive as the heart of the biblical narrative. Wright's seminal work, *The Mission of God*, not only served as a synthesis to the concerns of an earlier generation, but also gave new impetus to biblical research from the perspective of the mission of God.[31]

This new hermeneutical lens seeks to reclaim all of Scripture for God's missional purposes. George Hunsberger helps us to grasp the contours of this approach by distinguishing four streams in missional hermeneutics.[32] First, if Scripture's story is a story about God on redemptive mission in the world, then reading it within this *framework* is natural and legitimate. Second, Scripture

---

28. See also the recent WEA publication on *The Church in Mission: Foundations and Global Case Studies*, ed. Bertil Ekström (Pasadena: William Carey, 2016). This volume contains several studies from a European evangelical perspective on missional ecclesiology. Cf. Gabriel Monet, *Église émergente: être et faire Église en postchrétienté* (Berlin: Lit Verlag, 2014), for the French-speaking context; Robert Badenberg and Friedemann Knödler (eds), *"Missional": Embracing a Paradigm Shift for Missions* (Nuremberg: VTR, 2015), for the German speaking context and broader.

29. This can be compared with the large quantity of literature on the "missional church" that has emerged from the North American context over the past thirty years.

30. See David J. Bosch, "Towards a Hermeneutic of 'Biblical Studies and Mission,'" *Mission Studies* 3.2 (1986), 65–79; James Brownson, *Speaking the Truth in Love. New Testament Resources for a Missional Hermeneutic* (Harrisburg: Trinity Press, 1998); Richard Bauckham, "Mission as Hermeneutic for Scriptural Interpretation," *Currents in World Christianity Position Paper* 106 (1999), www.christianstudylibrary.org/article/mission-hermeneutic-scriptural-interpretation.

31. Wright, *Mission of God*.

32. George Hunsberger, "Mapping the Missional Hermeneutics Conversation," in *Reading the Bible Missionally*, ed. Michael Goheen (Grand Rapids: Eerdmans, 2016), 45–67.

functions as a tool that God uses to form his people to bear witness, among other things, to who God is and to his purposes in the world. Third, all reading of Scripture takes place in a particular social and missiological location, so readers bring their missiological questions to bear on the biblical text. Fourth, Scripture shows us how to engage each cultural context critically through the *matrix* of the gospel. It is believed that these four currents in missional hermeneutics are needed to give a full account of what Scripture teaches about mission and the implications for the way mission is lived out in various contexts.

In the past mission studies lost the interest of Bible scholars, but this missional turn in hermeneutics has brought renewed interest among biblical scholars for a more robust biblical theology of mission. It has already generated several doctoral dissertations in Europe.[33] The body of literature engendered by this field of research testifies to its importance for both biblical scholars and missiologists. The extensive bibliography put together by Michael Goheen and Tim Davy on the website of the Centre for the Study of Bible and Mission shows that evangelical scholars are heavily involved in this renewed reading of Scripture for the sake of mission.[34] Evangelicals are discovering that the Bible does have things to say about mission that past generations did not notice.

Missional Theology and Ethics

The impact of the theology of God's mission on theological discourse and ethics is noteworthy. First of all, for some time there has been discussion among evangelicals about "missional theology."[35] In 2014, at a colloquium held by the Tyndale Fellowship Christian Doctrine group, prominent evangelical systematic theologians and missiologists discussed "the central question of what it means to *do theology* for the sake of mission."[36] This resulted in the publication of *The End of Theology: Shaping Theology for the Sake of Mission*. This conversation seeks to reclaim all of theology for the purpose of mission by

---

33. See Peter F. Penner, *Missionale Hermeneutik. Biblische Texte kontextuell und relevant lesen* (Neufeld: Edition Wortschatz, 2012); Tim Davy, *The Book of Job and the Mission of God: A Missional Reading* (Eugene: Pickwick, 2020); McTair Wall, *Le débat sur l'herméneutique missiologique à la lumière de l'utilisation lucanienne de l'Ancien Testament* (Doctoral dissertation, Vaux-sur-Seine, 2021). See also the monographs on different parts of the Bible from an exegetical and missiological perspective in the bibliography in the next note.

34. See https://bibleandmission.org.uk/missional-hermeneutics-bibliography/.

35. See Paul G. Hiebert and Tite Tiénou, "Missional Theology," *Missiology: An International Review* 34.2 (2006), 219–38.

36. Jason S. Sexton and Paul Weston, "Introduction," in Sexton and Weston (eds), *The End of Theology: Shaping Theology for the Sake of Mission* (Minneapolis: Fortress Press, 2016), xxii.

reframing evangelical theology through a "missional lens": what they believe about God, creation, human beings, the problems with and hope for the world, etc. John Franke puts the question in this way, quoting Andrew Kirk:

> If theology is to serve the life of the church and its witness to the gospel, and if we assume that "the church can exist as truly itself only when dedicated to the mission of God, a burning question ensues: How should one reinvent theology and theological education so that they flow naturally for an integral perspective on God's consistent will and activity in the world?"[37]

The need to recalibrate theological education in light of the mission of God and the church has recently been emphasized in the second Manifesto of the International Council of Evangelical Theological Education (ICETE). Under the direction of the Swiss Bernhard Ott, who drafted the Manifesto, evangelicals affirm the need to place God's mission at the heart of theological education.[38] Thus, the Manifesto calls theological educators and institutions to refocus their attention on the major raison d'être of theological education: preparing leaders to better serve the redemptive purposes of God.

Finally, in the wake of the holistic shift in bearing witness to the gospel, "missional ethics" have been receiving much-needed attention. Here, the focus lies on reclaiming all of ethical life for missional purposes, as believers seek to embody and display the good news of salvation through the way they live lives that are transformed into the image of Christ in the power of the Spirit. This is about whole-life discipleship. The idea is that believers need to *become good news* in an age when the gospel has become bad news. In a time when people are losing hope, showing others what it means to be "whole" and balanced, to live in peace and in harmony with others, and to respect God's creation, have become priorities. It is part of the "great commission" to teach disciples to "embody" the teachings of Jesus (Matt 28:19–20). Many, including Christopher Wright and N. T. Wright, have given voice to this need to develop "missional

---

37. John R. Franke, *Missional Theology: An Introduction* (Grand Rapids: Baker, 2020), 62. See also the critical review of this book by Jim Dahl, https://trainingleadersinternational.org/jgc/154/missional-theology-an-introduction.

38. "ICETE Manifesto II: Call and Commitment to the Renewal of Theological Education," *Evangelical Review of Theology* 47.3 (2023): 253–73. For a brief introduction to the Manifesto, see Bernhard Ott, "Shaping the Future of Theological Education: Introducing the ICETE Manifesto II," *Evangelical Review of Theology* 47.3 (2023): 250–52.

ethics" in evangelical missiology.³⁹ The recent doctoral dissertation of Martin Salter, *Mission in Action*, is a major contribution in this direction.⁴⁰

In summary, the theology of God's mission has become an integral part of the landscape of evangelical missional thinking. Some have seen this theology as a "trojan horse" in evangelical missiology, with the potential of liberalizing influences,⁴¹ but others see it as a "gift" that God has given to evangelicals, through the historical process of theologizing, to reform their missiology and to realign it with some forgotten biblical and theological foundations. The end result of all of this appears to be a general movement toward a more balanced and nuanced evangelical missiology.

Future Trajectories

We have argued with Bebbington that mission is the lifeblood of evangelicals, yet the understanding of what that mission constitutes has clearly developed over the past fifty years. In light of this, we would like to suggest a few perspectives for ongoing evangelical missiological thinking and practice, especially in continuity with the reflection on holism and the impact of the theology of the mission of God.

First, the Swiss missiologist, Hannes Wiher, observes that younger Europeans are becoming more holistically oriented in their worldview.⁴² If this is true, then we need a more holistic approach to mission in the European context which balances past tendencies toward a more minimalist conception of missional identity and engagement, and resonates with newer concerns in society that are more socially oriented. However, embracing a "maximalist" understanding of mission will mean that evangelicals energetically preserve the heartbeat of mission which has characterized them from the start. That is, calling others to be followers of Christ and to embrace the salvation that he brings, gathering them into communities of Jesus's disciples, with baptism as a hallmark of their discipleship and teaching them to embody the gospel

---

39. See Wright, *Mission of God*, 357–93; N. T. Wright, "Reading the New Testament Missionally," in Goheen, *Reading the Bible Missionally*, 175–93.

40. Martin C. Salter, *Mission in Action. A Biblical Description of Missional Ethics* (London: Apollos, 2019).

41. Helmut Rosin, *Missio Dei: An Examination of the Origin, Contents and Function of the Term in the Protestant Missiological Discussion* (Leiden: IIMO, 1972).

42. Wiher, *Holistic Mission*, 50–63. Lausanne's recent report confirms this when it suggests that Europeans are no longer able to make a "distinction between the person and their opinion" (*State of the Great Commission Report*, 424).

as good news, as well as continuing to make disciples of others. This implies that missiologists need to explain to newer generations how more traditional missional emphases relate both biblically and theologically to newer ones, such as social justice and creation care.[43] In so doing, they will need to abandon the "either/or" binary logic of either doing evangelism and church-planting or showing the love of Christ through good works. The hard work of connecting these in the overall proclamation of the good news of the kingdom of God is required in each generation.

Elsewhere, I have suggested that the heart of mission is about disciples and communities of disciples bearing witness to and embodying the "good news of the kingdom" in Christ, in view of calling others to embrace that reign in every area of their lives.[44] Indeed, this can take many forms, including the believers' love for God's creation, social justice and the well-being of the whole person. These can serve as bridges to calling others to turn to Christ and embrace his just, loving and righteous reign. Calling others to repentance and faith in Christ through evangelism is also a call to embrace the good news of his kingdom reign. Showing others what embracing that reign may look like, in embodied form, is also a form of witness, albeit an indirect call to follow Jesus.

Second, despite the significant impact of the mission-of-God theology on evangelical missional identity, the notion itself still needs further biblical and theological articulation from an evangelical perspective.[45] That being said, one fruitful way of deepening the understanding of Europeans of their missional identity is learning to read Scripture through a missional lens. This can help the emerging generation to rediscover what Scripture has to say about their missional identity and best practices as God's people sent out into the world. The work of Christopher Wright and others needs to be taken up in each context in order to get an even richer understanding of the missional teaching of all of Scripture. Seeing that there is a "social location" aspect in all readings of Scripture, people in every context have something to say about what they discern as missionally relevant in the text.

---

43. In my analysis, the recent documents of the Lausanne Movement in preparation of the fourth Lausanne Congress in Seoul, including the Seoul Statement itself, need ongoing work to make this clearer.

44. McTair Wall, "La notion de mission dans l'œuvre de Luc: un regard des sciences bibliques," in *Mission intégrale, volume 2: Regards historiques, philosophiques, bibliques et théologiques*, ed. McTair Wall (Charols: Excelsis, 2023), 85–130.

45. Thomas Schirrmacher, *Missio Dei: God's Missional Nature* (World of Theology Series 10; Bonn: Culture and Science Publishing, 2017), 17. Chris Wright's *Mission of God* has already started this reflection but, as John Flett demonstrates in *Witness of God*, there is still much work to be done.

Conclusion

We are in a period of deconstruction of many past conceptions of the world, ourselves and various heritages. Instead of reacting against this wave of deconstructionism, I recommend surfing this wave and reconsidering our core beliefs and practices by returning to Scripture. This may indeed be a new move of the Spirit to help us navigate the troubled waters of late modernity. Recapturing the sense of evangelical missional identity is vital for the future of evangelical Christianity in Europe. As European societies drift away from their Christian past and heritage, evangelicals are called to reclaim all of Scripture, all of theology, all of life, all of the life of the church as instruments of God's mission to the new Europe.

There is a specificity about European missiology that sets it apart from other approaches that tend to be managerial and pragmatic. A deep thoughtfulness characterizes the European approach, which is probably related to the rich philosophical and theological heritage that is part of the European identity and experience. These need to inform the future course of our missional reflection and practices.

Bibliography

Bebbington, David W. *The Evangelical Quadrilateral: Volume 1: Characterizing the British Gospel Movement.* Waco: Baylor University Press, 2021.

———. *The Evangelical Quadrilateral: Volume 2: The Denominational Mosaic of the British Gospel Movement.* Waco: Baylor University Press, 2021.

Gantenbein, Jean-Georges. *Can the West be Converted? Towards a Contextual Theology for the West.* Lexington: Lanham, 2021.

Kuzmic, Peter. "Mission in Europe." In *Toward the Twenty-First Century in Christian Mission. Essays in Honor of Gerald H. Anderson.* Edited by James M. Phillips and Robert T. Coote. Grand Rapids: Eerdmans, 1993.

Lausanne Movement, The. *State of the Great Commission: A Report on the Current and Future State.* 2024. An online version at https://lausanne.org/report/europe.

Memory, Jim. *Europe 2021: A Missiological Report.* www.ecmi.org/de/europe-2021-a-missiological-report.

Schirrmacher, Thomas. *Missio Dei: God's Missional Nature.* World of Theology Series 10. Bonn: Culture and Science Publishing, 2017.

Wiher, Hannes. *Holistic Mission: An Historical and Theological Study of Its Development. 1966–2011.* World of Theology Series 25. Bonn: Culture and Science Publishing, 2023.

———, ed. *Evangelism in Europe.* Nuremberg: VTR, 2018.

Wright, Christopher J. H. *The Mission of God: Unlocking the Bible's Grand Narrative.* Downers Grove: IVP Academic, 2006.

9

British Evangelicals

Towards a Public Theology of Racial Justice

Israel Oluwole Olofinjana

Introduction

One of the most contested cultural questions of our time is: what does it mean to be human and Black?[1] Many racial incidents give rise to this question, but most important for our context is the question: how have UK evangelicals engaged slavery and racial justice? They have a long history of engagement with slavery and racial justice,[2] but today not all understand their mission in this area. Contemporary British evangelicals are ethnically diverse, but we

---

1. Since slavery, colonisation and neo-colonisation, Black people have been asking this question. See Kate Coleman, *Being Human: A Black British Christian Woman's Perspective* (Whitley Lectures; Oxford: Whitley Publications, 2006) and Joe Kapolyo, *The Human Condition: Christian Perspectives Through African Eyes* (Carlisle: Langham Global Library, 2013).

2. The words "race" and "racial justice" are contested and not everyone uses or accepts the terms. Their usage in this essay is rooted in the understanding that God created one human race and therefore "racial justice" is used with a New Testament nuance of reconciliatory justice. Some Christians prefer the term "ethnicity" which, they argue, is based in Scripture, and have suggested using "ethnic justice," "inter-ethnic justice" or "intercultural justice" in place of "racial justice." Yet these terms have not (yet) gained recognition. See the section on understanding racial justice below, and Richard Reddie, *Race for Justice: The Struggle for Equality and Inclusion in Britain and Ireland* (Oxford: Lion Hudson, 2022); Ben Lindsay, *We need to Talk About Race: Understanding the Black Experience in White Majority Churches* (London: SPCK, 2019); and Jason Roach and Jessamin Birdsall, *Healing the Divide: How every Christian Can Advance God's Vision for Racial Unity and Justice* (Epsom: Good Book Company, 2022).

have not managed to reflect this adequately in our theology and practice.³ I will therefore argue for the need to develop a new ecclesiology of radically inclusive communities and intercultural churches to combat the sin of racism in church and society.

Historical Engagement with Slavery and Racial Justice
Nineteenth Century

Probably the first engagement of British evangelicals with racial justice was the campaign to end the slave trade. This campaign was developed by the Clapham Sect, a group of reformers from different established churches. The Act to end the slave trade in 1807 was championed by William Wilberforce (1759–1833), a key member of parliament, but we need to acknowledge the contributions of others, such as the African ex-slaves Ignatius Sancho (1729–1780), Olaudah Equiano (1745–1797) and Ottobah Cugoano (1757–1791), who were part of the Abolitionist movement. Drawing on their personal experiences of slavery, these three wrote books on the evils of enslavement which aided the abolitionists' campaigns.[4]

The conference which led to the founding of the worldwide Evangelical Alliance (EA) in 1846 was marked by long discussions on the subject of slavery. The conference lasted from 19 August to 2 September and the slavery discussions took place from 28 August till 1 September. At the heart of the debate was whether slaveowners could be members of this new alliance. The British and Anti-Slavery Society had written to the London provincial committee of the proposed alliance in February 1846, urging them not to invite American slave holders to the conference. The letter described the situation, ordeal and commodification of the slaves in America and how all Christian denominations were complicit in this barbaric economy. At the conference, the presence of a Jamaican Wesleyan Holiness preacher, Revd E. Frasier, had great impact as he described the inhuman conditions of African slaves before the debates on

---

3. British evangelicals include Reformed believers, Anglicans, Baptists, Pentecostals, charismatics, Presbyterians, Methodists and others. They are diverse ethnically, with African Caribbean Pentecostal and Holiness churches, African Pentecostal churches, South Korean churches, South Asian churches, Spanish speaking Latin American churches, Portuguese speaking Latin American churches, Chinese churches and others.

4. Ignatius Sancho, *The Letters of the late Ignatius Sancho, An African*, www.gutenberg.org/cache/epub/66908/pg66908-images.html; Olaudah Equiano, *The Interesting Narrative of the Life of Olaudah Equiano* [1789], www.gutenberg.org/files/15399/15399-h/15399-h.htm; Quobna Ottobah Cugoano, *Thoughts and Sentiments on the Evil and Wicked Traffic of the Slavery and Commerce of the Human Species* [1781] (London: Penguin, 1999).

slavery started.[5] Subsequently, John Howard Hinton, secretary of the Baptist Union, proposed that slaveholders should not be allowed to become members of the EA. This was before the emancipation of slaves in the USA, and several American evangelicals objected. In the end the compromise was reached that the EA would be an affiliation of autonomous regional networks rather than an integrated international organization.

When the British evangelicals met in November 1846 to set up a British EA, the question came up whether slaveowners or shareholders in companies connected to slaveholding overseas could be members. Hinton and others proposed that they should be barred but sadly their motion was dropped. When the American EA was founded, slaveholders were barred from membership, which impacted the work for years because they lost support from the Southern states.[6]

Late Twentieth Century

In the mid-1970s, evangelical Christians formed the *Evangelical Race Relations Group* which consisted mainly of White Christians. The group was later rebranded *Evangelical Christians for Racial Justice* and included Black and Asian Christians. This group sought to engage and educate the church through biblical theology and a sociological and historical analysis of racism. Around this period appeared one of the first serious studies on race by an evangelical Christian;[7] in the 1990s two further such volumes appeared.[8]

Through the ministry of Philip Mohabir (1937–2004) and Clive Calver, in 1984 the *West Indian Evangelical Alliance* (renamed the *African and Caribbean Evangelical Alliance* or ACEA in 1989) was formed to bridge the gap that existed between White evangelical Christians and Black Pentecostal churches. Describing the pioneering work of Philip Mohabir, Hugh Osgood sees two reasons why the West Indian EA was formed: the fragmentation among Black Pentecostal churches and the polarization between Black majority churches

---

5. Evangelical Alliance, "Report of the Proceedings of the Conference held at Freemasons Hall London 1846," London 1847, 217–18.

6. Ian Randall and David Hilborn, *One Body in Christ: The History and Significance of the Evangelical Alliance* (Carlisle: Paternoster, 2001), 136.

7. Patrick Sookhdeo, ed., *All One in Christ: A Biblical View on Race* (London: Marshall, Morgan & Scott, 1974).

8. Paul Grant and Raj Patel (eds), *A Time to Speak: Perspectives of Black Christians in Britain* (Nottingham: Russell, 1990) and Joel Edwards (ed.), *Let's Praise Him Again: An African-Caribbean Perspective on Worship* (Eastbourne: Kingsway, 1992).

and White evangelical churches.[9] The best-known leader of the ACEA was its first General Secretary, Joel Edwards (1951–2021), who later became the first Black General Director of the EA UK in 1997. The ACEA was very successful in serving the African and Caribbean Windrush community and their descendants. Operating independently from the EA, it managed to connect the EA with Black Pentecostal churches and leaders.

In 2010 the EA received a prophetic challenge from some senior Black church leaders that it needed to engage with the ethnic and cultural diversity of the UK church. As a result, it set up the *One People Commission* in 2013, to build on the pioneering work of the ACEA, to re-imagine it for a new context, to engage the breadth of ethnic and cultural diversity of British Christianity, and to ensure that the EA was ethnically diverse in its structures. The *One People Commission* therefore started with the strapline of celebrating ethnic diversity whilst promoting unity.

Research on Race: Towards an Evangelical Theology of Racial Justice

The brief history above illustrates that British evangelicals have at different points engaged with slavery and racial justice, but inconsistently and not very deeply. Today not all evangelical Christians and churches are actively engaged in the concerns of racial justice. One of the consequences is a lack of serious scholarship, research and robust theology on racial justice from an evangelical perspective, so that today anyone who wants to engage the concerns of racial justice has to explore a Black liberation theological framework.[10]

One of the few recent research projects on racial justice within the evangelical constituency is an Irish handbook which seeks to understand the experience of and attitudes towards welcome and integration, racism and discrimination in Irish churches.[11] The latest piece of research on racial justice by UK evangelicals is *Attitudes and Practices Towards Race within the UK Evangelical*

---

9. Hugh Osgood, *Evangelical and African Pentecostal Unity: Balancing Principles and Practicalities in Britain around the Millennium* (Eugene: Pickwick, 2024), 24.

10. James Cone, who is regarded as its founding father, defined Black Theology as "a theology of liberation because it is a theology which arises from an identification with the oppressed Blacks of America, seeking to interpret the gospel of Jesus in the light of the Black condition. It believes that the liberation of the Black community is God's liberation." James H. Cone, *A Black Theology of Liberation, 20th Anniversary Edition* (Maryknoll, New York: Orbis, 2004), 4–5. Black Theology also exists in the context of Southern Africa to address the apartheid system. We also now have a thriving Black British Theology in the UK.

11. *From Every Nation? A Handbook for a Congregation's Journey from Welcome to Belonging*, Churches in Ireland, 2021, www.irishchurches.org/cmsfiles/From-Every-Nation-.pdf.

Church, a report commissioned to inform the strategic work of the EA in this area.[12] The aim of this report is to better understand the participants' experiences of and attitudes towards race in order to inform the strategy of the EA, to develop a robust evangelical theology on racial justice and to encourage all Christians to take seriously the gospel call for racial justice.

The present chapter is largely based on data from this report, as it highlights problems around race relations within evangelical churches.[13] The four areas investigated were: understanding racial justice, experiences of racism in the church, responses to racial injustice and repairing relationships through reparative justice. The data was drawn primarily from a survey of nine hundred and sixty-four respondents in the EA's extended network, of whom one hundred and fifty-five were people with a Majority World background.[14] It also included a further survey of attendees at the EA Council in 2022: seventy-six attendees of which twenty-two were from a Majority World background. Interviews were conducted with twenty-six senior evangelical leaders, of whom fifteen were from the Majority World. Lastly there was a focus group of eighteen young leaders from a Majority World background.

Key Findings from the Research

1. Nine in ten respondents (91 percent) felt welcome at their church. This proportion did not vary by ethnicity.

2. At the same time, most respondents from a Majority World background (51 percent) had experienced discrimination in church at some point in their lives. Just under three in ten (29 percent) said they experienced discrimination multiple times a year.

3. Respondents said that the most common barriers to churches pursuing racial justice were competition for churches' time and a sense that racial justice was not relevant to their context – most

---

12. *Attitudes and Practices Towards Race within the UK Evangelical Church*, Evangelical Alliance internal Document 2024. Not in the public domain. Working for the EA, I lead the One People Commission and the research commissioned by the EA was carried out by my team with the help of an independent research company. The Evangelical Alliance did some earlier research on race in the late 1990s and early 2000s.

13. *Attitudes and Practices*, 2024.

14. "Majority World" as used here denotes people of African, African Caribbean, Asian, Latin American and Oceanian heritage who were either born in the UK or migrated at some point. It is also used of people of mixed heritage.

frequently because of a lack of diversity in their local area. However, young people from a Majority World background saw other barriers, including an unwillingness to acknowledge the need for justice, a lack of representation on church leadership teams, and uncertainty about whether church leaders were pursuing justice from the right motives.

4. Respondents were divided over reparative justice, but people from the Majority World were not much more favourable than White respondents: 47 percent were favourable towards it, 24 percent had views that were neither favourable nor unfavourable, and 29 percent were unfavourable. This compared to 40 percent, 30 percent, and 29 percent (respectively) for White British respondents – a small enough gap to fall within the research's margin of error.[15]

Understanding Racial Justice

A key question the research raised is: what is an evangelical understanding of racial justice and what concerns should this address? What does the Bible say around issues of justice and is there a biblical template for addressing racial justice? A casual perusal of Scripture reveals that the Bible has much to say on the theme of justice. The Hebrew word for justice, *mishpat*, appears more than four hundred times in the Old Testament. A related word is righteousness, *zedakah*, which appears around five hundred and forty times! Both words express the character of God as the one who acts justly and therefore wants his people to act and live rightly.

A theological theme in Scripture that can help evangelicals develop a biblical understanding of racial justice is reconciliation (2 Cor 5). That God in Christ was reconciling us back to God and all things to himself is at the heart of the gospel message (Col 1:15). In Ephesians 2, Paul explains that the gospel is about reconciling humanity to God and uniting divided humanity in a new *ecclesia* of Jews and Gentiles. The New Testament church community, working towards healed relationships between Jews and Samaritans, and Jews and Gentiles, is a template for racial reconciliation today.

Some in the evangelical community are reluctant to use the term racial justice because of its connotations and affiliation to a secular notion of social justice, others because we are still using the word race, despite its rootedness

---

15. *Attitudes and Practices*, 2024.

in the Enlightenment social construct of categorizing humanity. Therefore an evangelical biblical theology on racial justice has to start with the understanding that God created one human race. But is it possible to use the term racial justice with a biblical understanding of reconciliation? For this reason the Reconciled Church,[16] with exponents such as Owen Hylton (Brixton) and Rosie Hopley, prefers the term racial reconciliation to emphasize the New Testament ministry of reconciliation.

To shift our understanding of racial justice away from a binary of Black and White, as important as that is, and to locate the discourse on racial justice within intercultural theology (with a cross-cultural focus as opposed to merely social justice), I have suggested the term intercultural justice. Intercultural justice brings an angle of World Christianity to our understanding of racial justice by recognizing the experiences of not only Africans and African Caribbeans, but Asians, Latin Americans and people of mixed heritages, arguing for the need to create radical inclusive communities that can address racial injustices. In this definition of intercultural justice, note the centring of the experiences of people with a Majority World background. This is because in the survey, experiences of people from Majority World background were more likely to shape their understanding of racial justice than experiences of White British respondents.

Seventy-one percent of the participants in the survey defined their understanding of racial justice as equality between ethnicities. Yet I want to suggest that in order to achieve racial justice we need more than equality: we will also need equity. Equality assumes that we are all starting from the same position, but that is not usually the case. We need equity to level our starting positions.

Experience: Race and Racism in the Church?

It is encouraging that the research shows that 91 percent of the participants across all ethnicities felt welcomed at their churches. The church in Britain has journeyed a long way in terms of how we welcome people from other nations. I suspect we have learnt something from the Windrush experiences of the 1940s–1960s, when many African-Caribbean migrant Christians did not feel welcomed in our churches. It is interesting to observe the current efforts of British churches to welcome Hong Kong and Ukrainian migrants. The Baptist

---

16. A group of charismatic church leaders interested in how local churches can work towards multicultural ministries and reconciliation.

Union, for example, has appointed a Hong Kong leader to help the denomination receive migrants from Hong Kong.

This improvement and encouragement in welcoming must not be substituted for creating a sense of belonging, because the research revealed that 51 percent of people from a Majority World background had experienced racism in our churches and that 29 percent experience racism more than once a year. This is shocking but not surprising for anyone who has paid attention to the issues of race and racism in the churches. Before the death of George Floyd, there were many conversations about the need for British churches to go the extra mile in tackling racism. Many leaders from a Majority World background felt ignored to the extent that some have completely stopped calling us to action. Since the death of George Floyd there is renewed interest in talking about and addressing racism in churches, church structures and organizations. Perhaps a way to begin to address racism in our churches is to recognize that welcoming is not enough. We need to create a process that leads from welcoming to belonging and finally integration. What can this process look like?

Welcoming is the first step in our hospitality, never the end result. Welcoming is intentionally creating spaces and contexts for new people to feel comfortable in our fellowship. It goes beyond offering tea and biscuit to someone on a Sunday morning. Belonging goes deeper still, as it intentionally creates spaces and contexts for new people to begin to express who they are. If welcoming is about making strangers feel comfortable, belonging is about identity. Do migrants, people seeking asylum and refugees feel they can honestly share some of their struggles in our churches or do they sense that they will be stereotyped, judged or misunderstood? Can people from a Majority World background discuss the racism that they face both at church and society in our house groups? Creating a sense of belonging sometimes disrupts our comfort because we are not seeking to assimilate new people, we are seeking to understand where they are coming from.

Responses: How Can Churches Address Racism?

It is encouraging that half of the respondents in our survey had talked or prayed with a friend at church about issues around racial justice. This demonstrates that people in our churches are interested in the subject. More than 35 percent of the respondents have listened to a sermon on the subject whilst 30 percent had read a book on it. However, only 33 percent felt racial justice was a focus for their churches. Could it be that our churches have not yet centred this conversation? Some of the barriers to racial justice mentioned by young people from a Majority World background shed light on this. These included unwillingness to acknowledge the need for racial justice, tokenism, concern that discussing racial justice might cause division, the idea that racial justice is not biblical, the perception that racial justice is too political, and lack of representation on leadership teams.

Before discussing how churches become radically inclusive, it is worth commenting on other reasons why some churches might not see racial justice as important. The pandemic and post-pandemic realities have left church leaders exhausted. Some are trying to survive whilst others are trying to keep the church going. Churches may not see racial justice as a priority if they are located in a completely White British rural area. Whilst this may be the current reality of some, it is important to start to prepare for when that area might become more ethnically diverse. The migratory trends in the UK show that people are moving out of urban centres due to inflation. Areas that are predominantly White British today could soon become ethnically diverse.

A current initiative of my work at the EA are the Intercultural Church Conversations, which developed as a result of our vision of intercultural unity, intercultural churches and intercultural justice. The intercultural church strategy is to help promote an intercultural model of church in the UK that goes beyond a multicultural church. But what is the difference between a multicultural church and an intercultural church? In the words of Kate Coleman, the founding director of Next Leadership:

> In cross-cultural churches, one culture is often considered "the norm" and all other cultures are compared or contrasted to this dominant culture, which is viewed as superior (the others are treated as inferior and often "exist" in survival mode). In multicultural churches several cultural or ethnic groups live alongside one another, but each cultural group does not necessarily have meaningful interactions with others. They tend to focus on representation with less powerful groups in survival mode.
>
> "Inter" conveys the idea of sharing, reciprocity, and equality. In these churches, there is robust contact between cultures and a deep understanding and respect for all cultures. Intercultural communication focuses on the mutual exchange of ideas and cultural norms and the development of deep relationships. In an

intercultural church, no one is left unchanged because everyone learns from one another and grows together.[17]

Churches will have to journey through the stages of cross-cultural and multicultural in order to develop an intercultural church. This requires intentionality from the church leadership and it has to be accepted as part of the vision of the church. The leadership must centre the process and communicate to the congregation that the church will journey in this direction. An important step in the process is developing an intercultural leadership, first to model intercultural visibility to the church as a prophetic vision, second to drive and sustain the vision, and third to encourage welcoming, belonging and integration.[18]

In order to develop an intercultural church, racial justice must be at the centre of our discipleship framework.[19] This requires that we encourage churches to develop preaching series on racial justice, encourage house group discussions on the subject and develop worship and liturgies around the theme of racial justice. The resources for the annual Racial Justice Sunday in February could prove useful in reflecting on justice themes.[20] A final requirement is investment in equipping and training church leaders to be able to discuss the subject. By engaging in all the above practices, we will be integrating racial justice into our discipleship framework and working towards developing an intercultural church.

Repair: How Can the Church Repair Relationships?

Perhaps the most controversial part of the research concerns reparative justice. This topic received a mixed reaction both from White British respondents and people of a Majority World background. Many respondents mentioned problems with reparative justice, such as, how do you implement it, who gives the money and how do you determine who receives reparations?

---

17. Kate Coleman, *Metamorph: Transforming your Life and Leadership* (Birmingham: 100 Movement Publishing, 2024).

18. For further resources on intercultural churches, see Ben Aldous, Idina Dunmore and Mohan Seevaratnam, *Intercultural Church: Shared Learning from New Communities* (Oxford: Grove Books, 2020) and Osoba Otaigbe, *Building Cultural Intelligence in Church and Ministry* (Milton Keynes: Author House, 2016).

19. Israel Olofinjana, *Discipleship, Suffering and Racial Justice: Mission in a Pandemic World* (Oxford: Regnum Studies, 2021).

20. Racial Justice Sunday is organized and resourced by Churches Together in Britain and Ireland. Because this is an ecumenical body, some evangelicals will not engage in it.

These responses probably betray the association of reparative justice with monetary values. However, we can also conceive reparative justice in terms of repairing relationships, akin to the New Testament teaching on reconciliation. There is currently an important secular conversation on reparative justice in Britain: families who have profited from slavery are giving back what was stolen, institutions such as museums are returning stolen artefacts, and the Royal family has commissioned research into aspects of royal history that are tainted by slavery. Whilst there are several resources,[21] there is a lack of biblical and theological resources on the subject in the UK context. The UK church is still trying to work out what its position ought to be in these conversations. The Church of England is debating a suggestion to increase their £100 million reparations fund to one billion Pound and the backlash highlights the volatile nature of this conversation. The current lack of biblical resources on the subject leaves many evangelical Christians wondering what the Bible says about reparative justice.

A good place to start for evangelicals is the theme of restitution in the Old Testament. Restitution was a system set in place to administer justice after the theft of livestock and properties, returning them to their rightful owner (see Exod 22:1–6; Lev 6:4–5; Num 5:5–10; 2 Sam 12:6; Ezek 33:14–15 and Luke 3:10–14). Whilst it could be argued that this was an Old Testament practice, the New Testament does contain the example of the story of Zacchaeus, who offered to repay anyone he had exploited. What is crucial in this story is that Jesus did not demand that Zacchaeus should repay what he had stolen: Zacchaeus demonstrated the fruits of repentance by intentionally offering to repair the damage he had done.

Another point to consider in this debate is that the term reparative justice sounds to many like a form of retributive or punitive justice. Yes we need to understand reparative justice as a means to repair damaged relationships that requires holistic healing, repairing and addressing the past so that reconciliation, healing and peace can occur in the present. This approach will be holistic because it concerns not only financial, but also spiritual, psychological, social and spiritual restoration from a traumatic past.

Lastly, I suggest that the discussions of 1846, referred to above, can inform how we enter that conversation today. Can we once again listen to marginal voices as we enter the debate on how we can repair the damages of the past?

---

21. E.g. Eleasah Louis Phoenix, ed., "We will Repay: A Biblical Case-Study for Reparations," https://ctbi.org.uk/wewillrepay/.

Conclusion

This chapter is a first attempt to develop an evangelical theology and practice regarding racial justice, using the key findings from the EA research on race. Whilst British evangelicals have a rich history of engaging with these issues, this has not (yet) translated into systematic theological insights that can enable evangelical churches to address the sin of racism in church and society. The effect is that some evangelical churches today see the issue of race and racial justice as either wokeness or left-wing politics and therefore as something the church should not be involved with. I have provided theological reflection and commentary on the four areas of the research findings, that is, understanding of racial justice, experiences of racism, responses to racism and reparative justice. This chapter is not the final word on the subject but a contribution to an ongoing discussion among British evangelicals.

Bibliography

Attitudes and Practices Towards Race within the UK Evangelicals. Evangelical Alliance UK internal document, 2024.

Coleman, Kate. *Metamorph: Transforming your Life and Leadership.* Birmingham: 100 Movement Publishing, 2024.

———. *Being Human: A Black British Christian Woman's Perspective.* Whitley Lectures. Oxford: Whitley Publications, 2006.

Edwards, Joel, ed. *Let's Praise Him Again: An African-Caribbean Perspective on Worship.* Eastbourne: Kingsway Publications, 1992.

Kapolyo, Joe. *The Human Condition: Christian Perspectives Through African Eyes.* Carlisle: Langham Global Library, 2013.

Lindsay, Ben. *We Need to Talk About Race: Understanding the Black Experience in White Majority Churches.* London: SPCK, 2019.

Louis, Eleasah Phoenix, ed. *We Will Repay: A Biblical Case-Study for Reparations.* Racial Justice Advocacy Forum, Baptists Together and Churches Together in England, 2024. https://ctbi.org.uk/wewillrepay/.

Olofinjana, Israel. *Discipleship, Suffering and Racial Justice: Mission in a Pandemic World.* Oxford: Regnum Studies, 2021.

Osgood, Hugh. *Evangelical and African Pentecostal Unity: Balancing Principles and Practicalities in Britain around the Millennium.* Eugene: Pickwick, 2024.

Otaigbe, Osoba. *Building Cultural Intelligence Church and Ministry.* Milton Keynes: Author House, 2016.

Reddie, Richard. *Race for Justice: The Struggle for Equality and Inclusion in Britain and Ireland.* Oxford: Lion Hudson, 2022.

10

The Elephant in The Room

Sexual Ethics and the Boundaries of Evangelicalism

David Sandifer

Introduction

At a recent European conference on evangelicalism, two presenters gave strikingly different assessments: one was encouraged by the present diversity, including theological diversity, and said that this was a source of strength; another reflected that deep theological differences within evangelicalism were untenable, like rowers rowing in opposite directions on the same boat, and would need to be resolved sooner or later.

It is possible, of course, that these two speakers were not contradicting each other but responding to different theological issues. Yet the question of the boundaries of evangelicalism is a vexing one and has been so for a long time.[1] However, since the advent of the "New Evangelicalism" (or "Neo-evangelicalism") in the 1940s there has been at least a rough consensus about the core features of evangelicalism, the authority of Scripture and priority of evangelism, first and foremost. Key documents such of the Lausanne Covenant (1974) formalized these distinctives. Recently, however, a strain has been placed

---

1. In the fundamentalist/modernist controversy of the 1920s, the "modernist" party was represented by "progressive evangelicals" like Harry Fosdick, and that it was precisely for this reason that "Fundamentalism" was the term adopted by conservatives to differentiate themselves.

on evangelical unity and questions have arisen around the boundaries of evangelicalism on account of sexual ethics, and LGBTQ issues in particular. While this is happening all over the world to some degree, it is most pronounced in North America and especially in Europe.

This chapter seeks to address two questions: first, whether a traditional sexual ethic constitutes a boundary marker for evangelicalism; and second, if yes (as will be argued), what this means for how evangelical groups and churches define their beliefs.

Two clarifications are in order. In the first place, the approach taken in the first part is primarily historical. No attempt will be made to argue for a traditional perspective on sexual ethics. Others have done this voluminously and it would be outside the scope of this chapter even to summarize these arguments.[2] Rather, the question which will be engaged is simply whether, historically speaking, a traditional approach to sexual ethics can be said to be a constitutive aspect of evangelicalism. Second, any discussion of sexual ethics, and of LGBTQ issues in particular, obviously has profound pastoral dimensions. Again, I will not attempt to engage these, not because they are not important – they are of course crucial to a faithful Christian response – but because they are outside my narrow purpose.

Background: "Affirming" Evangelicalism

Until fairly recently, there was a functional unanimity among evangelicals on questions of sexuality. When liberal theologians began to question traditional sexual norms in the 1960s, they found no support from evangelicals. None, for example, aligned with the situation ethics advocated by John A. T. Robinson in *Honest to God* (1963).[3] Similarly, ever since historic Protestant denominations in Europe and the USA opened the door to co-habitation and homosexuality in the 1970s and 1980s,[4] evangelicals within these groups have been dissenters. Thus when Robert Gagnon defended a traditional sexual ethic in his encyclopaedic *The Bible and Homosexual Practice*, the sparring partners he had in view were liberal theologians (like some of his fellow faculty at

---

2. For a general defence of the traditional Christian sexual ethic, see in particular Denis Hollinger, *The Meaning of Sex: Christian Ethics and the Moral Life* (Grand Rapids: Baker Academic, 2009) and Gerald Hiestand and Tod Wilson (eds), *Beauty, Order and Mystery: A Christian Vision of Human Sexuality* (Downers Grove: IVP Academic, 2017). The reference work with respect to homosexuality remains Robert Gagnon, *The Bible and Homosexual Practice: Texts and Hermeneutics* (Nashville: Abingdon, 2002).

3. John A. T. Robinson, *Honest to God* (London: SCM, 1963).

4. For instance, in John S. Spong's *Living in Sin?* (San Francisco: Harper & Row, 1988).

Presbyterian Theological Seminary, where he formerly taught), not "progressive evangelicals."[5] Even a left-leaning evangelical like Tony Campolo, who had a reputation for pushing the boundaries of evangelicalism, voiced strong support for a traditional sexual ethic throughout the 1990s.[6] At least until the early 2000s, a traditional view on matters of sexuality was an unquestioned marker of evangelicalism, both in relation to the larger culture and to more liberal forms of Christianity.

This began to change in the early 2010s. In 2012, a young man by the name of Matthew Vines, who identified as evangelical, gave a church presentation which made the case that the Bible did not condemn committed same-sex relationships. The video of his presentation went viral, being viewed nearly a million times.[7] Strikingly, Vines' arguments were the same ones which evangelicals had been refuting for two decades or more – yet they quickly gained traction amongst younger evangelicals of the internet generation. In 2014, Vines followed up his video with a book, *God and the Gay Christian*,[8] and went on to head an organization, the cheekily named Reformation Project, dedicated to shifting evangelical opinion on the subject of homosexuality. While its website does not advertise itself as "evangelical," it states, "our beliefs are grounded in our commitment to the authority of the Bible and orthodox theology" and "we love the Bible and revere it as the Word of God, inspired by God and authoritative for Christian life and practice."[9]

In 2013, New Testament scholar James Brownson published *Bible, Gender, and Sexuality: Reframing the Church's Debate on Same-Sex Relationships*.[10] While Brownson is not a self-proclaimed evangelical (and does not teach at an evangelical institution), he was viewed as a relatively conservative scholar and his apology for committed same-sex relationship was a reversal of his earlier position. His book has become an important text for affirming evangelicals. In a similar vein, Baptist theologian and ethicist David Gushee released his change-of-heart account.[11] While Gushee now identifies himself as "post-evangelical," he considered himself an evangelical at the time the book was published and

---

5. Gagnon, *Bible and Homosexual Practice*.

6. See for example his *20 Hot Potatoes Christians Are Afraid to Touch* (Nashville: Thomas Nelson, 1993), 15, where his discussion of AIDS clearly references homosexual acts as sinful.

7. Matthew Vines, "The Gay Debate: The Bible and Homosexuality," www.youtube.com/watch?v=ezQjNJUSraY.

8. Matthew Vines, *God and the Gay Christian* (Colorado Springs: Convergent Books, 2015).

9. "Our Values," The Reformation Project, https://reformationproject.org/values/.

10. James Brownson, *Bible, Gender, and Sexuality: Reframing the Church's Debate on Same-Sex Relationships* (Grand Rapids: Eerdmans, 2013).

11. David Gushee, *Changing Our Mind* (Canton: Read The Spirit Books, 2014).

his treatment, like Brownson's, has been influential in evangelical circles. (His ethics textbook is the main text in at least one European evangelical seminary today.[12]) In 2016, following years of speculation that his position had shifted, Tony Campolo released a statement affirming same-sex marriage.[13] This was perhaps not terribly surprising for a speaker and writer who had often enjoyed being something of the *enfant terrible* of evangelicalism; but the endorsement which former *Christianity Today* editor David Neff gave him was more so, when he posted on his Facebook page that he thought Campolo was "on the right track."[14]

Here in Europe, Michael Diener, a pastor and former chairman of the German Evangelical Alliance, in 2021 released *Raus aus der Sackgasse!* ("Get out of the dead end"),[15] a book urging "evangelical and pietistic" churches to adopt an affirming stance. Stefan Pahl, the former chairman of Willow Creek Germany, who now sits on its Executive Committee, provided an approving blurb for the book, stating that he would "give the book to his three children." Finally, in 2024 Richard Hays recanted his earlier position on homosexuality in a book co-authored with his son.[16] Again, while Hays is probably not an evangelical *per se*, he is one of the most respected biblical ethicists writing today (his *Moral Vision of the New Testament* is a reference work) and evangelicals had previously leaned on the support that he had given to a traditional reading of the Scriptures.[17]

Similarly, some notable evangelical organizations and churches have either softened their stance on sexuality or explicitly taken an affirming position, both in Europe and in the USA.

---

12. David Gushee, *Introducing Christian Ethics: Core Convictions for Christians Today* (Canton: Front Edge, 2022).

13. Tony Campolo, "Tony Campolo: For The Record," 8 June 2015, www.tonycampolo.org/for-the-record-tony-campolo-releases-a-new-statement/.

14. *Christianity Today* found this so significant that it immediately published an editorial in rebuttal: Mark Galli, "Breaking News: 2 Billion Christians Believe in Traditional Marriage," ChristianityToday.com, 9 June 2015, www.christianitytoday.com/2015/06/breaking-news-2-billion-christian-believe-in-traditional-ma/.

15. Michael Diener, *Raus aus der Sackgasse! Wie die pietistische und evangelikale Bewegung neu an Glaubürdigkeit gewinnt* (Ostfildern: Adeo, 2021).

16. Christopher Hays and Richard Hays, *The Widening of God's Mercy: Sexuality within the Biblical Story* (New Haven: Yale University Press, 2024).

17. Richard Hays, *The Moral Vision of the New Testament: A Contemporary Introduction to New Testament Ethics* (San Francisco: HarperOne, 1996). Hays devoted a chapter (16) in this book to homosexuality, where he offered a robust traditional reading of the New Testament passages.

In 2022, in Germany a new organization was launched, Coming In, at a conference with the same name. It described itself as started by people who "work in evangelical or conservative communities" and who "dream of a Christian community in which everyone is welcome, whether lesbian, gay, bi, trans or queer."[18] In a similar vein, Inclusive Evangelicals was started in the UK in 2023 to bring together "evangelical Christians . . . who believe an open and including welcome of same-sex relationships can be held with biblical integrity."[19] In the Netherlands, Mozaïek, a large and fast-growing charismatic church with sites across the country, includes small groups devoted to LGBTQ persons. One of these advertises that "we find equality and acceptance in every aspect important" and that "you are like God made you and that is good."[20]

In 2023 the large Crossroads Church in Atlanta, pastored by Andy Stanley, hosted a conference on homosexuality which included speakers taking an affirming position and a same-sex couple. Stanley dedicated a sermon to the issue shortly afterwards, in which he simultaneously re-affirms Crossroads' adherence to a traditional view and defends the decision to include the same-sex couple as speakers at the conference:

> This is why Justin and Brian were invited, the two married gay men at the center of all the controversy. And I'm sure that you've read all about that. And here's the thing about Brian and Justin: their stories and their journeys of growing up in church and maintaining their faith in Christ and their commitment to follow Christ all through their high school and college and singles and all up to the time that they were married, their story is so powerful for parents of gay especially kids, that it's a story gay parents and gay kids need to hear.[21]

In 2022, the Christian Reformed Church, an evangelical denomination in the USA, endorsed a traditional position as part of its confession.[22] Prior to this, around a third of the faculty at its flagship institution, Calvin University, had

---

18. "Was genau ist Coming-In?" ComingIn.de, https://coming-in.de/.

19. "Who we are," InclusiveEvangelicals.com, www.inclusiveevangelicals.com/about.

20. "Love To Meet LGBTQ," 055. Mozaiek.com, https://055.mozaiek.nl/communities/love2meet/love2meet-lgbtq.

21. Andy Stanley, "I love my church," Sermon preached at Northpoint Community Church, 1 October 2023, https://sermons.love/andy-stanley/16592-andy-stanley-i-love-my-church.html.

22. Yonat Shimron, "Christian Reformed Church Brings LGBT Stance Into Faith Statement," ChristianityToday.com, 18 June 2022, www.christianitytoday.com/2022/06/christian-reformed-church-crc-lgbt-stance-calvin/.

issued a statement pleading for the denomination not to take this step, since the faculty is required to subscribe to the church's confession. A compromise was found when the board of the university allowed professors to publicly disagree with the sexuality part of the denomination's confession.[23]

While these writers, churches and organizations still represent a minority within evangelicalism, both in Europe and in the USA, "evangelical" and "LGBTQ-affirming" are no longer mutually exclusive. Moreover, some (many?) evangelical churches in Europe have adopted a kind of "don't-ask-don't-tell" policy: while formally continuing to hold a traditional position, this is rarely if ever taught from the pulpit or publicly affirmed, and no effort is made to ensure that church members either hold to this view or live by it; indeed, the assumption will often be that the congregation will be divided and only those in leadership roles expected to subscribe to a traditional understanding.[24]

How should we respond to this significant shift within evangelicalism? More specifically, should a traditional sexual ethic constitute a boundary marker for evangelicalism?

Sexual Ethics As a First-Order Issue for Evangelicalism

The argument in favour of seeing traditional sexual ethics as a necessary constitutive element of evangelicalism is simple, almost simplistic, yet it needs to be made. It can be summarized this way: a) Evangelicalism is situated within historic orthodox Christianity. b) A traditional sexual ethic is a non-negotiable element of historic orthodox Christianity. Let us look at each of these points in turn.

Evangelicalism is Situated within Historic Orthodox Christianity

Defining "evangelicalism" is both difficult and controversial; some have suggested that it is too varied historically, theologically, geographically and sociologically to admit of any unitary definition.[25] Yet many agree that in fact there

---

23. "Board of trustees retains faculty who disagree with CRCNA on LGBTQ+ relationships," *Chimes*, 1 November 2022, https://calvinchimes.org/2022/11/01/board-of-trustees-retains-faculty-who-disagree-with-crcna-on-lgbtq-relationships/.

24. It is difficult to estimate how many European evangelical churches have adopted this approach. In the Netherlands, it would seem from anecdotal evidence that it is common.

25. Thus Nathan Hatch, one of the most respected historians of American evangelicalism, famously argued that "there is no such thing as evangelicalism"; see Nathan Hatch, "Response to Carl F. H. Henry," in Kenneth S. Kantzer and Carl F. H. Henry (eds), *Evangelical Affirmations* (Grand Rapids: Zondervan, 1990), 97.

is a "stable core" to evangelicalism and have attempted to provide a definition that will encompass it. By far the most influential of these is David Bebbington's, which has become known as the "Bebbington Quadrilateral" and contains four characteristics: biblicism, crucicentrism, conversionism and activism (evangelism, mission more broadly, and social action).[26]

One of the few alternative attempts that has gained traction is the one Timothy Larsen proposed and to which he half-seriously refers as the "Larsen Pentalateral,"[27] since it contains five elements, three of which are adaptations of Bebbington:

1. An orthodox Protestant movement
2. In the tradition of eighteenth-century Great Awakening/Evangelical Revival
3. Biblicism
4. Crucicentrism
5. Conversionism and evangelism[28]

The advantage of Larsen's definition, in addition to being embedded in a historical context, is that it makes explicit what the Quadrilateral assumes (and is perhaps contained within "biblicism"), namely that evangelicalism is an "orthodox Protestant movement."[29] Historically, evangelicalism has undeniably fallen within the bounds of orthodox Christianity (at least in its mainstream expressions) and its most influential leaders have understood the movement in this way. This was true of its earliest leaders, the Wesleys and George Whitefield, who saw their mission in part as a restoration of orthodoxy, in particular

---

26. David Bebbington, *Evangelicalism in Modern Britain: A History from the 1730s to the 1980s* (London: Unwin Hyman, 1989), 2–17. The book has been in print ever since.

27. Timothy Larsen, "Defining and Locating Evangelicalism," in *The Cambridge Companion to Evangelical Theology*, ed. Timothy Larson (Cambridge: Cambridge University Press, 2007), 1.

28. Larsen, "Defining," 1–14.

29. While this is not the place to pursue this at length, both definitions are open to improvement, as they leave out arguably key aspects of the movement. Furthermore, any adequate definition must operate *differentially* with respect to the larger historical reality of Protestantism. In a paper presented to the FEET Conference in 2022, I argued for an alternative five-point definition, namely that evangelicalism is an orthodox and Protestant Christian movement (which as such affirms both biblicism and crucicentrism), and characterized by:
    Conversionism (centrally)
    Missionalism (evangelism and social action)
    Experientialism ("vital religion")
    Consecrationism ("practical religion," or the expectation of changed lives)
    Trans-denominationalism (resulting in particular in a new conception of the church-state relationship).

in response to the rising influence of Socinianism (Unitarianism) and Deism during their time. In fact, when the term "evangelical" was deployed as a label in the eighteenth century (then used more or less interchangeably with "Methodist"), many in the movement were uncomfortable with it, as they did not wish to be seen as a party, but simply as "vital," "serious" or even "real" Christians.[30] In more recent times, some evangelical theologians have even argued that evangelicalism is *nothing but* historic orthodox Christianity, with John Stott in particular stating that it is "nothing other than the historic Christian faith: original, biblical, apostolic Christianity"[31] and J. K. A. Smith opining "what does the term 'evangelical' get you that the term 'Catholic' doesn't?"[32] While these approaches may be unhelpfully imprecise from a historical point of view, they do highlight a core aspect of historic evangelicalism: it is situated within orthodox Christianity.[33] This claim is reinforced by the fact that, while evangelicalism has no creeds in a formal sense, the primary confessions which evangelicals have sometimes used as boundary markers, such as the Lausanne Covenant and the statement of faith of the World Evangelical Alliance, have been at pains to re-articulate the core tenets of orthodox Christian theology.

A Traditional Sexual Ethic is a Non-negotiable Element of Historic Orthodox Christianity

From the birth of Christianity, orthodox Christian teaching has given pride of place to ethical living as a marker of authentic Christianity ("orthopraxis") and to standards of sexual conduct in particular. In Acts 15 the decision of the Jerusalem Council includes in its very short list of requirements for gentile believers that they should "abstain from sexual immorality" (Act 15:29). One of the oldest Christian texts outside of the New Testament documents, the *Didache*, likewise gives significant attention to sexual morality as an expres-

---

30. See, for example, the full title of William Wilberforce's enormously popular evangelical apology: *A Practical View of the Prevailing Religious System of Professed Christians, in the Middle and Higher Classes in this Country, Contrasted with Real Christianity* (London: Robert Napper, 1797).

31. Michael Reeves and John Stott, *The Reformation: What You Need to Know and Why* (Peabody: Hendrickson, 2017), 31.

32. J. K. A. Smith, "An Evangelical Manifesto?," 7 May 2008, https://jameskasmith.com/an-evangelical-manifesto/.

33. Thus offshoot movements such as "Oneness" (or "Jesus-only") Pentecostals, who deny the Trinity, while sometimes described as "evangelical," should properly be classified along with heterodox groups such as the Jehovah's Witnesses.

sion of "the way of life" contrasted with "the way of death." It appears early in the list of commandments:

> And the second commandment of the Teaching; You shall not commit murder, you shall not commit adultery, you shall not commit pederasty, you shall not commit fornication, you shall not steal, you shall not practice magic. . . .[34]

The historian Kyle Harper has documented the central importance given to sexual morality in the early church, as well as its counter-cultural significance:

> For the early Christians, a rigorous sexual morality was integral to its spiritual project, which was to move through a world that was always ebbing away and toward the immaterial and transcendent God.
>
> It was not the austere sexual morality itself that set Christians apart from the world so much as its central place within an effort to redefine how humanity ought to live in a created but fallen order. This transforming vision was something new and altogether estranging—in antiquity and ever since.[35]

The early church fathers consistently denounced homosexual practice in particular, with condemnations from Athenagoras, Tertullian, Clement of Alexandria, Origen, Cyprian, Hippolytus, Novatian, Basil of Caesaria and John Chrysostom.[36] Augustine wrote that "shameful acts which are contrary to nature, such as the acts of the Sodomites, are everywhere and always to be detested and punished."[37] Medieval theologians renewed these strictures, with Hildegard of Bingen asserting that "a man who sins with another man as if

---

34. *The Teaching of the Twelve Apostles, Commonly Called the Didache*, trans. by Cyril Richardson, in *The Library of Christian Classics: Vol. 1, Early Christian Fathers*, ed. Cyril Richardson (Philadelphia: Westminster Press, 1953), 148–56, 149.

35. Kyle Harper, "The First Sexual Revolution: How Christianity Transformed the Ancient World," *First Things* 279 (January 2018), 41–46. See also Kyle Harper, *From Shame to Sin: The Christian Transformation of Sexual Morality in Late Antiquity* (Cambridge: Harvard University Press, 2016).

36. For a thorough but compact summary of the unanimity of church teaching on homosexuality, see James Spiegel, "A Great Cloud of Moral Witness," *Touchstone Magazine*, Jan/Feb 2018.

37. Augustine, *Confessions*, trans. Henry Chadwick (Oxford: Oxford University Press, 1991), 3:8:15 (46).

with a woman sins bitterly against God" and Thomas Aquinas declaring that of the "sins against nature" sodomy is, except for bestiality, "the most grievous."[38]

In a comprehensive survey, Donald Fortson and Roland Grams argue that the witness of the church on sexual ethics has not only been consistent across the ages but also central to its vision of the Christian life:

> One of the primary things handed down in the Christian church over the centuries is a consistent set of ethical instructions, including specific directives about sexual behavior. The church of every generation from the time of the apostles has condemned sexual sin as unbecoming a disciple of Jesus. At no point have any orthodox Christian teachers ever suggested that one's sexual practices may deviate from biblical standards.[39]

Of particular interest to evangelicals, as heirs of the Reformation distinctives, is the stance of early Protestant leaders and churches. These in no way differed from the historic teachings of the Catholic Church on this point. Thus Martin Luther stated:

> The heinous conduct of the people of Sodom is extraordinary, inasmuch as they departed from the natural passion and longing of the male for the female, which was implanted into nature by God, and desired what is altogether contrary to nature. Whence comes this perversity? Undoubtedly from Satan, who, after people have once turned away from the fear of God, so powerfully suppresses nature that he blots out the natural desire and stirs up a desire that is contrary to nature.[40]

Likewise, John Calvin's views on both fornication and homosexuality reiterated the traditional proscriptions of the church: of the former, he wrote that the one who sins in this way "break the body of our Lord Jesus Christ into as

---

38. Hildegard of Bingen, *Scivias*, and Thomas Aquinas *Summa Theologica* (II-II, 154, 12), in Spiegel, "Cloud."

39. Donald Fortson and Roland Grams, *Unchanging Witness: The Consistent Christian Teaching on Homosexuality in Scripture and Tradition* (Nashville: B&H Academic, 2016), 27.

40. Martin Luther, "Lectures on Genesis: Chapters 15–20," in *Luther's Works Volume 3*, ed. Jaroslav Jan Pelikan, Hilton C. Oswald and Helmut T. Lehmann (Saint Louis: Concordia, 1999).

many pieces as he can"[41] and of the latter that "this crime is one of the most abominable that there is. It is clearly punished by the Holy Scriptures."[42]

In the case of homosexual acts, both Luther and Calvin appear to be hesitant even to speak of them, on account of their depravity. Thus Luther prefaces his comments with the following:

> Moses proceeds with a description of a terrible sin. I for my part do not enjoy dealing with this passage, because so far the ears of the Germans are innocent of and uncontaminated by this monstrous depravity; for even though this disgrace, like other sins, has crept in through an ungodly soldier and a lewd merchant, still the rest of the people are unaware of what is being done in secret.[43]

As Kevin DeYoung has noted, when Question 87 of the Heidelberg Catechism states that "No unchaste person, no idolater, adulterer, thief, no covetous person, no drunkard, slanderer, robber, or the like will inherit the kingdom of God," this is an obvious paraphrase of 1 Corinthians 6:9–10, and "the like" refers to the categories of persons omitted, in particular those who commit homosexual acts.[44] In his commentary on this question, Ursinus, the chief author of the Catechism, refers to those lusts which are "contrary to nature and of the devil."[45] Similarly, the *Westminster Larger Catechism* lists sodomy amongst the sins prohibited by the seventh commandment.[46]

The Reformation was, to be sure, primarily a movement of theological, not moral, reform, yet moral purification was always also in view: it not only channelled the same moral commitments that had long been part of the church's teaching, it also heightened the importance of adhering to them, as seen in Luther's elevation of marriage as a way to battle concupiscence and in the

---

41. John Calvin, *Sermons on the Ten Commandments*, trans. B. W. Farley (Pelham: Solid Ground Christian Books, 2011), 173, quoted in Balázs Magyar, "Punishment and forgiveness of sexual crimes: A special reference to sodomy in Calvin's theology," *Verbum Eccles*. (Online) 43.1 (2022), http://dx.doi.org/10.4102/ve.v43i1.2626.

42. John Calvin, *Ioannis Calvini opera quae supersunt omnia, volume 59*, edited by G. Baum, E. Cunitz, E. Reuss and A. Erichson (Brunsvigae: C. A. Schwetschke, 1863–1900), 69, quoted in Magyar, "Punishment."

43. Luther, "Genesis."

44. Kevin DeYoung, "Does the Heidelberg Catechism Have Anything To Say About Homosexuality," The Gospel Coalition, 16 March 2012, www.thegospelcoalition.org/blogs/kevin-deyoung/does-the-heidelberg-catechism-have-anything-to-say-about-homosexuality/.

45. Ursinus, *Commentary on the Catechism*, 592, quoted in DeYoung, "Heidelberg." That the Christian Reformed Church granted "confessional status" to its condemnation of homosexual acts in 2022 was based on this interpretation of the Heidelberg Confession.

46. *Westminster Larger Catechism*, Question 139.

Puritan emphasis on fighting sin and maintaining a clean conscience. This same orientation was a marker of early evangelicalism: the strength of Methodism were its societies, where members met weekly to confess their sins to each other, and leading evangelical luminaries such as William Wilberforce and Hannah More devoted enormous energies to the "reformation of manners" for society as a whole and committed Christians in particular.[47] Sexual purity was a central concern of this movement, as evidenced, for example, in the work of the Society for the Suppression of Vice.[48]

Without question, then, a traditional sexual ethic has been an important and incontrovertible aspect of the church's moral teaching since its birth. With respect to homosexuality, Fortson and Grams found not only consensus in the church's teaching over the centuries, but *unanimity*: they were unable to locate a single Christian writer prior to the twentieth century who conferred approval on homosexual acts.[49] When in 1968 the Metropolitan Community Church was founded in California as a church which affirmed homosexual relationships, it was because even the most liberal denominations at the time did not do so – all the changes across denominations which have taken place in this respect have occurred since then.

It is for this reason that N. T. Wright, writing in 2009 following the revisionist stance taken by the American Episcopal Church, accused it of "formalizing schism" by rejecting "chastity, as universally understood by the wider Christian tradition."[50] Similarly, Wolfhart Pannenberg, though by no means an evangelical, understood the significance of the changes being proposed with respect to sexual ethics:

> Here lies the boundary of a Christian church that knows itself to be bound by the authority of Scripture. Those who urge the church to change the norm of its teaching on this matter must know that they are promoting schism. If a church were to let

---

47. See Wilberforce, *A Practical View*. For an excellent overview of the moral reform efforts of evangelicals in early nineteenth-century Britain, see Herbert Schlossberg, *The Silent Revolution and the Making of Victorian England* (Columbus: Ohio State University Press, 2000).

48. See Michael Roberts, *Making English Morals: Voluntary Association and Moral Reform in England, 1787–1886* (Cambridge: Cambridge University Press), 73–86.

49. Fortson and Grams, *Unchanging Witness*, 141, 376. One can assume that this conclusion would have been taken up as a challenge by revisionists and that if there were any "affirming" stance to be found in the history of the church prior to the late twentieth century, this would have been unearthed and magnified to make the counterclaim.

50. N. T. Wright, "The Americans know this will end in schism," 14 July 2009, www.fulcrum-anglican.org.uk/articles/the-americans-know-this-will-end-in-schism-by-tom-wright-full-version.

itself be pushed to the point where it ceased to treat homosexual activity as a departure from the biblical norm, and recognized homosexual unions as a personal partnership of love equivalent to marriage, such a church would stand no longer on biblical ground but against the unequivocal witness of Scripture. A church that took this step would cease to be the one, holy, catholic, and apostolic church.[51]

It is not too much, then, to refer to the traditional position as the "orthodox" one on sexuality matters. Some have pushed back against using the word orthodox in this way, arguing that the terms "orthodoxy" and "creedal orthodoxy" in particular should be reserved for beliefs relating to the nature of God and core gospel doctrines as expressed in the major creeds.[52] However, this is too narrow a use of the word: while "creedal orthodoxy" is obviously more restricting by definition, "orthodox" beliefs simply refers to those things which the church has always believed and taught, in the famous words of Vincent of Lérins, "everywhere, always, by all."[53] The traditional teaching on sexual ethics, and on homosexual acts in particular, clearly meets this test. If there is any lingering doubt on this in any reader's mind, then consider the following thought experiment: imagine that, at the time of Augustine, Aquinas, Calvin, Wesley or Spurgeon, there had existed a group of supposed Christians who practised same-sex marriage, is it conceivable that any of these leaders would have regarded this group as orthodox?

If evangelicals are orthodox Christians and if orthodox Christians affirm a traditional perspective on sexuality, then it follows that an orthodox perspective on sexuality is a non-negotiable aspect of evangelical teaching. In other

---

51. Wolfhart Pannenberg, "Revelation and Homosexual Experience: What Wolfhart Pannenberg says about this debate in the church," *Christianity Today*, 11 November 1996, 35–37, 37, www.christianitytoday.com/1996/11/revelation-and-homosexual-experience-what-wolfhart-pannenbe.

52. James K. A. Smith posted a much-discussed article making this argument: "On 'orthodox Christianity': some observations, and a couple of questions," 4 August 2017, http://forsclavigera.blogspot.com/2017/08/on-orthodox-christianity-some.html.

53. "All possible care must be taken that we hold that faith which has been believed everywhere, always, by all," Vincent of Lérens, *For the Antiquity and Universality of the Catholic Faith Against the Profane Novelties of All Heresies*, trans. C. A. Heurtley, in *Nicene and Post-Nicene Fathers, Second Series, Vol. 11*, ed. Philip Schaff and Henry Wace (Buffalo: Christian Literature Publishing, 1894), revised and edited by Kevin Knight www.newadvent.org/fathers/3506.htm, II.6.

words, it is a "first-order issue," that is, an issue about which definitions and boundaries are necessary.[54]

A Call for Clarity
Positions (not) Taken

If an orthodox view of sexuality is an irreducible part of an evangelical identity, how should evangelicals respond to individuals and groups claiming to be both evangelical and to have an affirming perspective? It goes without saying that no one can be prevented from calling themselves "evangelical," any more than anyone be kept from calling themselves "Christian." But equally, it is important to bring clarity to this issue which is causing increasing confusion. Currently things are in a muddle: some churches and institutions have adopted clear statements; some have put out reports or statements which, while not binding on their members, point to an orthodox position; and some have not yet taken a stance.

The Lausanne Movement is in the first category. Its *Cape Town Declaration* (2010) states that "all pastors should set an example of sexual chastity and faithfulness . . . and teach clearly and often that marriage is the exclusive place for sexual union."[55] Its *Seoul Statement* (2024) strengthens this by including a detailed section on human sexuality, and homosexuality in particular, affirming an orthodox position.[56] In 2016, InterVarsity Christian Fellowship (IVCF), the American branch of the International Fellowship of Evaneglical Students (IFES), released *A Theological Summary on Human Sexuality*, which espouses an orthodox position on sexuality and attracted much criticism as a result, including a story in *Time*.[57] The IVCF statement is significant in that it clarifies that employees are expected to adhere to a traditional position and live in accordance with it. The IFES itself does not have any public position

---

54. Al Mohler popularised the terminology of first-order, second-order and third-order issues in his 2005 article, "A Call for Theological Triage and Christian Maturity," https://albertmohler.com/2005/07/12/a-call-for-theological-triage-and-christian-maturity/. "First-order issues" are those which define the boundaries of orthodox Christianity, "second-order issues" typically define the boundaries between Christian denominations and "third-order issues" are matters of personal conviction that should not create any boundaries at all.

55. Lausanne Movement, *The Cape Town Commitment*, 5B, https://lausanne.org/statement/ctcommitment.

56. Lausanne Movement, *The Seoul Statement*, 59–70, https://lausanne.org/statement/the-seoul-statement.

57. "Top Evangelical College Group to Dismiss Employees Who Support Gay Marriage," *Time*, 6 October 2016, https://time.com/4521944/intervarsity-fellowship-gay-marriage/.

on sexuality-related issues. The European Leadership Forum in 2015 added a *Statement on Sexuality and Marriage* to its doctrinal statement, which affirms an orthodox stance and requires those in leadership roles to adhere to it.[58]

The UK Evangelical Alliance (the original Evangelical Alliance) in 2012 released a document titled *Biblical and Pastoral Responses to Sexuality*, which states that "sexually active lesbians and gay men" should "see the need to be transformed and live in accordance with biblical revelation and orthodox church teaching"; but its Basis of Faith, which prospective members must affirm, does not mention marriage or sexuality. More recently, the European Evangelical Alliance (EEA), the umbrella organization for the various European Evangelical Alliances, issued a statement affirming that "the place where God has intended us to live out our sexuality is within a covenant relationship with a person of the opposite sex" and offering guidance to European EAs and member groups on addressing sexuality and gender issues. On the other hand, most of the European EAs have no statements on sexuality. The World Evangelical Alliance, which groups the Evangelical Alliances worldwide, does not have an official statement on marriage or sexuality. However, in 2014 it put out a statement criticizing new Ugandan laws on homosexuality and in this context stated that "as evangelicals, we affirm that God created marriage to be solely between one man and one woman" and that "we are not condoning homosexual behavior."[59]

Over the last fifteen years, a number of evangelical denominations and evangelical groupings within larger denominations, both in Europe and the USA, have clarified their stances on sexuality matters, while others continue to debate the merits of doing so. There are too many cases to detail here, but the stance of the Evangelical Group of the General Synod, the official evangelical grouping within the Synod of the Church of England, is worth noting: in 2019 it added an "Additional Declaration" to its statement of faith, which affirms "the unchangeable standard of Christian marriage between one man and one woman as the proper place for sexual intimacy and the basis of the family."[60]

---

58. "ELF Doctrinal Statement," European Leadership Foundation, https://euroleadership.org/sites/default/files/2023-08/ELF%20Doctrinal%20Statement-Evangelical%20Affirmations.pdf.

59. "WEA Issues Brief Statement Concerning Sexuality, Justice and Christian Witness," WorldEA.com, 20 March 2014, https://worldea.org/news/15812/wea-issues-brief-statement-concerning-sexuality-justice-and-christian-witness/.

60. Evangelical Group of the General Synod, "EGGS Basis of Faith," www.eggscofe.org.uk/uploads/5/5/6/3/5563632/eggs_basis_of_faith_nov_2021.docx.

This resulted in some members leaving and in the creation of a new, affirming, "Evangelical Forum" within the General Synod.[61]

In the current situation, evangelical churches and organizations may be said to fall into four broad categories with respect to their stance on sexuality and marriage:

1. Affirming: those that have taken an explicitly revisionist position
2. Ambiguous: those that have taken no position or contradictory positions, so that their stance in unclear
3. Implicitly orthodox: those that have taken no position but give the impression of maintaining an orthodox stance
4. Explicitly orthodox: those that have explicitly issued some kind of statement affirming an orthodox position

Because of the importance given to marriage and chastity in both Scripture and historic Christian teaching, and because this teaching is under increasing pressure both from the surrounding culture and from some Christians, including some claiming to be evangelicals, it is vital for evangelical churches and organizations who have not yet done so to adopt a clear public stance. The argument for doing so can be expressed in the form of a syllogism:

Major premise:
If a biblical teaching is both important and non-negotiable, and is actively questioned or rejected by some Christians, then faithful Christian churches and organizations must publicly and explicitly affirm it.

Minor premise:
The biblical teaching on sexuality is both important and non-negotiable, and is actively questioned or rejected by some Christians.

Conclusion:
The biblical teaching on sexuality must be publicly and explicitly affirmed by faithful Christian churches and organizations.

This position faces objections from some who maintain an orthodox position on sexuality but are hesitant about having a public statement. There is not sufficient space to respond to these in detail, but it is worth highlighting

---

61. Nikki Groarke, "General Synod: A Pragmatic View from the Middle Ground," https://viamedia.news/2021/11/11/5234/.

these concerns and providing a brief counterargument. (However, even if these objections were stronger than they are, they do not provide *defeaters* for the argument above.)

Frequent Objections with Brief Responses

Here follow responses to some common objections to the thesis that Christian churches and *organizations* ought to have a clear public stance on sexuality issues:

1. It gives too much importance to morality and/or sexuality

It is the Western culture which has given too much importance to sexuality and distorted its meaning; faithful Christians must respond both for the sake of witness and discipleship.

2. It will exclude some individuals, churches and organizations that presently identify as evangelical

Hopefully, it will instead encourage them to move in a more orthodox direction; if not, it is still better to have clarity than inclusion at the cost of orthodoxy.

3. It will lead to further policing and division about secondary matters

As argued here, sexual ethics is not a "secondary matter"; there is no reason for this to be a slippery slope toward division.

4. It will scare away non-Christians, especially young people

This is possible but there is no gain in attracting people to a sub-Christian faith; and it may well equally, if not more, *draw* people in who are hungry for the truth and for Christians who are willing to stand for it.

5. It will attract unwanted legal attention

Of course we should not deliberately court legal troubles and we should be wise in how we express ourselves. Yet if publicly affirming Christian teaching should lead to prosecution, then we should not be afraid of persecution nor assume that this will be harmful to our witness or ministry. The history of the church has often proven otherwise.

On the other hand, there are additional strong supporting reasons for having clear public statements in support of the orthodox position:

1. It is part of our faithfulness to Christ (cf. Rev 2:20)
If we are to be faithful to the "faith once received," a biblical sexual ethic is part of the package and we will be held accountable for how we uphold it.

2. It is part of the purity of our witness to the world (Phil 2:15–16)
Christian faithfulness has always included a counter-cultural component. This is part of what sets us apart from the world and points the world to Christ. We cannot conceal aspects of our calling which are most likely to offend and still maintain the purity of our witness.

3. It is part of our duty to protect the sheep and not lead others into sin (Matt 18:6)
Many Christians today are deeply influenced by the world's thinking on matters of sexuality, beginning with children and young people. We have a charge from Christ to protect them from false notions which will lead them astray. Pastors and other leaders will be emboldened to teach clearly on these matters when organizations and churches have a clear stance.

4. It strengthens our unity with other orthodox Christians around the world (and eases the burden of some experiencing persecution)
Many Christians around the world are looking with dismay on the apparent equivocation of Western Christians on matters of sexuality, a stance which sometimes tars them and brings unwarranted persecution. We have a responsibility to take a clear stand alongside faithful Christians around the world.

5. It provides protection for smaller churches and organizations, which can draw strength from the clear stance of larger groups
It is more difficult for smaller churches and groups to issue statements, both for practical reasons and for fear of being singled out. When larger organizations take a clear stance, not only does it provide an example but smaller groups can associate with them for cover.

6. By ignoring the issue we are postponing the inevitable and will only make it more painful
It is likely that the cultural and legal pressures on churches and groups will only become stronger in the years to come; the later a clear stance is attempted, the more difficult it will become. (It may also become impossible within a given group, if the revisionist position comes to predominate.)

Conclusion

A traditional sexual ethic does indeed constitute a boundary marker for evangelicalism. Therefore, given the current pressures and confusion around these questions, evangelical churches and organizations should have an explicit and public statement about marriage and sexuality. The forms which these statements take may vary: some may be short, some long; they may involve a change to a doctrinal statement or an addition to one; they may be expressed in the form of a separate paper or document, though care should be taken in this case to clarify how authoritative the document is; or they may involve subscription to an existing document or statement of another organization (such as the Lausanne Seoul Statement). Some concerns about "not poking the beast," given a contentious cultural and sometimes legal environment, are warranted: care should be taken that statements are well crafted, that they faithfully express biblical teaching and emphasis, and point to God's love for us expressed in his good purposes. Longer statements should also reflect pastoral concern and love for those struggling with various sexual temptations. And it is sensible to be informed about the legal climate in one's jurisdiction, to avoid needlessly triggering a challenge. Yet these concerns should not be allowed to paralyze us from adopting the clarity which is required of faithfulness. Indeed, the more evangelicals and other orthodox Christians are willing to unify in strong biblical witness to truth in these matters, the less individual churches and groups are likely to be targeted. Self-censorship is not only unfaithful, it is likely, in the longer term, to achieve the opposite of its aim.

Addendum: Sample Statements on Sexuality by Evangelical Organizations

> The place where God has intended us to live out our sexuality is within a covenant relationship with a person of the opposite sex.

European Evangelical Alliance ("LGBTQ+ rights: Responding to a Changing World")[62]

> Sexual intimacy between a husband and wife is beautiful; it is a sacred expression of what it means to be one flesh – "bone of my bones and flesh of my flesh." It follows that any sexual expression outside of this special marriage relationship – whether extramari-

---

62. See www.europeanea.org/wp-content/uploads/2019/01/LGBTRights_Responding-to-a-Changing-World.pdf.

tal, premarital, or same-sex union – is a distortion of God's gracious gift.

InterVarsity Christian Fellowship ("A Theological Statement on Human Sexuality" – statement not publicly available)[63]

> We believe that the term "marriage" has only one meaning and that is marriage sanctioned by God which joins one man and one woman in a single, exclusive union, as delineated in Scripture (Gen 2:18–25).
>
> We believe God intends sexual intimacy to only occur between a man and a woman who are married to each other (1 Cor 6:18; 7:2–5; Heb 13:4). We believe God has commanded that no intimate sexual activity be engaged in outside of a marriage between a man and a woman.

European Leadership Forum (statements 2 and 3 of "Marriage and Sexuality" Addendum)[64]

> We affirm . . . that according to God's design, marriage is a unique and exclusive covenant-relationship between one man and one woman, who commit themselves to a lifelong physical and emotional union of mutual love and sharing (Gen 2:24; Matt 19:4–6).
>
> Furthermore, the biblical teaching is consistent that covenant marriage is the only legitimate context for sexual intercourse. Sex outside the bounds of marriage is declared to be a sinful violation of the Creator's design and intent . . .
>
> All the biblical references to sex between persons of the same sex lead us to the inescapable conclusion that God considers such acts as a violation of his intention for sex and a distortion of the Creator's good design, and therefore, sinful. However, the gospel assures us that those who have, by ignorance or knowingly, given into temptation and sinned, will find forgiveness and restoration

---

63. IVCF has not made its position paper, produced in 2015, publicly available, though it did issue a news release summarizing its position, see https://intervarsity.org/news/intervarsity-reiterates-theology-human-sexuality. In addition, the statement has been made available by others, see www.scribd.com/document/326684433/InterVarsity-Christian-Fellowship-Theology-of-Human-Sexuality-Paper.

64. See https://euroleadership.org/sites/default/files/2023-08/ELF%20Doctrinal%20Statement-Evangelical%20Affirmations.pdf. The European Leadership Forum uses as its statement of faith the Evangelical Affirmations document which came out of the Consultation on Evangelical Affirmations conference co-sponsored by the National Association of Evangelicals in 1989. However, in 2015, the ELF added a separate statement on "'Marriage and Sexuality."

of fellowship with God through confession, repentance, and trust in Christ.

Seoul Statement, Lausanne Movement (from paragraphs 59, 60 and 68)[65]

We believe God designed marriage as a unique conjugal relationship joining one man and one woman in a single, exclusive, life-long union, and God intends sexual intimacy to only occur within that relationship.

The Alliance Defending Freedom ("Alliance Defending Freedom Doctrinal Distinctives"[66])

Bibliography

Brownson, James. *Bible, Gender, and Sexuality: Reframing the Church's Debate on Same-Sex Relationships*. Grand Rapids: Eerdmans, 2013.

Campolo, Tony. *20 Hot Potatoes Christians Are Afraid to Touch*. Nashville: Thomas Nelson, 1993.

Diener, Michael. *Raus aus der Sackgasse! Wie die pietistische und evangelikale Bewegung neu an Glaubürdigkeit gewinnt*. Ostfildern: Adeo, 2021.

Fortson, Donald, and Roland Grams. *Unchanging Witness: The Consistent Christian Teaching on Homosexuality in Scripture and Tradition*. Nashville: B&H Academic, 2016.

Gagnon, Robert A. J. *The Bible and Homosexual Practice: Texts and Hermeneutics*. Nashville: Abingdon Press, 2002.

Gushee, David P. *Changing Our Mind*. Canton: Read The Spirit Books, 2014.

———. *Introducing Christian Ethics: Core Convictions for Christians Today*. Canton: Front Edge Publishing, 2022.

Harper, Kyle. "The First Sexual Revolution: How Christianity Transformed the Ancient World." *First Things: A Monthly Journal of Religion and Public Life* 279 (January 2018): 41–46. www.firstthings.com/article/2018/01/the-first-sexual-revolution.

———. *From Shame to Sin: The Christian Transformation of Sexual Morality in Late Antiquity*. Cambridg: Harvard University Press, 2016.

Hays, Christopher, and Richard B. Hays. *The Widening of God's Mercy: Sexuality Within the Biblical Story*. New Haven: Yale University Press, 2024.

---

65. See https://lausanne.org/statement/the-seoul-statement.

66. See https://adflegal.org/about-us/careers/statement-of-faith/; the ADF is a legal defence group which has been involved in many court cases relating to religious rights around the world, including in Europe (for example, with Paivi Rasanen in Finland). Originating in the USA, their international branch is located in Vienna.

Hays, Richard B. *The Moral Vision of the New Testament: A Contemporary Introduction to New Testament Ethics*. San Francisco: HarperOne, 1996.

Larsen, Timothy. "Defining and Locating Evangelicalism." Pages 1–14 in *The Cambridge Companion to Evangelical Theology*. Edited by Timothy Larson. Cambridge: Cambridge University Press, 2007.

Magyar, Balázs D. "Punishment and Forgiveness of Sexual Crimes: A special reference to sodomy in Calvin's theology." *Verbum et Ecclesia* 43.1 (2022). https://verbumetecclesia.org.za/index.php/ve/article/view/2626/6005.

Vines, Matthew. *God and the Gay Christian*. Colorado Springs: Convergent Books, 2015.

Part 2

Evangelicals in Various Countries

11

Evangelicalism in Austria

Frank Hinkelmann

Prehistory

In Austria, one can only speak of an evangelical movement after World War II.[1] At the same time, one cannot assess the Austrian evangelical movement in isolation from previous historical developments. Rather, the evangelical movement is directly linked to the history of European and North American Christianity in the context of Pietism, revivalism and the emergence of new Protestant denominations during the nineteenth century, in the German speaking world frequently called free churches.[2] These pietistic groups as well as the free churches, alongside other new groups, were to become the main sources of the evangelical movement that emerged after World War II. They all held to theological convictions in agreement with the basic principles of the evangelical movement which had already found a platform in the Evangelical Alliance since the nineteenth century.[3]

---

1. For the history of the Evangelical movement in Austria, see Frank Hinkelmann, *Die Evangelikale Bewegung in Österreich. Grundzüge ihrer historischen und theologischen Entwicklung 1945–1998* (Bonn: Verlag für Kultur und Wissenschaft, 2014).

2. Frank Hinkelmann, "Transkonfessionelle und transnationale Netzwerke im Umfeld von Pietismus, Erweckungsbewegung und Freikirchen im ausgehenden 18. und im 19. Jahrhundert und ihre Verbindungen nach Österreich," *Jahrbuch für die Geschichte des Protestantismus in Österreich* 138 (2022): 13–61. The British church historian W. Reginald Ward, for example, speaks of an "evangelical awakening" with regard to the Protestant emigrants from Salzburg; see Ward, *The Protestant Evangelical Awakening*, 2nd ed. (Cambridge: Cambridge University Press, 2002), 93–115.

3. Frank Hinkelmann, *Geschichte der Evangelischen Allianz in Österreich. Von ihren Anfängen im 19. Jahrhundert bis in die Gegenwart*, 2nd revised ed. (Bonn: Verlag für Kultur und Wissenschaft, 2012).

Beginnings (1945–1961)

The emergence of the evangelical movement in German-speaking countries under the term "evangelical" and not "evangelisch" (protestant) must be understood in the context of the emergence of the neo-evangelical movement in North America. The latter was as a countermovement to fundamentalism and found organizational expression in the founding of the National Association of Evangelicals at the beginning of the 1940s in the USA; it also had a rapid influence on further developments in Europe.[4]

Unprecedented Denominational Diversity

An important player in the first phase of the evangelical movement was a group that had already been active in the interwar years, the Austrian People's Mission (Volksmission). This organization had been established through the evangelistic efforts of the Lutheran minister Max Monsky and continued to exist in numerous cities, albeit with increasing autonomy and independence from its founder. Soon after the war, the place of Monsky was taken by Lydia Haman in Salzburg. Haman had already been in charge of the Volksmission in Salzburg before the war. When the Nazi regime collapsed in 1945, new opportunities arose in American-occupied Salzburg. The following years saw the "heyday of the Salzburg Volksmission."[5] Looking back on this time, Haman wrote:

> The influx of refugees [ethnic Germans who had lived in Eastern Europe before, FH] began, especially ethnic Germans. Believers and unbelievers were looking for the word of life. Our hall often couldn't hold the people. We really felt the stirrings of the spirit – miracles and signs happened, the sick were healed and the desperate were given new courage.[6]

As early as October 1947, Haman also opened a missionary school with the aim to train young women as religious teachers, parish helpers, as missionaries for Austria and abroad, and for youth ministry. Ten years later, forty-four women had already graduated. It proved to be strategically important that

---

4. On the introduction of the term "evangelical" in German-speaking countries, see Frank Hinkelmann, *Evangelikal in Deutschland, Österreich und der Schweiz. Ursprung, Bedeutung und Rezeption eines Begriffes* (Bonn: Verlag für Kultur und Wissenschaft, 2017).

5. Hannelore Reiner, *Das Amt der Gemeindeschwester am Beispiel der Diözese Oberösterreich. Entstehung, Funktion und Wandel eines Frauenberufes in der Kirche* (Wien: Evang. Presseverband, 1992), 167.

6. Lydia Haman, *Großes hat der Herr getan* (Ebensee: Franz Swoboda, 1973), 45.

Haman secured the support of the Lutheran Church. Her sphere of influence soon extended across Austria. Annual Holiness Conferences were held in Salzburg and youth conferences were organized in different parts of the country, which were attended by hundreds of young people every year.

In addition to these pietistic groups, we need to mention free church denominations, primarily the ones that had already been active before the war and had established congregations. The Methodist Church had suffered greatly during the war and its membership had fallen to around six hundred in 1945. It was primarily ethnic German refugees who brought new life to the Methodist Church in Austria as there were a number of Methodists among the refugees, including four ministers. These refugees also began with a social and evangelistic work in various refugee camps and in turn new Methodist congregations were planted.

Another existing denomination were the Baptists, who also experienced strong growth in their congregations in the post-war years, again partly due to ethnic German Baptist refugees, but also due to the mission-mindedness of their congregations. By 1950, around one hundred and fifty baptisms had taken place in Vienna alone and in subsequent years a number of Baptist congregations were planted in various parts of the country.

Like no other denomination the Pentecostal movement benefitted from the influx of ethnic German refugees. Members of ethnic German Pentecostal congregations from Yugoslavia fled to Austria and soon reached out in evangelism, while at the same time gathering their fellow believers from their old homeland. As early as 14 December 1946, the Federation of Free Christian Churches of Philadelphia Austria was founded. The missionary zeal for Austria among these young Pentecostal churches is all the more remarkable as many of them only regarded Austria as a stopover on their way to North America or Brazil. Contemporary witnesses described these first post-war years as a time of revival. In the summer of 1947 alone, seventy-six baptisms were carried out in Upper Austria and the number of church members rose to around 1,800 in 1948–1949. However, at the beginning of the 1950s the Pentecostal movement lost entire congregations, numerous families and eight of its preachers to emigration; the number of members fell to around three to four hundred in 1954.

In the early 1950s, the arrival of missionaries from the German Missionshaus Bibelschule Wiedenest, a missionary agency of the German Open Brethren, led to a church planting ministry in Styria. The Wiedenester missionaries endeavoured to achieve three main goals through their ministry: "1. to bring the gospel to the ignorant so that they may be saved. 2. to keep the saved together so that biblically orientated local churches grow. 3. to continually place the local churches in the responsibility of the church as a whole."[7]

With the beginning of mission work by the Mennonite Brethren Church, we experienced a phenomenon that was of great and lasting importance for the further development of the evangelical movement in Austria. For the first time, North Americans discovered Austria as a mission field that they could not only support financially, but to which they could send missionaries for evangelism and church planting. North American evangelicals discovered Europe as a mission field as they brought aid in the post-war period. To this was added a theologically motivated urgency: they encountered a nominal Christianity that was not professing and which needed to be evangelized. The founder and leader of the European Christian Mission, Gans Pertel Raud, wrote in 1946:

> Let us not be rendered confused or idle because people in Europe have forms of religion. Without salvation through Christ Jesus set forth in the Holy Scriptures, they are unsaved. No provision of civilisation, or learning, or religious profession is a substitute for the gift of God which is eternal life through Jesus Christ our Lord.[8]

A little later, he clarified his view of the spiritual situation in Austria:

> Turning to Protestantism, we find that the Lutheran Church has the most adherents. Evangelical believers in Christ constitute a scarcely perceptible number; and there is, consequently, little true gospel witness in the country. Austria for centuries has been without the Word of God and without the knowledge of evangelical Christianity, knowing only the religious formality and false hopes of the Roman Catholic system.[9]

Further non-denominational foreign mission agencies also started ministering in Austria, focusing first and foremost on evangelism. Among those were the German Mission for South-East Europe, which later became Evangeliumsdienst, a Dutch ministry called the Internationale Gemeenschap van Christenen, later known in Austria as the Dutch Mission, as well as the International Miners' Mission, which all began to send missionaries to Austria in the 1950s.

---

7. Anonymous, "Österreich," *Offene Türen* 39.5 (1959): 23.

8. G[ans]. P[ertel]. Raud, *Inside Facts on Europe* (New York: European Christian Mission, 1946), 25.

9. G[ans]. P[ertel]. Raud, *Inside Facts on Europe*, 117.

Unprecedented Evangelistic Efforts

> There is evangelism back and forth in Austria. The Lord is breaking ground. But there is too little evangelism, too haphazard. And, above all, there is still too little supporting, too little victorious certainty of faith behind it, too little authority based on His unbroken Word and His redeeming blood and too little persistent, determined, comprehensive prayer of the faithful.[10]

In a report on a conference on evangelism in Carinthia in 1950, the Lutheran minister Steffen Meier-Schomburg emphasized the urgency of the missionary task in light of the eschatological dimension: "The doors are still open, but nobody knows how much longer" – a widespread element of evangelical piety and mission motivation at the time.

> The doors in Austria are still wide open. However, the last elections have shown that they can quickly close again. Those who do nothing for Austria today will remember the word of God in 1 Peter 4:17 when this country's time of grace has come to an end. But let us take advantage of the day of salvation![11]

The evangelical movement of the 1950s hardly reflected theologically on evangelism but simply practised evangelism: street evangelism, Bible distribution, a tent wagon mission, large-scale tract distribution and the organization of evangelistic rallies were on the agenda in this first phase of the evangelical movement.

Unprecedented Cooperation Between Evangelical Groups

Increasingly, the need for cooperation beyond denominational boundaries became evident and the Evangelical Alliance became the rallying point for evangelical agencies and churches. In its statement of faith, a viable formula was found which enabled Christians from different denominational backgrounds to meet and the Alliance increasingly formed a platform for joint evangelistic campaigns. Missionaries from abroad were often familiar with the Evangelical Alliance from their home countries and were happy to build on these experiences of inter-church cooperation.

---

10. Steffen Meier-Schomburg, "Evangelisation in Österreich!" in *Stimmen aus Österreich* 2.11 (1950): 2.

11. Georg Lorenz, "Die Missionslage in Österreich," *Offene Türen* 36.6 (1956): 18.

In the mid-1950s, the Evangelical Alliance was joined by a new initiative aimed at full-time Christian workers across all denominations. The Kingdom of God Workers Conference (Reichsgottes-Arbeiter-Tagung) was initiated by Lydia Haman. What began in 1955 soon became a permanent institution. Evangelical workers in mission agencies, evangelical churches and fellowships found a platform to get to know each other, for networking and for mutual encouragement.

However, the early 1950s also saw a split in the evangelical movement: on the one hand, the Pentecostal movement and on the other, the pietist and free-church groups, historically characterized by a critical attitude towards the Pentecostal movement.

Internationalization (1961–1981)

The 1960s and 1970s saw further development in the evangelical movement in two ways. Proven and new ways of evangelism were pursued, and new mission agencies, especially from North America, joined the agencies already active in Austria.

Proven and New Ways of Evangelism

Mission and evangelism continued to play a central role among evangelicals. While the focus during the first fifteen years after the war lay more on an evangelistic penetration of the country, a change in strategy took place since the beginning of the 1960s. Larger scale evangelistic rallies came to the fore.

The first large-scale evangelistic rally took place in Vienna in 1961, led by the German evangelist Anton Schulte, founder and director of the New Life (Neues Leben) mission agency. At the invitation of the Viennese Evangelical Alliance, Schulte conducted a three-and-a-half week evangelistic campaign in the Vienna City Hall with three objectives: "1. To win those far away to faith in Christ. 2. To revitalise and deepen the local churches. 3. To have an impressive witness throughout the city."[12] This rally exceeded all previous events in terms of numbers. The advertising budget alone totalled at least fifty-four thousand German Marks, plus around twenty-five thousand Marks for renting the Vienna City Hall. An invitation to the rally was sent to all seven hundred and sixty Viennese households, "which also contained a clear testimony of Christ."[13]

---

12. Karl Zedlacher, "'Feldzug des Glaubens' in Wien," *Weckruf* 12.9–10 (1961): 14.
13. Anonymous, "Feldzug des Glaubens in Wien," *Neues Leben* 6.11 (1961): 6.

The total number of visitors was around fifty thousand, with the final meeting attracting the highest number of visitors at around four thousand. Several hundred people sought pastoral counselling and around two hundred and fifty people attended a follow-up meeting with Anton Schulte. In addition, 14,455 Bibles were distributed and sold during these weeks. This Vienna Crusade of Faith was the starting signal for numerous further large-scale evangelistic rallies in the following years, also predominantly led by German evangelists, such as the Essen evangelist Wilhelm Busch, the Nuremberg minister Kurt Heimbucher and Dr Gerhard Bergmann.

In addition to traditional forms of evangelism, new approaches and strategies for evangelism were adopted. For the first time music was used as an evangelistic tool.[14] In 1967, for example, music evenings were organized in Judenburg and Knittelfeld, at which the singer Franz Knies performed arias, chorales and "gospel songs" and gave testimony of his personal faith in between. Films were also well received as a new form of evangelistic work. It was the Billy Graham Evangelistic Association that produced and made available films for evangelistic use. In 1973, there were two hundred and sixty-eight screenings, which were attended by around eleven thousand five hundred mostly young people. In 1965, the New Life mission agency carried out a "literature campaign" in Vienna, which it described as one of the "most difficult and laborious tasks" that the mission agency had ever carried out.[15] Some one hundred and fifty distributors delivered an evangelistic magazine entitled *Neues Leben* to all five hundred and seventy thousand households in Vienna.

Further new impetus for evangelism through literature came in 1973 with the founding of the Austrian branch of Every Home for Christ (Evangelium in jedes Haus). As a first major campaign, an evangelistic leaflet including an invitation to an evangelistic rally with the Janz team was distributed to all one hundred and four thousand households in the greater Linz area with the help of one hundred to one hundred and twenty Christians in November 1974. Between April and November 1975, 270,800 households were reached, and 541,600 "printed messages" were handed out. The achievements of Evangelium in jedes Haus in the 1970s were remarkable. Within three years of its founding, more than 50 percent of all Austrian households was reached with an evan-

---

14. Cf. Frank Hinkelmann, "Evangelisation im Land von 'Sound of Music'. Musik als evangelistisches Tool in der freikirchlichen Gemeindegründungsarbeit der 1960er bis 1980er Jahre in Österreich," in *Polyphone Klangräume*, ed. Eberhard Werner and Elmar Spohn (Nuremberg: VTR, 2022), 39–47.

15. Anonymous, "Literaturfeldzug in Wien," *Neues Leben* 10.6 (1965): no page.

gelistic tract. By 1980, the percentage of households reached had risen to 68.5 percent. In 1980 alone, this amounted to 159,402 (1979: 106,411) households. The total number of tracts distributed by the end of 1980 was 3,530,272.

Established and New Missionary Agencies and Initiatives

The 1960s also saw endeavours by new mission agencies. In particular North American agencies began to send missionaries to Austria, contributing to the internationalization of the evangelical movement. These agencies included the Greater Europe Mission (GEM) and the American The Evangelical Alliance Mission (TEAM). The staff of TEAM reached its peak number, twenty-six, in 1977; they focused on various church planting activities in the greater Vienna region. William Wagner, himself a missionary of the Mission Board of the Southern Baptist Convention in the USA, estimated that in 1977 there were over three hundred foreign missionaries in forty-three different agencies, most of whom were working independently and without denominational connections.[16]

In addition, Austrian branches of international ministries were established, such as Trans World Radio (Evangeliumsrundfunk) and the Fellowship of Evangelical Students (Österreichische Studenten Mission). The Salzburg Mission Agency, which had collapsed and slipped into insignificance following Lydia Haman's death in 1977, was replaced by a new group targeting the evangelical groups within the Lutheran Church: the Torchbearers – Schloss Klaus (Missionsgemeinschaft der Fackelträger – Schloss Klaus). Camps were to become a focal point of the ministry of Schloss Klaus, with work among confirmands an increasingly important second pillar of its ministry.

Proven Church Growth Focus and New Church Planting Initiatives

In the 1960s and 1970s, a church planting movement characterized the independent evangelical congregations, mainly initiated by the foreign agencies described above, while the topic of church growth came to the fore among evangelical congregations in the Lutheran Church. Subsequently, new evangelical congregations emerged, especially in the metropolitan area, but also in a number of regional centres. Particularly in urban areas, where secularization

---

16. William L. Wagner, *New Move Forward in Europe. Growth Patterns in German Speaking Baptists in Europe* (Pasadena: William Carey Library, 1978), 103–5.

was more rapid and visible than in the countryside, these church planting efforts met with a positive response.

Denominational Narrowing and Institutionalization (1981–1998)

Three things describe the development of the evangelical movement in the 1980s and 1990s: a denominational narrowing of the term "evangelical," a consolidation of evangelical free church congregations as well as growing institutionalization.

A Denominational Narrowing of the Term "Evangelical"

The Association of Evangelical Churches in Austria (ARGEGÖ) was founded in 1981.[17] The ARGEGÖ saw itself neither as an evangelical association of churches as such nor as an umbrella organization of evangelical Christians, but rather as a working group of evangelical congregations. However, its founding led to a narrowing of the term evangelical, which is also evident in the name, which omitted the descriptive attribute "free church." Thus, the naming implied that only free-church congregations with a similar view of Scripture were to be regarded as evangelical. The ARGEGÖ grew strongly in the following years. In addition to the annual training week with up to two hundred participants, faith conferences were organized. The Pentecostal youth meetings also developed into a permanent institution with between three hundred and nine hundred participants.

In the 1980s the evangelical-free church congregations grew rapidly: "The total number of members increased by 230%, the number of congregations by 210% and the number of ministers by 120%."[18] Existing denominations, such as the Pentecostal movement, Baptists and Mennonites, also experienced constant, albeit slower, growth during this period; but it was primarily the young independent churches planted by foreign missionaries that grew rapidly.

While in the 1980s mainly congregations and church plants closely linked to the ARGEGÖ originated, this changed in the 1990s. Now it was mainly neo-charismatic churches that were planted throughout the country, including

---

17. Frank Hinkelmann, "The Association of Evangelical Churches in Austria. A Free-Church 'Ecumenism'. Its Prehistory, Founding and Further Development," *Religion in Austria* 8 (2022): 237–78.

18. Mary Lawson, ed., *Christian Handbook for Austria: Churches and Mission* (London: Marc Europe, 1991), 8.

several Vineyard churches, churches of the Foursquare movement, churches of the South African His People movement, today's Life Church Movement as well as house churches. Five independent charismatic churches later merged to form the Elaia Christian Churches denomination.

In addition, the Baptist congregations and the Pentecostal movement experienced strong growth during the 1990s. This was a result of the arrival of Romanian migrants since the mid-1980s; they formed their own Romanian-speaking congregations within the unions. In addition, the Pentecostal Church of God (Cleveland) emerged as a further, independent denomination, albeit Romanian-speaking.

The second half of the 1980s also saw the first of several conflicts between the leadership of the Lutheran Church in Austria and parts of the evangelical movement, which led to sharp confrontations and subsequently strengthened and accelerated the evangelical-free church tendency to denominationalize the term "evangelical." The Lutheran leadership began to take rigorous action against free-church congregations that used the term "evangelisch" (Protestant) in their self-designation, as they claimed name protection for the term "evangelisch."[19] Congregations were demanded to refrain from using the term "evangelisch" as part of their name, for fear of legal action against them. Despite international protest and mediation efforts, no compromise could be reached. The free-church congregations concerned decided against legal action, thus abandoning the use of the term "evangelisch." Instead they sought and found a new term – evangelical – as self-designation.

In 1991, several previously independent evangelical-free churches endeavoured to establish a Federation of Evangelical Churches in Austria (Bund Evangelikaler Gemeinden or BEG) under association law.[20] However, the Lutheran Church opposed the establishment of the BEG and as a result the authorities in Vienna prohibited its founding for the time being. A lengthy dispute followed but in 1992 the Federation of Evangelical Churches in Austria was founded. For the first time, an Austrian denomination – originally triggered by the name conflict with the Lutheran Church over the term "evangelisch" – had the term "evangelical" in its name and thus contributed to a denominational reinterpretation of the term "evangelical" in Austria.

---

19. Cf. Frank Hinkelmann, "'Evangelisch' in Österreich. Der Konflikt zwischen Evangelischer Kirche und Freikirchen um die Verwendung des Begriffs evangelisch," *Freikirchenforschung* 29 (2020): 106–28.

20. For the history of the BEG, see Frank Hinkelmann, "The Federation of Evangelical Churches in Austria: Origins, Foundation, Structure, Development and Theological Position (1991–2013)," *Religion in Austria* 9 (2024): 183–237.

Consolidation

Alongside the disputes, a growing consolidation of the evangelical movement began, again, initially predominantly among free church groups. This consolidation can be observed in three areas: theological training and education, leadership development and the trend towards having one's own church premises. Training institutions such as Biblical Education on Site (Biblische Ausbildung am Ort), the later Evangelical Academy in Vienna (EVAK) as well as the Ampflwang Bible School, later Wallsee and a few years later the Institute for Theology and Church Growth (ITG), which grew out of this work, were established. Special emphasis was placed on equipping lay leaders.

Congregations that had only been founded during the 1970s and 1980s and had previously either rented church premises or met in public event halls, gradually moved towards having their own church premises. Congregations left the pioneering phase and entered a consolidation phase.

A development of socio-political importance for the evangelical movement in Austria was that the "Kultusamt" in the Ministry of Education, responsible for all cultural affairs including religion, created a new legal form between a mere NGO structure and that of a recognized religious society: the state-registered religious denomination. Free-church denominations had already sought to be recognized as religious societies in the past, but their applications had always failed. Finally, on 20 July 1998, the Federation of Baptist Churches in Austria, the Pentecostal movement and the Federation of Evangelical Churches in Austria were granted the status of a state-registered religious denomination. Despite all justified criticism of the act, for the first time the law offered evangelical free church denominations the possibility of relative state recognition, which went beyond registration as an NGO. This recognition also changed the public perception of the denominations concerned.

Institutionalization

The increasing institutionalization of the evangelical movement during the 1980s and 1990s was reflected in a growing number of independent, evangelical and at the same time interdenominational charities targeting specific groups. For example, Family Life Mission, Team F. – New Life for Families and Christian Family Work were ministries that promoted marriage and family. In the area of children's and youth work, Scripture Union (Bibellesebund) and the Child Evangelism Fellowship (Kinder-Evangelisations-Bewegung), which had already been active in Austria for some time, got legal registration in the early

1980s. It should not be overlooked that the various free church denominations and the ARGEÖ also had their own children's and youth networks.

Breaking Out of Isolation

During the 1990s, there were signs of a slow but steady opening and a break-up of denominational camps within the evangelical movement in Austria. Various factors played a role here. The role and significance of the ARGEÖ were weakening, primarily due to the founding and development of the BEG, which grew over the years and which established its own structures and committees. It was precisely these member congregations of the BEG that had originally initiated the work of the ARGEÖ, which now decided to focus on the BEG instead of the ARGEÖ. Due to a heavy workload, key staff were increasingly faced with the question of which committees they wanted to focus on. From then on, the BEG took priority for most of them.

Parallel to this development, the Austrian Evangelical Alliance overcame its crisis of the 1980s. In the 1990s, the Alliance board also addressed the question of tension between the evangelical movement and the Pentecostal and charismatic movements. As the umbrella organization of all evangelicals, the EA approached the Pentecostal movement and, despite some opposition, there was an increasing opening. At the Alliance Council meeting in spring 1996, two pastors from the Pentecostal movement were admitted to the Austrian Alliance Council and in 1998 a Pentecostal pastor was elected to the Alliance Board. Today, the Pentecostal and charismatic movements are fully integrated into the EA and form an important wing of the evangelical movement.

The Twenty-First Century – A Preliminary Assessment

The previous section already showed a gradual erosion of intra-evangelical divisions and a gradual broadening of the definition of the term evangelical in the sense of a denominational, free-church understanding. However, further developments can be observed.

State Recognition

For several decades, various free church denominations had unsuccessfully tried to obtain full state recognition as a religious body. New movement in this matter came in 2009 on the initiative of the Catholic episcopal commission Justitia et Pax in cooperation with the evangelical-ecumenical group Round

Table – Path to Reconciliation (Runder Tisch – Weg der Versöhnung), whereby the support of the Roman Catholic Cardinal of Vienna, Christoph Schönborn, has to be emphasized.[21] Subsequently, a joint working group consisting of representatives of various free churches and experts in Austrian religious law was set up.[22] After several years of negotiations, the Free Churches in Austria (Freikirchen in Österreich), consisting of five evangelical denominations, were fully recognized on 26 August 2013.[23]

Diaspora Communities

As in many other European countries, diaspora congregations are emerging in Austria, either joining existing denominations or forming their own.[24] At present the Romanian Pentecostal Church of God forms the largest free church with around eighteen thousand members.[25] Other denominations, like the Pentecostal movement, also have an African and an international branch. Numerous other migrants have joined Austrian, German-speaking congregations of various denominations. It is likely that over 50 percent of the approximately sixty thousand evangelicals in Austria now have a migrant background – including Germans and Swiss.[26]

A Concluding Summary

The history of the evangelical movement in Austria over the past eighty years is one of major developments. At the end of World War II, evangelicals were mainly to be found in the Lutheran Church and in a few free churches in the country's larger cities. Today, evangelical Christians are not only to be found

---

21. Hans-Peter Lang, "Freikirchen auf dem Weg zur staatlichen Anerkennung," in *Meilensteine auf dem Weg der Versöhnung. 20 Jahre „Ökumene der Herzen" am Runden Tisch für Österreich*, ed. Johannes Fichtenbauer, Lars Heinrich and Wolf Paul (Vienna: Self-publishing, 2018), 265–74.

22. Frank Hinkelmann, "Das Anerkennungsverfahren der 'Freikirchen in Österreich' und der Beitrag der "Steuerungsgruppe"," in *Die gesetzliche Anerkennung der Freikirchen in Österreich: Ein ökumenisches Gesamtkunstwerk*, ed. Christine Mann and Armin Wunderli (Religion und Bildung 6; Vienna: LIT-Verlag, 2023), 61–101.

23. For the entire recognition process, see the anthology Mann and Wunderli (eds), *Gesetzliche Anerkennung*.

24. The most detailed overview in Frank Hinkelmann, *Kirchen, Freikirchen und christliche Gemeinschaften in Österreich. Handbuch der Konfessionskunde* (Vienna: Böhlau, 2016), 151, 163, 165, 249–78.

25. Information provided by the Romanian Church of God.

26. Assessment based on the author's own research.

in congregations scattered throughout the country – including in rural areas – but also in a wide range of different churches and denominations. Numerous evangelical ministries have been established and form an active part of today's evangelical movement, whose umbrella organization is the Evangelical Alliance. The high proportion of migrants among the evangelicals is striking, and this also applies explicitly to leadership positions. It remains to be seen to what extent it will be possible to make missionary impulses from the diaspora fruitful for the entire evangelical movement.

Bibliography

Haman, Lydia. *Großes hat der Herr getan*. Ebensee: Franz Swoboda, 1973.

Hinkelmann, Frank. "The Association of Evangelical Churches in Austria. A Free-Church 'Ecumenism'. Its prehistory, Founding and Further Development." *Religion in Austria* 8 (2022): 237–78.

———. *Evangelikal in Deutschland, Österreich und der Schweiz. Ursprung, Bedeutung und Rezeption eines Begriffes*. Bonn: Verlag für Kultur und Wissenschaft, 2017.

———. "'Evangelisch' in Österreich. Der Konflikt zwischen Evangelischer Kirche und Freikirchen um die Verwendung des Begriffs evangelisch." *Freikirchenforschung* 29 (2020): 106–28.

———. *Die Evangelikale Bewegung in Österreich. Grundzüge ihrer historischen und theologischen Entwicklung 1945–1998*. Bonn: Verlag für Kultur und Wissenschaft, 2014.

———. *Geschichte der Evangelischen Allianz in Österreich. Von ihren Anfängen im 19. Jahrhundert bis in die Gegenwart*. 2nd rev. ed. Bonn: Verlag für Kultur und Wissenschaft, 2012.

Lang, Hans-Peter. "Freikirchen auf dem Weg zur staatlichen Anerkennung." Pages 265–74 in *Meilensteine auf dem Weg der Versöhnung. 20 Jahre "Ökumene der Herzen" am Runden Tisch für Österreich*. Edited by Johannes Fichtenbauer, Lars Heinrich and Wolf Paul. Vienna: Published by the author, 2018.

Lawson, Mary, ed. *Christliches Handbuch für Österreich. Kirchen und Mission*. London: Marc Europe, 1991.

Mann, Christine, and Armin Wunderli, eds. *Die gesetzliche Anerkennung der Freikirchen in Österreich. Ein ökumenisches Gesamtkunstwerk*. Religion und Bildung 6. Vienna: LIT-Verlag, 2023.

Wagner, William L. *New Move Forward in Europe. Growth Patterns in German Speaking Baptists in Europe*. Pasadena: William Carey Library, 1978.

12

Evangelicalism in Croatia

Danijel Časni

Historical Introduction: Two Groups of Protestants

Croatia is a country of about four million inhabitants which was part of the Kingdom of Serbs, Croats and Slovenes from 1918 until 1929 and part of Yugoslavia from 1929 until 1991. Evangelical Christianity in Croatia needs to be seen in the context of the Reformation and the later spiritual awakening movements. The Protestant churches in Croatia have their roots in the Reformation of the sixteenth century and fall into two large groups. Stanko Jambrek defines these two as "Protestant churches" and "Churches of reformed heritage or evangelical churches." The first group includes the Lutheran Church, the Reformed Calvinist Christian Church, the Protestant Reformed Christian Church, the Evangelical Church of Vadeze and the Methodist Church.[1] The second group includes Baptist churches, Pentecostal churches, the Brethren Church, Church of Christ, Church of God, independent charismatic churches and some free churches with an evangelical perspective that are not part of the Evangelical Alliance.

This second group forms evangelical Christianity in Croatia and these "free churches" find their roots in the tradition of the radical Reformation.[2] They first appeared in the former Yugoslavia in the second half of the nineteenth century in the form of the activities of international Bible societies and Baptist missionaries, preachers and distributors of the Bible. Significant meetings of

---

1. Ankica Marinović Bobinac and Jerolimov Dinka Marinović, *Vjerske zajednice u Hrvatskoj* (Zagreb: Prometej, 2008), 109–89.

2. Stanko Jambrek, *Crkve reformacijske baštine u Hrvatskoj* (Zagreb: Bogoslovni institut, 2003), 16.

Baptist believers were noted in the 1870s in Zagreb and Daruvar. The first Pentecostal churches in Croatia were organized in the 1920s. Several evangelical denominations now operate under the auspices of the Pentecostal movement in Croatia, including the Evangelical Pentecostal Church, the Church of God and the Alliance of Christ's Pentecostal Churches. During the 1980s, a charismatic movement emerged in Croatia, which in many ways followed the Pentecostal movement. Since then, about twenty independent charismatic communities have been founded and some of them are organized as the Union of Churches Word of Life.[3]

Cooperation Between Evangelicals Before 1980

In Croatia, during the 1960s evangelicals were mostly gathered in Baptist, Pentecostal and Brethren churches, between which there was little cooperation. The common goal that connected the Christian communities with each other was evangelism. At the 1966 Congress on World Evangelism in Berlin, where the main speaker was Billy Graham, among the delegates from Croatia were Josip Horak and Branko Lovrec. They met with Graham and invited him to visit Yugoslavia.[4] For Croatia, where the Catholic Church had a majority of believers, the opinion of the Roman Catholic Cardinal of Boston, Richard Cusing, was important: he praised the outline and content of Billy Graham's sermon and he encouraged Catholics to listen to Graham. As a personal friend of the late President John F. Kennedy, the cardinal had a great influence and his encouragement of the Catholic faithful to listen to Graham's sermons was significant.[5] In Berlin, the Baptist churches were represented by Josip Horak and Franjo Klem. An interview with them enables us to sense the atmosphere in the evangelical churches in the sixties. When asked whether there was already any cooperation between Protestant churches in the field of evangelism, Klem expresses himself negatively, while Horak points out some modest cooperation with Methodists in Vojvodina (Serbia) and with Lutherans in Zagreb (Croatia).[6]

That greater cooperation between different churches is possible was shown by the evangelistic campaign of Billy Graham, which was held in July 1967; the local organizers were Josip Horak and Branko Lovrec from Zagreb Baptist Church. There was even a meeting in the premises of the Catholic Archdioc-

---

3. Stanko Jambrek, *Reformacija nekad i danas* (Zagreb: Biblijski Institut, 2017), 143–44.
4. "In conversation with Billy Graham in Berlin," *Glasnik* 11–12 (1966): 174.
5. "They said," *Glasnik* 11–12 (1966): 177.
6. "Interview with Josip Horak and Franjo Klem," *Glasnik* 11–12 (1966): 185–86.

esan Seminary in Zagreb. Believers from evangelical, Pentecostal, Brethren, Baptist, Orthodox and Catholic Churches gathered to evangelize. Thanks to the extraordinary cooperation of Horak with Bishop Dutsch from the Evangelical Church, on 8 July an evangelistic meeting was held in the Evangelical Church in Gundulićeva Street with more than fifteen hundred people present. It was the first such gathering in a socialist country.[7]

Christian organizations and associations such as Youth for Christ, which sent its student groups to visit churches, had an important influence on the development of evangelical thought in the former Yugoslavia. For many years, Trans World Radio also broadcast radio programmes through their Monte Carlo and Bonaire transmitters, spreading the gospel to the peoples of Yugoslavia. In addition, the Greater Europe Mission supported missionary work, especially work in the field of education through the Evangelical Biblical Institute, which had its headquarters in Vienna.

As president of the Baptist Church Alliance in Yugoslavia, Josip Horak was present at the largest meeting of Christians in history, which was attended by 1,200,000 people of different denominations and organized by Campus Crusade for Christ: EXPLO 1974 in Seoul. Horak later said that "these meetings in Korea will remain unforgettable in my memory, because then I felt a part of heaven already here on earth. I saw rivers of blessing." Encouraged by this congress, Horak set out to develop such a spirit of unity and cooperation among the churches in Yugoslavia.

Also in 1974, Zagreb Baptist Church organized a seminar for Christian leaders and Christian workers with Bill Bright as a speaker, the founder and president of Campus Crusade for Christ. The gathering brought together sixty representatives from the Baptist, Pentecostal, Brethren, Methodist, Evangelical, Roman Catholic and Orthodox Churches. The goal of the seminar was to strengthen the personal spiritual life of the participants and to find new ways of transmitting the gospel. Attention was also paid to church organization and management.[8]

The 1974 Congress for World Evangelization in Lausanne was attended by leaders from four different Croatian churches: the above-mentioned Josip Horak; the Baptist preacher Branko Lovrec; the president of the Pentecostal Association, Ludvig Üllen; Peter Kuzmič; Martin Hovan as representative of the Methodist communities; and the representative of the Lutheran Church,

---

7. "God loves you," *Glas evanđelja* 7–8 (1967): 99–100.
8. "Seminar for Christian leaders and spiritual workers," *Glas evanđelja* 4 (1974): 29.

pastor Vlado Deutsch.⁹ When the Lausanne Committee organized a subsequent consultation in Thailand in 1980, the delegates were the Baptists Horak and Lovrec and the Pentecostals Kuzmič and Boris Arapovič.

Towards Evangelical Association

On the initiative of the Biblical Theological Institute in Zagreb, the Voice of the Gospel in Zagreb and the Baptist Theological School in Novi Sad, a seminar entitled "The Nature and Mission of the Church" with John Stott as keynote speaker was organized for Christian leaders, preachers, pastors and associates from 11–13 April 1980 in Novi Sad. It was the first interdenominational meeting on the premises of the Baptist School of Theology and it brought together representatives from Baptists, Pentecostals, Evangelicals, Methodists, Calvinists and Open Brethren. Together they reflected on Stott's teaching on topics such as: God's Church is one body; evangelizing through the local church; ideals of pastoral ministry; the unity and diversity of the church; and characteristics of a Spirit-filled church. The event fostered greater understanding and better relations between the members of the various Protestant churches. They concluded that it was necessary to organize similar meetings and also to establish a formal body, an organization that would strive to maintain the unity of all evangelical Protestant churches in order to make the name of Jesus Christ known throughout our country through the work of our churches. The conviction was that a time was ahead that would show how seriously we had taken the Bible's message and how much we were willing to work together to communicate the Christian truths that bind us together into one body.[10]

The formation of a formal organization did not have to wait long. In December of the same year, John Stott visited the Baptist Theological School in Novi Sad again and held a seminar attended by about one hundred and fifty Christians from seven different denominations. They discussed the foundations of evangelical Christianity and the necessity of cooperation between evangelical Christians. Stott explained how evangelical Christians differ from other Christians in terms of convictions about the Bible, salvation and evangelism. In addition to the seminar, a preliminary meeting was held under the leadership of the Baptists Stjepan Orčić and Branko Lovrec, and Peter Kuzmič from the Pentecostal Church. It was decided to proceed with the establishment of an evangelical organization that received the official name of *Council*

---

9. "Why Lausanne 74?," *Glas evanđelja* 3 (1974): 18.
10. "John R. W. Stott in Yugoslavia," *Glas evanđelja* 2 (1980): 16.

of Evangelical Christians in Yugoslavia (SEK). The coordinating committee defined the activities of the SEK in six points and published a statement on the cooperation of evangelical Christians in Yugoslavia.[11] On the same occasion, a group of young people discussed the responsibilities and tasks of evangelical Christians. They pointed out that evangelical Christianity was too closed in on itself and needed to begin evangelizing. They also argued that evangelical Christianity in Yugoslavia felt like something imported in "Western packaging" and that it was necessary to build its own evangelical identity based on the local culture. The necessity of mutual acquaintance and cooperation of all Christian churches in the country was strongly emphasized.[12]

The plan to create a single body that would unite the Protestant evangelical Christians did not meet with everyone's approval. After the founding of the SEK, there were disagreements regarding cooperation with other evangelical denominations among the leaders of the Union of Baptist Churches, due to certain difficulties in the past. They expressed concern that any cooperation at this level would be detrimental to the work in their own communities. A special session of the Federal Committee of Baptist Churches on 16 May 1981 demanded that the signatories of the SEK, Branko Lovrec and Stjepan Orčić, should resign from the SEK.[13] Lovrec and Orčić responded that they had been involved in the establishment of the SEK in a personal capacity, out of their own convictions, and they indeed stayed on in a personal capacity.[14] This incident shows that although high-ranking Baptist leaders were involved in inter-church meetings, even on behalf of the Alliance, there was no unified federal position on cooperation with other Protestant, let alone Catholic or Orthodox structures. Apart from occasional meetings at lectures, receptions, symposiums and joint prayer gatherings, stronger cooperation did not happen.[15]

Despite these disagreements about cooperation, further conferences and evangelistic campaigns were held, to which representatives of different Christian denominations were invited. Thus, in April–May 1983 the Baptist Church in Novi Sad held an interdenominational seminar on the topic of evangelism, with the speakers Leighton Ford and Gottfried Osei-Mensah, who then held

---

11. "Cooperation of evangelical Christians," *Glas evanđelja* 5/6 (1980): 26–27.

12. "Evangelical Christians together," *Iskre* 2 (1981): 19–21.

13. Lovrec was the editor of the *Glas Evanđelja* (*Voice of the Gospel*) and the director of the publishing house *Duhovna Stvarnost* (*Spiritual Reality*). Orčić was the director of the Baptist Theological School.

14. "Gospel Christian Counsel Statement," *Glas evanđelja* 1–2 (1981): 20.

15. Ruben Knežević, *Pregled povijesti baptizma na hrvatskom prostoru* (Zagreb: SBC u RH, 2001), 114–15.

the roles of President and Executive Secretary of the Lausanne Committee for Evangelism. Osei-Mensah was encouraged and happy to see interethnic cooperation in Yugoslavia between Christians: Serbs, Croats, Macedonians, Albanians, Hungarians, Montenegrins and other nationalities worked together. He counselled that the gospel unites despite ethnic differences. He advised that if the brothers were ready to accept the theological framework, this could be the beginning of the Lausanne Commitment in Yugoslavia, because evangelism unites.[16]

During the 1980s, several international and interdenominational parachurch organizations began missionary activities in Yugoslavia, including Croatia, such as Campus Crusade for Christ, Teen Challenge and STEP, an evangelical student movement that was active in organizing student conferences called "Catch the Rhythm" and connecting students from different churches. However, despite cooperation between the churches, the work of the SEK did not yield results.

On the initiative of Peter Kuzmič, in June 1987 the *Association of Evangelical Religious Ministers* was founded. It began with sixty members who were pastors, preachers and religious workers from the Pentecostal, Baptist, Church of God, Church of Christ and Christ Church of Bethany denominations.[17] Its aim was to help evangelical ministers in full-time church employment with their specific problems. Peter Kuzmič was elected as president, Stevan Mađarac as secretary, Veljko Bogdanović as treasurer, and Josip Jendričko and Pavao Moguš as members of the executive; in 1989, Branko Lovrec and Giorgio Grlj were added as reinforcement. The Association has sections for theological education, for the press and information, for Christian ethics, for work with young people and students, and for "women's work." At the 1989 Assembly in Osiek, it was accepted that the Association should be the initiator and sponsor of projects such as the promotion of Christian business ethics, the promotion of medical ethics and social engagement.[18]

According to the model of the Croatian Association, in March 1990 the *Association of Evangelical Religious Ministers in the Socialist Republic of Serbia* was founded in Belgrade, whose members are priests, preachers and others from various Protestant denominations. The first executive was composed of Stojšić Lazar as president, Mitrović Stojan as vice-president, Strajać Dragoslav

---

16. "Novi Sad Seminar of Evangelism 29.04.–2.05.83," *Glas evanđelja* 2 (1983): 10–16.
17. Stanko Jambrek, *Evandeoski pokret. Zbornik radova* (Zagreb: PEV, 1997), 36.
18. "Association of Evangelical Religious Ministers," *Glas evanđelja* 4 (1989): 31.

as secretary, Drobina Josip and Stojić Tihomir.[19] This Association later changed its name to *Protestant Evangelical Association in Serbia* (PEUS).

One Hundred Years of Theological Education

As in other countries, in Yugoslavia theological schools have often been places for the development of unity and evangelical communion. With the increase of believers after World War I, there was a need to train Christian workers. The first initiative for education appeared among the Baptists in 1923, when Nikola Dulić organized a two-week seminar for Sunday school teachers and a conference for the training of mission workers in Novi Sad.[20] In 1940, the Baptist Theological Seminary opened in Belgrade but stopped work due to the war. On the initiative of Josip Horak, Franjo Klem and Adolf Lehotski, it was re-established and began its ministry in Zagreb in 1954. Two years later it moved to Daruvar and finally in 1957 to Novi Sad, where it is still active today.[21] By 1974, forty-four diplomas had been awarded, and seventy students had attended the classes. Franjo Klem handed over the position of school director to Stjepan Orčić.[22] Although the seminary was a Baptist college, believers from other denominations, such as the Pentecostal preacher Dragutin Volf, also studied there. Volf saw the need for permanent education of the believers of his own denomination and organized the publication of a manual for correspondence studies.

In the 1970s, other theological colleges were founded. In 1972, the Pentecostal Church founded the Biblical Theological Institute in Zagreb, which operated until 1978. It was opened again in 1984, when it moved to Osijek. At the end of the 1980s, the institute became an interdenominational and international school with students from all over Eastern Europe and the Soviet Union. In those years, it changed its name to Evangelical Theological Seminary and remains active to this day.[23] It played an important role in the development of evangelical Christianity, especially in Croatia but also throughout Central Europe. At the initiative of the Greater Europe Mission, the Evangelical Biblical

---

19. "The Association of Evangelical Religious Ministers in the Federal Republic of Serbia was founded," *Izvori* 3–4 (1990): 15.

20. Davor Peterlin, "Theological Education among Croatian Baptists: A Socio-Historical Survey," *The Baptist Quarterly* 5 (2000): 243.

21. English website www.btsns.org/.

22. "New Graduates of the Theological School," *Glas evanđelja* 4 (1974): 15.

23. See www.evtos.hr/.

Institute was founded in Zagreb in 1974; today it is in Krapina and in 1999 it changed its name to Theological Biblical Academy.

In Zagreb in 1976 the Faculty of Theology Matthias Flacius Illyricus was founded, which connected Protestants and evangelical Christians. The founders were the Lutheran Church and the Baptist Church Union of Yugoslavia. This faculty currently operates as part of the Centre Matija Vlačić Illyricus of the University of Zagreb and is the highest ranked Protestant college in the Republic of Croatia. The faculty has members of various Protestant and evangelical communities in Croatia, and it enabled part-time study.[24]

The Bible School of the Church of Christ in Zagreb was founded in 1990 with the purpose of training believers for church service. In 2000 the school became the Institute for Biblical Studies; in 2006 it changed its name to Biblical Institute and has been operating to this day. Several hundred students of different denominations studied here and continuously promoted ecumenical and evangelical openness and unity in Christ.

The Division of Yugoslavia; National Evangelical Alliances

With the dissolution of Yugoslavia in the period from 1991 to 2003, six independent republics (Slovenia, Croatia, Bosnia and Herzegovina, Montenegro, Serbia and Macedonia) and two autonomous provinces (Vojvodina and Kosovo) were created, and in 2008 Kosovo became an independent republic. Due to the resulting Homeland War (1991–1995), there was much less communication between the evangelicals in the different republics. The communication between the churches in Croatia and Serbia even broke down completely; only after the end of the war in 1995 relations gradually normalized.

There was no Evangelical Alliance in Yugoslavia before 1991, the SEK trying to act as one. The Bosnian Evangelical Alliance was formally established in 2003 and the founding assembly was in 2013, when it became a member of the European Evangelical Alliance (EEA) and the World Evangelical Alliance. The Bosnians started a legal battle for registration in 2007 and were recognized in 2023 under the name Protestant Evangelical Alliance in Bosnia and Herzegovina.[25]

---

24. "Competition for enrollment," *Glas evanđelja* 2 (1976): 31.

25. Notes from a conversation with Saša Nikolinović and Tomislav Dobutović on 8 January 2025.

In Serbia there exists the above-mentioned Evangelical Alliance Serbia (PEUS), which is not a member of the EEA.[26] There is also another, unregistered group, The Evangelical Protestant Initiative; its basis of voluntarism makes it difficult for it to be very active.[27]

Today, the cooperation between the various groups of evangelicals in the former Yugoslavia is satisfactory when they are organizing large international gatherings and conferences. Special meetings such as the Balkan Learning Community bring together Evangelical Alliances from Croatia to Greece. Otherwise there are contacts between the Alliances but no extensive cooperation. The latest gathering took place in Albania in February 2024, bringing together evangelical Christian leaders from Albania, Greece, Bosnia and Herzegovina, Bulgaria, Montenegro and Croatia.

The Evangelical Alliance in Croatia

In April 1992 Croatia got its own Evangelical Alliance. At the session of the Association of Evangelical Religious Ministers, more than thirty preachers and other ministers from six evangelical Protestant churches (Baptist, Evangelical Pentecostal, Church of Christ, Church of God, Church of Christ Bethany and Christian Church of Agape) decided to transform the Association into the Council of Protestant Evangelical Christians, which would bring together evangelical Christian denominations, local communities, church institutions and organizations. The aims were a more appropriate joint appearance of the evangelical churches in society and a more comprehensive and better promotion of the evangelical worldview. The establishment of the Council also opened the way for direct connections and cooperation with similar organizations in Europe and the rest of the world.[28] The new organization, also known as the Protestant Evangelical Alliance (PEV), was duly founded in May 1992 in Zagreb,[29] right in the middle of the Homeland War. Thus, from the beginning of the creation of the Republic of Croatia, the PEV was involved in social issues, especially those related to religious rights. The founding committee consisted of Branko Lovrec (Baptist), Peter Kuzmič (Pentecostal) and Mladen

---

26. Cf. www.peus.rs.
27. Notes from a conversation with Samuilo Petrovski on 8 January 2025.
28. "On the way to creating the Council of Evangelical Protestant Christians," *Izvori* 5 (1992): 11.
29. "Appeal of the Protestant Evangelical Alliance," *Izvori* 6 (1992): 20. The Association of Evangelical Religious Ministers was disbanded. The Croatian EA is thus known both as Protestant Evangelical Alliance (PEV) and as the Council of Protestant Evangelical Christians.

Jovanović (Church of Christ) as the presidency; members were Endre Langh (Reformed Calvin Church), Josip Jendričko (Church of God), Giorgio Grlj and Stevo Dereta (both Baptist). The committee was entrusted with drafting a constitution in accordance with the new socio-political and religious situation in Croatia. The PEV would try to unite the churches of Reformed heritage as an advisory body.[30]

As a result of the fact that in 1991 some Protestant and evangelical churches in Croatia – the Baptist Union, the Church of God, the Lutheran Church, the Evangelical Pentecostal Church and the Reformed (Calvinist) Church – became members of the Conference of European Churches (CEC),[31] the cooperation between church leaders and believers became even better.

The General Assembly of the EEA in May 1992 accepted the PEV into membership, giving this body international credibility.[32] In May 1994, the PEV assembly entitled "Time for Peace and Hope" was held in Bizovac. The need for evangelical Christians to connect and cooperate was emphasized. A seat on the presidency was left for a representative of the Evangelical (Lutheran) Church if they would join the PEV. Nine committees were established: for theological issues and ecumenical dialogue, for social ethics and social issues, for the coordination of humanitarian work, for the media, for religious education, for publishing, for relations with foreign media, for conferences and evangelism, and for youth and student work. A decision on whether to establish a committee for women's work was left to the women. It was decided that there would be an annual PEV Day on the Sunday before 31 October, when funds would be collected for the work of the PEV.[33]

The next PEV Assembly was held in June 1995 in Crikvenica under the theme "The Church in the Social, Religious and Own Environment." In view of the continuing wars, a reconciliation commission was set up.[34] On Reformation Day, the PEV organized and encouraged joint performances, services, seminars and forums, as well as work on the development of religious education in Reformed churches. In 1995, the evangelistic campaign ProChrist of Billy Graham in Essen (Germany) was broadcast live in six Croatian cities.

---

30. Mladen Jovanović, "The Evangelical Perspective of Unity and the Contribution of the Protestant Evangelical Alliance to the Unity of Christians in Croatia," *Kairos* 2.1 (2008): 80.

31. See https://ceceurope.org/who-we-are/member-churches.

32. "Protestant Evangelical Alliance in Europe," *Izvori* 11–12 (1992): 20.

33. "PEV Assembly," *Izvori* 7–8 (1994): 23.

34. "Protestant Evangelical Alliance – Crikvenica 95," *Izvori* 7–8 (1995): 20–21.

On the occasion of the 150th anniversary of the World Evangelical Alliance in October 1996, the PEV organized a scholarly conference in Zagreb with speakers from different Christian churches. On that occasion the representative of the Evangelical (Lutheran) Church in Croatia, Vladimir Šporčić, noted with regret that his church had still not joined the PEV.[35] Unfortunately, even today the Lutheran Church is not yet a member of the PEV, and in the meantime the Reformed (Calvinist) Church has withdrawn from membership.

The PEV participated in the organization of the Billy Graham School for Evangelism held in November 1997 in Stubičke Toplice. This brought together a large number of participants from Baptist, evangelical and Christ Churches, which was significant for the development of good mutual relations and cooperation. In 2003, evangelicals in membership with the PEV signed an *Agreement with the Government of the Republic of Croatia* on issues of common interest, which regulated their legal statute and approved financial resources from the state budget for their smooth functioning. In 2016, the PEV organized seminars and consultations on church growth in cooperation with the Lausanne Committee. It held a Day of Prayer and was the organizer of the celebration of the 500th anniversary of the Reformation in 2017.

The Current Situation
Evangelicals and Other Christians

Despite various efforts, the relationship between the evangelicals and other Protestant groups is weak. It is only visible through the joint gathering for prayer for the Week of Prayer for the Unity of Christians in January and through the joint work of the Association for Religious Freedom. There should be more joint initiatives between evangelicals and other Protestants in the future and a joint celebration of Reformation Day on 31 October could be a positive step in that direction.

The same is true for the relationship with the Roman Catholics, who are the majority religious community in Croatia, making up 79 percent of the population.[36] On the initiative of the Karizma Association, in August 1987 an all-Christian conference for spiritual renewal, Karizma 87, was organized in a Roman Catholic Church in Siget (Zagreb), with the purpose of gathering Christians of good will in the love and spirit of Christ to pray, get to know

---

35. "PEV Symposium," *Izvori* 1–2 (1997): 36–37.
36. See https://dzs.gov.hr/vijesti/objavljeni-konacni-rezultati-popisa-2021/1270.

each other and celebrate together. The speakers were the Protestant preachers Derek Prince, Rune Brannstorm and Slobodna Gajicki.[37]

Numbers

The number of evangelicals in Croatia in 2022 is 0.15 percent of the population, or between five thousand eight hundred and six thousand four hundred people,[38] but when one considers their social engagement, humanitarian work, education, publishing and church activities, the impression in society is that there are ten times as many evangelicals. Thanks to the dedicated work of the board of the Association for Religious Freedom, which includes members of various religious groups, full freedom of religion exists in Croatia.

Ten years ago, the number of evangelical Christians was over seven thousand, but this decreased because many churches predominantly had elderly members. In addition, after Croatia's entry into the European Union many young people in their twenties and young married couples with children emigrated to Western European countries. Today in Croatia there is almost no evangelical church from which someone has not moved to Western Europe. In this way, many churches were left without their young pillars. The consequences of these displacements will become visible in the rural churches in the next ten years.

In the last decade the world has witnessed many wars and as a result an increase in refugees around the world. Although Croatia was on the route that migrants from Syria (2011–2024) and Afghanistan (2001–2021) took, only a small number of them stopped in Croatia to ask for asylum. Currently less than twenty immigrants are involved in local Christian communities. On the other hand, the war in Ukraine has resulted in an increased number of refugees who have found their temporary home in Croatia. From 24 February 2022 to April 2024, Croatia granted temporary protection to 24,965 displaced persons from Ukraine.[39] Yet it is estimated that fewer than fifty Ukrainians have become involved in local evangelical congregations.

---

37. "Charisma 87," *Iskre* 7–8 (1987): 19.

38. According to research CRBUH 1990–2020 of the Biblical Institute in Zagreb.

39. See https://n1info.hr/vijesti/cak-42-milijuna-ukrajinaca-raseljeno-diljem-eu-evo-koliko-ih-je-u-hrvatskoj-i-koja-prava-imaju/.

Issues of Identity

The evangelical Christians in Croatia are currently divided on the issue of identity. Some describe themselves as evangelical Protestants while others do not want to have anything to do with mainline Protestantism. The baptism of believers on the basis of a personal confession of faith is becoming an important issue, because the question is being asked whether traditional Protestants, who have mostly been baptized as young children, can legitimately consider themselves as evangelical Christians. One group of evangelicals is arguing for an inclusive approach to this issue, one which is based on conversion not on baptism, and on the importance of the gospel in everyday Christian life. This approach can keep traditional Protestant *wjwerniks* included. In 2023 the Evangelical Theological Society in Croatia began consultations in order to contribute to the resolution of these issues and to build unity. Traditionally, the most important element for Croatian evangelicals has been to perceive evangelicalism as a theological movement and not as a confessional affiliation.

While in traditional Protestant churches it is common to ordain female pastors, this was not the case in the evangelical churches. Occasionally, prominent female leaders served as deaconesses, usually under the umbrella of their husbands who performed pastoral ministry. Today, women are slowly being introduced into the ministry of some evangelical churches, but these are exceptions, and it is to be expected that it will take a decade for any major developments to occur.

Regarding the current state of evangelical Christianity in Croatia, Thellman notes that

> . . . the Lausanne movement is concrete evidence of the reality of evangelicalism as a growing global movement that, while certainly not homogeneous, nor limited to a singular or even a few denominations or traditions, still maintains distinct unifying characteristics across various denominations, traditions, and cultures, as well as the varieties of theology and praxis noted above.[40]

Evangelicals in Croatia are mostly gathered around the PEV, which unites a significant number of them on a denominational basis. Given that the evangelical movement is based on the gospel which is "the power of God for salvation to everyone who believes" (Rom 1:16), it is hoped that other Christian churches and individuals who agree with the basic tenets of evangelical Christianity will

---

40. Gregory S. Thellman, "A Future Imbued with Hope: Reflections on Global Evangelical Christianity and the Croatian Context," *Kairos* 16.2 (2022): 131–43.

join the PEV, so that this evangelical family in Croatia will include members of other Christian denominations.

Bibliography

Bloesch, Donald G. *Osnove evanđeoske teologije* 1. Novi Sad: Dobra vest, 1989.
Bobinac, Ankica Marinović, and Dinka Marinović Jerolimov. *Vjerske zajednice u Hrvatskoj*. Zagreb: Prometej, 2008.
Jambrek, Stanko. *Evanđeoski pokret. Zbornik radova*. Zagreb: PEV, 1997.
———. *Crkve reformacijske baštine u Hrvatskoj*. Zagreb: Bogoslovni institut, 2003.
———. *Reformacija nekad i danas*. Zagreb: Biblijski Institut, 2017.
Knežević, Ruben. *Pregled povijesti baptizma na hrvatskom prostoru*. Zagreb: SBC u RH, 2001.
Peterlin, Davor. "Theological Education among Croatian Baptists: A Socio-Historical Survey." *The Baptist Quarterly* 5 (2000): 239–59.
Thellman, Gregory S. "A Hopeful Future: Reflections on Global Evangelicalism and the Croatian Context." *Kairos* 16.2 (2022): 97–110.

13

Evangelicalism in the Czech Republic

Pavel Černý

Historical Development

Just to speak of the evangelical identity in our language is not always clear. For many years, we were using the word "evangelical" – in Czech *evangelický* – to describe all Protestants. In the second half of the twentieth century, mainly in opposition to theological liberalism, we started using the word "evangelical" to describe just a part of the Protestants. The word "evangelical" had the meaning of a theologically conservative yet missiologically minded segment of Protestantism. We started to translate "evangelical" as *evangelikální*. Before that more common word to identify evangelicals, the word "revivalism" was used, meaning "Christians touched by spiritual awakening." This distinction links evangelical Christians in our country with the Great Awakening of the eighteenth and nineteenth centuries.

At the beginning of the seventeenth century our country consisted of 90 percent Protestants, influenced by several waves of Reformation, and only 10 percent Roman Catholics. After losing the battle against the Habsburgs and the Catholic League in 1620, a very cruel and severe Counter-Reformation began. Many leaders were executed or exiled; many families had to emigrate, losing their property. As a part of the Austro-Hungarian Empire, the Bohemian Kingdom became a country of just the Roman Catholic confession. After one hundred and fifty years of this Counter-Reformation, the percentages were reversed: it was 90 percent Roman Catholics and only 10 percent Protestants, who were functioning underground. The Patent of Tolerance issued in 1781 brought limited possibilities for three confessions: the Lutherans, the Calvinists and the Greek Orthodox. The Unity of the Czech Brethren (*Unitas Fratrum*) remained forbidden.

Later our country was touched by German Pietism and the great revivals of the nineteenth century. Some local revivals broke out and new contacts with foreign missionaries were developed. Presbyterian missionaries from the Free Church of Scotland entered via Saxony and Poland while Congregational missionaries of the Boston Board of Mission came from the United States. These missionaries wanted to strengthen the spiritual life of the Lutheran and the Reformed Churches. Unfortunately, those two churches were hit by the theological liberalism of the nineteenth century. People who experienced repentance of their sins, spiritual conversion and new spiritual life by following Jesus Christ mostly found no understanding and acceptance in the established Protestant denominations, which led to the beginning of illegal worship services. Some pastors from the established churches tried to stop these unofficial meetings, sometimes even calling in the police. At that time, the World Evangelical Alliance (British Branch) sent a delegation to the emperor in Vienna to intercede and ask for the protection of the newly planted house fellowships.[1] The Evangelical Alliance was the first ever large unity movement to speak up for religious freedom in Europe. This help from abroad had good results and the Habsburg Austro-Hungarian Empire became less rigid in its religious politics. There were also some foreign influences on the acceptance and practice of the Protestant Patent (1861) and the new state Constitution (1867). The complicated relationship between the established churches and revival groups continued to lead to the founding of the new evangelical denominations. In 1880, the Free Reformed Church was established, uniting some local revivals in Eastern Bohemia, the work of the Scottish Presbyterian mission from Wroclaw and the American congregational mission in Prague, Brno and in other places. The *Unitas Fratrum* or the Unity of Brethren, better known as the Moravian Church, had been functioning abroad since the revival movements in the eighteenth century, as a worldwide missionary movement from the settlement of the mostly Moravian refugees in Germany. These refugees were helped by Count Nikolaus Ludwig Zinzendorf and they settled in Herrnhut and surrounding villages. Other Czech exiles set up their homes in the Berlin area. At home, the Moravian Church was founded in 1880 under the name Unity of the Brethren; the Baptist Church was founded in 1884 and the

---

1. In 1879, five representatives of the Evangelical Alliance from abroad visited the emperor in Vienna to negotiate; see M. Košťál et al. *Sto let ve službě evangelia 1880–1980* (Praha: Rada Církve bratrské, 1981), 22.

Evangelical Methodist Church in 1921. These churches developed as evangelical denominations which stressed independence from the state and were not financially supported by it.

It would be a mistake to overlook the evangelicals in the mainline denominations, such as the Lutheran church and the Reformed (Calvinist) Church. In both churches, *collegia pietatis* were functioning like *ecclesiolae in ecclesia*. Some pastors endorsed pietistic spirituality, prayer life and solid biblical teaching. The influence of the revival penetrated local church life. There were different joint initiatives in social work and in the ecumenical Unity of Constance, which commemorated the martyrdom of Jan Hus, the Czech Reformer who was burned at the stake during the Council of Constance in 1415. The heritage of the Czech Reformation was accepted by the old and new denominations and further developed. Several denominations used the name "brethren." In our context this word has nothing to do with the "Plymouth Brethren" but it is a link to the original *Unitas Fratrum*, founded in 1457 and destroyed by the Counter-Reformation. The last bishop of this church, Jan Amos Comenius, was expelled from his country and became a famous European pilgrim. The heritage of the Reformation was linked to the local reformation represented originally by the Hussite movement and the Unity of Czech Brethren. To this soil the heritage of the Lutheran and Calvinistic Reformations was added.

Complete freedom of religion in our country came at the end of World War I, when modern Czechoslovakia came into being. All churches enjoyed religious freedom and space to develop their mission. Mainline churches operated as state churches whereas smaller evangelical denominations functioned as free churches independent of the state.

This freedom was brutally ended by World War II, which brought some limits to church ministry while some church workers were put into concentration camps. Unfortunately, the end of the war did not bring freedom. The Yalta agreement (1945) brought our country in the Soviet Union sphere of influence. In 1948, the Communist revolution occurred, led by Soviet advisors and KGB agents. Immediately, atheist propaganda was pushed in all schools, media and professions. Many pastors and priests were persecuted and even arrested; all monastic orders were disestablished. The state introduced new church laws in 1949, forcing the churches to accept strict state control. These laws also changed the status of free churches as all churches had to receive state money for their pastors' wages. These wages were kept very low in order to limit the number of pastors. The church laws put all churches, including the Roman Catholics, on the same level, persecuted and limited in their activities and outreach. Some congregations were closed by the authorities, the social work of all denominations was taken over by the new regime, and many church buildings and other properties were confiscated. The International Bible Society printed Bibles for the Czech churches. During certain periods, the printing of Bibles was forbidden and Bibles along with other Christian literature were smuggled into the country.

Nevertheless, ecumenical potential developed. The pressure led evangelical pastors and the pastors and priests of other churches to support each other. Roman Catholic priests were sharing prison cells with evangelical pastors, praying together, reciting Bible texts together and helping each other to survive. This explains the distinctive shape of the Czech ecumenism which is characterized by close cooperation among the clergy of different confessions and their churches.

The Contemporary Situation

The Velvet Revolution of 1989 brought a miraculous change. Almost overnight, the churches – used to limitations and persecution – were given full religious freedom. It was like a dream and most churches soon took the opportunity to develop their activities and mission.

The evangelical churches started denominations and some which had been operating underground during totalitarianism were registered, among which the Pentecostal Church. Until 1989, the evangelical movement was separated from the worldwide movement, but now the borders were open and many visitors from the West came to see the church situation and to help. Some American and West European churches sent short-term and long-term missionaries to our country. Evangelicals were quick in founding Christian printing houses and starting social ministry and Christian schools. Many of these things were done well, but many things were developed too hastily. Because of the new challenges of mission, Christian workers needed more training. For this reason, a new faculty of theology, theological seminaries and Bible colleges were established. The evangelical denominations started church planting programmes. In some denominations, the number of congregations has doubled since 1989.

It is interesting that the former free churches retained the cooperative relationship with the state. During the time of Communism, the evangelical denominations were part of the Ecumenical Council of Churches. After the liberation, all churches kept their membership in it and newly founded denominations even joined this ecumenical body. There are several reasons for this. The Ecumenical Council of Churches gave all denominations the opportunity to broadcast worship services via the state television and radio. Later, openings arose to send chaplains to the army and to start prison chaplaincy and hospital ministry. Churches started to renew social ministry and opened church schools. These projects would not have been possible for just one isolated denomination. Another reason for staying in the ecumenical body was the long process of reaching an agreement with the government to rectify the injustices of Communism. An extremely large number of buildings, fields, forests and other property was confiscated by the state during the time of the Communist government, most of it belonging to the Roman Catholic Church. The Ecumenical Council of Churches and the bishops' conference worked closely together and after twenty years a restitution agreement was agreed and some injustice partly solved.

As a result, the majority of the evangelical churches do not function as "free churches" (completely separated from the state): the cooperative model with the state is being further developed from both sides. The churches are independent and there are no state churches anymore, but the model of voluntary cooperation with state institutions is accepted.

Evangelical Identity

From a theological point of view, the evangelical identity of the churches has survived the turbulent times. The Czech evangelical movement always wanted to respect and develop the heritage of the Reformation. Personal conversion to Christ, new birth by the Holy Spirit, regeneration and assurance of salvation were emphasized. Even during the time of persecution, evangelism through personal witness, small secret Bible camps, house groups and evangelistic worship services continued. The authority of the Bible was held in reverence. The evangelical denominations were able to cooperate with Christians from the mainline churches.

Since the revolution, the evangelical movement has been enriched by the charismatic movement and the Pentecostal Church. The charismatic movement penetrated most denominations; some charismatic Christians stayed in their denominations while others joined newly planted independent churches. Of course, there were some tensions, but churches learnt how the different ecclesiological models can live side by side.

The need to increase the number of pastors, elders, counsellors, youth leaders and social workers led to the establishment of new theological schools, but we now see that too many theological institutions and Christian publishing houses were founded. The evangelical churches learnt that in the Czech

Republic, there is no reason to duplicate activities and to establish separate institutions for the work of Reformed evangelicals, Christians from the radical reformation (Baptists, etc.), charismatics and Pentecostals. Over the years, the Czech evangelicals have learned how to cooperate in a positive way.

In the 1970s and 1980s, the term "revival Christianity" ceased to be used and was replaced by the term "evangelical" for two reasons. First, the church does not experience revival all the time: there are only special periods with God given spiritual renewal. Second, the growing cooperation with the worldwide church helped us to identify with the worldwide evangelical movement.[2] In 1974 two pastors, one from the mainline Czech Brethren Evangelical Church and one from the evangelical denomination Church of the Brethren, attended the Lausanne Congress.[3] Their reports were well-received. From time to time, some pastors were given opportunity to study theology abroad, because the Communist government wanted to pretend that religious freedom existed by allowing some pastors to travel to the West. In the opposite direction, some leaders of evangelical churches in the West were given permission to visit Czech churches, but it was obvious that these contacts were carefully monitored by the secret police.

In 1980, the Church of the Brethren (*Církev bratrská*) invited Rev. Dr John Stott to the country. Probably because it was known that he was a chaplain to Queen Elizabeth, Stott got permission to speak at the pastors' conference and to preach in three congregations. He was received with great enthusiasm as a guest from the Church of England. His lectures at the pastors' conference and his sermons in the worship services touched the hearts and minds of the local pastors and church members. Many people said, "This is our theology too." It was a big surprise that a clergyman from the Anglican church could be so close to our evangelical theology and understanding of the Bible and his visit helped to strengthen the evangelical movement. After the Velvet Revolution of 1989, John Stott returned several times to lecture at conferences and preach in churches. In 1991, his visit encouraged the start of the Czech Evangelical Alliance[4] as well as theological education at the newly founded Evangelical Theological Seminary in Prague.[5] The Fellowship of European Evangelical

---

2. The evangelical Christians belong through the local Evangelical Alliance to the European and the World Evangelical Alliance. There is a cooperation with the Lausanne Movement for world evangelism and with other evangelical bodies.

3. Their names were Rev. Dr Cyril Horák and Rev. Dr Miloslav Košťál.

4. See https://ea.cz/en/home/.

5. See https://etspraha.cz/en/home.

Theologians enabled close contact of Czech pastors and theologians with European theologians through conferences, guest lectures and literature.

But the relations between the different wings of the evangelical movement were not always peaceful. The rise of the charismatic movement brought tensions. At first, it was not clear if charismatics and Pentecostals were evangelicals too. It took some years of negotiation and cooperation to overcome prejudices. In 1993, the first extensive cooperation between the evangelicals took place through the European satellite evangelistic campaign of Billy Graham. It was overwhelming to see Reformed and Lutheran evangelicals cooperating with charismatics and even with Roman Catholics who were happy to cooperate with the evangelicals. We learnt the important theological lesson that evangelicalism is a uniting movement and that various churches can keep their own ecclesiology and theological emphases whilst still working together.

Czech evangelicalism has some special characteristics. The heritage of the Czech Reformation is still alive and as a result Czech evangelicalism is not rigid from a confessional point of view. The Bible is the measure of our faith and life. There are fundamentalists in every denomination, but our definition of the authority of the Scripture has never been one-sided. When we say that the Bible is the word of God and has the highest authority, we add that the Bible is also the word of men and needs interpretation. We have never used the word "inerrancy" for the authority of the Bible, as many Americans do. The word of God needs exegesis and hermeneutics to be preached and taught. Our evangelical movement is in line with the Lausanne Commitment on the authority and the power of the Bible.[6] The Lausanne Commitment is well accepted by many evangelicals from the whole ecumenical spectrum.

Another issue was introduced by foreign missionaries, some of whom were quite radical in their eschatology, strongly pushing premillennialism. It surprised them that most Czech evangelical pastors are amillennialists and only very few are premillennialists or postmillennialists. It is possible to say that millennialism is not a dividing point among Czech evangelicals. Another point of division is the understanding of Reformed Theology. Many evangelicals put much emphasis on Reformed Calvinistic theology; the Heidelberg Catechism and the *Confessio Helvetica Posterior* are widely accepted. Originally, the form of Calvinism represented by the Synod of Dort (1618–1619) and the so-called "Tulip" (the five points of Calvinism) were not even known in our country. The teaching of some foreign church workers and the literature that they translated

---

6. "... the only written Word of God, without error in all it affirms," John R. W. Stott, *Making Christ Known: The Lausanne Covenant* (Carlisle: Paternoster, 1996), 13.

and printed have caused some very sharp divisions. Some evangelicals are more focused on predestination, some are more Arminian. This posture may have its roots in the Czech Reformation in the fifteenth and sixteenth centuries. The theologians of the old Unity of Brethren refused to define what the Bible calls a mystery: we humans are unable to break into the mystery of predestination. Most Czech evangelicals believe in predestination for salvation, but this mystery has not been revealed to us so we are not dogmatic at this point.

A very similar approach can be seen regarding the Lord's Supper. The presence of Christ in the eucharist is considered as real in the Holy Spirit. There is no way to define exactly Jesus's presence in celebrating the Lord's Supper, although we are sure that he is present there in some way. Eucharistic hospitality is practised among evangelicals across the evangelical denominations but also with mainline churches. Lutherans, Anglicans, Reformed, charismatics and Pentecostals can celebrate the Lord's Supper together and have communion with Christ and among themselves. A helpful way to celebrate together is to remember the context of the Passover meal.

Marks and Characteristics of the Evangelical Movement

We can use different marks to identify the evangelical movement which is present in the Czech Republic in all churches including in Roman Catholicism. For instance, the Catholic Charismatic Conference is very popular and evangelicals from different denominations participate. Most of its teaching can be recognized as evangelical. Instead of emphasizing differences in teaching between Roman Catholics and evangelicals, we support each other in Christian ethics and social work. We have learnt to cooperate ecumenically.

We are aware of many attacks on the evangelical identity. Secular circles attack us because of evangelical support in the USA for the questionable morality and character of Donald Trump. Trumpism and the conservative opposition to abortion, gender issues and the LGBT+ agenda open us up to criticism from secular society. From ecumenical circles, there are regular accusations against Czech evangelicals concerning fundamentalism. Some mainline Christians still do not distinguish between evangelicalism and fundamentalism. Quite often, it is said that evangelicals do not distinguish the different literature styles of the Bible and always interpret the Bible literally. It is important to explain our positions and to be engaged in ecumenical dialogue. In recent years, the presidency of the Ecumenical Council of Czech Churches was filled by evangelical leaders. It is interesting that they were able to build a bridge between Protestants and Roman Catholics. A growing number of evangelical theologians have completed PhDs at various universities to be better equipped for ecumenical dialogue and for teaching and writing theology.

Our country as a whole is not experiencing a spiritual revival but some evangelical churches are growing. This is in contrast to the situation of the mainline churches, many of which are rapidly diminishing in numbers. The publication of good quality evangelical books is also important for building the evangelical identity.

What is the Evangelical Identity in Our Situation?

To describe the marks of an evangelical, we could use the famous Bebbington quadrilateral,[7] which includes:

1. Conversionism – the belief that the lives of people need to be changed.
2. Activism – the expression of the gospel in daily life.
3. Biblicism – particular regard for the Bible.
4. Crucicentrism – an emphasis on the sacrifice of Christ on the cross.

These characteristics describe the identity of the majority of the evangelical movement.

John Stott helpfully explains that "the evangelical faith is *not a recent innovation*, a new brand of Christianity."[8] I find this emphasis very important. In ecumenical dialogue, it is worthwhile to present the evangelical movement not as a recent innovation, but as a form of Christianity which has its roots in the Reformation and tied to the Christian heritage of the first five centuries. These five centuries provide common ground for the unity of all Christianity. *The Nicene Creed* or *The Niceno-Constantinopolitan Creed*, amended in 381 AD, and the older and shorter *Apostles' Creed*, are the most comprehensive elements for Christian unity. In our ecumenical context, we must not allow others to regard evangelicals as an innovation or even a new sect. As Stott also emphasizes, "the evangelical faith is *not a deviation from Christian orthodoxy*."[9]

---

7. David W. Bebbington, *Evangelicalism in Modern Britain: A History from the 1730s to the 1980s* (London: Hyman Unwin, 1989), ix.

8. John Stott, *Evangelical Truth: A Personal Plea for Unity* (Leicester: IVP, 1999), 16; italics original here and in subsequent quotations.

9. Stott, *Evangelical Truth*, 17.

The evangelicals in the Czech Republic are in line with Stott's claim and agree with the characteristic of the movement stated by Alistair McGrath:[10]

1. The supreme authority of Scripture as a source and knowledge of God and a guide to Christian living.
2. The majesty of Jesus Christ both as incarnate God and Lord and the Saviour of sinful humanity.
3. The lordship of the Holy Spirit.
4. The need for personal conversion.
5. The priority of evangelism for both individual Christians and the church as a whole.
6. The importance of the Christian community for spiritual nourishment, fellowship and growth.

In *10 Great Ideas from Church History*,[11] Mark Shaw shows that the evangelical movement is deeply rooted in the Reformation and he describes the direct connections to Martin Luther, John Calvin and others.

The third claim of John Stott is that "the evangelical faith is *not a synonym for fundamentalism* for the two have a different history and a different connotation."[12] Despite the respectable history of "The Fundamentals," today we must clearly distinguish ourselves theologically from contemporary fundamentalism. There are several clear differences, the most important of which is that the evangelical movement understands the Christian mission as a result of the *Missio Dei*. The mission of God is not only expressed in evangelism, but it is always connected to social work (*diakonia*) and God's interest in law and justice, as Christopher Wright shows.[13] Our evangelism must always be connected with social ministry and most evangelical churches accept this. When designing a new church building, for example, it is necessary not only to think about worship services, but to include something for the community,

---

10. Alister E. McGrath, *Evangelicalism and the Future of Christianity* (Downers Grove: IVP, 1995), 55–56. This characteristic is also used by authors such as J. I. Packer, G. M. Marsden and D. Bloesch.

11. Mark Shaw, *10 Great Ideas from Church History* (Downers Grove: IVP, 1997); Czech translation *Deset významných idejí církevních dějin: Kořeny evangelikální tradice* (Brno: CDK, 2001).

12. Stott, *Evangelical Truth*, 19.

13. Christopher J. H. Wright, *The Mission of God: Unlocking the Bible's Grand Narrative* (Nottingham: IVP, 2006).

such as a gym, club rooms or spaces for social activities for various generations or English classes.

Our preaching must be based on solid exegesis and hermeneutics, and show appropriate respect for other Christian traditions and for the emotions of different seekers. In our country with its high percentage of non-Christians, we must stress the dialogue with other Christian groups.

Unlike some fundamentalists, the evangelical movement must not be anti-intellectual. We need a high standard of theological education for church workers as well as for church members. The evangelical movement in our country has largely left behind its separatist ecclesiology and confessionalism. As pointed out above, the Czech evangelicals are active within the ecumenical movement and most of them have no problem cooperating with churches with a different ecclesiology and a different confession. Evangelical churches do not dogmatize about the eschatological hope because dispensationalism has only ever been present at the margins.

As evangelicals and activists, we need to deepen our spirituality, in line with our historical Christian heritage which offers many models of mystics and pious people who have had a deep connection with God in the Spirit. Our struggle is to present evangelicalism as a large and broad movement, including the diverse emphases and spiritualities of so-called Reformed evangelicals, Lutherans, charismatic evangelicals and Pentecostals. Our unity is not based on a particular doctrine, but on the high authority of the Bible, on regeneration, conversion, fulfilment with the Spirit and ecumenical thinking. Despite many problems, historical and theological misunderstandings, and the political and intellectual misuse of the name evangelical, we believe that evangelicalism can still be an important correction to theological liberalism, fostering mission and making an ecumenical bridge between Protestantism, Catholicism and Orthodox Christianity. The movement needs to be flexible in developing and accepting different ecclesiological models. A strict confessionalism can be a great obstacle to unity and common mission in contemporary Europe. Mission today must be done ecumenically. There are many possibilities to cooperate in everything that is not against the Scripture. The evangelical movement needs to be enriched from the sources of early Christianity and the Reformation. To be reformed does not mean to repeat (re-live) the Reformation, but to be *ecclesia reformata, semper reformanda* (the reformed church [is] always to be reformed). It means to stay open to new expressions of our faith, new ecclesiology, new forms of worship, new ways of evangelism and social ministry. The evangelicals must be open to investigate and try new ways of life and work, because not everything has been revealed to us yet. We remain pilgrims and seekers: "For now we see in a mirror dimly, but then face to face. Now I know in part; then I shall know fully, even as I have been fully known."[14]

The Czech scholar of religious studies, Zdeněk Vojtíšek, is correct when he argues that evangelicals have had relative success in pluralist societies.[15] The adjustment of evangelicalism to the conditions of a pluralist society has had an impact on other Christian and even non-Christian religious traditions. Vojtíšek is convinced that evangelicalism may help others to survive or even to prosper in the conditions of the contemporary world. Ecclesiological, liturgical and evangelistic freedom is a good precondition for learning from others, contextualizing the gospel and developing new forms of church life and ministry. I consider evangelicalism to be a Christian tradition based on orthodox biblical Christianity, but creative and radical in its application. As John Stott has said, we should be conservative in doctrine, guarding the deposit (1 Tim 6:20; 2 Tim 1:14), but radical in application, asking awkward questions of the establishment and reverencing no sacred cows.[16] The word evangelical may carry with it some baggage of problems, mistakes and misunderstandings, but we are unable to find a better name in the Czech language. For this reason I agree with Justin Welby, the former Anglican archbishop of Canterbury, who said,

> I'm perfectly happy to be called "evangelical" with a small "e." "Evangelical" in many parts of the world is a sort of tribal name and has gotten a lot of baggage in the last 30 or 40 years, in the UK as well. I'm evangelical because I believe that the Bible, properly interpreted, is the final source for matters of faith and practice . . .[17]

Bibliography

Adlof, Alois. *Nástin dějin*. Praha: Křesťanský spolek mladíků, 1905.
Constantineanu, Corneliu, and Peter Penner, eds. *Central and Eastern European Bible Commentary*. Carlisle: Langham Global Library, 2022.

---

14. 1 Corinthians 13:12 (ESV).

15. Zdeněk Vojtíšek, "Evangelikalismus – Protestantské křesťanství přizpůsobené situaci náboženského pluralism" in *Lidé města / Urban people* 16.1 (2014): 23–66, https://lidemesta.cuni.cz/LM-836-version1-vojtisek.pdf.

16. John R. W. Stott, *Balanced Christianity: A Call to Avoid Unnecessary Polarization* (London: Hodder and Stoughton, 1978), 27–28.

17. Paul Handley, "ACC-17: Welby candid, and not in camera," *Church Times*, 2 May 2019, www.churchtimes.co.uk/articles/2019/3-may/news/world/acc-17-welby-candid-and-not-in-camera.

Košťál, Miloslav, ed. *Sto let ve službě evangelia 1880–1980*. Praha: Rada Církve bratrské, 1981.

McGrath, Alister E. *Evangelicalism and the Future of Christianity*. Downers Grove: IVP, 1995.

Nešpor, Zdeněk, T., and Vojtíšek Zdeněk. *Encyklopedie menších křesťanských církví v České republice*. Praha: Karolinum, Univerzita Karlova, 2015.

Shaw, Mark. *10 Great Ideas from Church History: A Decision-Maker's Guide to Shaping Your Church*. Downers Grove: IVP, 1997.

Stott, John R. W. *Balanced Christianity: A Call to Avoid Unnecessary Polarization*. London: Hodder and Stoughton, 1978.

———. *Evangelical Truth. A Personal Plea for Unity*. Leicester: IVP, 1999.

Wright, Christopher J. H. *The Mission of God: Unlocking the Bible's Grand Narrative*. Nottingham: IVP, 2006.

14

Evangelicalism in France

Sébastien Fath

Introduction: The French Evangelical "Coming-out"

Evangelical Protestants in France are relatively unknown in the country. These born-again Christians are still often confused with evangelists – people specializing in evangelism. Sometimes they may even be identified as a cult.[1] However, times are changing, not only because of news related to the cultural and political scene in Brazil and the USA. After being understudied for a long time, evangelicals are now an important focus for French researchers and journalists. This evangelical "coming-out" started a generation ago, mainly because of the steady growth of French evangelical churches. Having remained a tiny minority until the end of World War II, French evangelical demographics increased from around fifty thousand in 1950 to at least around 1,100,000 in 2024. In Greater Paris alone, there are now four Pentecostal megachurches.[2] We will describe the five episodes in the history of the French evangelicals, the first of which lasted from their birth to the Revolution of 1849.

"Not recognized." Evangelicals in the Margins (1800–1849)

Prior to the French Revolution of 1789, Protestants used to be persecuted and banned from the kingdom, but during the first half of the nineteenth century they could take root again in their homeland as a small minority. At

---

1. Slimane Zeghidour, "Les évangéliques, la secte qui veut conquérir le monde," dossier du *Nouvel Observateur*, n°2051 du 26 février 2004.

2. These megachurches are Rencontre Esperance (downtown Paris), Paris Centre Chrétien, Impact Centre Chrétien and Église MLK (Paris suburbs).

that time, the European context was still one of religious stability, in which identities were linked to geographic territories and collective heritage. The state regulated the special relationships it intended to nurture with the main recognized religious denominations.

In this context, the reintegration of French Protestants took two forms. Derived from the Concordat (1801), the first form is the public recognition granted by the state to Reformed Protestants and Lutherans. Through the *articles organiques* (legal national agreement signed in 1802 with Napoleon), these Protestants benefited from an official status. The second form is "non-concordatarian." Other Protestants, including a few evangelicals, did have a right to exist and worship, but they did not benefit from any kind of official recognition. This lack of recognition exposed them to difficulties in obtaining the right to assemble, in a context in which the freedom of association was not yet guaranteed. This second category of "non-recognized" Protestants, numerically weaker than the first, was later influenced by the Geneva Revival.[3] This continental wave of revival boosted an awakening, relaunching evangelistic activity, biblical training, new missions and conversions. International evangelical support, mainly from Switzerland, Great Britain and even the USA, also contributed to the evangelistic work in France. Since the beginning of the nineteenth century France was an important strategic target for evangelical missionary work. "An evangelized France would stimulate all intelligent classes in Europe," wrote Adoniram Judson in 1832, pleading for the start of a new Baptist outreach in the country of Victor Hugo.[4]

During this first phase of Protestant reintegration in France, evangelism met with strong social and cultural resistance. The first evangelical groups, including some very active Methodists and Baptists, suffered from isolation and discrimination. Yet in spite of many challenges, the "non-recognized" Protestants succeeded during this period in affirming the traits of a new religious culture, one based on choice rather than tradition, on the community of believers (professing churches) rather than on a mass institution, on local democracy rather than on vertical authority. French-speaking Protestant networks such as the Evangelical Society (Société Evangelique), created in 1833, were very actively at work. On French soil, they came up against a narrowly

---

3. Jean Decorvet, Tim Grass and Kenneth J. Stewart (eds), *The Genevan Reveil in International Perspective* (Eugene: Pickwick, 2023).

4. Adoniram Judson, Letter to the American Missionary Committee (Howard Malcom), quoted in "Baptist Churches in France (from a correspondent)," *Baptist Quarterly* 14 (1951–1952): 184.

compartmentalized pluralism, largely dominated by Catholicism, which tended to relegate "non-concordatarian" Protestants (mainly evangelicals) to the margins of the religious game, in a form of legal and cultural ghetto.

Starting to Multiply (1849–1921)

The year 1849 marked a turning point. At the beginning of the Second Republic, the so-called "free" evangelical churches separated from the state-recognized Reformed body. Three years after the founding of the Evangelical Alliance in London, French evangelical Protestants entered into a new phase. The creation of the Union of Free Churches brought new dynamics. The pastors of this new Union openly joined the existing tiny evangelical circles. Several of them were skilled leaders, rooted in the French Reformed tradition, combined with an evangelical distinctiveness. Among them were Frederic Monod (1794–1863) and Agenor de Gasparin (1810–1871), while notable women like Emilie Mallet (1794–1856) and Albertine de Broglie (1797–1838) also actively participated in new social work and missionary impulse in France and French-speaking Europe.[5] Networking increased, along with pastoral training and evangelism, between growth and dispersion. Yet full freedom was still not granted: during the reign of Napoleon III (1851–1870) some evangelical places of worship were even closed by the police, like in Chauny and La Fère (Aisne), and some pastors and evangelists were arrested.

The year 1875 marked a further turning point. With the rise of the long-lasting Third Republic, religious freedom for the non-Concordatarians, previously very precarious, became a reality. No more chapels were closed by the police, no more pastors were targeted only because they were preaching and evangelizing. The right to believe was granted.[6] At the same time, after a split the evangelicals in the Reformed Churches became autonomous (1872), consolidating a Protestant evangelical voice which was gaining confidence. Meanwhile, the proselytizing activity of Baptists, Methodists, Free churches and Brethren communities continued and was reflected in the appearance of new denominations like the Open Brethren and the Salvation Army. But the dream of protestantizing France, which had been cherished until World War I, failed. Protestants (evangelicals or not) remained in the ultra-minority, with

---

5. Michèle Miller Sigg, *Birthing Revival. Women and Mission in Nineteenth-Century France* (Waco: Baylor University Press, 2022).

6. Patrick Cabanel, *Le droit de croire. La France et ses minorités religieuses, XVIe-XXIe siècle* (Paris: Passé Composé, 2024).

less than 0.5 percent of the overall population, and evangelicals were widely dispersed, without a core network.

Building Strong Networks (1921–1965)

After World War I the diversification of the French evangelical landscape continued and they entered their third phase. They also became a recognized part of the religious landscape, as a distinctive Christian offer.[7] The Pentecostal movement, carried mainly by the Assemblies of God (ADD), became a new big player.[8] This pluralization was accompanied by much more active networking which built bridges between the various evangelical groups. The creation of strong networks became a priority and evangelistic efforts were coordinated. In 1921 Reuben and Jeanne Saillens founded the Bible Institute of Nogent, based near Paris. This ambitious Bible Institute, designed to train missionaries, evangelists and pastors, played a pioneering role in bringing various denominations together. French evangelicals from very diverse church backgrounds learned to study and work together.[9] This networking was stimulated by Reformed reunification (1938), leading to the creation of the French Reformed Church (Eglise Réformée de France). This process produced a polarizing effect on the French Protestant landscape because it accentuated the distinct evangelical identity that was based on conversion and believers' churches.

After World War II the global trend toward more cooperation increased. One fruit of this process was the creation of the Evangelical Information and Action Center (CEIA) in 1948. Organized like an annual fair, this event became, year after year, the largest meeting point for evangelical churches, bookstores, missions, agencies, other Christian ministries, schools and Christian music producers. A few years later, the French Evangelical Alliance (AEF) was relaunched (1953). An Association of Professing Churches (AEP) was also founded in 1957. The AEF gathers individuals but the AEP only churches.

---

7. Sébastien Fath, *Du ghetto au réseau, Le protestantisme évangélique en France (1800–2005)*, new ed. (Geneva: Labor & Fides, 2005), 2018.

8. Alexandre Antoine, *Une socio-histoire des Assemblées de Dieu en France (1909–1968); Naissance et développement d'un mouvement pentecôtiste de Réveil* (PhD Dissertation, Ecole Pratique des Hautes Etudes, Paris 2022).

9. Anne Ruolt, *A l'ombre du grand cèdre, Histoire de l'Institut Biblique de Nogent, 1921–2021* (Nogent: IBN Editions, 2021).

This Cold War period became also the golden age for American evangelical missionaries in France.[10] The increased unity for common evangelical goals also enabled two Billy Graham campaigns. Graham's first major campaign in France took place in Paris between 5 and 9 June 1955. An average of eight thousand spectators came every evening and two thousand decisions – or profession of faith – were made.[11] This rally was characterized by its spectacular dimension, meticulous organization and rather tumultuous media coverage. "The preacher boy," as the French press called him, created a sensation in the so-called City of Light. The secular press oscillated between curiosity and mockery. "The angel Gabriel in an overcoat" was scorned,[12] Graham was seen as the "Gospel's Pin-up Boy,"[13] the "evangelical mission's Stakhanov," "conversion's Barnum,"[14] "the fisher of dough,"[15] the "atomic evangelist," "Charm's preacher," "Buffalo Billy circus"[16] and "exporter of fundamentalism."[17] Sarcasm was flowing, but what remained is that evangelicalism made the headlines in France for the first time.

Graham's second campaign followed a similar logic. It took place from 12 to 26 May 1963 in different cities in the country: Montauban, Douai, Paris, Nancy, Toulouse, Lyon and Mulhouse. In Paris, Graham's preaching and meetings took place under a large tent at the Porte de Clignancourt. It is estimated that about forty-five thousand persons gathered there to hear the American evangelist and that twelve hundred commitments were made, with name and address handed in by the persons who had gone forward at the altar call. The meetings in the rest of the country gathered large numbers as well. The Graham committee estimated that about sixty thousand people were reached by the campaigns. Without the strong networks among the French evangelicals, these two large campaigns would have been impossible.

---

10. Allen V. Koop, *American Evangelical Missionaries in France, 1945–75* (Lanham: University Press of America, 1986).

11. This term is used to define the "decision" to follow Jesus expressed by someone hearing Billy Graham, when they come to the altar after the call made by the evangelist, in order to testify that they are willing to convert. The evangelistic journal of the Billy Graham organization is called *Decision Magazine*.

12. Christiane Château, *France Soir*, 4 June 1955.

13. "Billy Graham, le '"pin up boy"' de l'évangile," *L'Aurore-Paris*, 30 June 1954.

14. *Samedi Soir*, 24 June 1954.

15. Edgar Schneider, *France Soir*, 7 June 1955.

16. Valentine de Coincoin, "Barnum-Christ," *Le Canard Enchaîné*, 29 May 1963.

17. *L'Humanité*, 18 September 1986.

Becoming a Centre of Gravity within French Protestantism (1965–2000)?

During the last half of the twentieth century French evangelical churches and missions continued to evangelize, while other churches chose other paths, assuming that proselytizing had become out of date. The evangelical strategy seems to have paid off: from World War II to the end of the century professing evangelical churches multiplied their membership approximately sevenfold. This increase happened at the same time that a strong secularization process took place elsewhere. Roman Catholicism declined and French sociologists spoke about a "Christian heritage in disgrace."[18] The evangelical growth rate far exceeded that of the French population. It happened in all evangelical groups, but it was most evident among charismatics[19] and Pentecostals.

The growth was accompanied by a maturation of the evangelical networks built previously and by an increased offer of theological training, with the creation of two faculties, the Free Evangelical Faculty of Vaux-sur-Seine (1965) and the Free Reformed Faculty of Aix-en-Provence (1974).[20] In the 1980s and the 1990s, French evangelicals became more and more noticed by the mainstream French media and they were often described as a new driving force of French Protestantism: younger, more practising, more visible and more vibrant.

It is in this context that the third and final campaign by Billy Graham in France took place on 20–27 September 1986 at a grandiose venue, the Palais Omnisport at Bercy, downtown Paris. During this campaign, Graham was even able to meet the French socialist president, François Mitterrand, making headlines for this very reason. Prepared over a period of at least three years, since the June 1983 meeting at the temple de l'étoile (L'Etoile Chapel) in Paris,[21] this campaign was organized by the committee Mission France, led by honorary president Pierre Chaunu (a famous French Reformed historian and Sorbonne University professor) and executive president André Thobois (president of the French Baptist Federation and vice president of the French Protestant Federation). Before the campaign, a survey was conducted on behalf of Mission France among a panel of one thousand and nine French individuals over the

---

18. Guy Michelat, Julien Pottel and Jacques Sutter, *L'héritage chrétien en disgrâce* (Paris: L'Harmattan, 2003).

19. Evert Veldhuizen, *Les protestants charismatiques en France, émergence, dynamique et intégration d'un mouvement (1968-1988)* (Paris: Olivétan, 2024).

20. This Faculty later changed its name to Faculté Jean Calvin (John Calvin Faculty).

21. Seventy pastors and lay leaders met on the occasion and decided to create the Mission France committee, which was officially launched in June 1984. *Mission France, Une nuée de témoins* (Fontenay-sous-Bois: World Wide Publications, 1985), 5.

age of eighteen. It revealed that, while 52 percent of the respondents identified as believers, only 11 percent practised regularly.[22] For French evangelicals as well as for the Billy Graham Association, these results left room for improvement! A total of over one hundred thousand people came to listen to the American evangelist in Paris, whereas in the thirty-one locations in the rest of the country two hundred thousand people are estimated to have listened to Graham's message (with the help of the TELECOM 1 satellite). Of these people, seven thousand made a commitment of faith according to Graham's statistics, a very small proportion (lower than one per thousand). In absolute numbers, this was the evangelist's most important impact, but in proportion the ratio was lower than the ratio reached in 1963 and 1955. However, such rallies as this cannot be considered as the main growth booster for the evangelical movement. Most of the evangelistic work was done through individuals and local churches.

At the end of the twentieth century the French evangelicals did not yet form one percent of the population. But with their number reaching four hundred thousand believers, compared with fifty thousand fifty years before, some observers considered these born-again Christians as the new centre of gravity of French Protestantism.

Enlarging Boundaries: French Evangelicals, "Hub" of a "Francophone Revival" (2000–2025)

The fifth phase begins at the turn of the millennium and is marked by "divine connexions" of a new kind.[23] France and the world were experiencing the Internet revolution, a technological turning point in terms of communication and relationships. With the internet coming into every home in the 2000s and the subsequent rise of the social networks (Facebook, Instagram, WhatsApp, TikTok etc.) in the 2010s, evangelical churches are rethinking their ways and their "identity mix." They still claim to be communities of converts, but they are also becoming a community of the connected, with the help of strong French-speaking internet portals and media like TopChrétien, ICNews and EMCITV.

Three trends are emerging in the first quarter of the twenty-first century: creolization, charismatization and mutualization. These three movements fuel new French-speaking dynamics. From West Africa (Ivory Coast, Congo, Cameroon, Benin), a French-speaking evangelical awakening unfolded during this

---

22. See the newsletter of Mission France, "L'évangile à Bercy," 11 September 1986, 2.
23. Eric Celerier, *Connexions divines* (Paris: Première Partie, 2016).

period, with strong connections with Quebec and the Caribbean. Francophone Black Africa, where thousands of new converts joined evangelicals, Pentecostals and the Prophetic Churches every day, has become a major mission player, including evangelistic outreaches in the suburbs of Paris and in the main French cities.[24] The Maghreb, and particularly Algeria, is also influenced by these new trends. Several networks are reaching out to evangelize the North African population, both across the Mediterranean and among the immigrants in France. This is the case with the Evangelical Ministry among the Arabic-speaking Nations, created in France in 1980. More recently, the Association of North African Christians, chaired by pastor Karim Arezki (with an Algerian background), and the Union of North African Christians of France, chaired by pastor Saïd Oujibou (with a Moroccan background), succeeded in mobilizing thousands of North African Christians in France.

Many large transnational French-speaking evangelical ministries are appearing, like Impact Christian Centre (Impact Centre Chretien), led by pastor Yvan Castanou and his wife Modestine. These new networks, often reinforced by megachurches – like the ICC Royal City, inaugurated in Croissy-Beaubourg in 2023 – do have branches all over the former French colonial empire. Since the beginning of the twenty-first century France has become the "hub" of a larger francophone evangelical revival. Pastor Eric Celerier and his wife Muriel have been key players. He created the TopChretien, a large website and digital media service connecting the French-speaking Christians all over the world as early as 1999. After that year this very creative web mission developed first the Jesus.net Alliance and then the IC News media group.[25] All these tools are used by millions, bringing internet users to a closer experience of the Christian faith.

Evangelical Protestantism in continental France has continued to experience sustained growth during this time and today it exceeds the number of one million believers, which means evangelicals today form more than 1.5 percent of the French population. Two main sources feed the trend: former Roman Catholics and immigrants, the latter mainly coming from the wider African francophone world. Some former Muslims do also join, along with a few former Jewish believers and purely secular people. According to an IPSOS survey (2017), a majority of 62 percent of the French evangelicals are born in

---

24. Close to Pentecostal and charismatic churches, Prophetic Churches are characterized by a religious authority focused on prophecy. A pastor has to be a prophet.

25. Sébastien Fath, "Eric Celerier, pasteur de la francophonie," Fil-info Francophonie, Regardsprotestants, 28 June 2021, www.infochretienne.com.

an evangelical family, but 38 percent of them do come from other backgrounds, including fully secular. Welcoming several megachurches and transnational ministries, evangelical France is repositioning itself at the heart of the French-speaking evangelical and postcolonial network.

These French converts stand out by a high rate of social involvement. According to the same 2017 IPSOS survey data, 30 percent of the French evangelicals surveyed were involved in a charitable association, compared to 21 percent for other Protestants and 10 percent (three times less) for Roman Catholics.[26] They include several flagships of social action such as the Salvation Army, which is recognized in France as a charity of public utility. In terms of local political investment, we find them in town halls and municipal councils, like Franck Meyer, mayor of Sotteville-sous-le-Val (Seine Maritime) and president of the Protestant Committee for Human Dignity (CPDH), an influential evangelical network, with a conservative line, committed to ethical issues. In terms of national political commitment, the evangelical mark is more discreet, but it is found in parliament, in the senate, through the regular involvement of the Pentecostal pastor Thierry Le Gall, who is a parliamentary chaplain and the author of a book in which he recounts his journey, his challenges and his areas of activity.[27]

Last but not least, at the interface with public authorities, since 2010 evangelical Protestants have stood out through the effectiveness of the National Council of Evangelicals of France (CNEF), which is recognized by the Office of Religious Affairs (Ministry of the Interior). This umbrella network is the fruit of a long process of reconciliation between two evangelical blocks: on the one hand the Pentecostals of the Assemblies of God and on the other hand the French Evangelical Federation. Overcoming their conflicting views about the role of the Holy Spirit, both sides decided to build a bridge and join in a new representative structure.[28] It paid off. Led since 2022 by the Baptist pastor Erwan Cloarec, the CNEF succeeded to gather a majority of the French evangelical constituency. It has worked to pool resources and is committed to a two-dimensional impact: first, it aims at the general public and political actors, in particular through explanatory brochures. Second, it operates

---

26. IPSOS, Survey on Protestants, October 2017 (commissioned by the French Protestant Federation), www.reforme.net/les-dossiers-reforme/un-sondage-exclusif-sur-les-protestants-500-ans-apres-la-reforme.

27. Thierry Le Gall, *Un avenir, une espérance, Chroniques d'une aumônerie parlementaire protestante évangélique* (Paris: Cerf, 2022).

28. Stéphane Lauzet, *Bâtir des ponts. Regards sur l'origine du CNEF (1995–2010)* (Charols: Excelsis, 2024).

towards evangelical circles, through training sessions for local churches, as in 2021 during the implementation of the CRPR law which became known as the "separatism law" and was designed to address the challenge of radical religion.[29]

The CNEF is not the only network through which evangelicals work together. The main French Protestant umbrella is the French Protestant Federation (FPF), created in 1905, of which several evangelical bodies are part. But although their share is growing within the FPF council, they remain a minority, mingled in a larger Protestant family. When most French evangelicals want to express their distinctive voice, it is channelled through the CNEF, not through the FPF.

French evangelicals have no affinity for centralized institutions, far from the field; they are more comfortable in local management and the implementation of engagement dynamics in the working-class neighbourhoods, small towns and the countryside. In an IFOP survey commissioned by Protestant Family Associations in 2012, 4 percent of Lutherans and French Reformed Protestants said they were local elected officials, compared to 8 percent of evangelical Protestants.[30] This data reveals that evangelicalism is more politically involved locally than other Protestants.

Conclusion: The French Paradox

Although a majority of French evangelicals are doing well in terms of church planting, some groups are struggling. Some French evangelical churches do have to close, others are confronted by sectarian drifts, including sexual abuse. However, on a national scale French evangelicals are strongly on the rise in a society that is getting more secular year after year. This is the French paradox: the rise in secularism seems to go along well with the rise of evangelicalism. Religion and secularism are not necessarily opposed.[31] In 2023 the National Institute of Demographic Studies and the National Institute of Statistics and Economic Studies released a large study about religious affiliation in France

---

29. Nancy Lefevre, "French Secularism and the Fight Against Separatism. From the 1905 laïcité of separation to the 2021 laïcité of surveillance." *International Journal for Religious Freedom* 14.1/2 (2021): 69–84.

30. *Enquête auprès des Protestants*, IFOP survey for the Associations des Familles Protestantes (AFP), June 2012, www.ifop.com/wp-content/uploads/2018/03/2074-1-study_file.pdf.

31. Philippe Portier and Jean-Paul Willaime, *Religion and Secularism in France Today* (Abingdon: Routledge, 2022).

today.[32] Here are the main results: in 2019–2020, 51 percent of the French population aged eighteen to fifty-nine in mainland France declared that they had no religion. Increasing over the past ten years, this religious disaffiliation impacts 58 percent of people without migratory ancestry, 19 percent of immigrants arriving after the age of sixteen, and 26 percent of the descendants of two immigrant parents. While Roman Catholicism remains the leading religion, its decline is considerable. Only 29 percent of the population declares to be Catholic. Islam is claimed by a growing number of faithful (10 percent) and holds its place as the second largest religion in France. The number of people declaring another Christian religion is also increasing, reaching 9 percent. This very important number of "other Christians" surprised many observers.[33] French evangelicals are not the only ones to be part of these "other Christians." They may comprise 1.5 percent, or even a little bit more, but are far away from 9 percent of "other Christians." However, they are continually growing and attracting youth.

How to explain the paradox of this religious growth in a society which is more and more secularized? The main reason may be the powerful mix the evangelicals offer to the French population, combining strong values and beliefs with a bottom-up believer's community. The "family-like" social bond offered by French evangelical churches is based on lay involvement (men and women) and shared, gospel-based belief and practices. Roman Catholics who are tired of a pyramidal institution driven by men only sympathize with this alternative offer. They switch from the old-fashioned model of an identity through tradition and institution, to the trendy model of a chosen identity within a community of converts. This model seems to fit better with democracy and the consumer society. Secular people who are struggling with loneliness and anxiety find in these close-knit communities reasons to love and to be loved. The secular age described by Charles Taylor is not easy to handle.[34] The impact of neoliberalism on the working class leaves some individuals and families hopeless. It seems that the French paradox of a strong secular trend getting along with a rise of evangelicalism suggests to us that there may be a future for a renewal of Christianity in Europe. Seeking hope and community, a part of today's youth is longing for a faith based upon choice instead of tradition,

---

32. TEO 2 Survey (INSEE and INED, France), released in January 2023, www.insee.fr/fr/statistiques/6793308?sommaire=6793391.

33. This group of 9 percent includes Orthodox and Oriental Christians, Lutherans and Presbyterians, Prophetic and postcolonial churches, non-denominational Christians and also "internet Christians" with no particular affiliation.

34. Charles Taylor, *A Secular Age* (Cambridge: Harvard University Press, 2007).

association instead of institution, and a socialized experience of personal conversion instead of identity politics.

Bibliography

Antoine, Alexandre. *Une socio-histoire des Assemblées de Dieu en France (1909–1968); Naissance et développement d'un mouvement pentecôtiste de Réveil*. PhD Dissertation. Ecole Pratique des Hautes Etudes, Paris 2022.

Cabanel, Patrick. *Le droit de croire. La France et ses minorités religieuses, XVIe–XXIe siècle*. Paris: Passé Composé, 2024.

Decorvet, Jean, Tim Grass and Kenneth J. Stewart, eds. *The Genevan Reveil in International Perspective*. Eugene: Pickwick, 2023.

Fath, Sébastien. *Du ghetto au réseau, Le protestantisme évangélique en France (1800–2005)*. New edition. Geneva: Labor & Fides, 2005, 2018.

———. "Evangelical Protestantism in France: An example of Denominational Recomposition?" *Sociology of Religion* 66.4 (2005): 399–418.

Koop, Allen V. *American Evangelical Missionaries in France, 1945–75*. Lanham: University Press of America, 1986.

Lauzet, Stéphane. *Bâtir des ponts. Regards sur l'origine du CNEF (1995–2010)*. Charols: Excelsis, 2024.

Lefevre, Nancy. "French Secularism and the Fight Against Separatism. From the 1905 laïcité of separation to the 2021 laïcité of surveillance." *International Journal for Religious Freedom* 14.1/2 (2021): 69–84. https://ijrf.org/index.php/home/issue/view/vol14/36.

Miller Sigg, Michèle. *Birthing Revival. Women and Mission in Nineteenth-Century France*. Waco: Baylor University Press, 2022.

Portier, Philippe, and Jean-Paul Willaime. *Religion and Secularism in France Today*. Abingdon: Routledge, 2022.

15

Evangelicalism in Germany

Frank Hinkelmann

Prehistory

In Germany, one can only speak of an evangelical movement since the end of World War II in 1945.[1] At the same time, this movement has to be understood in light of its rich legacy of previous renewal movements. It is directly linked to the history of European and North American Christianity in the context of Pietism,[2] awakenings and revivals[3] and the emergence of free churches[4] during the nineteenth century. Therefore, the main pillars of the evangelical movement that emerged after World War II were the pietistic groups, the free churches and the Evangelical Alliance.[5] They held to positions of faith that were in agreement with the basic theological convictions of the evangelical movement and together with the Evangelical Alliance they had already formed a platform

---

1. On the history of the evangelical movement in Germany cf. Friedhelm Jung, *Die deutsche Evangelikale Bewegung. Grundlinien ihrer Geschichte und Theologie* (Bonn: VKW, 2011). Gisa Bauer focuses on the relationship of the evangelical movement to the Protestant Church in *Evangelikale Bewegung und evangelische Kirche in der Bundesrepublik Deutschland. Geschichte eines Grundsatzkonflikts (1945 bis 1989)*. (Arbeiten zur Kirchlichen Zeitgeschichte. Reihe B: Darstellungen 53; Göttingen: Vandenhoeck & Ruprecht, 2012).

2. Cf. Martin Brecht et al. (eds), *Geschichte des Pietismus*. 4 vols (Göttingen: Vandenhoeck & Ruprecht, 1993–2004).

3. Cf. L. Tiesmeyer, *Die Erweckungsbewegung in Deutschland*. 4 vols (Kassel: Ernst Röttger, [1902–1907]); Stephan Holthaus, *Heil – Heilung – Heiligung. Die Geschichte der deutschen Heiligungs- und Evangelisationsbewegung (1874–1909)* (Gießen: TVG Brunnen, 2005).

4. Cf. Karl Heinz Voigt, *Freikirchen in Deutschland (19. und 20. Jahrhundert)*. Kirchengeschichte in Einzeldarstellungen III/6 (Leipzig: EVA, 2004).

5. Cf. on the Evangelical Alliance Erich Beyreuther, *Der Weg der Evangelischen Allianz in Deutschland* (Wuppertal: Brockhaus, 1969).

that had been promoting cooperation across denominational boundaries since the nineteenth century.

The Beginning

The emergence of the actual evangelical movement in the German-speaking countries,[6] which also appeared under the term "evangelical" instead of "evangelisch" (Protestant), has to be understood in the context of the rise of the neo-evangelical movement in North America as a countermovement to fundamentalism. At the beginning of the 1940s, the neo-evangelicals formed the National Association of Evangelicals (NAE) in the USA. The NAE would soon influence further developments in Europe in general and in Germany in particular, especially in the person of Billy Graham.[7] As Fritz Laubach wrote in the early 1970s, ". . . the evangelical impulses that are noticeable in Germany today have jumped over like a spark from America" with explicit reference to the "New Evangelicals in North America."[8]

Graham held his first "crusade" in Germany in June 1954 and the secular media reported widely on the event. In June 1954, the weekly *Der Spiegel* even dedicated a cover story to Graham under the headline "Religion for mass consumption: God's advertising expert Billy Graham"[9] and the weekly *Die Zeit* reported under the headline "Billy Graham converted 20,000 Berliners."[10] In

---

6. Cf. on the introduction of the term "evangelikal" in German: Frank Hinkelmann, *Evangelikal in Deutschland, Österreich und der Schweiz. Ursprung, Bedeutung und Rezeption eines Begriffes* (Bonn: Verlag für Kultur und Wissenschaft, 2017); Jung, *Evangelikale Bewegung*, 22–49; and Frank Hinkelmann, "'Reizwort evangelikal' – und warum es sich trotzdem lohnt, am Begriff 'evangelikal' festzuhalten" in *Die begründete Einheit der Evangelikalen Bewegung. Christlicher Glaube in den Herausforderungen unserer Zeit*, ed. Martin Grünholz and Frank Hinkelmann (Petzenkirchen: VGTG, 2025): 75–110.

7. On Graham and his ministry in Europe and Germany, see Frank Hinkelmann, "Graham, Franklin William 'Billy'" in *Biographisch-Bibliographische Kirchenlexikon XL* (Nordhausen: Bautz, 2019), 300–28; Uta Andrea Balbier, "German Protestantism between Americanization and Rechristianization, 1954–70" in *Zeithistorische Forschungen/Studies in Contemporary History*. Online-Ausgabe 7 (2010), H. 3, https://zeithistorische-forschungen.de/3-2010/4402; Uta Balbier, *Altar Call in Europe. Billy Graham, Mass Evangelism and the Cold-War West* (New York: Oxford University Press, 2022); Matthias Dvorak, *Die Evangelisationsbewegung der Deutschen Evangelischen Allianz nach 1949* (Gießen: Unveröffentlichte Hausarbeit, 1998), 29–75; Wilhelm Brauer (ed.), *Europas Goldene Stunde. Stimmen zum Besuch Billy Grahams aus Kirche, Presse und Gemeinde* (Wuppertal: Brockhaus, [1955–1956]).

8. Fritz Laubach, *Aufbruch der Evangelikalen* (Wuppertal: Brockhaus, 1972), 83. All translations from the German are mine.

9. *Der Spiegel* 25 June 1954, 1, 21–26.

10. Elke von Merveldt, "Billy Graham bekehrt 20 000 Berliner. Der amerikanische Evangelist im Olympia-Stadion – Würstchen, Coca-Cola und Posaunen," *Die Zeit* 01.06.1954, 2.

general, it is remarkable how much space media such as *Der Spiegel* devoted to reporting on both Graham's ministry and on his person. Overall, the reports are surprisingly favourable, even if a dash of polemic was occasionally allowed. A short report from 1966 stated:

> William Franklin ("Billy") Graham, 47, American Baptist preacher (nicknamed "God's machine gun"), revealed during a sermon at the Atlanta Press Club (US state of Georgia) that God is not dead. Proof: "I spoke to him this morning."[11]

The two German rallies in 1954 took place with around forty thousand visitors in Düsseldorf's Rhine stadium and with around eighty to ninety thousand visitors in the Olympic stadium in Berlin.[12] A year later, Graham spoke again in Germany, this time in Frankfurt, Mannheim, Stuttgart, Nuremberg and Dortmund.[13] Initially, the German Evangelists' Conference under the leadership of Wilhelm Brauer acted as organizer, some representatives of the Evangelical Alliance taking a leading role from the outset.[14] From the early 1960s at the latest, the German Evangelical Alliance (DEA) assumed sole overall responsibility as organizer.[15] This was also the time when the term "evangelical" was introduced into the German language. Peter Schneider, Billy Graham's translator and later the General Secretary of the DEA, claimed to have coined the term "evangelical" in his translation of a speech by Graham, when he translated the English term "evangelical" not as "evangelisch" (Protestant) but as "evangelical" (German: evangelikal) in order to prevent the term "evangelical" from being equated with the Protestant Church.[16]

In the 1960s, not only was the term "evangelical" introduced into the German church landscape, but the Evangelical Alliance, as the main organizer of the Billy Graham rallies, increasingly moved into the foreground of the (Christian) public. It remained not only a grassroots movement, but it increasingly became a network and umbrella organization of evangelical groups; an evangelical movement with the Evangelical Alliance as its "rallying point"

---

11. *Der Spiegel* 14 March 1966, 157.
12. Cf. Wilhelm Brauer, "Ein Heroldsruf über Europa" in Brauer, *Europas goldene Stunde*, 11–12.
13. Cf. Wilhelm Brauer, "'Wenn Gottes Winde wehen . . .' Ein Gesamtbericht über Dr. Grahams Deutschlandbesuch im Juni 1955" in Brauer, *Europas goldene Stunde*, 50–54.
14. The DEA was initially quite critical of Graham's rallies and sent several observers to London in 1953 in order to get a first-hand impression of the rallies there. Cf. Dvorak, *Evangelisationsbewegung*, 32.
15. Cf. Laubach, *Aufbruch*, 83–85.
16. Cf. Hinkelmann, *Evangelikal*, 22–23.

had emerged.[17] Fritz Laubach wrote in 1972: "One thing is clear: there is also an evangelical movement in Germany, which is crystallizing mainly in the Evangelical Alliance. Things are still in flux."[18] Friedhelm Jung coined the term "Alliance evangelicals" to refer to this oldest and strongest branch of the evangelicals.[19]

Building Its Own Structures

In order to understand the developments that, from the second half of the 1960s onwards, led to the evangelical movement establishing its own structures and, in some cases, deliberately creating parallel structures to existing structures in the Protestant Church, it is important to consider the theological-historical developments during the 1960s, which were primarily reflected in the theological debate with Rudolf Bultmann's demythologization programme[20] and the theological course of ecumenism.[21] As a Protestant inner-church countermovement to theologically liberal positions, the confessional movement "No Other Gospel" (*Bekenntnisbewegung "Kein anderes Evangelium"*) was founded in March 1966.[22] A further branch of the evangelical movement thus came into being, which was to form the "confessional evangelical" branch.[23] Well-known proponents of this group were theologians such as Peter Beyerhaus,[24]

---

17. Cf. Bauer, *Evangelikale Bewegung*, 642–43.

18. Laubach, *Aufbruch*, 10–11. Cf. early publications on the relationship between evangelicals and the Evangelical Alliance: Rolf Scheffbuch, "Evangelikal: Ein neuer Begriff für eine neue Sache," *Licht & Leben* 84 (1973): 140–41; Ulrich Betz, "Evangelikale in Deutschland. Skizze einer neuen geistlichen Bewegung im deutschen Protestantismus," *Ökumenische Rundschau* 22 (1973), 309–19; Peter Schneider, "Was ist evangelikal? Versuch einer Klärung," *Neues Leben* 19 (August 1974), 5.

19. Cf. Friedhelm Jung, *Was ist evangelikal?* ideaDokumentation (Dillenburg: Christliche Verlagsgesellschaft), 18.

20. Cf. Bauer, *Evangelikale Bewegung*, 259–423.

21. Cf Peter Beyerhaus, *Christliches Zeugnis in unsere Zeit. Der Glaubenskampf der Bekennenden Gemeinschaften in Deutschland in Deutschland in autobiographischer Perspektive dargestellt*. Vol. 1 (Nürnberg: VTR, 2015).

22. On the history of the Bekenntnisbewegung cf. Roger J. Busch, *Einzug in festen Burgen? Ein kritischer Versuch, die Bekennenden Christen zu verstehen* (Hannover: Lutherisches Verlagshaus, 1995); Friedhelm Jung, "Die Entstehung der 'Bekenntnisbewegung ›Kein anderes Evangelium‹,'" in *Die evangelikale Bewegung in Württemberg und Westfalen. Anfänge und Wirkungen*, ed. Siegfried Hermle and Jürgen Kampmann (Bielefeld: Luther-Verlag, 2012), 63–73; Bauer, *Evangelikale Bewegung*, 389–423; Jung, *Evangelikale Bewegung*, 94–153.

23. Cf. Friedhelm Jung. "Was ist evangelikal?" 31–38.

24. Cf. Frank Hinkelmann, "Beyerhaus, Peter Paul Johannes," in *Biographisch-Bibliographisches Kirchenlexikon* XLIII (Nordhausen: Bautz, 2021), 170–216.

Paul Deitenbeck,[25] Gerhard Bergmann[26] and Georg Huntemann.[27] This is not the place to present and appraise the history and work of the *Bekenntnisbewegung* in detail; we can only refer to the literature already mentioned. However, these theological disputes and increasing polarization brought with them another result that had lasting and formative consequences for the German evangelical movement: the establishment of its own evangelical structures. This phase saw the founding of numerous theological training centres, such as today's Adelshofen Theological Seminary,[28] the Brake Bible School[29] and the Bergstrasse Bible School,[30] from which today's Giessen School of Theology[31] emerged. These and other training institutions joined forces in 1963 by establishing a "Society of Educational Institutions Faithful to the Bible" (*Konferenz bibeltreuer Ausbildungsstätten*).[32] In the field of missions, the "Working Group of Evangelicals Missions" (*Arbeitsgemeinschaft Evangelikaler Missionen* [AEM]) was founded.

The German AEM was founded in 1974 after the German Evangelical Mission Council had fought hard in the 1960s over the understanding of the Bible. Because of the perceived politicisation of the understanding of mission there, conservative evangelical mission organisations came together in 1968 to form the "Conference of Evangelical Missions" and organised their own conferences from 1969.[33]

---

25. Cf. Kl[aus] v. Orde, "Deitenbeck, Paul (1912–2000)" in *Evangelisches Lexikon für Theologie und Gemeinde*, 2nd ed. vol. 1, 1346–48.

26. Cf. Michael Kotsch, *Gerhard Bergmann – Der deutsche Billy Graham. Evangelist und Verteidiger der Bibel* (Niederbüren: Esras.net, 2021).

27. Cf. Frank Hinkelmann, "Huntemann, Georg" in *Biographisch-Bibliographische Kirchenlexikon* XLVIII (Nordhausen: Bautz, 2024), www.bbkl.de/index.php/frontend/lexicon/H/Hu/huntemanngeorg-80680.

28. Cf. Otto Riecker, *Mit 60 fing mein Leben an*, 2nd ed. (Neuhausen: Hänssler, 1996).

29. Cf. Stephan Holthaus, *Gott ist treu. Die Geschichte der Bibelschule Brake* (Bielefeld: CLV, 1995).

30. Heute BibelStudienKolleg.

31. Cf. Stephan Holthaus, *Unglaublich. Impressionen von Gottes Wirken in 50 Jahren FTH* (Gießen: Freie Theologische Hochschule, 2024).

32. Cf. H[orst]. Afflerbach, "Konferenz bibeltreuer Ausbildungsstätten (KBA)" in *Evangelisches Lexikon für Theologie und Gemeinde*, 2nd ed. vol. 2, 2033–34.

33. D[etlef]. Blöcher, "Arbeitsgemeinschaft Evangelikaler Mission (AEM)" in *Evangelisches Lexikon für Theologie und Gemeinde*, 2nd ed. vol. 1, 398–404; Laubach, *Aufbruch*, 90–93.

Today, the AEM is the largest umbrella organization of mission agencies with over 100 member organizations and around 4,000 missionaries sent out.[34]

Separate institutions in the media sector followed suit. *Evangeliumsrundfunk* (ERF), an evangelical radio station and partner of Trans World Radio, was founded in 1959. It has been producing and broadcasting radio and television programmes as ERF Medien e. V. to this day.[35] In 1970, idea was founded,[36] initially understood as an information service of the Evangelical Alliance, but which established itself as a separate organization in 1972. idea began as a press service and was soon also published in English

> ... and summarised the most important German evangelical news for abroad. This was supplemented by the approximately monthly themed issues of "ideaDokumentation." From 1978, "ideaSpektrum," the magazine that has since established itself as the leading evangelical periodical, appeared once a week. As early as 1981, "ideaSpektrum" had over 4,000 regular subscribers. The magazine was very quickly able to conquer and consolidate its monopoly position on the evangelical magazine market.[37]

With a circulation of over twenty thousand copies, ideaSpektrum is the German Christian print medium with the highest distribution.[38] Other evangelical organizations worth mentioning at this point, which emerged primarily in the 1970s and are still active today, include the *Arbeitskreis für evangelikale Theologie* (AfeT),[39] where evangelical theologians meet, the *Arbeitskreis für evangelikale Missiologie* (AfeM), which was renamed the *Evangelischer Arbeitskreis für Mission, Kultur und Religion* e. V. – Missiotop in 2015,[40] in which mission-related issues are discussed at an academic level and which also publishes its own journal, as well as the *Institut für Islamfragen* e. V. (IfI),[41] which researches the relationship between Christianity and Islam. In the area

---

34. Blöcher, "Arbeitsgemeinschaft," 400.
35. Cf. Hanni Lützenberger, ... *aber Gottes Wort ist nicht gebunden. Evangeliums-Rundfunk: Auftrag und Dienst* (Wetzlar: ERF-Verlag, 1977); Horst Marquardt, *Meine Geschichte mit dem Evangeliums-Rundfunk. Warten – Wunder – Wellen* (Holzgerlingen: Hänssler, 2002); Laubach, *Aufbruch*, 87–90.
36. Cf. J[oachim]. Cochlovius, "Allianz, Evangelische in Deutschland (Werke und Einrichtungen)" in *Evangelisches Lexikon für Theologie und Gemeinde*, 2nd ed. vol. 2, 120.
37. Bauer, *Evangelikale Bewegung*, 644.
38. As of 2017. Cf. Cochlovius, "Allianz," 120.
39. Cochlovius, "Allianz," 117.
40. Cf. Cochlovius, "Allianz," 119.
41. Cf. Cochlovius, "Allianz," 120–21.

of relief and humanitarian work, *Hilfe für Brüder* e. V.[42] was founded in 1980 on the initiative of the DEA and the AEM, from the latter in turn *Christliche Fachkräfte International* e. V (CFI) was founded in 1984.[43] *Hilfe für Brüder* e. V. and CFI have been operating together under the umbrella brand Coworkers for the last couple of years.

Even though the confessional movement No Other Gospel contributed to the shaping of the German evangelical movement through its theological engagement in the 1960s and 1970s, which in turn motivated the introduction of evangelical parallel structures in the church sector, its influence on the evangelical movement waned in the 1990s, partly due to internal conflicts.[44] Despite this fact, one thing was successful: "The DEA increasingly profiled itself as a 'rallying point for evangelicals.'"[45]

Reconciliation

The emergence of the Pentecostal movement at the beginning of the twentieth century led to a split in the evangelical camp in Germany. A decisive role in this development was played by the Berlin Declaration of 1909, in which leading representatives of the popular church community movement had distanced themselves from the Pentecostal movement emerging out of their groups. They had even come to the conclusion that the Pentecostal movement was of demonic origin and therefore "from below," as was the terminology used.[46] This historic split among evangelicals meant that in Germany the Pentecostal movement and, since the 1970s, the charismatic movement were excluded from participating in the Evangelical Alliance, the rallying point of the evangelical movement. In this respect the situation in Germany differed from that in most other countries where an Evangelical Alliance existed. But Friedhelm Jung was surely correct when he noted:

---

42. Cf. Cochlovius, "Allianz," 120.

43. Cf. Cochlovius, "Allianz," 119.

44. Cf. Frank Lüdke, "Evangelikales Christentum" in Markus Mühling (ed.), *Kirchen und Konfession* (Grundwissen Christentum 2; Göttingen: Vandenhoeck & Ruprecht, 2009), 165; Hinkelmann, "Beyerhaus," www.bbkl.de/index.php/frontend/lexicon/B/Be/beyerhauspeter-85452.

45. Bauer, *Evangelikale Bewegung*, 638.

46. R[olf]. Hille, "Berliner Erklärung" in *Evangelisches Lexikon für Theologie und Gemeinde*, 2nd ed. vol. 1, 771–73; cf. the wording of the Berlin declaration as well as further documents on the issue at www.glopent.net/iak-pfingstbewegung/Members/GerhardBially/berliner-erklaerung.

The Pentecostal churches and especially the charismatic groups in the Federal Republic of Germany should definitely be counted as part of the evangelical movement, not only because Pentecostals and charismatics describe themselves as "evangelical," but also because of their basic theological position, which largely coincides with that of the German Evangelical Alliance (DEA).[47]

Yet it was not until the 1990s that the Evangelical Alliance and representatives of the Pentecostal movement came closer together, resulting in July 1996 in a joint declaration in Kassel, which led to a common understanding and cooperation.[48] Today, the decades-long split between the Pentecostal movement and the Evangelical Alliance has been completely overcome and Pentecostal leaders and churches are fully integrated into the Evangelical Alliance. The Pentecostal evangelicals form a third important pillar of today's evangelical movement, especially due to the growth of the Pentecostal movement.

The Independent Evangelicals

In addition to the three branches of the German evangelical movement mentioned above, a fourth branch has emerged since the 1980s that has hardly been recognized to date but can no longer be overlooked due to its size and dynamism. These are the independent evangelicals, whose theology is strictly evangelical but who do not feel connected to any of the three previous evangelical branches. They include both the churches of repatriated Russian-Germans and the churches that cooperate in the Conference for Church Planting (*Konferenz für Gemeindegründung*), which are characterized by a Darbystic type of piety and a strong missionary impetus.[49] Independent Brethren churches that have not joined the Christusforum should also be included. I call this independent fourth branch of the evangelical movement the "free evangelicals" and I will now discuss its three components.

When they arrived in Germany, many of the Russian-German re-settlers often felt that the local congregations they found were not Bible-orientated enough. This problem was compounded by their different cultural background, so that many Russian-Germans did not find a spiritual home in any of the existing congregations and free churches (with the exception of the Baptist Union)

---

47. Jung, *Evangelikale Bewegung*, 153.
48. Cf. Hille, "Berliner Erklärung," 772–73, www.ead.de/fileadmin/DEA_Allgemein/Stellungnahmen/KasselerErklaerung96.pdf.
49. Jung, *Evangelikale Bewegung*, 167–68.

and instead decided to establish their own congregations. These congregations are organized in various associations.[50] "A survey of Protestant churches and free churches in the late 1990s revealed that fifteen of the twenty-five best-attended Protestant services in Germany were of Russian-German free church congregations."[51] Due to the steady influx of ethnic German repatriates, their congregations experienced rapid growth until the mid-1990s, but this levelled off at an annual growth rate of ten percent by the early 2000s.[52] Unfortunately, there are no more recent figures available.

The Darbystic "Conference for Church Planting" was founded in 1977 and around two hundred churches feel connected to it, both recently established congregations and longstanding Darbyst Brethren fellowships.[53] The exclusive Brethren congregations should also be mentioned here. Jung estimates the number of both groups together at around twenty to thirty thousand believers.[54] Holthaus characterizes these free evangelical groups as follows:

> They clearly distance themselves from the Roman Catholic Church. They reject the Pentecostal and charismatic movements and criticise the new, more open course of the Evangelical Alliance. It remains to be seen to what extent some of these groups can be labelled "evangelical." At least in Germany, their weight is not insignificant.[55]

Globalization

We now turn to a final branch of the evangelical movement, which I call "migrant evangelicals." Although there have been ethnic congregations in Germany in the past, they have seen extraordinary growth in recent years. The total number of Christians with a migration background in Germany is estimated at around ten million.[56] While many of these ethnic congregations of migrants

---

50. E.g. the *Bruderschaft der Christengemeinden* (Brotherhood of Christian Churches), the *Vereinigung der Evangeliums-Christen-Baptistengemeinden* (Association of Evangelical Christian Baptist Churches), the *Bund Taufgesinnter Gemeinden* (Federation of Baptist Churches) and the *Arbeitsgemeinschaft evangelikaler Gemeinden* (Association of Evangelical Churches). Cf. Jung, *Evangelikale Bewegung*, 168–70.
51. Jung, *Evangelikale Bewegung*, 169.
52. Jung, *Evangelikale Bewegung*, 171.
53. Jung, *Evangelikale Bewegung*, 172.
54. Jung, *Evangelikale Bewegung*, 172–73.
55. Holthaus, *Evangelikalen*, 50.
56. Cf. www.hanns-lilje-stiftung.de/aktuell/news/2019/2019_10_18.

in the Pentecostal church have joined the Association of Pentecostal Churches, the majority remain independent and are often not in contact with German congregations. It is quite difficult to record these congregations statistically, as there is often a lack of data and information.

> The entire spectrum of global Protestantism is reflected in around 2,000 to 3,000 Protestant migrant congregations in Germany with around 100,000 to 300,000 members. These figures can only be roughly estimated because new congregations are being founded every week. About half of these churches were founded by pastors from Africa . . . and about a quarter by Asian church leaders . . . Increasingly, Arabic and Farsi-speaking congregations are forming.[57]

Overall, the figure of two to three thousand migrant congregations in Germany seems to me to be far too low. In terms of classification, the Evangelical Church in Germany (EKD) provided a helpful typology of migrant congregations:

1. "Established denominational diaspora congregations" create a spiritual and socio-cultural home for the community from one denomination and one region of origin. Most European Protestant congregations belong to this category . . . They were often founded by the churches of origin.

2. "Free church mission congregations" invite migrants to the Christian faith who come from countries that hinder Christian mission. These include China, Vietnam, Iran, Turkey and the Arab states. They are supported by German and international mission agencies.

3. "Reverse mission churches" are charismatic Pentecostal or African-independent churches with strong links to their mother churches in Africa or Korea. They see themselves as international churches that also want to reach Germans in a missionary way.

4. "Independent, non-denominational new mission churches" also come from Central and West Africa and are similar to type 3. They

---

57. Gregor Etzelmüller and Claudia Rammelt, "Migrationskirchen: Internationalisierung und Pluralisierung des Christentums vor Ort" in *Krisen – Aufbrüche – Transformationen. Zur Sozialität der Evangelischen Kirche*, ed. Traugott Jähnichen et al., (Jahrbuch Sozialer Protestantismus 12 Leipzig: EVA, 2019), 217–18.

have emerged here as independent congregations and have little contact with their churches of origin.[58]

An important question for the future will be to what extent the evangelical movement will succeed in integrating migrants into the German evangelical movement. As Rolf Hille already wrote in 2007:

> The evangelical movement has great opportunities, not least if it utilises its global network. Evangelical groups in the traditional churches in the West should allow themselves to be infected by the missionary open-mindedness of the growing churches in Africa, Asia and Latin America. This could blow away the dust of ecclesiastical resignation.[59]

The Twenty-First Century: Assessing the Current State

Since its emergence in the 1960s, the German evangelical movement has developed into a permanent fixture in Protestantism with a representative body in the Evangelical Alliance, which represents large sections of the evangelical movement in Germany. The largest group within the evangelical movement are the so-called Alliance evangelicals. While the so-called confessional evangelicals were initially in second place in terms of numbers, their influence has declined rapidly since the 1990s. Their place has been taken by the so-called Pentecostal evangelicals, who, together with the free evangelicals and the migration evangelicals, form the other large branches of today's evangelical movement.

It remains difficult to establish the numbers. In the year 2000, Friedhelm Jung wrote:

> Previous studies on the German evangelical movement assumed that a total of around one million evangelical Christians can be expected. The alliance evangelicals number around 500,000, the confessional evangelicals 300,000 and the Pentecostal evangelicals around 200,000. The growth of the evangelicals has been fuelled primarily by the influx of evangelical immigrants. The fourth branch of the evangelical movement described above, the

---

58. Cf. https://internationale-gemeinden.de/was-verstehen-wir-unter-einer-internationalen-gemeinde/.
59. Rolf Hille, "Global Player," *Christliches Medienmagazin pro* (1.2007), 11.

independent evangelicals, unites around 300,000 believers, so that today a total of around 1.3 million evangelicals can be assumed.[60]

In the past twenty-five years, the positions have shifted again. The number of confessional evangelicals has decreased drastically during this period, while the number of Pentecostal evangelicals has certainly grown significantly. The *Evangelisches Sonntagsblatt*, for example, puts the number of Pentecostal evangelicals in Germany in 2021 at eight hundred and fifty thousand,[61] a figure that seems inflated to me. In addition, we lack reliable data for the migration evangelicals. The total number of evangelicals cited in 2007 varied between 1.3 million[62] and 1.4 million.[63] More recent data is not available – apart from the significantly inflated figure of 2.5 million evangelicals from the World Christian Database.[64] The EAD itself endeavours to be cautious about current figures.[65]

With regard to the future prospects of the evangelical movement in Germany, I would like to conclude with the words of Stephan Holthaus from 2007, which have lost none of their relevance to this day:

> It will therefore be necessary for the future of the evangelical movement in Germany to work on its own identity. The diversity of forms of piety and church backgrounds must not lead to the commonalities no longer being visible. Concentrating on the essential elements of biblical teaching is the only way in which evangelicals can gain relevance in society as a whole. The Bible, conversion, church and mission as its four basic pillars must once again come more into focus. . . . The theological centre of the evangelicals is also at risk. The range of views here has now become so wide that there are serious concerns about the cohesion of the

---

60. Jung, *Evangelikale Bewegung*, 173.

61. Cf. www.sonntagsblatt.de/artikel/pfingstkirchen-pfingstbewegung-fakten-evangelische-kirche#:~:text=In%20Deutschland%20ist%20die%20Pfingstbewegung,die%20insgesamt%20850.000%20Mitglieder%20haben. The World Christian Database even estimates 1.25 million Pentecostals and 1.282 million Evangelicals in Germany in 2020. (The World Christian Database differentiates between Pentecostals and evangelicals, see Kenneth R. Ross, Annemarie C. Mayer and Todd M. Johnson (eds), *Christianity in Western and Northern Europe* (Edinburgh Companion to Global Christianity; Edinburgh: Edinburgh University Press, 2024), 111.

62. Peter Strauch, "Wo steht die Evangelikale Bewegung?," *ideaSpektrum* 1/2 (2007), 22.

63. Stephan Holthaus, "Die Evangelikalen: Plädoyer für einen fairen Umgang," *Christliches Medienmagazin pro* 1 (2007), 5. Holthaus also spoke in the same year of 1.3 million, see Holthaus, *Evangelikalen*, 20.

64. Cf. Ross et al., *Christianity*, 111. I have added the numbers given for evangelicals and Pentecostals.

65. Email from the chair of the EAD, Reinhardt Schink, to the author dated 6 September 2024.

movement. Familiarity with the Bible has also decreased rather than increased. Even basic theological and ethical convictions are no longer familiar to some. The future of the movement as a whole will depend not least on whether this development can be halted and a lively, healthy theology restored.[66]

Bibliography

Balbier, Uta Andrea. "German Protestantism between Americanization and Rechristianization, 1954–70." In *Zeithistorische Forschungen/Studies in Contemporary History*. Online-Ausgabe 7 (2010), H. 3. https://zeithistorische-forschungen.de/3-2010/4402.

Bauer, Gisa. *Evangelikale Bewegung und evangelische Kirche in der Bundesrepublik Deutschland. Geschichte eines Grundsatzkonflikts (1945 bis 1989)*. Arbeiten zur Kirchlichen Zeitgeschichte. Reihe B: Darstellungen 53. Göttingen: Vandenhoeck & Ruprecht, 2012.

Betz, Ulrich. "Evangelikale in Deutschland. Skizze einer neuen geistlichen Bewegung im deutschen Protestantismus." *Ökumenische Rundschau* 22 (1973): 309–19.

Beyreuther, Erich. *Der Weg der Evangelischen Allianz in Deutschland*. Wuppertal: Brockhaus, 1969.

Hinkelmann, Frank. *Evangelikal in Deutschland, Österreich und der Schweiz. Ursprung, Bedeutung und Rezeption eines Begriffes*. Bonn: Verlag für Kultur und Wissenschaft, 2017.

Holthaus, Stephan. *Heil – Heilung – Heiligung. Die Geschichte der deutschen Heiligungs- und Evangelisationsbewegung (1874–1909)*. Gießen: TVG Brunnen, 2005.

———. *Die Evangelikalen. Fakten und Perspektiven*. Lahr: Verlag der St. Johannis-Druckerei, 2007.

Holthaus, Stephan (ed.). *Die Evangelikalen – wie sie wirklich sind. Daten und Fakten, die jeder kennen sollte*. idea-Dokumentation 3/2011. Bonn: VKW, 2011.

Jung, Friedhelm. *Die deutsche Evangelikale Bewegung. Grundlinien ihrer Geschichte und Theologie*. 4th ed. (= 3rd ed. 2001). Bonn: VKW, 2011.

Laubach, Fritz. *Aufbruch der Evangelikalen*. Wuppertal: Brockhaus, 1972.

Voigt, Karl Heinz. *Freikirchen in Deutschland (19. und 20. Jahrhundert)*. Kirchengeschichte in Einzeldarstellungen III/6. Leipzig: Evangelische Verlagsanstalt, 2004.

---

66. Holthaus, *Evangelikalen*, 96–97.

16

Evangelicalism in the Republic of Ireland

Patrick Mitchel

Introduction

David Bebbington, concluding his study on evangelicalism in modern Britain, wrote that "nothing could be further from the truth than the common image of evangelicalism being ever the same."¹ In this vein, the story of evangelical Christians in Ireland provides an example of how a religious identity adapts to, and is influenced by, its changing political and social context.² Broadly speaking, three historical phases in that story can be identified. The first was "Protestant and British"; the highpoint of evangelical political influence in nineteenth century Ireland.³ The second was "Identity in Opposition"; evangelical experience of exclusion by twentieth-century "moral monopoly" Catholicism in the newly independent Irish state.⁴ A third phase, "Post-Christendom

---

1. David W. Bebbington, *Evangelicalism in Modern Britain: A History from the 1730s to the 1980s* (London: Unwin Hyman, 1989), 271.

2. In this chapter, "Ireland" refers to the twenty-six-county Republic of Ireland and does not include the six counties of Northern Ireland that lie in the United Kingdom.

3. Key works include Desmond Bowen, *The Protestant Crusade in Ireland 1800–70* (Dublin: Gill & Macmillan, 1978); Miriam Moffett, *The Society for Irish Church Missions to the Roman Catholics, 1849–1950* (Manchester: Manchester University Press, 2010); and Irene Whelan, *The Bible War in Ireland: The "Second Reformation" and the Polarization of Protestant-Catholic Relations, 1800–1840* (Dublin: Lilliput Press, 2005).

4. For discussion of this period see Patrick Mitchel, "Evangelicals and Irish Identity in Independent Ireland: A Case Study" in *Irish Protestant Identities*, ed. M. Busteed, F. Neal and J. Tonge (Manchester: Manchester University Press, 2008), 155–70; Patrick Mitchel, "Evangelical Diversity" in *Evangelicals in Ireland*, ed. R. Dunlop (Dublin: Columba Press, 2005), 140–69.

Diversity," is the focus of this chapter and refers to today's socially liberal and increasingly heterogenous Ireland. As we shall see, the context and character of contemporary Irish evangelicalism is markedly different to that of phases one and two.

Since the 1990s Ireland is experiencing dramatic religious, social, economic and political upheaval, resulting in a remarkable transformation of culture and society.[5] Two changes have particularly impacted the experience of Irish evangelicals: the sudden and shocking advent of Irish post-Christendom and the onset of significant religious diversity. Each is discussed in turn below, followed by reflections on challenges facing evangelicals in contemporary Ireland.

The Collapse of Catholic Ireland

Crawford Gribben concludes that Christian Ireland is "dead and gone, and Catholic politicians buried it."[6] The fact that few people would disagree with his assessment is testament to the pervasive and stunning Irish experience of secularization.[7] While liberalization was inevitable and had been signposted by the decriminalization of same-sex relationships in 1993 and the narrow passing of divorce in a national vote in 1995,[8] the moral authority of the Catholic Church collapsed in the light of one horrendous abuse scandal after another, coupled with the exposure of flagrant hypocrisy by leading clerics.[9] When faced with mounting allegations in the 1990s, ecclesiastical responses followed a repeated pattern of denial and cover-up.[10] In 2011, Enda Kenny, then Taoiseach (Prime

---

5. See for example Tom Inglis, *Moral Monopoly: The Rise and Fall of the Catholic Church in Modern Ireland*, 2nd ed. (Dublin: University College Dublin Press, 1998); Dairmaid Ferriter, *The Transformation of Ireland 1900–2000* (Dublin: Profile Books, 2005); Micheál MacGréil, *Pluralism and Diversity in Ireland: Prejudice and Related Issues in Early 21st Century Ireland* (Dublin: Columba Press, 2011); and Sara O'Sullivan, *Contemporary Ireland: A Sociological Map* (Dublin: UCD Press, 2016).

6. Crawford Gribben, *The Rise and Fall of Christian Ireland* (Oxford: Oxford University Press, 2021), 205.

7. For detailed discussion see Gladys Ganiel, "Ireland After Secularization" in *The Oxford Handbook of Religion in Modern Ireland*, ed. Gladys Ganiel and Andrew Holmes (Oxford: Oxford University Press, 2024), 323–40.

8. The Divorce Referendum of 1995 was passed by 50.28 percent to 49.72 percent.

9. For detailed analysis see Carolyn M. Warner, "Benevolent Secularism and the Recalibration of Church–State Relations in Ireland in the Aftermath of the Clergy Child Sex Abuse Scandals," *Journal of Church and State* 62.1 (2020): 86–109; doi:10.1093/jcs/csz092.

10. A seminal television programme was Mary Raftery's "States of Fear" on RTE exposing the horrors of institutional "care." See also Mary Raftery and Eoin O'Sullivan, *Suffer the Little Children: The Inside Story of Ireland's Industrial Schools* (London: Continuum, 2001); Hugh Turpin, *Unholy Catholic Ireland: Religious Hypocrisy, Secular Morality, and Irish Irreligion*

Minister), announced the bitter dissolution of a relationship that had shaped the nation since independence. In a scathing Dáil (Irish Parliament) speech in which he responded to the Cloyne Report on sexual abuse,[11] he accused the Vatican of an attempt to

> frustrate an inquiry in a sovereign, democratic republic as little as three years ago, not three decades ago. And in doing so, the Cloyne report excavates the dysfunction, the disconnection, the elitism that dominate the culture of the Vatican today. The rape and the torture of children were downplayed or managed to uphold, instead, the primacy of the institution, its power, its standing, and its reputation . . . I want to make it clear, as Taoiseach, that when it comes to the protection of the children of this State, the standards of conduct which the Church deems appropriate to itself, cannot and will not, be applied to the workings of democracy and civil society in this republic.[12]

Symptoms of life in post-Catholic Ireland abound. Mass attendance, comfortably above 90 percent in the 1970s, was at 27 percent before COVID-19 but is now lower.[13] According to a former Archbishop of Dublin it is down to 2 percent in some inner-city areas of the capital.[14] One of the fastest growing groups identified in the 2022 census is those with "no religion," with 736,210 persons in this category representing over 14 percent of the population and an increase of 63 percent since the 2016 census, and of 187 percent since 2011.[15] In the 2022 census 69 percent of people identified as Roman Catholic, a 10 percent drop from 2016, a downward trend set to continue. Vocations have virtually collapsed, with St Patrick's College Maynooth, the ecclesiastical centre

---

(Stanford: Stanford University Press, 2022); and James Gallen, "The Abuse Crises in the Irish Christian Churches" in Ganiel and Holmes, *Oxford Handbook*, 378–95.

11. The Cloyne Report was the result of an investigation by a commission in the Catholic Diocese of Cloyne.

12. Enda Kenny, "Dáil Motion: Commission of Investigation Report in the Catholic Diocese of Cloyne," 20 July 2011, https://en.wikisource.org/wiki/D%C3%A1il_Motion:_Commission_of_Investigation_Report_in_the_Catholic_Diocese_of_Cloyne.

13. Iona Institute, *Mass Going During and After the Pandemic*, https://ionainstitute.ie/wp-content/uploads/2020/09/MASSGOING-COVID_Survey.pdf.

14. Patsy McGarry, "Mass Attendance to Drop One-Third by 2030," *Irish Times*, 21 January 2016, www.irishtimes.com/news/social-affairs/religion-and-beliefs/mass-attendance-in-dublin-to-drop-by-one-third-by-2030-1.2504351.

15. Central Statistics Office (CSO), www.cso.ie/en/releasesandpublications/ep/p-cpp5/census2022profile5-diversitymigrationethnicityirishtravellersreligion/religion/. See also Hugh Turpin, "The Rise of 'No Religion'" in Ganiel and Holmes, *Oxford Handbook*, 561–78.

of Catholic Ireland, now being the sole surviving seminary in the country, with a fraction of its past intake of students. Remarkably, Ireland became the first country in the world to legalize same-sex marriage via a decisive majority in a 2015 referendum. This followed the introduction of civil partnership for same-sex couples in 2010. Positive attitudes towards LGBTQ+ inclusion, coupled with fluid understandings of gender identity, are also increasingly influential.[16] More significantly, given that a deep-rooted religious and emotional opposition to abortion was a core value of Catholic Ireland, a 2018 referendum was passed with a two-thirds majority allowing unrestricted abortion up to twelve weeks gestation or later in exceptional circumstances.[17] Widespread public celebrations afterwards were a stark reminder of how far and fast liberal values had displaced Christian beliefs about the sanctity of all life. It is likely that legislation on euthanasia will continue this trend.[18]

Care is needed not to caricature here; it is not as if Catholicism is no longer significant in Irish culture[19] nor has personal faith "disappeared."[20] Nevertheless, the reality is that a large (especially younger) section of the population now perceives Christianity as an *obstacle* to social progress. Elsewhere I have written of how a post-Christendom liberal secular democracy espouses values (pluralism, equality, tolerance, choice and separation of church and state) that it believes will lead to a healthier, fairer and more advanced society than that of the past. Each value stands in *contrast* to what Christianity is perceived to

---

16. A Gender Recognition Act was passed in 2015 enabling a person to apply to have their preferred gender recognized by the state. In 2017 Leo Varadkar became Ireland's first openly gay Taoiseach.

17. These circumstances include "a serious risk to the life or serious harm to the health of the pregnant woman" or the expectation that the foetus is likely to die within twenty-eight days of birth. See the Health (Regulation of Termination of Pregnancy) Act 2018, www.irishstatutebook.ie/eli/2018/act/31/enacted/en/print.html.

18. As I write, a "Dying with Dignity 2020" Bill aimed at making provision for "assistance in achieving a dignified and peaceful end of life" is currently at the Third Stage of consideration before Dáil Éireann.

19. At an institutional level the Church still runs, with state funding, nearly 90 percent of state primary schools; it is a major owner of healthcare facilities; and it is a key provider of voluntary organizations delivering disability provision and one quarter of acute care hospitals in the country. Warner, "Benevolent," 105. At a personal level, "being Catholic" now equates more to cultural heritage rather than to commitment to the institutional church. See Tom Inglis, "Being Catholic in Ireland" in Ganiel and Holmes, *Oxford Handbook*, 361–77.

20. In research on religious practice in contemporary Ireland, Ganiel identified the rise of what she terms "extra-institutional religion": people practising their faith outside, or in addition to, the institutional Catholic Church. Gladys Ganiel, *Transforming Post-Catholic Ireland: Religious Practice in Late Modernity* (Oxford: Oxford University Press, 2016).

represent.²¹ As Colin Marshall memorably put it, with the demise of Christendom, religion tends to be viewed "as a trivial, if not malign, influence in political life . . . it is no longer accepted that Christian theology trades in public truth; it simply articulates the beliefs of a minority of 'cognitive deviants' in the population."²²

Migrant Christians

The second significant change in Irish religious culture has been the arrival of Christians into the state from all over the world. Around 40 percent of non-Irish born immigrants are non-Catholic, especially those from Asia and Africa.²³ The 2022 census recorded nearly 632,000 non-Irish citizens, 12 percent of the population. The Irish experience of immigration has been distinct in its rapidity and lateness. By 2022 there were over one hundred thousand Orthodox Christians (Greek, Coptic and Russian) in Ireland, an increase of 65 percent in six years and of 128 percent since the 2011 census.²⁴ Putin's war on Ukraine led to over one hundred thousand Ukrainian refugees arriving in Ireland between February 2022 and February 2024,²⁵ many of whom are committed believers. Evidence is anecdotal, but I have been told several stories of small rural evangelical churches more than doubling in size overnight with the arrival of Ukrainian or African Christians due to the Irish government policy of decentralizing its international protection centres.²⁶ Many churches now have congregants from twenty or thirty nationalities, drawn from India, Latin

---

21. Patrick Mitchel, "Sex, Truth and Tolerance: Some theological reflections on the Irish Civil Partnership Bill 2010 and challenges facing Christians in a post-Christendom Culture," *Evangelical Quarterly* 84.2 (2012), 155–73.

22. Colin Marshall, "What Language Shall I Borrow?; The Bilingual Dilemma of Public Theology," *Evangel* 24.2 (2006): 45–52, here 47–48.

23. Vladimir Kmec, "Minority Religions and Immigration in Ireland" in Ganiel and Holmes, *Oxford Handbook*, 522–41, here 524. In the 2022 census the number of people who identified as Black or Black Irish-African was 67,546, up 17 percent from 2016. A further 8,699 people identified as Black or Black Irish-any other Black background, up 28 percent since the previous census. An Asian or Asian Irish-Chinese ethnicity was recorded by 26,828 people, up 38 percent. There were 44,944 people who identified as Asian or Asian Irish-any other Asian background and the number of people who selected the Mixed or Other categories was 64,992. See www.cso.ie/en/releasesandpublications/ep/p-cpp5/censusofpopulation2022profile5-diversitymigrationethnicityirishtravellersreligion/ethnicgroupbackground/.

24. See www.cso.ie/en/releasesandpublications/ep/p-cpp5/censusofpopulation2022profile5-diversitymigrationethnicityirishtravellersreligion/religion/.

25. See https://emn.ie/new-data-on-arrivals-from-ukraine-in-csos-latest-release-3/.

26. In 2024 there were forty-eight of these centres in Ireland, see www.hiqa.ie/sites/default/files/2024-01/IPAS-FAQs.pdf.

America (especially Brazil), numerous African countries (especially Nigeria), China, Romania, the Philippines, India, South Korea and so on. A significant proportion of these migrants bring their (predominantly Pentecostal) faith with them. Some have formed migrant communities and others become part of established churches; both developments are discussed below.

Migrant Churches and Networks

There are good reasons why immigrants form their own religious communities. They provide a familiar and welcoming relational network with others who share the same ethnic, national, denominational background and, most crucially, a common language.[27] The work of Abel Ugba among Pentecostal African immigrants is illustrative in this regard.[28] Ugba writes that their arrival "represented dramatic and innovative changes [to the] religious landscape of Ireland"[29] with migrant churches functioning as "dynamic community institutions and the fulcrum of social and cultural activities of many African immigrants."[30] Yet even he, as an African, was an "outsider within," mainly due to his non-Pentecostal convictions. These sorts of factors lie behind why Nick Park, executive director of the Evangelical Alliance Ireland (EAI), writes of a *hidden* "religious revolution" taking place "under our noses." He tells the story of tourists and Irish people walking by a historic church in Dublin's city centre, blithely unaware that inside the building is packed with nine hundred Romanian Pentecostal worshippers.[31] However, over time some migrant churches have become highly visible. For example, in West Dublin one of the most ambitious church buildings constructed in Ireland in decades is called Betina, a Romanian Pentecostal church. The 1,200-seater building, largely built and funded by the community themselves at a cost of over €8 million, was officially opened in September 2022 by Leo Varadkar, the local member of parliament, then Tánaiste (Deputy Prime Minister) and twice Taoiseach of

---

27. Kmec, "Minority Religions," 523.

28. Abel Ugba, *Shades of Belonging: African Pentecostals in Twenty-First Century Ireland* (Trenton: Africa World Press, 2009).

29. Abel Ugba, "Researching African Immigrant Religions: Boundaries, Belonging, and Access" in *African Traditions in the Study of Religion, Diaspora and Gendered Societies*, ed. Ezra Chitando, Afe Adogame and Bolajo Bateye (London: Routledge, 2016), 85–98, see 2.

30. Ugba, "Researching African," 3–4.

31. Nick Park, "A Religious Revolution is Taking Place in Ireland," *Irish Times*, 25 May 2017, www.irishtimes.com/opinion/a-religious-revolution-is-taking-place-in-ireland-1.3092198.

Ireland.³² The symbolism of such an event is remarkable given the religious history of independent Ireland.

Such Christians have helped to transform a formerly homogenous religious landscape.³³ Most churches near main population centres have become ethnically diverse in a manner that was inconceivable even in the 1990s. The current membership of the Irish Council of Churches, formed in 1923 and comprised of a range of Protestant denominations, now includes various strands of Orthodox communions such as the Malankara (Indian) Orthodox Church,³⁴ alongside predominantly Nigerian Pentecostal denominations such as the Redeemed Christian Church of God (RCCG) and the Cherubim and Seraphim Church.³⁵ The first RCCG parish in Ireland dates back to 1998. By 2017 there were around two hundred parishes (individual churches) of various sizes in the Republic,³⁶ with an overall membership of probably over ten thousand.³⁷

Two other examples of migrant church networks, among many, help to illustrate contemporary diversity.³⁸ The Chinese Gospel Church of Ireland

---

32. Varadkar served as Taoiseach from June 2017 till June 2020 and from December 2022 till March 2024, see www.irishtimes.com/ireland/social-affairs/2022/09/25/new-church-for-romanian-community-in-ireland-officially-opened/.

33. Mimi Kelly, "Ireland" in Michael Wilkinson (ed.), *Brill's Encyclopedia of Global Pentecostalism* (Leiden: Brill, 2021), 332–34, who notes that the 2008 *Directory of Migrant-led churches and Chaplaincies*, produced by the All-Ireland Churches Consultative Meeting on Racism, listed some 361 faith communities.

34. See www.irishchurches.org/members/indian-orthodox-church. https://indianorthodoxuk.org/parishes/ireland.

35. The website of the latter says that "The first church was inaugurated in Ireland in 1998 and now has seven branches with over 600 members in Dublin, Limerick, Galway and Cork." See www.irishchurches.org/members/cherubim-and-seraphim.

36. See www.vox.ie/001/2017/4/11/the-changing-face-of-christianity-in-ireland.

37. In 2012 there were 118 parishes with an estimated membership of seven thousand, see www.irishchurches.org/members/redeemed-christian-church-of-god. In 2011 my wife and I attended the annual Holy Ghost service in City West in Dublin. Ganiel estimates twenty thousand attended making it probably the largest non-Catholic religious gathering in the history of the state. Ganiel, *Transforming*, 159. For further reading see her chapter on The Jesus Centre in Dublin, the national headquarters of the RCCG in Ireland.

38. Examples include Christ Apostolic Church (CAC), a Nigerian denomination consisting of congregations in Dublin, Drogheda, Dundalk, Cavan, Galway and Midleton in Co. Cork; and Christian Congregation in Ireland, an international, Pentecostal and non-denominational fellowship, comprizing mostly of Brazilians (www.ccirl.ie/). Brazilian churches which have established branches in Ireland include Snowball Church Ireland (Bola de Neve Irlanda, see https://linktr.ee/snowballchurchireland) and Lagoinha Church (see www.facebook.com/lagoinhadublinchurch/?locale=nl_BE). The Indian Pentecostal Church of God established itself in Ireland in 2006. Its primary constituency are Malayalam speaking Keralite nurses and their families who arrived in Ireland in significant numbers since 2000, see www.ipcireland.org/about-us/.

(CGCI) traces its origins to the early 1980s.[39] The Chinese population in Ireland expanded rapidly during the "Celtic Tiger" years of the early 2000s and in 2022 there were 26,828 people recorded with an Asian or Asian Irish-Chinese ethnicity in Ireland, up 38 percent since 2016.[40] The church has two communities with significant premises in the centre of Dublin and in Esker House, Lucan, west of Dublin, with seven others in development.[41] Evangelical in its identity, the mission of the church is primarily to "reach out to the Chinese community in our local community, in Dublin and to further parts of Ireland."[42] Word International Ministries Ireland (WIN-Ireland) is a network, developed since the early 2000s, of primarily Filipino Christians, many of whom are employed by the Irish health-care system.[43] The church's own history shows the attractive power of worshipping with fellow believers from one's own culture above that of assimilation into other local churches:

> Initially attending different Christian churches already in existence in Dublin, now they sought each other – Filipinos in a strange land, hoping to ease their homesickness even by just hearing their own tongue spoken, or finding a common affiliation when they meet someone from their hometown. Previously strangers, their faith and culture have brought them together.[44]

The history also tells a typical story of moving from one temporary home to another, of sharing rented premises with other migrant congregations (Romanian and African), to finally purchasing its own premises in a Dublin industrial estate, appointing formal leadership, establishing new congregations[45] and building formal links with Filipino believers internationally. The church's primary mission is to reach out to the wider Filipino community in Ireland but they welcome believers from other cultures.

However incomplete, this colourful kaleidoscope of contemporary migrant evangelical and Pentecostal faith in Ireland represents a welcome contrast to twentieth-century Catholic-Protestant oppositional dualisms. As noted, some

---

39. See https://cgci.ie/history/.
40. See www.cso.ie/en/releasesandpublications/ep/p-cpp5/censusofpopulation2022profile5-iversitymigrationethnicityirishtravellersreligion/ethnicgroupbackground/.
41. These are in Portlaoise, Carrick-on-Shannon, Dundalk, Bray, Tullamore and Carlow. I am grateful to Dr. Tommy Kyaw Tun for this information.
42. See https://cgci.ie/history/.
43. See https://wordinternationalireland.com/about/.
44. See https://wordinternationalireland.com/about/our-church-history/.
45. Churches have been established in three towns: Carrickmacross, Cavan and Kildare.

of these churches see their mission as serving primarily their own ethnic communities (e.g. CGCI and WIN-Ireland) whereas others also hope to reach a secular Ireland with the gospel. A stated aim of the RCCG, for example, is to have a local church within five minutes' drive of everyone in Ireland. It prefers to describe itself as an international or multicultural church rather than a Nigerian one and evangelism is one of its top priorities. When asked about his vision for Ireland, Pastor Tunde Adebayo-Oke, leader of the RCCG in Ireland replied:

> I'm encouraged about the future. My vision is very simple, for the church and for Ireland, that Jesus will take over. I want to see the atmosphere changing, and I want people to appreciate who Jesus really is. People need to know that Jesus did not come to condemn but to love. I want His love to be widespread and to introduce Jesus to the nation. John 3:16 sums up that vision![46]

Missiologists have coined the phrase "reverse-mission" to describe the phenomenon of missionaries and communities of believers from the former "mission fields" of Africa, Asia and Latin America now "doing mission" in the post-Christian "sending countries" in Europe and North America.[47] It is, perhaps, too early to tell if and how this vision of RCCG and other migrant churches will be fulfilled. There are certainly major obstacles to be overcome, not least those of profoundly different religious cultures.[48] Ugba's work suggested that despite a God-given mission to reintroduce Christianity to Europeans, African migrant-led churches primarily represented places for self-definition, social empowerment and relative economic mobility where believers had refuge from the precariousness and insecurities of immigrant life.[49] Similarly, in the United Kingdom, research into the RCCG by Babatunde Adedibu concluded that their "parishes are better described as migrant sanctuaries. These parishes have not been able to translate their missionary drive to membership within the indigenous Caucasian population." Nevertheless, Adedibu argues that "even if the mission out of Africa is not yielding many new converts amongst the indigenous Caucasian population," the presence of African Christians within British church culture has irreversibly changed the religious landscape, drawing "new

---

46. Olajide Jatto, "The Changing Face of Christianity in Ireland," *VOX* April-June 2017, www.vox.ie/001/2017/4/11/the-changing-face-of-christianity-in-ireland.

47. For an introduction to the theology of reverse mission see Israel Oluwole Olofinjana https://israelolofinjana.wordpress.com/2013/06/13/theology-of-reverse-mission/.

48. See Ganiel, *Transforming*, 161–64 for discussion of RCCG evangelism in Ireland.

49. Ugba, *Shades of Belonging*.

imaginative boundaries."⁵⁰ His words resonate for Ireland as well. Vladimir Kmec adds that migrant churches in Ireland can also provide "opportunity to engage in intercultural interactions, which encourages migrants' sense of belonging to the society in which they live."⁵¹ Integration is not homogenous, much depends on personal motivation and language skills.

Migrants in Previously Established Churches

Adedibu's "new imagined boundaries" include the impact of migrant believers *in* previously established evangelical communities. There is little evidence that the disintegration of Catholic Ireland was resulting in growth among Protestant/evangelical church communities. Further research would be required, but it seems as if migrant Christians have helped existing churches *maintain* their numbers as well as contributing welcome new life and cultural diversity. For example, despite the arrival of migrant believers, the Presbyterians have only held their numbers steady at just below twenty-three thousand between 2011 and 2022, as has the Church of Ireland at just below one hundred and twenty-five thousand. The Methodists declined by over 18 percent in the same period to 5,106 and the Baptists experienced a marginal increase to just over four thousand in 2022.⁵² The number of people identifying as Apostolic or Pentecostal also stayed virtually unchanged between 2011 and 2022 at 13,500.⁵³

Useful insights into the impact of migrant believers in non-denominational churches are contained in a 2017 EAI census and survey of "Christian Churches Beyond the Traditional Four Main Denominations."⁵⁴ In a report published

---

50. Babatunde Adedibu, "Missional History and the Growth of the Redeemed Christian Church of God in the United Kingdom (1988–2015)," *Journal of the European Pentecostal Theological Association* 36.1 (2016): 80–93, DOI: 10.1080/18124461.2016.1138631.

51. Vladimir Kmec, "'Transnational and Local: Multiple Functions of Religious Communities of EU Migrants in Dublin," *Journal of the Irish Society for the Academic Study of Religions* 5 (2017): 20–39, 20.

52. Broadly speaking, Irish Baptists and the great majority of Irish Presbyterians are conservative evangelicals. The picture is more mixed in Anglican and Methodist circles, but evangelicals form a strong strand within both.

53. See www.cso.ie/en/releasesandpublications/ep/p-cpp5/census2022profile5-diversitymigrationethnicityirishtravellersreligion/religion/.

54. Evangelical Alliance Ireland, *A Census and Survey of Christian Churches Beyond the Traditional Four Main Denominations* (Dublin: EAI, 2018). The self-confessedly "clumsy" title was used because it was inaccurate to call such churches "independent" (many belonged to networks) or "new" (c. 57% were under fifteen years old, but some were long established). The four main denominations are Church of Ireland, Presbyterian Church in Ireland, the Methodist Church in Ireland and the Roman Catholic Church.

in 2018, they identified five hundred and four "non-mainstream" churches in the Republic. Such communities tend to be strongly evangelical. Of the one hundred and eighteen which participated in the survey, c. 19 percent were predominantly African, c. 56 percent self-described as ethnically diverse and about one fifth described themselves as predominantly Irish. Various networks were represented including the following:

- The Assemblies of God Ireland were formed in 2006 and renamed Christian Churches Ireland (CCI) in 2016. It is a growing network of Pentecostal churches across the island of Ireland with over thirty churches in the Republic which self-describe as "Bible loving, evangelical, pentecostal."[55] Consistent with global trends, and partly due to immigration, such Pentecostal churches tend to be the fastest growing constituency within the broad Irish evangelical community in Ireland today. Some of these communities are of significant size and are typically multiethnic. St Mark's in Dublin has five satellite churches in the greater Dublin area. One of the largest member churches is Open Arms in Newbridge, County Kildare, founded in 2015. It has about four hundred and fifty people meeting regularly on a Sunday morning from over thirty different nationalities and a new church plant in Dublin of about two hundred and fifty people planning to open a new multi-million euro building in 2025.[56] Ganiel devotes a chapter to Abundant Life in Limerick city.[57] It is a good example of a Pentecostal/charismatic congregation with origins dating back to 1979 during the "phase two" era of oppositional Catholic–evangelical identities.[58] Most original members were ex-Roman Catholics but the church has been transformed by immigration to become a multiethnic multinational congregation with its own "state of the art Life Centre venue" in the city centre.[59] Ganiel notes that, while most churches tend to assume a passive approach, Abundant Life "strives not just to accommodate diversity, but to celebrate it . . . [this is] most impressively demonstrated in its diverse leadership team, where one ethnic group does not hold

---

55. See https://ccireland.ie/about/.
56. Thanks to John Startin for this information.
57. Ganiel, *Transforming*, 119–36. Abundant Life belongs to the CCI network, see https://ccireland.ie/project/abundant-life-church/.
58. See https://abunlife.com/who-we-are/history.
59. See https://abunlife.com/who-we-are/history.

significantly more power than others."⁶⁰ Anecdotally, there are signs that some large migrant Pentecostal churches are beginning to seek affiliation with CCI and so connect themselves with an established Irish network.
- Other Pentecostal networks include established ones like Elim Ministries Ireland with 14 churches in the Republic as well as Solid Rock, part of the Church of God (Cleveland) denomination and pastored by Nick Park of EAI.[61]
- The Association of Baptist Churches in Ireland has about thirty congregations in the Republic.[62] One of the most diverse is Grace Bible Fellowship in Dublin city centre which has a remarkably global congregation as well as a sister Romanian congregation.

While the EAI research focused on independent churches, denominational churches with an evangelical ethos have also experienced significant diversification in their membership. One such is Emmanuel Church in Dublin city centre. Belonging to the Church of Ireland, Emmanuel was planted in 2007 and describes itself as having "a rich diversity of age and culture that reflects the make-up of a multi-ethnic Dublin." It roots its mission in God's plan "through the Gospel, to call for himself a new people from every nation and language."[63]

Tullamore Presbyterian Church, County Offaly, is a rural example worth noting. It is the first, and to date only, Presbyterian congregation to receive a "Church of Sanctuary" award in 2022 due to its work in providing welcome and hospitality to refugees and asylum seekers. This work began in 2009 with volunteers helping families with young children living within the inadequate confines of a nearby direct provision centre.[64] The church later provided a meeting space for Hazara refugees from Afghanistan, an initiative that developed into an international welcome centre that has offered hospitality to families taking up residence in the town. William Hays, the minister of the church, comments that

---

60. Ganiel, *Transforming*, 136.

61. Solid Rock has large churches in Drogheda and Dublin, with over forty nationalities represented in the former (https://churchofgod.org/), the latter describing itself as "a vibrant multicultural/multigenerational family-oriented community of Christians from all social backgrounds," see www.facebook.com/solidrockdublin.

62. See www.baptistsinireland.org/churches.

63. See www.immanuelchurchdublin.org/about-us/our-story/.

64. Ireland's system of direct provision has been widely condemned by human rights organizations. For numerous articles see www.irishtimes.com/tags/direct-provision/.

Along with families from Afghanistan and Syria, people from Russia, China, Iran, Sudan, Libya, Brazil, Germany, France, Poland, Latvia, Lithuania, Ukraine, Italy, India and Turkey find a warm welcome at the centre . . . Like most Irish county towns, Tullamore is an astonishingly diverse place for its size and rural context. For example, a discussion a few years ago. . . . revealed that the 44 different families present comprised 22 different ethnicities and nationalities. This has meant that in order to simply be a local church working within our parish we had to learn to be a community that reaches out and provides a welcome space for people of many different nationalities and backgrounds.[65]

Concluding Reflections

In a course on faith and culture I ask students which Ireland they would prefer to live in – that of Christendom or post-Christendom. No student has yet preferred to live in the past, despite it being a simpler time of moral certainties. While that is a small and unscientific survey, it echoes the attitude of Irish society in general. Yet, if preferable to the past, life in a diverse post-Christendom culture raises challenges for evangelicals to negotiate and it is with these that we conclude.

Negotiating Post-Christendom

The missiologist David Smith describes Christian experience in post-Christendom as one of "liminality."[66] By this he means an experience of uncertainty, without clear boundaries or direction. This is an apt image in Ireland where old assumptions have been discarded and believers are negotiating an unfamiliar landscape. For example, in 2010 the EAI decided to endorse the proposed legislation to establish Civil Partnerships for same-sex couples. Other evangelicals and conservative Catholics strongly disagreed.[67] Later the EAI stood against the same-sex marriage and abortion referenda. Today, some strands in Pentecostalism appear to be adopting a confrontational posture to secularism around issues of education, gender and religious liberty: "We must not retreat

---

65. William Hays, "A Place of Sanctuary," *The Presbyterian Herald*, June 2023, https://issuu.com/presbyterianireland/docs/presbyterian_herald_june_2023/s/25132157.

66. David Smith, *Mission After Christendom* (London: Darton, Longman & Todd, 2003).

67. For more detailed analysis see Mitchel, "Sex, Truth, Tolerance."

from our culture or society, but rather reclaim them in Jesus Name!"[68] The Presbyterian Church in Ireland has hit the national headlines more than once around decisions to enforce its teaching on marriage, generally being depicted as "hard line" in the Irish media.[69] Such an ambiguous and unsettling context requires, I suggest, theological reflection on at least two levels.[70]

First, Irish evangelicals can broadly welcome the arrival of post-Christendom. It continues to open up an Irish religious landscape that was previously characterized by high walls and impermeable boundaries, leading to new opportunities for mission.[71]

Second, evangelicals in Ireland need to be realistic about their marginal status. Christians have no special right to expect the state to legislate in accordance with their morality. This means neither a naïve longing for a new form of Christendom nor cultural detachment. Rather than trying to "re-take" the culture, they should support the construction of a pluralistic society where difference is tolerated and which provides as much justice and compassion and social stability as possible.[72] An authentically Christian theology will not be self-centred but will lead to concern for matters of public life and the wellbeing of human society.[73]

Negotiating Diversity

Ireland's relatively new experience of significant religious diversity poses challenges to both migrant and established churches. A question for the former is how effectively they can be bridges, enabling their members to adapt and flourish in their host Irish culture. This will become a more pressing issue as

---

68. See www.christianvoice.ie/about.

69. Patsy McGarry, "Deep Rifts Over Presbyterian Church's Hard Line on Same Sex-Sex Marriage," *Irish Times*, 21 October 2019, www.irishtimes.com/news/social-affairs/religion-and-beliefs/deep-rifts-over-presbyterian-church-s-hard-line-on-same-sex-marriage-1.4057050.

70. The following points are drawn from Mitchel, "Sex, Truth Tolerance."

71. One example of this is the growth of the Alpha course in Ireland (and internationally). In Ireland in 2023, over 5,800 people took part in Alpha courses, with broadly equal participation across Catholic and Protestant churches. Such cooperation across boundaries around reading the Bible and emphasis on personal faith was unimaginable in Christendom Ireland. Thanks to Dominic Perrem for this information.

72. For fuller discussion see John Stackhouse, *Making the Best of It: Following Christ in the Real World* (New York: Oxford University Press, 2008), 300–6.

73. For a recent articulation of this sort of approach, setting forth a case for liberal democracy, see Tom Wright and Michael F. Bird, *Jesus and the Powers: Christian Political Witness in an Age of Totalitarian Terror and Dysfunctional Democracies* (London: SPCK, 2024).

second and third generations grow up acculturated in Irish society and shaped by Western values.

But perhaps bigger challenges face the longer established majority White churches. Despite the fact that Ireland is known globally as the country of a "one hundred thousand welcomes,"[74] xenophobia is increasingly prevalent. As I write this, close by a hostile anti-immigration march is making its way down Dublin's O'Connell Street,[75] which was itself the scene of violent anti-migrant riots in November 2023.[76] The riot in Dublin preceded similar wide-scale right-wing riots across the UK during 2024 and was symptomatic of a rising antagonism against immigrants across Ireland, frequently taking the form of burning out potential housing centres for migrants or asylum seekers.[77] In the wake of violence and hate-filled rhetoric online, these words of one migrant are surely shared by many:

> Ireland doesn't feel comfortable, let alone safe, for me right now. . . . There is a numbness that I feel too, a numbness stemming from exhaustion, exhaustion from speaking ad nauseam, about the collective fear many ethnic minorities have and currently are expressing and experiencing right now across Ireland.[78]

In such a context, the reasons why most migrants tend to stay away from Irish majority churches should give pause for thought: a cold reception, racist attitudes, dissatisfaction with superficial relationships, and the exclusion of immigrants in decision making.[79] Evidence suggests that few such churches have yet thought seriously and theologically about the task of developing authentically inter-cultural church communities. "Inter-cultural" here has a specific meaning distinct from multi-cultural (the presence of multiple cultures). Inter-cultural communities are "characterized by the genuine mutual

---

74. The Irish expression is *Céad Míle Fáilte*.

75. Colman O'Sullivan, "19 People Arrested As Protests Held in Dublin City Centre," *RTE News*, 20 September 2024, www.rte.ie/news/dublin/2024/0919/1470910-dublin-protests/.

76. Elaine McCallig, "Dublin's Dark Side," 27 November 2023, www.tortoisemedia.com/2023/11/27/dublins-dark-side/.

77. Elaine McCallig, "Ireland Is Turning Violently Against Migrants," 19 July 2024, www.tortoisemedia.com/2024/07/19/ireland-is-turning-violently-against-migrants/.

78. Jesuit Centre for Faith and Justice, "Reading the City Centre Riots: Thoughts, Feelings and Reactions of the Dublin Community Co-op," *Working Notes 95: The Voices of the North-East Inner City*, 4 June 2024, www.jcfj.ie/article/reading-the-city-centre-riots-thoughts-feelings-and-reactions-of-the-dublin-community-co-op/.

79. Kmec, "Minority Religions," 525.

exchanges of ideas and the development of deep relationships of mutual dependency."[80]

One positive development in this regard is the setting up of Intercultural Ministries Ireland to facilitate an "increasing number of our brothers and sisters in Christ from the global church making Ireland their home engaging with and enriching the wider Irish church and its witness."[81] Another development emerged from a 2021 survey sponsored jointly by the Irish Council of Churches/Irish Inter-Church Meeting, *VOX* magazine and the EAI, called "Exploring Race and the Churches in Ireland." It led to the production of *From Every Nation? A Handbook for a Congregation's Journey from Welcome to Belonging*.[82] This handbook contains both practical and theological resources for local congregations. The authors are aware that development towards intercultural church involves more than pragmatic changes: it involves a posture of listening, learning and engaging with the Other. Such a process will likely challenge people's assumptions about what is "normal" regarding race and church practice. For example, in a conversation about race, Gerard Chimbganda, a Zimbabwean pastor in Dublin, comments that

> Diversity must not be white-controlled, otherwise it becomes purely a PR exercise for white people to say, "We've done this for black people." Inclusion means you are breaking the barriers; allowing people of colour to contribute and to rise. There has to be real reconciliation . . . It is about a deep transformation of how we think, how we relate and how we talk.[83]

The good news is that there are deep theological and historical resources in Christianity for precisely this sort of task. Jesus Christ is Lord of all and from its inception the Christian faith has been inherently and radically intercultural. The New Testament reminds us that we are all migrants, called to live as strangers in a foreign culture (1 Pet 2:11). As the centre of global Christianity continues to move South and believers from the Global South continue to arrive in the West, euro-centric Christendom assumptions will continue to

---

80. I am grateful to Nathaniel Jennings of Intercultural Ministries Ireland for this definition; see www.interculturalireland.org/.

81. See www.interculturalireland.org/about-6.

82. Irish Council of Churches and the Irish Inter-Church Meeting, *From Every Nation? A Handbook for a Congregation's Journey from Welcome to Belonging* (Dublin: Irish Council of Churches, n.d.).

83. Gerard Chimbganda, "I'm Black and I'm Proud," *VOX*, July-September 2018, www.vox.ie/001/2018/7/10/im-black-and-im-proud. Chimbganda was in conversation with Richard Carson, CEO of ACET Ireland.

crumble.[84] This development has long been foreseen and welcomed by those involved in global mission. The Seoul Statement from the fourth Lausanne Congress in 2024 talks of the "spectacular diversity" shaped by the "distinctive cultures and unique contextual challenges" in global Christianity, adding that

> In the church catholic, no human culture can claim preeminence. All human cultures must bow in submission before the God of all wisdom and as they do so, they each make their contribution to our understanding of Scripture and proclamation of the gospel. In this way, God unites us together to declare and display his glory in all our diversity.[85]

Such words invite evangelicals in Ireland to embrace God-given unity in diversity. This is no easy task in a volatile political climate. It calls for intentionality, hospitality, love, respect and friendship. But perhaps the courageous pursuit of such a vision can provide a foretaste of God's kingdom where one day believers "from every nation, from all tribes and peoples and languages" will stand "before the throne and before the Lamb."[86]

Bibliography

Ganiel, Gladys. *Transforming Post-Catholic Ireland: Religious Practice in Late Modernity.* Oxford: Oxford University Press, 2016.
———. "Ireland After Secularization." Pages 323–40 in *The Oxford Handbook of Religion in Modern Ireland.* Edited by Gladys Ganiel and Andrew Holmes. Oxford: Oxford University Press, 2024.
Gribben, Crawford. *The Rise and Fall of Christian Ireland.* Oxford: Oxford University Press, 2021.
Inglis, Tom. *Moral Monopoly: The Rise and Fall of the Catholic Church in Modern Ireland,* 2nd ed. Dublin: University College Dublin Press, 1998.
Kmec, Vladimir. "Minority Religions and Immigration in Ireland." Pages 522–41 in *The Oxford Handbook of Religion in Modern Ireland.* Edited by Gladys Ganiel and Andrew Holmes. Oxford: Oxford University Press, 2024.

---

84. It is estimated that by 2050, 77 percent of Christians will live in the Global South. Gina A. Zurlo, Todd M. Johnson and Peter F. Crossing, "World Christianity and Mission 2020: Ongoing Shift to the Global South," *International Bulletin of Mission Research* 44.1 (2020): 8–19; https://doi.org/10.1177/2396939319880074.

85. The Lausanne Movement, Seoul Statement para. 31. https://lausanne.org/statement/the-seoul-statement.

86. Revelation 7:9 NRSV.

———. "Transnational and Local: Multiple Functions of Religious Communities of EU Migrants in Dublin." *Journal of the Irish Society for the Academic Study of Religions* 5 (2017): 20–39.

Mitchel, Patrick. "Evangelicals and Irish Identity in Independent Ireland: a case study." Pages 155–70 in *Irish Protestant Identities*. Edited by M. Busteed, F. Neal and J. Tonge. Manchester: Manchester University Press, 2008.

———. "Sex, Truth and Tolerance: some theological reflections on the Irish Civil Partnership Bill 2010 and challenges facing Christians in a post-Christendom Culture." *Evangelical Quarterly* 84.2 (2012): 155–73.

Ugba, Abel. *Shades of Belonging: African Pentecostals in Twenty-First Century Ireland*. Trenton: Africa World Press, 2009.

Warner, Carolyn M. "Benevolent Secularism and the Recalibration of Church–State Relations in Ireland in the Aftermath of the Clergy Child Sex Abuse Scandals." *Journal of Church and State* 62.1 (2020): 86–109.

17

Evangelicalism in Italy

Leonardo De Chirico

Introduction

From a religious viewpoint, Italy is traditionally linked to Roman Catholicism more than to the Protestant Reformation or with present-day evangelicalism, in the Counter-Reformation expression epitomized by the Council of Trent (1545–1563), and its pervasive presence in culture and national life. The religious icon of the country is St Peter's Square in Rome and Italian identity is often connected with Roman Catholicism as if the two were synonymous. The evangelical population equals one percent, the second largest religious minority after Islam. Most of the evangelical churches are small congregations, made up of faithful believers with few resources and in survival mode. Yet, these congregations are all alive in spite of the important shifts in society and culture.

The first part of this chapter offers a historical sketch of the evangelical presence in Italy, from the (missed) Reformation to today's realities, while the second part highlights some of the opportunities and challenges that Italian evangelicals face as they live in a layered society, somewhat squeezed between strong Roman Catholic and secular influences.

Historical Sketches of the Evangelical Presence

In the Italian peninsula, the spiritual, cultural and ideological influence of Roman Catholicism has been basically unchallenged since the inception of papal power. Yet this does not mean that the reforming waves that swept over Europe did not reach the Italian peninsula. In fact they had a significant – though not lasting – impact.

Before and after the Reformation

The renewed interest in religious matters that characterized the sixteenth century was preceded by various personalities and movements who are often seen as forerunners of the Reformation.[1] Arnold of Brescia (c.1090–1155) called on the Church to renounce property ownership; Peter Waldo (c.1140–c.1205) refused to obey a papal ban forbidding him to preach a simple gospel message marked by voluntary poverty; Girolamo Savonarola (1452–1498) spoke most strongly against the corrupt clergy. These and other men paved the way for an appreciation of the need for renewal in the morality and the teaching of the Church.

In addition, the background of the Renaissance, with its emphasis on the need to recover the sources of classical culture, made the reading of the Bible *ad fontes* a practice of the intellectual élites, most of whom were lay people, who would debate topics of religious interest outside of ecclesiastical contexts. While small in scope, these developments in Italy represented a conscious re-appropriation of resources that could be used against the ignorance, corruption and superstitions of the early sixteenth-century clergy.

An outstanding book written in Italy is worth mentioning because it reflects widespread evangelical concerns. It is the single most famous and significant work of Italian renewal, the *Beneficio di Cristo* (*Benefit of Christ*). The book first appeared in Venice in 1543 and quickly became a bestseller. Within six years, forty thousand copies were sold in Venice alone before it was forbidden and put on the Church's Index. Its dependence on the teaching of Juan de Valdés (1509–1541) has been widely recognized and interpreters have also noted its indebtedness to John Calvin's *Institutes*.

Confronted with the need to take a stand, many sympathizers of the *Beneficio di Cristo* tried to maintain a formal allegiance to the Roman Catholic Church while cultivating their own interest behind the scenes. Because this reforming movement in the sixteenth century did not go beyond personal inclinations, it did not take ecclesiastical roots: the various Protestant circles did not become established churches.[2] John Calvin called these Italians "nicodemites." However, after 1542 some of these believers paid the price of death or exile in order to maintain their Protestant faith: Bernardino Ochino

---

1. For an overview on this section see S. Caponetto, *The Protestant Reformation in Sixteenth-century Italy* (Kirksville: Thomas Jefferson University Press, 1999).

2. Historians such as M. Firpo and others call these sixteenth-century movements the Italian "evangelical movement" because it did not become an organic part of the continental Reformation; see e.g. /www.jstor.org/stable/20565664.

(1487–1564), Pietro Paolo Vergerio (1498–1565), Jerome Zanchi (1516–1590) and Peter Martyr Vermigli (1499–1562). The latter wrote *Loic Communes*, which makes him equal to John Calvin and Heinrich Bullinger, whose *Loci Communes* (*Common Places*) were standard works for generations of Protestant pastors. These Italian Protestant theologians contributed significantly to the cause of the Reformation worldwide but were practically unknown in their own country until a few years ago.

The Protestant movement was prevented from taking roots in Italy due to internal and external causes. As already noted, it was fragmentary in nature, incapable of organizing itself in ecclesiastical structures, too limited in time and, although spread over the country, lacking a significant breakthrough in any of the major cities. The main external reason was the violent opposition by the authorities of the Roman Church. This included factors and defining moments such as the Inquisition, through which Protestants endured physical and psychological torture, even execution, and the gradual influence of the Index of Prohibited Books, which banned unauthorized translations of Scripture and writings such as the *Beneficio*. The reaction of the Catholic Church thus prevented the spread of the gospel renewal movements. It also incorporated some of its concerns into its life patterns, for example by setting a higher bar for the moral and intellectual standard of priests, although theologically accommodated to fit the Roman system.

The Reformation in Italy has been studied by scholars especially after the unification of the country in 1861. These renewal movements were seen as forerunners of the *Risorgimento*, the cultural and political shift that energized the formation of the nation state over against the prerogatives of papal power. However, these historical studies have tended to downplay the theological and spiritual significance of the Reformation because they were more interested in the heterodox nature of Italian evangelicalism and its historical intricacies.[3]

Recent interpretations of the Italian Reformation have stressed more radical features of the sixteenth-century Protestant movement. It was shaped by a series of cultural disconnections that prevented its consolidation and resulted in its ultimate disintegration:

1. a "social" disjuncture: the members of the movement were prone to hide their convictions from public while cultivating them in private;

---

3. L. Felici, ed., *Ripensare la riforma protestante. Nuove prospettive degli studi italiani*, (Torino: Claudiana, 2016).

2. a "personal" disjuncture: it was difficult for them to adhere to codified patterns of belief while they were pursuing religious interests based on personal curiosity;

3. a "structural" disjuncture: they saw freedom and authority as opposites, instead of appreciating the new relationship suggested by the mainstream Reformation.

Many Italians were opposed to the Catholic Church and rejected the Roman system as authoritarian, but as free thinkers they were not prepared to accept the emphasis which the Reformation placed on the authority of the Word of God over that of the church.[4]

New Openings in the Nineteenth Century

As a result of the Counter-Reformation, for centuries lay people were not allowed to read the Bible in the Italian vernacular language. The irony (or better: the tragedy) of our country is that it was regarded as a highly religious nation and people, with deeply rooted religious traditions, but that it lacked access to be Bible and was therefore almost totally ignorant of the Word of God. The main concern of evangelicals throughout the centuries has been the circulation of the Bible, the encouragement to read it, and the provision of various means to put the Bible at the centre of church, family and personal life.

Eventually, after the unification of the country in 1861, the outstanding literary and theological output that is Giovanni Diodati's translation of the Bible into Italian (1607) reached the Italians. Bible distribution was the main vehicle of the evangelization of the country which was the work of national movements such as the Waldensians (a medieval group which eventually sided with the Protestant Reformation) and the Brethren (a nineteenth-century grassroots movement characterized by Bible reading and the priesthood of all believers), as well as of mission societies which mainly came from the United Kingdom and the USA. It was through these missionary efforts that Italian branches of the Baptist and Methodist denominations were formed. All these churches and agencies showed a significant degree of evangelistic zeal when, faced with religious and cultural opposition, they were able to plant churches throughout the country.[5] However, although they all related to one another at some level,

---

4. P. Bolognesi, "La ricezione di Calvino nell'Italia del Cinquecento," in *Calvino ieri e oggi in Italia*, ed. P. Bolognesi and A. Olivieri (Roma: Aracne, 2010), 94–95.

5. G. Spini, *Studi sull'evangelismo italiano tra Otto e Novecento* (Torino: Claudiana, 1994).

they never managed to completely overcome their "silo" mindset: each of them pursued its own projects with little sharing of resources or long-term planning. The modest evangelical expansion at the turn of the century ran aground in the diatribes of Latin individualism and the lack of an overall vision that was capable of distinguishing essential from secondary points.

At the beginning of the twentieth century the Pentecostal movement made important inroads and soon became the largest evangelical presence in the country.[6] Mainly through the restless work of Italian converts who had migrated to the USA and now came back to their native cities and villages, Pentecostal congregations were formed, especially in Sicily and other Southern regions. The Pentecostals were the primary targets of the opposition from the Fascist regime against all minorities. In 1935 the Fascist government defined Pentecostal spirituality as a "threat to the purity and sanity of the race." Disruptions of services and imprisonment of leaders followed.[7] However, this negative attitude did not stop the growth of Pentecostal churches. It was only after the end of World War II and the fall of Fascism that the stigma on Pentecostals began to be questioned in the public opinion and overcome in the national legislation.

Protestants and Evangelicals in the Twentieth Century

After the war a new season of freedom and opportunities began. Italian Protestants had to re-affirm their presence in the country in a minority situation; each denomination had to re-organize its internal operations and re-launch its missionary efforts. Since the nineteenth century Italian Protestantism had reflected the denominational differentiations that are a feature and a child of the Reformation. However, in the post-war years, Italy also witnessed the emergence of two separate poles within Protestantism: the historic Protestants and the evangelicals.

The Waldensian Church joined the World Council of Churches at its establishment (Amsterdam 1948). Stemming from the same theological platform of ecumenical Protestantism, after a first attempt in 1965, the Federation of Evangelical Churches in Italy (FCEI) was formed in 1967. It brought together many historic Protestant expressions in the country: the Waldensians, Methodists,

---

6. F. Toppi and D. A. Womack, *Le radici del Movimento pentecostale in Italia* (Roma: ADI-Media, 1989).

7. See my chapter, "La persecuzione religiosa nei bozzetti autobiografici di Roberto Bracco," in *Libertà religiosa e minoranze*, ed. G. Long (Torino: Claudiana, 2007), 93–99.

Baptist Union and Lutherans. Influenced by Barthian theology and with a conciliatory attitude towards Roman Catholicism, the FCEI became the national expression of the World Council of Churches. Because of theological uneasiness about the theological "openness" and the incumbent liberalism that they detected in FCEI circles, many "conservative" or "biblical" evangelicals (such as the Assemblies of God, the Brethren movement and many free churches) did not join the FCEI. They represented the majority of the Protestants in the country. For this reason the "E" in the name FCEI is confusing.

Meanwhile, the international evangelical world urged the Italian evangelicals not to remain isolated but to participate in the evangelical "resurgence" that was taking place after the war. It was at the European Congress on Evangelism which Billy Graham convened in Amsterdam in 1971 that a decisive event occurred. The large Italian delegation, made up of pastors and evangelists from Pentecostal and free churches, very much appreciated being together, not only in terms of fellowship but also in term of closer collaboration. In the words of Elio Milazzo, first president of the Italian Evangelical Alliance, "in Amsterdam the desire was expressed to continue a relationship that otherwise would have lasted only a few days."[8] The connections between the participants at the Amsterdam Congress were further strengthened by the Lausanne Congress on World Evangelization and in November 1974 gave rise to the establishment of the Italian Evangelical Alliance.[9]

At the 1974 Lausanne Congress, there was a report on Italy by Franco Bono which addressed the situation of the evangelicals in Italy; this report provides an interesting perspective on how the evangelicals saw themselves at that time.[10] The primary need was that of evangelism: evangelism through books and printed matter, evangelism through radio, evangelism through the local church and evangelistic campaigns. The report confirms that the South of the country was more evangelized than the North and that the greatest response to the gospel was obtained from the younger and older generations, while middle-aged people seemed to show more resistance. The report goes on to record a "lack of unity, cooperation and communication among Italian evangelicals," something already observed in previous decades. The harvest

---

8. G. Moretti, "Intervista ai Presidenti Bensi e Milazzo," *Idea* IV/2 (1979): 6–12.

9. The story of the early attempts to establish the Italian Evangelical Alliance to the 1974 constitution is told by G. Ciccone, *Unità evangelica, difficile ma possibile. Dal sogno di Paolo Geymonat alla costituzione dell'Alleanza Evangelica Italiana* (San Giovanni Teatino: Evangelista Media, 2014).

10. J. D. Douglas (ed.), *Let the Earth Hear His Voice. A Comprehensive Volume on World Evangelization* (Minneapolis: World Wide Publications, 1975), 1392–93.

is great, few are the workers, who are sometimes competing. The spirit of competition must be countered by the spirit of evangelical unity. Another need identified by the report is training. Many believers were self-taught and lacked basic theological training. This report depicts the situation at the time but also provides a helpful background to the issues and challenges which evangelicals are facing today.

Although even today not all evangelicals are formally associated with the Italian Evangelical Alliance, there is a sense in which Italian Protestantism is roughly characterized by a bipartition: a historic Protestant/ecumenical wing represented by the FCEI and an evangelical wing, which includes Pentecostals, that finds a common platform in the Italian Evangelical Alliance. This situation seems to exist in many European countries, so Italy is no exception.

Evangelicals in Italy Today: Issues and Challenges

After the Protestant Reformation had been suffocated by the powerful Roman Catholic Church, the evangelical community in Italy was always a small, persecuted minority until the second half of the twentieth century.[11] Having learned to survive, congregations are generally made up of believers with a robust faith who nonetheless tend to be inward-focused and suspicious of others. However, these difficult conditions did not prevent the gospel from spreading, especially in the southern regions of the country. Massimo Introvigne, the leading Italian sociologist of religion, writes:

> Among Italian citizens, the first religious minority is the Protestant one, with 435,000 faithful. The Italian Protestants are divided into over a hundred different denominations. Those that belong to the "historical" communities which are part of the World Council of Churches – Waldensians, Lutherans, Reformed, Methodists, Baptists – have been reduced to 14.2% of the total, while a solid absolute majority is made up of Pentecostals (72%).[12]

Here are some challenges that evangelicals face.

---

11. This and the next paragraph are based on an interview with the author by The Gospel Coalition in 2015, see www.thegospelcoalition.org/article/the-gospel-in-italy/. Used with permission.

12. M. Introvigne, *Enciclopedia delle Religioni* (Torino: Elledici, 2013).

Encouraging yet Limited Signs of Growth

The faithful evangelical witness of past generations in difficult circumstances is inspiring. The gradual growth of cooperative effort – for instance, in advocating for religious freedom or social work – is also encouraging. Substantial evangelical books are increasingly being translated into Italian, especially from Anglo-American authors (such as Don Carson, Tim Keller, John Piper, John MacArthur and Mark Dever) but also French (e.g. Henri Blocher) and Latin American (e.g. Augustus Nicodemus). In addition, conferences and training initiatives are available for Italian believers. The publisher GBU, which is affiliated with the International Fellowship of Evangelical Students (IFES), has produced many volumes of the commentary series "The Bible Speaks Today" which provide much-needed tools for teachers and preachers. In 2007 the *Dictionary of Evangelical Theology*, a nine-hundred-page volume with more than six hundred entries, was edited by Italian theologians and had to be reprinted in 2012, something that was unthinkable even a few years ago.[13]

There is also a growing desire to see a shift away from the survival mentality of the past to a missional mindset for the glory of God and the good of the nation. Without denying the struggles and problems, there is a sense of a coming momentum for the gospel. Efforts to help the Italian evangelical church from abroad have largely tended to either bypass national Italian church leadership or support independent individuals. Italian evangelical churches are now becoming more credible partners in promoting the gospel in the country.

The Italian theologian Pietro Bolognesi rightly argues that evangelicals are facing three main challenges: identity, unity and training.[14] In the situation of a struggling minority, our Christian *identity* has been largely defined not by who we are but by who we are *not* (not Roman Catholic, not theologically liberal, not culturally secular). The general public perception has been that evangelicals are a cult. There is thus a need to better grasp our evangelical identity based on core gospel essentials rather than on the features of a subculture. Recently two important resources were made available: collections of evangelical documents and statements from bodies like the World Evangelical Alliance and the Lausanne Movement on topics like mission, biblical interpretation, creation

---

13. P. Bolognesi, L. De Chirico and A. Ferrari, eds., *Dizionario di teologia evangelica* (Marchirolo: EUN, 2007).

14. A lecture given by P. Bolognesi, "Prospettive per la formazione teologica in Italia" at Rome Trastevere Baptist Church on 20 January 2001. See also his "Is There an Evangelical Vision? Reflections from an Italian Perspective," *European Journal of Theology* 13.2 (2004): 103–9.

care, education and public theology.¹⁵ The fact that they were published by a major Catholic publishing house meant that they are now circulating beyond the evangelical public, so that they are becoming a meaningful "identity card" for the evangelical movement.

Then there is *unity*. In the short history of Italian evangelicalism, secondary distinctives have produced too much fragmentation. Generally speaking, the Italian evangelicals still need to learn to do together what is biblically possible, knowing that most of the challenges ahead of them (such as public witness, church planting and quality training) cannot be faced at a local or denominational level alone. This has been a standing challenge since the re-opening of the country after the unification in 1861.

Finally there is *training*. In struggling and small churches, formation has not been seen as a priority. Most leaders in churches and para-church ministries are self-taught and self-trained. Cultural engagement is often shallow if not absent. This situation will not improve without a generation of leaders who are better equipped for ministry and if the level of gospel fluency and competence is not increased. Moreover, "ordinary" believers, most of whom are first generation evangelicals, need to be better prepared for how to be faithful and missional in their vocations.

Rebalancing the Church–Parachurch Relationship

In the history of Italian evangelicalism, missionary agencies and parachurch ministries have become the protagonists of mission work, showing a considerable ability to operate independently of, or unrelated to, the life of local churches. Compared with the reality of local churches and denominations, the latter have gradually become more introspective, localized and not always able to cultivate a missionary vision worthy of the name. The role of local churches and denominations has diminished, that of the mission agencies has grown, often reversing the burden of responsibility and the roles of each. In the reality of the contemporary evangelical church, too often the relationships between churches and "missions" have been reversed, with the latter becoming the central focus of initiatives. The churches became (and in some cases already were) basically passive. This situation has created ecclesiological imbalances with negative consequences for the overall health of the evangelical witness. What

---

15. P. Bolognesi, ed., *Dichiarazioni evangeliche. Il movimento evangelicale 1966–1996*, (Bologna: EDB, 1997) and *Dichiarazioni evangeliche II. Il movimento evangelicale 1997–2017* (Bologna: EDB, 2017).

took place was not collaboration but replacement; not synergy, but autonomy; not partnership, but competition or mutual indifference.

To remedy this, we would do well to listen to the *Lausanne Covenant* (1974) which invites us to rethink the relationship between churches and missionary agencies in the spirit of collaboration in the gospel: "We urge the development of regional and functional cooperation for the furtherance of the Church's mission, for strategic planning, for mutual encouragement and for the sharing of resources and experience" (par. 7).[16]

It is evident that parachurch agencies are called to assist the church/local churches in the promotion of gospel work in a spirit of mutual sharing of gifts and collaboration. The Italian evangelical church/churches must reappropriate their role in God's plan without delegating the mission to others. They themselves need to be directly committed to it. The relationship between churches and missionary organizations must be rebalanced so that the primary responsibility for carrying out the missional task rests with the churches and the role of the para-ecclesial agencies is limited to supporting that work.

The Promise and Challenge of Diaspora and Migrant Churches

As already indicated, evangelicals form about one percent of the Italian population, but this percentage only includes Italian citizens. Over the last two decades, the phenomenon of immigration has also become reality in Italy and the future of the country cannot realistically be imagined without immigrants. By the middle of the twenty-first century foreigners in the country, excluding those who will become Italian citizens, will be over 10 million with an incidence between 16 and 18 percent of residents and these changes are mainly due to immigration. Out of the current 5.3 million resident migrants, some one hundred and forty-five thousand are evangelical Christians.[17]

Some immigrants adhere to "new religions" but many others are contributing to a restructuring of the ethnic and cultural composition of Italian Christianity, not least of evangelicalism, because many immigrants from Latin America, Africa, China, the Philippines and Europe (mainly Romania) come from evangelical or Pentecostal backgrounds.[18] This increasingly significant

---

16. *Lausanne Covenant*, https://lausanne.org/statement/lausanne-covenant#cooperation-in-evangelism.

17. See www.ismu.org/immigrati-e-religioni-in-italia-piu-della-meta-degli-stranieri-e-di-religione-cristiana-comunicato-stampa-10-7-2024/.

18. See G. Rizza, "Chiese, etnie e pluralità," *Studi di teologia* – Suppl. n. 7 (2009): 16–25.

presence of evangelicals of foreign origin is a new phenomenon in Italian Protestantism. On the one hand, foreign-language evangelical communities have been established almost everywhere in the country; on the other hand, evangelical immigrants have gradually integrated into Italian-speaking communities, where they are taking on increasingly important roles. It is not just the numerical increase in the evangelical minority in Italy, but a contribution that introduces theological sensitivities – such as leadership styles and church practices – and ways of conceiving the church which are changing the shape of evangelicalism and whose real significance will only be assessed in future years.

Religious Liberty

The Italian Constitution deals with religious groups hierarchically: article 7 deals with the Catholic Church, which is represented by the Vatican, a sovereign state; article 8 deals with other religious groups which have signed an agreement with the state. There are eight such Protestant groups at the moment, which include the Waldensians/Methodists, Lutherans, Baptist Union, Assemblies of God, Seventh-day Adventists and the Apostolic Church. Some evangelical denominations, such as Elim churches and Consulta Evangelica, are asking for a similar agreement but the state is slow to take the matter forward. Others, such as the Brethren, do not want to sign any agreement with the state because of their ecclesiological convictions. Currently less than ten percent of the non-Catholic congregations have such an agreement with the state. Muslims are asking to be offered an agreement but for political reasons the government does not want to proceed. Considering that Italian society is increasingly multi-confessional, one would expect an increase in the number of new agreements rather than a decrease.

The only national laws on freedom of religion or belief date from the fascist period (1929–1931). Despite the fact that the Constitutional Court has removed some elements of these laws, they remain in force and are a continuing challenge for all religious minorities. In recent decades, discussions between the government and representatives of religious communities about a new law on freedom of religion or belief have failed. The absence of such a law affects Italian society as a whole and is allowing religious discrimination in several social contexts such as places of worship, recognition of religious officials, assistance in hospitals, chaplaincy and public broadcasting.

The inauguration of new places of worship and even the keeping open of existing ones remains difficult due to the unfair nature of regulations that were avowedly created to impede the opening of new places of worship. This situation has not only affected the Islamic community, this law has also had an impact on evangelical churches and other Christian communities.

One of the challenges in the laws that date from the fascist era is the concept of "non-catholic religious leader" (*Ministro di culto acattolico*). In recent years, independent churches and small denominations have found it extremely difficult to get their ministers recognized by the state. The procedure for recognition is slow and, in most cases, unsuccessful. The threshold to obtain recognition has become even higher because in 2012 the Council of State (*Consiglio di Stato*), a legal-administrative consultative body, recommended that a religious community must have a minimum of five hundred members for its pastor to be accredited. Non-recognized pastors are unable to carry out activities such as celebrating marriages or visiting prisoners and sick people in hospitals. Their churches remain unregistered.

The worrying trend of Catholic confessionalism has increased over the last few years. In state schools, only catholic teachers are allowed to teach religion – and they teach the Roman Catholic catechism. These teachers are chosen by bishops but paid by the taxpayers. Government bodies are still more inclined to confirm and allow privileges to the Catholic Church in many areas, such as the tax-system and the funding of building churches. The national broadcaster (RAI) has a Vatican department which daily provides the nation with all kinds of information about the pope and the Roman Catholic Church; almost nothing is done to inform about other churches and religious pluralism.

Although Italy is a secular state, the government often looks to the Roman Catholic Church for support for its policies; equally, the Catholic Church often tries to influence Italian politics. The Roman Catholic Church does not generally support freedom of religion at the national level and has a defensive attitude in trying to keep its huge privileges in terms of public funding and political support. At the popular level, there is much cynicism about the church and religion in general, as is the case in the rest of Europe. Yet because the cultural climate is sceptical, there are many opportunities to introduce the gospel based on the virtuous circle of evangelical truth, evangelical community and evangelical culture. Evangelical church life and culture is key to this goal because it combines believing and belonging, proclamation and service, the personal and the communal, creative contextualization and obedience to the word of God.

Bibliography

Bolognesi, Pietro, and Leonardo De Chirico. *Il movimento evangelicale*. Brescia: Queriniana, 2002.

Bolognesi, Pietro, ed. *Dichiarazioni evangeliche. Il movimento evangelicale 1966–1996*. Bologna: EDB, 1997.

———. *Dichiarazioni evangeliche II. Il movimento evangelicale 1997–2017*. Bologna: EDB, 2017.

Bouchard, Giorgio. *Chiese e movimenti evangelici del nostro tempo*. Torino: Claudiana, 2006.

De Chirico, Leonardo. "Il movimento evangelicale." Pages 329–73 in *Conosciamo i fratelli. Corso breve di ecumenismo*. Edited by T. F. Rossi. Roma: Centro Pro Unione, 2016.

Ferrario, Fulvio, and Pavel Gajewski. *Il protestantesimo contemporaneo*. Roma: Carocci, 2007.

18

Evangelicalism in Norway

Lars Dahle

Introduction

Situated in the north-western corner of Europe with a very long coastline, Norway together with Denmark and Sweden constitutes the Scandinavian region. The stereotypes of the Nordic countries are many: "Technologically advanced, but also inheritors of a brutal pagan past; first to take up the Reformation but also first to ride the waves of secularization, peaceful social democrats, and fearsome religious warriors."[1] As with any stereotypes, their relationship to reality is ambiguous. Today, Norway is well-known globally as a secular nation with oil riches, beautiful scenery and the Nobel peace prize. Some cultural observers are also aware of Norway's strong Christian heritage.

Historically, evangelical faith had a significant impact on Norwegian society and culture at large, and Norwegian evangelicals have contributed in various ways to global evangelicalism. These aspects will be explored in this chapter, alongside some historical and contemporary trends related to Norwegian evangelicalism.

I am using *evangelical* and *evangelicalism* in line with widely accepted definitions. First, in conceptual terms, evangelicalism may be defined as centred around some key convictions: "I still believe that emphases on cross, Bible, conversion, and activism reflect the reality of the evangelical movement eve-

---

1. Mark Hutchinson, "Evangelicals in Northern Europe," in *Evangelicals around the World. A Global Handbook for the 21st Century*, ed. Brian C. Stiller, Todd M. Johnson, Karen Stiller and Mark Hutchinson (Nashville: World Evangelical Alliance, 2015), 372.

rywhere, always, and by all."[2] Second, in historical terms, evangelicalism in Britain and the United States may be located as orthodox Protestantism "in the tradition of the global Christian networks arising from the eighteenth centuries revival movements associated with John Wesley and George Whitefield."[3] As we will see below, evangelicalism in Norway largely fits into this conceptual and historical framework. However, in the Norwegian context, the international impulses are due to a combination of influences from continental Pietism in an earlier phase and Anglo-American revivalism in a later phase.[4]

The Wider Story of Christianity in Norway

The history of evangelicalism in Norway is set within the broader story of Christianity in Norway. Four factors may be highlighted in this history: a millennium with Christian faith and values, the Lutheran Reformation heritage, the pivotal role of Hans Nielsen Hauge and the secularization process.

A Millennium with Christianity

The Christian faith came to Norway during the Viking age through a complex combination of personal and political influences and initiatives. The year 2024 marked the one thousand-year-jubilee of the first Christian laws (*kristenretten*) of Norway. According to tradition, these laws were affirmed at a national legal assembly (*Mostratinget*) in 1024:

> The introduction of these Christian Laws began an extensive and radical social upheaval – "from a society of power to a society of law." It marked the beginning of a new era, with a stronger consideration for the people and the legal protection of individuals. In our modern society, we still see traces of these Christian Laws, which have been both a fundament for developing the Church of Norway and contributed to the shaping of the Norwegian legal

---

2. David W. Bebbington, "The Evangelical Quadrilateral: A Response," in *Evangelicals: Who They Have Been, Are Now, and Could Be*, ed. Mark A. Noll, David W. Bebbington and George M. Marsden (Grand Rapids: Eerdmans, 2019), 187.

3. Timothy Larsen, "Defining and Locating Evangelicalism," in *The Cambridge Companion to Evangelical Theology*, ed. Timothy Larsen and Daniel J. Treier (Cambridge: Cambridge University Press, 2007), 1.

4. For the overall historical description of Christianity in Norway since the early nineteenth century, I am especially indebted to Helje Kringlebotn Sødal, *Norsk kristendomshistorie 1800–2020. Fra selvsagt tro til mangfold* (Oslo: Cappelen Damm Akademisk, 2021).

system. In this perspective, Mostratinget 1024 was an important event that started significant change processes in Norway, which is why we celebrate this as a national jubilee for Norwegian laws.[5]

Thus, the long era of Christendom in Norway had begun, with strong links between church and state. At its best, the emerging national legal systems and cultural traditions were influenced by genuine Christian faith and values, whereas too often abuse of power and mixed theologies became deeply challenging.

The Heritage of the Reformation

The Lutheran Reformation was introduced top-down by the monarchs in the Nordic countries. Nevertheless, it had a deep long-term societal impact. We may describe the Reformation heritage in Norway in theological, cultural and legal terms. Theologically, Lutheranism became the normative framework for Norwegian church doctrine, liturgy and devotional life for centuries. The five *solas* of the Magisterial Reformation became the dominant theological worldview: *sola Scriptura, sola fide, sola gratia, solus Christus* and *soli Deo gloria*. Alongside this shared Reformation theology were the confessional Lutheran doctrines on Law and Gospel and the sacraments of infant baptism and the Holy Communion, as well as a dominant traditional role for the Lutheran minister.

Culturally, Lutheran theology and piety had a strong influence on the arts, literature and everyday life. However, the notion that post-Reformation Norwegian society was dominated by a monocultural Lutheranism needs to be nuanced by supplementary perspectives as well as oppositional voices from below. Nevertheless, a key consequence is that "the material, if not the immaterial, religious landscape of Scandinavia still has the imprint of Christian religion – in its multivocal, diverse versions."[6]

The Norwegian constitution of 1814 established a state church, with "the Evangelical-Lutheran Religion" as the official religion.[7] Even though religious freedom was gradually introduced in the nineteenth and twentieth centuries, due to the combined influence of Lutheran revivalism, evangelical nonconformism and liberalism, the formal ties between state and church were

---

5. See https://moster2024.no/info/information-for-english-speakers.

6. Arne Bugge Amundsen, "Religious Heritage in the North: Monocultural or Multicultural?," *Approaching Religion* 13.2 (2023): 18.

7. See The Constitution of the Kingdom of Norway.

not dissolved until 2012, when the Church of Norway became a distinct legal entity as "a national folk church." This dissolution has been referred to as "the biggest change to the Church since the Reformation."[8]

Hans Nielsen Hauge

Many historians would consider lay preacher, revivalist, and entrepreneur Hans Nielsen Hauge (1771–1824) as one of the most important personalities in the formation of a modern Norwegian society. Through his preaching throughout Norway, his publications and the initiation of networks of "Haugian friends," Hauge had a deep impact on religious life across geographical regions and social classes. This influential national Haugian revival emerged despite strong opposition from many Lutheran ministers and government officials. The lack of religious freedom, with The Conventicle Act prohibiting lay ministry, resulted in a long imprisonment for Hauge.

Closely linked to Hauge's ministry as a revival preacher was his role as pioneer and motivator in various fields of entrepreneurship: "Hauge was part of a large Pietistic and Lutheran tradition with British Puritan inspiration in his entrepreneurial activities. He was influenced by Martin Luther's understanding of the biblical concept of calling or vocation."[9] There are still significant traces of this entrepreneurship tradition across religious, industrial, social, political, and educational sectors. Thus, Hauge and the Haugian revival had a remarkable broad impact across Norway. After the annulment of The Conventicle Act in 1842, the Haugians "went on to be organized in other lay Christian organizations, such as outer and inner missions and the temperance movement."[10]

The Contemporary Context

A unifying characteristic of the nineteenth century across Scandinavia was the presence of widespread evangelical grassroot movements. Before intro-

---

8. See https://www.loc.gov/item/global-legal-monitor/2017-02-03/norway-state-and-church-separate-after-500-years/.

9. Truls Liland and Ola H. Grytten, "The Inspiration from Hauge: An Introduction," in *In the Legacy of Hans Nielsen Hauge: Entrepreneurship in Economics, Education and Politics*, ed. Ola H. Grytten and Truls Liland (Bergen: Bodoni Forlag, 2021), 14. See also Truls Liland, John Daniel Andersen and Jan Inge Jenssen, "Perspectives on Christian Revivals and Societal Change," *European Journal of Theology* 33.2 (2024): 215–40.

10. Jostein Garcia de Presno, "From the Will of God to the Will of Hauge: Institutionalization of beliefs and practices in the Norwegian Haugian movement," *Scandinavian Journal of History* 49.4 (2024): 483–84.

ducing these outer and inner mission movements in Norway, we will include a brief description of major transitions to contemporary Norwegian secular and pluralistic society.

From the 1880s and onwards, secular thought was gradually introduced in the academy, the arts and the media, and the educational sector, with naturalism and positivism as key influences. More recently, secular humanism has become an attractive worldview option. The secular influence is also seen in the current prominence of secular-rational and self-expression values in Scandinavia at large.[11] Alongside these fundamental changes in beliefs and values, as in many other Western European countries, Norwegian society at large has been shaped by a strong secularization process with increasing marginalization of Christian institutions, beliefs and behaviour.[12] The combined effects of an increase in migration, global media consumption and international travel in recent decades have also resulted in an accelerated pluralism, with citizens facing competing worldviews.

In terms of religiosity and religious legislation, Norway has changed "from a denominational state to a state with a pluralistic religious policy."[13] Some core issues emerge in this new context: Does neutrality refer to worldview neutral or value neutral? Should secularism be inclusive and non-doctrinal or exclusive and doctrinal? How should we understand the difference between liberal rights and liberal values?[14] These issues are being discussed and negotiated within the evangelical community and in society at large.

The Evangelical Heritage in Norway

Three of the significant movements which contributed towards creating a Norwegian evangelical heritage were the establishment of prayer houses, the founding of foreign mission societies and the gradual emergence of influential non-conformist evangelical groups.

---

11. According to https://www.worldvaluessurvey.org/WVSContents.jsp.

12. See Lars Dahle, "Western Europe – Marginalization of Christians through Secularization?," in *Freedom of Belief and Christian Mission*, ed. Hans Aage Gravaas, Christof Sauer et al. (Oxford: Regnum, 2015), 382–94, www.ocms.ac.uk/wp-content/uploads/2021/01/Freedom_of_Belief_and_Christian_Mission-Final-WM.pdf.

13. Robert Lilleaasen, "Religion in Norway between National Legislation and Local Politics," *European Journal of Theology* 31.1 (2022): 111.

14. Lilleaasen, "Religion in Norway," 111.

The Lutheran Prayer Houses

A series of influential evangelical revivals characterized the nineteenth century, which gradually led to the establishment of more than two thousand prayer houses across Norway and the founding of several inner mission networks and societies. The specific nature and function of the prayer house as an evangelical institution is well described by Kristin Norseth:

> A prayer house means, in its most straightforward sense, "a house for prayer." The term is used for freestanding meeting houses where there are religious and social activities run by individuals or local associations that are associated with national, Lutheran lay movements for foreign missions and home missions, which work within the bounds of the Lutheran state Church of Norway. In the Norwegian context, the term "prayer house" therefore has confessional implications: A prayer house – *et bedehus* – is always Lutheran. The statutes of the prayer houses confirm, more or less without exception, that all activities within and beyond the prayer house should be run "in compliance with the Evangelical Lutheran Church's confession." The prayer house served not only for edification, but it also aided in the fight against "sectarianism," liberal theology, and secularisation.[15]

The first prayer houses were built in the 1840s and 1850s, after the annulment of The Conventicle Act. The meetings were usually organized and led by non-ordained local leaders. Sunday evenings were often preferred, to avoid competing with the local Sunday morning parish service. Itinerant revivalist preachers were frequently invited to speak, but the local groups would meet on a regular basis to pray and to share their testimonies. Increasingly, the prayer houses also became arenas for a wide variety of social activities, often with specific religious intentions such as faith education, discipleship ministry and support for the foreign mission societies. As a revival and renewal movement within an established church, the Norwegian prayer house movement is a clear manifestation of the classic pietistic principle *ecclesiolae in ecclesia* ("little churches within the church").[16]

The religious and societal influence of the prayer houses gradually diminished in the era after World War II due to the overall transition to a largely

---

15. Kristin Norseth, "The Prayer House as Promised Land," in *Tracing the Jerusalem Code: Volume 3: The Promised Land. Christian Cultures in Modern Scandinavia (ca. 1750–ca. 1920)*, ed. Ragnhild J. Zorgati, Anna Bohlin and Therese Sjøvoll (Berlin: De Gruyter, 2021), 167.

16. See www.britannica.com/topic/ecclesiolae-in-ecclesia.

secular and pluralistic society. However, the prayer house movement is currently being revitalised in some areas, especially in the Norwegian "Bible Belt" (the southern and western coastal strip).[17]

The Lutheran Foreign Mission Movement

In the latter part of the nineteenth century Norway probably sent out more Christian missionaries *per capita* than any other country in the world. This was largely a result of the formation of several missionary societies. The first of these was the Norwegian Missionary Society (NMS), founded in 1842. In the pioneering phase, NMS sent out missionaries to Zululand (South Africa) and Madagascar. Many other similar initiatives followed, such as The Norwegian Church Ministry to Israel (1844), The Santal Mission (1867, now: Normisjon) and Norwegian Lutheran Mission (1891).

The foreign mission movement had a deep, long-term impact in Norway both at the local level and the national level. Locally, thousands of dedicated mission support groups were established with regular meetings in private homes or in prayer houses; many of these groups were only for women. Nationally, mission magazines were established, some with large audiences. "The number of subscribers to the Norwegian missionary journal *Norsk Missionstidende* increased from 2,000 in the 1850s to 6,500 in the 1870s and 10,000 in 1885. By comparison, in the 1870s the leading secular newspaper in Norway, *Morgenbladet*, had 2,000 subscribers."[18] Through this foreign mission movement, supporters became part of a global evangelical community and mission shaped their view of the wider world:

> By default, the mission was the primary mediator between Norwegians and the non-European world. It had a decisive influence on the formative process of Norwegian attitudes towards Africa and Africans, at a time when the idea of modern press coverage was lacking. Missionaries created the Norwegian picture of "the Other."[19]

---

17. For a historical analysis, see Bjørg Seland, "Det norske bibelbeltet. Geografiske og kulturhistoriske perspektiv," *Historisk tidsskrift* 99.2 (2020): 128–43; https://doi.org/10.18261/issn.1504-2944-2020-02-04.

18. Roald Berg, "The missionary impulse in Norwegian history," *Studia Historiae Ecclesiasticae* 36.1 (2010): 5.

19. Berg, "The missionary impulse," 8.

It is fascinating to note that, during "the high era of foreign mission" in Norway, "evangelical missionaries were culture heroes, hymned in the press, celebrated authors, and subjects of portraiture"![20]

The Non-Lutheran Evangelical Heritage

In 1845, three years after the law against lay preaching had been abolished, the Dissension Act (*Dissenterloven*) was passed. This allowed "free churches" to establish themselves in Norway:

> The law, which made religious individualism a legal principle, allowed persons above the age of 25 (age of majority) to abandon the state church and take up membership in free Christian congregations. This was an important step towards dismantling the state monopoly on religion. It was also a decisive legal invention, which detached membership of the Norwegian state church from Norwegian citizenship. An immediate consequence was that a number of Free Churches were founded in the following decades. Most of them were small local groups and were comprised of between a couple of hundred to 1000 members.[21]

From these humble beginnings, the non-Lutheran evangelical constituencies have grown steadily, both in numbers, confidence and in terms of theological and missional strength. Today, denominations such as the Pentecostals, the Baptists and the Norwegian Covenant Church represent significant streams within Norwegian evangelicalism.

Evangelical Contributions from Norway

Many Norwegian evangelicals have made significant contributions to the wider evangelical community, both in Europe and globally. This is especially evident in the areas of global evangelical mission, evangelical student work and the Lausanne Movement.

---

20. Derek R. Peterson, "Review of Kristin Fjelde Tjelle. *Missionary Masculinity, 1870–1930: The Norwegian Missionaries in South-East Africa*," *The American Historical Review* 120.2 (2015): 755–56, doi.org/10.1093/ahr/120.2.755.

21. Anne Stensvold, "Paving the Way for Pentecostalism: A Historical Exploration of Post-Reformation Revivals in Norway," in *Charismatic Christianity in Finland, Norway, and Sweden*, ed. Jessica Moberg and Jane Skjoldli (Palgrave Studies in New Religions and Alternative Spiritualities; Cham: Palgrave Macmillan, 2018), 31.

Contributions to Evangelical Global Mission

We identified the foreign mission movement above as a major characteristic of Norwegian evangelicalism. This has resulted in many significant contributions to global mission. We may illustrate this by highlighting four influential individuals who represent different missional communities, eras and emphases. One of the best-known missionaries in the nineteenth century was Lars Dahle (1843–1925). He served as a pioneer missionary in Madagascar for seventeen years, with broad and lasting impact. His pioneering approach seems to have been modelled on William Carey's classical missionary model. Dahle later served for more than thirty years as General Secretary of the NMS, expanding its work while being a prolific writer and a public voice. He was well connected internationally and led the Norwegian delegation at the 1910 Edinburgh World Missionary Conference.[22]

Many female missionaries from Norway had remarkable ministries. Annie Skau Berntsen (1911–1992) was a missionary nurse sent out for The Norwegian Missionary Association. "Sister Annie" served in Shaanxi (China) from 1938 to 1950. When all missionaries were expelled from China, she moved to Hong Kong where she co-founded the tuberculosis sanatorium Haven of Hope Hospital. After her retirement in 1978, sister Annie and her diaconal ministry became very popular nationally, when she was profiled as a warm-hearted evangelical entrepreneur on the Norwegian version of *This is Your Life* in 1985.[23]

Media involvement has been a prioritised tasks for many Norwegian evangelicals, with evangelical-ecumenical Sigurd Aske (1914–1991) as a leading entrepreneur. Having served as a Lutheran missionary in China and Japan until 1957, Aske became involved with the Lutheran World Federation (LWF) in Geneva, with special responsibility for broadcasting. Aske's most significant achievement was establishing Radio Voice of the Gospel in Ethiopia, considered as the first major independent radio station in Africa. He also pioneered strategic Christian media initiatives in Norway.[24]

The Pentecostal evangelist Arild Edvardsen (1938–2008) was also a media entrepreneur, with an extensive national and international media ministry. He considered his calling to be worldwide evangelism through national witnesses and national churches. This was achieved mainly through funding indigenous

---

22. See Lars Dahle, "Lars Dahle," in *Kristne strateger*, 146–53. Dahle was my great-grandfather.

23. See Ingunn Folkestad Breistein, "Annie Skau Berntsen," in *Kristne strateger*, 292–301.

24. See Jon Magne Lund, "Sigurd Aske," *Norsk Biografisk Leksikon* (2005), https://nbl.snl.no/Sigurd_Aske.

workers who served with local partners, an approach which Edvardsen pioneered in Norway. He participated actively in international charismatic networks, with special connections to the United States and South Korea. Edvardsen and his ministry *Troens Bevis* were widely known in Norway and beyond.[25]

Contributions to Evangelical Student Work

Two Norwegian leaders had a central role in the founding phase of the International Fellowship of Evangelical Students (IFES). At an early preparatory evangelical student work conference in Norway in 1934, theology professor and inner mission leader Ole Hallesby (1879–1961) gave the opening address with three key themes which are "hallmarks of Norway's unique contribution to [IFES]":[26]

> The first is the importance of personal spiritual and devotional life, including personal reading of God's word, prayer, and clear beliefs. The second theme is the belief that our faith is not just a set of doctrines but something we must live out. The third is an attitude of humility and friendship.[27]

Hallesby's devotional classic *Prayer* (1931) has had a global impact in IFES circles and beyond.

The other prominent Norwegian evangelical leader during the IFES founding phase was theologian and pastor Carl Fredrik Wisløff (1908–2004). He proposed an international evangelical network of Christian Unions at a preparatory meeting in the mid-1930s, partnered with Hallesby when the IFES was formally established in 1947, had a deep concern throughout for the IFES Doctrinal Basis and later became IFES President (1967–1979).[28]

Several evangelical leaders have followed in the footsteps of Hallesby and Wisløff and continued the strong Norwegian IFES involvement in various leadership roles.[29]

---

25. See Helje Kringlebotn Sødal, "Aril Edvardsen," in *Kristne strateger*, 322–31.
26. See https://nkss.no/greetings-from-general-secretary-of-ifes-tim-adams/; see also Timothée Joset, *The Priesthood of All Students: Historical, Theological and Missiological Foundations of a Global University Ministry* (Carlisle: Langham Global Library, 2023), chapter 3.
27. See https://nkss.no/greetings-from-general-secretary-of-ifes-tim-adams/.
28. See Egil Sjaastad, *Carl Fr. Wisløff. Presten som ble misjonsfolkets professor* (Kristiansand: Portal, 2016).
29. Two examples could be highlighted: Anfin Skaaheim as IFES President (1979–1984) and Tor Erling Fagermoen as IFES Regional Secretary for Europe (2015–2021).

Contributions to the Lausanne Movement

When the International Missionary Council joined the World Council of Churches (WCC) in the early 1960s, the Norwegian Missionary Council was one of the few national partners which decided to stay independent, due to widespread theological scepticism towards the WCC. This historical background provides a key reason why the first Lausanne Congress (1974) and the subsequent movement were warmly embraced by many evangelicals in Norway. A wide spectrum of evangelical leaders became involved with Lausanne, including bishops in the Church of Norway, leaders of Lutheran mission organizations, and church and mission leaders from non-Lutheran contexts. This original enthusiasm paved the way for a broad Norwegian involvement in subsequent Lausanne Congresses, consultations and networks up until the present day. This includes various leadership contributions, especially in missiology, within issue networks such as tentmaking and media engagement, and in mentoring for younger leaders.[30]

The Evangelical Community in Norway

A significant merger happened in 2001, when the Norwegian Lausanne Committee, the Norwegian Evangelical Alliance and the Norwegian Missionary Council established Norme (Norwegian Council for Mission and Evangelism). Membership of Norme is usually regarded as a hallmark of the evangelical identity of a denomination or organization. Currently, forty-three Norwegian mission organizations and denominations are members of Norme.[31]

As concluding reflections, I would like to highlight some significant current trends in the evangelical community in Norway:

- During the last decade, the evangelical community within the Church of Norway has been weakened. This is largely due to a majority move towards theological liberalism, as illustrated in a dominant progressive view of same-sex marriages.
- Several Lutheran mission organizations are in a transformational stage, where local fellowships in prayer houses are establishing more

---

30. Key missiologists include Knud Jørgensen, Tormod Engelsviken and Rolf Kjøde. In terms of issue networks, Berit Helgøy Kloster and Steinar Opheim have been central in tentmaking, alongside Lars Dahle in media engagement. Ole-Magnus Olafsrud has pioneered mentoring and leadership development for younger leaders.

31. See https://norme.no/medlemsorganisasjoner/.

independent local churches. Many would consider this as a revitalization of the traditional prayer house movement.
- The non-Lutheran evangelical denominations are becoming more influential in the evangelical movement in Norway. Some local churches in these denominations are experiencing considerable church growth.
- A broad spectrum of evangelical church leaders has focused on church planting as a key missional task. Norway is leading the way in Europe, especially through the M4 Europe network with the vision to "ignite church planting movements across Europe."[32]
- Increasingly, many young Christians seem more spiritually open and more courageous than earlier generations. Christian apologetics is being rediscovered as a key resource for discipleship and evangelism in a secular and pluralistic society, across generations.[33]
- Many migrant churches are growing in numbers, experience and confidence. They are increasingly becoming significant mission partners of ethnic Norwegian churches, with Lausanne as a key platform.

As evangelicals in Norway, we would do well – in view of the picture presented above – to heed the wise advice in the chapter on "Re-evangelizing Europe" in *The State of the Great Commission* report:

> We need to focus on restoring truth, reshaping morality, rebuilding community, reconnecting digitally, respecting creation, and regarding demography.[34]

Bibliography

Amundsen, Arne Bugge. "Religious Heritage in the North: Monocultural or Multicultural?" *Approaching Religion* 13 (2023) 2:6–20. https://doi.org/10.30664/ar.130637.

Berg, Roald. "The missionary impulse in Norwegian history," *Studia Historiae Ecclesiasticae* 36 (2010) 1:1–13. https://core.ac.uk/download/pdf/43167535.pdf.

Dahle, Lars, Margunn Serigstad Dahle and Knud Jørgensen. "Introductory Chapter: Evangelical Perspectives on Mission – from Lausanne to Cape Town." Pages 1–10

---

32. The Norwegian Lutheran pastor and entrepreneur Øivind Augland is "the founder and visionary leader" of M4 Europe, see https://m4europe.org/our-story.

33. Originally inspired by the European Leadership Forum, the Veritas Conference partnership has been especially significant for the apologetics renaissance in Norway, see www.veritasnorge.no.

34. Cf. https://lausanne.org/report/europe (2024).

in *The Lausanne Movement. A Range of Perspectives*. Edited by Margunn Serigstad Dahle, Lars Dahle and Knud Jørgensen. Oxford: Regnum, 2014. www.ocms.ac.uk/wp-content/uploads/2021/01/The_Lausanne_Movement-Final-WMF.pdf.

Garcia de Presno, Jostein. "From the Will of God to the Will of Hauge: Institutionalization of beliefs and practices in the Norwegian Haugian movement." *Scandinavian Journal of History* 49 (2024) 4:471–92. https://doi.org/10.1080/03468755.2024.2332284.

Hutchinson, Mark. "Evangelicals in Northern Europe." Pages 372–77 in *Evangelicals around the World. A Global Handbook for the 21st Century*. Edited by Brian C. Stiller, Todd M. Johnson, Karen Stiller and Mark Hutchinson. Nashville: World Evangelical Alliance, 2015.

Liland, Truls, and Ola H. Grytten. "The Inspiration from Hauge: An Introduction." In *In the Legacy of Hans Nielsen Hauge: Entrepreneurship in Economics, Education and Politics*. Edited by Ola H. Grytten and Truls Liland. Bergen: Bodoni Forlag, 2021.

Lilleaasen, Robert. "Religion in Norway between National Legislation and Local Politics." *European Journal of Theology* 31.1 (2022): 92–113. https://doi.org/10.5117/EJT2022.1.006.LILL.

Norseth, Kristin. "The Prayer House as Promised Land." Pages 163–88 in *Tracing the Jerusalem Code: Volume 3: The Promised Land. Christian Cultures in Modern Scandinavia (ca. 1750–ca. 1920)*. Edited by Ragnhild J. Zorgati, Anna Bohlin and Therese Sjøvoll. Berlin / Boston: De Gruyter, 2021. https://doi.org/10.1515/9783110639476-010.

Stensvold, Anne. "Paving the Way for Pentecostalism: A Historical Exploration of Post-Reformation Revivals in Norway." In *Charismatic Christianity in Finland, Norway, and Sweden*. Edited by Jessica Moberg and Jane Skjoldli. Palgrave Studies in New Religions and Alternative Spiritualities. Cham: Palgrave Macmillan, 2018. https://doi.org/10.1007/978-3-319-69614-0_2.

Sødal, Helje Kringlebotn. *Norsk kristendomshistorie 1800–2020. Fra selvsagt tro til mangfold*. Oslo: Cappelen Damm Akademisk, 2021.

Sødal, Helje Kringlebotn, ed. *Kristne strateger*. Oslo: Cappelen Damm Akademisk, 2023.

19

Evangelicalism in Portugal

Timóteo Cavaco

Introduction

The history of Protestantism in Southern Europe presents a complex tapestry of religious, cultural and social dynamics. While the Reformation predominantly shaped northern Europe, its influence in southern European countries, particularly Portugal, has often been overlooked. This chapter explores the development of Protestant movements within the southern European context, focusing on Portugal, which is a peculiar case. By analysing the similarities and dissimilarities in the evolution of the Protestant churches across the region, we seek to illuminate the unique interplay of historical events, theological developments and socio-political factors that have shaped Protestantism in Portugal. In doing so, the chapter contributes to a deeper understanding of the religious transformation in Southern Europe and its ongoing relevance in contemporary society.

It is essential to begin with two key premises. First, the focus of comparison is not all of Southern Europe, but the principal Catholic-majority countries in this area: Portugal, Spain, France and Italy. Second, this chapter treats the terms "Protestantism" and "Evangelicalism" as synonymous. This approach is justified by the particular historical development of Protestantism in Portugal, a subject that will be examined in detail in the last section of the chapter.

Portugal within Southern Europe

While there are similarities in the reception and development of Protestantism across the rest of Southern Europe, Portugal's religious landscape exhibits distinctive features. In order to provide context, I will first present some relevant data on the current state of affairs before delving into the historical analysis.[1]

Portugal presents surprisingly high levels of religious belonging and even practice. According to 2021 data, the number of inhabitants of Portugal who identify themselves as Roman Catholic still exceeds 80 percent,[2] which compares with 74.5 percent in Italy,[3] only 57 percent in neighbouring Spain[4] and 47 percent in France.[5] This show that in the other three countries secularism has caused much greater erosion in the Christian field. Another dissimilarity has to do with the fact that in Portugal, Christian minorities are clearly the second religious group, with almost 5 percent of the population (about half of these are Protestant/Evangelical), while Muslims account for less than 0.5 percent of the population.[6] By contrast, in Spain (4.9 percent)[7] and in France (4 percent)[8] Islam is clearly the second largest religious group, while in Italy (3.7 percent) Muslims are the third religious group, slightly behind the joined group of non-Catholic Christians, but substantially higher than the Protestants/Evangelicals in the country.[9]

Although in recent decades the number of people without religion (atheists, agnostics, believers without religion) has increased significantly in Portugal, to 14 percent in 2021,[10] this figure is well behind Spain (42 percent)[11] and

---

1. See also the chapter by Elsa Correia Pereira in this volume.

2. Out of a total of 8,781,900 respondents, 7,043,016 stated that they belong to the Catholic religion. This figure does not include residents of Portugal under the age of 15, nor individuals who chose not to answer the question on religious affiliation. The total population of Portugal, according to the same census, is 10,343,066 people ("Censos 2021").

3. "2022 Report on International Religious Freedom: Italy," *U.S. Department of State*, www.state.gov/reports/2022-report-on-international-religious-freedom/italy.

4. "Share of the Spanish population who consider themselves Catholic from 2011 to 2024," *Statista*, www.statista.com/statistics/992681/share-of-catholics-in-spain.

5. "2022 Report on International Religious Freedom: France," *U.S. Department of State*, www.state.gov/reports/2022-report-on-international-religious-freedom/france.

6. "Censos 2021." The non-evangelical half consists of Orthodox believers, Jehovah's Witnesses, Mormons, Adventists and "others" (non specified).

7. "Religious affiliation of the population in Spain as of 2022," *Statista*, www.statista.com/statistics/1338534/number-adherents-religions-spain.

8. "2022 Report . . . France."

9. "Number of Italian citizens belonging to religious minorities in Italy in 2022," *Statista*, www.statista.com/statistics/579495/italian-citizens-belonging-to-religious-minorities-italy.

10. "Censos 2021."

11. "Share of non-religious people in Spain from 1980 to 2023," *Statista*, www.statista.com/statistics/1419110/share-of-non-religious-people-in-spain.

France (34 percent)[12] and slightly behind Italy (15.3 percent).[13] The Roman Catholics are intensely polarized whereas the less than 6 percent religious minority is very fragmented and fundamentally concentrated in the urban centres, mainly due to migratory factors.[14]

Protestants in Portugal before the Nineteenth Century

At the end of his life, king Manuel I (1469–1521) sought to keep the ideas of Martin Luther (1483–1546) away from our country. Soon Portuguese diplomacy was closely following the religious events in northern and central Europe. Pope Leo X sent a bull to king Manuel in March 1521, exhibiting his concern that Luther's ideas would penetrate Portugal[15] and in April the Portuguese king wrote to the German emperor Charles V, his brother-in-law, asking him to eradicate what he considered to be "such a great wickedness."[16] The letter implied that Manuel's concerns were not only religious or theological, but mainly political.

No Protestant community was formed in Portugal in the sixteenth century due to three factors: the centralization in the crown of literary production, the intense religiosity of the population and the ecclesiastical leaders, and highly effective repression by the Inquisition which was established in 1536. Manuel Travassos (c.1543–1571) was among the first Portuguese Lutherans sentenced to death.[17] On the other hand, in the overseas Portuguese territories several Protestant communities were founded, such as those of French Huguenots in the Guanabara Bay (1557) and Dutch Calvinists in Brazil (1630–1654). In the Far East the first Bible translation into Portuguese appeared in 1681, made by João Ferreira de Almeida (c.1628–1691), a Portuguese man who was a Reformed missionary and pastor in Java. This translation is unique as

---

12. "2022 Report ... France."
13. "2022 Report ... Italy."
14. For further information see Alfredo Teixeira (ed.), *Religião, Território e Identidade: Contextos Metropolitanos* (Lisboa: Imprensa Nacional, 2023).
15. Isabel M. R. Mendes Drumnod Braga, "Ecos do problema religioso além Pirenéus no Portugal moderno," *Estudos em homenagem a João Francisco Marques* 1 (2001): 229–49, 232.
16. Paulo Drumond Braga, "Carta de D. Manuel I a Carlos V sobre a rebelião de Lutero (1521)," *Itinerarium* 145 (1993): 41–43, 42.
17. See for details Isaías da Rosa Pereira, "O processo de Manuel Travassos na Inquisição de Lisboa (1570–1571)," *Anais da Academia Portuguesa da História* 23.1 (1975): 117–56.

it is the only Bible translation into a leading European language prepared in a colonial context.[18]

After six decades of union with the Spanish crown (1580–1640), Portugal regained its independence. From that moment communities of Protestant foreigners began to be established as a bargaining chip for the support that Protestant countries gave to consolidate the Portuguese independence from Spain.[19] However, for the next three centuries there is no evidence that Protestant ideas or practices reached Portuguese citizens and Protestantism continued to be seen as a religion of foreigners. This means that the beginnings of Portuguese Protestantism in the first decades of the nineteenth century had little connection with missionary efforts in previous centuries or from abroad. The religious recompositing of Portugal in the nineteenth century includes a "Reformation without Protestantism" in the exact sense of the term. There were never any Lutheran Churches in our territory, not even within the Protestant movement.

Nonetheless, Protestantism is still often seen as a foreign phenomenon. This is based on the assumption that foreign entities planned a mission to Portugal in the nineteenth century, which does not correspond to reality. Initially, Protestantism was helped by foreigners, mainly the British, who acted on their own initiative or responded to requests of Portuguese or other foreigners already settled in Portugal, but without formal support from foreign missionary entities. It is due to this perception that Protestantism is still not entirely assimilated by the social fabrics.

With rare exceptions, Portugal only began to be genuinely considered as a mission territory by Protestant entities at the turn of the twentieth century. An exception to this pattern was the British and Foreign Bible Society, which has operated in Portugal since 1809. However, its British leaders did not see its activities as a "Protestant mission" because, in their view, making the Bible available to believers and even non-believers was a service to all.[20]

---

18. See further Luís Henrique Menezes Fernandes, *Diferença da cristandade: A controvérsia religiosa nas Índias Orientais holandesas e o significado histórico da primeira tradução da Bíblia em português (1642–1694)* (PhD thesis, São Paulo: Universidade de São Paulo, 2016).

19. Tom-Eric Krijger, "An Extraterritorial Privacy Zone? Dutch Protestants and Their Embassy Chapel in Early Modern Portugal," *Tijdschrift voor Sociale en Economische Geschiedenis* 18.3 (2021): 41–74, 46.

20. Rita Mendonça Leite, *Livro, Texto e Autoridade. Diversificação religiosa com a Sociedade Bíblica em Portugal (1804–1940)* (Lisboa: Imprensa Nacional, 2019), 43.

Protestantism in Portugal since 1830
Nineteenth Century

The year 1834 marks the beginning of organized Protestant presence in Portugal. It was Vicente Gomez y Tojar (1796?–1878), born in Granada, Spain, who pioneered the Portuguese evangelical movement. Little is known about the family background and early years of Gomez, who studied medicine as well as theology and philosophy. At a young age, he became a parish priest in the diocese of Malaga and then a member of its cathedral chapter. Later he moved to Gibraltar, then to Tangier and finally to the already independent Brazil, where he remained until 1830. It is not known when he began to relate to the Protestant faith, but this transition was undoubtedly linked to his liberalism and his relationship with the British. In 1833, Gomez, married to the English Ann Pratt, travelled to Lisbon to practice medicine and religious action. In July 1834, without the support of any church or missionary organization, he began acting as a Bible Society correspondent. On 10 November 1839, the "Chapel of the Promulgation of the Holy Gospel of Our Lord Jesus Christ" was inaugurated, with one hundred and ten people attending. On 8 April 1841, the bishop of London received Gomez into the Church of England. In its early years, the Portuguese authorities tolerated this Protestant community in Lisbon, but the introduction of the Criminal Law (1852) resulted in the prohibition of its meetings and the dispersion of the congregation. Nonetheless, this church remained in existence until 6 December 1870.[21]

From the 1870s onwards, Protestantism consolidated and became a reality in Portuguese society. Numbers were small, but lasting structures were gradually created. Human and financial support, mainly from Great Britain, provided the emerging churches with resources for their consolidation. Buildings were purchased or even built from scratch and in most cases they were adapted to the communities' religious and liturgical needs. They allowed Sunday schools (for biblical and spiritual training) and daily schools (for literacy of children and adults) to open. Friendships among young people were stimulated through the creation of groups of the Young Men's Christian Association (*Associação Cristã da Mocidade* – ACM), with an emphasis on spiritual reflection but also intellectual stimulation and care of the body through physical exercise and

---

21. Timóteo Cavaco, "1834: The institutionalization of Protestantism in Portugal," in *The Global History of Portugal: From prehistory to the modern world*, ed. Carlos Fiolhais, José Eduardo Franco and José Pedro Paiva (Brighton/Chicago/Toronto: Sussex Academic Press, 2022), 292.

healthy behaviour. The first ACM group in Portugal was established in 1894 by the Methodist Alfredo Henrique da Silva (1872–1950).[22]

The first interaction of Portuguese Protestantism with the movement of the Evangelical Alliances, which had begun in London in 1846, also dates from this period. In 1849 Vicente Gomez was the first in Portugal to become a member of the Evangelical Alliance and he received its support from 1853 onwards. At a conference in Madrid in April 1878 the Hispano-Lusitanian Evangelical Alliance was formed. The following year, the first Universal Week of Prayer was held in Portugal between 5 and 12 January 1879.[23]

Twentieth Century

The forces in the country that saw Protestantism as a denationalizing movement and therefore pernicious to Portuguese society were seemingly overcome at the formal level with the creation of the Portuguese Protestant Association (*Associação Protestante Portuguesa* – APP). This was established on 31 July 1909 as the national agency of the Evangelical Alliance of London, with individual members who came from different churches such as the Episcopalians, Congregationalists and Presbyterians. As far as we know, however, the APP was completely inactive.[24] In the context of World War I the church leaders attempted to form a new organization that would federate the evangelicals in the country. It was only in 1919 that the bases of the future Portuguese Evangelical Alliance (*Aliança Evangélica Portuguesa* – AEP) were established. On 14 and 15 November 1921, the first plenary commission of the AEP met, made up of Episcopalians, Methodists, Presbyterians, Congregationalists and Baptists.[25]

From the scarce statistical data available, it can be concluded that a gradual growth in the number of believers marks the first century of Protestantism in Portugal. In 1906, there were fifty-three national communities, belonging to the Baptist, Episcopal, Congregationalist, Darbyist, Methodist and Pres-

---

22. Timóteo Cavaco, "O associativismo cristão para além das fronteiras confessionais," in *Religião e cidadania: protagonistas, motivações e dinâmicas sociais no contexto ibérico*, ed. António Matos Ferreira, João Miguel Almeida (Lisboa: Universidade Católica Portuguesa, 2011), 607–17, 611–12.

23. Timóteo Cavaco, *Aliança Evangélica Portuguesa: 100 anos de história e comunhão – das origens à atualidade* (Lisboa: AEP – Edições e Produções, 2022), 30–31.

24. Cavaco, *Aliança Evangélica Portuguesa*, 49.

25. Cavaco, *Aliança Evangélica Portuguesa*, 94.

byterian "rites," as well as more than thirty evangelical elementary schools.[26] About sixty years later, in 1967, the available information points to about four hundred local churches, including Assemblies of God, as well as cooperative organizations, periodicals, publishers and bookstores, education, charity, evangelical clinics, camps and scouts.[27] Subsequently, in the second half of the 1970s, there was a "first leap," which was caused by the influx of people that inhabited the Portuguese-speaking African nations until they acquired their independence; there were more Protestants in these regions than in mainland Portugal. A "second leap" can be perceived from the end of the 1990s onwards, when migration brought many believers to Portugal from various evangelical tendencies, mainly from Brazil.

Protestantism and Evangelicalism: Distinct Traditions or Shared Roots?

After several decades of conflict that had begun during the monarchy and culminated in the establishment of the Republic in 1910, the military coup of 1926 brought some degree of pacification to Portuguese society. This coup led to the establishment of a civil dictatorship which relied on military support throughout its nearly fifty-year existence. Portugal only became a democracy in the last quarter of the twentieth century.

This new authoritarian regime reestablished the institutional and social presence of the Catholic Church, which had been marginalized since 1910. The government did not formally repress or persecute religious minorities, which were almost exclusively Protestant churches and organizations.[28] But its authoritarian nature restricted individual and collective liberties, rights and guarantees, and so hindered the growth of religious expressions that did not align with its ethos or with what it regarded as the "religious tradition" of Portuguese society. Additionally, promoted mostly by Catholic clergy, a deeply ingrained collective spirit resurged, especially in rural areas, that viewed religious "difference" as a threat to national unity.[29] This sentiment was consistently

---

26. Trindade Coelho, *Manual Político do Cidadão Português* (Lisboa: Parceria A. M. Pereira, 1906), 391–99.

27. *Prontuário Evangélico*. 3rd ed. Lisboa: Movimento Promotor de Evangelização, 1967.

28. Paula Borges Santos, *A segunda separação: A política religiosa do Estado Novo (1933–1974)* (Coimbra: Almedina, 2016), 239–40.

29. João Francisco Marques, "Antiprotestantismo: A oposição crítica ao Protestantismo pelo catolicismo em Portugal," in *Dança de demónios: intolerância em Portugal*, ed. António Marujo and José Eduardo Franco (Lisboa: Temas e Debates / Círculo de Leitores, 2009), 203–63, 250.

reflected in political discourse, as the regime was aligned with the nationalist spirit that pervaded many other European countries at the time.

The government's legal protection of the Catholic Church became even more evident in 1940, with the signing of a Concordat between the Holy See and the Portuguese state. This agreement granted the Catholic Church near-exclusive privileges, not only in mainland Portugal but also in its African and Far Eastern colonies, particularly in education. This situation significantly hampered the efforts of Protestant missions, which had been establishing themselves in "Portuguese Africa" since the late nineteenth century. As the most consolidated and widespread religious minority in the country, Protestantism bore the brunt of this exclusion and the resulting discrimination. Nevertheless, some Protestant communities also became accommodating to the regime, viewing it with a certain degree of complacency. It is important to understand that from 1926 to the end of World War II, during which Portugal remained neutral, the country was relatively closed to external influences and consequently, so were its religious communities, including the extremely small Protestant community. This dual isolation – of the country from international affairs and of Protestantism within Portuguese society – might explain why the evangelical churches in Portugal were shielded from theological and ecclesiological disputes elsewhere. As such, the churches in Portugal were not subject to the debates between "liberal" and "conservative" factions.

This situation began to change after the war, with the influx of missionaries from American, Brazilian and European organizations and denominations from the late 1940s onward. This influx brought with it doctrinal divisions, particularly following the establishment of the World Council of Churches (*Conselho Mundial de Igrejas* – CMI) in 1948. The ideas that were debated internationally now circulated in Portugal as well and evangelical leaders were aware of these disputes. However, the community's fragile position vis-à-vis the state and its relative isolation allowed the main Protestant communities to remain united under the aegis of the Evangelical Alliance (AEP) until the early 1970s, a situation that is unique in Western Europe. For this reason, it is difficult to pinpoint the moment when a clear distinction emerged between what could be called the "Protestant world" and the "evangelical world" in Portugal. In fact, the Portuguese language does not have an exact translation for "evangelicalism."

Despite the apparent institutional unity of the Portuguese Protestants, missionaries with ties to the ecumenical movement abroad integrated into the sphere of the AEP. Unlike in North America and most European countries, these distinctions did not affect the cooperation among the Portuguese churches. This can be seen from the fact that various initiatives which were aligned with the conservative sector in the USA were generally embraced by the Portuguese Protestants. Examples include the arrival in 1949 of movements such as the Child Evangelism Fellowship (*Aliança Pró-Evangelização de Crianças*) and Scripture Union (*União Bíblica*), as well as Youth for Christ (*Mocidade para Cristo*) in 1950. All three were widely accepted across the evangelical churches. On the other hand, movements associated with the ecumenical movement, such as the Portuguese branches of the YMCA (ACM, 1894) and the World Student Christian Federation (*Movimento Académico Cristão*, 1947) were also accepted and integrated by all churches, even though the International Fellowship of Evangelical Students (*Grupo Bíblico Universitário* – GBU) did not yet have a branch in Portugal. The Bible Society (*Sociedade Bíblica* or SB, 1809) and AEP (1921) also served as common platforms for the entire Portuguese Protestant community.

However, until the 1960s there was no formal body that could be considered a true federation of evangelical churches, with decisions made by their representatives. Despite strong debates in the AEP from the late 1940s onwards, between those advocating for maintaining an individual membership base and those calling for a representative structure, the argument prevailed that amending the by-laws of the AEP could lead to its dissolution by the Portuguese dictatorial government, which could use any excuse to impose strong measures. Churches with synodal governance structures – such as the Presbyterians, Methodists and Anglicans – contested the exclusive individual membership base, and as their demands were not met, in 1971 they formed the Portuguese Council of Christian Churches (*Conselho Português de Igrejas Cristãs* – COPIC), which was clearly aligned with the World Council of Churches.[30] However, even after the establishment of COPIC, some members of churches that formed it remained individual members of the AEP and were deeply involved in its activities. One example is Augusto Esperança (1928–2018), who served as the General Secretary of the Bible Society (SB) from 1969 and was simultaneously president of the AEP from 1967 to 1972, during the very period when COPIC was established, even though he was a well-known and distinguished pastor of the Presbyterian Church, one of the COPIC's founding members. Thus, COPIC did not view itself as a secessionist movement but rather claimed to fill a gap that had existed since the formation of the first Protestant communities in Portugal over a century earlier. For this reason,

---

30. Manuel P. Cardoso et al., *Uma caminhada ecuménica: 25 anos de testemunho e serviço em Portugal* (Figueira da Foz: Conselho Português de Igrejas Cristãs, 1996).

joint initiatives continued, such as a general meeting of evangelical workers sponsored by World Vision in 1969, and a visit and campaign of the American evangelist John Haggai to Lisbon in 1970, organized by the Christian Businessmen's Movement, in 1972. There were even plans for a campaign by Billy Graham, which ultimately did not take place due to the military coup on 25 April 1974 that finally paved the way for full democratization in Portugal. Nevertheless, the preparations for these events involved leaders from all churches, including those that had already formed COPIC and were thus associated with the World Council of Churches and the international ecumenical movement.

After 1975 the distance between the AEP and COPIC gradually widened. In that year, the AEP amended its by-laws to allow churches and other evangelical organizations to affiliate with it. As a result, each church had to choose between belonging to the AEP or COPIC. From 1990, as part of a broader overhaul of its by-laws, the AEP required that its individual members were also members of a church within the sphere of the AEP, thus severing the few institutional ties that still existed with COPIC.

For the past thirty years the AEP and COPIC have operated as entirely separate entities, but there is a peaceful and respectful dialogue between them. Moreover, collaborative spaces have continued to exist over the years, as seen in the establishment of the Evangelical Broadcasting and Television Committee (*Comissão Evangélica de Rádio e Televisão*) in 1986,[31] which enabled the broadcast of evangelical programmes on public television and radio channels. The founding of the Evangelical Educational Action in Public Schools Committee (*Comissão para a Ação Educativa Evangélica nas Escolas Públicas*) in 1990[32] allowed evangelical students in public schools to receive religious education. Organizations like the SB, which is independent either from AEP or COPIC, and others that are members of the AEP, have continued to include members from churches affiliated with COPIC.

Concluding Remarks

In conclusion, the emergence of "Portuguese Protestantism" brought the loss of influence of the dominant Roman Catholic Church, but the fragile Protestant communities could not imitate the hegemonic presence and well-established organizational structure of the Catholics. Thus, Protestants were perceived as threatening the territorial uniformity of the nation. The diffusion of Protestant

---

31. Cavaco, *Aliança Evangélica Portuguesa*, 182.
32. Cavaco, *Aliança Evangélica Portuguesa*, 184.

theological and cultural ideas was closely associated with the process of religious differentiation that the country witnessed from the nineteenth century. Thus, while sixteenth-century Protestantism in central and northern Europe disputed the spaces already filled, conquering or losing them, Protestantism in Portugal contributed to dissolving the fabrics built over centuries of nationality. This resulted in the construction of a capillary network of Protestant communities that lacked uniformity and was based on family nuclei and other social groups. This mechanism explains the process of construction of Protestant places in contemporary Portugal.

There are currently almost two thousand Protestant local communities in Portugal for a total membership of nearly three hundred and forty thousand people, which is less than 4 percent of the country's population. On the other hand, there are almost four thousand five hundred Catholic parishes serving 81 percent of the total population. This means that the Protestants are dispersed and atomized, which has undoubtedly created and stimulated the perception of a disunited and schismatic people, while the Catholic religious community is still very dense.

Bibliography

"2022 Report on International Religious Freedom." *U.S. Department of State.* www.state.gov/reports/2022-report-on-international-religious-freedom/.

Cardoso, Manuel P. et al. *Uma caminhada ecuménica: 25 anos de testemunho e serviço em Portugal.* Figueira da Foz: Conselho Português de Igrejas Cristãs, 1996.

Cavaco, Timóteo. "O associativismo cristão para além das fronteiras confessionais: limites e relevância." Pages 607–17 in *Religião e cidadania: protagonistas, motivações e dinâmicas sociais no contexto ibérico.* Edited by António Matos Ferreira, João Miguel Almeida. Lisboa: Universidade Católica Portuguesa, 2011.

———. *Aliança Evangélica Portuguesa: 100 anos de história e comunhão – das origens à atualidade.* Lisboa: AEP – Edições e Produções, 2022.

"Censos 2021: População residente com 15 e mais anos de idade por local de residência à data dos Censos e religião." *Instituto Nacional de Estatística.* www.ine.pt/xportal/xmain?xpid=INE&xpgid=ine_indicadores&indOcorrCod=0012311&contexto=bd&selTab=tab2.

Coelho, Trindade. *Manual Político do Cidadão Português.* Lisboa: Parceria A. M. Pereira, 1906.

Escobar, Samuel. "Orígenes del movimiento de Sociedades Bíblicas y su contexto misionológico." *Revista Lusófona de Ciência das Religiões* 4.7–8 (2005): 21–30.

Espírito Santo, Moisés. *Origens do cristianismo português: Precedido de A deusa síria de Luciano.* 3rd ed. Lisboa: Universidade Nova de Lisboa, 2001.

Fiolhais, Carlos, José Eduardo Franco and José Pedro Paiva, eds. *The Global History of Portugal: From Prehistory to the Modern World*. Brighton/Chicago/Toronto: Sussex Academic Press, 2022.

Krijger, Tom-Eric. "An Extraterritorial Privacy Zone? Dutch Protestants and Their Embassy Chapel in Early Modern Portugal." *Tijdschrift voor Sociale en Economische Geschiedenis* 18.3 (2021): 41–74.

Marques, João Francisco. "Antiprotestantismo: A oposição crítica ao Protestantismo pelo catolicismo em Portugal." Pages 203–63 in *Dança de demónios: intolerância em Portugal*. Edited by António Marujo and José Eduardo Franco. Lisboa: Temas e Debates/Círculo de Leitores, 2009.

Prontuário Evangélico. 3rd ed. Lisboa: Movimento Promotor de Evangelização, 1967.

Santos, Paula Borges. *A segunda separação: A política religiosa do Estado Novo (1933–1974)*. Coimbra: Almedina, 2016.

20

Evangelicalism in Romania

Marcel Măcelaru

Introduction – The Evangelicals of Romania

The Romanian evangelicals historically comprise believers of Pentecostal, Baptist and Brethren convictions. They have a rich and complex history, rooted in revival movements of the nineteenth and twentieth centuries. Emerging from broader Protestant awakenings, these groups share a commitment to biblical authority, personal faith and evangelistic mission. Their journey has been marked by persecution, underground resilience and post-Communist expansion, leading to the well-defined denominations that exist today. The 2021 census recorded 544,062 evangelicals, almost 3.5 percent of the country's total population. Among them, approximately 75 percent are Pentecostals, primarily members of the Christian Pentecostal denomination The Apostolic Church of God; 19 percent are Baptists, affiliated with the Christian Baptist denomination; and 6 percent Brethren.[1] Together, these groups form the Romanian Evangelical Alliance, a platform for interdenominational cooperation and representation established in 1990.[2]

However, these census figures do not fully reflect the reality, nor does the Romanian Evangelical Alliance represent all evangelicals of Romania. Members of independent churches that are neither affiliated with a denomination

---

1. The census data is at www.recensamantromania.ro/rezultate-rpl-2021/rezultate-definitive.

2. See Iosif Țon, "Ce este și cum a început Alianța Evanghelică din România," in *Creștinul și biserica*. AlfaOmega.TV, 29.01.2015; https://alfaomega.tv/sectiuni-tematice/romania-puls-spiritual/3813-ce-este-si-cum-a-inceput-alianta-evanghelica-din-romania-de-iosif-ton. For the history of the Romanian Evangelical Alliance, see Bogdan Emanuel Răduț (ed.), *Alianța Evanghelică din România: istoric și documente* (Craiova: SITECH, 2015).

nor part of the Alliance were not included in the census. Instead, they were listed under "Christian," which often defaulted to "Orthodox" due to Romania's cultural and historical association with Eastern Orthodoxy. Additionally, the census did not account for Romanian evangelicals living abroad, particularly in Western Europe, where over eight hundred Romanian evangelical communities exist,[3] and North America, which hosts a similarly strong Romanian evangelical presence. Yet both the diaspora and the independent churches are integral to the story of Romanian evangelicals. The former maintains strong theological, financial and, in many cases, organizational ties with evangelicals in Romania whereas the latter contribute significantly to the vitality of Romanian evangelicalism, fostering spiritual renewal, local outreach and innovative ministry models that complement and diversify the broader evangelical landscape.

The historical overview below is a story of faith under pressure, endurance through persecution and transformation in freedom. The survival of the evangelicals under Communist repression, their growth following the 1989 Revolution and their global expansion through migration all reflect the resilience and adaptability of the movement.

Early Foundations and Identity Formation Until 1918

The roots of Romanian evangelicalism date back to the nineteenth century, when distinct evangelical communities began to emerge under the influence of wider shifts in European and subsequently North American Christianity.[4] The theological identity of Romanian evangelicals was shaped by three major influences: Pietism, the Anabaptist tradition and Western Protestant missions.[5] The new theological emphases introduced in the region included the emphasis on the authority of Scripture, the centrality of Christ's redemptive work,

---

3. On the Romanian evangelical diaspora, see Daniel Martin, "Evanghelicii români în diaspora europeană: Identitate, provocări și contribuții," in *Omul Evanghelic*, ed. Dănuț Mănăstireanu and Dănuț Jemna (Iași: Polirom, 2025, forthcoming).

4. For a comprehensive history of evangelical beginnings in Romania, see Dorin Dobrincu, "Sub puterea Cezarului: o istorie politică a evanghelicilor din România (a doua jumătate a secolului al XIX-lea – 1989)," in *Omul evanghelic: o explorare a comunităților protestante românești*, ed. Dănuț Mănăstireanu and Dorin Dobrincu (Iași: Polirom, 2018), 37–243.

5. See Dănuț Mănăstireanu, "Identitatea evanghelicilor români: Rădăcini, actualitate, perspective," in Mănăstireanu and Dobrincu, *Omul evanghelic*, 244–96; but also Dănuț-Vasile Jemna, "Criza de identitate a omului evanghelic român," in Mănăstireanu and Dobrincu, *Omul evanghelic*, 297–328.

personal conversion and active evangelism.⁶ Romanian evangelicals adapted these transnational religious currents to their own social and cultural context. For example, the pietist spirituality provided a foundation for the underground house churches which functioned in parallel with the "authorised" communities that gathered for worship on Sundays. The Anabaptist practice of faith baptism was embraced despite the influence of the dominant Eastern Orthodox tradition. And the Western Protestant missions provided an example of evangelism that was adjusted to fit the needs of a growing revivalistic movement in Romania.

The regions of Transylvania and Banat became focal points for early evangelical activity, benefiting from historical Protestant influences and exposure to Western missionary efforts. However, evangelicals met with cultural resistance and suspicion, as their emphasis on individual faith commitments and evangelistic outreach challenged the deeply ingrained Orthodox traditions that defined Romanian religious life. Yet despite opposition from religious and state authorities,⁷ evangelicals established small but resilient communities, marked by strong theological convictions, communal solidarity and a vision for transformation.

Baptists

The first evangelicals to emerge in Romania were the Baptists, who trace their origins to the mid-nineteenth century.⁸ The first recorded Baptist baptism took place in 1856 in Bucharest, performed by Heinrich Meyer, a Hungarian missionary. The movement initially spread within the German and Hungarian communities in Transylvania and Banat, areas with historical connections to Lutheran and Reformed traditions. A significant figure in this early period was Karl Johann Scharschmidt, a German carpenter who, along with his wife

---

6. For the theological stance of evangelicals in Romania, see Eugen Matei, "Teologia evanghelicilor români: rădăcini și perspective," in Mănăstireanu and Dobrincu, *Omul evanghelic*, 421–57.

7. On the persecution of evangelicals, see John Tipei, "Persecution of the Romanian Church in the Twentieth Century: A Historical and Theological Perspective," *Plērōma* 6.1 (2004): 71–102.

8. For the history of the Baptists, see Alexa Popovici, *Istoria baptiștilor din România: 1856–1989* (Oradea: Făclia, 2007); Samuel Bâlc, "Istoria baptiștilor din România: între relevanță, ignoranță și speranță," *Jurnal teologic* 20.2 (2021): 37–52; Marius Silveșan, "Istoriografia Bisericii Baptiste din România în secolul XX," in *După 25 de ani: evaluări și reevaluări istoriografice privind comunismul*, ed. Cosmin Budeancă and Florentin Olteanu (Iași: Polirom, 2017), 224–44; Marius Silveșan, "O scurtă istorie cronologică a baptiștilor din România," *Timotheus* 4.1 (2017): 185–212.

Augusta, arrived in Bucharest in 1856. Scharschmidt actively preached Baptist teachings among the German-speaking population, establishing the first informal Baptist gathering in the capital. He later communicated with Johann Gerhard Oncken (1800–1884), a key figure in German Baptist missionary work. By the 1870s, Baptist communities had begun forming in Banat, Crișana and parts of Transylvania, often comprised of ethnic Germans and Hungarians. Oncken collaborated with Hungarian and German Baptists in Oradea and Arad, training local leaders and evangelists. Iosif Seres and Gheorghe Toth played crucial roles in expanding the Baptist movement among ethnic Romanians. In 1884, they planted the first Romanian Baptist church in Păuliș (Arad County), which marked the beginning of a distinct Romanian Baptist identity.

These Romanian Baptists faced persecution from the authorities, aligned with the Orthodox Church, who viewed them as a foreign sect that threatened national religious unity. Converts to Baptist teachings often encountered ostracism, economic penalties and even physical violence. In some cases, Baptist gatherings were raided by authorities and pastors were arrested or fined. The Orthodox Church, closely tied to the Romanian national identity, denounced Baptists as a heretical and foreign influence, reinforcing state opposition.[9]

In 1912, the Baptist Union of Romania was formally established in Bucharest to coordinate the activities of the growing network of churches. The Union trained pastors, printed religious literature and advocated for legal recognition. By 1918, Baptist communities had spread beyond their original ethnic enclaves and were gaining traction among ethnic Romanians.

Brethren

The Brethren movement in Romania began taking shape in the 1870s and 1880s,[10] with early gatherings emerging in Bukovina and Moldova. These communities were primarily influenced by the Plymouth Brethren movement, which had spread from Ireland and England to Germany and Switzerland before reaching Romania. The movement gained traction through Swiss and German preachers who sought to promote simple, Bible-centred worship, inde-

---

9. On the oppression of Baptists, see Daniel Mitrofan, *Pigmei și uriași: file din istoria persecutării baptiștilor* (Oradea: Cristianus, 2007).

10. On the early history of the Brethren movement, see Gheorghe Modoran, "Istoria Bisericii Creștine după Evanghelie din România," *TheoRhēma* 8.1 (2013): 109–38; Gheorghe Modoran, "Contextul religios și factorii favorizanți ai apariției confesiunilor neoprotestante în teritoriile românești," *TheoRhēma* 8.2 (2013): 79–103; Bogdan E. Răduț (ed.), *Din istoria creștinilor după Evanghelie: culegere de documente* (Târgoviște: Editura Cetatea de Scaun, 2016).

pendent from state or clerical authority. The first Brethren groups in Romania formed around small house churches. A significant development was the arrival in 1899 of E. H. Broadbent, a British missionary. He was struck by the absence of evangelical preaching in Romanian and issued an appeal for missionaries. This call was answered by Francis Berney, a Swiss missionary affiliated with the Free Christian Assemblies of Switzerland. Berney arrived in Bucharest in 1899 and began holding meetings in his home, soon drawing a small following of Romanians and expatriates. In 1901, the first Brethren baptisms were performed in Bucharest. Berney's wife, Madeleine, contributed to the mission by opening a Bible school for girls, teaching both biblical studies and practical skills such as sewing and knitting.

The Brethren movement quickly expanded beyond Bucharest. Berney's associate Charles Aubert and the German Hermann Köning established a congregation in Constanța, and the Swiss Johann Bührer settled in Ploiești. Other missionaries expanded the movement in Transylvania, particularly among the German and Saxon populations in Brașov, Râșnov and Codlea. The 1921 Romanian Bible translation by Dumitru Cornilescu (1881–1975), sponsored by the British and Foreign Bible Society, became crucial for evangelical believers. Cornilescu, originally an Orthodox deacon, embraced Brethren theology and his clear and accessible translation helped unify and solidify Brethren communities.[11]

Despite opposition from the Orthodox Church and Romanian authorities, the Brethren continued to spread their faith. In 1909, Berney was expelled from Romania, forcing the movement to rely on local leadership. The preachers Grigore Constantinescu Fotino, Ion Petrescu and Gheorghe Giuvelea carried forward the Brethren message. By 1916, Brethren communities had taken root in Bucharest, Ploiești, Brașov, Vulcan, Cisnădie and Iași, with smaller groups in rural areas. During World War I many of its male members were drafted into military service, leading to a temporary stagnation in church activity. However, the war also created opportunities for outreach, as Brethren believers were exposed to new communities and spread their faith.

---

11. On Cornilescu's Bible and its influence, see Emanuel Conțac, *Cornilescu: Din culisele publicării celei mai citite traduceri românești a Sfintei Scripturi* (Oradea: DECENU.EU, 2024); Emanuel Conțac, "O perspectivă istorică asupra traducerilor Bibliei circulate în spațiul evanghelic românesc," in Mănăstireanu and Dobrincu, *Omul evanghelic*, 359–84.

Pentecostals

Before World War I the Pentecostal movement did not yet exist as an organized denomination, but scattered spiritual experiences and early adherents laid the groundwork for its later development.[12] An early Pentecostal influence came through Filaret (Filat) Rotaru from Udești, Suceava County, born in 1895. Rotaru emigrated to the United States in 1911, where he had a powerful spiritual experience involving divine healing following a serious work accident. After being baptized in water and receiving the baptism in the Holy Spirit, he returned to Romania in 1917. While serving in the Romanian army he began preaching the "full gospel" message in Udești, which led to the formation of a Pentecostal congregation in 1922.

Some historical accounts attribute early Pentecostal experiences in Vicovul de Sus, Suceava County, from 1918 to Nișu Constantin, a Romanian soldier who came into contact with Pentecostal Russians. In Transylvania, early Pentecostal manifestations occurred among ethnic Germans in 1919. A woman named Rezi (Theresia) reportedly began speaking in tongues during a prayer meeting, an event later explained to her by a Pentecostal believer from the United States. This remained a local phenomenon at the time. Only after World War I Pentecostalism took shape as a recognizable movement.

Interwar Expansion and Institutional Development

The interwar period (1918–1944) was an era of growth, organization and institutional consolidation for Romanian evangelicals.[13] The Great Union of 1918 unified Transylvania, Banat, Crișana, Maramureș and Bukovina with the Kingdom of Romania, significantly altering the religious and cultural landscape. As these newly incorporated regions contained well-established Protestant communities, the evangelical movement expanded its reach, particularly among ethnic Romanians. However, this period also presented challenges, as evangelicals faced nationalist policies and legal restrictions imposed by the Orthodox-dominated government. Despite these obstacles, the interwar years saw the establishment of theological institutions, publishing houses and

---

12. Valeriu Andreiescu, *Istoria penticostalismului românesc. Volumul I: Evanghelia deplină și puterea lui Dumnezeu* (Oradea: Casa Cărții, 2012), 31–50; Ciprian Bălăban, *Foc din cer: Un secol de penticostalism românesc* (București: Plērōma / Cluj-Napoca: Risoprint, 2022), 11–50.

13. Paul E. Michelson, "The History of Romanian Evangelicals, 1918–1989: A Bibliographical Excursus," *Archive Moldaviae* 9 (2017): 191–233; Iemima Ploscariu, "The Word Read, Spoken, and Sung: Neo-Protestants and Modernity in Interwar Romania," *Central Europe* 18.2 (2020): 105–21.

denominational leadership structures, enabling evangelicals to strengthen their communities.

Baptists

During the interwar years, the Baptist movement in Romania experienced significant demographic growth,[14] particularly in the regions of Crișana and Banat, where Hungarian[15] and German Baptists had been active since the nineteenth century. The incorporation of these regions into Greater Romania facilitated the expansion of Romanian-language Baptist churches, as local mission efforts intensified. Crucial milestones were the formation of the Baptist Union of Romania and the first Baptist Congress, both in 1920, which brought together communities across Romania. The cities of Oradea and Arad became centres for Baptist organization and theological training. In Oradea, the Baptist Theological Seminary was established in 1921, initially functioning in Buteni before relocating first to Arad and later to Bucharest under the leadership of Constantin Adorian, the first president of the Baptist Union.[16] Other key figures in this period included Ioan Socaciu,[17] who played a crucial role in

---

14. Daniel Bărnuț, "Perspectivă a literaturii religioase interbelice cu privire la comunitățile de credincioși baptiști din Banatul montan – cercetare cantitativă Foaia Diecezană 1920–1925," *Jurnal teologic* 22.2 (2023): 89–98; Mihaela Bucin, "Sanda Mateiu: un model interbelic de resurecție spirituală," *Plērōma* 20.2 (2018): 117–32; Teodor-Ioan Colda, "Baptiștii din România după Marea Unire de la 1918, între entuziasmul realizării idealului național și tragediile persecuției religioase," in *Studii de istorie eclesiastică*, ed. Marius Oanță (Craiova: SITECH, 2018), 121–35; Emanuel Jurcoi, "Uniunea Tineretului Baptist din România (1925–1947)," *Jurnal teologic* 20.1 (2021): 146–58; Marius Silveșan, "Baptiștii din România între regimul de autoritate monarhică al lui Carol al II-lea și regimul de democrație populară," in Oanță, *Studii de istorie eclesiastică*, 137–70; David Natanael Tătar, "Evoluția istorică a lucrării de tineret din bisericile baptiste din România în perioada interbelică," *Jurnal teologic* 22.2 (2023): 99–109.

15. Cf. Mihaela Bucin, "Baptiștii români din Ungaria, aleșii care trăiesc ca străini (1 Petru 1:1)," *Jurnal teologic* 16.1 (2017): 25–48.

16. See Octavian D. Baban, "Note despre înființarea Seminarului Baptist din București: paradigmele libertății și credinței la început de secol XX, în România," *Jurnal teologic* 20.1 (2021): 39–71; Ioan Bunaciu, *Umblând pe ape printre stânci* (self-published, București 2009); Daniel Gherman, "Institutul Teologic Baptist la o sută de ani de la înființare în comparație cu alte școli ce au trecut de pragul secolului de la fondare," *Jurnal teologic* 20.2 (2021): 25–36; Emanuel Jurcoi, "Educația fetelor baptiste în perioada interbelică la Seminarul Teologic Baptist din București și la James Memorial Training School (1921–1941)," *Jurnal teologic* 20.2 (2021): 53–67; Daniel-Marius Mariș, "Relația dintre Seminarul Teologic Baptist și Biserica Creștină Baptistă 'Golgota' din București," *Jurnal teologic* 20.2 (2021): 5–23; Daniel-Marius Mariș, Teodor-Ioan Colda, "In Memoriam Profesor Vasile Talpoș (1942–2021): 'Un păstor al păstorilor,'" *Jurnal teologic* 20.2 (2021): 88–95; Marius Slivesan, "Institutul Teologic Baptist din București la un secol de vocație teologică (1921–2021)," *Jurnal teologic* 20.1 (2021): 118–45.

17. See Marius Silveșan, "Ioan Rose Socaciu (1889–1959)," *Jurnal teologic* 20.2 (2021): 69–79.

pastoral training, and Vasile Berbecar, who contributed to the development of theological education. Alexa Popovici, an influential Baptist historian and leader, strengthened the movement by documenting its history and advocating for religious rights. To further support theological training and doctrinal dissemination, the Baptist Union launched the magazine *Farul Mântuirii* (*The Lighthouse of Salvation*), which became essential for Baptist theological discourse and church organization. The 1930 census shows that there were 60,562 Baptists in Romania.[18]

Despite this progress, Baptists faced persistent opposition from Orthodox authorities and the Romanian state, which viewed them as foreign and a threat to national unity. In 1927 a parliamentary decree, influenced by Orthodox leaders such as Bishop Grigore Comșa of Arad, sought to restrict Baptist religious activities and label them as sectarian. While Baptists secured partial legal recognition, their rights remained limited and in many parts of the country they could not conduct public worship or own church property.

By the 1930s, the Baptists had successfully expanded beyond their Hungarian and German ethnic origins, with increasing numbers of ethnic Romanian converts joining both rural and urban congregations. This growth was met with renewed government pressure during the authoritarian rule of King Carol II (1938–1940) and the dictatorship of Ion Antonescu (1940–1944), when new restrictions were imposed on "sectarian" movements, including Baptists. Baptist leaders and pastors were frequently harassed or arrested, and church properties were confiscated. In 1942, a decree sought to outlaw Baptist activities entirely, forcing many congregations underground.

The Baptist movement demonstrated remarkable resilience, maintaining strong ties with international Baptist organizations and continuing its theological training and evangelistic work in secret. The Baptist Union of Romania played a vital role in advocating for religious freedom and its leaders engaged in diplomatic efforts to ease government restrictions.

---

18. See https://insse.ro/cms/files/publicatii/pliante%20statistice/08-Recensamintele%20despre%20religie_n.pdf.

Brethren

During the interwar period the Brethren movement in Romania saw substantial growth, particularly in Moldova, Bukovina and parts of Transylvania.[19] They maintained a decentralized, non-hierarchical structure, operating mainly through house churches and Bible study groups. Their emphasis on biblical literacy and lay leadership allowed them to sustain their movement despite periodic state restrictions. Unlike Baptists, who established theological seminaries, the Brethren relied on informal theological education through house churches, itinerant teachers and discipleship-based Bible study gatherings. The 1921 Cornilescu Bible translation, mentioned above, played a crucial role in drawing new converts to the movement, as it allowed individuals outside traditional Orthodox structures to engage directly with Scripture.

International connections were another key factor in the development of the Brethren. The visits to Romania of E. H. Broadbent facilitated theological training and provided the Brethren with access to Christian literature and doctrinal resources. Francis Berney maintained contact with Romanian Brethren throughout the period, contributing to their doctrinal stability and organizational resilience.

Brethren communities flourished in key locations including Ploiești, Rădăuți and Suceava, where they established informal Bible training gatherings, often led by itinerant preachers rather than formally trained pastors. Despite their relatively smaller numbers compared to Baptists and Pentecostals, the Brethren remained focused on missionary work and the autonomy of local gatherings. While Baptist and Pentecostal migrants began establishing churches in North America, Brethren communities remained focused on Europe, receiving doctrinal and financial support from Western European Brethren assemblies. These connections supplied Christian literature, theological training and logistical support, strengthening the movement despite state opposition.

While their flexible organizational model allowed them to navigate state-imposed restrictions more easily than the Baptists, the Brethren still faced suspicion and occasional governmental interference. By the late 1930s, as Romania's political climate grew more authoritarian, Brethren communities, like other evangelical groups, encountered increasing restrictions, but their

---

19. Bogdan E. Răduț, "De la Carol II la Petru Groza: statutul juridic al Creștinilor după Evanghelie în perioada regimurilor autoritare (1930–1947)," in Oanță, *Studii de istorie eclesiastică*, 171–85; Bogdan E. Răduț, "Opinii asupra istoricului Bisericii Creștine după Evanghelie din România reflectate într-o scrisoare particulară din 1946," in Oanță, *Studii de istorie eclesiastică*, 187–200; Răduț, *Din istoria creștinilor după Evanghelie*; Dobrincu, "Sub puterea Cezarului"; Modoran, "Istoria Bisericii Creștine după Evanghelie din România."

emphasis on house churches and discreet Bible study meetings enabled them to survive and continue spreading their faith.

Pentecostals

During the interwar period, the Pentecostal movement was the newest and most controversial evangelical group in Romania.[20] Pentecostalism emerged officially in 1922, facing immediate resistance from both the Orthodox Church and state authorities. The movement began with Gheorghe Bradin (1898–1969),[21] a former Baptist from Păuliș, Arad County, who became convinced of Pentecostal teachings after corresponding with Romanian Pentecostals in the United States. He received a letter from Pavel Budean, a Romanian believer in Ohio, who introduced him to Pentecostal literature, particularly a brochure called *Adevărul Biblic* (*The Biblical Truth*), which discussed Spirit baptism and divine healing. Bradin and his wife Persida began hosting prayer meetings in their home and in September 1922 they formally established a Pentecostal church in Păuliș, with approximately 30 members by the end of the year. The movement was further influenced by Petru Pernevan, a Baptist who had returned from the USA after witnessing Pentecostal revivals there, and by Constantin Sida, who also encouraged Pentecostal ideas among Romanian migrants.[22]

Pentecostal beliefs spread rapidly despite harsh opposition. Early Pentecostal groups emerged in the regions of Suceava, Bihor and parts of Banat, where returning migrants who had encountered the Azusa Street Revival introduced the movement. By the late 1920s, Pentecostal congregations had expanded throughout the regions of Crișana and Transylvania, despite being officially

---

20. For Pentecostal interwar history, see Andreiescu, *Istoria penticostalismului românesc*, 51–202; Ciprian Bălăban, *Istoria Bisericii Penticostale din România (1922–1989): instituție și harisme* (Oradea: Scriptum, 2016), 15–80; Ciprian Bălăban, "Începuturile Mișcării penticostale în România," *Plērōma* 21.2 (2019): 111–29; Trandafir Șandru, *Biserica Penticostală în istoria creștinismului* (București: Editura Bisericii lui Dumnezeu Apostolice Penticostale, 1992), 123–47; Trandafir Șandru, *Biserica lui Dumnezeu Apostolică Penticostală din România* (București: Editura Cultului Penticostal – Biserica lui Dumnezeu Apostolică din Republica Socialistă România, 1982), 26–34; Trandafir Șandru, *Trezirea spirituală penticostală din România* (București: Institutul Teologic Penticostal, 1997).

21. See Pavel Riviș-Tipei, "1922–2007: 85 de ani de la înființarea primei biserici penticostale din România," in *Cuvântul Adevărului* 18.12 (2007): 3–9.

22. On Pentecostal leadership during this period, see Ciprian Bălăban, "Conducerea Bisericii Penticostale în perioada 1922–2012: președinți ai organizațiilor penticostale și ai Cultului Penticostal din România," *Plērōma* 14.2 (2012): 107–33.

outlawed by the state in 1925. Pentecostals faced police raids, fines and arrests for conducting unauthorized religious meetings.[23]

Because Pentecostals placed a strong emphasis on healing, spiritual gifts and prophecy,[24] they attracted further scrutiny from both religious and civil authorities. The government viewed their ecstatic worship and emphasis on miraculous healings as dangerous and subversive. Many Pentecostals were imprisoned, fined or exiled, and their literature was confiscated. Bradin himself was interrogated by authorities multiple times.

Although still not recognized by the state, the Pentecostal movement also sought to develop theological education. By the late 1930s, Bible schools began operating informally in Arad and Oradea, aiming to train new leaders for the rapidly growing congregations.[25] These schools were often forced to function in secret due to constant surveillance and confiscation of their literature. Gheorghe Bradin and Eugen Bodor played a crucial role in sustaining these underground theological initiatives.[26]

Pentecostals also used publications to educate their communities and spread their teachings. In 1929, they began publishing *Cuvântul Adevărului* (*The Word of Truth*), which was circulated secretly. Bradin's writings also played a role in shaping Pentecostal doctrine, with his materials distributed through underground networks despite government censorship.[27] Despite intense persecution, the movement grew rapidly, establishing a strong underground network. By the early 1940s, it had gained thousands of adherents.

Survival and Adaptation under Communism

The Communist era in Romania (1945–1989) was a period of intense persecution and hardship for evangelical communities, as the state sought to suppress all forms of religious expression that did not align with its atheistic ideology.

---

23. See Florin Pop, *Pionieri penticostali pe meleaguri bistrițene* (Beclean: Holy Fire Press, 2022); Florin Pop, *Enciclopedia ilustrată a bisericilor penticostale din județul Bistrița Năsăud* (Beclean: Holy Fire Press, 2022).

24. See Ciprian Bălăban, "Concepția penticostală românească despre Botezul cu Duhul Sfânt (1922–1989)," *Plērōma* 14.1 (2012): 232–48; Ciprian Bălăban, "Gândirea eshatologică penticostală românească în perioada 1922–1989," *Plērōma* 12.2 (2010): 173–209.

25. Ciprian Bălăban, "O incursiune în istoria învățământului teologic penticostal românesc," *Plērōma* 18.1 (2016): 111–26.

26. Ciprian Bălăban, "Represiunea pentru 'misticism' a pastorului Eugen Bodor," *Plērōma* 20.2 (2018): 87–116.

27. Ciprian Bălăban, "Publicații penticostale românești din perioada 1922–1989," *Plērōma* 15.2 (2013): 123–36.

Evangelicals faced confiscation of properties, restrictions on worship and constant surveillance by the feared Securitate, the infamous secret police. Despite these challenges, they displayed remarkable resilience and adaptability, finding creative ways to sustain their faith and communities. Underground networks, clandestine worship and the smuggling of Bibles became essential practices, enabling evangelicals to preserve their identity and mission. This era also forged a theology of suffering and hope, rooted in the conviction of God's faithfulness amidst trials. By the end of the Communist regime, Romanian evangelicals had not only survived but also strengthened their communal bonds.

State Repression

Seeking to control all aspects of religious life, the government confiscated church properties, including buildings used for worship, education and administration, leaving many congregations without physical spaces to gather. Evangelical institutions, such as seminaries and publishing houses, were either closed or brought under state control, severely limiting their ability to train leaders and disseminate theological resources. The Securitate closely monitored evangelical leaders and congregations, infiltrating communities with informants and cracking down on any activities perceived as a threat to the regime.[28]

In 1948, the Communist regime placed all religious communities under strict state supervision, requiring them to seek official recognition or be banned. Evangelical denominations were forced to comply with government-imposed restrictions and those who refused were declared illegal. Even when recognized as legal denominations, evangelicals faced severe pressure from the state, which sought to control their leadership and restrict their activities. Leaders of the Baptist Union who resisted state interference were arrested or forced into exile. Many Baptists, including influential figures such as Alexa Popovici, documented the increasing state repression in publications produced by the Romanian Baptist diaspora. The Baptist theological seminary was also heavily monitored and students suspected of anti-Communist activities were expelled.[29]

---

28. Ciprian Bălăban, "Reflectarea activității lui Richard Wurmbrand în dosarele Securității," *Plērōma* 19.2 (2017): 121–36.

29. See Daniel Mitrofan, *Pași: Cultul Creștin Baptist din România în perioada comunistă*, https://carteapasi.wordpress.com; Marius Silveșan, *Bisericile Creștine Baptiste din România: între persecuție, acomodare și rezistență (1948–1965)* (Târgoviște: Editura Cetatea de Scaun, 2012–2013); Marius Silveșan, "Identitatea baptistă și comunismul în România," in *Identități*

The legal recognition of Pentecostalism came in 1950, when the *Biserica lui Dumnezeu Apostolică din România* (The Romanian Apostolic Church of God) became the first Pentecostal denomination in the country. Still it was heavily scrutinized due to its emphasis on spiritual gifts, which the regime viewed as subversive.[30] Pentecostal leaders such as Gheorghe Bradin,[31] Pavel Bochain,[32] Trandafir Şandru[33] and Teodor Codreanu[34] were frequently interrogated,[35] while Pentecostal publications, including *Cuvântul Adevărului*, faced censorship. Pentecostal gatherings were infiltrated by informants and some leaders were pressured to collaborate with the regime.[36]

The decentralized and non-institutionalised Brethren movement was particularly vulnerable to repression. Because they refused to adopt a formal hierarchical system, the authorities viewed them with suspicion, often labelling them as a sectarian movement hostile to the socialist state. Many Brethren communities were denied legal status and had to meet in secret.

The state's strategy of repression included extensive surveillance by the Securitate, the confiscation of evangelical church buildings and the imprisonment of pastors and lay leaders. Some congregations were forcibly disbanded, with members dispersed or pressured to renounce their faith. Evangelical publishing houses were closed and access to Bibles and Christian literature was limited. Public expressions of faith were also restricted and even private gatherings were subject to surveillance. Pastors and lay leaders were frequently targeted for harassment, arrest and imprisonment, creating a climate of fear and uncertainty. The regime's atheistic propaganda sought to undermine evangelical theology, portraying it as backward and incompatible with the ideals of social-

---

sociale, culturale, etnice şi religioase în communism, ed. Cosmin Budeancă and Florentin Olteanu (Iaşi: Polirom, 2015), 386–402.

30. See Pavel Riviş-Tipei, "1922–2007: 85 de ani de la înfiinţarea primei biserici penticostale din România (2)," *Cuvântul Adevărului* 19.1 (2008): 4–7.

31. See Bălăban, "Represiunea pentru 'misticism' a pastorului Eugen Bodor," 87–116.

32. See Corneliu Constantineanu, "Bochian, Pavel," in *Brill's Encyclopedia of Global Pentecostalism Online*, ed. Michael Wilkinson, Connie Au et al. (Leiden: Brill, 2019), http://dx.doi.org/10.1163/2589-3807_EGPO_COM_043801.

33. See Corneliu Constantineanu, "Şandru, Trandafir," in Wilkinson, *Encyclopedia of Pentecostalism*, http://dx.doi.org/10.1163/2589-3807_EGPO_COM_043793.

34. See Corneliu Constantineanu, "Codreanu, Teodor," in Wilkinson, *Encyclopedia of Pentecostalism*, http://dx.doi.org/10.1163/2589-3807_EGPO_COM_043799; Florin Pop, "Codreanu Teodor (n. 1928 - d. 2004)," in Florin Pop, *Miracole: o abordare biblică, istorică şi contemporană* (Beclean: Holy Fire Press, 2020), 99–117.

35. See Bălăban, "Conducerea Bisericii Penticostale," 107–33.

36. On collaboration with the Communist regime, see Vasilică Croitor, *Răscumpărarea Memoriei* (Medgidia: Succeed, 2010).

ism. The evangelicals adapted to the challenges by turning to underground networks and small house churches, demonstrating remarkable resilience. This era of repression shaped a generation of leaders and congregants whose faith was deeply forged in adversity.

Strategies for Resilience

The Romanian evangelicals developed creative and courageous strategies to sustain their faith and communities. Underground worship became a cornerstone of their survival, with small groups gathering secretly in homes or secluded locations to pray, study Scripture and worship. These clandestine meetings fostered deep relational bonds and a sense of shared mission, enabling evangelicals to remain spiritually vibrant despite external pressures. Clandestine theological education flourished. Pastors and lay leaders conducted informal training sessions in hidden settings, equipping a new generation of leaders.

Diaspora support played a crucial role: evangelical communities abroad, particularly in Western Europe and North America, provided financial assistance and smuggled Bibles and other religious materials into Romania. Evangelical literature served as a powerful tool for resilience, helping communities maintain their theological identity. Printed materials, often produced secretly or imported by the diaspora, offered encouragement and doctrinal clarity. Together, these strategies enabled Romanian evangelicals to persevere through decades of persecution, emerging from the Communist era as a deeply rooted and spiritually resilient community.

Demographic Resilience

The Romanian evangelicals demonstrated remarkable demographic resilience, ensuring the continuity and growth of their communities. High birth rates played a significant role in this growth, reflecting a theological emphasis on the value of family and children as blessings from God. Evangelical communities prioritized mutual support and cohesion, fostering strong networks of care and accountability that bolstered their ability to navigate societal and governmental pressures. These close-knit relationships helped preserve the faith across generations, ensuring that the core values and theological distinctives of evangelicalism were passed down.

Migration to urban centres also shaped the demographic landscape of Romanian evangelicals. The state's industrialization policies prompted significant population shifts from rural areas to cities, bringing evangelical families into closer proximity with diverse religious and cultural influences. While these relocations posed challenges, such as the need to adapt to new social environments, they also provided opportunities to expand the evangelical presence in urban areas. Urban congregations became hubs of spiritual vitality and evangelistic outreach, connecting believers from various regions and fostering a broader sense of unity within the movement.

Post-Communist Revival and Global Expansion

The fall of Communism in 1989 ushered in a new era of freedom and opportunity for Romanian evangelicals,[37] allowing them to rebuild their institutions, expand their influence and reconnect with the global evangelical movement.[38] With the removal of state restrictions, evangelical churches experienced a rapid revival, establishing seminaries, publishing houses and missionary organizations. This period also saw the rise of diaspora contributions, as Romanian evangelicals living abroad provided crucial financial and theological support, fostering connections with global missions and intercultural partnerships. Additionally, evangelicals embraced cultural renewal, constructing modern worship spaces and producing literature that reflected both their historical legacy and contemporary aspirations. The post-Communist period has been characterized by remarkable growth and global engagement, positioning Romanian evangelicals as significant contributors to both local and international Christianity while navigating the challenges of secularization and generational change.

---

37. On the role of the evangelicals in the fall of Communism, see Bogdan E. Răduț, "Contribuția și perspectiva evanghelicilor români asupra revoluției române din decembrie 1989," *Arhivele Olteniei* 30 (2016): 203–16.

38. H. H. Drake Williams, III, "Romania Thirty Years After the Fall of Communism: Retrospect and Prospect," *Journal of Global Christianity* 6.1 (2020): 5–13; Valeriu Andreiescu, *Istoria penticostalismului românesc. Volumul II: Lucrările puterii lui Dumnezeu* (Oradea: Casa Cărții, 2012); Otniel Bunaciu, "Church and State in an Eastern Orthodox Context," *Jurnal teologic* 10 (2011): 14–23; Marcel Chirilă Botezatu, "Evanghelizarea în Biserica Penticostală din România: Studiu de caz sociologic," *Jurnal teologic* 21.2 (2022): 49–75; Vlad Bogdan Cristian, "Mișcări religioase moderne în spațiul românesc: sunt cultele evanghelice din România din punct de vedere istoric neoprotestante?," *Acta Marisiensis: Seria Historia* 4 (2022): 27–43; Daniel Fodorean, "'Biserica Online': analiză și perspective," *Jurnal teologic* 21.1 (2022): 65–92; Daniel Fodorean, "Primul model românesc de fuziune bisericească: Biserica Baptistă germane și o Biserică Baptistă română din București," *Jurnal teologic* 23.3 (2024): 74–91; Pavel Riviș-Tipei, "1922-2007: 85 de ani de la înființarea primei biserici penticostale din România (3)," *Cuvântul Adevărului* 19.2 (2008): 4–7.

Post-1989 Developments

After the fall of Communism in 1989, evangelical communities that functioned underground quickly gained legal recognition, enabling them to openly practise their faith and organize their communities. Confiscated buildings were reclaimed and new places of worship established. Seminaries and Bible schools were reopened or founded anew, revitalizing theological education and equipping leaders.[39] Publishing houses were also established, producing materials that helped foster a renewed sense of identity and purpose.

This revival extended beyond institutional rebuilding to include a renewed focus on missions and public engagement. Romanian evangelicals embraced their freedom to evangelize and expand their reach, both within the country and abroad.[40] Organizations were established to address spiritual and social needs, including education, poverty alleviation and community development. Public engagement also became a hallmark of the post-1989 era, with evangelicals advocating for ethical leadership, reconciliation and social justice in Romania's evolving democratic society. Evangelicals thus became active participants in shaping the nation's moral and spiritual landscape while reconnecting to the broader global Christian movement.[41]

Diaspora and Global Influence

Romanian evangelical diaspora communities in Europe and North America have played a pivotal role by funding the construction of churches, the establishment of seminaries and the production of literature. Many diaspora leaders returned to Romania to share their expertise. Diaspora communities also fostered collaboration with global missions and participated in intercul-

---

39. See Marcel Măcelaru, "The Context of Theological Education in Eastern Europe: Past, Present, Future," in *Re-Imagining Theological Education*, ed. Marcel Măcelaru, Corneliu Constantineanu and Romulus Vasile Ganea (Cluj-Napoca: Risoprint / București: Plērōma, 2016), 35–54.

40. Cf. Marcel Măcelaru, "Witnessing Christ in Eastern Europe: An Assessment of Context," in *Proclaiming Christ in the Power of the Holy Spirit: In the Face of Major Challenges*, ed. Wonsuk Ma (Tulsa: ORU Press, 2020), 375–86.

41. Cf. Marcel Măcelaru, "Holistic Mission in Post-Communist Romania: A Case Study on the Growth of the 'Elim' Pentecostal Church of Timișoara (1990–1997)," in *Mission in Central and Eastern Europe: Realities, Perspectives, Trends*, ed. Corneliu Constantineanu, Marcel Măcelaru, Anne-Marie Kool and Mihai Himcinschi (Regnum Edinburgh Centenary Series 34; Oxford: Regnum, 2016), 327–44; republished as Marcel Măcelaru, "Holistic Mission in Post-Communist Romania: A Case Study on the Growth of the 'Elim' Pentecostal Church of Timișoara (1990–1997)," in *Pentecostal Mission and Global Christianity: An Edinburgh Centenary Reader*, ed. Younghoon Lee and Wonsuk Ma (Regnum Studies in Mission; Oxford: Regnum, 2018), 305–22.

tural theological dialogues. Romanian evangelicals became active partners in international missionary efforts, bringing their distinct perspectives and experiences to global Christianity. Many diaspora churches are involved in cross-cultural mission projects in Africa and Asia, bringing to the mission field a holistic understanding of their role, as is evident in the way both spiritual and material needs are addressed. This collaboration enriched both Romanian and global evangelical movements, as Romanian churches benefited from exposure to diverse theological traditions and methodologies, while contributing their resilience and depth of faith forged under persecution. Intercultural theological exchanges further strengthened ties between Romanian evangelicals and the broader Christian community, enhancing their ability to engage with complex contemporary challenges and expand their influence on the global stage. These interactions cemented the diaspora's role as both a bridge to the international evangelical world and a vital source of support for Romanian evangelicalism.

Contemporary Challenges and Future Directions

Romanian evangelicals witnessed significant growth,[42] but now face a range of challenges, requiring them to balance theological identity with adaptation to a secularizing society.[43] The historical denominations – Baptist, Pentecostal and Brethren – have fostered both vibrancy and fragmentation, necessitating greater interdenominational cooperation to maintain a unified voice. Generational divides have emerged, with younger evangelicals, influenced by globalization, prioritizing inclusivity and social engagement, while older generations emphasize traditional theological and worship. Addressing these differences through mentoring and dialogue is essential for the movement's future.

Romanian evangelicals continue to play an important role in politics and society, advocating for religious freedom, ethical leadership and social justice.

---

42. The Pentecostals increased from 220,842 in 1992 to 404,475 in 2021. According to the censuses of these years, the Baptists and the Brethren stagnated or decreased in numbers. However, the 2021 census does not account for the thousands that have migrated to Western Europe and North America during this period. The numbers are available at: https://insse.ro/cms/files/publicatii/pliante%20statistice/08-Recensamintele%20despre%20religie_n.pdf and www.recensamantromania.ro/rezultate-rpl-2021/rezultate-definitive.

43. Cf. Marcel Măcelaru, "Burdens of Identity – On Christian Existence in a Post-Christian World," in *Values of Christian Relationships*, ed. Corneliu Constantineanu, Georgeta Raţă and Patricia Runcan (Puterea de a fi altfel 3; Bucureşti: Editura Didactică şi Pedagogică, 2014), 169–74; Marcel Măcelaru, "Naming the Issue in Contemporary Contexts. Part 4: Eastern Europe," in *Whole-Life Mission for the Whole Church*, ed. Mark Greene and Ian Shaw (ICETE Series; Carlisle: Langham Global Library, 2021), 80–84.

Their history of resisting oppression has shaped their commitment to transparency, integrity and reconciliation, particularly in efforts to heal divisions left by totalitarian rule. Evangelicals are also pursuing a vision for renewal by deepening theological engagement, fostering leadership development and leveraging cultural tools such as literature, architecture and education. Evangelical publishing remains vital, providing biblical insights into contemporary ethical dilemmas, while seminaries and schools integrate faith with academic excellence to prepare leaders for the modern world.

Conclusion

The history of the Romanian evangelicals is a testament to their resilience and their commitment to biblical authority, personal faith and active engagement in society. Each historical phase reveals their adaptability and steadfastness in the face of immense challenges. Their role in shaping Romanian culture, ethics and religious freedom is significant, offering a legacy of moral leadership, reconciliation and societal renewal. Through their advocacy for justice and their theological depth, evangelicals have contributed to the broader Christian witness, extending their influence far beyond national borders.

Looking to the future, Romanian evangelicals can build upon this legacy by addressing issues such as the impact of diaspora communities, architectural innovations in church design and evolving demographic trends. By integrating historical lessons into contemporary strategies, evangelicals can navigate challenges such as secularization, generational divides and denominational fragmentation while fostering unity and vision for the future. With a continued focus on theological education, cultural engagement and global partnerships, Romanian evangelicals are well-positioned to expand their impact and contribute meaningfully to the spiritual and cultural renewal of both Romania and the global Christian community.

Bibliography

Bunaciu, Otniel. "Church and State in an Eastern Orthodox Context." *Jurnal teologic* 10 (2011): 14–23.

Măcelaru, Marcel. "Burdens of Identity – On Christian Existence in a Post-Christian World." Pages 169–74 in *Values of Christian Relationships*. Edited by Corneliu Constantineanu, Georgeta Rață and Patricia Runcan. Puterea de a fi altfel 3. București: Editura Didactică și Pedagogică, 2014.

———. "Holistic Mission in Post-Communist Romania: A Case Study on the Growth of the 'Elim' Pentecostal Church of Timişoara (1990–1997)." Pages 327–44 in *Mission in Central and Eastern Europe: Realities, Perspectives, Trends*. Edited by Corneliu Constantineanu, Marcel Măcelaru, Anne-Marie Kool and Mihai Himcinschi. Regnum Edinburgh Centenary Series 34. Oxford: Regnum, 2016. Also pages 305–22 in *Pentecostal Mission and Global Christianity: An Edinburgh Centenary Reader*. Edited by Younghoon Lee and Wonsuk Ma. Regnum Studies in Mission. Oxford: Regnum, 2018.

———. "Naming the Issue in Contemporary Contexts. Part 4: Eastern Europe." Pages 80–84 in *Whole-Life Mission for the Whole Church*. Edited by Mark Greene and Ian Shaw. ICETE Series. Carlisle: Langham Global Library, 2021.

———. "The Context of Theological Education in Eastern Europe: Past, Present, Future." Pages 35–54 in *Re-Imagining Theological Education*. Edited by Marcel Măcelaru, Corneliu Constantineanu and Romulus Vasile Ganea. Cluj-Napoca: Risoprint / Bucureşti: Plērōma, 2016.

———. "Witnessing Christ in Eastern Europe: An Assessment of Context." Pages 375–86 in *Proclaiming Christ in the Power of the Holy Spirit: In the Face of Major Challenges*. Edited by Wonsuk Ma. Tulsa: ORU Press, 2020.

Michelson, Paul E. "The History of Romanian Evangelicals, 1918–1989: A Bibliographical Excursus." *Archive Moldaviae* 9 (2017): 191–233.

Ploscariu, Iemima. "The Word Read, Spoken, and Sung: Neo-Protestants and Modernity in Interwar Romania." *Central Europe* 18.2 (2020): 105–21.

Tipei, John. "Persecution of the Romanian Church in the Twentieth Century: A Historical and Theological Perspective." *Plērōma* 6.1 (2004): 71–102.

Williams, H. H. Drake, III. "Romania Thirty Years After the Fall of Communism: Retrospect and Prospect." *Journal of Global Christianity* 6.1 (2020): 5–13.

21

Evangelicalism in French-Speaking Switzerland

Monique Cuany

Introduction

In the ecclesiastical landscape of French-speaking Switzerland the word "evangelical" (*évangélique*) technically refers to two different entities. On the one hand, it describes the *Église évangélique réformée de Suisse* (EERS), which consists of most cantonal Protestant Reformed churches of Switzerland.[1] It is thus synonymous with the word "Protestant" and has been used in this way since the Reformation. On the other hand, "evangelical" qualifies a specific movement across a wide range of Protestant denominations and churches, including some parishes of the Reformed churches.[2] In popular consciousness and the media, the word "evangelical" tends to be more narrowly associated with churches which are not cantonal churches and are thus "free churches."

This chapter deals with evangelicals in the second sense. It begins with a brief statistical overview of evangelical Christianity in Switzerland, more specifically in the French-speaking part of the country. The second part then discusses the historical root of this type of Christianity in Switzerland. Finally, the last part outlines recent developments in the evangelical movement in French-speaking Switzerland since the 1950s.

---

1. Église évangélique réformée de Suisse, www.evref.ch/fr/organization.

2. For example, this is how the website of the chaplaincy services at the University Hospital of Lausanne defines evangelicals: www.chuv.ch/fr/dso/dso-home/pratique-clinique/pratiques-religieuses-en-milieu-hospitalier/a-lhopital/christianisme/eglises-evangeliques/description-des-eglises-evangeliques.

Evangelicals in the Swiss Religious Landscape

Historically, the religious landscape in Switzerland has been dominated by the Roman Catholic Church and the cantonal Reformed churches. Over the last fifty years, however, this religious distribution has changed significantly. According to the Federal Statistical Office (FSO), the proportion of both Roman Catholics and, more significantly, of Reformed Protestants, has fallen sharply, while that of people declaring no religious affiliation is rapidly increasing.[3] In 2022, the FSO gave the following figures: Roman Catholics 32.1 percent; Reformed Protestant 20.5 percent; other Christian communities 5.6 percent; Muslim communities 5.9 percent; no religious affiliation 33.5 percent. Thus, while over half of the population (58 percent) still identifies with a Christian confession,[4] the overall trend is towards a diversification of religious beliefs, a pluralization also observable within the Christian confessions, especially in Protestantism.[5]

Among these statistics, the exact proportion of evangelical Christians is difficult to determine. The latest estimates give the range of 2–3 percent of the Swiss population,[6] which represents about two hundred and fifty thousand people, of whom forty-two thousand reside in the French-speaking part of Switzerland.[7] Around one third of evangelicals who are attending a free church also consider themselves to be members of an official Reformed church.[8] The proportion of evangelicals who are only members of an official Reformed church is estimated at 5–10 percent.[9]

---

3. FSO: www.bfs.admin.ch/bfs/fr/home/statistiques/population/langues-religions/religions.html.

4. This proportion reached almost 97 percent in 1970.

5. Christophe Monnot, *Croire ensemble. Analyse Institutionnelle du paysage religieux en Suisse* (Geneva: Seismo, 2013), 46–47.

6. See Jörg Stolz, Olivier Favre and Emmanuel Buchard, "La compétitivité du milieu évangélique en Suisse," in *Le phénomène évangélique: Analyses d'un milieu compétitif*, ed. Jörg Stolz, Olivier Favre, Caroline Gachet and Emmanuel Buchard (Geneva: Labor et Fides, 2013). Monnot (*Croire*, 47) estimates them at 2 percent, but he notes that evangelical communities represent near to 25 percent of all religious communities in Switzerland. Elsewhere, Favre and Stolz gave the range of 2–4 percent: see Favre and Stolz, "Les évangéliques: des chrétiens convaincus dans un monde de plus en plus sécularisé," in *La nouvelle Suisse religieuse, Risques et chance de sa diversité*, ed. Martin Baumann and Jörg Stolz (Geneva: Labor et Fides, 2009), 140. The website of the Swiss Evangelical Alliance gives the number of 3 percent of the population, https://evangelique.ch/faq/.

7. These are the numbers of the Swiss Evangelical Alliance: https://evangelique.ch/faq/.

8. On double affiliation, see Olivier Favre, *Les Églises évangéliques de Suisse: Origines et identités* (Geneva: Labor et Fides, 2006), 305.

9. Favre and Stolz, "Les évangéliques," 141.

Regarding the number of (free) communities of evangelicals in Switzerland, an essay first published in 2007 gave the number of about fifteen hundred evangelical (free) churches, of which twelve hundred were grouped into about forty denominations or federations, the remainder being fully independent.[10] The largest evangelical denominations in Switzerland are the following: Église Viva Suisse (formerly Chrischona), the Salvation Army, the Free Evangelical Churches (*Freie Evangelische Gemeinden*), the Swiss Pentecostal Mission (*Schweizerische Pfingstmission*), the Evangelical Methodist Church (*Evangelisch-methodistische Kirche*), the *Evangelische Gemeinschaftswerk* (EGW) and the *Gemeinde für Christus*.[11] The largest French-speaking federation is the *Fédération Romande des Églises évangéliques* (FREE) with about four thousand five hundred members in around fifty congregations.[12]

Turning more specifically to French-speaking Switzerland, a study published in 2020 estimates the number of evangelical free churches to be over four hundred.[13] It is noteworthy, however, that the density of evangelical churches differs greatly between different cantons. Thus, the cantons of Vaud and Geneva – which have a long-time Protestant heritage – have the largest number of evangelical churches, with respectively one hundred and forty-two and one hundred and five churches. At the other end, the cantons of Fribourg, Jura and Valais – which are of Roman Catholic heritage – count respectively twenty, fourteen and thirteen evangelical churches.[14] In terms of churches per ten thousand inhabitants, however, it is the French-speaking part of the canton of Bern which has the largest number of evangelical free churches, with over five churches per ten thousand inhabitants.[15]

---

10. Favre and Stolz, "Les évangéliques," 141. The essay was first published in German in 2007.

11. According to Favre and Stolz, "Les évangeliques," 141, these denominations all count more than ten thousand members or supporters.

12. La FREE: https://lafree.ch/a-propos. The number of Baptists is very small.

13. Nirine Jonah, *L'implantation d'Églises: une étude en Europe francophone* (Romanel-sur-Lausanne: Sripsi, 2020), 16.

14. According to statistics, 88 percent of all evangelical free churches in French-speaking Switzerland are situated in Protestant cantons, while 12 percent are situated in Catholic cantons. Jonah, *L'implantation*, 41.

15. See Jonah, *L'implantation*, 22–26. In some places in the canton of Bern, evangelicals represent up to 12 percent of the population. Favre and Stolz, "Evangéliques," 142.

The Origins of Evangelical Christianity in Switzerland

Exploring the origins of "evangelicalism" or "evangelicals" in Switzerland – like all historical studies of evangelicalism – is a complex exercise. To begin with, because this particular "trend" or "type" of Christianity cuts across many churches and denominations, it involves the historical analysis of a great number of individuals, groups, movements and actions, as well as the identification of their connections and shared traits, both synchronically and diachronically. While several studies have focused on different aspects or groups of evangelical history, this type of in-depth and global historical studies of Swiss evangelicalism is still in the making.[16]

More fundamentally, the answer to the question of the origins of evangelicalism in Switzerland depends largely on how one defines "evangelicalism" and on the main characteristics one associates with this movement. For example, if we consider the insistence on a personal confession of faith and voluntary membership of a professing community as the key distinctive evangelical characteristic, then the Swiss Anabaptists of the sixteenth century, who held many core beliefs of the Reformers, but also advocated a strict separation between church and state, represent an expression of Christianity that has several interesting analogies with many twenty-first-century Swiss evangelicals.[17] However, the motivation for such a personal engagement among the Anabaptists of the sixteenth century was not a particular emphasis on personal agency in the modern sense, but the creation of a community where true brotherly love and justice could be practised thoroughly.[18] We can thus wonder whether this is exactly the same phenomenon as the "conversionism" often associated with modern evangelicals.[19] One could add that other traits which historians

---

16. A brief overview of this history can be found in Favre, *Origines*, 63–87. More in-depth studies specifically on the rise of evangelicalism in the nineteenth century include: Jean Decorvet, Tim Grass and Kenneth J. Stewart (eds), *The Genevan Réveil in International Perspective* (Eugene: Pickwick, 2023); Marc Lüthi, *Aux sources historiques des Églises évangéliques: L'évolution de leurs ministères et de leurs ecclésiologies en Suisse Romande* (Geneva: Je sème, 2003); and Timothy C. F. Stunt, *From Awakening to Secession: Radical Evangelicals in Switzerland and Britain, 1815–35* (Edinburgh: T&T Clark, 2000).

17. Several studies trace the root of Swiss evangelicalism to the Anabaptists in the sixteenth century, for example Favre, *Origines*, 63–87; and Favre and Stolz, "Les évangéliques," 143. Today, the great majority of evangelicals in Switzerland do indeed hold to a strict separation of church and state as did the Anabaptists. Historically or genealogically, however, only a small fraction of evangelicals in Switzerland today can trace their roots to this type of Christianity.

18. Neal Blough, *Histoire, identité et dialogue. Réforme et réformes radicales* (Charols: Excelsis, 2022), 39.

19. The fourfold criteria of conversionism, activism, biblicism and crucicentrism were first advanced in David W. Bebbington, *Evangelicalism in Modern Britain: A History from the 1730s to the 1980s* (London: Unwin Hyman, 1989).

have regularly associated with evangelicals, such as "missional," "pragmatic," "revivalist" and "transdenominationalism," did not yet characterize the Anabaptists in the sixteenth century.[20] Many societal and political developments would be necessary before these characteristics could become important traits in evangelical Christianity.

Conversely, historically, those who have been described as "evangelical" have not always been so primarily because of their conversionism or because of their advocacy of the separation of church and state. For example, during the *Réveil* of Geneva, which gave a crucial impetus to the Swiss evangelical movement in the nineteenth century, the "evangelicals" were largely characterized by a "return" to the doctrines of the Reformation in reaction to the natural religion that prevailed in Geneva at the time. Although conversionism also played a crucial role in the *Réveil*, what distinguished "evangelicals" during that time and in fact often during the nineteenth century was the fact that they held to the "orthodox" Reformation teachings on biblical authority and salvation by grace through faith, over against "liberal Protestantism."[21]

Roots of Evangelical Christianity in Switzerland
The Protestant Reformation (Sixteenth Century)

Historically and theologically, the evangelical movement in Switzerland can trace part of its roots to the Protestant Reformation of the sixteenth century. It was at that time that several of doctrines which have historically been central to the evangelicals, such as the centrality and authority of the Bible, the primacy of grace and faith, and the priesthood of all believers, were for the first time clearly formulated. Furthermore, in the evangelical revivals and development of the nineteenth century, the reaffirmation and reappropriation of several of these doctrines played a key role. The Reformed Church became the official church in several Swiss cantons or cities in the sixteenth century – including Zurich, Bern, Basel, Schaffhausen, Neuchâtel, Vaud and Geneva – and is still recognized as the state church in most cantons today, next to the Catholic

---

20. Despite their popularity, Bebbington's criteria are not without their problems, and other key characteristics have been proposed. See for example Mark A. Noll, "Noun or Adjective? The Ravings of a Fanatical Nominalist," in *Evangelicals: Who They Have Been, Are Now, and Could Be*, ed. Mark A. Noll, David W. Bebbington and George M. Marsden (Grand Rapids: Eerdmans, 2019), 164–69; and John G. Stackhouse, *Evangelicalism: A Very Short Introduction* (New York: Oxford University Press, 2022).

21. See Jean Decorvet, "Introduction to the Genevan *Réveil*," in *The Genevan* Réveil *in International Perspective*, 5–10.

Church. This period also saw the rise of Anabaptism, a movement associated with the radical Reformation, which gave birth to various groups, including the Mennonites, who today are a significant evangelical presence in some parts of Switzerland.

Anabaptism grew out of a split with the Reformation of Zwingli in Zurich in 1525. Dissatisfied with the progress of the Reformation in Zurich, a group of radicals formed around Konrad Grebel. Although they largely shared Zwingli's doctrinal views and his "biblicism," the first Anabaptists – called the "Swiss Brethren" – rejected infant baptism and demanded a radical separation of church and state. They were unconvinced that the entire population of Zurich would adhere to the Reformation and thus defended an alternative church project, based on the voluntary participation of only those who were prepared to commit themselves to it. This would ensure the creation of a *truly Reformed* church in which people would be committed to living the pure gospel in a community of brotherly love and church discipline.

The Anabaptists were violently persecuted from the outset. Some of them fled abroad, giving rise to various groups such as the Mennonites, Amish and Hutterites. However, despite the persecution, some of the Swiss Brethren remained in Switzerland, first in Zurich, then in the canton of Bern, particularly in the Emmental and the Jura regions. Only in 1848 the first federal constitution guaranteed freedom of religion and the Anabaptists were allowed to freely practise their faith. Today, the Mennonite churches are an important evangelical presence in the Emmental and Jura regions, counting two thousand members regrouped in fourteen communities (2007).[22]

Pietism (Eighteenth Century)

As in various other regions of Europe, Pietism was an important influence in the rise of evangelicals in Switzerland. This movement, with its emphasis on a personal experience of "new birth" and the ensuing commitment to ecclesial and societal change, began to influence parts of the Reformed Church in Switzerland at the beginning of the eighteenth century.[23] Viewed as a second "reformation" and going back to the teachings of the Reformers, the movement

---

22. Favre and Stolz, "Les évangéliques," 143.

23. Rudolf Dellsperger and Stefan Röllin, "L'influence du piétisme et des Lumières sur les confessions," in *Histoire du christianisme en Suisse. Une perspective œcuménique*, ed. Lukas Vischer, Lukas Schenker, Rudolf Dellsperger and Olivier Fatio (Genève/Fribourg: Labor et Fides/Saint-Paul, 1995), 174.

nonetheless carried a new emphasis on personal commitment and feelings.[24] Another characteristic of Pietism was that it touched people from all strata of society, thus putting a renewed emphasis on the involvement of the laity in ecclesiastical life, a characteristic often associated with evangelicals.[25]

Conventicules appeared in all Protestant cities, first in the churches in Bern, Zurich, St-Gallen and Schaffhausen and in the Grison, and later in Basel, Neuchâtel and Geneva. Although some pietists did separate from state churches, most attempted to spread renewal within it. Thus, for example, Samuel Lutz in Bern, Daniel Willi in the Grisons, and Hieronymus Annoni in Basel worked to bring renewal within the Reformed Church. All three were friends of Nicolaus von Zinzendorf, whose Moravian societies, under his direction, did not separate from the church.[26] Zinzendorf himself visited Geneva in 1741, and the Moravian community of close to seven hundred persons which was created would prove an important impulse in the early stages of the Genevan *Réveil*.[27]

The Birth of the Evangelical Movement (Nineteenth Century)

It is the nineteenth century which marks the birth of the evangelical movement in French-speaking Switzerland. During this period, a series of revivals – with centres in Geneva, Basel and Bern – led to renewals within established churches and to the creation and import of new churches and denominations. Furthermore, this century saw the birth of "evangelicalism" as an international movement intersecting diverse churches and denominations. Important societal and political changes in Switzerland during this century both enabled and influenced these developments in the Protestant landscape.

The *Réveil* in Geneva, which affected not only French-speaking Switzerland, but also many parts of Western Europe and beyond, has been deemed to "mark the rise and development of modern Evangelicalism in francophone Europe" and provides an important insight into this history.[28] It began as a revival among theological students under Moravian and British influences, chief among which was that of Robert Haldane (1764–1842), a Scottish Congregationalist who taught privately in the evening on the Epistle to the Romans. Uniting pietistic conversionism and Reformed orthodoxy, the revival took

---

24. Dellsperger and Röllin, "L'influence," 174–77.
25. Dellsperger and Röllin, "L'influence," 177.
26. Dellsperger and Röllin, "L'influence," 178–79.
27. Decorvet, "Introduction," 13.
28. Decorvet, "Introduction," 10.

the form of dissidence against the rationalist teaching of the faculty of theology at the university of Geneva and the state church combined with a strong reaffirmation of the faith of the Reformers. This did not prevent theological diversity among evangelicals, including on subjects such as state-church relations, church government, biblical prophecy and the relationship of the church to society.[29]

Although not all those who were "réveillés" left the national church, the revival did lead to the creation of the first independent church in 1818, and later to the creation of new denominations such as the *Église évangélique libre de Genève* in 1849. What happened in Geneva set the tone for other parts of French-speaking Switzerland, such as the cantons of Vaud and Neuchâtel, eventually leading to the creation of the *Église évangélique libre vaudoise* in 1847 and an *Église évangélique Indépendante* in Neuchâtel in 1873.[30]

Apart from the creation of free churches, several denominations from the British Isles also expanded in French-speaking Switzerland during the nineteenth century. Thus, the preaching of John Nelson Darby in Geneva and the canton of Vaud led to the creation of Darbyst communities in the 1840s, until some of them broke away and formed the *Assemblées et Églises évangéliques de Suisse romande* (AESR). The first Methodist churches appeared in 1856 in Lausanne and Zurich;[31] later, this denomination developed mainly in German-speaking Switzerland.[32] The Salvation Army first met with fierce resistance but was able to expand freely since the 1890s.[33]

The *Réveil* did more, however, than bring renewal to established churches and lead to the creation of new churches and denominations. It was accompanied by many "practical innovations" and an unprecedented zeal and development of missions and philanthropic activities, echoing the "activism" associated with the rise of evangelicalism in the Anglo-Saxon world.[34] For example, this time saw the foundation of numerous biblical and mission societies, such as the famous *Mission de Bâle* (Basle Mission), created in 1815 by a supporter of

---

29. Decorvet, "Introduction," 8.
30. Decorvet, "Introduction," 20.
31. Favre, *Origines*, 330.
32. Victor Conzemius and Olivier Fatio, "Le nouvel État fédératif et le Kulturkampf (1848–1880)," in *Histoire du Christianisme en Suisse*, 223.
33. Conzemius and Fatio, "Nouvel État," 224.
34. See Bebbington, *Evangelicalism*. The practical innovations also pertained to hymnology, catechesis and theological education. Decorvet, "Introduction," 8.

the *Réveil* in Basel, Christian Friedrich Spittler.[35] As to philanthropic activities, they pertained to almost all sectors of social life. For example, among the associations started by evangelicals during this period we find the Red Cross, founded in 1863 by two fervent adherents of the *Réveil*, Henry Dunant and Gustave Moynier,[36] the world's first secular nursing school, "La Source," which was founded in Lausanne in 1859 by a woman near to the free churches, Valérie Boissier or the countess Agénor de Gasparin, and the Blue Cross, which was founded in 1877 by pastor Louis-Lucien Rochat.[37] As these examples show, not just pastors, but many lay people, among whom an abundance of women, were involved in these actions.

Another consequence of the *Réveil* was the foundation, in 1847, of the French-speaking Evangelical Alliance (Alliance Evangélique Romande, AER) in Geneva.[38] With Henry Dunant – one of the founders of the Red Cross – as its secretary from 1852 till 1859, the Alliance was the Swiss counterpart of the Evangelical Alliance founded in London in 1846. This first cross-confessional alliance aimed to unite evangelical Christians and to evangelize together. The existence of this "Evangelical Internationale" and the extensive contact between evangelicals in Switzerland and abroad significantly helped to shape and influence missionary and philanthropic activity.

Developments since the 1950s
Multiplication and Diversification

Evangelicalism continued to develop during the first part of the twentieth century, but the multiplication and diversification of evangelical churches became significantly more pronounced from the 1950s, both geographically and in density.[39] For example, according to the website of the Intercantonal centre for information on religious beliefs (*Centre intercantonal d'information sur les croyances*), there were nine evangelical communities in the canton of Geneva

---

35. Victor Conzemius and Olivier Fatio, "De la République helvétique à la Confédération de 1848," in *Histoire du Christianisme en Suisse*, 202.

36. On this subject, see Monique Cuany, "The Réveil and Charitable Activities: Education, Care, and Society," in *The Genevan Réveil*, 437–60.

37. Conzemius and Fatio, "Nouvel État," 226–27.

38. In the German speaking part of Switzerland, a branch developed, first informally, and then formally since 1873. Both branches merged in 1875, becoming the Swiss Evangelical Alliance.

39. Jean-François Mayer, *L'évolution des chrétiens évangéliques et leur perception en Suisse romande* (Romanel: La Maison de La Bible, 2016), 24; Favre and Stolz, "Les évangéliques," 140.

in the nineteenth century and an additional four were created in the first half of the twentieth century. From 1950 to 1999, however, the map shows a total of thirty-nine new communities, and after 2000, twenty-one new communities were founded.[40]

Furthermore, while evangelicals used to be found mainly in cantons with a Protestant tradition, they are also now represented – although still much less – in territories of Catholic heritage. This is the result both of conscious efforts to plant churches in new areas and of the increased mobility of the population.[41] For example, before 1980 there was no French-speaking evangelical church in the canton of Fribourg, but today, there are several – both of Swiss and international origins – and new communities continue to appear regularly.

Ethnic Churches

One of the sources of the growth and diversification during the last decades has been the development of ethnic churches or, more broadly, international churches. This development is the result of the increased migration since the 1980s, a migration which has benefited both evangelical and Roman Catholic Christianity because it led to the creation of many churches from Asian, African and Latin-American origin.[42] These communities tend to concentrate in large urban centres, such as Geneva, Lausanne, Bienne and Fribourg in French-Speaking Switzerland.[43] It should be noted, however, that the influence of this migration does not only translate in new ethnic churches, but has also led to a remarkable increase in ethnic diversity in many evangelical churches of Swiss origin.[44]

---

40. Centre intercantonal d'information sur les croyances, https://info-religions-geneve.ch/carte/.

41. Mayer, *L'évolution*, 25.

42. Mayer, *L'évolution*, 24.

43. Unfortunately, there is no detailed study on this phenomenon in Switzerland. In 2007 Favre noted over fifty ethnic communities in Geneva alone, with a membership ranging from a few dozen to several hundred. In a private communication (13/12/2024), Nirine Jonah indicates that, based on his study, ethnic churches probably represent 25 percent of all evangelical churches in French-speaking Switzerland.

44. Mayer, *L'évolution*, 63. Sébastien Fath observes a "creolization" of francophone evangelical Christianity that shows the influence especially of African Christianity in France, Belgique and French-speaking Switzerland. Sébastien Fath, "Les mutations contemporaines de l'identité protestante évangélique francophone (France, Suisse, Belgique)," *Théologie évangélique* 16.2 (2017): 3–35.

Charismatization

Echoing a word-wide trend, another evolution in recent decades has been the increase of charismatic or Pentecostal congregations and a greater openness to charismatic influences among many evangelicals.[45] Pentecostalism entered Switzerland at the beginning of the twentieth century, first through German and British evangelists like Jonathan Paul, Smith Wigglesworth, George Jeffreys and Douglas Scott. Although it was first influential inside established churches, it finally led to the creation of new churches and denominations such as, in French-speaking Switzerland, the *Églises évangéliques de Réveil* (1935) and the *Église évangélique apostolique* (today *Mouvement Plus*) in the 1950s.

The two charismatic waves, first in the 1950s–1960s, and then starting at the end of the 1970s, further led to the creation and importation of new charismatic and Pentecostal churches, such as the International Christian Fellowship (ICF) or the Vineyard Christian Fellowship in the 1970s, but also recently to the creation of Gospel Centers from the movement Gospel Wave, C3, SOS churches and other international churches such as Hillsong in Geneva, or The New International Church in Bienne.[46] The rapid development of ethnic churches since the 1980s, with the appearance of missionaries or preachers from the South – whether from Latin America or Africa – also contributes to this charismatization.[47]

The charismatization of evangelical Christianity is also discernible beyond the actual charismatic and Pentecostal congregations. Indeed, although studies estimate that about a third of evangelicals in Switzerland are charismatic,[48] the distinction between charismatic and non-charismatic evangelical is less pronounced than it once was, and many so-called classical evangelicals are more open to charismatic impulses.[49]

All these factors have contributed to a diversification of the international influences on Swiss evangelicalism, and, although popular media still tend to

---

45. Mayer, *L'évolution*, 24. On the "charismatisation" of evangelicalism in Francophone areas, see Fath, "Mutations," 10–17.

46. These churches are often imports or extensions of movements from abroad, whether in Sweden, Australia, America, Nigeria or Kenya, and tend to work within their own networks.

47. Favre, *Origines*, 90–91.

48. Sociological studies on evangelicals in Switzerland usually classify them in three subclasses: charismatics, conservatives and moderates (or classical evangelicals). According to recent studies, moderates represent about a half of all evangelicals, charismatics a third, and conservatives 10 to 13 percent. Favre and Stolz, "Les évangéliques," 137–38.

49. Fath, "Mutations," 17.

associate it with a type of Christianity *à l'américaine*, the tendency is towards multiple international influences.⁵⁰

Resource Sharing and Common Representation

Despite their disconcerting diversity, recent decades also saw evangelicals multiply common initiatives and share resources at a new level. Although this type of collaboration and association has existed since the birth of Swiss evangelicalism in the nineteenth century, the growth of evangelicalism, globalization, and the numeric revolution all contributed to this evolution.⁵¹

In recent decades this collaboration has taken diverse forms, from common worship services or Alpha courses to the organization of events bringing together thousands of evangelicals, such as the *Jour du Christ*, ONE and the *Rencontre de Jeunesse* (RJ). The creation or restructuring of pan-evangelical media is another example of the sharing of resource with the aim of greater efficiency and quality. Thus, the merger of the magazines *Christianisme au XXIe siècle* (created in 1871) and *L'Avènement* (created in 1989) led to the creation of *Le Christianisme aujourd'hui*. Broadly evangelical websites, which aim to share resources, teaching and evangelism, have also multiplied. Created in 1999 by a French man (Eric Célérier) and a Swiss woman (Estelle Martin), *TopChrétien* has become the largest francophone evangelical website, reaching 1.7 million visitors per month in 2016.⁵² The creation of the *Haute Ecole de Théologie* (HET-PRO), a professing Protestant theological school, is another example of a trans-denominational project carried by evangelicals of diverse persuasion and by the evangelical wing of the Reformed Church.

In addition to these initiatives, efforts of "institutional" collaboration reached a new height with the creation of the *Réseau évangélique Suisse* (RES) in 2006.⁵³ According to some estimates, the RES currently regroups up to 80–90 percent of the evangelicals in French-speaking Switzerland and has thus reached the unprecedented achievement of representing a great proportion of evangelicals despite their diversity.⁵⁴ Several churches, however, are still not linked to the RES; chief among these are many ethnic or international

---

50. Mayer, *L'évolution*, 40–42.
51. On several of the examples listed below, see Fath, "Mutations," 18–23.
52. Fath, "Mutations," 21.
53. The RES is the result of a merger between the AER and the Fédération Romande d'Églises et Oeuvres Evangéliques (FREOE); website: https://evangelique.ch/portrait/.
54. Fath, "Mutations," 23.

churches. The RES is playing an important role in offering a representative structure for evangelicals in society. It has contributed to a better understanding of evangelicals in the media and has been an important credibility factor, as the fragmentation and diversity of evangelicals still continues to perplex observers.[55] The RES and its working groups also produce researched and balanced responses to social issues. However, the great diversity of evangelicals is likely to remain a challenge for the RES in the future, because the actions and positions of some groups are likely to affect the image of all evangelicals.[56]

Evangelicals and Society

With the growth of evangelicalism and the decrease of the influence of traditional religion, in an increasingly secular and pluralist world, the evangelical presence has become more normal and visible in Switzerland. In this context, evangelicals have also sought to be both more involved in society and societal issues, and to gain more recognition as a religious community.[57]

One way in which this has been done is by seeking state recognition as communities of public interest. Several evangelical federations have undertaken such procedures, such as the *Fédération évangélique vaudoise* (FEV) and the *Fédération évangélique neuchâteloise*. Evangelicals are divided on this issue, however, and several groups are opposed to such undertakings.[58] More broadly, the relationship to society and involvement in public life are likely to remain enduring points of disagreement among Swiss evangelicals.

Bibliography

Decorvet, Jean, Tim Grass, and Kenneth J. Stewart, eds. *The Genevan Réveil in International Perspective*. Eugene: Pickwick, 2023.

Fath, Sébastien. "Les mutations contemporaines de l'identité protestante évangélique francophone (France, Suisse, Belgique)." *Théologie évangélique* 16.2 (2017): 3–25.

Favre, Olivier. *Les Églises évangéliques de Suisse, origines et identités*. Geneva: Labor et Fides, 2006.

———, and Jörg Stolz. "Les évangéliques: des chrétiens convaincus dans un monde de plus en plus sécurlarisé." Pages 134–50 in *La nouvelle Suisse religieuse, Risques et*

---

55. Mayer, *L'évolution*, 78.
56. Mayer, *L'évolution*, 71.
57. Mayer, *L'évolution*, 63–64.
58. Mayer, *L'évolution*, 49; Jörg and Stolz, "Les évangéliques," 148–49; Favre, *Origines*, 102–3.

chance de sa diversité. Edited by Martin Baumann and Jörg Stolz. Geneva: Labor et Fides, 2009.

Jonah, Nirine. *L'implantation d'Églises: une étude en Europe francophone*. Romanel-sur-Lausanne: Scripsi, 2020.

Mayer, Jean-François. *L'évolution des chrétiens évangéliques et leur perception en Suisse romande*. Genève: Réseau Évangélique Suisse, 2016.

Stolz, Jörg, Olivier Favre, Caroline Gachet and Emmanuelle Buchard. *Le phénomène évangélique, analyses d'un milieu compétitif*. Genève: Labor et Fides, 2013.

22

Evangelicalism in German-Speaking Switzerland

Stefan Schweyer and Paul Bruderer

Swiss Reservation against the Label "Evangelical"

The evangelical movement in Switzerland cannot be studied by tracking the use of the term "evangelical"[1] because many in Switzerland refrain from using the label "evangelical" for themselves or for a specific group.[2] Unlike in Austria, there is no denomination in Switzerland that uses the term evangelical in its title. The Swiss Evangelical Alliance uses the German word *evangelisch* rather than *evangelikal* in its name and recommends that media avoid the term *evangelikal* and instead speak of *evangelische Christen*. The reason for this Swiss reluctance to use the label "evangelical" is probably the desire to avoid associations with fundamentalism, American evangelicalism and sectarianism.[3] We will nonetheless use the standard international terms such as "evangelicalism" in this chapter.

---

1. For the English word "evangelical," the German language has two words, *evangelikal* and *evangelisch*. *Evangelisch* refers to the movement started by the Reformation and the churches associated with it, while *evangelikal* refers more to the revivalist dynamics within Protestantism. When we use "evangelical," we mean what *evangelikal* denotes, despite the German *evangelisch* being the preferred term in the Swiss context. In some places the German word will be used when important.

2. On the use of the term in Switzerland, see Frank Hinkelmann, *Österreich und der Schweiz. Ursprung, Bedeutung und Rezeption eines Begriffs* (Bonn: Verlag für Kultur und Wissenschaft, 2017), 59–85.

3. Fritz Imhof, "'Evangelikal' – geliebt und gehasst." *Chrischona Panorama* 1 (2011): 9.

Historical Highlights

The history of the evangelical movement in Switzerland is closely intertwined with the international history of the evangelical movement,[4] whereby the founding of the Evangelical Alliance in London (1846) and the Lausanne Conference on World Evangelization (1974) can be considered the two most important global milestones. In the middle of the nineteenth century revivalist movements (including some puritan and pietist impulses) as well as ecclesiastical and social developments brought leaders of Protestant churches and groups together to form the Evangelical Alliance. This was a response to at least three challenges: the increasing fragmentation of Protestant Christianity into denominations; the rise of modernist thought and biblical criticism; and the social challenges of industrialization and globalization. The emergence of the Evangelical Alliance in England inspired the founding of a national alliance in French-speaking Switzerland in 1847 and in German-speaking Switzerland in 1873. The *Schweizerische Evangelische Allianz* (SEA) campaigned for religious freedom, for example in 1882 for the freedom of the then persecuted Salvation Army and in 1918 for the right of free assembly. In 1919, the Evangelical People's Party and the Association of Independent Churches were born out of circles close to the Alliance.

The American "New Evangelical" Billy Graham led rallies in Switzerland in 1955 and 1960. The 1974 Lausanne Congress, the Lausanne Commitment and the Lausanne Movement have played a key role in shaping the evangelical movement in Switzerland. A direct result of the Lausanne Congress was the founding of the Swiss Association for Evangelization which later became idea Schweiz.

The Evangelical Alliance and the Lausanne Movement offered Protestant Christians and communities, who could not identify with the socio-political course and theological orientation of the World Council of Churches, alternative platforms for communication, networking and cooperation. The network-like structure and ecclesial openness made it possible for people to pray, believe and work together even when they held different views on issues such as water baptism or baptism in the Holy Spirit. Among the national milestones were the national "Christ Days" (German: Christustage) which the Swiss Evangelical Alliance helped organize and which can be seen as both an expression and a source of inspiration for the evangelical movement. The first Christ Day took

---

4. Cf. Thorsten Dietz, *Menschen mit Mission. Eine Landkarte der evangelikalen Welt* (Witten: SCM R. Brockhaus, 2022), 15–52.

place in 1980 in the capitol Bern, the seventh and for the time being last Christ Day took place in Bern in 2010.

Institutions in the Context of the Evangelical Movement

Institutions are important for the evangelical movement because they act as hubs for the evangelical communication network, thus serving to reinforce and make evangelical convictions and values plausible.[5] Moreover, parachurch organizations enable experiences of unity beyond the local communities. Precisely because evangelicalism is not defined by a common ecclesiology or by common church structures, parachurch structures are important in uniting churches. We will discuss some.

The Schweizerische Evangelische Allianz (SEA)

The most important institutions of the evangelical movement in Switzerland are the SEA and its sister organization in the French-speaking part of the country. Around four hundred and eighty state and independent churches belong to the SEA and are organized in almost seventy local and regional sections.[6] Around one hundred and thirty organizations are collective members of the SEA. According to its own figures, the SEA network represents around two hundred thousand people. Specialists and organizations work in sixteen working groups in order to represent specific concerns in churches, congregations and also in the public sphere.

Church Networks and Associations

The SEA, its working groups and the local sections consist of state churches and independent churches. The Forum of State Churches (German *Landeskirchenforum*) is a working group of the SEA which brings together parishes and ministers from the Reformed state churches who share the convictions of the evangelical movement. The independent churches which were close to the Evangelical Alliance organized themselves into the Association of Independent

---

    5. Fabian Huber and Jörg Stolz, "Das evangelikale Milieu," in *Handbuch Evangelikalismus*, ed. Frederik Elwert (Bielefeld: Transcript, 2017), 275–87, 282–83.
    6. We use the term "state church" to denote *Landeskirche* and the term "independent church" to denote *Freikiche*, even though the English terms do not quite fit the respective church forms in Switzerland.

Churches (German: *Freikirchenverband*) in 1919 and today they call themselves Freikirchen.ch. These churches regard the Lausane Commitment, together with the Apostles' Creed, as their theological basis.[7]

Media

In the media landscape, several organizations are close to the Swiss evangelical movement. The Swiss branch of the German *Evangeliumsrundfunk* (ERF) was founded in 1973 and has been known as ERF Schweiz since 2008. The television programme *Fenster zum Sonntag* has been produced since the 1990s and is broadcast on national television channels, among others. The SEA and Freikirchen.ch are supporting organizations of ERF Schweiz. In 1986, the SEA founded idea Schweiz, which publishes the weekly magazine IDEA. The mission statement of Idea Schweiz includes communicating "the activities of Christians who are guided by the faith of the Evangelical Alliance and the Lausanne Commitment."[8] Since 2000, the Association Livenet, which is committed to the basis of faith of the European Evangelical Alliance and supported by the SEA, operates websites such as livenet.ch and jesus.ch.

Evangelism and Mission

Numerous evangelistic and missionary organizations have developed around the missionary dynamics of the Lausanne Movement, two of which are mentioned here as examples. Campus Crusade for Christ has been active in Switzerland since 1973. With currently eighteen working groups, the organization aims to "carry God's love holistically into the various areas of society."[9] Founded in 1972, the *Arbeitsgemeinschaft Evangelischer Missionen* (aem) is an umbrella organization of around thirty internationally active missionary organizations and sees itself as part of the SEA. In 2020, a process called Future Mission was initiated to improve the cooperation between independent churches, organizations and institutions for theological training.

---

7. On the relationship between free churches and the evangelical movement in Switzerland, see Stefan Schweyer, *Freikirchliche Gottesdienste. Empirische Analysen und theologische Reflexionen* (Leipzig: Evangelische Verlagsanstalt, 2020), 28–40.

8. See www.ideaschweiz.ch/ueber-uns. All translations from German are ours.

9. See www.cfc.ch/ueber-uns/wir.

Youth Work

Among the collective members of the SEA we mention as an example the Bund *evangelischer Schweizer Jungscharen* (founded in 1974), the fourth largest youth organization in Switzerland with groups in around two hundred and fifty churches. The association Adonia has been offering musical and sports camps since 1979 and also runs a publishing house. Adonia describes itself as an "independent organization based on the Evangelical Alliance."[10] One of the largest Christian youth events in Switzerland is the "Praisecamp," which is held over new year. Since 2002 Praisecamps have been held at irregular intervals and are coorganized by the SEA, Freikirchen.ch, Campus Crusade for Christ and others.

Theology

The evangelical movement has given birth to numerous theological seminaries.[11] The motivation was on the one hand to offer an alternative to programmes that adhere to biblical criticism, and on the other hand to serve as an opportunity for people without a university degree to qualify for service in mission and the church. Some of these theological seminaries are collective members of the SEA:

- The pietist-influenced *Theologisches Seminar St. Chrischona* (tsc, founded 1840)
- The *Seminar für biblische Theologie* in Beatenberg (sbt, 1934)
- The *Theologisch-Diakonische Seminar* Aarau (TDS Aarau, 1960) with its focus on social care
- The *Staatsunabhängige Theologische Hochschule* Basel (STH Basel, 1970), now accredited as a university institute
- The *Institut für gemeindeorientierte* Weiterbildung (IGW, 1991), which focuses on missional theology
- The International Seminary of Theology and Leadership (ISTL, 2005), which is characterized by a strong practical orientation.

The seminaries sbt, ISTL and IGW are accredited by the evangelical European Council for Theological Education (ECTC). With the exception of tsc, the seminaries listed here were from the outset interdenominational institutions. Some are more strongly rooted in the milieu of the independent churches (sbt,

---

10. See www.adonia.ch/ueber-uns.
11. Cf. Dietz, *Menschen mit Mission*, 172–202.

IGW, ISTL), while others are more consciously oriented towards both state and independent churches (TDS Aarau, STH Basel).

Politics

Switzerland has two political parties with an explicitly Christian profile: the Evangelical People's Party (German: *Evangelische Volkspartei*, EVP), which emerged from the SEA in 1919, and the Federal Democratic Union (German: *Eidgenössisch-Demokratische Union*, EDU), founded in 1975. There are also many organizations that are involved in socio-political issues, such as the Stop Poverty initiative which emerged from the international Micah movement and is committed to achieving the UN Sustainable Development Goals from a Christian perspective, and the SEA working group Christian Public Affairs, which aims to promote the political involvement of Christians.

In line with the original impulses of the evangelical movement, the institutional evangelical landscape in Switzerland has a network character. Numerous programmes are organized by parachurch institutions or joint working groups rather than by individual churches, associations or denominations. These interdenominational organizations enable people from state churches and independent churches to work together strategically. The basis of faith and the system of membership of the SEA provide both the foundation and the framework for these forms of cooperation.

Theological Orientation

The basis of faith of the Swiss Evangelical Alliance provides the theological basis for cooperation between many evangelical organizations.[12] It is not intended to serve as a common confession, because the confessional commitment should

---

12. The wording of the basis of faith was last amended in 2020, when the SEA adopted the wording of the 2018 version of the basis of faith of the German Evangelical Alliance but moved the article on the Bible from the last to the second position. Compared to the previous German version of the basis of faith of the European Evangelical Alliance, some aspects have been newly included, in particular the concept of humanity with an emphasis on human dignity and gender duality (Art. 3) as well as a more holistic view of mission, which integrates aspects of social action and welfare with the proclamation of the gospel (Art. 7); see European Evangelical Alliance, *EEA Glaubensbasis*, www.europeanea.org/wp-content/uploads/2019/11/2019-11_EEA-basis_of_faith_german.pdf.
This chapter uses the numbering and version of the SEA.

lie with the churches and organizations of origin.[13] It is rather understood as a summary of those theological convictions that make it possible to act together as Christians. Such actions take place expressly on the basis of a particular worldview,[14] which on the one hand accepts and supports the reality of a religiously pluralistic society (notably freedom of faith and conscience) and on the other hand distinguishes evangelical Christianity from other worldviews such as atheism and heresies within Christianity.[15]

The basis of faith integrates the classic evangelical theological beliefs of the Bebbington quadrilateral with the emphasis of the Lausanne Movement on holistic, integral mission. Bebbington's four core convictions (a high view of the Bible, the cross as central for salvation, the necessity of conversion and the call to mission)[16] can all be found in the basis of faith.[17] In addition, the basis of faith contains central theological statements that distinguish it from heresies (the Trinity of God, article 1) and anthropological insights that are significant for ethics (man and woman created in the image of God, article 3).

In addition to this basis of faith, the SEA recognizes the founding texts of the Lausanne Movement in its statutes, specifically the Lausanne and Cape Town Commitments.[18] The explicit reason for this is their emphasis on holistic, integral mission.[19] The SEA thus distinguishes itself to some extent from forms of evangelicalism that overemphasize the afterlife at the expense of the here and now and could therefore have a tendency of withdrawal from the world. Through its connection to the Lausanne Movement, the SEA is strengthening its missionary profile, the fourth point of the Bebbington quadrilateral.

With respect to holistic mission, the explicit focus is on the call to social action which must not be seen as a disguised strategy for evangelism. However, holistic mission does not only concern the social dimension, but the entire spectrum of human and creaturely existence. It therefore includes politi-

---

13. Schweizerische Evangelische Allianz, *Wegleitung zur Glaubensbasis der Schweizerischen Evangelischen Allianz 2022*, www.each.ch/wp-content/uploads/2022/05/220517_Hinleitung_SEA-Glaubensbasis-1.pdf, 1.

14. *Wegleitung zur Glaubensbasis*, 2.

15. *Wegleitung zur Glaubensbasis*, 3.

16. Bebbington, *Evangelicalism in Modern Britain*, 2–3.

17. See especially the articles 2, 4, 5 and 7.

18. Schweizerische Evangelische Allianz. *Statuten (mit Glaubensbasis). Gemeinsam besser.* 2021, www.each.ch/wp-content/uploads/2022/05/Statuten_mit_Glaubensbasis.pdf, Art. 4.

19. Schweizerische Evangelische Allianz. *Wegleitung zur Glaubensbasis der Schweizerischen Evangelischen Allianz*, 1; Schweizerische Evangelische Allianz. *Hintergrund zu den Dokumenten der Lausanner Bewegung. 2022*, www.each.ch/wp-content/uploads/2022/05/220517_Hintergrund_Lausanner-Bewegung.pdf, 1 and 3.

cal, economic and ecological commitment.[20] These other dimensions are not explicitly mentioned in the basis of faith but are addressed in the Cape Town Declaration. Within these parameters, a diversity of theological convictions is possible that nevertheless share common spiritual life (especially prayer) and common action. This becomes visible and tangible when one considers the diversity of organizations and associations that we have mentioned.

Evangelicals in Switzerland thus clearly heard the call of the Lausanne Movement to turn to the world in a missionary fashion and the conversations at Lausanne 1974 and Manila 1989 about the relationship between culture, society and the gospel. The Swiss discussed appropriate contextualization for the proclamation of the gospel, forms of worship and church community. While impulses from the Seeker Church movement were taken up in the 1990s, the postmodern context and the associated questions of a new contextualization of church and gospel received greater attention from the 2000s onwards.[21]

Fluidization of the Evangelical Scene

Because evangelicals do not identify themselves through church or institutional affiliation, but primarily through a particular theological orientation that leads to common action, they have a fundamental openness to Christians from other organizations and traditions who have a similar orientation.

Ecumenical Encounters with the Roman Catholic Church

In the 1990s ecumenical encounters with the Roman Catholic Church began. During this time, the charismatic movement in the Roman Catholic Church gained traction through the person of Urban Camenzind, who preached and ministered in many revivalist church services. From the 2010s onwards, many Christians in independent churches began to attend conferences and listen to the podcasts of the House of Prayer in Augsburg, Germany, with its Catholic leader Dr Johannes Hartl. In 2012, the Centre for Faith and Society (German: *Zentrum für Glaube und Gesellschaft*) was founded at the Catholic University of Fribourg with a focus on ecumenical relations. Through its media work and annual study days in particular, the centre contributes to interdenominational networking, including networking with evangelical circles.

---

20. Cf. Wright, *Mission of God's People*, chapters 3 and 6.
21. Todjeras, *Emerging Church*.

To mark the 500th anniversary of the Reformation, the SEA published a paper on its relationship with the Roman Catholic Church and on the possibilities, opportunities and limits of cooperation. The paper signals that the SEA is open to the membership of Roman Catholic individuals and to the guest status of Roman Catholic parishes in local sections. The paper also recommends the cooperation of all Christian churches and congregations at local level.[22]

Post-Evangelicalism

The years 2000 to 2015 saw two distinct developments, which overlap in such a way that it is difficult to distinguish them. On the one hand, an increasing emphasis on holistic mission to the world;[23] on the other, the movement towards post-evangelicalism,[24] in which theological and ethical convictions that were previously undisputed in large parts of the evangelical movement were questioned and revised. After 2015 the post-evangelical movement gained momentum and began to differentiate itself more clearly from evangelical beliefs and forms of church; individuals began to distance themselves publicly from their evangelical origins.

An example is a podcast from autumn 2018 in which David Jäggi, at that time head of studies at IGW and pastor in a Chrischona congregation, outlined his path from a pre-critical understanding of the Bible (for him the area of fundamentalism and evangelicalism) to a post-critical understanding.[25] Jäggi did not use the term post-evangelical but "progressive." He emphasized that he wanted to take the good things from the earlier phases of his faith with him into the next phase. It seems that in this period attempts were still being made to keep evangelicalism and post-evangelicalism together.

Yet after around 2020 clear and complete distancing from the evangelical scene became more frequent. In October 2020, Jäggi described himself as a former evangelical.[26] Eveline Baumberger, who currently heads RefLab together

---

22. Schweizerische Evangelische Allianz. *Arbeitspapier: Verhältnis der Schweizerischen Evangelischen Allianz SEA zur römisch-katholischen Kirche. 500 Jahre nach der Reformation.* 2017, www.each.ch/wp-content/uploads/2017/05/170505_Arbeitspapier_Katholiken_17.pdf.

23. For an example from the evangelical movement in Switzerland, see Roland Hardmeier, *Kirche ist Mission. Auf dem Weg zu einem ganzheitlichen Missionsverständnis*, 2nd ed. (Schwarzenfeld: Neufeld, 2020).

24. Cf. in principle Dave Tomlinson, *The Post-Evangelical* (London: SPCK, 2014); Patrick Todjeras, "'Post-evangelikal' – eine Verständigung," *Pastoraltheologie* 110 (2021): 59–79.

25. Unfortunately, the recordings are no longer available online. The recording mentioned here is available privately.

26. See www.reflab.ch/ausgeglaubt-was-christlich-special-mit-thorsten-dietz.

with Manuel Schmid, identified with ex-evangelicals and post-evangelicals in 2021.[27] Martin Benz, a pastor at the Vineyard church in Basel and a lecturer at the IGW for many years, provides a detailed argumentation for post-evangelicalism in opposition to classical evangelicalism. In his book *Wenn der Glaube nicht mehr passt* (English: *When Faith Doesn't Fit Any More*), he openly confesses to having left evangelicalism behind.[28] According to his blog, evangelical faith is "often characterized by many fears and threatening scenarios: fear of God, fear of the devil, fear of sin, fear of judgement, fear of the end times, fear of hell and a fear-mongering style of evangelism."[29] Negative experiences in the evangelical scene seem to be an important driver of the post-evangelical movement.

For people with evangelical roots, The RefLab project of the Reformed Church of Zurich is a key centre for post-evangelical theological reflection in Switzerland from its beginnings in 2019. The Mennonite Education Centre Bienenberg is developing into a second such hotspot, not least due to the appointment of Martin Benz in 2023. Discourse in the post-evangelical setting often revolves around central theological topics such as the understanding of revelation, the doctrine of God, the theology of the cross, sexual ethics and the pastoral handling of doubt, differing opinions and developments in faith. The theological convictions that are held in post-evangelical contexts can be in considerable tension with the worldview and theological orientation laid down in the basis of faith of the SEA, for example the theology of the cross, where the basis of faith includes substitutionary atonement and Jesus's sacrificial death (art. 4), or in sexual ethics, where the basis of faith states the duality of the sexes (art. 3). This shows that we are probably dealing with a new phenomenon that cannot simply be integrated into the previous evangelical setting. Evangelical networks therefore need to address the question of how to deal with convictions within their own ranks that are no longer compatible with the basis of faith. In view of global trends with upheavals and splits in denominations and churches (such as the Anglican Church and the United

---

27. See www.reflab.ch/hilfe-ich-werde-wieder-fromm.

28. "Personally, I have packed my bags from the conservative-evangelical or fundamentalist thought patterns in which I was at home for many years. The old town became too narrow for me." For Benz, "old town" is a reference to evangelical. In the image of the relocation, he had ended up "in a new neighbourhood, so to speak," outside the evangelical world. See Martin Benz, *Wenn der Glaube nicht mehr passt. Ein Umzugshelfer* (Neukirchen-Vluyn: Neukirchener, 2022), 45.

29. See www.movecast.de/mc-116-was-glaubt-man-wenn-man-postevangelikal-ist-teil-9-angstfrei-glauben.

Methodist Church), it cannot be ruled out that Switzerland will see similar developments and new coalitions.

Loss, Shift and Sharpening of the Evangelical Profile

As the previous descriptions show, the evangelical movement in Switzerland has become more fluid. This liquefaction can be interpreted in different ways.

a) Some see it as a problematic loss of identity and are concerned that core beliefs are being sacrificed. This view leads to new demarcations, for example in the case of the Swiss branch of "The Last Reformation" movement, initiated by Torben Søndergaard. This movement seeks to promote true Christianity and true discipleship as a response to the "deceptions" in which many Christians live. "The Last Reformation" thinks that many rely on church structures and have a false understanding of what it means to be a Christian.[30] For this reason, the movement criticizes ecumenical relations.[31] It is no coincidence that the Swiss protagonists were unable to continue their pastoral ministries within Swiss independent churches because the tensions were too big.[32] Thus "The Last Reformation" is an example of a movement that originated in the evangelical movement, but has detached itself from evangelical networks and from the principles and convictions of evangelicalism.

b) The tendency towards fluidity can also be interpreted as a shift in profile. This type of shift happens when Christians use classic evangelical positions as bogeymen in order to disassociate themselves from them. Liquefaction in this case is therefore not about an expansion of evangelical convictions, but about a decisive change in theological orientation. Occasionally, such views can be found among post-evangelicals, especially in the area of sexual ethics, where evangelical convictions are now declared to be a "sin."

c) Finally, the liquefaction can also be interpreted as a sharpening of profile. The idea here is that dialogue with other churches and theological positions can help recognize potential evangelical one-sidedness. According to this view, theological openness leads to a deepening of the understanding of the Christian faith. Where the other two interpretations focus on loss and displacement,

---

30. See www.pioneertrainingschool.ch/home/die-letzte-reformation.

31. For example www.jesus-reformation.ch/die-grosse-gefahr-falscher-einheit/; www.jesus-reformation.ch/category/die-irrlehren-der-roemisch-katholischen-kirche-und-der-orthodoxen-kirchen.

32. See www.jesus-reformation.ch/wer-wir-sind. Lukas Stolz was a pastor in a Free Evangelical Church (German: *Freie Evangelische Gemeinde* FEG), Joel Salvisberg in a Bewegung-Plus church.

this perspective seeks to retain evangelical truths and integrate them into a more sustainable and robust theological concept. This perspective is the one we favour and seek to explore in greater depth in the following considerations.

Bibliography

Bartholomä, Philipp, and Stefan Schweyer. *Gemeinde mit Mission. Damit Menschen von heute leidenschaftlich Christus nachfolgen. Grundlagen und praktische Impulse.* 3rd ed. Gießen: Brunnen, 2024.

Benz, Martin. *Wenn der Glaube nicht mehr passt. Ein Umzugshelfer.* Neukirchen-Vluyn: Neukirchener, 2022.

Dietz, Thorsten. *Menschen mit Mission. Eine Landkarte der evangelikalen Welt.* Witten: SCM R. Brockhaus, 2022.

Hardmeier, Roland. *Kirche ist Mission. Auf dem Weg zu einem ganzheitlichen Missionsverständnis.* 2nd ed. Schwarzenfeld: Neufeld, 2020.

Hinkelmann, Frank. *Evangelikal in Deutschland, Österreich und der Schweiz. Ursprung, Bedeutung und Rezeption eines Begriffs.* Bonn: Verlag für Kultur und Wissenschaft, 2017.

Huber, Fabian, and Jörg Stolz. "Das evangelikale Milieu." Pages 275–87 in *Handbuch Evangelikalismus.* Edited by Frederik Elwert. Bielefeld: Transcript, 2017.

Imhof, Fritz. "'Evangelikal' – geliebt und gehasst." *Chrischona Panorama* 1 (2011): 9.

Schweyer, Stefan. *Freikirchliche Gottesdienste. Empirische Analysen und theologische Reflexionen.* Leipzig: Evangelische Verlagsanstalt, 2020.

Todjeras, Patrick. "'Post-evangelikal' – eine Verständigung." *Pastoraltheologie* 110 (2021): 59–79.

———. *"Emerging Church" – ein dekonversiver Konversationsraum. Eine praktisch-theologische Untersuchung über ein anglo-amerikanisches Phänomen gelebter Religiosität.* Göttingen: Vandenhoeck & Ruprecht, 2020.

Tomlinson, Dave. *The Post-Evangelical* [1995]. London: SPCK, 2014.

23

Evangelicalism in Ukraine

Sergii Sannikov

Introduction

Historically, religion has played an important part in the political and social life in Ukraine. Finding itself on the civilization fault line between aggressive Western Catholicism and similarly aggressive Russian Orthodoxy, in the sixteenth and seventeenth centuries Ukraine sought its identity in Greek Catholicism, Orthodox Fraternities, and partly in Protestantism.[1] In this way the Ukrainians tried to find a *via media* between Catholicism and Byzantine Orthodoxy, although it did not always work. The country's centuries-long religious and political struggle for independence has formed a deeper religious awareness in this ethnic group than in the inhabitants of other Eastern European countries.[2] According to the latest polls, 58 percent of the people considered themselves believers in 2000; in 2010–2023 this number ranged between 70 and 74 percent.[3]

At the beginning of 2024, most Ukrainians considered themselves Orthodox (c. 60 percent). Some 11 percent were Greek Catholic and 1.4 percent of the population identified themselves as Protestant and evangelical.[4] This means

---

1. Ho-woog Kim and Jun-ki Chung, "History of Protestantism in Ukraine," *Theological Quarterly*, 83 (2023), 469.

2. For example, Orthodoxy was brought from the Byzantine Empire to Russia ready-made, so the people often perceived the faith as an obligatory civic ritual.

3. Ю. Якименко, *Українське суспільство, держава і церква під час війни. Церковно-релігійна ситуація в Україні-2023* (Київ: Razumkov Center, 2023), 4. [Y. Yakimenko, *Ukrainian Society, State, and Church During War. Church And Religion in Ukraine in 2023* (Kyiv: Razumkov Centre, 2023)], 4.

4. Yakimenko, *Ukrainian Society*, 34.

that there are about half a million evangelicals in Ukraine. This is a rather large number, but, unfortunately, this group is fragmented due to the strong influence of fundamentalism, which emerged under the influence of nineteenth-century dispensationalist and holiness movements. A distinctive fundamentalist understanding of Scripture emerged which associated the authority of the Bible with its perfect factual truthfulness. The American debate over the inerrancy and infallibility of the biblical text did not affect Eastern European evangelicals, but Harriet Harris accurately described this type of fundamentalist: "fundamentalist reasoning implies that it is the text that reveals the truth about God, not Jesus himself as he actually lived and died and rose again."[5]

The fundamentalist tradition always leads to a division into "others," and the term "others" most often means "not like us," because it seems like a way to keep yourself clean. Separation from all and presenting themselves as the sole possessors of truth was actively supported by Soviet society and continues in post-Soviet society. It is not surprising that evangelical groups in Ukraine have been susceptible to this mindset and have tried to avoid contact with one another, thinking that this way preserves their identity.

Eastern European Evangelicals are characterized by a conservative approach to many ethical issues and values. Most evangelicals, especially Baptists and Pentecostals, oppose even alcohol consumption and smoking, as well as (together with most European evangelicals) abortion, and same-sex marriage. Sometimes the battle against LGBT is manifested not only in the proclamation of traditional Christian values, but also in demonstrations attempting to ban such communities.

Who are the Evangelicals in Ukraine?

In Ukraine, the term "evangelicals" as a unifying concept is unknown to a broad public. A generic term more often used is "evangelical Christians," although, in its narrow sense, this is the name of a denomination which will be introduced below. Therefore, there is a certain ambiguity about the term "evangelicals": sometimes it is used to mean the denomination of the Evangelical Christians (also called Prokhanovites after their famous leader), at other times it indicates the broader movement that holds to the principles described in the classical work of David Bebbington: conversionism, activism, biblicism and crucicen-

---

5. Harriet A. Harris, *Fundamentalism and Evangelicals* (Oxford: Oxford University Press, 2008), 304.

trism.⁶ Since this article speaks of the Ukrainian context, we will use the word "evangelicals" for evangelical Christians in the broad sense of the term.

Unlike other European countries, Ukraine has never had a national Evangelical Alliance. Ukrainians love freedom and individualism and see themselves as a part of the European family. This reflected on the character of the evangelical Christians as well. There have been many attempts to create an Evangelical Alliance. In 1904 Ivan Prokhanov, the leader of the Evangelical Christians, established the Evangelical Union as a forerunner of the Evangelical Alliance, but it existed only for four years. Other causes of the failure to unite the evangelical movement aside from fundamentalism are the mutual resentments among the evangelical denominations that were caused by mutual proselytism and unjustified defamation at the early stages of their existence. A final factor with lasting effect was the forced unification of all Ukrainian evangelicals by the state between 1944 and 1990. But at the end of the 1990s, the situation began to change and attempts were made to bring the evangelicals closer together so that they could assert their interests before the state and the international community. These attempts began at the level of denominational leaders. In 2005, the Council of Evangelical Protestant Churches of Ukraine (CEPCU) was formed by Baptists, Pentecostals, charismatics and Seventh-day Adventists. Later, the Reformed Church and the evangelical part of the Lutheran Church joined the CEPCU, which now unites twelve religious associations which recognize each another as evangelicals. This means that the local churches which belong to these associations practise the values highlighted by Bebbington at least to some degree. And although the evangelical movement in Ukraine remains fragmented and confessional, there are clear tendencies towards efficient interaction and mutual fraternal help. It is the CEPCU that represents the Ukrainian evangelicals internationally.

According to the statistics provided by the State Service for Ethnopolitics and Freedom of Conscience in Ukraine, as of 1 January 2024, Baptists, Pentecostals, charismatics and Seventh-day Adventists – which comprise the core of the evangelical movement – had 8,127 registered congregations with a total of over four hundred thousand members.⁷ There are also no less than one hundred thousand other evangelicals including unregistered groups. Although this

---

6. David W. Bebbington, *Evangelicalism in Modern Britain: A History from the 1730s to the 1980s* (London: Hyman Unwin, 1989), 2–17.

7. 3,251 Baptist congregations belonging to various unions and associations, 2,781 different Pentecostal congregations, 1,067 Charismatic congregations and 1,028 Seventh-day Adventist congregations.

number of believers is rather impressive for Eastern Europe, the evangelicals remain marginalized in the religious life of the society, although scholars view them as an influential minority.

Stundism

The forerunner of the modern evangelical movement in Ukraine was the so-called Stundism, a group which originated in the nineteenth century. In 1818, the four Gospels were published in Ukraine for the first time, in 1822 followed by the publication of the New Testament in the generally known Russian language. These books were actively distributed among common people and their reading brought a wave of spiritual awakening. At the same time, German colonies in the south of Ukraine experienced an evangelical revival among the Lutherans and Mennonites in the spirit of neo-Pietism. When the first Ukrainian believers who were searching for God encountered this German neo-Pietism, they started to form their own Bible study groups, the core of which was comprised of those who had experienced the transformation of life. Since these groups met for one hour, similar to the German Pietists called Stundists, they became known under the same name.[8]

Initially the Stundists did not want to leave the Orthodox Church, but hostility of the priests who deprived them of their Bibles and hymnbooks as well as pogroms and lynchings, often started by fellow-villagers, made the Stundists realise that they were different. They began leaving the Orthodox Church and forming their own congregations.

A careful study of the New Testament convinced the Ukrainian Stundists of the necessity of the adult baptism, but the majority of their German mentors held to the idea of infant baptism. Still, the Ukrainian Stundists were able to find like-minded people in the one of the Mennonite groups. In the summer of 1869, Abraham Unger, a Mennonite pastor, came to Old Danzig and baptized Efim Tsymbal. This baptism was the beginning of an organized evangelical movement in Ukraine.

Two years later, the congregation under Tsymbal's leadership consisted of fifty-eight baptized members. It was with this community that the preaching of the gospel and the all-Ukrainian mission began. The German Johann Gerhard Onken, the "Father of Continental Baptists," travelled through the South of Ukraine in 1869 and played an important role in the establishment of the evangelical principles in the Stundist movement. Oncken visited the German

---

8. The German word Stunde means hour.

Baptist Church in Odessa and the Mennonite colonies in Khortitsa, ordained ministers and guided the Ukrainian Stundism in the Baptist direction.

The First Steps of the Evangelical Movement

The first Stundist and Baptist congregations in the south of Ukraine were very mission-minded: they fully or partially supported dozens of evangelists whom they sent to other parts of the country. Ukrainian religious scholar Victoria Liubashchenko states that the fact that the beliefs of the Stundists were unsophisticated made them popular among common people. They were ardent biblicists who based all their arguments on the Bible.[9] In the 1880s Ukrainian Stundism completed its transition to an Oncken-type Baptist movement and spread throughout Ukraine. Vasiliy Pavlov, a graduate of Oncken's seminary in Hamburg and pastor in Odessa, played an important role in the institutionalization of the congregations.

The 1890s saw the formation of the first congregations of the Evangelical Christians. This denomination had begun among the Russian aristocracy in St. Petersburg in 1874 thanks to the preaching of Lord Granville Radstock. Initially, the groups in Ukraine had little structure, but when Ivan Prokhanov returned from abroad in 1898, he became the leader of the movement and organized them according to the Baptist model. Later, the Evangelical Christians were also established in Crimea, but most of their congregations were in big cities. Since the headquarters was in St. Petersburg, where most activities took place, the Evangelical Christians had little impact on Ukraine as such. Yet the influence of Prokhanov was strong. He prepared and published collections of sheet music for evangelical songs, many of which are still sung, and at the Second Congress of the Baptist World Alliance in 1911 he was elected one of the six vice-presidents.

From the beginning, there were tensions between the congregations of the Evangelical Christians (Prokhanovites) and the Baptists. These were to some degree caused by some secondary doctrinal differences, but to a greater extent by disagreements between the leaders. The various attempts to unite them usually resulted in a bigger schism. The Baptists were marked by a stricter church organization and hierarchy, obligatory laying on of hands on church members after baptism, and the ordination of ministers.

---

9. Вікторія Любащенко, *Історія протестантизму в Україні: Курс лекцій* [Victoria Liubashchenko, *History of Protestantism in Ukraine: Series of Lectures*] (Kyiv: Prosvita, 1996), 232.

Thanks to missionaries from Germany, the first groups of Seventh-day Adventists were established in German colonies in 1886; ten years later there were already about 800 Adventists among the indigenous population.

Suffering and Growth: Evangelicals in the Twentieth Century

Before 1905 all evangelicals were persecuted by the government which did not recognize any religious groups outside the Orthodox Church. According to the law, all citizens of the Empire were Orthodox. The evangelicals were imprisoned, sentenced to hard labour and exiled to the farthest corners of the Empire. But because of the revolution, in 1905 Emperor Nicholas II issued a decree which allowed all so-called "sectarians" to exist legally. This decree marked a stage of relative freedom and a fast growth for the evangelicals. Yet when World War I broke out, they were again viewed with suspicion and seen as spies of Germany, against which the Russian Empire went to war.

The final years of this war had a negative effect on the evangelicals. Besides, the Treaty of Riga (1921) ceded the western areas of Ukraine (Galicia and Volyn) to Poland while Ukraine became a part of the Soviet Union. According to Victoria Liubashchenko, by the beginning of the Soviet era there were about 50,000 Baptists, a similar number of Evangelical Christians and several thousand Adventists in Eastern Ukraine.

After the Civil War (1917–1922) the religious life of Ukraine was enhanced by a new component: the Pentecostal movement. Its beginning was connected with the ministry of Ivan Voronaev, who came as a missionary of the Assemblies of God to Odessa in 1921. Being a great preacher and organizer, he started the first Pentecostal church in less than a year, which consisted mainly of former Baptists and Evangelical Christians. This created considerable tension and hostility towards the Christians of Evangelical Faith (CEF), as the followers of Voronaev called themselves. Inspired by the new ideas of the baptism of the Holy Spirit and the sign of tongues, the Pentecostal congregations were active in missionary work and in 1926 the All-Ukrainian Union of Christians of Evangelical Faith was established, which included three hundred and fifty churches and about seventeen thousand believers.

Almost at the same time that Voronaev's movement began in Eastern Ukraine, the Pentecostal movement began in Western Ukraine, then part of Poland, as some peasants who had worked in the USA and had become Pentecostals returned to their villages. They travelled and preached the new teaching. In 1929 two missionaries of the Assemblies of God established the Eastern European Mission, which organized the work among the Ukrainians in Poland. The All-Polish Union of Christians of Faith, Evangelical (CFE, formed in 1928) included over three hundred congregations with twenty-five thousand members in 1939. The Pentecostals of Eastern Ukraine differed from the ones in the west of the country in that they practised foot washing before the Lord's Supper.

Before the Soviet Union annexed Western Ukraine in 1939, the evangelical movement was able to develop in relative freedom there. When the Union of the Baptists and the Evangelical Christians (Prokhanovites) merged in 1923, both denominations included about two thousand active evangelists. The union did not last long, however, because misunderstandings between the Prokhanovites and the Baptists led to a split in 1927.

Evangelicals and Militant Atheism

The history of the evangelicals in Ukraine is truly dramatic. According to Walter Sawatsky, before Stalin's persecutions began in 1929, there were no less than three thousand congregations of Evangelical Christians and Baptists and over five thousand Adventist believers in Ukraine. In 1918–1926, nine hundred and six new churches with a total of thirty five thousand members were planted.[10]

The Soviet decree *On Religious Associations* (1929) led to intense anti-religious propaganda and drastic restrictions of the freedom of conscience. Religious freedom was limited to the performance of rituals and any propagation of one's views was strictly forbidden. This measure was immediately followed by persecution of believers, who were often accused of espionage and counterrevolutionary activities. In 1929 the leaders of all evangelical unions were arrested, Bibles were confiscated and the evangelical periodicals were closed down. From 1935 not only the leaders but all believers were called enemies of the people. They were sent to labour camps and sentenced to death; often even the wives and minor children of evangelical leaders were arrested. By 1936, almost all Protestant churches in the USSR were deprived of registration and their prayer houses were confiscated. Yet clandestine worship services, usually led by women, continued to be held in private homes; baptisms and the Lord's Supper were performed in secret.

During World War II, under pressure from the Western allies, the Soviet government agreed to legalize religious life and some church leaders were

---

10. Walter Sawatsky, *Soviet Evangelicals since World War II* (Eugene: Wipf and Stock Publishers, 2007), 42.

released. The state decided to unite all evangelicals in one union so that it would be easier to control them. Thus on 14 October 1944 the All-Union Council of Evangelical Christians-Baptists (ACECB) was formed. This allowed many congregations to get legalized and to restore their numbers. According to Soviet religious scholar Lev Mitrokhin, by the 1960s the Baptists were a well-organized church with congregations in almost every region of the country and some 10,000 people a year joining on average. At that time the ACECB included about half a million people in over five thousand churches.

The forced unification was especially painful for the Pentecostals, who had to renounce the requirement of baptism by the Holy Spirit with the sign of speaking in tongues. According to the official statistics, over twenty five thousand congregations with four hundred thousand members joined the ACECB. But in the beginning of the 1950s, many Pentecostal churches refused the state registration and left the ACECB to create the clandestine Union of Independent Christians of Evangelical Faith which established the Union of the unregistered CFE churches in Kharkiv in 1956.

In the 1960s, a dissident movement began among the Evangelical Christians-Baptists. The renunciation of the registration and necessity to go underground were caused by the autocratic management of the local churches enforced by the state, especially the requirement to ban children from attending worship services. Under various pretexts over three hundred churches of the Evangelical Christians-Baptists were closed down. An Initiative Group, led by Gennadiy Kriuchkov and Alexei Prokofiev, was transformed into the Council of Churches of Evangelical Christians-Baptists in 1965. Sawatsky points out that by that time about 13 percent of the believers supported this movement, which included only about 155,000 members.[11] But ACECB leaders began to admit and correct their mistakes and after 1966 most congregations rejoined the original union.

The Ukrainian evangelicals, both Pentecostals and Baptists, saw considerable growth in the 1970s. After 1974, the Soviet policy towards the evangelicals changed. They were allowed more freedom and they experienced a considerable transformation. Many clandestine Baptist and Pentecostal congregations began to register as independent churches. In the middle of the 1980s, the state started the liberalization policy which ended with the so-called Perestroika (restructuring) and the disintegration of the Soviet Union in 1991. In February 1990, the ACECB was dissolved, and separate confessional evangelical bodies were formed.

---

11. Sawatsky, *Soviet Evangelicals since World War II*, 222.

Attempt to Work Together: Evangelicals in Independent Ukraine

The first decade of Ukraine's independence saw a rapid growth of evangelical churches due to the unprecedented interest in religion after seventy years of atheistic propaganda. Billy Graham's visit to Kiev in 1988 can be considered the beginning of such growth. More than 15,000 people gathered for his campaign. The streets around the stadium were filled with people. About a quarter of those present came up front following his call to repentance. It was a time of great spread of the good news. Many were inspired by the Lausanne Movement, which they got to know at the Second Lausanne Congress in Manila (1989), which they managed to attend even before the disintegration of the Soviet Union. They came back not only inspired, but also equipped with projectors and the *Jesus* movie that they began to use actively for evangelism.

In the beginning of the 1990s, Western missionaries brought the charismatic movement to Ukraine; it soon reached young Pentecostals and Baptists. It consists of various groups, which grew fast during the first years of their existence and each have their own leader. These groups are known for their highly emotional, ecstatic nature, openness to society, mission and ecumenism.

Theological institutions have played a major role in the development of the evangelical movement in Ukraine. Until 1989, the Soviet Union had only one institution for pastors – Bible courses in Moscow – but after independence, seminaries, Bible schools and training centres at various levels were organized in Ukraine with the help of mainly American partners to train ministers. By 1997 there were about fifty such centres in Ukraine and the Euro-Asian Accreditation Association was established to streamline their activities. In the beginning it included 30 Ukrainian theological schools from almost all evangelical denominations and became virtually the only platform for evangelicals to contact and interact with each other. Thanks to the developed system of standards and participation in the international organization ICETE, theological education was stabilized and proved to be an excellent tool for training ministers for the many new churches that were planted after independence. Currently, according to official statistics, there are 146 registered evangelical educational institutions in Ukraine, but there are still many churches without ordained pastors because most of the training programmes are oriented towards training lay ministers.

The political events of the last decade, and especially Russian aggression, have prompted the formation of Ukrainian evangelical public theology. Ukrainian Evangelical Theological Seminary (Kyiv) published several issues of the journal *Christiyanska Dumka* devoted to analysing the relationship between the Church and civil society. Special attention began to be paid to theological reflection on political processes. Thus, in December 2023 in Bucha (Kyiv region) was organized a broad conference on the theme *Identity, Ethnicity, Nation* on the materials of which was published the journal *Bogomyslie* (vol. 34; #1, 2024). This journal included articles not only by Ukrainian Protestants, but also by evangelical-oriented Orthodox and Catholic theologians. The turbulent political events of recent years have contributed to the shift of evangelicals from separatism to cooperation, as well as rethinking of the hermeneutical approaches to the participation of believers in public and political life. It means many believers began to read the biblical texts differently, seeing in it a call to active participation in the public life of society, and realizing the need to a clearly defined social doctrine.

Great opportunity for public demonstration of activities, for rapprochement and partnership among the evangelicals were the preparations for the 500th anniversary of the Reformation which was celebrated in Ukraine both nationally and locally. A Thanksgiving Day in Kiev in 2017 was attended by over 500,000 people. This collaborative work bore good fruit, because after the many public and private activities the number of evangelicals grew from 0.8 percent of the population in 2017 to 2.2 percent in 2018, although already in 2019 it decreased to 1.5 percent. Because of the war and as a result of active social work, the number increased from 1.5 percent in 2021 to 3.7 percent in 2022, but in 2023 it dropped again to 1.4 percent.[12] This flux shows both the effectiveness of the partnership in preaching the gospel and social work, and the inability of the churches to consolidate the results and to organize systematic work with the new converts.

Cooperation: Evangelicals during the Russian Aggression

Russia's war against Ukraine began in 2014 with the annexation of Crimea and part of the Donbas and became an open military aggression on 24 February 2022. It brought much hardship to the whole nation.

The war gave a powerful impetus to the collaboration of the various evangelical groups.[13] Joint work and partnership began primarily in the area of the provision of humanitarian aid to both civilians and soldiers. During the

---

12. Якименко, *Українське суспільство, держава і церква під час війни. Церковно-релігійна ситуація в Україні-2023*, 34. [Yakimenko, *Ukrainian Society, State, and Church During War. Church And Religion in Ukraine in 2023*].

13. Olena Panic gives many testimonies of how evangelicals, thanks to their beliefs, courageously met the Russian aggression. Olena Panych, "Ukrainian Evangelicals and the War," *Review of Ecumenical Studies* 15.3 (2023): 459–77; https://doi.org/10.2478/ress-2023-0029.

first two and a half years of the war, over 700,000 tons of humanitarian aid and much equipment have been delivered through evangelical churches. The participation of the evangelicals in military chaplaincy was especially fruitful. The Ukrainian Church of Christians of Faith, Evangelical, alone had 166 chaplains in 2023. Besides full-time chaplains, volunteer chaplains also play an important role in providing spiritual care. Ministers from various evangelical groups work together to help soldiers both at the front, in hospitals and in rehabilitation centres.

Russia's aggression has given an impetus to the new theological tendencies in the evangelical churches. There is a noticeable shift from pacifism to a just war theology and support for the army. According to the All-Ukrainian Union of Churches of Evangelical Christian Baptists, over three hundred of their pastors and deacons are serving in the army. Valentin Siniy notes that sermon topics have changed: they have become more relevant and understandable for non-believers. There is noticeable openness to society, commitment to prophetic ministry, proclamation of truth and social justice. There is a higher level of patriotism, a changed attitude to physical disability and counselling, and an understanding of the role of psychologists due to post-traumatic stress.

At the same time, the war has brought many spiritual problems. One of the most complicated ones is rejection of and resentment towards Russian evangelicals with whom Ukrainians enjoyed close fraternal relationship before the war. Historically, the two groups saw each other as brothers and sisters. Today anger and hatred of everything Russian – language, culture, literature, music, and so on – is cultivated in society and involuntarily adopted by the evangelicals. One of the reasons for this anger is that in the occupied areas about one hundred church buildings of the Union of Evangelical Christian Baptists alone have been destroyed or confiscated, and one hundred and ten churches have been closed.

The situation is exacerbated by the fact that the Russian evangelicals, who live under totalitarianism, are afraid and unable to show any support and compassion to their Ukrainian brothers and sisters. Many of them are so affected by the unscrupulous Russian propaganda that they actively defend the war on social media. Some have even joined the army to fight against Ukrainians. It is not yet clear how reconciliation, forgiveness and mutual acceptance of Russian and Ukrainian evangelicals can possibly happen in the future.

Conclusion

The Ukrainian evangelicals have had a hard history and their journey is not over yet. Society has often seen them as illiterate fanatics. They have shared in the constant hardships and sorrows of the Ukrainian people. The struggle for sovereignty, its attainment in the seventeenth century and its loss because of inner conflicts, wars, devastation, the Bolshevik terror, the exile or execution of all evangelical leaders in the twentieth century, the attempt to build an independent state in the twenty-first century, the renewed Russian aggression – all these things have brought the Ukrainian evangelical movement to marginality and confessionalism. But the last thirty years have provided a unique historical opportunity to learn to serve the Lord in partnership and mutual understanding, respecting one another and making efforts to build the kingdom of God.

Bibliography

Brik, Tymofii, and Jose Casanova. "Thirty Years of Religious Pluralism in Ukraine." Pages 249–82 in *From 'the Ukraine' to Ukraine. A Contemporary History*. Stuttgart: Wilson Center, 2021.

Kim, Ho-woog, and Jun-ki Chung. "History of Protestantism in Ukraine." *Theological Quarterly*, 83 (2023): 465–78.

Klingsmith, Scott. "Evangelicals in Eastern Europe." Pages 364–71 in *Evangelicals around the World*. Edited by Brian Stiller. Nashville: Thomas Nelson for the World Evangelical Alliance, 2015.

Liutkevicius, Eugenijus. "Transformation of Evangelicalism: The Ukrainian Case." Birmingham: University of Birmingham, 2020. http://etheses.bham.ac.uk/id/eprint/10347.

Long, Esther Grace. *Identity in Evangelical Ukraine: Negotiating Regionalism, Nationalism, and Transnationalism*. Lexington, Kentucky: University of Kentucky, 2005. https://uknowledge.uky.edu/gradschool_diss/358/.

Panych, Olena. "Ukrainian Evangelicals and the War." *Review of Ecumenical Studies* 15 (3) (2023): 459–77. https://doi.org/10.2478/ress-2023-0029.

Sawatsky, Walter. *Soviet Evangelicals since World War II*. Eugene: Wipf and Stock Publishers, 2007.

Wanner, Catherine. *Communities of the Converted: Ukrainians and Global Evangelism*. Ithaca: Cornell University Press, 2019.

Wilson, Andrew. *The Ukrainians: Unexpected Nation*. New Haven: Yale University Press, 2022.

Любащенко, Вікторія. *Історія протестантизму в Україні: Курс лекцій*. Київ: Просвіта, 1996 [Victoria Liubashchenko. *History of Protestantism in Ukraine: Series of Lectures*. Kyiv: Prosvita, 1996].

Якименко, Ю. *Українське суспільство, держава і церква під час війни. Церковно-релігійна ситуація в Україні-2023*. Київ: Razumkov Center [Y. Yakimenko. *Ukrainian Society, State and Church During the War. Church And Religion in Ukraine in 2023*. Kyiv: Razumkov Centre, 2023].

24

Evangelicalism in the United Kingdom

David Hilborn

"Gospel People"

The great British evangelical statesman John Stott (1921–2011) was clear about the primary provenance of the movement he helped so much to sustain and reinvigorate in the later twentieth century. Having played a leading role in the landmark global Lausanne Congress of 1974, and in the reconnection of evangelism with social action that it spurred, Stott insisted in 2013 that "the evangelical faith is not a recent innovation, a new brand of Christianity which we are busy inventing. On the contrary, we dare to claim that evangelical Christianity is original, apostolic, New Testament Christianity."[1]

Stott here emphasized the derivation of the term "evangelical" in the New Testament word *euangelion*,[2] and this cardinal focus on the gospel or good news of Christ, and on the missional imperatives implicit in it, should never be overlooked in any account of evangelical identity, whether in the British, European or global context.[3] In this more foundational sense of the term, it is possible

---

1. John Stott, *Evangelical Truth* (Carlisle: Langham Global Library, 2013), 1. On the Lausanne Congress of 1974, Stott's contribution to it and the movement that stemmed from it, see Brian Stanley, *The Global Diffusion of Evangelicalism: The Age of Billy Graham and John Stott* (Downers Grove: IVP Academic, 2013), 151–79.

2. For example, T. C. Hammond, *What is an Evangelical?* (London: Church Pastoral Aid Society, 1959), 6–13; Martyn Lloyd Jones, *What is an Evangelical?* (Edinburgh: Banner of Truth, 1992 [addresses given in 1971]), 34–35.

3. Derek Tidball and John Martin echo Stott's prioritizing of the pre-denominational, trans-national, biblical foundations of evangelicalism: Derek Tidball, *Who Are the Evangelicals?*

to trace discernibly "evangelical" traits in various figures and movements that pre-dated the eighteenth century, even while most church historians agree that its origins as a more distinct socio-religious phenomenon lie in Britain and America in the 1730s.[4] On each of these accounts, however, evangelical Christianity emerges as neither a church as such nor a particular Christian polity, but a dynamic movement of congregations, networks and individuals – one aligned with a core cluster of theological convictions and devotional emphases, but otherwise structurally adjustable and missionally adaptive.[5]

Precursors of Full-Blown Evangelicalism

While Martin Luther's challenge to the Roman Catholic Church is often cast as the "beginning" of the Protestant Reformation, there were significant precedents for his protest, not least in Britain. Inasmuch as Luther's *95 Theses* (1517) were impelled by prioritizing Scripture over tradition and divine grace and justification by faith over works of the law,[6] they reflected commitments anticipated in the work of the Oxford scholar John Wycliffe (1329–1384). Known as *doctor evangelicus*, Wycliffe critiqued clerical corruption, attacked the Catholic doctrine of transubstantiation, and instigated an English translation of the Latin Vulgate Bible.[7] These concerns were echoed in the so-called Lollard movement's critiques of indulgences and priestly privilege,[8] while Wycliffe's ideas were more directly passed on by the various Bohemian scholars who stud-

---

Tracing the Roots of Today's Movements (London: Marshall Pickering, 1994), 11; John Martin, *Gospel People? Evangelicals and the Future of Anglicanism* (London: SPCK, 1997), 8–14.

    4. D. W. Bebbington, *Evangelicalism in Modern Britain: A History from the 1730s to the 1980s* (London: Unwin Hyman, 1989), 1–2, 20–27; Kenneth Hylson-Smith, *Evangelicals in the Church of England, 1734–1984* (Edinburgh: T&T Clark, 1988), 1–13.

    5. I am using the terms "Britain" and "British" here to describe the national and geographical region I am addressing, which is the United Kingdom. "Britain" is etymologically traceable to a pre-Christian descriptor for the islands off the north-west coast of the European continent now more formally referred to as the "British Isles." These "British Isles" include the island of Ireland, but since 1921–1922 that has been divided into two separate jurisdictions: the Republic of Ireland and Northern Ireland. Only the latter forms part of the United Kingdom with Great Britain, where Great Britain comprises the nations of England, Scotland and Wales.

    6. Tryntje Helfferich (ed.), *The Essential Luther* (Indianapolis: Hackett, 2018), 8–20.

    7. John Stacy, *John Wycliffe and Reform* (London: Lutterworth Press, 1964).

    8. Anne Hudson, *The Premature Reformation: Wycliffe Texts and Lollard History* (Oxford: Clarendon Press, 1988).

ied under him at Oxford to the Prague-based reformer Jan Hus (1369–1415), whose writings in turn had a strong impact on Luther.⁹

Just as Luther would be inspired by Wycliffe's example to produce his groundbreaking German Bible of 1534–1545, another British theologian-translator, William Tyndale (1494–1536), completed his New Testament in English while exiled in 1525 at Worms – the very city that had hosted the 1521 Diet at which Luther's writings had been investigated, and from which an edict had been issued that had consolidated Luther's excommunication. Although King Henry VIII declared the independence of the English church from papal control in 1533 to secure the dissolution of his first marriage to Catherine of Aragon and the legitimation of his second to Anne Boleyn, he was hardly sympathetic to Luther's reforms. Indeed, fearing that Tyndale's work would be a conduit for them, he ordered his kidnap and execution near Brussels in 1536.¹⁰

Despite these precedents, the term "evangelical" was not attached regularly to a distinct party or tendency within the church until it began to be identified with Luther's teachings. Indeed, its first recorded use with this sense in the English context dates from 1531, when Henry's Chancellor Thomas More applied it disparagingly to Tyndale and to Tyndale's "evangelical brother" Robert Barnes, who had fled to Wittenberg to evade More's censure.¹¹ The term was later extended to the Reformed stream of Protestantism associated with Ulrich Zwingli, John Calvin and their followers – a stream given particular succour in the English context by Henry's child heir Edward VI.

On acceding to the throne in 1547, Edward mandated his Protestant-sympathizing archbishop Thomas Cranmer to produce the first two *Books of Common Prayer* (1549, 1552) as means of embedding the doctrines of the continental Reformers deep into English parish life. Significantly, both Diarmaid MacCulloch and Ashley Null in fact prefer the term "evangelical" as a descriptor of Cranmer's theology over either "Lutheran" or "Protestant" – in the former case because Cranmer drew from Reformed as well as Lutheran sources, and in the latter because "Protestant" gained more prominent use in

---

9. Matthew Spinka, *John Hus: A Biography* (Princeton: Princeton University Press, 1968), 36; 117; 312–39; John Wyclif, *Trialogus. Translated by Stephen Lahey* (Cambridge: Cambridge University Press, 2013), 21–31; Heiko A. Oberman, *Luther: Man between God and the Devil* (New Haven: Yale University Press, 2006), 54–66.

10. David Daniell, *William Tyndale: A Biography* (New Haven: Yale University Press, 2001).

11. Thomas More, *Confutation of Tyndale's Answer: Books 1–4. Modernized with Notes* by Mary Gottschalk, https://thomasmorestudies.org/wp-content/uploads/2020/12/Confutation-1-4-9-30-2020-2.pdf, Preface, 32.

England only under the reign of Edward's Catholic half-sister Mary following his premature death aged 15 in 1553.[12] The evangelical reforms applied by Cranmer and other English bishops like Hugh Latimer, Nicholas Ridley and Matthew Parker during and after Edward's reign were variously maintained and radicalized during the reign of Elizabeth I (1558–1603) in the form of Puritanism and Separatism.

Whereas Elizabeth sought a rapprochement of Catholic devotion with Protestant theology through a revised *Book of Common Prayer* in 1559 and the Thirty-Nine Articles of 1571, Puritans typically advocated for Presbyterian, Independent and Baptist ecclesiologies that they cast as heeding Calvin's insistence on a church formed "purely" according to what Scripture mandated, rather than on what Scripture either mandated or did not prohibit.[13] In Scotland these commitments were more fully realized under the leadership of Calvin's protégé John Knox (1514–1572), culminating in the constitution of the Presbyterian Church of Scotland in 1560–1561.[14]

Whereas many Puritans argued for reform from within the Church of England under Elizabeth's "supreme governorship," so-called Separatist groupings like the Brownists and Barrowists lobbied for what Robert Browne himself called "reformation without tarrying for any."[15] Since in practical terms this often meant dissenting from use of the *Book of Common Prayer* and resisting episcopacy, Separatists were regularly forced into exile – initially in Holland and then, from 1620, with the so-called Pilgrim Fathers in North America.[16] The Anglo-American axis of evangelicalism that resulted remains highly influential today, despite subsequent globalization of the movement.[17]

Puritan and Separatist aspirations were further intensified in the English Civil War, and in the experiment with republicanism that followed between

---

12. Diarmaid MacCulloch, *Thomas Cranmer: A Life* (London: Yale University Press, 1996) 18, 68, 153; Ashley Null, "Thomas Cranmer and Tudor Evangelicalism," in Michael A. G. Haykin and Kenneth A. G. Stewart (eds), *The Emergence of Evangelicalism: Exploring Historical Continuities* (Nottingham: Apollos, 2008), 221–51.

13. David D. Hall, *The Puritans: A Transatlantic History* (Princeton: Princeton University Press, 2019), 14–78; John Coffey, "Puritanism, Evangelicalism and the Evangelical Protestant Tradition," in Haykin and Stewart, *Emergence*, 252–77.

14. Hall, *The Puritans*, 78–108.

15. Robert Browne, *A Treatise of Reformation without Tarying for Anie* (Middleburgh, 1582) https://archive.org/details/atreatisereform00socigoog/page/n6/mode/2up.

16. Hall, *The Puritans*, 69–77, 206–51.

17. Mark Noll, David W. Bebbington and George Rawlyk (eds), *Evangelicalism: Comparative Studies of Popular Protestantism in North America, the British Isles and Beyond, 1700–1990* (Oxford: Oxford University Press, 1994).

1649 and 1660 under Oliver Cromwell and the short-lived tenure of his son, Richard. While that experiment did not last, the restored monarchy which emerged in the wake of it was subjected to greater parliamentary constraint through the so-called Glorious Revolution of 1688–1689, whose Bill of Rights codified principles of religious toleration that fostered greater freedom for "Dissenting" Protestant churches and thereby stimulated the confluence of diverse evangelical streams into the "evangelicalism" that is more formally recognized as such today.[18]

From "Evangelicals" to "Evangelicalism"? Eighteenth Century Revivals and the Coalescence of a Movement

The more permissive late seventeenth-century context described above in turn facilitated a phenomenon that came more explicitly to define evangelicalism – the phenomenon of religious revival, which emerged in both Britain and America during the 1730s. Indeed, while acknowledging the origins of evangelicalism in the Protestant Reformation, and while defining "evangelical religion" as a distinctively "Protestant movement," the leading historian of British evangelicalism, David Bebbington, argues that it developed into such a particular expression of Protestantism when focused through the dynamics of revival in this period that it merits separate identification in the capitalized terms "Evangelical" and "Evangelicalism" from that point onwards.[19]

I am somewhat more inclined than Bebbington to stress the continuities of evangelicalism with earlier British and continental Protestantism, and the placement of this chapter in a handbook of European evangelicalism certainly invites these continuities to be affirmed. As such, I will maintain "evangelicalism" in its uncapitalized form here, while readily acknowledging that Bebbington makes a compelling case for recognizing that British (and American) evangelicalism took on characteristics in the 1730s that had been far less prominent up to then in Protestantism as a whole. Indeed, it is true that until the 1730s, "evangelical" had more typically functioned as a synonym for generic Protestantism: indeed, the German term *evangelisch* had essentially functioned until then, as it still functions now, as a synonym for "Protestant."[20]

---

18. Michael R. Watts, *The Dissenters: From the Reformation to the French Revolution* (Oxford: Clarendon Press, 1978).

19. Bebbington, *Evangelicalism*, 1–2.

20. Only in the 1960s was the term *evangelikal* coined in German to distinguish the development of evangelicalism as defined by Bebbington. It subsequently developed on the Anglo-American axis described here, from the generic Protestantism denoted by *evangelisch*.

By contrast, Bebbington demonstrates that new emphases emerged within British evangelicalism from 1735 which not only modified its tenor and focus, but which enabled particular expressions of interdenominational and parachurch ministry that have continued to characterize it down to the present.

Bebbington's dating of the start of this "new phase" of British evangelicalism to 1735 is prompted by the emotive conversions or renewals of faith experienced that year by Howel Harris and Daniel Rowland in Wales, and George Whitefield in England, each of whom soon went on to lead many others to faith or renewed commitment.[21] In May 1738, Whitefield's friend John Wesley testified to his heart having been "strangely warmed" in a meeting at Aldersgate Street, London, such that he "did trust in Christ alone for salvation."[22] Wesley's brother Charles had had a similar experience the very same week, and both joined Whitefield in a ministry of itinerant preaching, evangelism, hymn-writing and "Methodist" organization that eventually spawned a "Free" church denomination distinct from their own Church of England.[23]

It is possible to recognize the providence of God in these chronologically proximate experiences of revival while also acknowledging that the Wesleys and Whitefield had been seeking such refreshment of faith for some time, and that John in particular had taken inspiration from German Moravians whose "Pietist" iteration of Lutheranism had developed related concerns for personal holiness and biblical formation from the 1660s onwards.[24] As it was, Whitefield's preaching in particular galvanized further such fervour in Cambuslang, Scotland in 1742.[25] Moreover, these revivals were paralleled in America, where from 1734 the Presbyterian minister and theologian Jonathan Edwards experienced and fostered a similar outpouring of spiritual passion and enthusiasm within and beyond his own Massachusetts congregation – one that became known as the First Great Awakening.[26]

---

21. Bebbington, *Evangelicalism*, 20–21.

22. L. Tyerman, *The Life and Times of the Rev John Wesley, M.A., Vol. 1* (London, 1871) 179–80, 233.

23. David Hempton, *Methodism: Empire of the Spirit* (New Haven: Yale University Press, 2005).

24. Douglas Shantz (ed.), *A Companion to German Pietism, 1660–1800* (Leiden: Brill, 2014); Emile Griffin and Peter C. Erb, *The Pietists: Selected Writings* (New York: Harper Collins, 2006).

25. Arthur Fawcett, *The Cambuslang Revival: The Scottish Evangelical Revival of the Eighteenth Century* (Edinburgh: Banner of Truth, 1971).

26. Bebbington, *Evangelicalism*, 20–27. "Awakening" tends to be more associated with American expressions of revival from Edwards onwards, while the term "Evangelical Revival" is more usually applied to such expressions in Britain.

Earle Cairns defines revival as "the work of the Holy Spirit in restoring the people of God to a more vital spiritual life, witness and work by prayer and the Word after repentance in crisis for their spiritual decline."[27] For Bebbington, the distinctive features of revival as a movement within broader Protestantism at this time were its more overtly affective displays of devotion, its stress on the outflow of justification by faith in holiness of life, and its emphasis on assurance of salvation.[28] Assurance is contrasted by Bebbington here with the uncertainty of many Calvinists in particular over whether or not they had been predestined to salvation.[29] Whitefield was a Calvinist whereas the Wesleys' Arminian theology placed more stress on refining and even perfecting faith to maintain salvation. Tensions arose between them as a result, yet their joint efforts in evangelism, and the many others they inspired in this "new" form of evangelicalism, mobilized a freshly collaborative spirit within the movement that, as we shall see, gained more formal expression in the century to come. As it emerged from the 1730s, however, Bebbington summarizes this "modern" iteration of evangelicalism in a "quadrilateral" that comprises: "*conversionism*, the belief that lives need to be changed; *activism*, the expression of the gospel in effort; *biblicism*, a particular regard for the Bible; and what may be called *crucicentrism*, a stress on the sacrifice of Christ on the cross."[30]

While the marks of biblicism and crucicentrism are in clear continuity with core Protestant theological emphases stretching back to Luther, the first two – conversionism and activism – flow more particularly from the reconfiguration of Anglo-American Protestantism through revival that Bebbington links to the Wesleys, Whitefield, Harris, Rowland and Edwards in this period. Certainly, by the dawn of the nineteenth century, Methodism in both its Wesleyan and Calvinistic expressions had not only grown and spread significantly within and beyond Britain; it had also spurred evangelical revival within the Church of England, and in "Free Churches" from Presbyterian and Congregationalist to Baptist and more.[31]

Although various scholars have attempted to modify or supplement Bebbington's quadrilateral, it remains the most influential and most widely cited

---

27. E. E. Cairns, *An Endless Line of Splendor: Revivals and their Leaders from the Great Awakening to the Present* (Eugene: Wipf and Stock, 1986), 22.

28. Bebbington, *Evangelicalism*, 20–27.

29. Bebbington, *Evangelicalism*, 6–7, 42–50. Cf. Joel R. Beeke, *The Quest for Full Assurance: The Legacy of Calvin and his Successors* (Edinburgh: Banner of Truth, 1999).

30. Bebbington, *Evangelicalism*, 3.

31. John Wolffe, *Evangelical Faith and Public Zeal: Evangelicals and Society, 1780–1980* (London: SPCK, 1995).

short definition of evangelicalism from the past fifty years.[32] A cogent addition to it, however, is that proposed by both George Marsden and John Stackhouse – namely, *trans-denominationalism*.[33] This becomes more particularly cogent as a descriptor for British evangelicalism as it developed from the early 1800s onwards, and spread in mission around the world.

Nineteenth- and Early Twentieth-Century Developments: Through the Lens of the British Evangelical Alliance

In the 1740s John Wesley called for a "national union of evangelical clergy" and Jonathan Edwards for "explicit agreement and visible union" between evangelicals. They would not see this vision fulfilled in their lifetimes, Wesley characterizing the many British evangelicals who failed to support it as a "rope of sand."[34] Progress in evangelical unity came later, however, from the growing zeal for world evangelism exemplified by the formation of the London Missionary Society (1795) and the British and Foreign Bible Society (1804), both of which were consciously interdenominational.[35] Evangelical unity was also a feature of the momentous efforts of William Wilberforce's Clapham Sect, and of Olaudah Equiano, Ottobah Cuguano and others through the same period to abolish the slave trade.[36] Similar transformative efforts in evangelical activism were evident at home, in the educational and factory reforms spearheaded respectively by Hannah More (1745–1833), the Seventh Earl of Shaftesbury (1801–1885) and others.[37]

---

32. Mark A. Noll, "One Word but Three Crises" in *Evangelicals: Who They Have Been, Are Now, and Could Be*, ed. Mark A. Noll, David W. Bebbington and George M. Marsden (Grand Rapids: Eerdmans, 2019), 1–13.

33. George M. Marsden, "Introduction: The Evangelical Denomination," in *Evangelicalism and Modern America*, ed. George M. Marsden (Grand Rapids: Eerdmans, 1984) vii–xvi; John G. Stackhouse Jr., *Evangelical Landscapes: Facing Critical Issues of the Day* (Grand Rapids: Baker Academic, 2002), 181–83. Also from Stackhouse, see "Generic Evangelicalism," in Kevin Bauder et al, *Four Views on The Spectrum of Evangelicalism* (Grand Rapids: Zondervan, 2011), 121.

34. Frank Baker, *John Wesley and the Church of England* (London: Epworth, 1970), 183, 191, 196.

35. Michael Gladwin, "Evangelicals and Mission in the Global South," in *The Routledge Research Companion to The History of Evangelicalism*, ed. Andrew Atherstone and David Ceri Jones (London: Routledge, 2019), 162–70.

36. Adam Hochschild, *Bury the Chains: The British Struggle to Abolish Slavery* (London: Macmillan, 2005).

37. Ian J. Shaw, *Evangelicals and Social Action: From John Wesley to John Stott* (London: IVP, 2021), 56–69, 85–99.

With these collaborative successes in mind, a group of British evangelical leaders including the Congregationalist John Angell James, the Presbyterian David King and the Anglican Edward Bickersteth organized a meeting for broader unity and common action in Liverpool in October 1845. Also prominent in the coordination of that event was Thomas Chalmers, who had led four hundred and seventy evangelical Scots Presbyterians in a secession from the Church of Scotland over the right of churches to choose their own ministers – a secession that resulted in the formation of the Free Church of Scotland. The Liverpool meeting endorsed a plan for the constitution of a "World's Evangelical Alliance" the next year, and in August 1846 over eight hundred attendees gathered in London to inaugurate that new body.[38] While positive coordination of world mission and the championing of religious freedoms for evangelicals at home and abroad were high on its agenda, the inaugural conference of the Alliance also reflected a more oppositionalist mood, with motions on combatting Sabbath-breaking, the sectarianism of the Plymouth Brethren, and the "dual encroachments of Popery and Puseyism."[39]

Although the ambitions of those who formed the Alliance were for a global rather than a purely British organization, only ten percent of those who attended the inaugural conference were from the United States and just six percent from continental Europe. The international structure envisaged for the new body was abandoned after a dispute between British and American participants over whether a slave holder could be a member of it.[40] The result was a loose network of autonomous regional Alliances that would gather every few years for a multilateral conference with little or no executive power. In November 1846, the "British Organization" of the Alliance was duly established at a conference in Manchester, growing from three thousand to six thousand members by 1859.

As Head of Theology at the UK Evangelical Alliance from 1997 to 2006, chair of its Theological Advisory Group from 2016 to 2024, and co-writer of its authorized history *One Body in Christ*,[41] in what follows I will present the

---

38. Evangelical Alliance, *Report of the Proceedings of the Conference (1846)* (London: Partridge and Oakey, 1847), 1–19; Appendix C– lxxvii–xcviii; Ian Randall and David Hilborn, *One Body in Christ: The History and Significance of the Evangelical Alliance* (Carlisle: Paternoster, 2001), 18–70.

39. "Puseyism" denoted the movement led by John Henry Newman, John Keble and Edmund Pusey that developed into Anglo-Catholicism. Randall and Hilborn, *One Body*, 37–38; W. S. F. Pickering, *Anglo-Catholicism: A Study in Religious Ambiguity* (Cambridge: James Clarke, 2008), 17–24.

40. Randall and Hilborn, *One Body*, 61–66.

41. Randall and Hilborn, *One Body*.

development of the British Alliance since 1846 as a useful lens through which to focus broader headline themes that have shaped British evangelicalism during that period, and that shape it now.

From shortly after its inception, the British Alliance petitioned governments around the world on religious liberty, just as in its own context evangelical and other Dissenters or "Non-Conformists" had been granted greater rights through the Religious Disabilities Acts of 1846, and just as the repeal of various Test Acts in the 1860s, 70s and 80s enabled them to hold key public offices and gain admission to Oxford and Cambridge Universities.

The publication of Charles Darwin's *Origin of Species* in 1859 prompted a debate on creation and evolution between the Bishop of Oxford, Samuel Wilberforce, and the biologist T. H. Huxley in June 1860. As William Wilberforce's son, Samuel's biblicist opposition to Darwin represented the majority evangelical view at that point, even if most commentators judged Huxley the winner. In time, British evangelical leaders like Chalmers and James McCosh proposed the compatibility of evolution with Scripture, even as others continued to oppose it.[42] Similar differences between evangelical advocates of theistic evolution and creationism persist within the UK and other Evangelical Alliances today: a survey conducted by the former in 2016 identified sixty percent of British evangelicals as affirming the compatibility of evolution with Scripture and forty percent as denying such compatibility.[43]

German higher criticism of the Bible also presented a challenge for British Evangelicals towards the end of the nineteenth century. The London-based Alliance was initially antagonistic, organizing rallies against it and related "infidelities" through the 1880s. The prominent Baptist evangelical C. H. Spurgeon spoke at these gatherings. By 1900, however, moderate biblical criticism on this pattern was becoming more acceptable among British evangelicals.[44] In relation to that, the doctrine of hell as eternal conscious punishment had come under increasing scrutiny in the wider academy and church, and certain British evangelicals questioned it, too. For instance, despite his creationism, Birks' *Victory of Divine Goodness* (1873) suggested some ultimate remission of

---

42. Randall and Hilborn, *One Body*, 103–11; David N. Livingstone, *Darwin's Forgotten Defenders: The Encounter between Evangelical Theology and Evolutionary Thought* (Vancouver: Regent College, 1997). Samuel Wilberforce had moved in a more Anglo-Catholic direction by 1860, but his biblical apologetic at the Oxford debate was still discernibly evangelical.

43. Evangelical Alliance, *21st Century Evangelicals: A Snapshot of the Beliefs and Habits of Evangelical Christians in the UK* (London: Evangelical Alliance, 2016), 9; www.eauk.org/church/resources/snapshot/upload/21st-Century-Evangelicals.pdf.

44. Randall and Hilborn, *One Body*, 111–19.

the suffering of the damned and thereby caused a split in the executive council of the British Alliance.[45]

Failure to form a unitary World Alliance in 1846 was, perhaps, a portent of later evangelical disagreements on how to approach the modern ecumenical movement. The roots of modern ecumenism are often traced to the pivotal Edinburgh World Missionary Conference of 1910. The Swiss-American theologian Philip Schaff had been a key advocate of internationalist, ecumenical evangelicalism, but his vision of structural unity diverged from others' focus on "invisible" oneness and the need to maintain the integrity of evangelicalism.[46] Indeed, R. J. Campbell's "New Theology" was opposed by a British Alliance pamphlet series in 1907 as a dangerous importation of continental liberalism.[47] Such concerns were also evident in the responses of more traditional evangelicals to what became known as Liberal Evangelicalism. Initially conceived by the Anglican A. J. Tait in 1906 as a means to greater cooperation with Anglo-Catholics, the Anglican Evangelical Group Movement (AEGM) he developed with fellow progressive evangelicals like T. Guy Rogers and Vernon Storr affirmed "the fundamental spiritual truths of Evangelicalism" while declaring that "old doctrines had to be set forth in modern language."[48]

These moves led to significant division. In 1922 conservatives in the Church Missionary Society broke away to form the Bible Churchmen's Missionary Society. In 1928, the AEGM launched an annual conference as an alternative to the more traditional, holiness-driven evangelicalism of the Keswick Convention, founded by Robert and Hannah Pearsall Smith in 1875. These intra-Anglican evangelical tensions were reflected in more interdenominational contexts, too. The university-based Student Christian Movement (SCM) came under liberal evangelical influence, and in 1928 the Inter-Varsity Fellowship (IVF) was formed at Cambridge by those convinced that SCM had compromised the gospel.[49]

Despite such intramural tensions, as the threat of fascism grew through the 1930s, the British Organization of the Alliance supported the German Confessing Church in its opposition to Hitler, and, despite the reservations of some about his "neo-orthodox" theology, hosted a tribute to Karl Barth when

---

45. Randall and Hilborn, *One Body*, 119–32.
46. Randall and Hilborn, *One Body*, 146–48.
47. Randall and Hilborn, *One Body*, 184–88.
48. David Hilborn, "Liberal Evangelicalism," in *New Dictionary of Theology – Historical and Systematic*, ed. Martin Davie, Tim Grass, Stephen R. Holmes, John McDowell and T. A. Noble, 2nd ed. (London/Downers Grove: IVP, 2016), 513–14.
49. Hilborn, "Liberal Evangelicalism," 513–14.

he visited London in 1937. During World War II itself, the British Alliance was at the forefront of various national prayer initiatives.[50]

Later Twentieth and Twenty-First Century Developments – Again through the Alliance Lens

Following the formation of the World Council of Churches in 1948, a resolution of the British Evangelical Alliance's Council declared its position towards the WCC to be one of "benevolent neutrality," echoing the polite caution that had accompanied its approach to Edinburgh 1910, and warning that "outward uniformity" should not be mistaken for its own long-standing commitment to "real spiritual unity."[51] A similar approach pertained at the global level in the post-War period, as the original vision for a World's Evangelical Alliance in 1846 was reconfigured through the formation of a World Evangelical Fellowship (WEF) at Woudschoten, Netherlands, in 1951. Consciously avoiding the strongly conciliar structure of the WCC, this new body featured significant British input, with John Stott speaking at its inaugural conference.[52]

However much they differed on formal ecumenism, British evangelicals were readier to collaborate *interdenominationally* in the post-War period for the cause of evangelism, sponsoring Billy Graham's highly popular Harringay Crusade of 1954, backing his return to London at Earls Court in 1966, and supporting his countrywide Mission England campaign of 1984, ten years after he had played a key role with John Stott in founding the Lausanne Movement.[53]

Tensions on ecumenism remained after the formation of the WEF, however, and the British Alliance sought to address these at a 1966 Assembly. The EA General Secretary, Gilbert Kirby, took a calculated risk in asking Stott and the prominent independent evangelical preacher and leader Martyn Lloyd-Jones to address the meeting. Lloyd-Jones was not only sceptical about the ecumenical movement, but had become increasingly critical of theologically "mixed" denominations, too.[54] The Anglican Stott was more favourable towards ecumenism and had consistently counselled loyalty among evangelicals in

---

50. Randall and Hilborn, *One Body*, 204–6.
51. Randall and Hilborn, *One Body*, 235.
52. Randall and Hilborn, *One Body*, 237–41; https://worldea.org/who-we-are/our-history/.
53. Randall and Hilborn, *One Body*, 208–31, 284; Brian Stanley, *The Global Diffusion of Evangelicalism: The Age of Billy Graham and John Stott* (Downers Grove: IVP Academic, 2013), 151–80.
54. John Brencher, *Martyn Lloyd-Jones (1899–1981) and Twentieth-Century Evangelicalism* (Carlisle: Paternoster, 2002), 83–115.

mixed churches. Lloyd-Jones called for a realignment of evangelicals into a new association, although historians debate whether this implied actual secession for those in more plural denominations. Stott retorted that Scripture and history opposed this view. The ensuing controversy deeply damaged the Alliance and accentuated divisions for years afterwards. In 1970, the Alliance hosted a tense conference on the doctrine of the church, at which Anglicans reconfirmed the denominational loyalty and ecumenical engagement they had upheld in a congress convened at Keele in April 1967 to take stock of the Stott–Lloyd-Jones dispute.[55]

The rise of the charismatic movement in the 1960s brought new impetus and fresh challenges to British evangelicalism, as it did elsewhere. By assimilating classical Pentecostal spirituality within more historic denominations, charismatics were affirming a devotional dynamic that had itself inherited much of the fervour of the Wesleyan holiness stream of evangelicalism.[56] Yet as it developed from the Los Angeles-based Azusa Street revival of 1906–15, classical Pentecostalism's more distinctive emphasis on the supernatural gifts or charismata of the Spirit also differentiated it in significant ways, either as a discrete stream within the broader evangelical family, or as a movement in its own right that might make common cause with evangelicalism while retaining its particular identity as Pentecostal.[57]

Another reason to regard Pentecostalism as distinctive within the broader gospel-centred coalitions represented by bodies like the Evangelical Alliance is the fact that many "first generation" African-Caribbean immigrants to Britain (1948–1970s)[58] were Pentecostal. The Black Majority congregations they established as part of the New Testament Church of God, the Church of God of Prophecy and the New Testament Assemblies, or as smaller, more independent communities, significantly changed the landscape of Christianity in Britain, as did evangelical churches formed by Asian, West African and other immigrant Christian groups.[59] Indeed, as we shall see, the New Testament Church of God

---

55. Randall and Hilborn, *One Body*, 246–56; Philip Crowe (ed.), *Keele '67: The National Evangelical Anglican Congress Statement* (London: Falcon Books/Church Pastoral Aid Society, 1967).

56. Peter Hocken, *Streams of Renewal: The Origins and Early Development of the Charismatic Movement in Great Britain* (Carlisle: Paternoster, 1997).

57. William Kay, *Pentecostals in Britain* (Carlisle: Paternoster, 2000), 1–54.

58. The first wave of Caribbean immigrants arrived on the *Empire Windrush* passenger ship in June 1948.

59. Babatunde Adedibu, "Introduction to Pentecostalism and Ecumenism," in *Anglicans and Pentecostals in Dialogue*, ed. David Hilborn and Simo Frestadius (Eugene: Wipf and Stock,

produced the Alliance's first non-White General Secretary. In subsequent years relationships with Pentecostal denominations and charismatic networks like the Fountain Trust would develop much further, but some Pentecostals did become active on the Alliance's Council from the late 1960s, under the leadership of A. Morgan Derham (1966–1968) and Gordon Landreth (1969–1982).[60]

While relatively brief, Derham's tenure was also distinguished by the establishment in 1967 of the Evangelical Alliance Relief Fund (TEAR Fund), a project whose growth allowed it within a few years to become an autonomous charity. The theological and practical integration of evangelism and social action modelled by TEAR Fund provided a template for core affirmations along the same lines that would distinguish the Lausanne Covenant seven years later.[61] The appointment in 1983 of the young British Youth for Christ leader, Clive Calver, as General Secretary of what would be renamed as the Evangelical Alliance UK (EAUK) further reflected this emphasis.

Calver's tenure at the Alliance was one of remarkable expansion: from one thousand individual members in 1983 to fifty-six thousand in the mid-1990s, and from less than one thousand churches to three thousand in same period – against a backdrop of tumbling church attendance as secularization gathered pace.[62] This growth owed much to Calver's assimilation of neo-charismatic "House Church" constituencies while maintaining the support of conservative evangelicals.[63] A keen student of the Alliance's history, Calver sought to build on the shared emphases of TEAR Fund and Lausanne: dynamic unity for more effective evangelism, and concerted social action. The Spring Harvest festival, conceived by Calver and others in the late 1970s and boosted greatly by the Alliance under his direction, epitomized the former, as did the Alpha Course developed by the influential charismatic EAUK member church Holy Trinity Brompton (HTB).[64] The latter emphasis was borne out by the founding of related African Caribbean and Asian Alliances and national Alliances in Scotland, Wales and Northern Ireland, by the establishment of the employment

---

2023), 37–42; *Coat of Many Colours: The Origin, Growth, Distinctiveness and Contributions of Black Majority Churches to British Christianity* (Gloucester: Choir Books, 2012).

60. Randall and Hilborn, *One Body*, 267.

61. Randall and Hilborn, *One Body*, 275–76, 287.

62. Randall and Hilborn, *One Body*, 283–308; cf. Callum G. Brown, *The Death of Christian Britain: Understanding Secularisation 1800–2000* (London: Routledge, 2nd ed. 2009).

63. Andrew Walker, *Restoring the Kingdom: The Radical Christianity of the House Church Movement* (Guildford: Eagle, rev. ed. 1988).

64. Andrew Atherstone, *Repackaging Christianity: Alpha and the Building of a Global Brand* (London: Hodder & Stoughton, 2022).

consultancy Evangelical Enterprise, and by the formation of Christian Action Networks for community engagement.[65] By 1996, the Alliance was confident enough to "lay the ghost" of 1966, and convened a successful Assembly in Bournemouth, as a prelude to Calver's moving to a new post in the United States.[66]

Aware of a growing need for theological reflection to mitigate division, Calver had formed an Alliance Commission on Unity and Truth among Evangelicals (ACUTE) in 1993. This body went on to address fresh and continuing theological tensions within and beyond British evangelicalism. In 1994, consultations were arranged on the so-called "Toronto Blessing" that had been promoted by HTB and others, and a statement was issued on this new wave of charismatic activity, which had been distinguished particularly by the phenomenon of "slaying in the Spirit."[67]

When I took over ACUTE as the Alliance's in-house theologian in 1997, I did so at the same time that Clive Calver's successor started in post. Joel Edwards had formerly served as General Director of African Caribbean Alliance and UK Director of the EAUK. As both a pioneer and exemplar of the Alliance's growing ethnic diversity, he was the first person of colour to lead the Alliance. A British New Testament Church of God pastor born in Jamaica, Edwards regularly spoke on BBC Radio and was appointed an ecumenical canon of St Paul's Cathedral. He later served as an advisor on the persecuted church for Christian Solidarity Worldwide. His work for Christian unity, anti-poverty and justice was recognized in the Queen's New Year's honours list in 2019 before he died of cancer in 2021.[68] By then the ten largest churches in London were "largely forms of either reverse mission or immigrant churches" and in high migration cities falling attendance figures had either slowed or even turned around thanks to the presence and growth of such churches.[69]

---

65. Randall and Hilborn, *One Body*, 283–93.

66. Randall and Hilborn, *One Body*, 305–7.

67. David Hilborn, "Introduction: Evangelicalism, the Evangelical Alliance and the Toronto Blessing," in *"Toronto" in Perspective: Papers on the New Charismatic Wave of the Mid-1990s*, ed. David Hilborn (Carlisle: Paternoster, 2001), 3–34.

68. Joel Edwards, *Lord, Make Us One – But Not All the Same! Seeking Unity in Diversity* (London: Hodder & Stoughton, 1999).

69. Mark Hutchinson, "Evangelicalism in Western Europe," in *Evangelicals around the World: A Global Handbook for the 21st Century*, ed. Brian C. Stiller, Todd M. Johnson, Karen Stiller and Mark Hutchinson (Nashville: Nelson, 2015), 387. Reverse mission is defined by Israel Olofinjana as "missionaries and pastors from a former mission field now ministering in Europe and North America"; see www.baptist.org.uk/Articles/372473/Theology_of_Reverse.aspx; also Israel Olofinjana (ed.) *Turning the Tables on Mission: Stories of Christians from the Global South in the UK* (Watford: Instant Apostle, 2013).

Under Joel Edwards' oversight, I coordinated the report *Faith, Hope and Homosexuality* (1998) – a long-requested articulation of the mainline evangelical position on what was becoming an increasingly fraught issue within a range of UK denominations.[70] *The Nature of Hell* followed in 2000, addressing an intra-evangelical debate about annihilationism versus eternal punishment in which John Stott had, somewhat controversially, inclined towards annihilationism – the view that the unredeemed are finally extinguished rather than forever punished in hell. The EA report concluded that annihilationism represented a "significant minority evangelical view" that fell within the parameters of the EA Basis of Faith.[71] A more detailed study on the Toronto Blessing and books on intergenerational church and mission, the prosperity gospel and evangelicals and social action followed.[72] In addition, a Public Policy Commission was formed in 1999 and issued reports on what was then termed transsexuality in 2000, and on the church's role in civic life in 2005.[73]

The fact that so many of these EAUK reports addressed the interrelationship of church, evangelism and social concern clearly reflects the legacy of the affirmation in the Lausanne Covenant two decades previously that while

> reconciliation with other people is not reconciliation with God, nor is social action evangelism, nor is political liberation salvation, nevertheless . . . evangelism and socio-political involvement are both part of our Christian duty. For both are necessary expressions of our doctrines of God and Man, our love for our neighbour and our obedience to Jesus Christ.[74]

Such reports likewise echoed the elaboration of Lausanne 1974 provided by a second Congress at Manila (1989), while anticipating subsequent such

---

70. ACUTE (Alliance Commission on Unity and Truth among Evangelicals), *Faith, Hope and Homosexuality* (Carlisle: Paternoster, 1998).

71. David Hilborn (ed.), *The Nature of Hell* (ACUTE; Carlisle: Paternoster, 2000).

72. Hilborn, *"Toronto" in Perspective*; David Hilborn and Matt Bird (eds), *God and the Generations: Youth, Age and the Church Today* (ACUTE; Carlisle: Paternoster, 2002); Andrew Perriman (ed.), *Faith, Health and Prosperity: A Report on "Word of Faith" and "Positive Confession" Theologies* (ACUTE; Carlisle: Paternoster, 2003); David Hilborn (ed.), *Movement for Change: Evangelical Perspectives on Social Transformation* (Carlisle: Paternoster, 2004).

73. Evangelical Alliance Public Policy Commission, *Transsexuality* (Carlisle: Paternoster, 2000); Evangelical Alliance, *Faith and Nation: Report of a Commission of Inquiry to the Evangelical Alliance* (London: Evangelical Alliance, 2005).

74. See https://lausanne.org/wp-content/uploads/2021/10/Lausanne-Covenant-%E2%80%93-Pages.pdf 1974, Section 5, 45.

global Lausanne Congresses at Cape Town (2010) and Incheon (Seoul, 2024), and the further expositions of holistic mission issued from them.[75]

Not all the theological work done by the Alliance in this period was outward facing, however. Indeed, its vocation to maintain intra-evangelical unity was severely tested in 2005 over the doctrine of atonement. Just as the historic Reformed model of penal substitution had been challenged by liberal Protestants in the nineteenth century and by Liberal Evangelicals in the early twentieth, the leading Baptist evangelical Steve Chalke critiqued it again in a 2003 book entitled *The Lost Message of Jesus*. Chalke and his co-author Alan Mann rejected this theology of the cross, arguing that it turns God from a loving Father into a vengeful tyrant, who "suddenly decides to vent his anger and wrath on his own Son." Echoing feminist theologian Rita Nakashima Brock, they added that some might thus construe this version of atonement as a "form of cosmic child abuse," even if Chalke and Mann did not directly describe it as such themselves. However, they did depict it as a "total contradiction of the statement 'God is love'" which "makes a mockery of Jesus' own teaching to love your enemies."[76]

More conservative evangelicals, in particular, reacted sharply to this[77] and the Alliance duly convened a symposium on it; the papers from that event were later published as *The Atonement Debate*. Although some contributors were more sympathetic to Chalke's concerns, others either stated or implied that his position was incompatible with the Basis of Faith of the EAUK.[78] Despite this, Chalke would not part ways with the EAUK over atonement, but over the question of same-sex relationships that had prompted ACUTE's first major publication a decade earlier.

That Alliance report, *Faith, Hope and Homosexuality*, was expanded and updated in 2012 under the new title *Biblical and Pastoral Responses to Homosexuality*.[79] Around the same time, Chalke began publicly to identify himself with what came to be known as an "affirming" or "including" evangelical

---

75. See https://lausanne.org/our-history.

76. Steve Chalke and Alan Mann, *The Lost Message of Jesus* (Grand Rapids: Zondervan, 2003), 182–83.

77. Steve Jeffrey, Mike Ovey and Andrew Sach (eds), *Pierced for Our Transgressions: Rediscovering the Glory of Penal Substitution* (Leicester: IVP, 2012).

78. Derek Tidball, David Hilborn and Justin Thacker (eds), *The Atonement Debate* (Grand Rapids: Zondervan, 2008); see especially my Introduction, 15–32, Chalke's paper, 34–47, and subsequent contributions from Joel Green (sympathetic, 153–70) and Garry Williams (critical, 172–91). Cf. www.eauk.org/about-us/how-we-work/basis-of-faith.

79. Andrew Goddard and Don Horrocks (eds), *Biblical and Pastoral Responses to Homosexuality* (London: Evangelical Alliance, 2012).

position on same-sex relationships and, latterly, on the broader spectrum of LGBTQ+ identities.[80] This liberalizing stream on sexuality and gender in evangelicalism reflected moves within mixed mainline British denominations like the United Reformed Church, the Methodist Church, the Church of Scotland and the Church of England to authorize or at least recognize and pastorally affirm faithful, stable same-sex partnerships.[81] Chalke's eventual departure from the EAUK over this issue paved the way for a series of "affirming evangelical" testimonies, papers and books from other British authors.[82] All the same, these did not deter the Alliance – now with Steve Clifford established as CEO and with ACUTE renamed the Theological and Public Policy Advisory Commission and then the Theological Advisory Group – from maintaining the classical evangelical position on marriage and sexual relations that it had affirmed previously. This was further reinforced in 2018, with an update of its 2000 *Transsexuality* report, now entitled *Transformed*. Here, as in *Biblical and Pastoral Responses*, the Genesis creation narrative was affirmed as speaking of "two distinct and compatible biological sexes" and as approving heterosexual marriage on this basis as the sole divinely ordained context for sexual relations.[83]

Conscious that British social attitudes and laws had shifted significantly towards more permissive acceptance of LGBTQ+ partnerships and identities since the 1990s, in the 2010s the EAUK recognized that its own more traditional pronouncements on this and other such moral issues might fall foul of increasing censure amidst the so-called "culture wars" – ideological stand-offs whose polarization was being stoked by the proliferation of social media. With this in mind, in 2016 the EAUK joined with the Lawyers' Christian Fellowship to produce *Speak Up*, a resource that advised evangelicals on the religious free-

---

80. Steve Chalke, *A Matter of Integrity: The Church, Sexuality, Inclusion and an Open Conversation* (Kindle Books, 2013).

81. "United Reformed Church approves gay marriage services," 9 July 2016, www.bbc.co.uk/news/uk-36756387; "Methodist Church allows same-sex marriage in 'momentous' vote," www.bbc.co.uk/news/uk-england-57658161; "Church of Scotland to allow same-sex marriages," www.bbc.co.uk/news/uk-scotland-61547729; "Church of England backs services for gay couples," www.bbc.co.uk/news/uk-67432854.

82. Jayne Ozanne (ed.), *Journeys in Grace and Truth: Revisiting Scripture and Sexuality* (London: Via Media/Ekklesia, 2016); Jayne Ozanne, *Just Love: A Journey of Self-Acceptance* (London: DLT, 2018); Vicky Beeching, *Undivided: Coming Out, Becoming Whole and Living Free from Shame* (London: William Collins, 2018); Marcus Green, *The Possibility of Difference: A Biblical Affirmation of Inclusivity* (Buxhall: Kevin Mayhew, 2018); David Ison, "Principles and Prodigals," in Ozanne, *Journeys in Grace*, 16–23; David Runcorn, "Evangelicals, Scripture and Same-Sex Relationships – an Including Evangelical Perspective," in House of Bishops, *Report of the House of Bishops on Human Sexuality* (London: Church House, 2013, 176–95).

83. See www.eauk.org/resources/what-we-offer/reports/transformed-understanding-transgender-in-a-changing-culture/transformed-the-resource, 12.

doms they continued to enjoy, while offering practical guidance on avoiding investigation and/or prosecution for the expression of their now more culturally dissonant views – not only on sexuality and gender but also in opposition to abortion, euthanasia and certain doctrines and practices of other religions.[84] This, in effect, was a significantly modernized form of the campaigning for religious liberty that the Alliance had prioritized at its inception in the 1840s.

In the same year in which *Speak Up* was published, two political events occurred which fuelled the same "culture wars" it had addressed. In a referendum held in June 2016, the UK voted by 52–48 percent to leave or "Brexit" from the European Union; then, in November, Donald Trump was elected President of the United States on a strong wave of support from White evangelicals – an outcome that, for many non-evangelicals, tied evangelicalism inextricably to right wing politics.

In March 2019 a special meeting of the Alliance Council was devoted to assessing the theological issues and consequences of Brexit, and of the variously "hard" and "weak" forms it might take. As for Trump, Gavin Calver, who succeeded Steve Clifford as CEO of the UKEA in 2019 after serving as its Mission Director, felt compelled to explain in the London *Times* that the social and political profile of evangelicalism in Britain was far less monolithic than many had inferred from the alignment of White American evangelicals with so-called "MAGA" Republicanism.[85]

Calver's pleas for differentiation between British and American evangelicalism were also prompted partly by an emerging American trend dubbed "exvangelicalism," whereby various typically younger evangelical worship leaders, pastors and evangelists had announced their departure from the movement – and sometimes from Christian faith altogether – in disillusionment at its perceived "captivity" to the Right, homophobia and/or misogyny.[86] In Britain, a movement identified as "post-evangelicalism" had gained some traction in the mid-1990s with certain similar concerns – albeit with more focus

---

84. Evangelical Alliance and Lawyers' Christian Fellowship, *Speak Up: The Law and Your Gospel Freedoms* (London: EAUK, LCF, 2016), www.eauk.org/what-we-do/initiatives/speak-up.

85. From Trump's slogan, "Make America Great Again" see www.thetimes.com/world/us-world/article/let-us-redefine-evangelism-after-the-trump-presidency-crnrlrzs6; www.christianitytoday.com/2021/02/evangelical-alliance-uk-trump-british-church-brexit-covid/. The voting patterns of Black evangelicals in both the 2016 and 2020 Presidential elections were almost the reverse of those seen among White evangelicals, see https://religioninpublic.blog/2021/03/29/the-2020-vote-for-president-by-religious-groups-christians/.

86. Sarah McCammon, *The Exvangelicals: Loving, Living, and Leaving the White Evangelical Church* (New York: St Martin's Press, 2024).

on the perceived intellectual shortcomings of evangelicalism rather than on its political affiliations, which tend to have been less partisan in the UK context.[87]

Another issue that has proved problematic for British evangelicalism in recent years is the number of alleged or proven cases of sexual, physical, psychological and pastoral or spiritual abuse[88] that have come to light in its midst. To be clear: such abuses are hardly unique to evangelicalism, or to British evangelicalism; this is a problem for the church as a whole rather than for evangelical churches and networks specifically.[89] Even so, several high-profile cases of religious abuse in recent times have arisen in evangelical contexts, not least in Britain. The 2024 Makin Report documented serial physical and pastoral abuses of young boys and men by the Anglican evangelical lay leader John Smyth, who died in 2018.[90] Makin's highlighting of procedural failures associated with the Smyth case led to the resignation of the evangelical Archbishop of Canterbury Justin Welby in late 2024. Shortly afterwards the former evangelical occupant of that post, George Carey, stepped down from licensed ministry amidst allegations of institutional failures related to an abuse case during his tenure.[91] Prior to these developments, the UK Christian Safeguarding agency Thirty-One: Eight was commissioned to review allegations of spiritual or pastoral abuse at Emmanuel Church, Wimbledon and the Crowded House, Sheffield – both prominent centres of evangelical ministry.[92] Moreover, in 2023 the Church of England Safeguarding Team and the Diocese of St Albans found that the leader of another such centre, Mike Pilavachi at Soul Survivor,

---

87. Dave Tomlinson, *The Post-Evangelical* (London: Triangle, 1995); Graham Cray et al., *The Post-Evangelical Debate* (London: Triangle, 1997); David Hilborn, *Picking Up the Pieces: Can Evangelicals Adapt to Contemporary Culture?* (London: Hodder & Stoughton, 1997).

88. "Spiritual abuse" is often preferred to "pastoral abuse" They are effectively synonyms, yet for reasons to prefer the former, see my taxonomy and explanation in Graham Nicholls (ed.), *Challenging Leaders: Preventing Pastoral Malpractice and Investigating Allegations* (Fearn: Christian Focus, 2023), 133–34 (also 11–16).

89. See www.theguardian.com/film/2016/jan/13/spotlight-reporters-uncovered-catholic-child-abuse-boston-globe; www.iicsa.org.uk/reports-recommendations/publications/investigation/anglican-chichester-peter-ball/case-study-2-response-allegations-against-peter-ball/c1-introduction-peter-ball-case-study.html; www.larche.org.uk/jean-vanier-report.

90. See www.churchofengland.org/media/press-releases/independent-review-churchs-handling-smyth-case-published; www.churchofengland.org/sites/default/files/2024-11/independent-learning-lessons-review-john-smyth-qc-november-2024.pdf.

91. See www.bbc.co.uk/news/live/cj505ygdp17t; www.bbc.co.uk/news/articles/cly2714w-gdno.

92. See https://thirtyoneeight.org/media/gk1dnt14/independent-lessons-learned-review-report_march-2021.pdf; https://thirtyoneeight.org/media/khzksimf/the-crowded-house-learning-review-full-report.pdf.

Watford, had engaged in coercion and inappropriate wrestling and massage with young males on his team.[93]

Various views have been advanced as to particular characteristics of evangelical theology and culture that might incline certain of its leaders to such abuses – from penal substitutionary atonement and biblical "literalism" to repressed sexuality[94] – but among the more cogent is the tendency of evangelicals to elevate skilled and successful preachers, teachers and ministers to a level of "celebrity" and power beyond which they might cease to become duly accountable.[95] To reiterate: abuse is a scourge in various streams of Christianity as well as in other religious communities. Yet if there *are* distinctive dynamics of evangelicalism that might more readily tempt some within it to perpetrate particular forms of pastoral or spiritual abuse, it is incumbent on responsible evangelical leaders to assess that possibility with humility and to model healthier patterns of leadership and ministry for the future.

Looking Ahead with Hope

The use of the Evangelical Alliance here as a lens through which to survey broader trends in British evangelicalism means that we can end with optimism for its future, even while taking note of the challenges it will face.

In 2013, the ethnically distinct Alliances formed under Clive Calver's leadership were brought into closer integration with each other, and with the Alliance as a whole, through the One People Commission (OPC). As it celebrated ten years of work to oppose racism and promote collaboration in 2023, the OPC committed itself to a "10-step roadmap to racial diversity and unity" that reflected the significant advances made by British evangelicals in these areas, while looking to the future with hope for further progress under its Nigerian-British director, Israel Olofinjana.[96] Alongside this, since 2016 the Great Commission project has sought to galvanize grass-roots mission and

---

93. See www.stalbansdiocese.org/news/soul-survivor-scolding-review-statement-response-september-2024/; www.churchofengland.org/safeguarding/safeguarding-news-releases/scolding-review-statement-lead-safeguarding-bishop.

94. Andrew Graystone, *Bleeding for Jesus: John Smyth and the Cult of the Iwerne Camps* (London: DLT, 2021); www.unadulteratedlove.net/blog/2021/11/5/the-abusive-toxic-culture-produced-by-the-evangelical-doctrine-of-penal-substitution; https://msmagazine.com/2018/09/27/evangelical-theology-supports-culture-sexual-abuse/.

95. Marcus Honeysett, *Powerful Leaders? When Church Leadership Goes Wrong and How to Prevent It* (London: IVP, 2022), 35–89; Nicholls, *Challenging Leaders*, 43–66.

96. See www.eauk.org/what-we-do/networks/one-people-commission/10-step-roadmap-to-racial-diversity-and-unity. [Editors: See Olofinjana's chapter in this book.]

church planting initiatives that are effective and attuned to changing cultural demands, while the Being Human programme has set ambitious goals around re-framing contested questions of sexual and social ethics within broader biblical paradigms of theological anthropology, divine providence and eschatology.[97] Not only do such initiatives further exemplify the reconvergence of evangelism and social action that the Lausanne movement has been mobilizing in worldwide evangelicalism since 1974; they also bear out the "original, apostolic, New Testament Christianity" in which John Stott saw evangelicalism rooted, and which we have seen exemplified here by a noteworthy lineage of British evangelical pioneers, churches and gospel ministries.

Bibliography

Atherstone, Andrew, and David Ceri Jones, eds. *The Routledge Research Companion to the History of Evangelicalism*. London: Routledge, 2019.

Bebbington, D. W. *Evangelicalism in Modern Britain: A History from the 1730s to the 1980s*. London: Unwin Hyman, 1989.

Haykin, Michael A. G., and Kenneth J. Stewart, eds. *The Emergence of Evangelicalism: Exploring Historical Continuities*. Nottingham: Apollos, 2008.

Noll, Mark A., David W. Bebbington and George A. Rawlyk, eds. *Evangelicalism: Comparative Studies of Protestantism in North America, The British Isles, and Beyond*. Oxford: Oxford University Press, 1994.

Noll, Mark A., David W. Bebbington and George M. Marsden, eds. *Evangelicals: Who They Have Been, Are Now, and Could Be*. Grand Rapids: Eerdmans, 2019.

Olofinjana, Israel. *Turning the Tables on Mission: Stories of Christians from the Global South in the UK*. Watford: Instant Apostle, 2013.

Randall, Ian, and David Hilborn. *One Body in Christ: The History and Significance of the Evangelical Alliance*. Carlisle: Paternoster, 2001.

Shaw, Ian J. *Evangelicals and Social Action: From John Wesley to John Stott*. London: IVP, 2021.

Stanley, Brian. *The Global Diffusion of Evangelicalism: The Age of Billy Graham and John Stott*. Downers Grove: IVP Academic, 2013.

Tidball, Derek, David Hilborn and Justin Thacker, eds. *The Atonement Debate: Papers from the London Symposium on the Theology of Atonement*. Grand Rapids: Zondervan, 2008.

---

97. See www.eauk.org/great-commission; www.eauk.org/what-we-do/initiatives/being-human.

Part 3

Sociological Analyses

25

Evangelicals in Central and Eastern Europe

The Case of Poland

Natalia Zawiejska

Introduction: Central and Eastern Europe

Geo-politically, Central and Eastern Europe (CEE) includes Poland, the Czech Republic, Slovakia and Hungary, whereas Croatia, Romania and Bulgaria have close affinity with it.[1] The principal basis for this identification is the shared historical experience of these countries, the period of socialist government after 1945. Yet East Germany (often included in Central and Western Europe) and the Baltic countries (with an affinity to Northern Europe) could also be included, as could Ukraine, which is often ascribed to Eastern Europe. In many cases, belonging to CEE is based on a blurred definition and the sense of not fitting fully into other categories, or of existing somewhere betwixt and between the North, East, South and West.[2] If these definitions of CEE seem problematic from an analytical point of view, there is heuristic potential in such blurring, as it allows for the tracing of several common features, despite

---

1. The research for this chapter was funded by the National Science Centre, Poland, under grant SONATA 17, number 2021/43/D/HS6/02274; it is based on long-term ethnographic research conducted from 2022 to 2024, and on several shorter field visits in 2016–2021.

2. Martin Müller, "In Search of the Global East: Thinking between North and South," *Geopolitics* 25.3 (2018): 734–55.

regional divergence. From the perspective of the social sciences, the most important aspects are the implications for reflection on the socio-religious formation and the socio-political transformation of this vast region.[3]

Scholarship has only recently started to pay attention to the socio-religious post-socialist transformation, looking beyond the outcomes of the policy of atheism and the religious revival that followed.[4] Many scholars agree that the analytical tools and heuristic frameworks created in the West are insufficient to apply to an exploration of CEE, or at least have to be rethought and reframed, as in the case of post-secular and postcolonial frameworks.[5] Others are trying to coin their own descriptive and analytical toolkits, as in the case of re-enchantment[6] or securitization and woundedness theorizations.[7] These various attempts are applicable to locating the evangelical movement in the socio-religious framework of CEE. Some countries of CEE have to be examined according to local histories and particular socio-political formations, and in many countries of the region evangelicals constitute a marginal minority. These evangelicals operate within the framework of a historically dominant mainstream religion, where religious pluralization is socially imagined as awkward and is often stigmatized, as is the case in Poland. The dominant, well-established and highly institutionalized religions manage the local religious habitus and often shape the administrative or legal framework for minority groups.[8] In several cases, the dominant religion is conflated with the state power and local governing structures, which often limits the activities of minority groups, including evangelicals.[9] In several cases, such as Poland, Bulgaria,

---

3. Irena Borowik, "The Religious Landscape of Central and Eastern Europe after Communism," in *The SAGE Handbook of the Sociology of Religion*, ed. James Beckford and N. Demerath (London: SAGE, 2007), 654–69.

4. Douglas Rogers, "Introductory Essay: The Anthropology of Religion After Socialism," *Religion, State and Society* 33.1 (2005): 5–18.

5. Irena Borowik, "The Concept of Public Religion in the Context of the Development of the Sociology of Religion: The Perspective of Central and Eastern Europe," in *Metamorphoses of Religion and Spirituality in Central and Eastern Europe*, ed. Sławomir H. Zaręba et al. (New York: Routledge, 2022), 33–45.

6. Agata Ładykowska, Viola Teisenhoffer and Alessandro Testa, "'Re-Enchantment' and Religious Change in Former Socialist Europe," *Religion* 54.1 (2024): 1–20.

7. András Máté-Tóth and Kinga Povedák (eds), *Religion as Securitization in Central and Eastern Europe* (Abingdon: Routledge, 2025).

8. Katarzyna Zielińska, "Lost between Caesar and God? Religion and Politics in Post-Socialist Europe," *East European Politics* 31.3 (2015): 361–63.

9. Agnieszka Pasieka, "Conflict and Coexistence of Church and State Authorities in (Post) Communist Poland," in *Atheist Secularism and Its Discontents*, ed. Tam T. T. Ngo and Justine B. Quijada (London: Palgrave Macmillan, 2015), 70–91.

Romania and Hungary, where the hegemonic religious power overlaps with nationhood and with the genealogies of national identity, evangelical identities are challenged as inadequate and foreign, or even suspicious.[10]

The fact that evangelicals are in a minority is clearly visible in statistics and quantitative data. Looking at selected examples of recent censuses in Poland, Slovakia, the Czech Republic and Hungary helps to show how evangelicals are located in the religious landscape. In Hungary, the number of Protestants is 1,155,253 and that of the dominant Roman Catholics is 2,643,855. At about 13 percent and 27.5 percent respectively, this is still less than 50 percent of the total population (9,603,634). Yet Protestants are more numerous here than in other countries of the region.[11] For instance, in the Czech Republic, where the Roman Catholic Church dominates at 741,019 adherents on a population of 10,524,167, the total number of Protestants is about 105,000.[12] In Slovakia, for 3,038,511 Roman Catholics, there are almost 430,000 Protestants, on a total population 5,502,265; thus Catholics form 55 percent and Protestants less than 8 percent of the Slovak population.[13] In Poland, Roman Catholic adherence is very high, with 27,121,331 on the total population of 38,036,118, which gives Roman Catholics over 71 percent, while all Protestants together count for just 0.29 percent.[14]

None of these censuses indicates clearly the number of evangelicals, which is much lower than the total number of Protestants in each country. But if in Hungary the number of evangelicals in relation to all Protestants is low, in Poland, this difference is not very significant, as evangelical Christianity is growing and has reached 0.2 percent of the population, dominating the Protestant landscape (all together 0.3 percent of the population).

The statistical data has to be read critically as, in relation to evangelicals, several blind spots hinder the collection of exact data and their interpretation. For example, in several censuses, a significant number of people did not respond to the question about religious affiliation and others declared no religious affiliation. These groups might include not only people who are

---

10. Agnieszka Pasieka, *Hierarchy and Pluralism: Living Religious Difference in Catholic Poland* (New York: Palgrave Macmillan), 153–55, 167–75; Cristian Sonea, "Ecumenical Convergences: Romanian Evangelicals Exploring Orthodoxy," *Religions* 12.6 (2021): 398.

11. Hungarian Central Statistical Office, "Census Hungary 2022," https://nepszamlalas2022.ksh.hu/en/.

12. Czech Statistical Office, "Census 2021," https://scitani.gov.cz/home.

13. Statistical Office of the Slovak Republic, "Census Slovakia 2021," www.scitanie.sk.

14. Główny Urząd Statystyczny, "Narodowy Spis Powszechny Ludności i Mieszkań 2021," https://spis.gov.pl/.

not involved with religion but also those who do not see themselves as a part of mainstream or institutionalized churches and organizations; they might be the category "other Christians" or simply "other" in some questionnaires. Such blind spots in the quantitative data hinder the understanding of current processes in the evangelical movement in the region and ethnographic studies might be of significant value to fill these gaps. In the sections that follow, an ethnographic account of the evangelical, and particularly the Pentecostal movement, in Poland will reveal the complexity of contemporary evangelicalism in the country. Poland is the largest country in the CEE region and, despite its particularities, might prove a useful case study.

Definitions, Identifications and Semantic Challenges

An important problem in relation to the Protestant movement in Poland is the low recognition of Protestants in the society. If the word "Protestant" is not completely unfamiliar, it is usually associated with Lutherans, Baptists, Methodists, Calvinists (Reformed) and Adventists. It is worth mentioning that the Evangelical Church of the Augsburg Confession, according to the last census, is represented by 65,407 members, the Pentecostal Church (Kościół Zielonoświątkowy) by 30,105 members, the Baptist Union by 5,181 members, the Seventh-day Adventists by 3,129 members and the Church of God in Christ by 2,007 members.[15] Many small evangelical communities are still not recognized by the society as Christians and are even seen as "sects." This might stem from "anticult" movements that were most visible in the Polish public sphere in the late nineties of the twentieth century.[16] In Kraków (Southern Poland), for instance, such an anticult organization still exists under the umbrella of the Roman Catholic Dominican Order and was called the Dominican Centre for Information on New Religious Movements and Sects (DCI).[17] Such units have been framing many new religious communities and New Religious Movements (NRMs) in pejorative terms as "sects." This has been polarizing the social perception of the difference between the Roman Catholic Church and religious "Others."

---

15. Główny Urząd Statystyczny, "Narodowy Spis Powszechny Ludności i Mieszkań 2021," https://spis.gov.pl/.

16. Zbigniew Pasek, "Wspólnoty ewangelikalne we współczesnej Polsce," in *Ewangelikalny Protestantyzm w Polsce u Progu XXI Stulecia*, ed. Tadeusz J. Zieliński (Warszawa-Katowice: Wydawnictwo Credo, 2004), 19.

17. Dominikańskie Centrum Informacji o Nowych Ruchach Religijnych i Sektach (DCI), https://sekty.dominikanie.pl/.

Similarly, the names first given to the Jehovah's Witnesses were *kociarze* or *kocia wiara*, which literally translated mean "cat's faith"; a clearly derogatory term. The Jehovah's Witnesses used to spread the word door to door, which might explain this popular name. Other non-Catholic Christian groups and communities then became associated with the name and many small evangelical groups still bear this stigma. Furthermore, many evangelical communities, particularly those who hold public evangelistic events or "street church" might be confronted by those who are disappointed by the local socio-religious habitus, moulded by the Roman Catholic Church. Therefore, by mistake or by generalized ascription, the public practices of some evangelicals are perceived in the light of social tensions around politicization and claims to control social life, as executed by the Roman Catholic Church, and suffer a negative social reception. The Polish public sphere is still largely seen as secular, despite its overwhelmingly post-secular shape. As a result, limits on the public display of religious convictions persist, shaping work environments, public institutions and social relations. Several evangelicals admit hiding their religious affiliation and convictions in public, in social relations and with their families, or report limited social space and acceptance for their religious convictions and beliefs, and sometimes discrimination on these grounds in the workplace.[18]

The frames and names given to evangelicals in Poland relate to the difficulty of estimating their exact number. If the number of all Protestants oscillates around 0.3 percent, evangelicals are even more marginal. According to self-estimates, evangelicals in Poland reach around 0.2 per cent of the population, which is about seventy thousand people. However, it is challenging to establish who is counted as an evangelical Christian and how many remain in the blind spot. The first point to be explored is proper naming. In Polish, the words *Ewangelik* (for a person) and *Ewangelicyzm* (for a group or formation) refer to Protestant and Protestantism respectively, mostly to the Lutheran and Reformed traditions.[19] The adjective *Ewangeliczny* stands for evangelicals, particularly when it is used in the phrase *Ewangeliczni chrześcijane* (literally: evangelic Christians). It is problematic that, while the etymology of the word *Ewangeliczny* derives from Greek *euangelion* and refers to the gospel ("good news"), the grammatical form in which it is used – adjective – should designate and characterize all Christians who are based and grounded in the gospel. In practice, however, there is a perceived tension between *ewangelicki* and

---

18. Fieldwork 2022–2024.
19. Tadeusz J. Zieliński, *Protestantyzm ewangelikalny. Studium specyfiki religijnej* (Warszawa: Wydawnictwo Naukowe Chat, 2014), 20.

ewangeliczny, pointing to different Protestant streams, the first to the sixteenth-century Reformation, the latter to the later pietist and revival tradition.[20] From the 1980s, the word *Ewangelikalny* ("evangelical") slowly started to be introduced from the English, aiming to clearly differentiate evangelicals from other Protestants. The word was promoted in academic circles and is now understood by some evangelicals.

However, there are further challenges. According to fieldwork conducted from 2022 to 2024, many evangelicals in Poland do not speak of themselves as evangelicals. Instead, they say "Christians" or "people who have a direct relationship with God" or refer to themselves as "Followers of Jesus," "Born again" and "New Creature." Several do not even consider themselves Protestants; some people do not fully understand what it means whereas others claim, "we do not have anything to protest against." Thus *Ewangelikalny* includes not only a variety of denominations and individuals who do not necessarily frame themselves as evangelical, but also charismatic Roman Catholics. The inclusion of the latter in the evangelical group in Poland will be discussed below.

The Polish Pentecostal movement faces similar definitional and semantic challenges. Pentecostalism is traditionally called *Ruch zielonoświątkowy*, which refers to the Polish name of Pentecost, *Zielone Świątki*, literally, "Green Holidays,"[21] a name deeply rooted in the spring holidays and local Christianized pagan traditions of the agricultural calendar. The word "Pentecostal" (*Pentekostalny*) is not universally understood, not even among evangelicals. This situation is confusing for foreigners coming to Poland. However, the word "Pentecostal" is gradually entering evangelical vocabulary. *Zielonoświątkowy*, when used to describe a particular form of spirituality, might also be applied to the Roman Catholic charismatic movement. This points to the fact that many Roman Catholics might be considered "born again" Christians, similar to the evangelicals who identify as non-Catholic.

At the same time, there are groups of individuals who do not belong to any kind of organized structure, constituting loosely attached groupings with a flattened leadership structure, who organize themselves as home groups, cells and home churches. These are hard to frame in terms of denominational belonging, as they are anti-denominational and mainly rely on the group authority and their own studies and intuition about the biblical accurateness of their beliefs and practices.

---

20. Zieliński, *Protestantyzm ewangelikalny*, 20–22.
21. Zbigniew Pasek, *Ruch zielonoświątkowy. Próba monografii* (Kraków: Nomos, 1992).

Summing up, the internal difficulties of identifying evangelicals and a complex spectrum of various auto-identifications contribute to the difficulty of establishing credible statistical data.

Relations and Connections: Unity, Discontinuity, Division

The evangelical movement in Poland is not only marginal but also very fragmented. Many evangelical churches arose or were significantly reconfigured in the late 1980s, particularly after the end of the Communist era in 1989, when the legislation for structuring and organizing religious institutions changed.[22] At that time, a wave of hope for a political, social and religious "new beginning" dominated the development of visions, plans for the future and the direction of change. The first decade after the transformation was difficult for Poland in terms of political instability and structural chaos at many levels of social life and the economy, but for Polish evangelicals this period was rich in new opportunities, with many international missionaries arriving and international connections forming.[23] However, divisions and separatist practices soon emerged.

Several factors determine the current fragmentation, one of which is the legal framework for religious organizations. According to Polish law, a religious organization can be officially recognized and registered if it has the certified signatures of at least a hundred followers – Polish citizens.[24] This high number dramatically affects both smaller evangelical institutions and foreign churches. As a result, many groups function informally and some opt to exist as charities (in Polish called foundation or association), although such a solution is not satisfying for most of them as they claim that "association is not a church."[25] Others function under the umbrella of larger, recognized religious institutions such as the Church of God in Christ (*Kościół Boży w Chrystusie*), the Pentecostal Church in Poland (*Kościół Zielonoświątkowy*) and the Church of God (*Kościół Boży*). The advantage of this practice is that it

---

22. Zbigniew Pasek and Wojciech Włoch, "Historia ruchu zielonoświątkowego i Odnowy Charyzmatycznej na ziemiach polskich," in *Historia Ruchu Zielonoświątkowego i Odnowy Charyzmatycznej. Stulecie Ducha Świętego 1901–2001*, ed. Vinson Synan (Kraków: Instytut Wydawniczy Compassion, 2006); Pasek, "Wspólnoty ewangelikalne," 13–50.

23. Lawrence Jones, "An American Pentecostal Mission to Poland in 1989," in *Christianity and Hegemony. Religion and politics on the Frontiers of Social Change*, ed. Jan Nederveen Pieterse (London: Bloomsbury, 1992), 273–301.

24. Sejm Rzeczpospolitej Polskiej, "Ustawa z dnia 17 maja 1989 r. o gwarancjach wolności sumienia i wyznania, Art. 31," https://isap.sejm.gov.pl/isap.nsf/.

25. Fieldwork October 2024.

aggregates various communities in the imagined network, creating shared identities and adherence policies. For several groups and communities, such arrangements guarantee administrative and functional safety. However, if the hosting institution limits the autonomy, secessions and abandonment occur. The acceptance of imposed authority is a challenge for many groups, including those of different cultural backgrounds or of a particular evangelical culture. For instance, cultural and structural misunderstanding became an issue in relations between Polish groups and the Ukrainian groups that flourished in Poland after the Russian invasion of Ukraine and the influx of war refugees. As a result, several Ukrainian communities ultimately resolved to remain unaffiliated and independent.[26]

Struggles over representation, authority and influence in the evangelical world have also been present in the Polish Evangelical Alliance, where the more established churches found it difficult to accept that the votes of less established and smaller denominations would carry equal weight. Such struggles remain in Polish evangelicalism; however, it is important to acknowledge recent attempts to find common ground over denominational divides. Here are examples of two such initiatives.

The first is *Wspólny Mianownik* ("Common Denominator"), an initiative that understands evangelicals as a broad spectrum and includes charismatic members of the Roman Catholic Church. The initiative started over five years ago in northern Poland. The main idea is to create a platform, an imagined common space, for people who aim in the same direction. This common space is framed by the leaders of Wspólny Mianownik.[27] The first is "Worship" which is intended to stress a commonality in worshipping God, in prayer and in studying God's word. The second is "Relationships." According to the leaders, the aim is to develop mutual relations between leaders and communities, rooted in a common identity, that is Jesus Christ. Third there is "Unity of generations," supported by the passage, "He will turn the hearts of the fathers to the children and the hearts of the children to their fathers; otherwise, I will come and strike the land with complete destruction" (Mal 3:24 CJB). And finally, "Unity," which should be a response to the words of Jesus: "That all of them may be one, Father, just as you are in me, and I am in you. May they also be in us so that the world may believe that you have sent me" (John 17:21 NIV).

---

26. Ganna Tregub, "Double minority: Ukrainian Pentecostalisms in Poland," *Zeszyty Łużyckie* 62.1 (2025) (forthcoming).

27. Fieldwork 2024.

During the Wspólny Mianownik conference in October 2024, which took place near Gdańsk in the north of Poland, these visions were also specified. Unity does not mean the acceptance of every practice, idea or innovation. Some leaders openly claimed that there are evangelicals, practices and innovations that should not be accepted or promoted, although nobody mentioned any by name. Nevertheless, the speakers at the conference were varied and included Baptists, Pentecostals and Roman Catholic charismatics. This mirrors the ongoing attempts at dialogue within the evangelical spectrum in Poland which manifest themselves in joint conferences, workshops and educational institutions, for instance.

The meeting considered an important problem that had emerged recently, the vertical differentiation, that is the generational change. Many evangelical communities in Poland that came into existence in the 1980s and 1990s have had the same leadership for decades. Well-established communities and churches do not tend to change, and the older leaders keep their positions, preventing younger members from exercising influence. Such stagnation often leads to the departure or resignation of those younger members who have a different vision, are inspired by international trends and are more sensitive to rapid cultural and social changes.

The other initiative that arose around 2018 is a platform for establishing evangelical common ground in Poland, excluding Roman Catholic charismatics. *Ewangeliczna Polska* ("Evangelical Poland") came into existence as an initiative of leaders of the Baptist Church in Poland, the Church of Christ in Poland,[28] the Church of Christians of the Evangelical Faith in Poland, the Church of Evangelical Christians in Poland, the Church of God in Christ[29] and the Council of the Free Christian Churches, many of whom are members of the Polish Evangelical Alliance.[30] The idea to establish the organization was inspired by experiences in France of the main coordinator, Andrzej Górski. Ewangeliczna Polska has a clear agenda: by 2050, evangelicals in Poland should be much more socially accepted and the number of evangelical Christians should rise to at least one percent of the population. These objectives should be attained through evangelism and church planting, training and development of leaders and staff, investing in the development of evangelical media and communication, establishing educational institutions at all levels, charitable and social projects, and discipleship.

---

28. Kościół Chrystusowy w RP, http://chrystusowi.pl/.
29. Kościół Boży w Chrystusie, a church which originated in Belarus, https://kbwch.pl/.
30. Ewangeliczna Polska, https://ewangeliczna.pl/.

The focus of this group goes beyond creating a space for mutual understanding and building on the "unity in diversity" paradigm. The idea behind it is expressed by the main motto "United for future generations,"[31] which means enhancing social impact and developing political influence. The fate of the Polish nation and state is important to the members of this group and they want to actively shape local socio-political reality. In October 2024, the annual meeting of Ewangeliczna Polska took place in Warsaw at the headquarters of the Pentecostal Church in Poland. One of the concluding plenary sessions was devoted precisely to "engagement." "We all gathered here are activists," said the speaker. Indeed, most conference participants were engaged in various projects, which were displayed on stands on Exhibition Day, when leaflets were also distributed. Evangelical activities are various social projects focused on men's identity and psychology, creating cultural or community centres, developing evangelical businesses linked to education and leisure, and social welfare projects. The exchange of experiences and getting to know each other played an important role at this meeting.

If the primary word that defines most Polish evangelicals is "relationship," understood as unmediated and personal contact with God, in the case of Ewangeliczna Polska relationships are also being forged horizontally. The structure of this initiative facilitates mutual cooperation and help despite differences. However, this does not include those who remain at the margins of these vast networks. The exclusion occurs both as a result of people's own reluctance, frequently rooted in mistrust and the conviction of not fitting into the Ewangeliczna Polska platform, and as a result of being neglected by others. For instance, the absence of migrant communities is well visible. While Operation Mobilisation (OM) presented a project for refugees and immigrants during the conference, it did not reflect the voice and visibility of such foreign communities.[32] Also, there were no foreign churches invited as speakers or presenters. Other factors explaining selective participation in Ewangeliczna Polska networks might be the tension between the socio-geographic centre and periphery and the social divisions. Poland is not a homogenous country in terms of welfare and development, and the distribution of economic and cultural resources varies. Therefore the costs of participation in the conference might be a barrier, particularly for peripheral communities and individuals from smaller cities, far from the capital Warsaw. Moreover, the majority of

---

31. Ewangeliczna Polska, "Wizja Rozwoju Ewangelicznego Chrześcijaństw w Polsce do 2050 r.," 2018, https://ewangeliczna.pl/wp-content/uploads/2019/11/Wizja-2050.pdf.

32. Operation Mobilisation in Poland, https://ompolska.org/.

participants represent the Polish middle class, acting from the perspective of their own social location. Therefore, several of my interlocutors who hesitated about Evangeliczna Polska saw it as having a particular socio-political agenda that is not universally supported. For these reasons, several evangelical communities and leaders are criticizing Ewangeliczna Polska for its elitist character. To many others, this initiative is still unknown.

Roman Catholic Charismatics: Brothers and Strangers

The charismatic movement in the Polish Roman Catholic Church should not be marginalized or ignored when mapping evangelicals in Poland. According to some authors, Roman Catholic groups are a primary source of new members for Pentecostal churches due to conversion from Catholic to Pentecostal[33] and a significant proportion of the current pastors of well-established evangelical communities were once, in the 1980s, members of Roman Catholic charismatic groups. But reconversions occur and there is ongoing tension between these two groups. On both sides there are groups and organizations eager to engage in dialogue (such as *Głos na Pustyni*, "The Voice in the Desert," representing the Roman Catholic Church),[34] but on both sides strong criticism can be heard of cooperation with "the other side," which is regarded as evidence of heresy.

The Roman Catholic charismatic movement in Poland began in the 1970s and has existed in at least two dimensions since then. First, "Light and Life" (*Ruch Światło Życie*, called also the Oaza movement) was set up by the priest Franciszek Blachnicki and inspired by the organization Campus Crusade for Christ. Second, the *Odnowa w Duchu Świętym* (Catholic Charismatic Renewal) started as a prayer group and constituted its first congregation in Warsaw a decade later.[35] Now the growth of the movement is incentivised by "New Evangelization" (*Nowa Ewangelizacja*), the evangelization agenda of the Roman Catholic Church, focused on transmitting the faith to people, environments, regions and even countries that were once baptized, so countries which have roots in the Christian faith but need revitalization of faith for various reasons. As such it was formalized in the second decade of the twenty-first century due

---

33. Konrad Siekierski, "Catholics in the Holy Spirit: The Charismatic Renewal in Poland," *Religion, State and Society* 40.1 (2012): 145–61; Ariel Zieliński, *W okolice schizmy; społeczności Ewangelikalne wywodzące się z katolickiego ruchu charyzmatycznego* (Kraków: Nomos, 2009).

34. Głos na Pustyni, Chrześcijańska Fundacja, https://glosnapustyni.pl/.

35. Andrzej Siemieniewski, *Ochrzczeni w jednym Duchu': Perspektywy integracji mistycyzmu pentekostalnego z Duchowością Katolicką* (Wrocław: Papieski Wydział Teologiczny, 2002); Pasek, "Wspólnoty ewangelikalne," 37–38.

to the engagement of Benedict XVI and is now focusing on re-evangelization and new ways of practising Christianity.

It is important that these charismatic groups flourish within the Roman Catholic Church, constituting one of the principal branches of spiritual renewal in the Church. Catholic charismatic events attract thousands of people. For instance, in 2021 a popular young lay person, Marcin Zieliński, founded "Rozpal Wiarę" (*Fuel the Faith*), a charity that is involved in, among other things, organizing mass evangelistic meetings combined with concerts and prayers for healing. These events, under the name *Chwała Mu* ("To Him the Glory"), have already taken place in Łódź in 2022 with ten thousand people participating, in Wrocław in 2023 with about twenty-five thousand people, and in Kraków in 2024 with about twenty thousand people.[36]

The charismatic movement in Poland proved the evangelistic potential of missionaries from the Global South. Before the COVID-19 pandemic, Father John Baptista Bashobora from Uganda led large evangelistic and healing events for great crowds, attracting sixty thousand people to the National Stadium in Warsaw.[37] These events attract very diverse people, both Catholics and Protestants, which again shows that there is a thin line between the denominations. However, in many Protestant evangelical communities, participation in such events is considered a "betrayal of faith."[38]

Migration

Migration recently became a challenge for Polish society. Under the Communist regime (1945–1989) Poland, once a diverse, pluralistic and multiethnic nation, was reframed as monoethnic, monolingual and monoracial. Due to the initial instability after the 1989 transformation, its demanding immigration policies and its unfavourable economic situation – at least in comparison to Western and Northern European countries – migrants did not see Poland as a desirable country. On the contrary, Polish people emigrated to Western Europe and the USA in large numbers. Yet this situation has changed recently and the country has started to attract professionals and students from African countries, India and various European countries as well. Moreover, with

---

36. Rozpal Wiarę, www.rozpalwiare.pl.

37. Natalia Zawiejska, "The Pentecostal Complex in Poland: Missionaries, Migrants, and Social Imaginaries," in Jörg Haustein and Michael Wilkinson (eds), *The Pentecostal World* (London: Routledge, 2023), 390–404.

38. Fieldwork 2024.

the ongoing war in Ukraine, both since 2014 and since the Russian invasion in 2022, Ukrainian immigrants and war refugees have appeared *en masse* in Poland. Equally, the crisis at the Polish-Belarusian border brought immigration to social attention.

The flow of immigration resulted in a constant growth in numbers of foreign evangelicals, refugee communities, Global South communities, and missionaries who started to appear and circulate in Poland. For evangelical "Others" coming to Poland, the language is the first barrier; therefore, instead of trying to join a Polish church or group, many join the international ministries that are created as part of the established churches in the large cities. Working under the umbrella of Polish institutions, migrant churches such as the Redeemed Christian Church of God (RCCG) and Ukrainian Pentecostal churches[39] are now present in the larger cities. Yet what is most visible in the Polish Pentecostal movement is that the White and Polish ethnocentric paradigm persists. Most events, including those focused on unity and referring to the creation of a common ground for evangelicals in Poland, do not take immigrants into consideration. Many existing communities are reluctant to integrate and share authority with migrants. If the situation is different anywhere, that should be seen as an exception rather than a rule.[40]

I will discuss two such exceptions. The first is in Lublin, in eastern Poland, where not long ago many African students appeared, attracted by the local university's study programmes in English, such as nursing. Churches serving this vast African community followed suit: RCCG, Calvary Apostolic Assembly, Apostolic Faith Mission and Zion Christian Church, originally from Zimbabwe. These churches only serve the African community, but two local churches do not reflect this pattern. One is led by a Polish couple, Alina and Beniamin Perenc, pastors who left the established church "Charisma" several years ago. They were both disappointed with its stagnant profile and wanted something different. The decision to initiate their own church, the Zion Church (*Kościół Syjon*)[41] coincided with the appearance of the first Africans, who were welcomed with great attention. The two pastors organized services, study groups, home cells and various church activities in which they engaged with the church members and devoted themselves to the growth of the community. The church is growing in a process of mutual learning. It became an exceptional case in

---

39. Tregub, "Double minority" (forthcoming).
40. Zawiejska, "The Pentecostal Complex," 390–404.
41. Zion Church, https://zionchurchlublin.pl.

which an African community is led by Polish pastors and not adapted to any particular African tradition.

Another example of integration is the International Christian Fellowship in Lublin,[42] which functions under the umbrella of the Polish evangelical church "Centre" (*Społeczność Chrześcijańska „Centrum" w Lublinie*). Its ministry is led by a pastor who is originally from Norway, Ronald Gabrielsen. Whereas this community is financially and structurally dependent on the Polish church, they are relatively autonomous in searching for connections and engaging with various projects. Together with other African communities, they recently organized the event "Joy in the City," a several-hour-long concert, where evangelism took place in the main square of the city. Such events are among the largest non-Catholic events taking place in the historic centre of Lublin, engaging city dwellers and various communities. Such practices point to another important dimension of evangelicalism in Poland, the cooperation with local governing structures and administration, which is still underdeveloped. Paradoxically, in Lublin, it is the foreign evangelical communities that managed to reach out on the streets and organize mass entertainment in a predominantly White city.

Both cases depict a situation in which immigrants are the source of a new evangelical force in Poland. They represent the few cases in which immigration was rethought and approached other than through the paradigm of diasporic communities and isolation strategies. Foreignness, otherness and immigration urgently need to be acknowledged and integrated into the Polish evangelical landscape because they are crucial for the future shape and development of the evangelical movement.

The research data also show the challenge of the presence of foreign international mission agencies and large institutions that operate in Poland, such as the Billy Graham Evangelistic Association and others. While they are happy to receive help and support from such institutions, several Polish leaders report unplanned dependency, imposition of authority and the moulding of the character of the local evangelical congregation according to the ideas of the international, mostly Western, institutions. For some church leaders and members these incursions into Polish evangelicalism constitute a threat to its local identity and are evidence of a lack of respect. For instance, a recent visit of Franklin Graham to Poland (2024) caused distinctly mixed feelings because large amounts of resources were invested in activities without full consultation with local leaders. As a result, several churches were sceptical about participation and did not fully promote Franklin Graham's "God Loves You Tour."

---

42. International Christian Fellowship in Lublin, www.icfl.eu.

Conclusion

Evangelicals constitute a minority of the population of Central and Eastern Europe, but as the example of Poland shows, identity struggles are still an important internal challenge. Paradoxically, the dominant position of the Roman Catholic Church does not stimulate internal consolidation of evangelicalism but in some aspects (Roman Catholic charismatics) contributes to the further blurring of the evangelical identity. Studying the dynamics and development of evangelical Christianity in Central and Eastern Europe may contribute to a greater understanding of both the local richness and the glocalized challenges of the evangelical movement, which may help the understanding of evangelicalism worldwide.

Bibliography

Cieślar, Oliwer. "The Pentecostal Movement in Poland and its Modern Social Context." *Journal of the European Pentecostal Theological Association* 36.1 (2016): 30–41.

Czech, Karolina. "Polish Evangelical Churches Contribution to Building a Civil Society." *Forum Pedagogiczne* 2.1 (2015): 213–25.

Gajewski, Wojciech, and Krzysztof Wawrzeniuk. "A Historical and Theological Analysis of the Pentecostal Church of Poland." *Journal of the European Pentecostal Theological Association* 20.1 (2000): 32–48.

Hacker, Randy. *North American Mission Agencies in Poland: A Study in "Partnership."* Master of Arts in Intercultural Studies Dissertation. Columbia: Columbia International University, 2013.

Pawłowski, Edward. "Poland." Pages 517–19 in *Brill's Encyclopedia of Global Pentecostalism*. Edited by Michael Wilkinson, Connie Au, Jörg Haustein and Todd M. Johnson. Leiden: Brill, 2021.

Siekierski, Konrad. "Catholics in the Holy Spirit: The Charismatic Renewal in Poland." *Religion, State and Society* 40.1 (2012): 145–61.

Zawiejska, Natalia. "The Pentecostal Complex in Poland: Missionaries, Migrants, and Social Imaginaries." Pages 390–404 in *The Pentecostal World*. Edited by Jörg Haustein and Michael Wilkinson. London: Routledge, 2023.

Zieliński, Tadeusz J. ed. *Ewangelikalny protestantyzm w Polsce u progu XXI stulecia*. Warszawa-Katowice: Wydawnictwo Credo, Baptystyczne Seminarium Teologiczne w Warszawie, 2004.

———. ed. *Władze Polski Ludowej a mniejszościowe związki wyznaniowe*. Warszawa-Katowice: Wydawnictwo Credo, Baptystyczne Seminarium Teologiczne w Warszawie, 2014.

———. *Protestantyzm ewangelikalny. Studium specyfiki religijnej*. Warszawa: Wydawnictwo Naukowe Chat, 2014.

26

Evangelicals in Portugal

Plural and Growing Communities

Elsa Correia Pereira

Introduction: Religious Freedom

Religious freedom in Portugal celebrated its fiftieth anniversary in 2024.[1] It was the fall of the dictatorial regime that allowed for the emergence of a political and public framework that embraced religious plurality. After a long journey, the Portuguese Law on Religious Freedom was ratified in 2001. According to experts, this law is one of the most comprehensive and extensive in Europe.[2] In 2019 the Portuguese Parliament even established 22 June as the National Day of Religious Freedom and Interreligious Dialogue to commemorate the day in 2001 when this law on Religious Freedom was ratified, thus recognizing it as of utmost importance for the country. Parliament unanimously approved of this commemorative day.[3]

Another step forward for religious diversity in Portugal, particularly for evangelicals, occurred during the most recent census in 2021. As the Portuguese Evangelical Alliance (PEA) commented in a statement,

---

1. The project which resulted in this chapter was funded by FCT - UI/BD/154276/2022.

2. José Vera Jardim, "The Portuguese Law on Religious Freedom is One of the Most Open in Europe," in *The Paths of Religious Freedom in Portugal*, ed. António Marujo (Lisbon: Assembly of the Republic, Collection of Images and Documents, 2023), 67–77.

3. Eduardo Ferro Rodrigues, "Message from the President of the Assembly of the Republic on the Occasion of the National Day of Religious Freedom and Interreligious Dialogue," 22 June 2019, www.parlamento.pt/Paginas/2019/junho/Dia-Nacional-liberdade-Religiosa.aspx.

> . . . this is the first time since the first general census of the Portuguese population was conducted in 1864 that the designation "evangelical" has been included as a religious affiliation category, which may help explain the significant increase in the number of respondents, given that in 2011 only 75,571 identified as "Protestant" (0.84 percent of respondents).[4]

The question about religious affiliation is the only one in the census that is optional and as a result, about 230,000 citizens did not answer it. Another 2.13 percent identified as evangelical. The number for religion is usually not broken down by gender, but for the purposes of our doctoral research, this breakdown was provided to us by the National Institute of Statistics of Portugal, showing that all Christian denominations have more women than men, while all non-Christian denominations have more men than women (except for Buddhism, where men and women are close to 50 percent each). This observation likely reflects migratory movements from other countries, with more men than women, bringing with them non-Christian religious affiliations.

This brings us to the fact that the theme of religion in Portugal is closely associated with immigration and the cultural diversity of the people who seek to live in the country. It also intersects with the arts, the media and the public sphere, social action, education and human rights, health, leadership and gender dynamics. We will explore some of these topics in the following paragraphs.

In this context of religious plurality, the PEA is trying to understand the plural reality inside the evangelical communities. In a study conducted in 2023, out of approximately three hundred and fifty evangelical church leaders in Portugal, 82 percent reported that their churches were growing and 53 percent indicated that attendance in their communities had increased in the post-pandemic period.[5]

---

4. Portuguese Evangelical Alliance, "Evangelicals in Portugal According to the 2021 Census," 30 November 2022, https://aliancaevangelica.pt/site/evangelicos-em-portugal-segundo-o-censos-2021/.

5. Portuguese Evangelical Alliance, "2023 Report – Evangelical Church in Portugal: A Close-Up View!," Office of Studies and Research, 6 June 2023. Earlier such studies were conducted in 2016 and 2020.

Consolidation and Expansion: Two Different Paths toward Growth

When we examine the dynamics of Portuguese evangelical communities today, we can identify two trends which are not necessarily mutually exclusive. Helena Vilaça describes these trends of closure and opening as follows:

> Although viewed as more conservative [than historical Protestants, ECP], evangelicals, due to their lesser emphasis on tradition and greater institutional fragility, exhibit greater plasticity [than any other Christian tradition, ECP] in terms of adapting to modernity. While it is true that many evangelical churches are in crisis due to crystallization and closure, younger generations, who are now more educated and possess cultural capital that gives them significant communicative ability, tend to establish new churches. Most of these are non-denominational; that is, they consider themselves evangelical Christians but are not bound (at least apparently) by the designation of their denomination. They have more neutral names, such as CCLX (Christian Community of Lisbon), Casa da Cidade [City House], Hillsong/City Christian Center, or Surf Church.[6]

But these trajectories of evangelical churches in Portugal are closely intertwined with the contemporary reality of international mobility. Christianity has become polycentric and is slowly decolonizing: missionaries move from South and East to North as well in the traditional opposite direction; it is growing in the Global South but shrinking in the North; and the number of denominations keeps increasing.[7] In the Northern Hemisphere, which was once the source of theology and missionary movements heading south, many churches with members from the Global South countries are now emerging. Gina Zurlo notes that in Portugal between 2000 and 2016, three hundred new evangelical churches were established and since 2005, more than twenty different denominations were imported from Brazil.[8] Although less reported, communities from Portuguese-speaking countries such as Angola, and from South Asian countries like Bangladesh, have established themselves in Por-

---

6. Helena Vilaça, "Religion in the City: Territories, Materialities, and Communication," *Sociology: Journal of the Faculty of Arts of the University of Porto, Thematic Issue – Social Processes and Sociological Issues* (2017): 20. Crystallisation means becoming static.

7. Lausanne Movement, "What is Polycentric Christianity?," in State of the Great Commission Report, Part 2: Context Shifts, https://lausanne.org/report.

8. Gina A. Zurlo, *Global Christianity: A Guide to the World's Largest Religion from Afghanistan to Zimbabwe* (Zondervan Academic, 2022), 238.

tugal just as in other developed countries in the Global North. Alongside this geographical mobility, we also have the social mobility mentioned earlier and the entrepreneurial characteristics of Generation Z. Those born between 1995 and 2010 do not follow rigid hierarchies and leaderships unquestioningly but rather those who earn their respect,[9] which means that they can be evangelical leaders or mentors from international contexts. Furthermore, Generation Z, which is entrepreneurial in the workplace – the generation of startups – is also entrepreneurial in their faith, not conforming to pre-formatted ideas of "doing church" from previous generations. They design their own faith community projects, heavily based on multimedia, imagery, champions or influencers, creativity, the arts, particularly music and online interaction.[10]

Migration, Media and Misunderstandings

We have seen that much of the religious diversity in Portugal, especially represented by non-Christian groups, is the result of immigration; yet the increase in evangelical Christian denominations is largely due to Brazilian immigration to Portugal. Because the public opinion (fuelled by sensationalist media reports) associates Brazil with the growth of evangelicals in Portugal, there seems to be a desire on the part of the media to explore the so-called "Evangelical Bench" in Portugal. In other words, there is an attempt to equate the influence of so-called conservative and far-right trends that academic studies and the media have been attributing to the politics of the former Brazilian president Bolsonaro with those evangelicals in Portugal who are involved in politics. The PEA has been regularly pressured with questions about any involvement with parties that are considered populist, such as Chega, or, in the 2024 elections, with National Democratic Alternative (ADN), to which the organization responds with its characteristic non-partisanship. The determination of the media to create links between Trump, Bolsonaro and André Ventura (Chega) or the ADN on the one hand and the evangelicals on the other is more an attempt to stereotype than to inform the public.

On the other hand, this determination is also common in academic research, which links politics to religion or vice versa. The reality is that there are no in-depth geopolitical or geo-religious studies in Portugal that actually

---

9. C. Valente, *Generation Z: Understanding and Inspiring Their Future* (Lisbon: Diário de Bordo, 2019), 79.

10. Elsa Correia Pereira, "Gender and Religion in Dialogue: The Example of Evangelical Churches" (2023), unpublished manuscript.

associate the electorate of these populist parties with the geographical location of evangelical potential voters in the country. Without this, it is not correct to make any kind of association.

When asked by the press,[11] the PEA has several times distanced itself from any partisan tendency, also through statements on its own website.[12] In fact, history shows that evangelicals in Europe, although they stem from movements which originated in the Protestant Reformation, have always insisted on distancing themselves from any relationship with the state and political power, unlike historic Protestants.

Like an Iceberg

Other "misunderstandings" that need to be clarified concern the questions who the evangelicals are, what defines and unites them, and what subgroups constitute them. In fact, with the massification of the internet, air travel, book publishing and other factors, it has become easier to "transport" theologies and ways of doing church, especially when there is no language barrier. This is the case with many denominations imported from Brazil, which maintain their networks of contact in their country of origin. The names of these denominations may correspond to the classic evangelical denominations that have existed in Portugal for over one hundred years, but they usually distinguish themselves by adding the name of their place of origin. For example: Assembly of God – Madureira Ministry (originating from this location in Brazil). These churches, with an international presence, have their own programmes, networks of contacts between communities in the country of origin, and their own theological schools and supervisors, so they do not rely on Portuguese institutional networks.

Portugal is often the launching platform for the spread of Brazilian-origin churches into other European countries, such as Italy. In other words, the European headquarters of a certain Brazilian-origin evangelical denomination or missionary movement are in Lisbon and the church expands to other European countries. An example of this is the Sara Nossa Terra denomination. Paulo Gracino Júnior has investigated this internationalization and transnationali-

---

11. Ana Taborda and Raquel Lito, "The Power of Evangelicals," *Sábado* 1049 (6–12 June 2024): 28–39.

12. Portuguese Evangelical Alliance, "Evangelicals and the Elections," 19 February 2024.

zation of churches.[13] From a theoretical point of view, we may agree with his perspective, as other authors also speak of transnationalism concerning other global evangelical denominations such as Hillsong (more on this later). The problem arises when Júnior refers to the Universal Church of the Kingdom of God (IURD) which is not considered to be either evangelical or Pentecostal by evangelicals because of its pyramidal governance structure.[14]

In Portugal, the historic Protestant denominations (Lusitanian Church, Methodist Church and Presbyterian Church) belong to the Portuguese Council of Christian Churches (COPIC) founded in 1971. These denominations have synodal governance. Those we consider evangelicals are the churches affiliated with the PEA or those that, while not affiliated, follow the same rules of faith and conduct and have a congregationalist model of governance. Among these evangelicals are classic denominations such as the Baptists, the Assemblies of God and the Brethren Churches, as well as many independent churches that are not always affiliated with the PEA. As there is freedom of association in Portugal since the Carnation Revolution of 1974, a group of people can perfectly well gather as a faith community without even being registered as such.

For this reason a member of the Study and Research Office of the PEA describes the Portuguese evangelical landscape as an iceberg.[15] The evangelical churches affiliated with the PEA correspond to the part of the iceberg above the water. At the waterline we have churches which, although not affiliated with the PEA, have been in Portugal for two or three decades and have therefore already built networks of sociability and partnerships with churches that have existed for longer. Under water we have the numerous more recent churches, with their own connections, projects, agendas and international networks, which we often do not know about. The National Registry of Non-Catholic Religious Entities (NRNCRE), which formalises churches that want to register for tax purposes, estimates that the number of evangelical churches is more than double that of those registered with the PEA.

---

13. Paulo G. Júnior, "Jesus Made in Brazil: Notes on the Transnationalization of Brazilian Pentecostalism to Portugal," Dossier: Pentecostalism in Brazil, *Horizonte*, Belo Horizonte, 9, 22, (July/September 2011): 416–45, https://periodicos.pucminas.br/index.php/horizonte/article/view/P.2175-5841.2011v9n22p416.

14. Like other churches from Brazil, IURD is seen as neo-Pentecostal, not due to an emphasis on the gifts of the Holy Spirit but for chronological reasons. The governance of these churches tends to be more autocratic, with the leader centralizing power and decision-making and little to no participation by the believers. This contrasts with the congregationalism of the Baptist Churches and Assemblies of God.

15. In private conversation.

In March 2023, the PEA had three hundred and sixty affiliated churches corresponding to seven hundred and nineteen places of worship.[16] Meanwhile, according to the NRNCRE, there were nine hundred and seventeen registered non-Catholic entities, of which 80 percent, so seven hundred and thirty-four, are with a high degree of certainty evangelical.[17] This number excludes Jehovah's Witnesses, Mormons (The Church of Jesus Christ of Latter-Day Saints), the Universal Church of the Kingdom of God and Maná, but possibly includes the Seventh-day Adventists, although they are not part of PEA. Many of these entities have a single tax identification number but various places of worship. The so-called local Protestant communities can have twenty or more meeting places per tax number.[18] Therefore, the total number of evangelical places of worship is not currently quantified. Lastly, there are older communities led by older citizens who do not agree with the registration of properties or any other assets in the name of the church, which they consider a violation of the separation of church and state. Given the previous information, it can be concluded that the number of evangelical churches and places of worship in our country is much higher than those registered, currently making it untraceable.

Social Geography

In the social geography of evangelicals, we see that new churches are springing up "like mushrooms" in locations which host large migrant populations, such as the larger cities (like Braga in Northern Portugal) and the outskirts of major cities. In such areas there may be four or more churches on a single street, all labelled "evangelical." This pluralism in the religious market in the Lisbon Metropolitan Area had already been reported in a 2019 study,[19] but since COVID-19 it has increased and spread throughout the entire country, transforming both urban and more rural areas – to the astonishment of local residents.

---

16. Source: Office of the PEA.

17. Source: Telephone interview with a member of the Board of the Commission for Religious Freedom, 2023.

18. For example, the Portuguese Union of Seventh-day Adventists (which might be considered as evangelical) has only one tax identification number for a hundred congregations; the Abundant Life Christian Centre has one number for twenty-one congregations; the Church of the Nazarene has fourteen congregations. There are also communities that register as non-profit associations but function as churches.

19. Alfredo Teixeira, ed., *Religious Identities and Social Dynamics in the Lisbon Metropolitan Area* (Lisbon: Fundação Francisco Manuel dos Santos, 2019).

The term "megachurches" is often associated with churches like Hillsong which, according to Cristina Rocha, have a sense of belonging to transnational urban landscapes and create a modern "attachment" or sense of community for their followers.[20] However, on the basis of its size and membership figures, I would not characterize Portuguese Hillsong as a "megachurch": that label is commonly used for churches with two thousand or more members. We can call Hillsong a "brand church" because the entire musical performance, attire, stage, lights, multimedia, musical production etcetera adhere to a "brand image" that is universally recognized and corresponds exactly to the "religious product" and global identity with which younger generations identify.

Some more recent churches do not fit under traditional labels because they are not Pentecostal in the sense of being recognized for operating the gifts of the Spirit, nor are they brand churches. We usually refer to them as independent churches, with all the fragility that this designation entails. Typically of medium size, they are characterized by concentrating on several features associated with other churches: modern music, freedom in dress, well-educated members, significant social intervention in the local community and an innovative theology. They deviate somewhat from institutional canons but maintain the principles of the evangelical faith such as the centrality of the Bible, the new birth, the Trinity and the fellowship of believers. Given their relatively recent origins, a taxonomy for them could be "New Evangelicals."

Evangelicals in Sports, Arts and Academia

More than twenty-five years ago, some "classic" Portuguese evangelical churches did not allow believers to play football or to perform in theatre or cinema, together with restrictions regarding code, makeup and hairstyle. However, with the emergence of numerous alternative churches and increased mobility, people are able to choose a church further from their residence if they are dissatisfied with their current church or need a specific religious service. There are reports of people (such as with teenage children) who belong to two churches in order to maintain a connection to their "old" church. In the morning, they might attend the church the family has always frequented and in the afternoon, they visit a community more aligned with their musical tastes or social preferences.

This mobility has forced church leaders to think of strategies not only to attract new members but also to retain current ones. Some social restrictions

---

20. Cristina Rocha, *Cool Christianity, Hillsong and the Fashioning of Cosmopolitan Identities* (Oxford: Oxford University Press, 2024), 128.

have been abolished or even reversed. For example, whereas a few decades ago the public prominence of a member in a field that could lead to "stardom," such as arts, sports or academia, was viewed with suspicion, today it is seen as a way to enhance the social relevance of the faith community, potentially giving it "status" and visibility among other communities. If a musician, athlete or professional belongs to a certain church, this is now considered an asset for that community, which may capitalize on their visibility to attract more followers. With a young and adaptable hierarchical structure, the image of champions or "ambassadors" of these churches helps to build their name in the religious scene.

Although it is not yet as visible in Portugal as elsewhere in Europe and around the world, the development of religious narratives based on scientific, theoretical and empirical foundations helps to dismantle stereotypes and to lend credibility to certain religious movements. Where academia once was predominantly a space for Catholics and some historical Protestants, the presence of evangelicals is becoming more noticeable across various fields of knowledge. This development is making concepts such as religious identity and community, and social transformation or social gospel more common in the study of faith, particularly the evangelical faith, thereby adding reliability to the movement and enhancing its credibility and reputation.

Social Action, Education, Environment and Human Rights Activism

Since the nineteenth century evangelical efforts to spread the faith in Portugal have not been limited to church planting but have included education, social action and healthcare. More recently, evangelical voices have joined activism for human rights and environmental issues. Global issues such as climate change, the environmental crisis, gender equality, fair distribution of resources and support for refugees are at the forefront.[21] Meanwhile, evangelical Christian communities and networks, often overlooked in the past, have emerged as significant catalysts for change, offering unique and inspiring responses to these and other pressing challenges both locally and globally.

Thus, despite secularism and the efforts of Western modernity to relegate religion and faith to the private sphere, social issues have been widely embraced by evangelical Christian communities, bringing evangelical Christian voices into the public sphere. It is therefore crucial to highlight the intersection

---

21. These issues are strongly promoted by the UN's 2030 Agenda for Sustainable Development Goals.

between evangelical responses to climate change, gender equality, peacebuilding, refugee support and other global concerns, demonstrating how faith can drive solutions to common problems in the public arena. Many evangelicals see the struggle for gender equality as a way to value human beings. On the other hand, environmental advocacy is intrinsically linked to the ethical and spiritual principles that guide the human relationships with creation. Faith-motivated social intervention represents the practice of a holistic vision of justice and moral and social responsibility taught by the gospel of Jesus.

Portuguese evangelicals have been active in these areas from the beginning, but the interest exploded in the multifaceted social responses of the twenty-first century. From supporting Portuguese-speaking communities in Africa, Brazil and Timor, to funding schools, primary health care and providing aid in goods, evangelical communities, with their characteristic voluntarism, have been actively involved. They spontaneously organize and support the communities in which they are located.[22]

After 25 April 1974, and with the arrival of approximately one million refugees from Portuguese-speaking African countries, evangelical communities provided social and spiritual support to thousands of people and continue to do so. Since 2015, the PEA, along with other European countries and the European Evangelical Alliance, regularly joins networks supporting refugees and combating human trafficking. It has actively participated in other networks such as the European Educators Christian Association. From 1990, the subject of Evangelical Moral and Religious Education is part of the curriculum of primary and secondary schools, offering students more than just the teaching of a religious confession. The teachers concerned bring to the school various activities, including theatre, music, sports and community support activities that benefit everyone involved: teaching staff and support staff, families, children and local charities.

The participation of evangelical communities in social action allows churches to participate in the life of the cities where they are established with wisdom and a sense of opportunity. Through parish social committees and local social action councils, they increase their understanding of the needs of the people around them. A master's thesis written in 2020 describes the

---

22. David Martin, *Reflections on Sociology and Theology* (Oxford: Clarendon, 1997), 81; David Martin, "Voluntarism. Niche Markets Created by a Fissile Transnational Faith," in *Religions in Movement: The Local and the Global in Contemporary Faith Traditions*, ed. R. W. Hefner, J. Hutchinson, S. Mels and C. Timmerman (New York: Routledge, 2013), 180–95; Grace Davie, "Religion in Europe in the 21st Century: The Factors to Take into Account," *European Journal of Sociology* 47 (2006): 271–96.

importance of evangelical social work and the need to create a federative network structure.[23]

The increasing higher education and academic resources of their members have helped evangelical churches to engage in more organized and institutionalized responses to the needs of their community. Evidence of this is the establishment in 2021 of Eunoia, a Christian Evangelical Social Federation, which has since grown to include more than thirty member organizations. A study by the PEA from 2023, entitled "Evangelical Church Up Close," notes the growing involvement of evangelical communities in social intervention, increasingly in an institutionalized context.

Post-COVID-19 Evangelicals: Mobilities and Changes

After COVID-19, we have a new world. This is also true for evangelical churches. Many had to find out quickly how to broadcast services online: how to record and edit, and how to deliver the word of God and worship songs into people's homes while keeping them united in faith. The use of social media, Zoom and other online tools was a challenge for smaller churches, especially those with older congregations. Some even resisted going online, particularly after it became possible to gather in person again. Yet other churches, despite returning to in-person services, continue to stream their Sunday meetings online. This can be beneficial for older people with mobility issues, those temporarily ill, and even those who have emigrated for work and wish to continue attending services in their home country. Streaming is widely reported as a powerful outreach tool.[24] Although numbers are not available, the social networks of various Portuguese evangelical denominations show an exponential increase in videos of services, music, church programme presentations, "activity reports" in video format and youthful creativity.

Another undeniable post-COVID-19 reality in Portugal was the explosive rise in immigration into the country: ". . . in 2018, there were fewer than 480,000 immigrants. By 2022, this number had risen to 800,000 and now exceeds one million. In just five years, Portugal has received more than double

---

23. Pedro Cartaxo, *Evangelical Solidarity Institutions and the Importance of Creating a Federative Network Structure* (Santarém: Institute of Polytechnic of Santarém: School of Management and Technology, 2020).

24. See https://lausanne.org/report/digital-ministry/proclamation-evangelism.

the number of immigrants."[25] Portugal was accustomed to immigrants from countries where Portuguese is the official language, which made integration much easier: Brazil and the Portuguese-speaking African countries Angola and Mozambique, but also Cape Verde, St Tome and Principe and Guinea Bissau. From the 1990s these people were followed by migrants from Eastern European countries, notably Ukraine and Romania, who were well received as cheap labourers. The immigrants concentrated in the major metropolitan areas, in Lisbon, Porto and the Algarve, where there are generally more jobs. In addition, people from South Asia (Nepal, Bangladesh, Pakistan, India . . .) arrived to work in agriculture.

But in the last five years the number of immigrants has more than doubled. They are now spread across the entire country, forever changing cultural, religious, social, linguistic and gastronomic landscapes. Braga, for example, once one of the most Catholic cities in Portugal, is now filled with groups of people from different countries who bring with them religious traditions, attire, customs, habits, music and languages. In the squares, people with diverse features, cuisines and clothing are seen. While this development poses a challenge for society at large, it also does for the church. An additional effort is needed to approach and understand the culture and religion of the others. It is important to recognize that interreligious dialogue is not ecumenism, and without healthy relationships and an understanding of the identity of the other, evangelism will be difficult. Interculturality and interreligious dialogue should, therefore, become mandatory subjects in the theological education of our churches.

The Portuguese church has warmly embraced evangelical brothers and sisters from other cultures. It has become common in the past five years for Portuguese churches to offer their facilities to other communities for their celebrations. For instance, groups of Nepalese, Indians, Ukrainians and Guineans celebrate their evangelical services on Saturdays, while the Portuguese do so on Sundays in the same facilities.

Interreligious Dialogue

The High Commissioner for Migration established the Working Group for Interreligious Dialogue in 2014. The PEA has actively contributed to this dialogue, both through interfaith radio programmes and through the Inter-

---

25. TV channel Sic Notícias, "Number of Immigrants in Portugal Soared in 2023," 27 May 2024, https://sicnoticias.pt/pais/2024-05-27-video-numero-de-imigrantes-em-portugal-disparou-em-2023-mais-de-um-milhao-residiam-no-pais-93dabccf.

religious Working Group on Religion and Health. Although the Law on Religious Freedom dates from 2001, public entities and the general population still require "religious literacy." For example, the Law recognizes chaplaincy services in hospitals and the army, not only from the majority Roman Catholic Church but from all religious confessions, but many on the ground are ignorant or negligent in this respect. For example, evangelical pastors are often denied entry to visit patients in hospitals outside regular visiting hours.

In 2023, the then President of the Assembly of the Republic proposed to the Working Group for Interreligious Dialogue the exhibition "The Paths of Religious Freedom in Portugal," which was indeed displayed in the atrium of the Portuguese House of Democracy for several months and in which the PEA actively collaborated.

In 2024, the 2012 "The Village of Religions" was repeated in Priscos – Braga. Organised by the Catholic Church, it involved various religious confessions, including the PEA, which had the opportunity to perform a concert, offer theatre for children and teenagers, hold devotional moments and host panels on social action and student movements, among other activities.

Internationalization, Interculturalism and Hierarchical Versatility

In the PEA study "The Evangelical Church Up Close" (2023), the increase in the number of different nationalities now comprising our evangelical communities across the country is clearly evident. This international mobility makes it urgent for Portuguese evangelical communities to connect, learn, share and strategically think about international evangelical networks such as the Lausanne Movement (1974) and the Ibero-American Missionary Cooperation (COMIBAM), which emerged in 1987. Due to the availability of the internet, multiple networks have developed that come together online to pray, discuss issues related to Christianity, evangelism and the development of evangelical churches. This is facilitated by the fact that evangelical churches have a relatively fluid hierarchy: membership is more about the involvement and voluntarism exhibited than formal registration, opening doors to a global faith movement.[26] This mobility and the influx of believers from other countries bring with them the need for church leaders to acquire intercultural dialogue and management skills. When the newcomers are integrated into local churches of Portuguese origin, they often wish to participate more actively in decision-making and church management. These multifaceted negotiations of managing places of

---

26. David Martin, *Pentecostalism – The World Their Parish* (London: John Wiley, 2001).

worship require communication skills and flexibility which the older generation of leaders in established churches may not have.

Regarding pastoral vocations, it is surprising how many young people are interested in pursuing a pastoral calling, either full-time or bivocational. In the PEA study "New Generations and Pastoral Ministry," 33 percent of the five hundred and twenty respondents stated that they consider pastoral ministry as a future option. However, thirty-six young people openly mentioned not pursuing this due to lack of support from family, the church and primarily due to financial constraints.

Effective Communication

Queen Esther in the Bible was both courageous and wise. Instead of rushing into the king's presence with the truth about her enemy, she invited the king to a feast, then to a second feast, and only at the right moment did she reveal the truth. The church carries the truth of God. But instead of communicating recklessly and overwhelming others, it must understand the "science of the times" (1 Chr 12:32 KJV), like the tribe of Issachar, and communicate it with wisdom and prudence. Knowing the right opportunities and the appropriate ways to communicate the truth can prevent conflicts, losses, confrontations and unnecessary battles. We must therefore ask the Holy Spirit to teach us where, how, with what, and to whom we communicate. We need to be a church with the "knowledge and understanding in all learning and wisdom" that characterized Daniel and his friends (Dan 1:17 GNV). Even though we live in a culture that seems to drift away from a social fabric that was steeped in the memory of God, it is our duty to seek the peace of the culture where the Lord has placed us and to pray for it to the Lord, for in its peace we will find peace (Jer 29:7, my paraphrase).

An important issue for all evangelicals is the deepening of theological studies, not only for pastors and leaders, but for everyone who wants to serve the church. Not in order to obtain an academic or ecclesiastical title, but to acquire the tools to be able to address today's complex issues, for which the word of God always has an answer, though it may not always be obvious. Those responsible for theological education institutions must continue to work towards increasingly qualifying students and, if possible, coordinating with government institutions to ensure that evangelical theological education is recognized by the state. We urgently need to revive the Christian culture of our country; formally recognized theological education will be a good way to achieve this.

Bibliography

Aliança Evangélica Portuguesa. "Report 2023 – The Evangelical Church in Portugal: A Close Look!" Office of Studies and Research, 6 June 2023. https://aliancaevangelica.pt/site/igreja-evangelica-em-portugal-vista-de-perto/.

Cartaxo, Pedro. *Evangelical Solidarity Institutions and the Importance of Creating a Federative Network Structure*. Instituto Politécnico de Santarém: School of Management and Technology, 2020.

Davie, Grace. "Religion in Europe in the 21st Century: The Factors to Take into Account." *European Journal of Sociology* 47 (2006): 271–96.

Jardim, José Vera. "Portuguese Religious Freedom Law is One of the Most Open in Europe." Pages 67–77 in *The Paths of Religious Freedom in Portugal*. Edited by António Marujo. Lisbon: Assembleia da República, Imagens e Documentos Collection, 2023.

Júnior, Paulo G. "'Jesus Made in Brazil': Notes on the Transnationalization of Brazilian Pentecostalism to Portugal." Dossier: Pentecostalism in Brazil. *Horizonte*, Belo Horizonte, 9, 22 (July/September 2011): 416–445. doi 10.5752/P.2175-5841.2011v9n22p416.

Martin, David. "Voluntarism. Niche Markets Created by a Fissile Transnational Faith." Pages 180–95 in *Religions in Movement: The Local and the Global in Contemporary Faith Traditions*. Edited by R. W. Hefner, J. Hutchinson, S. Mels, and C. Timmerman. New York: Routledge, 2013.

Rocha, Cristina. *Cool Christianity, Hillsong and the Fashioning of Cosmopolitan Identities*. Oxford: Oxford University Press, 2024.

Teixeira, Alfredo (ed.). *Religious Identities and Social Dynamics in the Lisbon Metropolitan Area*. Lisbon: Fundação Francisco Manuel dos Santos, 2019.

Vilaça, Helena. "Religion in the City: Territories, Materialities, and Communication." *Sociologia: Revista da Faculdade de Letras da Universidade do Porto, Thematic Issue - Social Processes and Sociological Issues* (2017): 12–27. https://repositorio-aberto.up.pt/bitstream/10216/108539/2/227646.pdf.

Zurlo, Gina A. *Global Christianity: A Guide to the World's Largest Religion from Afghanistan to Zimbabwe*. Grand Rapids: Zondervan Academic, 2022.

27

Evangelicals in Southern Europe

Sociological Perspectives

Sébastien Fath

Introduction: Out of the Ghetto?

"Make friends, become God's athletes, listen to his Word . . . Become missionary disciples."[1] These are words spoken in Portugal through a video screen by the French international footballer Olivier Giroud, in front of forty thousand young French pilgrims, gathered in Lisbon for the Catholic World Youth Days 2023. Never before had a self-proclaimed evangelical spoken in Portugal to such a young crowd.[2] Does this mean that the evangelical identity in Southern Europe got out of the ghetto to become mainstream? That remains to be seen. It is easy to connect Southern Europe with Christianity in general, "the world's largest religion" and the dominant religion on the northern shore of the Mediterranean Sea.[3] Just as easy as Southern Europe is connected with olive oil or its Roman heritage. Connecting Southern Europe specifically with evangelicalism is much more difficult. For a long time it seemed as if the

---

1. "Faites-vous des amis, devenez des athlètes de Dieu, écoutez sa parole . . . Devenez des disciples missionnaires. Assurez sereinement votre foi en Jésus, prenez Dieu dans votre vie. Invitez-le. Travaillez aussi à l'unité de tous les chrétiens." Olivier Giroud, *World Youth Days*, Lisbon (Portugal), Tuesday 1 August 2023.

2. Olivier Giroud, *Always Believe* (London: Pitch, 2021); French *Toujours y croire* (Paris: Plon, 2020) contains a chapter on his evangelical faith.

3. Gina A. Zurlo, *Global Christianity: A Guide to the World's Largest Religion from Afghanistan to Zimbabwe* (Grand Rapids: Zondervan, 2022).

Southern European "imagined community"[4] could not fit well with Born Again Christianity. However, time is changing and at the moment there are almost four million Southern European evangelicals – if we include France. They contribute to the European narrative of the twenty-first century in creative ways, although discreetly and rarely noticed by the wider public.

In order to study this Christian subculture, let us start with two definitions. How do we define evangelicals? These Christians are part of the large Protestant family, rooted in the time of the Reformation and the Revivals. They are often recognized as "hot prots," which means Protestants with strong convictions and evangelistic zeal. Along with David Bebbington, in his groundbreaking synthesis about Britain, we will recognize them through four characteristics.[5] Although they are challenged by non-historians,[6] these criteria are still useful[7] but they are to be used as Weberian ideal types: they do not work as essences, but as tools. They combine biblicism – the strong, normative authority of the Scriptures; crucicentrism – Christ the only way to salvation; conversionism – no one becomes a Christian by birthright, it is a religious personal choice to commit to Christianity; and activism. This activism of the convert goes through local churches operating as voluntary societies.

How do we define Southern Europe? The main distinctiveness of this part of Europe, apart from being Southern, is that the countries share the Mediterranean shore, either directly or indirectly (like Portugal or Serbia). Three blocks can be distinguished. The first block consists of France, Spain and Portugal with the principalities of Andorra and Monaco. The inclusion of France in this bunch is disputed,[8] but according to its history and geography, including France in Southern Europe does make full sense: the total length of the French Mediterranean coast is 1694km.[9] The second block is Italian speaking and includes Italy, San Marino, the Vatican State and Malta. The third block is

---

4. Cf. Benedict Anderson, *Imagined Communities: Reflections on the origin and spread of nationalism* (London/New York: Verso, 1983).

5. David W. Bebbington, *Evangelicalism in Modern Britain. A History from the 1730s to the 1980s* (London: Unwin Hyman, 1989).

6. Matthew Avery Sutton, "Redefining the History and Historiography on American Evangelicalism in the Era of the Religious Right," *Journal of the American Academy of Religion 2024*, lfae063; https://doi.org/10.1093/jaarel/lfae063.

7. David W. Bebbington, *The Evangelical Quadrilateral. Characterizing the British Gospel Movement* (Baylor: Baylor University Press, 2021).

8. Actually, France may be defined as part of Western and of Southern Europe at the same time.

9. Including Corsica, with 688 km.

the Balkan peninsula, including Albania, Bosnia, Croatia, Greece, Northern Macedonia, Serbia, Slovenia and part of Turkey.

In this European playground, marked by a religious-secular competition,[10] how does the very tiny evangelical minority relate to twenty-first century challenges? Almost ten years after the synthesis provided by Mark Hutchinson, it is time for some fresh reflections.[11] After a discussion of three sociological specifics of the Southern European evangelicals, a contemporary overview of these churches and networks will lead us to three main questions ahead.

The Wider Culture. Three Sociological Specifics

Southern European evangelicals did not fall from heaven. The history, economy, culture and politics of Southern Europe have had a great impact on their identity, distinguishing them from their Western, Eastern and Northern European brothers and sisters. From the wider context, three specifics may be highlighted.

Stigma: A Minority Amidst a Catholic/Orthodox Majority

Since the groundbreaking work of Erwin Goffman, we have known the sociological meaning of stigma.[12] Through words spoken repeatedly, in a social context marked by an imbalance of power, we can inflict a negative reputation on a person or group. It is like an invisible mark, which inflicts an inferiority complex on the dominated group. In all European countries, evangelicals have at one time or another been stigmatized, but this stigmatization has been most pronounced in Southern European countries. The main cause is that Protestantism never developed well in these countries. In Central, Western and Northern Europe, Protestant churches have experienced significant growth since the Reformation, but this was not the case in Italy, Spain, Greece, Serbia or Portugal. France is a semi-exception: Protestantism there developed well in the sixteenth and seventeenth centuries but then came to a terrible halt with the revocation of the Edict of Nantes. The lack of a strong and lasting Protes-

---

10. Jörg Stolz, Judith Könemann et al. (eds), *(Un)Believing in Modern Society. Religion, spirituality, and religious-secular competition* (London: Routledge, 2016).

11. Mark Hutchinson, "Evangelicals in Southern Europe," in Hutchinson et al., *Evangelicals Around the World, A Global Handbook for the 21st Century* (Nashville: Thomas Nelson, 215), 378–84.

12. Erving Goffman, *Stigma: Notes on the Management of Spoiled Identity* (Englewood Cliffs: Prentice-Hall, 1963).

tant presence in Southern Europe has been very detrimental to evangelicals, who are a branch of Protestantism, descended from the Reformation. Protestant counterparts do not always make things easier and it has happened that Reformed Protestants or Lutherans have persecuted certain evangelicals. But in most cases, the proximity of other Protestants was favourable to the evangelicals and allowed them to make themselves better understood. In Southern Europe, the absence of a strong Protestant presence has reinforced the stigma against evangelicals. In these countries, conquering "the right to believe"[13] has been a long, windy, stormy path, navigating between the accusation of being a "cult" and being a separatist threat.[14] These circumstances make it hard for sociologists and researchers to identify them: when asked about their identity, many of them may not reply "evangelical," sometimes for fear of stigma. They may reply "Protestant" or "Christian" in order to avoid being accused of being fringe or members of a cult.

Tradition: A Born-again Culture Facing the Roman Heritage

Another sociological specificity Southern European evangelicals have to face is the particularly heavy weight of tradition. The adage "people don't change their religion" was constantly used against evangelical Protestants in Southern Europe from the eighteenth to the mid-twentieth century. Tradition versus conversion. This phenomenon was not restricted to Southern Europe and can be traced also in other parts of Europe, but its emphasis is particularly strong in the Mediterranean countries due to three causes. The first cause is the dominance of the Catholic (or Orthodox, for Greece) framework. The second cause is the holistic Mediterranean social model in which community traditions are crucial. The third cause goes back to more ancient history: all the countries of Southern Europe were particularly marked by the Roman Empire. This Empire also left its mark on the rest of Europe, but to a lesser extent. The European countries bordering the Mediterranean experienced up to one thousand years of Roman-Latin civilization. One characteristic of this culture was the early appearance of writing. In Sweden, an example from

---

13. Patrick Cabanel, *Le droit de croire. La France et ses minorités religieuses, XVIe-XXIe siècle* (Paris: Passé Composé, 2024).

14. For the Greek case, see Philemon Bantimaroudis, "Media Framing of Religious Minorities in Greece: The Case of the Protestants," *Journal of Media and Religion* 6.3 (2007): 219–35; for the French case, see Nancy Lefevre, "French secularism and the fight against separatism. From the 1905 laïcité of separation to the 2021 laïcité of surveillance," *International Journal for Religious Freedom* 14.1/2 (2021): 69–84.

Northern Europe, the first written sources date from the eighth century AD. By contrast, in Italy – an example from Southern Europe – the first written sources date from the eighth century BC, introduced by Greek settlers. This very old and lasting historical anchoring has given the countries of Southern Europe a somewhat particular relationship to history. More than in Central or Northern Europe, history is an issue. And sometimes, being able to show historical records works as an identity marker in order to be legitimized. For citizens of Southern Europe, being able to identify the history of a group, especially if it is a minority and little known, is essential. This gives Southern European evangelicals a particular responsibility in relation to their history: being able to transmit this history means being able to better identify themselves and to better fit into the Southern European societies that are so fond of history.

Community: A Close-knit Family System

Thanks to demographers, we can identify a third sociocultural characteristic of the Southern European space: the family models that dominate society, nurturing a strong community culture. The French demographer Emmanuel Todd, a specialist in family models in Europe, argues that Southern Europe is much more marked than the rest of Europe by two dominant family models: the egalitarian nuclear family, on the one hand, and the community family, on the other.[15] The root family (French: *famille souche*), which is unequal, is less represented, as is the absolute nuclear family, defined as liberal and indifferent to equality. The two dominant demographic and family models in Southern Europe both emphasize equality. They historically favoured the rise of Communism, which at one point was indeed very strong: first in the Balkan countries, but also in Spain, France and Italy. These family models challenge the liberal model of individuals detached from their community and family ties. They promote social practices of sharing and conviviality. Thus, according to an OECD survey,[16] the French spend, on average, two hours and thirteen minutes eating and speaking around the table every day. By comparison, in Northern Europe, in a country like Sweden, people on average only spend one hour and fourteen minutes per day eating. It is one hour nineteen minutes in the United Kingdom, one hour thirty-five minutes in Germany. This indicator reveals different ways of socializing.

---

15. Emmanuel Todd, *The Explanation of Ideology: Family Structure and Social Systems* (London: Blackwell, 1985); Todd, *L'invention de l'Europe* (Paris: Seuil, 1990).

16. Organization for Economic Cooperation and Development Survey 2016.

Sociologically, Southern Europe tends to favour community and family,[17] which naturally has consequences in terms of evangelical establishment. The individualist model of "giving one's heart to Jesus" is not naturally familiar in societies where collective experience is valued. Yet other evangelical models, the ones which promote community integration, are closer to the demands of Southern Europeans.

Evangelicalism Today: A Fast-Growing Micro-Minority

In comparison to Western and Eastern Europe, there are few evangelicals in Southern Europe. They remain a micro-minority of less than four million worshippers. However, this is a fast-growing micro-minority. We look at the three main areas.

Portuguese, Hispanic and French Speaking Europe: Evangelicals Spreading out of the Ghetto

Portugal, Spain and France have in common that they once had a huge colonial empire. They also share a common Catholic past and a current phase of secularization that is marked by a tremendous decline in religious practice. Evangelicals, however, appear to be a growing minority, spreading out of the ghetto.[18] Around 1.7 percent of this part of Southern Europe may be evangelical in 2024, with a total number of approximatively 2.8 million believers. It was significantly less twenty years ago. Of the three former colonial powers, the evangelicals in Spain seem to be the fastest growing group. In 2023, 4,259 evangelical places of worship were counted in Spain.[19] The 1.4 million Spanish believers, including immigrants from Latin America and a significant Gipsy minority,[20] represent 2.9 percent of the Spanish population of 44 million.

France follows with about 1.2 million evangelical believers, who represent between 1.7 and 1.8 percent of the country's population, and almost 3,000

---

17. Francesc-Xavier Medina, "Looking for Commensality: On Culture, Health, Heritage, and the Mediterranean Diet," *International Journal of Environmental Research and Public Health*, 5 March; 18(5): 2605 [2-021]; doi 10.3390/ijerph18052605.

18. Sebastien Fath, "Evangelical Protestantism in France: An Example of Denominational Recomposition?," *Sociology of Religion* 66.4 (2005): 399–418.

19. David Goodwin, "Evangelical Christian Numbers on the Rise in Spain," *Christian Today*, 20 September 2023, www.christiantoday.com/article/evangelical.christian.numbers.on.the.rise.in.spain/140777.htm.

20. Manuela Cantoó-Delgado, ed., *Evangelical Gypsies in Spain, "The Bible is our Promised land"* (Lanham: Lexington, 2020).

places of worship, including several megachurches. To give a comparison, around 1950 only fifty thousand evangelicals could be counted in France. Within a strong secularist framework,[21] the French evangelicals appear to be the strongest example of religious re-composition: from identity by tradition – which is in dramatic decline – to identity by conversion. They probably share their growth rate with Islam; it is boosted by a particularly robust Pentecostal branch.[22]

Last but not least, after a difficult time in the first decade of the twenty-first century the Portuguese evangelicals are facing a very significant growth, boosted by many Brazilian immigrants. According to the last census, one hundred and eighty-seven thousand evangelicals could be counted in the country, representing 2.1 percent of the population and an estimate of thirteen hundred worship places.[23]

In these three countries the solid growth "out of the ghetto" seems largely to consist of two groups: a flux of former Catholics, joining evangelical circles more and more, and a flux from former colonies.

Balkan Europe: Challenges for a First-Generation Evangelical Movement

With Albania, Bosnia, Croatia, Greece, Northern Macedonia, Serbia, Slovenia and a part of Turkey, Balkan Europe presents a very different picture. In this part of Southern Europe, often marked by the weight of Orthodox churches, only a maximum of 0.4 percent of the population may be identified as evangelical. The qualification "micro-minority" applies to the full. Of the one hundred and fifty thousand evangelicals who live in Balkan Europe, around eighty thousand believers are in Serbia, many of them connected to wider networks,[24] forty thousand – maybe more – in Greece, eighteen thousand in Croatia, where a new society of theologians was created in 2018,[25] and eight thousand in Northern Macedonia. In most of these countries, pluralistic culture and democratic

---

21. Philippe Portier and Jean-Paul Willaime, *Religion and Secularism in France Today* (Abingdon: Routledge, 2022).

22. Alexandre Antoine, "Une socio-histoire des Assemblées de Dieu en France (1909–1968). Naissance et développement d'un mouvement pentecôtiste de Réveil" (PhD diss., Ecole Pratique des Hautes Études Paris, 2022).

23. Portuguese census, 2021.

24. Aleksandra Djurić Milovanović and Mirolad Djurić, "Transnational Evangelical Networks in Serbia and their Influence on Interethnic Relations," *Berkley Center for Religion, Peace and World Affairs*, Working paper July 2023.

25. Stanko Jambrek, "The founding of the Evangelical Theological Association of Croatia," *Kairos, Evangelical Journal of Theology* 16.2 (2022): 135–43.

practice have not been around for very long. The evangelicals in the Balkans are used to being seen as a cult, almost strangers in their own country.

However, things have been changing since the massive transformations that followed the collapse of the Soviet Union and its satellites. The growing influence of the European Union and its emphasis on freedom, democracy and pluralism is also part of an opening process. In twenty-first century Balkan Europe there is probably more space than ever before for evangelical witness. In September 2022, Evi Rodemann, chair of groups and gatherings for the Lausanne Younger Leaders Generation and director of the *LeadNow* ministry, released a report on a Balkan tour from 23 July to 12 August 2022. Here is an abstract:

> The team was struck by the resilience and faithfulness of the Balkan Christian leaders. Evangelical Christians in the Balkan region are primarily first-generation and many of the churches the team visited are the first evangelical church plants in the country, where growth has been very slow.[26]

The report mentions Kosovo, among other places: only 24 evangelical churches were counted in this country, 80 percent of which without any children's or youth ministry. With its mostly first generation, micro-minority of evangelicals, the Balkan part of Europe is one of the most challenging mission fields for twenty-first century European evangelicals.

Italian-Speaking Europe: Overcoming Isolation and Gated Identity

Last but not least, 1.2 percent of Italian-speaking Europe may be considered as evangelical, with Italy hosting roughly 1.3 percent of evangelicals, which amounts to eight hundred and thirty thousand evangelicals in 2024. In Malta, 4,516 Protestants were recorded in 2021, including a majority of evangelicals.[27] This part of Southern Europe seems to be half-way between the two other areas. The evangelical constituency is less significant than in Spain, Portugal or France, but the Italian-speaking evangelicals do not share the micro-minority status of their Balkan brothers and sisters.

---

26. Micaela Braithwaite, "A Journey of Encouragement through the Balkans. Traveling by caravan to encourage younger leaders," 26 September 2022, published on the Lausanne Movement website, https://lausanne.org/about/blog/a-journey-of-encouragement-through-the-balkans.

27. Malta census 2021. Not all people of Malta speak Italian, but a large majority do.

The Italian evangelicals are sustained by old revivalist branches like the Waldensian Evangelical Church, which was founded in the twelfth century and joined the Reformation in the sixteenth century, and by the Baptists, who started to form local churches in the 1860s. Since the beginning of the twentieth century they have also been strongly reinforced by a powerful Pentecostal revival[28] and much later by prophetic and charismatic churches boosted by immigration, like the Nigerian variety, studied by Annalisa Butticci.[29] In a very strong Catholic culture, the Italian-speaking evangelicals struggle to overcome isolation.[30] While some live in a kind of gated identity, including the many Nigerian believers who have a hard time connecting with existing Italian Christian networks, others engage in the national debate, like pastor Leonardo De Chirico (Breccia di Roma). In an interview in 2015, he said: "There's also a growing desire to see a shift from the survival mentality of the past to a missional mindset." De Chirico then quotes his colleague Pietro Bolognesi (*Istituto di Formazione Evangelica e Documentazione*) as saying, "We have three main challenges: (1) identity, (2) unity, and (3) training."[31]

Three Specific Challenges Ahead

The desire for unity expressed by Pietro Bolognesi does not only reflect an Italian concern. Among the challenges facing contemporary Southern European evangelicals, connecting and networking is certainly not the least.

Networking: Being Heard in Spite of Neo-Nationalism

Since the middle of the 2010s, Europeans are facing the rise of nativist populism.[32] In Italy, Georgia Meloni, serving as Prime Minister since October 2022, is leading the Brothers of Italy (Fratelli d'Italia), a nationalist conservative radical right-wing political movement. Another example is found with France, where the National Gathering (RN, "rassemblement national"), an extreme

---

28. Carmine Napolitano, *I Pentecostali in Italia* (Torino: Claudiana, 2021).

29. Annalisa Butticci, *African Pentecostals in Catholic Europe. The Politics of Presence in the Twenty-First Century* (Cambridge: Harvard University Press, 2016).

30. Kevin Madigan, *The Popes against the Protestants: the Vatican and Evangelical Christianity in Fascist Italy* (New Haven: Yale University Press, 2021).

31. Leonardo De Chirico interviewed by Ivan Mesa, "The Gospel in Italy," 25 November 2015, TGC US edition website, www.thegospelcoalition.org/article/the-gospel-in-italy.

32. Eirikur Bergmann, *Neo-Nationalism. The Rise of Nativist Populism* (Cham: Springer, 2020), 1–28.

right-wing movement, won the last European elections, with 31.37 percent of voters in favour of Jordan Bardella, the RN candidate. This conservative and neo-nationalistic movement had double the share of the vote of the candidate of the president's party, Valérie Hayer.

As evangelicals do not appear to be "traditional Christians" in the Southern nations of Europe, the rise of neo-nationalism is bad news for them. From the perspective of national tradition, they may be seen as a foreign threat and be silenced. For the scattered and tiny Southern European evangelical denominations and groups, networking is all the more needed. In Spain, the Federation of Evangelical Religious Entities of Spain, created in 1956, gained weight and influence since the beginning of the twenty-first century. In France, the National Council of French Evangelicals (*Conseil National des Evangéliques de France*), formally created in 2010, has to a certain extent succeeded in uniting a majority of French evangelicals and building bridges.[33] Many other Southern European countries have not yet managed to build such a representative body, although many federations and associations are slowly developing. One of the most successful networking efforts since the start of the new century in the field of media is, without doubt, the creation of *Evangelical Focus Europe*. Born in 2003 from a Spanish initiative, *Evangelical Focus* defines itself as a "news website with a Christian perspective on current issues in Europe." Its aim is to "build bridges between evangelical churches and all of society."[34] Providing a rich amount of content every day, Spanish-based *Evangelical Focus* is one of the best achievements of the networking and unifying effort undertaken by Southern European evangelicals.

Welcoming: Through Local Churches, Opening Arms to Newcomers from the Global South

As a result of their colonial history, Portugal, Spain and France share a common Southern European openness toward specific countries located in the so-called Global South. And because of its geography, Southern Europe as a whole is obviously the closest territory to be reached by migrants coming from the southside of the Mediterranean Sea. A strong flux of population and networks

---

33. Stéphane Lauzet, *Bâtir des ponts. Regards sur l'origine du CNEF (1995–2010)* (Charols: Excelsis, 2024).

34. "The project," *Evangelical Focus Europe*, https://evangelicalfocus.com/about-us.

link African countries and their postcolonial churches[35] with Mediterranean Europe.[36] Does immigration lead to a "changing soul of Europe"?[37] It leads at least to "new Christian geographies"[38] and it poses challenges to existing Southern European churches and networks. At a global level, the European Evangelical Alliance appears to be fully aware of the challenges and undertook many initiatives, like the "Refugee Campaign." Welcoming instead of rejecting is the main goal, addressing the politics of fear: "Together we can speak out, learn and make a difference. The Hope for Europe Refugee Campaign aims to combine Christians, churches, member- and specialist organizations to be the response to the asylum crisis in Europe."[39] In many transit areas like Greece,[40] the "moving faith" of immigrants fleeing poverty, hunger and civil war represents a challenge. In the responses of local churches we see two scenarios, depending on the context: either an increased diversity in the local churches, which operate as a melting-pot or a blended family. This diversity may be observed, for example, at the *Iglèsia Internacional de Barcelona* (International Church of Barcelona), a multicultural charismatic church located in the heart of the Catalan capital. The other scenario is that of separate growth of immigrant evangelical churches, with little or no contact between them and existing Southern European congregations. This may be the case of hundreds of Nigerian evangelical churches in Italy.

Inspiring: Raising Hope in the Continent with the Lowest Birth Rate

A current challenge for Southern European evangelicals is to raise hope in the continent with the lowest birth rate. To give a striking example, the tourist image of the "Italian mama" surrounded by a dozen children does not reflect the actual Italian birthrate, which has dropped to an alarming 1.2 percent

---

35. Sébastien Fath and Cédric Mayrargue, "New Christianities in Africa," *Afrique Contemporaine* 252.4 (2014): 13–26.

36. This applies also, at a slightly lesser extent, to South American countries.

37. Inger Furseth et al., *The Changing Soul of Europe: Religions and Migrations in Northern and Southern Europe* (London: Routledge, 2014).

38. Mar Griera, "New Christian Geographies: Pentecostalism and Ethnic Minorities in Barcelona," in *Sites and Politics of Religious Diversity in Southern Europe,* ed. Ruy Blanes and José Mapril (Leiden: Brill, 2013), 225–49.

39. "We believe that hope overcomes fear," European Evangelical Alliance, www.europeanea.org/the-refugee-campaign.

40. Darren Carlson, *Christianity and Conversion among Migrants. Moving Faith and Faith Movement in a Transit Area* (Leiden: Brill, 2021).

in 2023.⁴¹ In that same year, the Spanish birth rate hit its lowest level (1.19 percent) since records began in 1941; it dropped almost 25 percent in the last decade.⁴² It appears that the fabric of hope has disappeared from society. Sociologically, hope is related to the capacity to believe and invest in a better future.⁴³ Instead of doom and gloom, Southern European evangelicals could be presented as "hope factories" which relocalize the Good News. But are they *tangibly* relocalizing hope? The significant growth they are experiencing in some Southern European countries (Spain, Portugal, France) may lead, at least in some cases, to a positive answer, although the reasons behind the growth are diverse and not always easy to interpret.⁴⁴ Between tradition and emotion,⁴⁵ roots and wings, nationalism and Christian internationalism, Southern European evangelicals are at the crossroads.

Conclusion in Three Words: Exit, Voice or Loyalty

In a rapidly secularizing Southern Europe, torn between the politics of fear and the multiple offers of a free spiritual market, evangelical believers are facing the classic sociological options of exit, voice and loyalty.⁴⁶ Exit? Leaving the evangelical label is an option, following many Gen Z Christians on the other side of the Atlantic. A choice for "voice" means challenging evangelical networks and churches from within, with the help of many determined evangelical women around the Mediterranean Sea⁴⁷ and a willingness to hear the

---

41. Giorgia Orlandi, "Italy's falling birth rate is a crisis that's only getting worse," *Euronews* 10 May 2024, www.euronews.com/my-europe/2024/05/10/italys-falling-birth-rate-is-a-crisis-thats-only-getting-worse.

42. "Spanish birth rate hits lowest level since records began in 1941," Reuters, 21 February 2024, www.reuters.com/world/europe/spanish-birth-rate-hits-lowest-level-since-records-began-1941-2024-02-21.

43. Adrian Scribano, "The Sociology of Hope: Classical Sources, Structural Components, Future Agenda," *Society* 61 (2024): 1–8, https://doi.org/10.1007/s12115-023-00888-z.

44. At least three interpretations are competing: evangelical growth may be mainly due to a recycling of disappointed Catholics, tired of a vertical institution too hard to reform; or it may first be related to immigration coming from less secularized countries; or it is due to the need of a very secularized youth to find meaning and a safe, close-knit community.

45. Jean-Pierre Bastian, ed., *La recomposition des protestantismes en Europe latine. Entre émotion et tradition* (Geneva: Labor & Fides, 2004).

46. Albert Hirschman, *Exit, Voice, and Loyalty. Responses to Decline in Firms, Organizations, and States* (Cambridge: Harvard University Press, 1970).

47. Like Valérie Duval-Poujol in France (vice-president of the French Protestant Federation since 2018) or Carolina Bueno, who in 2022 became the first woman to lead the FEDERE (Evangelical Federation of Spain).

"muted voices."[48] A choice for loyalty may either mean an obedient passivity or an unflinching and creative faithfulness to the core of the gospel, promoting bloom instead of doom.

Bibliography

Bantimaroudis, Philemon. "Media Framing of Religious Minorities in Greece: The Case of the Protestants." *Journal of Media and Religion* 6.3 (2007): 219–35.

Fath, Sébastien. *Du ghetto au réseau, Le protestantisme évangélique en France (1800–2005)*. Geneva: Labor & Fides, 2005, new ed. 2018.

Furseth, Inger, Enzo Pace, Helena Vilaça and Per Pettersson, eds. *The Changing Soul of Europe: Religions and Migrations in Northern and Southern Europe*. London: Routledge, 2014.

Hutchinson, Mark, Todd M. Johnson, Brian C. Stiller and Karen Stiller, eds. *Evangelicals Around the World, A Global Handbook for the 21st Century*. Nashville: Thomas Nelson, 2015.

———. "Evangelicals in Southern Europe." Pages 378–94 in Hutchinson et al., *Evangelicals around the World, A Global Handbook for the 21st Century*. Nashville: Thomas Nelson, 2015.

Jambrek, Stanko. "Guidelines for the Future of Evangelical Christianity in Croatia." *Kairos: Evangelical Journal of Theology* 16.2 (2022): 111–42.

Kay, William K., and Anne Dyer, eds. *European Pentecostalism*. Leiden: Brill, 2011.

McLane, Merrill F. "Evangelicalism Among the Spanish Gypsies." *Journal of the Gypsy Lore Society* 4.2 (1994): 111–17.

Oro, Ari Pedro. "South American Evangelicals' Re-conquest of Europe." *Journal of Contemporary Religion* 29.2 (2014): 219–32.

Rodrigues, Donizete. "Ethnic and Religious Diversities in Portugal: The Case of Brazilian Evangelical Immigrants." Pages 133–48 in *The Changing Soul of Europe: Religions and Migrations in Northern and Southern Europe*. Edited by Furseth et al. London: Routledge, 2014.

---

48. Jim Memory, "Hearing the 'muted voices' at Lausanne Europe 20/21," *Vista 40, Networks, Lausanne Europe*, 30 January 2022, https://vistajournal.online/latest-articles/lausanne-europe-2021.

28

Evangelicalism in Northern Europe, Especially in Sweden

A Sociological Perspective

Per Ewert

Introduction

This chapter investigates the sociological position of evangelical Christians in northern Europe. Because Sweden stands out both globally and within this region, and because my own research has focused on this country, Sweden will be used as this chapter's prime example to illustrate the sociological aspects of evangelical Christianity in northern Europe. As Sweden captures several cultural patterns that appear in the whole Western world, it is also a useful model for understanding larger European patterns. Values that appear in the whole Western world are also found in the Nordic countries, only stronger. Values appearing in the Nordic countries appear even stronger in Sweden. Sweden and Northern Europe are thus exceptionally strong examples of the value changes that are taking place on the European continent and the English-speaking world.

The Nordic countries find themselves in a remote corner in the Inglehart-Welzel map of world values. Sweden, Norway and Denmark have the most secular-individualistic values in the world, with Finland and Iceland lagging only slightly behind. These countries are also part of the larger circle of Protestant Europe, with a stronger combination of self-expression- and secularism-

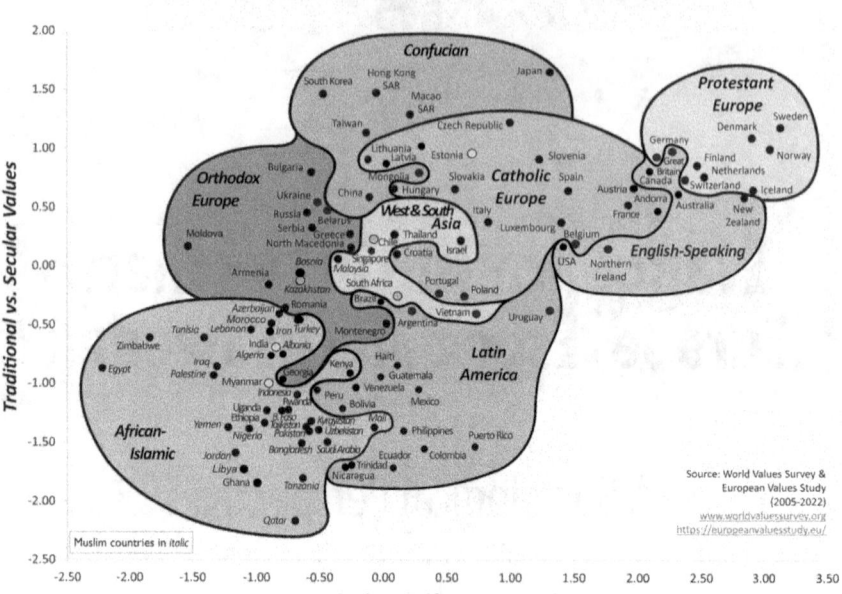

oriented values than any other religious-cultural clusters around the globe, with Sweden in pole position.

When Gallup asked in 2009, "Is religion an important part of your daily life?," Swedish and Danish citizens were among the top three nationalities which answered the question in the negative.[1] The share of the Swedish population that regards religion primarily as a negative societal force is also considerably higher than in other Western democracies.[2] Accordingly, Sweden displays a higher degree of individualistic values and opposition towards authority than any other Western nation.[3]

This pattern raises the historical question how this particular value-culture was shaped. Apparently, there are factors within Protestantism which make people incline towards expanding the personal focus of the faith towards putting the individual at the centre of everything. These factors appear to be

---

1. Steve Crabtree, "Religiosity Highest in World's Poorest Nations" (2010), https://news.gallup.com/poll/142727/religiosity-highest-world-poorest-nations.aspx.

2. "Is Religion A Force For Good In The World? Combined Population of 23 Major Nations Evenly Divided in Advance of Blair, Hitchens Debate" (Ipsos Reid, 2010), www.ipsos.com/sites/default/files/news_and_polls/2010-11/5058.pdf.

3. "World Values Survey and European Values Study joint survey round (2017-2020)," www.worldvaluessurvey.org/WVSEVSjoint2017.jsp, Q17.

prevalent in the Nordic countries, which for half a millennium had Lutheran state churches. There are also nation-specific reasons why the Nordic countries still took somewhat differing routes.[4]

This pattern also raises the question how secularized the Nordic countries are at present and what role evangelical Christianity still has in these countries. A first answer is that even though these nations share a largely similar heritage and culture, the situation still differs considerably between them. Iceland is geographically and culturally remote. Finland stands out because the religious sociology follows language lines more than elsewhere, with Swedish-speaking congregations separating from the majority Finnish-speaking population, and Orthodox groups present in the eastern, Russian-speaking parts.

The evangelical movement in Sweden and Norway is larger than in Denmark.[5] In Norway and Denmark, many of the evangelical revival movements arose within the Lutheran state church. Such movements occurred also in Sweden, but from the mid-1800s the revival movement in Sweden organized itself into free denominations. The pattern in Denmark and Norway may be described as elliptic: evangelical church members live their Christian lives both in the larger former state churches and in their local prayer houses or mission houses. Another Danish particularity is that the self-perception of the Danish Lutheran Church is that it is not a state church, but a "church of the people" (*folkekirke*), which is a very important part of their identity. This has created an "anarchic" dimension in the system since the 1800s, which gives biblically conservative movements extensive freedom within the state church. A practical consequence of this is that when same-sex marriage was introduced in Denmark, local Lutheran ministers were given the legal right not to take part.[6] Another consequence is that congregations have the right to choose an evangelical minister.

---

4. In my doctoral dissertation I investigated how Sweden's highly influential Social Democratic Party actively pushed the nation in a secular-individualistic direction; see Per Ewert, "Moving reality closer to the ideal: The process towards autonomy and secularism during the Social Democratic hegemony in 20th century Sweden" (VID Specialised University, 2022), https://vid.brage.unit.no/vid-xmlui/handle/11250/3039121.

5. The evangelical free churches in Denmark, including the Pentecostals, only have between three thousand and five thousand members. *Religion i Danmark* Aarhus University (2020), 8–10.

6. If the pastor refuses to perform the ritual, however, the bishop is obliged to refer the couple to another pastor who is willing to officiate. The free churches, Jews, Muslims and others have the option not to offer marriage rituals to couples of the same sex.

Evangelicalism among Individuals and Churches in Sweden

The secularization has strongly affected religious life in Sweden.[7] Church service attendance shrunk from 11 to 9 percent from 1988 to 2019, the last year before the pandemic, and during the same period the number of those who pray regularly decreased from 19 percent to 15.[8] However, the changes are not the same in each denomination. The politicized and theologically liberal Church of Sweden suffered the most serious losses. Between 1990 and the present, the attendance at its Sunday services shows a more or less straight downward line: from nine million to 2.5 million. The number will be zero sometime during the 2030s if nothing breaks the curve.[9]

Meanwhile, other denominations have also shrunk, but very unevenly. The evangelicals, understood as groups with a high view of the Bible, in fact increased in number. During the 2000s, the liberal denominations suffered the largest losses, while the Pentecostals grew slightly. When we compare different branches of free churches, the pattern becomes even clearer. Between 2000 and 2020, the number of congregations in the traditional free churches fell from 2,274 to 1,552, and those within the Lutheran church family fell from 571 to 358. But during the same period the number of non-denominational churches grew from 80 to 319. Many of the latter are new migrant churches, which typically have a strong evangelical and charismatic identity. While the total membership of the free churches declined during the 2000s, the share of the non-denominational churches grew from 1.4 to 6.6 percent of the total members.[10]

Magdalena Nordin and Torbjörn Aronson confirm a similar development for the period between 1980 and 2020. In the Stockholm region the number of local congregations actually increased by 40 percent, but the growth is spread very unevenly over the denominations. The number of Catholic and Orthodox churches grew, largely due to immigration; the older liberal Swedish denominations saw their number of congregations shrink, while evangelical churches

---

7. Some research separates between denominations and theological positions, but the largest repeated studies on values, habits and individual religiosity do not separate between denominations or even religions.

8. SOM-institutet, Gothenburg University, "Svenska trender 1986–2023" (2024), www.gu.se/sites/default/files/2024-04/Svenska%20trender%201986-2023_0.pdf.

9. Svenska kyrkan, "Svenska kyrkan i siffror" (2024), www.svenskakyrkan.se/statistik.

10. Øyvind Tholvsen, *Frikyrkoundersökningen: En rapport om frikyrkornas utveckling i Sverige 2000-2020*, Sveriges frikyrkosamråd (2021), https://vidare.nu/wp-content/uploads/2021/06/frikyrkoundersokningen-2021.pdf.

increased in number, with the fastest growth among Pentecostal churches – especially migrant ones, as can be seen in this table:[11]

Change in number of local churches in the Stockholm region 1980–2020 (Nordin/Aronson)

	1980	2020	Change in number of churches	Change in %
Church of Sweden	145	98	–47	–32
Older free churches[12]	147	94	–53	–36
International Protestant[13]	13	19	6	46
Classical Pentecostal	21	36	15	71
International Pentecostal	0	83	83	—
Other Pentecostal	12	37	25	200
Catholic	5	23	18	360
Orthodox	12	49	37	300

In another study Aronson has shown that this pattern also applies to the rest of the country. Here too, the trend towards internationalization is clear: among the 427 new congregations that were launched between 1974 and 2020 and still remain, over half were started by immigrants, typically with a conservative view on the Bible.[14] This is one of the most interesting religio-sociological trends of the last decades.

The denominational dividing lines are, however, not as clear today as they were half a century ago. Back then, the separation between evangelical and liberal groups was quite clear and roughly coincided with the separation between denominations. Nowadays this pattern has changed, not least in Sweden, as a reflection of the larger culture war in the West. On one hand, the secular-individualistic trend built around individual autonomy continues to strive for

---

11. Magdalena Nordin and Torbjörn Aronson, "A New Ecclesial Landscape: Changes in numbers of churches and international pentecostalism in Stockholm 1980–2020," *PentecoStudies* 22.1 (2023), 14–37, https://doi.org/10.1558/pent.26644.

12. That is, denominations stemming from the nineteenth-century revival movements, such as free Lutheran groups, Baptists and the Salvation Army.

13. That is, Swedish branches of European Protestant churches dating back to the eighteenth century, but also modern congregations with mother churches in the USA.

14. Torbjörn Aronson, "Tillväxten av nya pentekostala församlingar i Sverige 1974–2020," in *Pentekostalismen i Sverige på 2020-talet*, ed. Jan-Åke Alvarsson (Forskningsrapporter från Institutet för Pentekostala Studier; Skellefteå: Artos, 2021), 50.

cultural hegemony, with several Christian denominations, congregations and individuals having taken a liberal turn. On the other hand, we see a backlash, both inside and outside of church, against the progressive culture and its consequences. These two trends appear side by side, both in the whole West and in the Nordic countries. It becomes visible when evangelical groups take a public stand, but also in the general culture, where the progressive side has prevailed on several fronts in the culture war, but where a conservative counterreaction appears. There are signs in churches which point in the same direction. A Finnish study indicates that church attendance, personal prayer and belief in God has almost doubled during the 2000s among young men in Finland.[15] In Norway, the charismatic and evangelical free churches are drawing more young participants, and membership in the denominations outside the former state church rose by 10 percent between 2017 and 2023.[16] However, it may be too early to draw certain conclusions from these findings.

As the cultural divide shakes up society, it also goes straight through denominations, where some congregations and individual members lean towards a liberal view, and others within the same denomination towards a conservative view. This pattern of conflict appears within the historical churches, the liberal denominations, as well as within those that have traditionally viewed themselves as evangelical. As things stand at the moment, though, the growth among those parts of Christianity that hold on to a biblical foundation and a charismatic church life appears to compensate for the falling membership numbers elsewhere. However, the branches of the Protestant church tree are currently growing in and out of each other, and future denominational patterns appear uncertain.

Evangelical Visibility in Public Life

Despite Sweden's strongly secular culture – or possibly due to it – the evangelical movement has become remarkably visible during the 2000s, both in the sphere of the media, in the political debate and in education. There are now several Christian newspapers, of which two function as dailies. There are also at least four different TV stations that produce and broadcast evangelical TV

---

15. Santero Marjokorpi, "Against the odds, Finnish researchers find an increase in religiosity among young Finnish men," *Evangelical Focus*, 18 January 2024, https://evangelicalfocus.com/europe/25092/against-the-odds-researchers-find-an-increase-in-religiosity-among-young-finnish-men.

16. Ronnie Baraldsnes, "Ny vekkelsesbølge: Unge strømmer til frimenighetene," TV2, 18 November 2024, www.tv2.no/nyheter/innenriks/unge-strommer-til-frimenighetene/17102200/.

for a Swedish audience, while other evangelicals produce much-watched programmes for YouTube and other internet sites. One Swedish station, Himlen TV7, also has a strong position in Finland. In Norway, several Christian TV stations produce and broadcast via a satellite and so reach the general population.

In Sweden, thinktanks such as the Evangelical Alliance, the Clapham Institute, the apologetically focused Apologia and others are actively promoting evangelical views among the general public as well as in the church arena, sometimes in open contrast to the liberal strands of Christianity. The Swedish Evangelical Alliance is the formal representative of the Lausanne Movement and the other groups can be defined as more informal representatives of the ideas behind the Lausanne Covenant.

This said, it is often still challenging for Bible-believing Christians to get access to popular media. Most of the leading media outlets prefer more liberal Christians and act as gatekeepers against the presence of evangelicals in popular media. On the other hand, a conservative counterreaction is apparent against the ultra-progressive dominance in society. Which of these two trends will prevail in the long run is still an open question.

In politics, evangelical Christians who have achieved high political offices have regularly met harsh criticism. When Sweden's present-day minister of finance was appointed as minister for the first time, almost all questions asked were about her previous participation in evangelical circles, and the way for her to survive politically appeared to be to distance herself from this background. The present second deputy speaker of the Swedish parliament also met harsh criticism at her election.

In the judicial system, the prime examples of the conflict between the evangelical and the secular mindset have centred around the question of public expressions of a biblical position. After the Swedish anti-discrimination law was extended in 2003, the Pentecostal pastor Åke Green was sentenced to a month in prison for delivering a sermon on homosexuality. He was, however, later acquitted in all courts including the Swedish Supreme Court. As his case concerned a decisive ruling about the limits of freedom of religion and expression, the Supreme Court hearing was transmitted through national television – still a unique occasion in Swedish court history.

In 2022, the Finnish former minister of interior affairs and MP for the Christian Democrats, Päivi Räsänen, was also put on trial for expressing a biblical position on these matters. Both Green and Räsänen have also faced severe antipathy in secular media, while several Christian leaders have been hesitant to show their support. Räsänen was acquitted in two trials and is at the time of writing facing the final verdict of the Finnish Supreme Court.

These two examples illustrate that there is strong judicial support for a biblical view in the largest area of conflict in our time, but that the media and public prosecutors are still quite willing to put biblical views on trial.

In the area of education, Sweden made a secular and individualistic move during the 1960s. However, in the 1990s the first government in which Christian Democrats participated counter-reacted by introducing a national curriculum which applies until the present day and which states that Swedish schools shall be based on an ethic based on "Christian tradition and Western humanism." Nonetheless, research shows that due to the more secular tone of textbooks, teacher training colleges and the general culture, Swedish schools still have a negative attitude towards religion in general and Christianity in particular.[17]

The Nordic countries have systems for free schools which allows for the existence of confessional schools. In Sweden, a large wave of new schools was opened during the term in office of the above-mentioned government during the 1990s. Today, some sixty confessional schools exist, of which the vast majority are Christian, mainly evangelical. Finland has seventeen Christian schools. However, both in Sweden and the other countries there is pressure from the state to separate education and confession.[18]

Nonetheless, in the academy the Nordic countries allow the formation of Christian institutions for higher education whose funding is covered by the state. Some of these institutions stand on an evangelical foundation[19] but several have moved in a liberal direction,[20] which illustrates the challenge of cooperating closely with a secular political system.

Similar challenges are evident in the Swedish Agency for Support to Faith Communities. This support system was introduced in 1980 with the objective to create more equal opportunities between the state church and the free churches. With the help of increased financial resources, several denominations

---

17. Karin Kittelmann Flensner, "Religious Education in Contemporary Pluralistic Sweden" (Doctoral dissertation Göteborg University, 2015).

18. Lennart Nijenhuis, "Why Danish Christian teachers feel priviliged," *CNE News* 7 June 2024, https://cne.news/article/4301-why-danish-christian-teachers-feel-privileged; Evert van Vlastuin, "Christian school on the tightrope along the Gulf of Bothnia," *CNE News* 31 May 2024, https://cne.news/article/4276-christian-school-on-a-tightrope-along-the-gulf-of-bothnia.

19. E.g. the Lutheran institution Johannelund and the small charismatic Scandinavian School of Theology.

20. This particularly applies to University College Stockholm, the theological institution of the liberal free churches, while the counterpart of the more conservative denominations, the Academy for Leadership and Theology, struggles to maintain an evangelical direction in a secular environment.

enlarged their central administrative offices. This development has affected the identity of the denominations concerned as they followed the international trend that denominations gradually centralize, changing from "sect-like" to "church-like" and thereby also sliding from evangelical to more liberal positions.[21]

The Current Evangelical-Liberal Divide

The main divide across the whole Protestant world can be described as a split between evangelical Christianity, with Scripture as the final authority, and a liberal understanding which leans towards contextualizing the faith in accordance with the surrounding culture. In Northern Europe this divide has widened during the last few decades. The main change of position did not occur within evangelicalism but in the liberal-leaning groups which have moved even further towards an inner-worldly or secular position. This tension has been present as long as Christianity has existed. The increasing secularism of the last century has, however, widened the gap between biblical and secular, autonomous values. This period in history has thus increased the incentives for Christians to gradually adapt to the general culture.

Although the distinction between conservative and liberal groups is typically based on their differing views of the Bible, it often finds expression through specific contested issues. In the twenty-first century there is little doubt that the issue of relations, sexuality and marriage has become the watershed for this divide. Until recently, the entire Christian world was united in the view that human sexuality should be restricted to the monogamous, lifelong marriage between one man and one woman. Among theologically liberal denominations this view was gradually abandoned around the time of the sexual revolution. The first change concerned attitudes towards heterosexual relationships, with divorce becoming acceptable, but when homosexuality became increasingly accepted among the secular population around the turn of the millennium, liberal-minded groups within Christianity followed suit. The divide increased as states began to redefine marriage, making it even more difficult for Christian denominations to limit the conflict.

In our time a new feature within Protestant Christianity is that this ethical divide often runs right through denominations, rather than between them. This

---

21. The word "sect" here is used in an academic sense, signifying a Christian movement in a phase with a strong personal conviction and evangelistic focus, where congregations view themselves in opposition to secular culture and church establishment.

has led to Methodist and Baptist denominations splitting in many countries due to irreconcilable differences which ultimately rest on the question whether to be theocentric or humanist.[22] I see historical parallels between the current denominational reorganization and the rise of the Pentecostal movement in the early 1900s, when some groups within the established churches adopted this revival while others did not. As a result, some congregations remained in their denominations while others left. Similar divides also appeared within local congregations, where some members left for the new Pentecostal congregations while others remained. The current division over issued related to sexuality does not rest on people's individual experiences of the Holy Spirit but on a deep disagreement over sources of authority. This division appears hard to reconcile and it is therefore reasonable to expect that Protestant Christianity is facing a period of considerable restructuring, also in the Nordic countries.

A different contemporary division is the one that has arisen among various non-denominational organizations that are involved in missionary work. The Swedish Missions Council had gradually adopted an inner-worldly understanding of missionary work. As a reaction to this, in 2021 six organizations which explicitly adhere to the Lausanne Covenant formed the Swedish Evangelical Mission Alliance for missionary work both inside and outside Sweden.

A third area where denominational differences are considerable is that of membership. The Swedish free churches peaked in membership around 1950, at a time when the older, more liberal denominations in Sweden had already been following the international pattern of steady decline for some decades. In 2013 the two small denominations of Baptists and Methodists merged with the larger Swedish Mission Church to create the new Equmenia Church, which typically aligns itself with theological liberalism and has a continually negative membership curve. Among the free churches, only the Pentecostals are growing in Sweden, and mainly through the formation of migrant churches.

It may be repeated that, as we saw at the outset, on the values scale the Nordic countries are situated in the periphery of the world. The external pressure on Christian churches – including evangelical ones – has also been stronger in the Nordic countries than elsewhere, as is evident from the World Values Chart above which illustrates the very secular-individualistic culture in this region. Within evangelicalism these pressures have caused internal tensions between what may be called conservative evangelicals and progressive

---

22. The best-known example is the separation of the Methodists in the United Methodist Church and the Global Methodist Church.

evangelicals, with the positions of the latter group tending towards what has traditionally been called a liberal perspective.

Managing the Friction between Evangelical and Secular Culture

All interaction between Christian churches and secular culture involves friction. In order to diminish this friction, throughout history some churches have taken steps to reduce the differences between the biblical revelation and secular culture. The sharpest dividing line in our time is in the area of sexuality and marriage, most notably on LGBTQ issues.

This tension between biblical and secular has also led to open debates in various evangelical denominations in northern Europe, particularly in Baptist-related denominations. Some traditionally evangelical denominations have chosen to take a neutral stance, which in my opinion in practice equals a positive view on same-sex marriage and homosexuality. For example, in 2012 the Danish Baptists chose not to take a stand but to leave the matter to the local congregations.[23] On the other hand, some Norwegian denominations have used various strategies to reaffirm their biblical stance. At its 2024 synod, the Evangelical Lutheran Free Church of Norway gave the status of "central teaching" to a document that defends a classical view on marriage, cohabitation and sexuality, which means that all its ordained leaders are expected to follow the traditional teaching.[24] The Norwegian Baptist Union, in their turn, in 2020 decided with a large majority to preserve a biblical view on sexuality and to elect a more conservative leadership. This happened after a local congregation had elected a woman who was in a same-sex marriage to its church council.[25] In 2023, the same denomination even affirmed their stance further, establishing that the Baptist community does not approve of homosexual relations among leaders and members, and that congregations which do not abide with this stance should be suspended.[26] A final example is how the Methodist Church in Norway split after their decision to accept same-sex marriage. As a

---

23. Theological Forum in the Baptist Union of Denmark, *To Danish Baptist Churches on the Place of Homosexuals in the Church* (2012), https://drive.google.com/file/d/1AQsjqbWmgiJ0Y8WVMHrE4qcCWC_IWp1b/view.

24. "Synod protocol" 2024, https://frikirken.no/synoden2024/sak6, §6.

25. Stein Gudvangen, "Norwegian Baptists confirm conservative marriage stance," *Evangelical Focus*, 12 November 2020, https://evangelicalfocus.com/europe/8922/norwegian-baptists-confirm-conservative-marriage-stance.

26. "Norwegian baptists against same-sex relationships," *CNE News*, 7 September 2023, https://cne.news/article/3581-norwegian-baptists-against-same-sex-relationships.

consequence, some congregations with a traditional view joined the Pentecostal movement early 2025. Their move to a denomination with a different view of baptism illustrates how marriage has become the prime factor for choice of denomination, surpassing even views on the sacraments.[27]

In Sweden, evangelical congregations and denominations have used different strategies to handle the pressure. In 2023, the Evangelical Free Church published a much-debated report on LGBTQ issues. This denomination has traditionally described itself as standing on four legs: evangelical, baptist, missional and charismatic. The report, though, altered the order, with missional coming first and evangelical only third, with the argument that in order to reach present-day secular Westerners, the church needs to contextualize its teaching by accepting views from the surrounding culture. The tenor of the report led to a motion at the 2024 denominational congress which demanded the rejection of the report's conclusions and a clear stance for a traditional view. Over against this motion, the denominational board proposed to keep a traditional view on marriage, without however rejecting the report. At the congress, a third suggestion was raised, viz. to dismiss both these alternatives and let all congregations decide views themselves. This third alternative was clearly the least popular and in the final vote, the suggestion from the board won a majority.[28] At the time of writing, it remains unclear how this "middle" alternative will be interpreted. However, as the denominational board had previously decided not to expel a congregation which had changed their view of marriage, a practical tolerance towards a liberal view appears likely.

Of particular interest here is the Filadelfia Church in Stockholm, for many decades the largest local congregation in Northern Europe. In 2006, they hired a head pastor from a more liberal denomination, who introduced a more open stance towards secular society, in later years most notably towards homosexuality. In the meantime, between 2005 and 2022 the membership decreased from six thousand two hundred to three thousand six hundred. As a result, Filadelfia lost its position as Sweden's largest congregation, despite the fact that the Swedish Pentecostal movement as a whole is growing. This confirms the diverging membership pattern between evangelical and liberal congregations.

---

27. Herman Frantzen, "Metodistkirker bytter dåpssyn og går inn i Pinsebevegelsen," *Vårt land*, 10 January 2025, www.vl.no/religion/2025/01/10/metodistkirker-bytter-dapssyn-og-gar-inn-i-pinsebevegelsen.

28. Urban Thoms, "Vitt skilda åsikter inom EFK i debatt om kyrkans äktenskapssyn," *Dagen*, 26 May 2024, www.dagen.se/nyheter/2024/05/26/stor-spannvidd-i-asikter-nar-efk-debatterade-aktenskapssyn.

Conclusions

In sum, evangelical Christianity in Northern Europe experiences a situation of both pressure and possibilities. Evangelical groups and individuals take an active part in society in several ways. However, secular intolerance opposes groups which defend biblical values as superior to the secular-individualistic ideas which are particularly strong in this part of the world. Still, liberal brands of Christianity are gradually losing adherents whereas other Christian denominations are experiencing strong growth, particularly charismatic evangelical groups and the Catholic and Orthodox Churches.

On the surface, the current divide within Christianity deals with marriage and sexual ethics, but at a deeper level it reflects opposing views on the Bible as the ultimate authority in life and society. The main area of open conflict is how to respond to the rapidly changing sexual ethics of the secular society – whether to adapt to secular norms or to remain on a biblical foundation. This secular pressure is felt strongly by evangelical groups and the resulting divide goes right through most denominations, rather than between them. If denominational leaders wish to base their strategies on historical trends, they should know that the pattern is clear: groups which adapt to secular culture lose members while those which preserve an evangelical basis and an openness to charismatic Christianity grow. Therefore, even if biblical arguments were excluded from consideration and statistics were the sole tool for decision making, denominations ought to take caution before abandoning their biblical convictions. At this stage, the response of evangelicalism in Northern Europe appears to hang in a balance.

Bibliography

Ewert, Per. "Moving reality closer to the ideal: The process towards autonomy and secularism during the Social Democratic hegemony in 20th century Sweden." VID Specialised University, 2022. https://vid.brage.unit.no/vid-xmlui/handle/11250/3039121.

Gudvangen, Stein. "Norwegian Baptists Confirm Conservative Marriage Stance." *Evangelical Focus*, 12 November 2020. https://evangelicalfocus.com/europe/8922/norwegian-baptists-confirm-conservative-marriage-stance.

Kittelmann Flensner, Karin. "Religious Education in Contemporary Pluralistic Sweden." Doctoral dissertation, Göteborg University, 2015.

Marjokorpi, Santero. "Against the Odds, Finnish Researchers Find an Increase in Religiosity among Young Finnish Men." *Evangelical Focus*, 18 January 2024. https://

evangelicalfocus.com/europe/25092/against-the-odds-researchers-find-an-increase-in-religiosity-among-young-finnish-men.

Nordin, Magdalena, and Torbjörn Aronson. "A New Ecclesial Landscape: Changes in Numbers of Churches and International Pentecostalism in Stockholm 1980–2020." *Pentecostudies* 22.1 (2023). https://doi.org/10.1558/pent.26644.

"Norwegian Baptists against Same-Sex Relationships." *CNE News*, 7 September 2023. https://cne.news/article/3581-norwegian-baptists-against-same-sex-relationships.

Christensen, Henrik Reintoft, and Marie Vejrup Nielsen. *Religion i Danmark*. Aarhus University, 2020.

SOM-institutet, Gothenburg University. "Svenska Trender 1986–2023" (2024). www.gu.se/sites/default/files/2024-04/Svenska%20trender%201986-2023_0.pdf.

Theological Forum in the Baptist Union of Denmark. *To Danish Baptist Churches on the Place of Homosexuals in the Church* (2012).

Tholvsen, Øyvind. *Frikyrkoundersökningen: En Rapport Om Frikyrkornas Utveckling I Sverige 2000-2020*. Sveriges frikyrkosamråd (2021). https://vidare.nu/wp-content/uploads/2021/06/frikyrkoundersokningen-2021.pdf.

"World Values Survey and European Values Study Joint Survey Round (2017–2020) Results in % by Country (2020)" (2022). www.worldvaluessurvey.org/WVSEVSjoint2017.jsp.

29

Evangelicalism in Western Europe Today

Some Sociological Remarks

Jelle Creemers

Introduction and Aim

A plethora of facts and figures will not suffice to fairly present the diversity of the evangelical movement in Western Europe in the limited space of this chapter. My contribution, therefore, limits itself to one argument, which is based on a scrutiny of some recent sociological publications on the movement in this region. In going through some facts and analyses, it simply pleads for proud appreciation of the inner diversity of the evangelical movement.

We define Western Europe on the basis of a comparison of the German *Ständiger Ausschuss für geographische Namen* and the CIA World Factbook.[1] Both sources divide Europe into five regions, as was done at the 2024 FEET/EEA conference which has led to the present publication. In both sources, Western Europe consists of at least the United Kingdom, Ireland, the Netherlands, Belgium, France and Monaco. The sources differ on whether or not Luxemburg and Andorra are to be considered part of Western Europe. As I will not specifically discuss either of these small countries, nor Monaco, I leave this question open. Hence, this overview will focus on (recent sociological research

---

1. See for StAGN, Peter Jordan, "Großgliederung Europas nach kulturräumlichen Kriterien," *Europa Regional* 13.4 (2005): 162–73.

on) the evangelical movement in the five larger countries of Belgium, France, Ireland, the Netherlands and the United Kingdom.

Western Europe: Highly Secularized with Assertive Religious Minorities

When looking sociologically at the development of the evangelical movement in Western Europe – or anywhere in the world – we start by giving some attention to the social context within which the movement exists today. Mark Hutchinson, a leading researcher of global evangelicalism, describes Western Europe as presenting "the picture of, at one level, advanced high modern secularization, and on the other, the increasing diversity and assertiveness of minority religious cultures." This context has resulted, Hutchinson continues, in "the growth of Evangelicalism in most constituencies, both as a proportion of Christian constituencies, and in terms of overall numbers."[2] While we will put the *growth* statement in the second sentence in perspective later, Hutchinson offers a succinct and helpful analysis of the contemporary context of Western European evangelicalism in the first sentence, to which we turn first.

Hutchinson starts with a description of Western Europe as being highly secularized – which resonates with the classic secularization paradigm, of which this region is the prime example. We are well aware of the criticisms and alternatives to this paradigm which have been developed in the past decades, notably in what Rodney Stark and Roger Finke call "the new paradigm," based on an economic logic.[3] Still, one can hardly disagree that on the European continent the classic secularization thesis generally holds. In Western Europe the rise of modernity with its scientific optimism, differentiation of society and turn towards the self has created a highly secularized context, meaning at least a context in which irreligion is not just an option, as proposed by Charles Taylor, but a postulate for societal analysis.[4] Longitudinal research such as the European Values Studies demonstrates that irreligion (or the group of "religious nones") has been growing for decades and is still growing, as this table shows:

---

2. Mark Hutchinson, "Evangelicals in Western Europe," in *Evangelicals Around the World. A Global Handbook for the 21st Century*, ed. Brian C. Stiller, Todd M. Johnson, and Karen Stiller (Nashville: Nelson, 2015), 385.

3. See Rodney Stark and Roger Finke, *Acts of Faith: Explaining the Human Side of Religion* (Berkeley: University of California Press, 2000).

4. Cf. Charles Taylor, *A Secular Age* (Cambridge: Harvard University Press, 2007).

Percentage of people without religion ("nones")[5]

	1981-1984	2005-2010	2017-2020
Belgium	17.3	43.3	
France	28.8		57.1
Ireland	1.3	11.4	
Netherlands	38.1	47.4	61.3
United Kingdom	10.2		59.3

This secular context within which the evangelical movement seeks its place is often considered problematic by evangelicals and a serious challenge in view of their evangelistic endeavours. But it may also be a context that actually accommodates evangelical spirituality quite well – given the movement's attention to religious choice, its tendency to differentiate between world and church, and its focus on the individual (see also below).

The second part of Hutchinson's statement gives attention to the fact that minority religious cultures have grown in Western Europe, not only in diversity, but also in assertiveness. They have grown in their self-awareness and have come to better understand and argue for their place in society and their individual and group rights. This is clearly visible for the evangelical movement today in the countries under consideration, in some of which evangelicals were still considered heretics or sectarians less than thirty years ago.[6] In Belgium, after an emancipation process, in 2003 the evangelical churches were taken up in the officially recognized Protestant-evangelical religion, meaning they can benefit from different forms of state support. This recognition implies not only that they have a say in the organization of Protestant-evangelical religious education in primary and secondary schools, it also implies that evangelical churches can now have a pastor salaried by the state.[7]

---

5. Source: European Values Studies. See for these and more numbers Dominik Balazka, "Mapping Religious Nones in 112 Countries: An Overview of European Values Study and World Values Survey Data (1981-2020)" (Trent: Fondazione Bruno Kessler, 2020), www.researchgate.net/profile/Dominik-Balazka/publication/344176211_Mapping_Religious_Nones_in_112_Countries_An_Overview_of_European_Values_Study_and_World_Values_Survey_Data_1981-2020.

6. See e.g. Jelle Creemers, *"In de wereld, niet van de wereld": Strategische identiteitsbepalingen in de Vlaamse evangelische vrijkerkelijke beweging (1980-2022)* (Leuven: Evangelische Theologische Faculteit, 2022).

7. For more details, see Jelle Creemers, "All Together in One Synod? The Process of Structural Unification of Evangelical Free Churches in Belgium (1985-1998)," *Trajecta* 26.2 (2017): 275-302; Jelle Creemers, "Protestanten Verenigd Voor of Door de Staat? Onderhandelingen

In France, the CNEF (Conseil national des évangéliques de France) has in the past decades become a strong organization which currently represents over 70 percent of the Protestant-evangelical churches towards French society and the state. Their growing acceptance in the country of *laïcité* (secularism) is evident in the fact that its previous director, Clément Diedrichs last year was awarded the rank of Knight in the National Order of Merit for his service to the CNEF and thus to society, having been nominated by the French minister of Internal Affairs, Gérald Darmanin, and appointed by president Emmanuel Macron.[8] The growth of the CNEF is the example *par excellence* which brings home the main thesis of Sébastien Fath's 2005 monograph that the movement has moved from ghetto to network.[9] The implications of this development are currently being analysed by Constance Varoquier (GSRL-CNRS).[10] In the Netherlands and in the United Kingdom, the societal presence and influence of evangelicals has been known for some time. They play an important, even if not always appreciated, role in the sociopolitical sphere.

Note that these examples do not aim to argue that evangelicals are fully accepted in all Western European countries and contexts today. Believers from these countries can definitely provide ample examples of the societal and legal discrimination that is still there. But there is definitely ground for Hutchinson's statement that evangelical self-awareness and assertiveness have grown in this area.

Statistics on the Size of the Evangelical Movement

After these considerations of Hutchinson's premises, let us now turn to his subsequent claim, namely that the evangelical movement has grown in most constituencies. We will problematize his statement in two ways: first, by looking at some statistics; second, by asking some critical questions of definition.

As a minority interdenominational religious reality in all of the countries under consideration, it is very difficult to really say much about the size of the evangelical constituency. The numbers in the statistics below have come from several sources: first, we have taken over the 2010 data and projections of the

---

over de Afbakening van Een Erkende Eredienst in België (1999–2002)," *Tijdschrift Voor Religie, Recht en Beleid* 10.2 (2018): 5–18.

8. See www.lecnef.org/page/509713-missions-et-valeurs.

9. Sébastien Fath, *Du ghetto au réseau: Le protestantisme évangélique en France 1800–2005* (Geneva: Labor et Fides, 2005).

10. GSRL-CNRS: *Groupe Sociétés, Religions, Laïcités* is a research lab under the *Centre National de la Recherche scientifique*; see https://gsrl-cnrs.fr/.

World Christian Database (WCD) and of Operation World (OW). Second, in the fourth column we present the projections of the 2019 World Christian Database.[11] In addition, some other estimations are presented, which often come from local (evangelical) organizations or research institutes.

Percentage of evangelical Christians per country

Country	OW % 2010	WCD % 2010	WCD % 2020	Other
Belgium	1.2	0.4	Ev: 0.8 Ev+:[12] 3.4	
France	1.0	1.1	Ev: 0.5 Ev+: 2.0	2012: 0.7[13] 2023: 1.1[14]
Ireland	1.6	3.4	Ev: 3.5 Ev+: 11.9	
Netherlands	4.3	3.7	Ev: 3.4 Ev+: 5.9	2023: 1.7–2.2[15]
United Kingdom	8.8	19.3	Ev: 8.8 Ev+: 14.1	7.6%[16]

A quick look at these numbers leaves us with some important first impressions. Of course, we see that the numbers are quite diverse. Notably, the estimation of the number of evangelicals in Ireland and the United Kingdom in 2010 by Operation World is less than half of what WCD estimates. The difference cannot simply be attributed to different terminology or sampling methods, as in the same year the Operation World numbers in Belgium and in the Nether-

---

11. Data from the WCD and of OW (2010) are taken over from *Evangelicals Around the World. A Global Handbook for the 21st Century*, ed. Brian C. Stiller et al. (Nashville: Nelson, 2015), 362–63. Data from the WCD 2019 are taken from Todd M. Johnson and Gina A. Zurlo, *World Christian Encyclopedia* (3rd ed.; Edinburgh: Edinburgh University Press, 2020), 6.

12. Ev+ = Evangelicals + Pentecostals/charismatics.

13. The CNEF indicated that there were 460,000 evangelicals in France in 2012; see Hutchinson, "Evangelicals in Western Europe," 390.

14. The CNEF indicates that there are 745,000 Evangelicals in France, which amounts to 1.1 percent of the population. It is not clear whether the CNEF have their own calculations for this number or have used the WCD. See "Les Églises Protestantes Évangéliques en France. Livrette cartographique et statistique 2023" (CNEF, 2023), www.dropbox.com/scl/fi/31w8eittalmf313ag0k8p/CNEF_2023_Livret-cartographique-et-statistique.pdf?rlkey=o0yimxkhpke8x76axjwrcxove&e=1&dl=0.

15. Joris Kregting and Merijn Wijma, "Evangelische protestanten in tijden van secularisering," *Religie & Samenleving* 18.2 (2023): 59–86.

16. www.joshuaproject.net/countries/UK. The source of these estimates is unclear.

lands are considerably higher that the WCD numbers. This simple observation warns us to be very careful with these numbers.

Notwithstanding, we would argue that these figures allow at least some simple insights. First, as can be expected, the United Kingdom is estimated to count the largest percentage of evangelicals. Still, even in the United Kingdom almost all estimations keep the numbers well under 10 percent. Hence, as a first insight, these figures confirm what we said earlier: that in all countries under consideration the evangelical movement is a small to very small minority of the population. This is, we assume, true of all of Europe. Second, it seems that evangelical presence is more substantial in the historically Protestant countries of the United Kingdom and the Netherlands than in the historically Catholic countries of Belgium and Ireland (and France). This aligns well with recent sociological research which indicates that people convert to evangelicalism mostly from other Protestant backgrounds rather than from a Catholic or atheist background.[17]

Third, if we stick with one database, the WCD, which over the decades has hopefully kept its methodology intact, we can see that we need to make some reservations regarding Hutchinson's claim that the evangelical movement is growing, at least in the period between 2010 and 2020. In some of the countries under consideration, the evangelical movement seems to have declined in membership rather than grown – a tendency which is sometimes reversed when Pentecostal and charismatic churches are added. There is one notable exception to this in the WCD data, and that is Belgium. In Belgium, the evangelical movement is estimated to have *doubled* between 2010 and 2020. This, however, is not correct. The entry on Belgium in the WCD was written by Aaldert Prins, Geert Lorein and myself,[18] but the numbers were added by the editors – and we strongly disagree with their conclusion.[19] So, from what we see in the numbers under consideration, there seems to be, if not a decline, at least a stagnation of the numbers of evangelicals in Western Europe.

However, even if the numbers are not indicating growth, it may still be possible to say that in Western Europe today, and in its own way, the evangelical movement is thriving. This is an assessment we find in a considerable body of literature, including anthropological and sociological (see below). This assess-

---

17. See Paul Vermeer and Peer Scheepers, "Church Growth in Times of Secularization: A Case Study of People Joining Evangelical Congregations In The Netherlands," *Review of Religious Research* 63 (2021): 43–66.

18. Geert W. Lorein et al., "Belgium," in Todd Johnson and Gina A. Zurlo, eds, *World Christian Encyclopedia* (Edinburgh: Edinburgh University Press, 2020).

19. Any questions as to the details can best be directed to Aaldert Prins.

ment may refer to the growing acceptance in society, it may refer to the growing presence of migrant churches, it may refer to the growing social responsibility and upward mobility of evangelicals. In all of this, however, we have until now been speaking about the movement without having given any attention to a crucial, preliminary question: who are the evangelicals in Western Europe?

Self-Identification of Evangelicals in Western Europe

The evangelical movement being a religious movement and its leaders usually being theologians, there is a natural tendency to identify the movement first and foremost with a theologically based definition, such as Bebbington's quadrilateral which describes early evangelicalism in Britain or, building on this, Timothy Larsen's five-point definition.[20] While these definitions are absolutely valuable and necessary in view of demarcations of research and in view of identity politics, they are more problematic than we might think at first sight. The cause of this is that, as we all know, there is no pope or institution that can authoritatively say what evangelicalism is, not even Bebbington or Larsen.

From a sociological perspective, a theological definition is certainly not the most obvious starting point for analyzing a movement. Sociological research on group identities typically starts from a group's self-identification – in this case, those who self-identify as evangelicals. But of course this approach also comes with challenges. We briefly discuss three of these. First, there are – in churches and in personal perspectives – many who may well fit in the theological categories mentioned above, but who do not identify as evangelicals. They may prefer to identify as Pentecostals, charismatics, Reformed, Baptists or just as Christians. This complicates the selection of the target group. Second, there are those who identify as evangelical but who do not fit the aforementioned theological categories. A 2023 poll in Northern Ireland showed that 21 percent of the population self-identifies as evangelical.[21] This explains why the late preacher-politician Ian Paisley called Northern Ireland "the last Bastion of

---

20. D. W. Bebbington, *Evangelicalism in Modern Britain: A History from the 1730s to the 1980s* (London: Unwin Hyman, 1989). After twenty years this historical definition was discussed again in Michael A. G. Haykin and Kenneth J. Stewart (eds), *The Emergence of Evangelicalism: Exploring Historical Continuities* (Leicester: Apollos, 2008). For Larsen's definition, see Timothy Larsen, "Defining and Locating Evangelicalism," in *The Cambridge Companion to Evangelical Theology*, ed. Timothy Larsen and Daniel J. Treier (New York: Cambridge University Press, 2007), 1–14. See also the chapter by Hetty Lalleman in this volume.

21. See Gladys Ganiel and Emma Soye, "'The Last Bastion of Evangelicalism in Europe?' Evangelicalism and Religiosity in Northern Ireland," *Religions* 15.696 (2024): 8.

Evangelical Protestantism in Western Europe."[22] Notably, though, this group of people self-identifying as evangelicals includes 38 percent of practicing Catholics, and "of evangelicals aged 18–24, 64% were Catholic and just 25% were Protestant." Hence the question arises, how should one deal with self-identification in relation to theology and theological tradition(s)? Third, what to do with those who self-identify as evangelicals and who feel comfortable with the earlier mentioned theologically-based definitions, but who are not recognized as "evangelicals" by other "evangelicals"? It is not hard to see which hotly contested theological or ethical topics best demonstrate these frictions and challenges. William Stell, for example, points to people who in various ways affirm LGBTQ equality and consider themselves fully "evangelical," not *despite* their affirmations, but even claiming that their affirmations actually render them more faithful evangelicals than those who oppose LGBTQ inclusion.[23] Hence, while self-identification is a very useful starting point for sociological insights into a movement, it has its own problematic aspects.

So, when speaking about evangelical identity, the question must be taken seriously as to who is to decide who belongs to the evangelical movement. The only manner in which "evangelical" Catholics and LGBTQ-affirming "evangelicals" could be considered outside of the evangelical movement is by authoritative definitions, which typically *add to* the classic elements of the definition, such as ecclesial exclusions, ethical positionings, etc. Such definitions can only be enforced in particular power dynamics, in which the powerful or the majority decide on what is evangelical and what is not. But both matters, authoritative definitions and majority power dynamics, are clearly in conflict with the typical evangelical self-understanding as having no overarching authoritative structure or pope and with the claimed focus on *personal* responsibility in matters of faith and practice.

Evangelical Diversity as a Strength

Starting from self-identifications remains, so we would argue, a defensible and valuable starting point for sociological research on the evangelical movement in Western Europe. What such research – and in particular research on diversity – in Western European evangelicalism may mean and may teach us,

---

22. Quoted in Martha Abele Mac Iver, "Ian Paisley and the Reformed Tradition," *Political Studies* 35 (1987): 368.

23. See William Stell, "Queerly Evangelical: The Rhetoric of Inverted Belonging as a Challenge to Heteronormativity in Evangelical Theology," *Theology & Sexuality* 25.1–2 (2019): 62–80.

can be demonstrated well with reference to a 2024 research article by Paul Vermeer and Saskia Glas. From this article, I will draw some key insights, before moving to my conclusion.[24]

Vermeer and Glas state that in the Netherlands the number of evangelicals is not enormous – they estimate at 300,000–400,000. Still, Vermeer and Glas see that as a religious minority "evangelicals seem to thrive."[25] To dig into this thriving community more deeply, they analysed survey data on more than eleven hundred Dutch self-identifying evangelicals who filled out a questionnaire on matters of faith and practice. In their article, for which they analysed their data using latent class analysis, they come to identify five distinctive groups within this Dutch evangelicalism, which are on a continuum between orthodox and liberal in their beliefs. They label these groups as Proclaiming Orthodox (13%), Engaged Orthodox (23%), Spiritual Orthodox (26%), Seeking Orthodox (25%) and Questing Liberals (14%).[26] This continuum in beliefs aligns in practice with the attitude of these persons towards society, i.e. their desire to separate from or rather engage with their sociocultural environment.[27] Vermeer and Glas argue that the five types can be seen as concentric circles and they explain:

> The Proclaiming Orthodox are at the core and with each circumferential circle the tension with the sociocultural environment lessens and evangelicals become slightly less orthodox and more open to society. The Questing Liberals occupy the widest circle and are the most open to society as they value religious pluralism and have religious doubts the most and show the least support for core evangelical beliefs concerning monism, biblicism and creationism.[28]

Interestingly, the authors consider this diversity within Dutch evangelicalism the very reason why the movement is thriving: "... they possess the ability to find a perfect, or delicate, balance between distinction and engagement with

---

24. Paul Vermeer and Saskia Glas, "E Pluribus Unum? Constructing a Typology of Contemporary Dutch Evangelicals," *Journal for the Scientific Study of Religion* 63.2 (2024): 368–87.
25. Vermeer and Glas, 368.
26. Vermeer and Glas, 378–81.
27. This confirms the observation of Rodney Stark that "... religious groups basically differ with respect to the degree of tension with their sociocultural environment." Rodney Stark, *Why God. Explaining Religious Phenomena* (West Conshohocken: Templeton Press, 2017), 131–40.
28. Vermeer and Glas, "E Pluribus Unum," 384.

their sociocultural environment."[29] In sociological terms, the most orthodox, the Proclaiming Orthodox, tend to pull towards a "sectarian" stance and they need the Questing Liberals to pull towards social conformity and engagement. Inversely, the Questing Liberals should not become dominant over time, so Vermeer and Glas argue, because "this may interfere with the ability of the evangelical movement to maintain a distinctive religious identity."[30] Hence, the internal theological diversity within Dutch evangelicalism is, from a sociological perspective, very important in view of the movement's thriving.

Conclusion

I close with a simple conclusion. Looking at sociological numbers, data and research on the evangelical movement in Western Europe, we can say that the numbers may not be growing – certainly not in a spectacular way – but that the movement is growing in influence and may therefore be considered "thriving." At the same time, the movement is quite diverse, both when we look at them through the lens of theological diversity and on the basis of evangelicals' self-identification. It is therefore not surprising that sociological research by Vermeer and Glas shows that the movement is actually quite diverse in its perspectives on faith and on society. Their suggestion that this diversity may be the very reason for its thriving should, in our estimation, also be integrated in our considerations on our inner diversity from a theological perspective. A proper acknowledgement and appreciation of our own diversity may well be a strength, which enables evangelicals to stay away from both sectarian and self-destructive tendencies.

Bibliography

Bebbington, D. W. *Evangelicalism in Modern Britain: A History from the 1730s to the 1980s.* London: Unwin Hyman, 1989.

Creemers, Jelle. *"In de wereld, niet van de wereld": Strategische identiteitsbepalingen in de Vlaamse evangelische vrijkerkelijke beweging (1980–2022).* Leuven: Evangelische Theologische Faculteit, 2022.

Fath, Sébastien. *Du ghetto au réseau: Le protestantisme évangélique en France 1800 – 2005.* Geneva: Labor et Fides, 2005.

---

29. Vermeer and Glas, "E Pluribus Unum," 369.
30. Vermeer and Glas, "E Pluribus Unum," 384.

Ganiel, Gladys, and Emma Soye. "'The Last Bastion of Evangelicalism in Europe?' Evangelicalism and Religiosity in Northern Ireland." *Religions* 15.696 (2024): 1–19. https://pure.qub.ac.uk/en/publications/the-last-bastion-of-evangelicalism-in-europe-evangelicalism-and-r.
Hutchinson, Mark. "Evangelicals in Western Europe." Pages 385–93 in *Evangelicals Around the World. A Global Handbook for the 21st Century*. Edited by Brian C. Stiller, Todd M. Johnson and Karen Stiller. Nashville: Thomas Nelson, 2015.
Johnson, Todd M., and Gina A. Zurlo. *World Christian Encyclopedia*. 3rd ed. Edinburgh: Edinburgh University Press, 2020.
Kregting, Joris, and Merijn Wijma. "Evangelische protestanten in tijden van secularisering." *Religie & Samenleving* 18.2 (2023): 59–86.
Larsen, Timothy. "Defining and Locating Evangelicalism." Pages 1–14 in *The Cambridge Companion to Evangelical Theology*. Edited by Timothy Larsen and Daniel J. Treier. New York: Cambridge University Press, 2007.
Lorein, Geert W., Aaldert Prins, Jelle Creemers and Patrick Nullens. "Belgium." Pages 105–9 in *World Christian Encyclopedia*. Edited by Todd Johnson and Gina A. Zurlo. Edinburgh: Edinburgh University Press, 2020.
Stark, Rodney, and Roger Finke. *Acts of Faith: Explaining the Human Side of Religion*. Berkeley: University of California Press, 2000.
Taylor, Charles. *A Secular Age*. Cambridge: Harvard University Press, 2007.
Vermeer, Paul, and Saskia Glas. "E Pluribus Unum? Constructing a Typology of Contemporary Dutch Evangelicals." *Journal for the Scientific Study of Religion* 63.2 (2024): 368–87.

About the Authors

Paul Bruderer has been the pastor of the Viva Church Frauenfeld since 2001. In addition to his work as a lecturer in systematic theology at the Theologisches Seminar St. Chrischona in Basel and ethics at the International Seminary of Theology and Leadership in Zurich, he blogs about cultural apologetics and post-evangelicalism at DanielOption.ch.

Danijel Časni graduated from the Faculty of Graphic Arts and Economics, University of Zagreb, and the Evangelical Theological Seminary in Osijek. He received his doctorate from the Faculty of Theology, University of Ljubljana. He is a lecturer and researcher at the Biblical Institute in Zagreb and the ETS in Osijek.

Timóteo Cavaco is a scientist and historian who works at the Universidade Aberta, the Universidade Católica Portuguesa and the Seminário Teológico Baptista in Queluz, Portugal. Since 2023 he serves as the president of the Evangelical Alliance of Portugal.

Pavel Černý is the retired head of the Church of the Brethren and also a former President of the Ecumenical Council of Churches. Until now he serves as a pastor in Prague, as tutor in practical theology at the Theological Seminary and as chairman of the Czech Fellowship of Evangelical Theologians.

Jelle Creemers is professor and chair in the department of religious studies and missiology at the Evangelische Theologische Faculteit (ETF), Leuven. He is the director of the Institute for the Study of Freedom of Religion or Belief (ISFORB) at ETF Leuven and board member of the Flemish Evangelical Alliance.

Monique Cuany is professor of history of Christianity at the Haute École de Théologie (HET-PRO) in Saint-Légier, Switzerland. Her publications include pieces on the *Réveil* of Geneva, the Protestant Reformation and Early Christianity.

Lars Dahle is professor of systematic theology and Christian apologetics at NLA University College, Norway, and serves as director of the resource development ministry Damaris Norway. He was co-editor of *The Lausanne Movement: A Range of Perspectives* (2014) and is involved with the European Leadership Forum and Lausanne Media Engagement Network.

Leonardo De Chirico is pastor of the Church Breccia di Roma and lecturer in historical theology at the Istituto di Formazione Evangelica e Documentazione in Padova, Italy. He is author of several books, including *Engaging with Thomas Aquinas: An Evangelical Approach* (2024). He blogs on Roman Catholic issues from an evangelical perspective at www.vaticanfiles.org.

Per Ewert's doctorate is on the political process towards secular individualism in Sweden. He is the author of several books on Christianity and society, and he is director at the Clapham Institute, Sweden's leading Christian think tank. He regularly contributes to newspapers and magazines, and currently studies processes of change in free protestant denominations.

Sébastien Fath, a historian and social scientist, is research fellow at the National Centre for Scientific Research (CNRS). He wrote a synthesis of French evangelical history. His research focusses on evangelicalism in its transnational dimension. Currently the Afro-European dimension dominates in his work, including field research on the prosperity gospel in French-speaking Africa.

Tim Grass is a senior research fellow at Spurgeon's College, London, and an academic historian. A fellow of the Royal Historical Society, he has written widely on modern Christian history and on dialogue between evangelicals and Orthodox. He is a lay minister in the Church of England on the Isle of Man.

Martin P. Grünholz earned his doctorate in theology from the University of Fribourg (CH) in 2023. Since 2022 he is lecturer in systematic theology at the Biblical-Theological Academy at Forum Wiedenest. Before this he served in pastoral ministry in southern Germany for nine years. He is married with three children.

David Hilborn is academic dean of the London School of Theology, UK. He was previously principal of Moorlands College and of St John's College, Nottingham. Before that, he helped to establish St Mellitus College, London. He was head of theology at the Evangelical Alliance UK (1997–2006) and chaired its Theological Advisory Group (2016–2024).

Frank Hinkelmann is professor at the Faculty of Humanities and Social Sciences at the Aurel Vlaicu University of Arad, Romania. He is also the principal of Martin Bucer Seminary, a German-based evangelical seminary. His research focusses on European evangelicalism with a special concentration on Austria. He has authored several books.

Gert Kwakkel is professor of Old Testament at Theologische Universiteit Utrecht, Netherlands, and at Faculté Jean Calvin, Aix-en-Provence, France. His research focusses on the theology of the Old Testament and the prophets, especially Hosea. Since 2020, he chairs the executive committee of FEET.

Hetty Lalleman taught Old Testament for thirty-five years, most recently at Spurgeon's College, London, UK, where she is now a senior research fellow. Her specialisms are Jeremiah and Old Testament ethics. She worked as the community pastor of a Baptist church in Surrey and recently published a novel.

Pieter J. Lalleman is the editor of the *European Journal of Theology*. He taught biblical studies at Spurgeon's College in London for over twenty years, serving as academic dean for thirteen years. Until recently he was minister of a Baptist church in Surrey, UK.

Marcel Măcelaru is professor of theology and the founding director of the Ars Theologica Research Centre at Aurel Vlaicu University of Arad, Romania. He has published eighteen books and more than a hundred articles. His research interests include the history, identity and theology of his own Pentecostal denomination and of the evangelical community at large.

Patrick Mitchel is director of learning and senior lecturer in theology at the Irish Bible Institute in Dublin where he has worked for thirty years. He is author of books, articles and book chapters, particularly related to evangelicals in Ireland as well as New Testament studies. He is an elder in a Presbyterian church in Co. Kildare.

Israel Oluwole Olofinjana is an African public missiologist with a focus on intercultural justice. He is the director of the One People Commission of the British Evangelical Alliance, the founding director of the Centre for Missionaries from the Majority World and an honourary research fellow at the Queen's Foundation for Ecumenical Theological Education in Birmingham, UK.

Elsa Correia Pereira is a doctoral candidate who is finishing her thesis in sociology of religion on the role of women in free evangelical communities in Europe. For twenty years she worked for evangelical non-governmental organizations. She is responsible for the Peace, Reconciliation and Human Rights network of the Portuguese Evangelical Alliance.

Evert van de Poll is professor of religious studies and missiology at the Evangelical Theological Faculty in Leuven, Belgium, and visiting professor at the Faculté Libre de Théologie Évangélique in Vaux-sur-Seine, France. Having served as a pastor in the French Baptist Federation he now lives alternately in his native countries of the Netherlands and France. He is also a musician and composer.

David Sandifer has a doctorate in history from the University of Cambridge, UK. He is chair of the department of practical and intercultural theology and associate professor of practical theology and ethics at Tyndale Theological Seminary in Badhoevedorp, Netherlands. He previously served as a pastor in churches in the USA and Australia for nearly twenty years.

Sergii Sannikov received his doctorate in theology (Dr. Habil.) from the National Pedagogical Dragomanov University in Kyiv. He was a founder and from 1989 until 1997 the first president of Odesa Theological Seminary, Ukraine. For fourteen years he was executive director of the Euro-Asian Accrediting Association and for six years its president.

Stefan Schweyer studied theology in Basel and Chicago. He was pastor in a free church from 1994 to 2008. He completed his doctorate at the Evangelische Theologische Faculteit Leuven, Belgium in 2006 and his habilitation at the University of Fribourg, Switzerland in 2019. He has been a professor of practical theology at Universitäre Theologische Hochschule Basel since 2020.

Joshua T. Searle hails from North East England and is professor of mission studies at the Theologische Hochschule Elstal, Germany. A graduate of Oxford, Prague and Dublin, Joshua taught at Spurgeon's College for ten years. He was a missionary in Eastern Ukraine and founded Dnipro Hope Mission. He is an ordained pastor in the German Baptist Union and the author of several books and articles.

Cristian Sonea, a Romanian theologian, serves as professor at the Faculty of Orthodox Theology, "Babeş-Bolyai" University, Cluj-Napoca. He holds a habilitation in theology and a doctorate in missiology from the same institution. An ordained Orthodox priest, he currently serves St Andrew's parish in Cluj-Napoca. His academic and pastoral roles intersect in his commitment to both theological education and the mission of the church.

McTair Wall is the coordinator of the Network of European Francophone Evangelical Missiology and professor of missiology at the Faculté de Théologie Évangélique in Montreal, Canada. A specialist in the burgeoning field of missional hermeneutics, he is also affiliated with the Faculté Libre de Théologie Évangélique in Paris and lectures in French-speaking Africa.

Natalia Zawiejska works as an assistant professor at the Institute for the Scientific Study of Religion at the Jagiellonian University in Krakow. She developed experimental research on urban religion in Poland (RUM Project) and on the public presence and social formations of Pentecostalism in Poland. Her ongoing research is focussed on Angolan Pentecostalism.

Langham Literature and its imprints are a ministry of Langham Partnership.

Langham Partnership is a global fellowship working in pursuit of the vision God entrusted to its founder John Stott –

to facilitate the growth of the church in maturity and Christ-likeness through raising the standards of biblical preaching and teaching.

Our vision is to see churches in the Majority World equipped for mission and growing to maturity in Christ through the ministry of pastors and leaders who believe, teach and live by the word of God.

Our mission is to strengthen the ministry of the word of God through:
- nurturing national movements for biblical preaching
- fostering the creation and distribution of evangelical literature
- enhancing evangelical theological education

especially in countries where churches are under-resourced.

Our ministry

Langham Preaching partners with national leaders to nurture indigenous biblical preaching movements for pastors and lay preachers all around the world. With the support of a team of trainers from many countries, a multi-level programme of seminars provides practical training, and is followed by a programme for training local facilitators. Local preachers' groups and national and regional networks ensure continuity and ongoing development, seeking to build vigorous movements committed to Bible exposition.

Langham Literature provides Majority World preachers, scholars and seminary libraries with evangelical books and electronic resources through publishing and distribution, grants and discounts. The programme also fosters the creation of indigenous evangelical books in many languages, through writer's grants, strengthening local evangelical publishing houses, and investment in major regional literature projects, such as one volume Bible commentaries like *The Africa Bible Commentary* and *The South Asia Bible Commentary*.

Langham Scholars provides financial support for evangelical doctoral students from the Majority World so that, when they return home, they may train pastors and other Christian leaders with sound, biblical and theological teaching. This programme equips those who equip others. Langham Scholars also works in partnership with Majority World seminaries in strengthening evangelical theological education. A growing number of Langham Scholars study in high quality doctoral programmes in the Majority World itself. As well as teaching the next generation of pastors, graduated Langham Scholars exercise significant influence through their writing and leadership.

To learn more about Langham Partnership and the work we do visit **langham.org**

www.ingramcontent.com/pod-product-compliance
Lightning Source LLC
Chambersburg PA
CBHW071432300426
44114CB00013B/1408